Leisure and
Recreation
Management

Also published by E & FN Spon

Coaching Children in Sport: Principles and practice
2nd edition
Edited by M. Lee

Coastal Recreation Management: The sustainable development of
maritime leisure
T. Goodhead and D. Johnson

Drugs in Sport
2nd edition
D. Mottram

Economics of Sport and Recreation
2nd edition
C. Gratton and P. Taylor

Facilities Management: Theory and practice
K. Alexander

Introduction to Sports Biomechanics
R. Bartlett

Notational Analysis of Sport
M. Hughes and I. Franks

Physiology of Sports
Edited by T. Reilly, P. Snell, N. Secher and C. Williams

Sports Biomechanics
R. Bartlett

Sports Management and Administration
D. Watt

Understanding Sport: An introduction to the sociological and cultural
analysis of sport
J. Horne, A. Tomlinson and G. Whannel

Visual Perception and Action in Sport
K. Davids, M. Williams and J. Williams

Leisure and Recreation Management

Fourth edition

George Torkildsen

London and New York

First published 1983 by E & FN Spon, an imprint of Chapman & Hall

Second edition 1986
Reprinted 1990
Third edition 1992
Reprinted 1992, 1993 (twice), 1994, 1995, 1996 (twice), 1997, 1998

Fourth edition published 1999 by E & FN Spon
11 New Fetter Lane, London EC4P 4EE

Simultaneously published in the USA and Canada
by Routledge
29 West 35th Street, New York, NY 10001

Reprinted 2000

Reprinted 2001 by Spon Press

Spon Press is an imprint of the Taylor & Francis Group

Typeset in Century Old Style by Keystroke, Jacaranda Lodge, Wolverhampton
Printed and bound in Great Britain by TJ International Ltd, Padstow, Cornwall

British Library Cataloguing in Publication Data
A catalogue record for this book is available from the British Library

Library of Congress Cataloging in Publication Data
A catalogue record for this book has been requested

ISBN 0–419–22940–X

This fourth edition of the book is dedicated to my friend and colleague

GWYNNE GRIFFITHS

a former influential lecturer and consultant who worked with me on the first, second and third editions and from whom I gained insights, positive critique and always a readiness to be of help.

'Big Griff' will not mind sharing this dedication with two of our friends.

TED BLAKE died in March 1998. He was an inspirational management trainer, writer and presenter and arguably the greatest early influence upon the fledgling profession of leisure management in the UK.

ROGER QUINTON died in March 1998. He was a founding member of the leisure management profession in the UK and a truly gifted manager, leisure service director and consultant.

Contents

CONTENTS

Illustrations

ILLUSTRATIONS

Preface and acknowledgements

This book is written for people who are interested in exploring the fascinating world of 'leisure' and 'recreation' and its management. They may be students, lecturers or researchers, leisure executives, managers, recreation officers, supervisors or trainee managers. They may be organizers and administrators, policy makers, planners or leisure architects. They may be people on the 'fringes' of leisure, including community workers, teachers and many others.

My motivation in writing the first book in the early 1980s, carrying the same title, stemmed from a preoccupation with and overwhelming interest in leisure and recreation and its management. That motivation remains and, indeed, is enhanced. Having been involved for forty years as teacher, coach, manager, director, lecturer and consultant, and having been part of the movement towards the development of the community leisure centre and the emerging profession of leisure management, I have felt destined to write about it and try to keep it up to date.

I thank all who helped in any way in the writing of this and all previous editions and in the production of this edition, through their work, support, information, advice, patience or understanding. The book could not have been written without the accumulated knowledge and experience gained over many years from a wide range of sources and very many people. Thanks to them were recorded in previous editions.

For this edition, I record my grateful appreciation to my colleagues. Our young leisure researcher from New Zealand, Kay McDonald was of great assistance throughout the process. My administrative colleagues Jan Allen, Sue Tarling and Pat Kendall have been a constant source of cheerful and hard working support and encouragement. My business colleagues Ian Barclay and Jim Lynch lent their support providing positive feedback on some of the work.

To all and many more, thank you.

Chapter one

Introduction, structure and significance of the book

1.1 Introduction – leisure in a changing world

Leisure and Recreation Management, published in 1983, was the first book of its kind. The second edition, published in 1986, carried many changes, but the third edition, published in 1992, was in large measure written as a new book because of the changes and growth in the field of leisure management. The edition embodied both the old and new. New chapters were written, but the baby was not thrown out with the bathwater! Fundamental philosophies and principles upon which to plan and manage survived and through further research were strengthened. Importantly, the historical aspects and contexts also remained, relating to government, planning, leisure and management.

So why the new changes in this fourth edition? As Tom Peters, noted for his bestseller, *Passion for Excellence*, says, 'quality improvement is a never-ending journey'. The changes in this edition are equally dramatic and equally sensitive to planning and managing on sound principles; they are concerned with people, their needs in leisure and the role of the Leisure Manager. What leisure is and what it means to people are probably more important now than ever before and the influence of government and its agencies has never been more evident.

The fourth edition of *Leisure and Recreation Management* expands and improves upon previous editions, reflecting enormous changes over the past few years. Since the last edition, in the United

Kingdom, the coming to power of a Labour government, after eighteen years of Conservative rule, changes in legislation and the introduction of the National Lottery make for more profound effects on leisure provision and management.

The leisure about which I write is both individual and universal. Global conditions affect each country far more now than in the past; the world economic climate, for example, has an impact on every nation. Europe is in a period of turbulent change. The political map has been redrawn, with the break-up of the Soviet Union into separate republics and a united Germany. The Single European Market, the prospect of a single currency and the Channel Tunnel all herald substantial change and opportunity. While changes are largely political and economic, the leisure industry is part of the new Europe and the contracting world, as more people move across the globe. The entry of Disney into France, and the British government's Millennium Dome in London are projects of international importance, a far cry from a cosy home leisure industry.

The world of leisure and recreation planning and management in the United Kingdom also has changed substantially since earlier editions of the book and at a faster rate than anyone had forecast. This is as a result of economic and social changes, including government policy in relation to local authority expenditure; new technology; the growth in tourism; the growth of the service sector economy and the commercial leisure industry; and the growing expectations of people for healthier life styles, leisure fashion, facilities, services and choices.

To have *leisure*, to do the things we want to do, free from responsibilities or weighty obligations, is a dream most people have but few achieve. Yet, at least in the Western world, leisure opportunity for the majority in Western civilization is a reality.

There is a fast-emerging profession with the words 'Leisure' and 'Management' in its title, an industry employing approximately 2.5 million people in the United Kingdom. This book is concerned with both leisure and management and with the fusion between the two.

1.2 Is there a need to manage people's leisure and recreation?

This book seeks to answer some simple questions about a complex phenomenon, for example, what is leisure and recreation? How is it planned and provided for, managed and controlled? How can greater opportunities be provided through improved management? But why this concern? Is there a need to manage leisure?

The first thing that could be said about provision and management is that nature provides us, in the natural environment, with abundant resources for recreation, so much so that, one could argue, there is no need for expensive additional facilities, services, programmes and management. Nature has provided fields, woods, rivers, beaches and sunshine. We have the challenge of the mountains, winter snow, the seas and the sky. There is beauty to behold, solitude in the country and peace away from the crowds.

The second thing that could be said is that we, as individuals, or with families or among our friends, should be quite capable of providing for all our recreational needs and for those of our children, or those unable to care for themselves, without additional facilities, services, programmes and management. Nature has provided us with the means to survive, to seek and explore, to find, to grow and to multiply. Certainly, it has provided us not only with the desire to play and to find recreation, but also with the human capacity and resourcefulness so to do.

Yet the demand for man-made additional resources for leisure and recreation is greater now than it has ever been. Access to the countryside is increasingly limited; footpaths are being destroyed; and playing fields are sold for development. Opportunities are often needed for children just to learn how to play with other children. Indeed, the problem is so acute that it has required government, institutional and voluntary agencies to promote the concept of the 'child's right to play'. The International Year of the Child (1979) focussed attention on the plight of children in slums, in traffic-congested areas, in high-rise blocks of flats and in bad homes and housing conditions. Since that time over the four editions of this book, little has changed for the disadvantaged.

The energies of some young people, channelled into acts of needless violence or vandalism, are evidence of unsatisfied needs. Could leisure opportunities provide the adventurousness, the noise, the speed and independence that youth seeks and assist in meeting some of those needs? One could ask whether opportunities are also needed for adults, for families, for the lonely, the old, the handicapped and the delinquent to experience the satisfactions that leisure holds. Will such experience enhance their quality of life?

The assumption is made in this book that leisure and recreation and its planning and management must be concerned, first, with *people*, not just with resources, buildings and facilities, but with the question of human rights, the dignity and the uniqueness of the individual. It is from this standpoint that planning and management are debated and this thread, however tenuous, links discussion on principles, planning and management.

The book deals with approaches towards better management and performance. It is not, however, a technical textbook dealing with buildings, facilities, design, maintenance, catering, accounting, nor with many specialisms and technical matters. These aspects are covered by other specific publications and particularly by institutions. Instead, this book is concerned with the leisure 'software' – namely, the quality of the experience, the principles underlying provision and the 'people approach' to planning, managing, leading and programming. Aspects of operational management have been revised to encapsulate the greater awareness of 'quality' management and the need for efficiency in times of stricter accountability.

Leisure and recreation are made possible by means of a range of services and facilities, both indoor and outdoor, in and around the home, in the urban environment, in rural areas and in the countryside. A range of services and programmes is provided by the public, institutional, voluntary and commercial sectors to meet the diverse needs and demands of individuals, families, groups, clubs and societies.

Many demands are met through resources and equipment in the home. Some demands are met, in part, through outdoor facilities such as gardens and open spaces, allotments, play areas and sports grounds. Other demands are met, in part, through a range of indoor facilities for entertainment, art, music, drama, literary activities, education, sport and physical recreation, hobbies and pastimes.

This range of activity requires general and specialist facilities in the form of halls and meeting rooms, libraries, theatres, museums, sports and leisure centres, swimming pools, community centres, entertainment centres, pubs, clubs, cinemas, concert halls, craftrooms and workshops. Recreation in the countryside requires good road networks, maps and signposting, stopping-off points, scenic viewing points, picnic sites, car parking, camping and caravan sites, clean beaches and lakes, water recreation areas, walkways, footpaths, nature reserves and many others.

Demands are met, however, not just by providing facilities, but in attracting people to use and enjoy them, through services, management policy and management action. The range of facilities in urban areas and in the countryside is increasing, and becoming more sophisticated. With it come greater opportunities and greater problems – opportunities which should be seized and problems which leisure professionals must help to solve.

1.3 Significance of the book

The purpose of this book is to explore, describe, inform, challenge, improve and enhance leisure and recreation management. Three propositions are postulated:

1   providers of leisure services and facilities should be concerned with the *quality of experience* for the individual and not just with the quantity of facilities;
2   leisure *opportunity* can lead to satisfying recreation experiences, which have positive effects on the quality of life of individual people and hence the community; and
3   *management* exerts a powerful influence on both participation and non-participation.

Leisure planners, providers and managers are in key positions for creating resources and opportunities, which can help to enhance the quality of life for many people. However, little research has been undertaken relating to people's needs and leisure management and the implications upon the planning, development and operation of facilities. The complex network is an area yet to be adequately explored.

There have been significant changes since the last edition in the United Kingdom: the creation of the Department of National Heritage (now Department of Culture, Media and Sport); the National Lottery; the Citizen's Charter; recession and recovery; greater business realism; lessons from compulsory competitive tendering (CCT) in the public sector; private management of public facilities; leisure trends, particularly health and fitness; definitive planning guidance for the first time in sport and recreation; national training initiatives; and the burgeoning number of courses in leisure management and related subject areas.

In the public sector, there has been a sea-change in public sector management and plans are in hand to replace CCT with a system of 'Best Value'. Managers who can hold their own in a competitive market are expected to be smart enough to do much more with much less. Contract management and the setting up of non-profit organizations to manage public leisure facilities have been means of reducing revenue deficits.

The National Lottery is forcing those responsible for developing new facilities and who wish to make application for funds, to take a strategic view, to link with other agencies, to open their doors to the wider community and to appoint professional or competent amateur personnel. When the voluntary sector is taken into account, a massive market for new managers is revealed, which has hardly been tapped.

The commercial sector has witnessed a dramatic expansion in the range and number of leisure facilities, such as Family Entertainment Centres and expanded cinemas, tenpin bowling, bingo and fitness centres.

A results-driven culture has emphasized the need for business management; however, the book also demonstrates the need for management approaches which retain the fundamental belief that leisure and recreation are good for individuals and the community.

The book has as much, if not more, significance in 1999 than it did when it was first published in 1983, in maintaining bridges between a philosophy of leisure and best management practice.

1.4 Structure and changes to the book

Part one – Leisure and the needs of people

The first part of the book describes and explains three related phenomena: *leisure*, *play* and *recreation*, and the needs of people. The word 'leisure' is rarely used without invoking other words and concepts, the most frequent being 'sport', 'art', 'entertainment', 'recreation' and 'play'.

Furthermore, little attention has been paid to relating the tangents of play, recreation and leisure into a cohesive and usable whole. The three concepts are used on the one hand to explain three distinct phenomena, yet on the other hand they can also be used indiscriminately and are frequently interchanged. As a consequence, clear understanding is limited and reliance is placed on generalized assumptions. What better place to start a book than at the beginning, with the needs of children and the concept of play – the cornerstone of leisure. Through play, children develop their physical, intellectual, emotional and social ability. Denied play opportunity, children suffer and so does the society in which they grow. Yet, in most countries, including the United Kingdom, play is undervalued and provision for play is under-resourced.

Chapter two is extended substantially from previous editions, dealing with play and its implications for leisure services and containing a section on children growing up in a complex world and how play can help them to develop and cope with it. Chapter three deals with the concept of recreation: recreation experience and the implications for leisure services. The word 'recreation' is sometimes interchanged with 'play' but most people perceive it separately. There is more blurring of definitions with the word 'leisure', which is covered in chapter four. The chapter is expanded substantially from the last edition, drawing together play, recreation and leisure into a useable 'whole' for planning and management.

Public community services are said to be based on the needs of people. Yet policy makers, researchers, planners and managers have insufficient insights into people's needs. Clearly, the satisfying of people's needs through leisure opportunity is one of the principles behind providing services. What are the factors which attract people to participate in recreation, and what factors militate against participation? Are management policy and operation significant influences on people, either to attract or inhibit participation? Chapter five gives some perspectives on people's needs and some of the main factors which appear to influence and condition recreation activity choice.

Part two – Leisure trends, planning and government

The second part of the book consists of three chapters: trends in leisure; planning for leisure; and the role of government and national agencies. In recent years in the United Kingdom, the pace of change not only in leisure but in our quality of life generally has been rapid. We are now enjoying higher standards of living, with access to goods, services, activities and opportunities that in past years seemed unimaginable. Underlying this growth have been several major, and numerous other minor, trends related directly or indirectly to leisure and recreation. These are described in chapter six.

Chapter seven is concerned with the planning process. The planner's dream is to provide the right facilities, in the best location, at the right time, for the people who need them and at an acceptable cost. Leisure planning must therefore include knowledge of leisure and the needs of the community. My contention is that leisure managers should be involved in the process. This substantial chapter contains new material and new planning models, and predicts a movement towards leisure strategies and local leisure plans. This is an area of work crucial to future facilities and professionally links leisure to planning. In the last edition 'leisure' knew very little about planning and 'planning' knew little about leisure! The tide is turning – slowly.

Chapter eight is a new chapter dealing with central government and its agencies. The most significant change since the last edition of the book, indeed since it was first written, is the creation of a government department for leisure with a Secretary of State and a seat in the cabinet. The Department of National Heritage (DNH) was formed by the Conservative government in April 1992 and renamed Department of Culture, Media and Sport (DCMS) by the incoming Labour government in 1997. This department is so important that it warrants a separate chapter. Parallel with this, the most dramatic influence on the provision of facilities for leisure has been the introduction of the National Lottery.

There are a whole range of national, regional and local agencies which assist in providing for public leisure and recreation. They are often hybrids of public authorities, and whilst it is not their primary function to provide facilities, some of them do, and all influence provision through grants, loans, technical advice or support of some kind. The major agencies form a regional network of services.

Part three – The leisure providers

Chapters nine to eleven deal with the providers in the public, voluntary and commercial sectors. The public sector is facing a period of substantial change and this is described in chapter nine. Legislation during much of the 1980s and 1990s had the effect of tightening councils' budgets and loosening management control. CCT in particular had a dramatic effect. Local Management of Schools and the Children Act compounded the changes. On top of these has come a re-organization of local government in Great Britain, bringing Unitary Authorities into Scotland and Wales and some parts of England, and there has been a change of government in 1997. All these changes make complications and opportunities for Leisure and Recreation Management. Publication of the Local Government Bill has marked the first stage in the replacement of CCT with 'Best Value'.

The opportunities offered to people through the vast range of thousands of voluntary bodies in the UK represent collectively a massive contribution to leisure and recreation. The sector is dominated by a vast array of leisure and recreation clubs and associations. In many cases voluntary organizations are inextricably linked to public providers and public money. This is exemplified in the movement towards more 'Not for Profit Distributing Organizations' (NPDOs). Chapter ten looks into the voluntary aspects of leisure provision, the concept of volunteerism and management through charities and NPDOs.

Leisure provision in the commercial sector is covered in chapter eleven – the commercial sector is the most volatile. This chapter has, therefore, been almost completely re-written in view of massive changes since the last edition, which include the growth in Family Entertainment Centres, cinemas, fitness centres and the renaissance of tenpin bowling and bingo.

Part four – The management of leisure

The fourth focus of the book is the part which, traditionally, is accepted as 'management'. A person is appointed to a position of, say, manager of a leisure complex and is told to get on with the job and *manage*. Many believe that leisure and recreation management starts from there. This book takes a different view. It is suggested that far from starting with the facility, leisure management starts with the people it is intended to serve, along with their needs and an understanding of the 'product', the market place, the providers and the planning process.

Management, including marketing and programming, it is contended, is a continual, beginning-to-end process. The techniques of service and facility management, however, are an important and essential part of the process. In the third edition there was a chapter on organizational performance appraisal. This is not included here in view of the pending introduction of Best Value, which is described at the end of chapter nine.

The objectives of chapter twelve are to describe the principles of management, to consider some general management factors which apply to all managers, such as decision making and leadership, and to look at specific management tasks in the leisure setting. Good management is the means by which an organization can meet its aims and objectives, in a style that encourages good relationships within the organization and with customers. Good leadership and communication require an understanding of people – ourselves, colleagues and customers – and of people's motivation. Key aspects, such as decision making are included in this long, important chapter.

Chapter thirteen moves from general management to specific management and to programming of leisure services and facilities in particular. Managers must have sufficient knowledge of programming strategies, approaches and methods, in order to direct staff in achieving the aims and objectives of the organization. A programming planning process is devised.

Chapter fourteen explores the possibilities for improved marketing of services and products, particularly in the public sector. In the commercial world, marketing leisure products has proved to be an effective means of making greater profits. For services in the public sector could it mean greater success? Or are there institutional and ethical problems? Should public service marketing be processed in a different way? The concept of marketing is relatively simple: academics have made it something complex! The chapter unravels the mystique and provides a plan for marketing.

Chapter fifteen covers the planning and management of events which have become increasingly important skills for leisure managers. Events are an important part of any comprehensive leisure programme. Well organized, they can be a boon; badly organized, they can spell disaster and deter people from coming to such events in future. Leisure Managers must be capable of leading or controlling the planning and staging of events. The chapter gives practical help in planning and presenting events.

Chapter sixteen considers staffing. Staff are the most important resource in any leisure organization and its cost should be regarded as an investment rather than an expensive item of expenditure. The right staff need to be employed, trained, nurtured and enabled to perform well for their organizations and for themselves. The way in which staff are organized is a crucial factor in the performance and level of success of management. The principles of management which concern staffing are described; some of the problems of staffing within recreation services are highlighted, staffing structures are examined and legislation relating to staffing is described briefly.

Training for leisure management is receiving much attention from government, agencies and institutions. Chapter seventeen provides a broad overview of the training scene in the United Kingdom with some critical observations and challenging questions relating to leisure management as an emerging profession. The old ways of developing our managers were never very good. How much better are they now? Training has been a major growth factor since the last edition. The introduction of National Vocational Qualifications (NVQs) and National Training Organisations (NTOs) in the leisure sector have been influential. New legislation has been introduced adding to the changes.

A Leisure Manager is not someone who graduates from college with a certificate; there are no instant managers. Nor is he or she someone who, through years of experience, can operate an establishment efficiently, but has no knowledge about the effectiveness of the operation, nor the needs of the consumers. Rather, a Leisure Manager is a person, younger or older, who has evolved – with a mix of education and training inside and outside the job situation, and some experience – to become a person with motivation, ability and sufficient understanding to create and manage opportunities for people to experience leisure through a choice of activities, at whatever level is satisfying for them. Hence the bland statement that 'any good manager can manage anything' is not unequivocally supported. The first tenet of management is to know what it is you are managing. What business are you in?

Many employers equate management with administration and thus appoint administrators. While the good manager should be able to administer, organize and learn, administration is only one of the many functions of management. The emerging profession of leisure management is accumulating many good administrators. This book is written in the hope that it will also accumulate many good managers.

Finally, in chapter eighteen, all the strands of the book – leisure philosophy, planning, provision and management – are drawn together into a new theory and framework for community leisure services and facility management which provides the linkages and bridges the gap between theory and practice, born out of the belief that there is nothing more practical than a good theory – if you put it into practice!

Part one

Leisure and
the needs of
people

Chapter two

Play, children and the community

What better place to start a book about people and leisure, than at the beginning, with the needs of children and the concept of play – the cornerstone of leisure. Through play, children develop their physical, intellectual, emotional and social ability. Denied play opportunity, children suffer and so does the society in which they grow. Yet, in most countries, including the United Kingdom, play is undervalued and provision for play is under-resourced.

Children are described often as the citizens of tomorrow. However, children are the young citizens of today. The kind of adult citizens they will become will depend on how citizenship for life is cultivated. Children and young people under the age of 16 years make up 21 per cent of the population in the United Kingdom – under 5 years of age, 6.5 per cent and 5–15 years, 14.1 per cent. Northern Ireland has the highest proportion of children under 16, with over 25 per cent; England 21 per cent, Wales 21 per cent and Scotland 20 per cent.

This chapter is concerned with the concept of play. It draws out the characteristics of play behaviour and attempts to understand what it is and why people play.

First, play is introduced to show that on the one hand it appears to be a simple phenomenon – just play – yet on the other it is an extraordinarily complex one that can shape behaviour and the type of persons we become.
Second, play is placed in historical perspective from the ancient Greek civilization to modern times.

Third, some of the theories – classical, recent and modern – are described.

Fourth, this chapter is extended substantially from previous editions. It encompasses part of a former chapter dealing with play and its implications for leisure services. It also includes the problems of children growing up in a complex world and how play can help them to deal with it.

Fifth, the rights of the child enshrined in conventions of the United Nations and new duties and powers under the Children Act are described.

Sixth, play provision is now expanding rapidly in the commercial sector and the effects of new technology are raised.

Having studied this chapter, readers will be able to discern the special characteristics of play behaviour and its freedom of expression and inner-consuming nature. Readers will be able to appreciate its role in the learning and socializing process in the young and its potential in adult leisure, given the right climate in which to flourish. Readers will perceive similarities to recreation and leisure, yet there are cultural differences.

2.1 Play shapes human behaviour

Children benefit from play. Denied opportunities to play freely in a loving and supporting environment, they will suffer. Play opportunities can help to shape human behaviour.

> To play, children need opportunities, with time and space, free from constraints and dangers. When homes are cramped, overcrowded and without easy access to play areas, children's play is restricted; when their neighbourhoods are dominated by traffic and polluted in other ways, children are exposed to risks and may be deprived of their independence to play; when children are subject to abuse, bullying and violence, their freedom to play is affected; when children and their parents are under pressure from social, educational and economic factors, play time is marginalised or ignored; when children become inactive, they become less healthy and when denied play, they take longer to recover from ill-health and trauma or are permanently damaged.
>
> *A Play Strategy for Scotland* (March 1996, Dunfermline DC)

Every opinion canvassed in the *A Review of National Support for Children's Play and Recreation* [1] believed, unequivocally, that play held substantial benefits for children. Wholesome development ('holistic' was a word often used), social education and learning were mentioned most often. Physical development, motor skills and creativity were also recognized. Many of those consulted spoke of the misunderstanding of the word 'play', often almost derided as 'only child's play'. That play is not taken seriously and is under-funded was a theme which dominated most consultations. 'Children's play', therefore, appeared to be an inappropriate phrase to describe the development of social, emotional, creative, intellectual and physical skills and 'play' gave the impression that its only function is fun, rather than enjoyment in doing many things, often very seriously.

Our old family dog, Sherriff, typical of so many animals, appeared to be happiest (when not eating) at play – catching, fetching, teasing, playing games and having fun. The play of animals illustrates that play precedes culture and human civilization. Of all the animal kingdom, the latest of the species – human beings – play most of all.

The play of young children is experimental. Objects stimulate curiosity and the imagination. We have all observed the infant who is far more interested in the box than in the present inside. In the same way, children need opportunities for exploration of the environment, exploration of physical movements and the development of relationships with objects and with people.

Great discoveries have been made which help unravel the past. In tracing human development, anthropologists have found not only implements for work and survival, but also playthings – toys, dolls, hoops, rattles, marbles and dice. Long before the Hans Christian Andersen story of Pinnochio, our ancestors were inventive and creative toy makers. Playing musical instruments, dressing up in ornate costume, pageantry and dancing may have resulted from, initially, just playing, or having fun. In later times, scientific discoveries and inventions may well have been the outcome of playing with a hobby, with intense and absorbing enthusiasm.

2.1.1 Play in all walks of life

So people play and appear to have done so from the dawn of man and woman. Why do they? Is play the same phenomenon as recreation? Is it leisure? Why does one person choose one activity, and another something entirely different? To one, an activity may be play; to another, the same activity may well be drudgery. What determines the choice? Is it upbringing, ability, stature or status, education, employment, personality or the pressure of the social group or friends? Given the right ingredients, can choices be determined, predictions made and demands gauged? If so, major planning problems can be tackled realistically.

Play is a mystery and an enigma. It is understood yet misunderstood; known yet unknown; and tangible yet so internal to the individual that it is untouchable. Also it is utterly individual yet universal. The play of children is accepted, but the play of adults has perhaps a stereotyped image of muddy footballers on muddy pitches. However, play is not confined to the games of children, the sport of young men, the family outing or the Christmas party. Play can pervade all aspects of life; not just physical play, but also the play of the mind, the play of words and the play of communications with people. To Sebastian de Grazia [2]:

> The world is divided into two classes. Not three or five or twenty. Just two. One is the great majority. The other is the leisure kind, not those of wealth or position or birth, but those who love ideas and the imagination. Of the great mass of mankind there are few persons who are blessed and tormented with

this love. They may work, steal, flirt, fight, like all the others, but everything they do, is touched with the play of thought.

Play then can be evident in all walks of life, at home, at school, at work, in politics and unions, in religion, in business, in crime and vandalism, in international dealings and even in war. The film *Oh, What a Lovely War!* carried the caption 'the ever popular war game with songs, battles and a few jokes'. The problem with war is that for some it can be a game – it can be fun!

One of the distinguishing signs of the play world is its strict adherence to invented rules, which suspend the ordinary rules of real life. The attitudes encompassed in play rules carry over from the play world into the 'real' world. While boxers play to Queensberry Rules, soldiers play to the rules of the Geneva Convention and some criminals have a code of acceptable behaviour. Parliamentary and local government rules are cloaked in the playful seriousness of obligatory procedures, the 'Chair', the 'points of order' and the adherence to the 'laws of the game'. Sometimes, as with children's games, it would appear that the procedures are more important than the business itself. 'Fair play' is often play acceptable to the rules. In this context, it is curious to find how much more lenient society is towards the cheat than it is towards the spoilsport. As Huizinga [3] points out, the spoilsport shatters the play world and robs it of its illusion (*in lusio*, 'in play'); the game ends. (If I can't bat, I'll take my bat and go home.) The cheat, on the other hand, pretends to be playing the game and on the face of it acknowledges the magic circle, the rules; the game continues. Play is a complex set of behaviours – 'a million permutations of human behaviour'. Any situation or activity, it appears, can function for someone as a play activity if undertaken in the spirit of play.

Suffice it to say, at this point, that play, normally reserved for the playground and playing field, is indelibly printed upon the lives of boys and girls, men and women. It spans the frivolous and the utterly serious, the shallow and the deeply emotional. Play is in the very nature of human beings.

2.2 Play in historical perspective

The roots of play philosophy and theory reach back to ancient times. In some respects, the classical era of Greece was also one of the most enlightened. Although child labour was common, children had an important place in classical society. Play was given a valuable position in the life of children, according both to Plato and Aristotle [4,5]. Play and leisure gave an opportunity to develop. The primary force was education (*paideia*), inculcating qualities of responsibility, of honour, loyalty, pride and of beauty. The philosophical writings which remain indicate dedication to state and culture, the highest value being placed on productive citizenship. It is not surprising therefore to note that play (*paideia*, i.e. the same word as education) was considered an aspect of enculturation and cultural reinforcement.

Play to the Greeks was associated with childhood. Yet the citizenship of adult life and the appreciation of aesthetics, music, art, athletics, drama and poetry might be seen as the products of play. Today we tend to look at the opportunities for play as incorporating free choice, freedom from compulsion, often spontaneity. But the

Greek citizen was bound to social commitment. There was a belief in universal personality/character which was held to be true of all noble persons. Hence life's activities were structured to fulfil this ideal. Play, then, was part of the means of integrating people into Greek culture as children. The Ancient Greeks laid a foundation of thought regarding play that has endured to influence leisure and recreation today. The perfectability of human nature through play, its usefulness in mental, physical and social well-being and the necessity of social control were of great importance.

Later civilizations modified Greek attitudes towards play. The Roman culture exploited leisure and provoked a hedonistic philosophy, which abandoned the concepts of moderation and balance in play behaviour. The ensuing over-reaction to play left its mark on the cultures that followed. The church took strict moral control over play expression. There emerged a suspicion of 'play' as a social threat. The Middle Ages marked a period when there was no concept of childhood; children were viewed simply as small adults but with low status. Obedience to and passive acceptance of God's will characterized the ethos of these times; play, the active seeking of new experience, retained little place in the ideals of this world. The body was thought to detract from more spiritual activities, thus every effort was made to curb its impulses. The Reformation acted further to restrict play among those following its creeds. Work became all-important; consequently, play became separated from work behaviour, and was considered morally dangerous.

Important contributions in the eighteenth and nineteenth centuries to counteract the decline in play philosophy came from Rousseau, Froebel and Schiller. Rousseau, in his revolutionary text *Emile*, espoused the idea of the natural child – the child of nature; mankind should return to a state of nature marked by simplicity and freedom. Schiller [6] took a more aesthetic view of play, a new respect for play with a hint of Greek idealism: 'Man plays only when he is in the full sense of the word a man, and he is only wholly Man when he is playing.'

Froebel [7] continued this philosophical direction. Play is the highest expression of human development in childhood.

> Play is the purest, most spiritual activity of man at this stage. . . . A child that plays thoroughly, with self-active determination, perseveringly until physical fatigue forbids, will surely be a thorough, determined man, capable of self-sacrifice for the promotion of the welfare of himself and others.

Froebel emphasized a belief in self-esteem, self-determination and self-discipline. The Froebel Kindergarten was fashioned not only on age-related growth needs, but also on the need for opportunity for individual expression and spontaneity. During the nineteenth century, the early education movement produced a new interest in play which culminated in a number of theoretical propositions attempting to explain and justify play. The ideas of Rousseau, and reformist and revolutionary ideas, forced society to accept two major changes: a distinction between the child and the adult, and the acceptance of play as an end in itself.

2.3 The theories – why do people play?

As life is a mystery, so too is play. What explanation is there for the mystery?

2.3.1 Classical theories

Many attempts have been made to explain the nature and function of play. The history of classical play theory has become relatively well known. Five of these theories are better known than the rest and survive in the literature today: the surplus energy, instinct, preparation for life, recapitulation and relaxation theories.

Schiller [6] saw play as 'non-survival' – important, even aesthetic, but essentially purposeless. Spencer [8] added two components: imitation, together with a physiological explanation. The surplus energy theory, sometimes referred to as the Schiller–Spencer theory, describes play as the expenditure of over-abundant energy which is unused in the normal processes of life sustenance.

The instinct theory suggests that play is caused by the inheritance of unlearned capacities to behave playfully. But this theory explains little as it ignores the fact that people learn new responses that we classify as play.

Groos [9] proposed that the play of children was practice for life. The preparation theory, based on Darwinian thinking, states that play is caused by the efforts of the player to prepare for later life.

Play is explained in the recapitulation theory as an outcome of biological inheritance. It is another Darwin-influenced theory. Children are a link in the evolutionary chain from animals to man, experiencing the history of the human race in play activities. Stanley-Hall [10] believed that play patterns were instinctive, generic expressions and re-enactments of early man's activities – i.e. a recapitulation of racial development seen in water play, digging in the sand, climbing trees and in tribal gangs.

Urban life puts people under extreme strain. The relaxation theory propounded by Patrick in *The Psychology of Relaxation* [11] proposed that playful activity was caused by the need to find compensating outlets to allow relaxation and recuperation from the tension and stress of work.

Most of the early theories were based on instinct as motivation of human play and these theories now only survive when they are incorporated in other theories of play behaviour. So today we find that play is considered to be much more complex than earlier theories suggested. All the older theories have some small merit, seeming to explain some aspects of behaviour, but they are over-optimistic in their simplicity. Each is relevant to different sets of problems. They take no account of individual differences. Ellis [12] suggests: 'Old soldiers never die' and they linger on in the literature as 'armchair theories'. They seem to explain, albeit curiously, some aspects of human behaviour, but they have logical shortcomings and are not substantiated by empirical findings.

2.3.2 *Early twentieth-century theories*

In contrast to the classical theories, recent theories (after the turn of the twentieth century) are concerned with attempting to explain the differences between the play of individuals. Among the recent theories, the learning, developmental and psychoanalytic theories show that play contributes to the development of intelligence and a healthy personality. Children gain pleasure, overcome unpleasant experiences and develop mastery of their physical and social environment.

Some, like Huizinga [3], claim that play is justification in and of itself without further rationalization, but animals play as well as humans and this seems to indicate that it performs some survival function. In his analysis of theories, Ellis [13] lists five major recent theories, namely generalization, compensation, catharsis, psychoanalytic development and learning. Other theories view play as an all-embracing phenomenon: as an end in itself, as the basis of civilization and culture, as the roots of social behaviour, as a reflection of society.

Two of the theories – generalization and compensation – rely on the belief that people's play choices are a result of the nature of their work. People who perform work tasks well, and are satisfied by them, will tend to behave similarly during their leisure time. The compensation theory suggests that adults select their leisure activities to compensate for the tendency of the work situation to deny satisfaction of their needs. These theories are over-simplistic, too general and take no account of pre-school play.

The cathartic theories of play stem from classical Greece, where dramatic tragedies and some music were believed to purge the audience of their emotions. The belief was that giving vent to feelings and emotions releases them. Feshbach [14] questions the validity of the theory that the expression of aggression in a socially approved form will reduce the amount of socially disapproved aggressive behaviour. Aggression researchers are finding that frustration leads to heightened aggressive feelings, but that subsequent aggressive behaviour does not reduce aggression. Berkowitz and Green [15] indicate that 'aggression begets aggression'.

In the psychoanalytic theories of play concern for individual behaviour is clearly paramount. Interest stemmed from the observations of Freud [16], who observed that much play is motivated by pleasure. His ideas were later amended and formalized by Wälder [17] to show that play has multiple functions and cannot be explained by a single function; that work was expanded still further by Erikson [18]. Hence the psychoanalytic theory goes beyond the pleasure principle to explain the play of children that is related to experiences that are not pleasant. There are encounters that they cannot control which are often unpleasant. To Freud, the opposite to play is not what is serious, but what is real.

Psychoanalytic theory suggests that children consciously add actual elements from their environment to their fantasies, mixing reality and unreality into their play. Adults are seen as more constrained by society, emphasizing their grasp of reality and hiding their tendency to deal with unreality in play. Thus adults are left with covert fantasies.

Wälder [17] suggests that 'fantasy woven about a real object is however nothing other than play'.

The psychoanalytic methods of viewing the phenomenon of play led researchers like Melanie Klein to develop play therapy [19]. By playing out feelings, a child can bring them to the surface, get them out into the open, face them and learn to control or abandon them. When anxious, a child will prefer to play with items which are salient to the anxiety (e.g. hospitalized children prefer to play with toys relevant to the situation, namely doctors and nurses). However, the psychoanalytic theories are another set of partial theories, explaining only some aspects of play behaviour.

Erikson [18] extended the ideas of infant development to stages of mastery and life development, taking into account effects of the environment. Play has a developmental progression in which a child adds new, more complex under-standings about the world at each stage. He identified three stages: 'autocosmic' play concerns bodily play; the 'micro sphere' is playing with toys and objects; and the 'macro sphere' develops sharing. For the child, Erikson feels that play may be used to work through and master reality. The child finds identity through play. Infant play between mother and child is all-important; adult behaviour and attitude are also of great importance. He relates this interplay to ritualization; the ritual expression combines the elements of play and social tradition, providing individual identity in a structured and/or communal fashion.

The Swiss child psychologist Jean Piaget [20] deals with play as an aspect of intellectual development. The structure of intelligence is a function of two co-existing processes which operate together to produce adaptation to the environment. These processes he called assimilation and accommodation.

Assimilation is a process whereby the child imposes on reality his or her own knowledge and interpretations and thus often alters reality to fit what is known from previous experience. In contrast is the process of accommodation, whereby the child alters existing cognitive structures to meet the demands of reality. Hence the child modifies feelings and thoughts when confronted with an object which appears novel: what he/she thinks is known must be altered to match what is encountered in the environment.

According to Piaget the balance between assimilation and accommodation constitutes the basis of intelligence and all behaviour is the 'acting out' of this cognitive interplay. Play is characterized by the assimilation of elements in the real world without the balancing constraints of accepting the problems of accommo-dating them – i.e. the behaviour that occurs when assimilation predominates can be described as playful and when accommodation predominates behaviour is viewed as imitative. Hence play is manipulative. Children alter and restructure environment to match experience and existing knowledge: reality is altered; the child creates an imaginary play world.

Piaget believes that play eventually becomes a game played with rules and structure. Sutton-Smith [21] has raised many objections to this thesis. He believes that play remains important, does not become more realistic or rationalistic as intelligence develops, but remains symbolic, ritualistic and playful, even into adulthood. In essence, however, Piaget implies that play is the most effective aspect of early learning.

Thorndike, Hull, Skinner and others view play as learned behaviour, 'stimulus–response behaviour' [22]. A response has an increased probability of occurring if it is accompanied by a pleasant or reinforcing event. If play behaviour is learned behaviour, then the learning will occur as a result of a whole variety of 'reinforcers' and reinforcing systems, for example, parents, other children and other adults sharing the same cultural and environmental influences.

Empirical studies have been undertaken by Roberts and Sutton-Smith [23], an anthropologist and psychologist collaborating to study the role of games in various societies. They have shown that individuals in different cultures perceive games differently, depending on the values and attitudes prevalent, and that such games serve to relieve social conflict and consequently enhance socialization. They put forward a theory of conflict enculturation. Conflicts induced by social learning (e.g. obedience, achievement, responsibility training) lead to an involvement in 'expressive models', such as games, through which these conflicts are moderated, lessened and assuaged. A learning process occurs which has cultural value both to the players and to their societies. They tested the hypothesis by studying the difference in rearing patterns and games played by the children in three societies. Clear evidence was found for an association between the predominance of one type of game and a particular emphasis in the rearing patterns.

2.3.3 Play as self-justification

Jan Huizinga [3], a Dutch historian, in his masterly book *Homo Ludens*, presents the cultural approach to play: 'Play is older than culture, for culture, however adequately defined always presupposes human society, and animals have not waited for man to teach them their playing.' Huizinga showed play to exist in every aspect of culture. He defines play as follows:

> Summing up the formal characteristics of play we might call it a free activity standing quite consciously outside 'ordinary' life as being 'not serious', but at the same time absorbing the player intensely and utterly. It is an activity connected with no material interest, and no profit can be gained by it. It proceeds within its own proper boundaries of time and space according to fixed rules and in an orderly manner. It promotes the formation of social groupings which tend to surround themselves with secrecy and to stress their difference from the common world by disguise or other means.

To Huizinga, play is self-justified. It can be present in all aspects of life – i.e. in work, business, leisure, sport, art, literature, music, religion and even in war. He believed most former theories to be only partial theories, which justified play as a means to an end: play was seen to serve something which it is *not*, leaving the primary quality of play untouched. Moreover, civilization had compartmentalized play, had grown more serious, had put play into second place. For the full unfolding of civilization we cannot neglect the play element: 'genuine pure play is one of the main bases of civilization.' Observation of the play rules were nowhere more important than in relations between nations. Once the rules were broken, society would be in chaos.

Huizinga believed that to play we must play like a child. When, for example, the play spirit is lost from sport, sport becomes divorced from 'culture'. He gives no explanation as to why people play, but he does describe play vividly. One can deduce from his description a number of interrelated characteristics.

1   Play is a free, voluntary activity. There is more freedom in the play world than in the real world. We cannot play to order; if the player is forced to 'play', it changes its nature; it is no longer play.
2   Play is indulged in for its own sake. It is unproductive and nonutilitarian.
3   Play is not 'ordinary' or 'real'. The player steps outside real life into a temporary sphere. The player knows it is only pretending, yet it is often utterly serious.
4   Play has boundaries of space and time. It has its own course and meaning.
5   Play is creative. Once played, it endures a new-found creation: it is repeated, alternated, transmitted; it becomes tradition.
6   Play is orderly and creates order. Into an imperfect world and the confusion of life it brings a temporary, limited perfection.
7   Play is regulated. It has rules and conventions; they determine what 'holds' in the temporary world. The new legislation counts; deviation spoils the play.
8   Play is 'uncertain'. The end-result cannot be determined. When the result is a foregone conclusion, then the tension and excitement is lost.
9   Play is social. Play communities tend to become permanent social groupings even after the game is over (clubs, brotherhoods, gangs). Groups are often esoteric or secret: 'It is for us, not for others.' Inside the magic circle there are the laws and customs which suspend the ordinary rules of life.
10 Play, then, is symbolic.

Huizinga's theory is a philosophical one. Play exists, it has always existed; it is its own justification. But self-justification is something that cannot be measured. It gives insights but not explanations.

The French sociologist, Roger Caillois [24], in *Man, Play and Games*, has presented a socio-culturally based theory of play building upon the theory of Huizinga. Caillois critically analysed the definition and redefined play as activity which is free, separate, uncertain, unproductive, governed by rules or make-believe.

Caillois developed a unique typology of the characteristic games of a society. Games are a culture clue, helping to reveal the character, pattern and values of a society. The basic themes of a culture should be deducible from the study of play and games no less than from the study of economic, political, religious or family institutions. He claimed that the destinies of cultures can be read in their choice of games: 'Tell me what you play and I will tell you who you are.'

The choice of games will reflect the society. Caillois identified four general classifications of games:

agon (competition): the desire to win by merit in regulated competition;
alea (chance): the submission of one's will to the luck of the draw;
mimicry (simulation): assuming a strange personality;
ilinx (vertigo): the confusion that giddiness provokes.

Games in each of the four categories were put on to a continuum representing an evolution from childlike play (*paidia*) to adult play (*ludus*). The first of these encompasses the spontaneous, frivolous, exuberant play, the frolic and the romping. The second is more concerned with man the thinker; the pleasure is in resolving difficulties. It represents those elements in play whose cultural importance seems to be the most striking. Rules are inseparable from play, once play acquires an institutional existence.

According to Caillois, while the games reflect the functioning of a society, if corrupted, they indicate the weakness and potential dissolution of the culture. Although not completely explanatory, and often weak in accurate identifications of social expressions, Caillois's theory does illuminate another perspective for analysis of play.

2.3.4 Modern theories

There are few modern theories of play emanating from the last half of the twentieth century. Play is increasingly seen as a mixture of different elements. Ideas about play which have survived into the second half of the twentieth century include the biological function, the anthropological view, psychoanalytic theories, and play for learning and development. Two further theories have come into the frame – play as stimulus-seeking behaviour and play perceived in terms also of playfulness.

Studies of children's play behaviour are succinctly summarized in *Make Way for Children's Play* by Play Board [25] and general theories of play are described by Elizabeth Child [26]. Norbek [27] puts forward the biological case. Play is characteristic of biological immaturity; the young play much more than adults, but play is also a characteristic of adulthood. 'Through infantile play, members of a species acquire motor and other skills needed in adult life for survival. Young human beings, with a long period of immaturity, are aided in this process by provision of specific opportunities for play experiences.'

An anthropological view suggests that the 'ultimate human being' is the person with varied behaviour. Play, in its multiple forms, appears to hold a position 'of prominence and vital importance.' Play fosters a wide range of adult behaviour. In *Looking at Play* [28], Hughes and Williams include 'A biological model'. They examine the ways human beings develop flexibility and how this development is necessary for survival and evolution:

> In both instances, we suggest that PLAY is the mechanism by which flexibility is achieved. And by doing this, present an argument which states that play is a feature of human behaviour from birth to death, and is absolutely essential in forming the basis both for human survival and human development.

Play, then, is concerned with two integral and related parts of the human learning process:

It describes the way the body deliberately searches for, and locates stimuli – and in so doing, describes how it gains information concerning the nature of its world. It describes the means by which the brain assimilates and selects those stimuli which give it 'good' feelings (+ve effects), and how it pursues them. Without play as an interactive experience, learning would not take place and the human would not acquire the skills necessary for survival.

The psychoanalytic theories – Sigmund Freud's [29] coming to terms with unpleasant experiences and 'wish fulfilment' – have been expanded upon by a number of writers such as Erikson [30] and Wälder [31] and play therapists like Anna Freud [32] and Melanie Klein [33].

Barnett summarizes the learning theories of play in 'Cognitive correlates of playful behaviour' [34] citing Piaget, Ellis and Sutton-Smith [35]. Children learn to be resourceful within the environment 'purely as a consequence of self-directed play'. Empirical support for this notion was found by Sylva [36] and by Barnett [37] herself and free play was seen as necessary behaviour for survival.

It is through play and its function of aiding the child to explore the environment that the child learns the procedures required to solve problems posed by the environment in later life. Play appears to be directly related to the divergent thought processes of the child and thus serves as the stimulus for normal cognitive development.

Michael Ellis's book *Why People Play* [12] is one of the most comprehensive and thorough studies of play in modern times. Ellis believes that there is no way of reaching any 'pure' definition and that the most satisfying explanation of play involves an integration of three theories: play as arousal-seeking behaviour, play as learning and the developmentalist view of play. There is considerable evidence to support the view that play enhances learning and development. The third aspect – the drive for optimal arousal – is advanced by Ellis.

Ellis shows that evidence is accumulating to explain some behaviour in terms of a drive to maintain optimal arousal. He defines play in this context as 'that behaviour that is motivated by the need to elevate the level of arousal towards the optimal'. Put another way, play is stimulus-seeking activity that can occur only when external consequences are eliminated: 'When primary drives are satisfied the animal continues to emit stimulus-seeking behaviour in response to the sensoristatic drive. The animal learns to maintain an optimal level of arousal.'

Researchers in arousal theory find that it is the stimuli that are complex, incongruous or novel that lead to arousal. In addition, the stimuli must have the ability to reduce uncertainty or carry information to the individual. Too much uncertainty and too much novelty will not be optimally arousing. Some intermediate level of information flow is optimally arousing. When situations are too complex, they have no arousal potential, and at the other end of the scale when the outcome is highly predictable, there is little uncertainty and the arousal potential diminishes. For example, the crossword in *The Times* will have no arousal potential for the easy-crossword dabbler; the gifted player will not be stimulated by the novice opponent. The play 'spirit' for many adults is often the play of the mind. Reading a thriller, following the fortunes of a favourite team in the newspaper, reading up on the Stock Exchange, doing crosswords, playing *Trivial Pursuit*, problem-solving or just day-dreaming are all activities actively sought after by adults, in particular, who by virtue of their age have a richer store of experiences. However, stimulus-seeking behaviour means more than merely seeking exposure to any stimuli. The stimuli must have *arousal* potential. Knowledge seeking, for example, results in the reduction of conflicts, mismatches and uncertainties. Laughter, humour and smiling are created by situations such as novelty, surprise, incongruity, ambiguity, complexity – all of which possess arousal potential. Fun has arousal potential.

Play, then, to Ellis is stimulus-seeking behaviour, but not all such stimulus seeking is play. The behaviour that seems to be clearly nonutilitarian is play. This may appear to lead to an artificial divide between work and play but clearly such stimulus-seeking behaviour can be found in both work and play. The theory appears to handle the question of work and play equally well. Indeed, it questions the validity of separating work from play.

Thus Ellis provides an explanation for both special and individual motivation towards play, and also describes a researchable, physiological base for play. In terms of its value to people and society, play fosters individuality; it provides 'learnings' that reflect individual, unique requirements; and it prepares for the unknown. Play will not occur when the essential conditions necessary for play behaviour are absent. One of the most important aspects coming out of this work is the realization that people play when the content of their behaviour is largely under their control.

The psychologist J. Nina Lieberman [38], has studied a concept which she identified as 'playfulness' and has observed and measured it in infants, adolescents, and adults. It is her thesis that playfulness is related to divergent thinking or creativity and that it has an important bearing on how we approach leisure. The three major components of playfulness are spontaneity, manifest joy and sense of humour.

Spontaneity shows itself in physical, social and learning dimensions and is a unitary trait in the young child. In the adolescent and adult, two separate clusters emerged in her studies which were labelled academic playfulness and social emotional playfulness respectively. The characteristics of academic playfulness were alert, bright, enthusiastic, imaginative, inquiring and knowledgeable. The outstanding characteristics of social emotional playfulness were entertaining, extroverted, joking, light-hearted, witty, making fun of himself/herself. The latter was also given the overall label of 'bubbling effervescence'.

At the infant level Lieberman found that the more playful child was also the more creative boy or girl. This was expressed in fluency, flexibility, and originality of thinking. In terms of intelligence, we know that two-thirds of the population fall within the middle range of intelligence quotients; in the case of creativity, the evidence appears to suggest different degrees of endowment and in different areas, for example, in specific talents such as science, music, writing and painting. Playfulness can therefore be part of any individual's make-up. Moreover, because of its importance in a person's general approach to work and play, playfulness should, in Lieberman's submission, be encouraged and developed throughout the lifespan of people.

Assuming this to be the case, we have to ask ourselves how playfulness can be developed. To develop spontaneity, Lieberman believes that there needs to be emphasis on gathering and storing facts beginning as early as the pre-school level. Only if the child has a storehouse of knowledge is there a basis for parents and teachers to encourage playing with various permutations.

Manifest joy is the ability of showing pleasure, exuberance, friendliness and generally positive attitudes in everyday life. The joy that the adult shows at the child's growing competence will lead to the child's own sense of pleasure in his or her activities.

The ability of engaging in 'good-natured ribbing, gentle wit, creative punning, as well as poking fun at yourselves and others', Lieberman includes in the category sense of humour. To develop this, a climate needs to be created which encourages 'psychological distancing'. Evidence was found that the cognitively more mature children preferred less hurtful expressions of humour. Humour is dependent on mastery of the situation; mastery can then lead to fun in learning.

Following Lieberman's argument, as we continue to learn throughout our lifespan, we therefore need to practise the psychological distancing which allows us to take the task at hand seriously, but not ourselves; we need to free ourselves from being preoccupied with ourselves and with our own problems, in order to cope, to be resourceful and for leisure to function as one of the means towards what Maslow [39] terms 'self-actualization'. Maslow stressed the need for individuals to develop to their fullest degree of independence and creative potential.

The next logical step to ask is how playfulness can help in our approach to leisure. It seems self-evident that any individual whose approach to everyday living embraces spontaneity, manifest joy and sense of humour would be able to deal in a creative way with free time. It is apparent, though, that many individuals have these traits and are not aware of them, or do not realize the benefits of applying them to leisure. Other people will need actively to practise them in order to make them part of their everyday repertoire. To what extent we can discover ourselves, our skills and aptitudes and acquire the ability of stepping back and laughing at ourselves, is an area yet to be explored.

2.4 Play and its implications for leisure services

The uniqueness and worth of each individual is the cornerstone of our culture. Ellis [40] states: 'Ideologically a human is most human when at play, as defined by our culture.'

Play is activity, physical or mental, freely chosen and indulged in for its own sake. It has intrinsic value and personal meaning for each individual. Play is life vividly expressed. The motives and feelings of ordinary life are lived through quickly, in abstract, but without the everyday contingencies of anxiety and fear. The major outcome of play is a feeling of regeneration. One is revived. As Sutton-Smith puts it: '"vive" leads to revival. One judges he has had fun' [41].

The implications of play for leisure and recreation services could be profound, yet play does not appear to have a central place in the institution of leisure and recreation services other than children's playgrounds. However, if people's lives are enriched by play – physically, intellectually and spiritually – and if play raises the tone of life and brings colour into people's lives, then it is indispensable to the well-being of individual people, and also of society. Therefore leisure professionals need to create situations and promote those factors that give the opportunity for play to occur and limit those factors militating against it.

From theories must come practice. A well used acronym today in playwork, building on the work of Hughes and Williams, is 'SPICE' – an approach based on an understanding of the significance of flexibility and the potential benefits of adult intervention in the child's environment: Social interaction; Physical activity; Intellectual stimulation; Creative achievement and Emotional stability.

Children need stimulating play from the earliest age. In terms of social behaviour and of later school attainment, children benefit from playgroups and this early learning experience, involving parents, can be of great advantage to both child and parent. Parental involvement in the out-of-home activities of their children is not found to the same extent in most other forms of provision. The community also benefits as parents, particularly mothers, put to wider use the skills they have learnt in running groups for under fives.

Can Leisure Managers 'organize' programmes to produce optimally arousing situations, offer opportunities for innovative experience where individuals control the content of their behaviour? Can we implant into recreation programmes the necessary ingredients such as exploration, investigation, manipulation, creativity and learning? For example, graded levels of instruction lead to complexity and creative problem-solving; clubs of like-minded people act upon each other to provide necessary complexity, and well presented events produce the drama for heightened arousal and awareness.

Society has need of many more innovative and vital people. Yet extending playfulness contributes to non-conformity, and some communities may well wish to limit it. The playfulness of young people – in growing up and mixing, in noisy rebelliousness and in their experimentation and testing the limits of the system – may be difficult at times for parents, schools and society in general to cope with. Leisure opportunities can give room to unfold some of the necessary adventurous behaviour patterns, without the inhibiting everyday constraints.

Play, in common usage, is clearly understood. Activities are seen as playful, non-productive, not instrumental in the process of survival, just play. In societies with a strong streak of puritanism, play, by virtue of its being unrelated to survival and production of profit, stands outside and inferior to the processes of work.

Play is often assumed to be free, the player not motivated by the end-product of the behaviour. By this argument, play cannot be controlled, planned, forced and still remain play. However, we can never be totally free, for we are always controlled to some extent by our environment. In addition, there are many examples of play being motivated by the end-product.

We refer to sport as being played by players. The study of play causes us to ask the question: how much do players in sport really play? The importance of the outcome, the external rewards (points, trophies, titles, press photographs and status) may make it all too externally serious to play, particularly when, for example, going through a losing streak in the competitive league. External pressures may then sap the *playfulness* of play. It is easy to overstate the case, the spirit of play still abounds at all levels. Nevertheless, it seems clear that the product orientation of winning, rather than process-orientation of playing well, plus the imposition of structures not of one's own making, can change the nature of the play experience. For games to remain in the domain of play, players should become part of the process of setting up structures, rules and controls. Indeed, administrators and officials of sports and arts may also be players – playing as much as the participants themselves. In spectator sports play elements may well be seen as much on the terraces as on the court. Yet tribal loyalty and gang warfare at soccer matches illustrates the way in which the play spirit can be destroyed by taking the game out of the play world into the real world of 'dog eat dog'.

2.5 The right to play

This book contends that play should be part of our leisure throughout life. However, play in childhood is essential. Lloyd George, in launching the National Playing Fields Association in 1926, attached the highest priority to play:

> The right to play is a child's first claim on the community. Play is nature's training for life. No community can infringe that right without doing deep and enduring harm to the minds and bodies of its citizens. Much that is un-wholesome and dangerous to the nation, comes from the overcrowding and congestion of our towns and cities and, in particular, from the restrictions and frustrations to which they subject the lives of the boys and girls who grow up in them.

Children's play can help to determine the type of people they are and the type of adults they will become; therefore we need to provide a carefully considered and guided variety of activities (freely chosen) for their development. Appropriate public provision for play is of the utmost importance. What was appealing to children before, or even yesterday, may not be appropriate today. There is a genuine concern that play areas and equipment need a refreshing and innovative approach.

It is salutory to consider the statements of Lady Allen of Hurtwood in *Planning for Play* [42] and their validity today:

> The need for *places* where children can participate in natural play activities as individuals and in groups is a consideration which should be given a very high priority. There are so few places where children can be themselves. Most that is interesting and stimulating around where they live has dis-appeared under concrete or other cold and uninteresting material. Housing now is functional, practical and clinically designed. There are very few places, if any, where children can indulge in private fantasy and creative play which often is noisy and messy. In almost every country of the world children live through long, empty hours, and they are criticized when they fail to develop positive interests and activities that involve effort and skill. But what are they to do? In Britain, their age shuts them out from Youth Clubs; they have few places outside their homes where they can meet friends; their homes are

often too tidy or too crowded for exciting work that may be messy; gardens are virtually non-existent. These children have no alternative but to use the street, with all its perils and frustrations. City children of school age who play in the streets often suffer from aimless boredom, or else they invent interesting and exciting activities which land them in the juvenile courts where much commendable initiative and enterprise has to be squashed. Valiant efforts are made by voluntary organizations to encourage young people to help themselves, but government and local authorities lend almost no support and waste their opportunities. A sense of responsibility cannot be inculcated in the young if the chances to practise it are eliminated, and it is up to the planners to provide these chances. Not all the so-called 'youth problems' are the fault of the young.

Today, in Britain, the situation is little changed in many areas. 'Latch-key' children are commonplace. As more women are attracted back to work, the situation can only get worse, unless substantial help is given to children's play, in addition to caring and 'baby sitting'. We live in a time of social anxiety.

2.6 Growing up in an uncertain world of social anxiety

Children are growing up in a rapidly changing world of uncertainty, and parents, guardians, carers and teachers have increasing concerns about them. Social anxieties exist due to lack of parenting, child neglect and abuse, crime, drugs, a more hostile, unsafe environment with inner city and rural deprivation, traffic problems, the lessening of play opportunity for many children and a culture of material competition, lacking appropriate values. Anxiety exists because of the apparent increase in violence and crime, which is rife among some children and young people on the one hand, and on the other, the neglect and abuse which some children are subject to. Latch-key children are a specific concern.

There is general concern at the poor levels of health and fitness of children. Many spend hours in front of a television set, sometimes watching video nasties, and the hypnotic effect of video games and virtual reality provide not what is real, but unreal. The danger is in encouraging a generation of computer-game-literate children, with finger dexterity, but who may be unable to throw and catch a ball or interact socially and emotionally. Fear of child molestation means that children are ferried to and from school and to and from leisure centres to go home to computer games. Young people need to test the limits – they need to feel free, adventurous, risk-taking. For teenagers, the rave party is quite understandable. It is hard to test the limits in front of a video screen or on a boring piece of play equipment.

Fears have been expressed among concerned parents that children are beginning to think that materialism matters greatly: if they do not wear Reebok shoes, they will not have friends! Children may see their worth in what they own, wear and how they look. Creative play lifts children from being trapped at such a functional level and helps to give them confidence in their own worth.

The enjoyment of physical activity can be inculcated through children's play; those who take up exercise, sports and games in childhood are more likely to continue into adulthood; indeed, later life health problems are in some measure the fruits of lack of childhood playing, poor diet and other factors. The variety of activities available to children today is extremely wide, but many children are living an increasingly isolated existence – ferried to and from school, spending hours watching TV and being driven to the places to play and swim and then driven back again. 'Inactive children are likely to become inactive adults, increasing the risks of obesity and heart disease. Trends set in childhood and adolescence become established, with the results often being seen years later' (Sports Council (c. 1990) *Children's Exercise*, Health and Fitness Fact Sheet).

Research at the University of Exeter [43] showed that half the girls and over a third of boys aged 11–16 did not even experience the equivalent of a ten minute walk a week. Twenty per cent were above appropriate cholesterol levels. 'Children have surprisingly low levels of physical activity and many children seldom experience the intensity and duration of physical activity associated with health-related outcomes. Boys are more active than girls and girls' activity levels deteriorate as they move through secondary school.'

A child without access to play will develop problems. 'Play on Prescription' has been devised, whereby GPs, health visitors and social workers can refer children with development or behavioural difficulties to special play sessions designed to help with the acquisition of language, physical and social skills.

Over 3 per cent of the child population in the United Kingdom are disabled and many are neglected in terms of their right to play. In addition, there are many thousands of children in mainstream public sector schools who have 'statements' of special needs. The play movement spans play in all settings, and opportunities for play in hospitals and for sick and disadvantaged children, are of much importance. The national organizations Action for Sick Children and the National Association of Hospital Play Staff support and enhance play for those who are in hospital.

Marriages within the United Kingdom fell from 459,000 in 1971 to 331,000 in 1994, yet divorce rates rose dramatically. In 1993 *Relate* organized in the United Kingdom a 'Children in Crisis' campaign to raise money to train more counsellors because divorce was having 'a devastating effect' on children, and 150,000 would be affected that year. There are about 1.3 million lone parents in Britain, 90 per cent female, bringing up 2.1 million children. A large proportion of these children have no contact with their fathers. Many lack family guidance and the support of the extended family. Three-quarters of lone parents depend on social security benefits. Lone parents often find themselves isolated and without financial and emotional support.

2.6.1 Children's loss of freedom

One False Move – A Study of Children's Independent Mobility (1990) [44] showed that child fatalities from road accidents in Britain had nearly halved over two decades. The government claimed that the roads have become safer, but the authors look at the underlying causes. In 1971, 80 per cent of 7 and 8 year-old children were allowed to go to school on their own. By 1990, only 9 per cent did so. Road accidents have declined 'not because the roads have become safer, but because children can no longer be exposed to the dangers they pose'. Moreover, parents have been increasing the time they spend escorting their children, further contributing to traffic congestion. The authors claim that the increase in personal freedom and choice arising from widening car ownership has been gained 'at the loss of freedom and choice for children'. Motorized travel has been responsible for the decrease in children's independence.

> The rise in the volume of traffic and its accompanying noise, pollution, danger and unpleasantness have contributed to a feeling of insecurity owing to the continuing decline of street life and, at the same time, to a rise in the proportion of people outside the home who are strangers. As a result, the fear of molestation has increased, especially after dark. . . . In a finite world, if more space is taken by traffic, there will be less for other purposes.

Children's enforced isolation robs them of their freedom and the opportunity of developing friendship patterns and the skills of socialization. As Sandra Melville of Playlink said, 'it is no use complaining about unsocial children when we take away their means of socialising'. We asked our grandchildren what was the highlight of their weekend with us: 'going to the shops *on our own*'. It was an adventure. Children increasingly play apart. Barnardo's *Playing it Safe* reported on the restricted lives of children, as anxious parents struggle to keep them safe. Children spend less time playing out of doors. There is a loss of their informal space.

Children's loss of freedom contrasts with two important pieces of legislation about their rights as individuals and to which we now turn.

2.7 The public sector and play provision

Resources for children's play are provided by the public, institutional, voluntary and commercial sectors. However, there is very little co-ordination and play delivery is fragmented. In the public sector, there is only a partial understanding of play. Play is perceived in narrow terms, and there is limited broad based provision. Even those councils that have a strategy for play in the main perceive play narrowly as playgrounds with safety surfaces, holiday play schemes and, recently, After School Clubs. Despite this emphasis, Kids Club Network reported that only one primary school child in a hundred had a summer playscheme place in 1995. KCN projects a need for 10,000 after-school clubs by the year 2010. Save the Children's *No Place to Play* reported similar findings (only sufficient summer placements for 10–15 per cent); particularly disadvantaged were low income families.

The paradox is that councils have sincere and caring attitudes to the needs of people and children, yet the resources given are wholly inadequate to meet the needs. Local Authorities have a mandate under the Children Act 1989 to care for children in need, but are not obliged to provide *play* services. Education, Health and Social Services departments have statutory roles in providing for children, but not children's play, *per se*. Leisure Services are discretionary, Arts Councils and Sports

Councils do not embrace play, and The National Lottery Charities Board is directed to the 'caring' services.

Certain services, of which play is a prime example, cross departmental boundaries and also find themselves within a mix of public, private, voluntary and institutional settings. They, and with them deserving, disadvantaged people, can lose out because leadership and funding criteria are not drawn up with their overall needs in mind. Play services, particularly supervised open access play for all, falls between the gaps. There is a need for a corporate approach, a coherent approach. There needs to be a consciousness about children and their needs.

Far too often, play provision is seen as caring for children while parents go to work or being looked after in school holidays or within 'closed' systems such as organized teams and coaching, uniformed groups and structured schemes. This emphasis on 'closed' systems hides the fact that children and young people need 'open' play opportunities with appropriate levels of supervision. Of late, the playcare model has attracted funding from government, business and parents and it is said by some that this has led to a loss of play opportunities for some children. However, boundaries are becoming blurred, with playcare schemes expanding to include drop-in services and play projects, such as open access holiday play schemes, being used as a form of child care (see 2.8.1).

The problem is not limited to the United Kingdom. In Australia, for example, over the past two decades, the workforce participation of women with primary school children has increased from less than 40 per cent to more than 70 per cent, and 57 per cent of women work full time. 'Vacation care is sometimes used as a punching bag by parents trying to resolve tensions about the working mother issue' (*The Australian*, 12 February 1993).

2.7.1 *Play, sport and leisure*

Integrating play and sport has always been an issue; sport which is taken so seriously can lose the spirit of play for its own sake. Children's sport is currently enjoying greater prominence, resulting in play-based development programmes such as the Youth Sports Trust/Sports Council 'Top Play', linking schools and local authorities to ensure progression from school sport to clubs. Governing bodies of sport have successfully introduced national schemes such as Startrack Athletics, Short Tennis, Soft Cricket and many other sports initiatives for children in Gymnastics, Swimming, Football and Rugby and Mini Movers, Tumble Tots and Mother and Toddler Swimming.

Play can also be an important feature of the Arts and Libraries services. Using libraries for music making, model making, games, quizzes, special projects and story reading are being encouraged, but only in a few areas. In the same way, play and the Museum Service, play in the parks, learning about the ecology and many other elements deserve far greater emphasis.

2.8 The government and children's play

In 1984, an independent agency, The Association for Children's Play and Recreation Limited (Play Board), funded by government at £700,000 per year, was established. The company went into liquidation in March 1987, in protest at the proposal to subsume Play Board into The Sports Council. Then, the National Children's Play and Recreation Unit (NCPRU), 'hosted' by the Sports Council, was set up for six years and funded by government at an equivalent of £700,000 per year from 1987 to 1993. It was to be an arms-length autonomous unit, with the Sports Council as 'Accounting Officer'. Thus, along with the Sports Council, the unit was transferred from the Department of Environment to the Department of Education and Science (now DfE), and finally to the Department for National Heritage (DNH), now the Department of Culture, Media and Sport (DCMS).

The National Children's Play and Recreation Unit ceased to be funded on 31 March 1993 and was disbanded. The Sports Council took on certain functions with effect from 1 April 1993. Having seen these two ventures (Play Board and National Children's Play and Recreation Unit) fail to secure a long-term future, the National Playing Fields Association commissioned and published an independent report, *A Review of National Support for Children's Play and Recreation* [1].

Following the disbanding of the National Children's Play and Recreation Unit, the DNH focussed its attention, through the Sports Council, on three main areas – dissemination of information, training in playwork and playground safety. These were put out to tender. The National Playing Fields Association won all three tenders in an integrated bid and took on the contract with a limited budget of only £400,000 per year for an initial three years.

2.8.1 Children's services

Children's Services Plans became mandatory from 1 April 1996 for Social Services departments in an Order under Section 17 (4) of the Children Act 1989. Guidance was issued jointly by the Department of Health, the Department for Education and Employment, the Home Office and the National Health Service Executive. The guidance encourages local authorities to listen to children, carers and parents, to involve them in planning and to take their views seriously. (The UN Convention on the Rights of the Child would be a starting point.) A number of underlying principles were set out by the National Children's Bureau:

> planning for children must start from the whole needs of the child and the needs of the local community; planning should begin with an assessment of children's real needs, not with preconceived ideas about which services can be provided; children benefit from a combination of care, education, play and health; the views of children and young people must be taken into account at all stages of the process.
>
> National Children's Bureau, May 1996

The government *Out of School Childcare Initiative* [45] has stimulated the development of different models of childcare provision. One model has come to be known as 'playcare'. In playcare, children attend a club for a fixed time period and do not normally leave unless they are collected by a responsible adult. Playcare services have been the main focus of the Training and Enterprise Councils' (TECs') out-of-school childcare strategies.

However, there is another model of supervised play provision for school-age children: 'open access play', where children are free to come and go. The play services run by play associations have largely been open access. Both types of service provide for children of a similar agegroup (predominantly 5–12 years), both should have competent staff and both recognize parental concerns about safety and security. However, open access play places its emphasis on the *play experience* of children and their rights to freedom to choose to come and go. Playcare emphasizes the need to *look after* the children of working parents, sometimes disparagingly referred to as 'child sitting' services.

2.9 Rights of the child

Sixty-five years after Lloyd George's often quoted passage on the rights of the child to play, the United Kingdom government committed itself to two hugely important legal declarations and policies: the *United Nations Convention on the Rights of the Child*; and the *Children Act*.

In 1991, the British government committed itself to the terms of the United Nations Convention on the Rights of the Child. This means that the United Kingdom's laws and the ways in which children and young people up to the age of 18 are treated should meet the standards laid down in the Convention. The Convention should be implemented by every arm of government, both central and local. The United Nations Convention on the Rights of the Child is now the most successful international treaty, in that by 1997 it had been ratified by 186 UN member states, with only two outstanding – Somalia and the United States of America. UNICEF is aiming for 100 per cent global ratification by the turn of the millennium. As play is fundamental to human development, all the Convention's Articles can be said to be relevant, but the following can be highlighted:

- *Article 31* – the right to rest and leisure, play and recreation, full participation in cultural and artistic life.
- *Article 24* – the right to be as healthy as possible and to live in a safe, healthy and unpolluted environment.
- *Article 23* – the right of disabled children to be as independent as possible and to be able to take a full and active part in everyday life.
- *Article 17* – the right of access to a wide range of information, especially any which will make life better for them.
- *Article 12* – the right to express a view and to be heard.

Article 31 is an essential cornerstone for leisure and recreation managers. It emphasizes the necessity of allowing children and young people access to leisure opportunities and the importance of consulting them on areas of leisure provision which affect them:

Article 31

1   Every child has the right to rest and leisure, to engage in play and recreational activities appropriate to the age of the child and to participate freely in cultural life and the arts.

2   Member governments shall respect and promote the right of the child to participate fully in cultural and artistic life and shall encourage the provision of appropriate and equal opportunities for cultural, artistic, recreational and leisure activity.

Childhood is a time for nurturing and a time for growing and developing. However, citizenship has to be inculcated. It doesn't just happen. In order for young people to be involved and to participate in decision making and to grow into citizens with roles and responsibilities, they need to be – in the jargon of today – 'empowered'. If not, the idea of inculcating 'citizenship' remains a pipe dream.

Article 12 of the UN Convention gives young people a fundamental right to participate in all decisions that affect them and to have their views given 'due weight'. The report, *Encouraging Citizenship*, emphasizes the need of young people to be equipped with knowledge and skills to help them to be more independent and understand the place and roles of various agencies in society. The National Curriculum Council has recommended that schools lay the foundation for citizenship by 'helping students gain and understand essential information' and 'providing opportunities and encouragement to participate in school life'. A new agency, 'Article 12', is an organization run by and for children and young people. It was launched in November 1996. Its main aim is to get the voices of young people heard, an objective enshrined in Article 12 of the UN Convention.

Alan Levy, a QC specializing in child law, says Britain needs to appoint a special champion to defend the rights and interests of children:

Britain is failing its children. In January, the UN Committee on the Rights of the Child attacked the government's record on children. It pointed out breaches of the UN Convention – ratified by this country in 1991 – rightly criticising Britain for failing to improve children's health, education and living standards, and condemned our criminal justice system for laying too much emphasis on imprisonment and punishment for young offenders.

Guardian 6 June 1995

2.10 The Children Act

On 16 November 1989, the Children Act received the Royal Assent and it came into force on 14 October 1991. It can be perceived as a unifying Act, replacing in part or whole 55 other Acts of Parliament, one going back 100 years! The focus of the Act is upon 'children in need' and the central role of local authority Social Services

Departments, but the duties and powers contained in the Act cover the widest range of services, well beyond the scope of any one local authority department. Key principles include:

- the recognition of the child as having an important place in the family and the community
- the right of the child to be cared for in the context of the family
- local authorities have responsibility for ensuring this whenever possible
- local authorities must argue a coherent case for a court to make a care order. The courts will only agree if it is better for the child.
- consideration of preventative services
- provision of a range of day care facilities which must be provided for children in need, *but may also be provided for all children.*

Considered in this wider perspective, the Act encompasses the role of leisure and play services in its work with children and their families. While ultimate responsibility for the registration of personnel and services lies with Social Services departments, what is also clear is that there should be corporate planning for childcare and supervised activities. Four factors appear to be of importance for local authorities: a) children are at the focus; b) all departments are involved separately and collectively – no one department has a 'right' in comprehensive provision; c) as play is crucial in the development of children, play needs to be included with all children's services; and d) a multi-disciplinary understanding of the many elements of play and recreation is necessary.

The main implications of all these matters are that local governments should positively plan for children rather than taking a narrow departmental and traditional perspective. To ensure that there are a range of services and support systems for children and their families, the Children Act commands local authorities to carry out four main duties: to provide; to publish; to review; and to register. Registration applies to the service that is open for two or more hours, whether or not the children stay for a shorter period.

Leisure officers and playworkers provide a number of services, including creches and playgroups; day nurseries; play schemes; after-school 'clubs'; activities in leisure centres – 'Tumble Tots', 'Mini Movers', ballet, trampolining and swimming classes; activities in museums and art galleries; adventure playgrounds; commercial 'Kids Play' centres; playbuses; city farms; theme parks; play spaces in shops and supermarkets; and holiday schemes in libraries, theatres and sport centres. These 'persons' (people and organizations) may need to be reviewed, inspected and registered. In very many cases, staffing, volunteers, programmes, equipment and facilities will need increase or improvement to comply with mandatory requirements in the Act. In local authorities, with cutbacks in services and reductions in financial support to voluntary organizations, the strict provisions of the Act can be used as reasons for not continuing with past projects and programmes. Regrettably, this has happened in some authorities.

The 1995 Children (Scotland) Act was founded on the principles derived from the UN Convention on the Rights of the Child and places a duty on local authorities to safeguard and promote the welfare of children and young people under 18 who are 'in need' by providing an appropriate range and level of service, to publish information and to prepare Children's Services Plans every three years, including plans for play. The Act defines a child 'in need' broadly as one who is unlikely to achieve a reasonable standard of health or development, or is disabled or affected by disability unless services are provided.

Although the Act is primarily concerned with social care and protection, play provision is a 'relevant' service in that if children are deprived of play, they will not achieve a reasonable standard of health and development.

2.11 Education Acts

Educational establishments potentially offer the greatest source of facilities for children's play and recreation. Outside the school timetable, however, they are used for children's play and recreation in only a minority of cases. The new Education Acts have created a climate and environment which can dramatically change the role of physical education, play and sport in school, the links between schools and the community and the management of community recreation.

The Education (No. 2) Act 1986 encouraged greater community use of school facilities and the Education Reform Act 1988 has directed financial and management responsibility from local education authorities (LEAs) to the governors of individual schools and, through the National Curriculum, has restructured the content of the curriculum in all subjects.

Linking school and community has always made sound sense, but the theory is not matched by good practice, particularly in terms of children's play and even after-school clubs have to rely heavily on non-school facilities.

The Education (Scotland) Act 1980 gave local education authorities powers to establish, maintain and manage camps, outdoor centres, playing fields, swimming baths, play areas and play centres, as well as to organize play events during school holidays.

2.12 Children, adventure and the great outdoors

Jean Jacques Rousseau, the eighteenth-century philosopher sought a return to a simpler and more primitive way of life; children, in particular need to be free to play in natural surroundings. Alas, as we have seen, far from being more free, children are more constrained today.

Playing for Real [46] is a colourful story about children's play capturing memories of our own childhood – 'it's never too late to play . . . or too early, growing, pretending, sharing and caring, playing catch, building, performing, working with junk and high tech and making sense of the world'. The spirit of the book is captured in the foreword by Sue Townsend (author of the Adrian Mole diaries):

> When I was a child, I was a member of a gang. Our territory consisted of a derelict manor house and its grounds, a large neglected orchard, mixed woodland and a spinney which had a clear water brook running through it.

Each season had its own particular delights. In the winter, the gang would push old fashioned prams to the coal yards, load up and struggle back up the icy hill. In the summer, we picked apples and pears and blackberries; in the autumn we roasted chestnuts over bonfires and brewed tea in old saucepans. . . . Playing was a serious business, without knowing it, we were preparing to join the adult world.

The underlying premise of the book is that the right to play must be recognized, understood and acted upon, 'then children will really experience a society that provides for their freedom to play safely and creatively. Not just in the home and the playground, but in the school, the street, and everywhere else that children need to play . . . they call it play and, for them, the fact that it's crucial to their healthy development is incidental.'

Adventure play is important for children and young people. The adventure playground, although not enjoying the high profile of the 1960s and 1970s, is of significance to the play of children and young people. An adventure playground provides opportunities for children to choose the ways in which they play. It is a place where children of all ages, under 'qualified', friendly supervision, are free to do many things that they can no longer do in crowded urban developments, or at home. They can climb, dig, light fires, cook, camp, garden, play games, paint, dress up, or simply just talk and make friends. The adventure playground can be a place for learning and for making relationships.

Because adventure playgrounds provide space and materials for children to create their own play world, they try out many things and learn to develop confidence in their abilities. The lack of structure allows for variability, change and flexibility. But adventure playgrounds tend to end up looking like junk yards, and important as they are, they have developed a reputation in some areas as 'good for the children; but not in my back yard!' However, the principle of the freedom to choose is fundamental to quality play experiences. These principles are extolled by PLAYLINK (formerly London Adventure Playground Association).

I Know Someone Who's Afraid of Sunflowers is the title of a book by Earthkids in 1989 [47]. The book is essentially a guide to good practice in the provision of environmental play opportunities for children of pre-school age to age eleven.

Nature Areas for City People [48] is a guide to the establishment of community wildlife sites. Many towns and cities would benefit from the provision of nature areas, especially in built up areas, and during the past decade, hundreds of nature areas have been established. All can benefit from living and working in areas which retain a closeness to nature, none more so than children.

Children Today [49] explored issues of rural isolation in Devon:

In some villages, there is no common or public land for children to play on, and the thin scatter of rural populations makes it difficult for children to meet others of similar ages and interests. Public transport tends to be infrequent or non-existent, and parents worry if their children go cycling.

The term 'inner city' conjures up the idea of a set of problems which include poverty, unemployment, poor standards in health, education, transport and housing, decaying buildings, crime, drugs and lack of social and recreational facilities. However, those who live in inner cities are not the only people affected by such problems. In the Duke of Westminster's report [50], crime, social unrest and tensions were said to threaten rural communities, but 'countryside' and 'rural' are not words which evoke the notion of problems.

But the problems and deprivation exist there. They are in many respects comparable with those in the inner cities. The same interests are at stake and the suffering is as great, but they do not attract the same attention. Action for people in rural areas should be taken now and it should be of the same urgency and intensity as the action which was eventually taken for the inner cities. Rural areas still have some of the social stability and cohesion which have been lost from the urban areas; it is essential that the fabric and character of rural society are not destroyed by the pressures which are now eroding them.

2.13   Play – a lucrative market in the private sector

The public sector has always considered itself to be the guardian of children's play space. Indeed, in most towns, the play areas are safer than ever before and some have high 'play value', but many are not attractive to children or their guardians. Playgrounds in parks are isolated. Playgrounds in urban and rural settings can be the gathering grounds for vandalism, smoking, drinking and drug abuse – by children and young people. And they can be playgrounds for dogs and cats and rubbish dumps, too. Parents want safe, supervised playgrounds. Those who can afford it are prepared to pay for such a service. Perhaps we will have pay-and-play playgrounds? We already have indoor play provision on such a basis.

It is estimated that within a few years, there will be 700 major sites for indoor play involving the large corporates, brewers, motorway services and shopping malls. Whitbread has over sixty *Charlie Chalk Fun Factories*. Scottish and Newcastle has *Funky Forest*, Greenall's Premier House, *Jungle Bungle*. The £2m *Action Stations* at Lakeside shopping centre in Essex provide children with a wrist watch with receiver, transmitter, chip and battery to keep a check. First Leisure's *Planet Kids* has a Smart Card system. At Blockbuster's *Discovery Zone*, children and parents wear matching coded labels. *Alphabet Zoo* is working with university sports science to incorporate educational and mobility best practice. This rapid growth will probably see market saturation and the collapse of smaller operations.

Birthday parties used to be about bringing friends home and families preparing and doing things together. Then there were party venues and 'bring your own'. Now we have the all-inclusive party with mum and/or dad simply acting as taxi drivers. Leisure centres are reporting an increase in each of the last three years. In the commercial sector, this is big business, particularly the knock-on business. Whitbread uses it as a marketing tool to develop family welcome and drive sales during quiet periods. They train 'fun leaders'. Pizza Hut puts staff on special courses, particularly those who are bright, out-going and patient. The concept of 'hosting' emphasizes the positive attitude of children perceived and treated as guests – being special. They find that feedback and research are vitally important.

The commercial sector has seen the huge potential in children's play based on market analysis and a marketing mix including low-price all-in packaging. Local authorities have been involved in giving free or low-cost services for children's play and outdoor playgrounds. But the message is clear: parents and children would rather pay for services at a price they can afford, than have free services (which may even be more beneficial), but which they do not want. While the private sector finds business opportunity in activities for children, many of the 'creations' offer more opportunities for learning and healthy activity than a boring piece of play equipment.

We all know that learning is so much more achievable when we have an interest and when it is fun in the doing. The 'play way' is needed at all stages of life and particularly in childhood. 'Play makes learning irresistible.'

Recently, the Science Museum in London opened its £3.5m investment, *Interactions*, encouraging children to explore, be inquisitive, learn through doing, be entertained and to appreciate beauty. *The Garden* for children three to six years old has visual and tactile features; the *Water Zone* harnesses the power of water; children can make dams and pump water; in the *Construction Zone*, hard hats are worn. Interactivity between children, adults, objects and the environment illustrates the need for children to be involved – that play is not something apart. It is about learning, sharing, friendships, relationships. Play is also the door to an appreciation of the arts, reading and sports participation.

2.14　Fair play in our time?

There is an argument which goes something like this: children play; they have always done so; it is part of our human nature. Why are we so obsessed with providing for what comes naturally? Surely we can provide for our own children? True. Children will continue to play despite adults' best efforts to inhibit opportunity and make things difficult!

So, why provide? First, because lack of provision will reduce potential positive benefits – social, physical, emotional and educational. Second, because play opportunity is being eroded. Children are unable, in many instances, to find places where they can be themselves, where they can experiment, test themselves and each other and play with natural materials such as sand, mud and water and experience adventure. And third, because we believe in equity and fairness. We provide for adult leisure, sports and arts with millions of pounds of tax payers' money; why not a fairer share for children?

It is not just about money and provision, however. It is about changing attitudes. I read in *Fair Play* of the Mobile Play Project worker who had gathered children on a public open space only to face angry residents and hear: 'What are you attracting them here for, we've spent ten years chasing them off?' Compare that with the statement of Javier Perez de Cuellar, former UN Secretary-General, in 1987: 'The way a society treats children reflects not only its qualities of compassion and protective caring, but also its sense of justice, its commitment to the future and its urge to enhance the human condition for coming generations.' Clearly, play shapes human behaviour and helps create future citizens who, we hope, will be more child-friendly than we are to the present generation of children and young people.

After food and shelter, one of the greatest human needs is for peaceful co-existence. Play offers the opportunity for developing relationships. President Roosevelt said peace in the world will only come if we cultivate the 'science of relationships'. A Victorian maxim used to be 'the family that prays together, stays together'. I wonder if the maxim 'the family that plays together, stays together' has validity also.

Bill Gates of Microsoft fame, the richest businessman in America, says that the new technologies with instant vision, sound and tele-conferencing will mean that in the future we will not need to meet. Communication will be the skill of transmitting information. But where will be the sharing, the fellowship, the bonds which go to make up that word 'community'?

2.14.1　Play is with us for life!

Paul Bonel [46] reminds us that play is with us for life. Adults too need to play.

> Play begins at birth and continues until we die. For adults, it's perhaps more comfortable to call it sport or recreation, art or leisure, but at some level and to some degree, we all play. For children, it is natural and necessary; they call it play and, for them, the fact that it's crucial to their healthy development is incidental.

However, adults, rather than take the opportunities for play, seem destined to search for ways to make all our time useful. The inability to find meaning in activities, in themselves, appears to drive many of us towards escape, to amusement and entertainment, and some to drink. We even set up parties for contacts, have luncheon dates for contracts and we attend civic functions to be seen and to 'network'.

The study of play teaches managers that the important thing, whether with children or adults, is to invest considerable decision making power in the hands of the participants. This is why some people like to belong to small autonomous groups, where they can feel creative and identified, where they can be masters of their own destiny, even for a short period of their routine lives. Recreation programmers would be foolhardy to omit autonomous groups, clubs and associations from their recreation programmes.

Another lesson from the study of play is to resist the temptation of controlling, administering and providing 'on a plate'. The process of controlling the content of our behaviour ourselves is important for the play element to flourish. More emphasis must be given to participation, rather than outcomes, and to a much broader range of activities that provides intrinsically rewarding play.

A child's world should be a world filled with wonder and excitement. Most adults appear to be separated or exiled from this childlike world. Yet we all need freedom and motivation to choose things of joy and wonder – to have one foot in the child's world. Despite their class culture, the Ancient Greeks' idea that life should be lived as play had merit; when they said 'Whom the gods love die young', perhaps they meant, like Lord Stankey, that those favoured by the gods stay young until they die.

2.15 Summary – play

Play is important to the lives of people. It has personal meaning for each individual. Play behaviour appears to be possible in almost any life situation. It can be readily observed, particularly in children, but there is little agreement as to a definition or explanation of why people play. There have been many theories of play. Classical theories may appear to have some 'common-sense' wisdom, but for the most part, they are archaic and not very helpful, with many logical shortcomings. Among the recent theories the learning, developmental and psychoanalytic theories show that play contributes to the development of intelligence and a healthy personality. Children gain pleasure, overcome unpleasant experiences and develop mastery of their physical and social environment.

Why play? There is no precise answer. Some claim that play is justification in and of itself without further rationalization, but animals play as well as humans and this seems to indicate that it performs some survival function. In addition, play does seem to be arousal seeking behaviour, a seeking out of novelty, a preparation for the unknown and children, especially, learn and develop through play.

The descriptions and explanations of play have been in the past too simplistic or obtuse. They have been obscure because of our failure to recognize that play cannot be conceived as a simple concept. Play is a complex set of behaviours – 'a million permutations of human behaviour'. As play is utterly individual and play activity can be seen at any time and in all life situations, it follows therefore that almost any situation or activity can function for someone as a play activity if undertaken in the spirit of play.

There appear to be several accepted characteristics of play in the absence of an exact definition. Play is activity of any kind, mental or physical. Play is undertaken freely and usually spontaneously. It is fun, purposeless, self-initiated and often extremely serious. Play is indulged in for its own sake; it has intrinsic value; and there is innate satisfaction in the doing. This has implications on leisure policies. If, for example, one general principle encouraged play for sheer enjoyment or for the satisfaction in the doing, then no matter who wins, no one loses. When there is nothing to lose, we 'go for our shots' untroubled by the fear of losing. The freedom to act and be ourselves is illustrated by Hoffer [51]: 'Men never philosophize or tinker more freely than when they know their speculations or tinkering leads to no weighty results. We are more ready to try the untried, when what we do is inconsequential. It is highly doubtful whether people are capable of genuine creative responses when necessity takes them by the throat'. Necessity may not, then, be the mother of invention. Invention may be the result of the freedom afforded by leisure.

The study of play has taught us that the activity itself, rather than a useful outcome, is the motivating force. However, play does have important functions for learning, for social development and in co-operation in 'playing to the rules', as even the most simple of games teaches. Indeed, the play group, more than parents or teachers, appears to be the principal agent of learning to get on with each other. Play and games are vitally important in our culture.

Play transports the player, as it were, to a world outside his or her normal world. It can heighten arousal. It can be vivid, colourful, creative and innovative. Because the player shrugs off inhibitions and is lost in the play, it seems to be much harder for adults with social and personal inhibitions really to play. Playfulness is a very important part of 'healthy' and 'wholesome' living, and it has implications for leisure behaviour and opportunity. Those people whose living embraces spontaneity, manifest joy and a sense of humour are probably better able to deal with the freedom and choice that are present in leisure. Play most often refers to the activities of children or to the 'childlike' behaviour in grown-ups. In this chapter we have seen that all (young and old) can play, but as Millar suggests: 'Adults sometimes just play but children just play far more' [52].

What has play to do with leisure and recreation management? Everything, because play is the cornerstone. Take the play element out of the activities of actors, sportsmen and women, recreational players or people just enjoying their formal or informal leisure and the essence of the activity is lost. Chapters three and four take us on to the themes of recreation and leisure.

Notes and references

1   Torkildsen, G. (1993), *A Review of National Support for Children's Play and Recreation*, National Playing Fields Association, London.
2   de Grazia, S. (1962), *Of Time, Work and Leisure*, Doubleday, New York, p. 359.
3   Huizinga, J. (1955), *Homo Ludens*, Beacon Press, Boston, MA.
4   Plato (1900), *The Republic of Plato* (translated by John Davis and David Vaughan), A. L. Burt, New York.
5   Aristotle (1926), *The Politics of Aristotle* (translated by Ernest Barker), Clarendon Press, Oxford.
6   Schiller, F. (1965), *On The Aesthetic Education of Man*, Frederick Ungar, New York.
7   Harris, W. T. (1887), *The Education of Man* (edited by F. Froebel), D. Appleton, New York; see editor's preface.
8   See Lehman, H. S. and Witty, P. A. (1927), *The Psychology of Play*, A. S. Barnes, New York.
9   Groos, K. (1901), *The Play of Man*, Appleton, New York.
10 Stanley-Hall, G. (1920), *Youth*, Appleton-Century, New York.
11 Patrick, G. T. W. (1916), *The Psychology of Relaxation*, Houghton Mifflin, Boston, MA.
12 Ellis, M. J. (1973), *Why People Play*, Prentice-Hall, Englewood Cliffs, NJ.
13 Ellis, M. J. (1973), uses the classification of 'classical' and 'recent' theories put forward by Gilmore, J. B. 'Play: a special behaviour', in Haber, R. N. (ed.) *Current Research in Motivation*, Holt, Rinehart and Winston, New York, 1966.

14   Feshbach, S. (1956), 'The catharsis hypothesis and some consequences of interaction with aggressive and neutral play', *Journal of Personality, 24*, 449–62.

15   Berkowitz, L. A. and Green, J. A. (1962), 'Simple view of aggression', *Journal of Abnormal and Social Psychology, 64*, 293–301.

16   Freud, S. (1974), *The Complete Works of Sigmund Freud*, Hogarth Press, London.

17   Wälder, R. (1933), 'The psychoanalytic theory of play', *Psychoanalytic Quarterly, 2*, 208–24.

18   Erikson, E. G. (1950), *Childhood and Society*, Norton, New York.

19   Klein, M. (1955), 'The psychoanalytic play-technique', *American Journal of Orthopsychiatry*, 25, 223–37.

20   Piaget, J. (1962), *Play, Dreams and Imitation in Childhood* (translated by G. Gattengno and F. M. Hodgson), Norton, New York.

21   Sutton-Smith, B. (1966), 'Piaget on play: a critique', *Psychological Review*, 73, 104–10.

22   The authors' ideas are reviewed in Ellis, M. J. *Why People Play*, Prentice-Hall, Englewood Cliffs, NJ, 1973.

23   Roberts, J. M. and Sutton-Smith, B. (1962), 'Child training and game involvement', *Ethnology, 1*, 166–85.

24   Caillois, R. (1961), *Man, Play and Games*, Free Press of Glencoe, New York.

25   Play Board (1985), *Make Way for Children's Play*.

26   Child, E. (1985), *General Theories of Play*, Play Board.

27   Norbeck, E., (1979), 'The biological and cultural significance of human play: an anthropological view', in *Leisure Today*, JOPERD, October 1979.

28   Hughes, B., and Williams, H. (1982), 'Looking at play', *Play Times*, September 1–5, and see also Brown, F. (1990), *Working with Children – A Playwork Training Pack*, Leeds Metropolitan University.

29   Freud, S. (1974), *Beyond the Pleasure Principle*, Hogarth Press, London, who also published *The Complete Works of Sigmund Freud*.

30   Erikson, E. (1965), *Childhood and Society*, Penguin, Middlesex.

31   Wälder, R. (1933), 'The psychoanalytic theory of play', *Psychoanalytic Quarterly, 2*, 1933.

32   Freud, A. (1946), *The Psychoanalytical Treatment of Children*, Imago, London.

33   Klein, M. (1937), *The Psycho-Analysis of Children* (2nd edition), Hogarth Press, London.

34   Barnett, L. (1979), 'Cognitive correlates of playful behaviour', in *Leisure Today*, JOPERD, October 1979.

35   Sutton-Smith, B. (ed.) (1979), *Play and Learning*, Gardner Press, New York.

36   Sylva, K., 'Play and learning', in Tizard, B. and Harvey, D. (eds), *Biology of Play*, Heinemann Press, London, 1977.

37   Barnett, L. (1976), The contrast between play and other forms of learning in pre-school children's problem-solving ability. Unpublished doctoral dissertation, University of Illinois.

38   Lieberman, J. N. (1977), *Playfulness: Its Relationship to Imagination and Creativity*, Academic Press, New York.

39   Maslow, A. (1968), *Toward a Psychology of Being* (2nd edition), D. Van Nostrand, New York.

40   Ellis, M.J. (1973), *Why People Play*, Prentice-Hall, Englewood Cliffs, NJ, p.1.

41   Sutton-Smith, B. in the Education and Leisure Conference, Liverpool University, 1974; can be found in a Columbia University Paper, *An Ideology for Play*.

42   Lady Allen of Hurtwood (1968), *Planning for Play*, Thames & Hudson, London.

43   Armstrong, N. and McManus, D. (1994), 'Children's Fitness and Physical Activity, A Challenge for Physical Education', *British Journal of Physical Education, 25* (1), pp. 20–26.

44   Hillman, M., Adams, J., and Whitelegg, J. (1990), *One False Move*, Policy Studies Institute, London.

45   Andrews, K. and Vernon, G. (Education Extra) (1997), *Out of School Childcare Initiative – Succeeding Out of School*, Department for Education and Employment, London.

46   Bonel, P. (1993), *Playing for Real*, National Children's Play and Recreation Unit, London.

47   Earthkids Project (1989), *I Know Someone Who's Afraid of Sunflowers*, The Urban Wildlife Trust, Birmingham.

48   Johnston, J. (1990), *Nature Areas for City People*, Ecology Handbook 14, London Ecology Unit, London.

49   Collins, M., and Melchan, A. (1992), *Children Today, A National Overview*, National Children's Play and Recreation Unit, London, and idem (1992), *Children Today in Devon*, National Children's Play and Recreation Unit, London.

50   *The Problems in Rural Areas*, (1992), A report of recommendations arising from an inquiry chaired by His Grace the Duke of Westminster, DL.

51   Hoffer, E. (1963), *The Ordeal of Change*, Harper & Row, New York.

52   Millar, S. (1968), *The Psychology of Play*, Penguin Books, Baltimore, MD.

Recommended further reading

National Playing Fields Association (1998), *Legislation and Children's Play*, NPFA, London.

National Playing Fields Association and National Centre for Playwork Education (North East) (1998), *National Strategy for Playwork Education and Training*, NPFA, London.

The Children's Society and National Children's Bureau (1998), *The New Charter for Children's Play*, The Children's Society and the National Children's Bureau, London.

Chapter three

Recreation

The word 'recreation' is sometimes interchanged with 'play'. However, recreation is perceived by most people as different from play, which is associated mainly with children. There is more blurring of definitions with the word 'leisure' but that is the subject of the next chapter. Here we focus on recreation.

First, recreation is introduced and put into historical context to show that, like leisure and play, it is not a simple phenomenon and that confusion is evident in our definition and understanding of what it is. Second, the range of ideas and theories about recreation is reviewed very briefly. Third, the recreation experience is debated. Fourth, a discussion and synthesis of ideas is attempted, which differentiates between recreation as an institution and as a process. Fifth, the implications for leisure services are noted, and sixth, the principles of recreation are perceived in the context of management. A summary of findings and issues relevant to community recreation is presented.

Having studied this chapter, readers will be able to understand the conceptual aspects and the make-up of recreation and appreciate their relevance in leisure planning and management. What will become clear to the reader is that recreation is perceived by most people as the organized leisure activities for personal and social benefits; yet for the professional manager, recreation must be perceived also as having intrinsic value.

One of the key learning points is that programmes and activities should give potential participants a wide choice of opportunity to enable them to experience satisfactions and benefits which, in turn, help to meet individual needs. A further insight into what these needs are can be found in chapter five, dealing specifically with the needs of people.

3.1 Recreation: an overview

The history of the organized recreation movement in the United Kingdom and in the United States is well documented, showing early developments in the late nineteenth and early twentieth centuries. There has been a close association between the recreation movement and the development of industrial society.

Many recreation theories view the concepts of play and recreation as one and the same thing. Others take the position that they are different entities. However, the view that recreation is adult activity and play is children's activity has been predominant.

The word 'recreation' stems from the Latin *recreatio*, 'restoration to health'. Hence traditionally the term has been thought of as a process that restores or recreates the individual. The historic approach in defining recreation has been to consider it as an activity that renews people for work, an approach which has obvious limitations.

While some definitions refer to recreation as *restoration*, most focus on it as a form of activity. Others, while corroborating the activity approach, apply the condition to it of social acceptance. Most view the activity as unobligated. For example, the *Dictionary of Sociology* defines recreation as 'any activity pursued during leisure, either individual or collective, that is free and pleasureful, having its own immediate appeal, not impelled by a delayed reward beyond itself'. Hutchinson [1] supports the social acceptance theory; recreation is 'a worthwhile, socially acceptable leisure experience providing immediate, inherent satisfaction to the individual who voluntarily participates in activity'.

Some authors look to recreation as being morally 'sound' and 'mentally and physically upbuilding'. Romney [2] believes that recreation is not a matter of motions, but rather emotions: 'It is a personal response, a psychological reaction, an attitude, an approach, a way of life.'

Many recent definitions, however, do not regard recreation as being the opposite of working, nor as being morally sound or even as being activity at all; Avedon [3], and Gray and Greben [4], for example, look to recreation as providing personal well-being.

It is evident that there is considerable confusion both in a definition and an understanding of recreation. While it would be easy to say 'it is whatever you think it is', that is hardly a means of explanation. The confusion that does exist was portrayed dramatically in an editorial in *Parks and Recreation* [5], which listed approximately two hundred words or phrases describing how recreation was perceived by different people!

3.2 Recreation theories

It is clear that recreation, like leisure and play, is a far from simple concept to grasp and to understand. Indeed, hundreds of writers have attempted so to do and the literature is filled with a plethora of theories, a fact which cannot be escaped or ignored. There follows a brief summary of some of the definitions, which represent the range of ideas. More important, however, is the possibility that each description has some element of 'truth', which can aid our appreciation of what it is we are dealing with.

Hundreds of theories of recreation exist. They do not fall into any clear or logical categories. Most of them embrace a large number of interrelating elements, such as need-serving, satisfying experiences, associated with activity, of value to society, and so on. Most theories, too, appear to overstress values, outcomes and 'wholesomeness'. The research is so confused and overlapping that an attempt is made below simply to highlight some of the main approaches to an understanding.

3.2.1 Recreation as needs-serving

Slavson [6] describes recreation as a 'need-serving experience'. Whatever the choice of recreation, each individual seeks to satisfy some inner need. Recreation is a response to pleasure cravings. But such a description concerns what recreation does, not what it is. Jacks [7] defines recreation as the 're-creation of something that gets damaged in human beings . . . the repair of human damage where it is repairable, and the prevention of it in the rising generation'. This also is an inadequate definition, in that it mixes biological need with social need.

Nash [8] also sees recreation as a means for satisfying the human need to express inner urges and drives. He evaluates activity in terms of the degree of creative social contribution. Recreation, therefore, serves both individual and society. Nash's romantic view of recreation is captured in his equating happiness within terms of recreation activity:

> The happy man paints a picture, sings a song, models in clay, dances to a call, studies the stars, seeks a rare stamp, builds a cabin, raises pigeons, digs in the desert, romps with his grandchild, reads the Koran, dreams of rushing rivers and snow-capped peaks . . . he has a hundred things yet to do when the last call comes.

3.2.2 Recreation as leisure-time activity

By far the most widespread definitions and the ones most acceptable to providers of recreation services are that recreation is simply those activities in which people participate during their leisure. For example, the Neumeyers [9] define recreation as an activity, either individual or collective, pursued during one's leisure time.

The problem with this traditional view of recreation as activity is that it is heavily slanted in certain preconceived directions. Indeed, so much so, that to many people recreation is synonymous with *physical* recreation and sport. In addition, providers tend to provide for activities and feel they are providing for recreation, without knowing which activities are the most appropriate and whether they are meeting the needs of people. Moreover, there is no universally accepted definition of what constitutes people's leisure.

The Sports Council report, *Professional Training for Recreation Management*, describes recreation as 'the purposeful use of leisure time' [10]. Other official documents refer to it as 'the wholesome use of leisure time'. A Countryside Recreation Research Advisory Group report defined recreation as 'any pursuit engaged upon in leisure time, other than pursuits to which people are normally "highly committed"'. Such a narrow view excludes the notion of recreation activities as 'serious leisure' (see Section 4.8 on 'casual' and 'serious' leisure).

3.2.3 Recreation as value to individual and society

Recreation has been dogged by having to live up to a standard of high moral and social value for the 'good' of the individual and society. The moral connotations are held strongly by many writers, such as Miller and Robinson [11], Meyer and Brightbill [12], Butler [13] and many others.

Miller and Robinson see recreation as the process of participation in leisure from a specific perspective of leisure values. Play is free, happy and expressive behaviour that contributes to childhood development. Recreation does not necessarily contain play, but must always have a particular value framework related to appropriate and satisfying use of leisure.

Meyer and Brightbill propose that recreation contains the following characteristics and these contribute to fulfilling human needs – i.e. action, variety of form, motivation towards enjoyment, engagement during leisure, voluntary participation, universality, purposefulness, flexibility, creation of by-products. Recreation is also an attitude of mind regarding leisure behaviour and has a direct influence on those factors which create personality. It can produce feelings of well-being, satisfactions, pertaining to positive identity, growth, creativeness, balanced competition, character, mental capacity, dignity of the individual, physical conditioning, socialization and a coping attitude!

Not surprisingly, Meyer and Brightbill view recreation as a social force. But such value orientations placed on recreation are questionable. Such descriptions may well overstress presumed recreational benefits, and resulting services based on such presumptions might repel people rather than attract. However, there is no shortage of supporters for such an orientation. Butler takes a similar view; he sees recreation as a force influencing people's lives, and as a system of services which provide 'wholesome' experience, to counteract disruptive social influences.

It is logical to perceive that from this value orientation 'wholesome' individual recreation will lead to recreation as an influence for social 'good'. From their viewpoint, community recreation is a means for improving and maintaining societal cohesion and the quality of life; its development is dependent on social participation. Hence community recreation is a system of services for wholesome, positively sanctioned activities.

3.2.4 *Recreation as a re-creation*

Most theorists have concentrated on the value of recreation, and the outcomes of recreation. They have not addressed themselves to the recreation experience itself. Shivers [14], in *Principles and Practices of Recreational Services*, focusses attention on 're-creation', although he treats play and recreation as virtually synonymous. Building on a theme of homeostasis (the process by which the body continues to produce the chemical balance necessary to maintain life; the process by which equilibrium is maintained), Shivers builds up to a definition of recreation based on the construct 'psychological homeostasis' – i.e. the satisfying of psychological needs, the process of mental balance.

He reasons that if homeostasis is the condition that motivates behaviour, it must also serve as the motivational stimulus for recreation. When there is imbalance, we move towards re-balance in which harmony and accord between self and the environment are found. Shivers claims that this balance may be restored through recreation. Recreation is 'any consummatory experience, non-debilitating in character' [15]. It produces unity and harmony within the individual. The unity of mind and body (*psyche* and *soma*) brought about at the time of 'consummation' is recreation. The distinguishing feature is its consuming and absorbing quality. It has the power to seize and hold one's attention to such an extent that the very meaning of subjective time and environment disappears from view. In this respect, it fulfils the need for psychological homeostasis. Hence the individual experiences a balance or temporary harmony at the point of complete fulfilment from which stems a feeling of *re-creation*, or re-birth. This realization of totality (i.e. complete integration by the individual within himself or herself) is the recreational focus.

The basic difference between recreational value and recreation itself is in time rather than degree. Recreational value will be noted after the consuming experience has occurred, whereas recreation itself occurs at the time of the experience. This unity of mind and body Shivers describes as the 'unity concept' of recreation.

This theory has value, in that it focusses our attention on what actually happens. However, there are a number of problems, for example, such complete absorption is rarely achieved and the theory raises the question of whether every satisfying experience is recreation. However, if recreation is essentially an *experience*, it is central to the provision of recreation services. Yet very little is known about the 'experience', what it is and what it does for people. Furthermore, planners and providers have come far in the development of recreation facilities, programmes and services with so little understanding of the result that they are trying to produce!

There have been some investigations into people's perceptions of recreation and the experiences they encounter but the findings have no scientific validity and further studies are needed. One piece of research elicited from college students, via self-reporting techniques, the most significant and memorable recreation experiences they had ever had. The results were reported by Gray [16] (Table 3.1). Reactions to personal 'recreation experiences' indicate that recreation is a highly significant component of total life experience. It also suggests that activities that do not generate some of these kinds of feeling may fail to produce a recreational result.

TABLE 3.1 What is this thing called recreation?

- Heightened or reduced sensitivity to temperature, colour and smell
- Time distortion: 'time stood still', 'an hour seemed like a minute'
- Anticipation and expectation
- Escape: 'getting away from it all'
- Novelty; the sense of 'for the first time' brings freshness and uniqueness
- Relaxation, including release from social convention and personal demands
- Self-testing; challenge; and achievement, competence and self-worth
- Improved self-image: 'In the end we all experience only ourselves'
- Feeling a part of nature; beauty and awe
- Heightened appreciation and unusual perception
- Culmination; a turning point; reward for extended preparation; a watershed life event
- Heightened insight; perspective clarity; illuminating experience; flashes of insight
- Order; regularity; clear and precise limits; rules
- Introspection; sorting out of life experience; release from sensory overload, contemplation; and communication with oneself
- Communion; love; friendship and identification with a group (perhaps the strongest single motivation for many recreation activities is the wish for social response)
- Personal development; learning; and extension of ability
- Refreshment; personal renewal; and recovery of powers
- Common experience; shared hardships; and teamwork
- Risk; apprehension; fear – being frightened is a part of the extraordinary experience
- Unity of mind and body; grace, co-ordination
- Feelings of excitement, freedom, control, power, creativity, inner peace, harmony, reward, competence; recreation experiences are a powerful stimulus to emotional response

Note: The table is an abridged selection and adaptation from *Parks and Recreation* [16]

3.3 Recreation – any kind of satisfying experience?

In broad terms, recreation can be considered as activity and/or experience. But is recreation *any* kind of satisfying experience? If so, recreation then becomes all of life's satisfying experiences. While philosophically this might be supported, in practical terms such a scope could make it far too wide and all-embracing to deliver and manage recreation services. Taking Shivers's belief that recreation is any consuming non-harmful experience, it could be interpreted as everything and nothing as far as recreation management is concerned.

Gray and Pelegrino [17] have adopted a similar definition, which is psychological in nature; recreation is defined in terms of a person's experiences:

> Recreation is an emotional condition within an individual human being that flows from a feeling of well-being and satisfaction; it is characterized by feelings of mastery, achievement, exhilaration, acceptance, success, personal

worth and pleasure. It reinforces a positive self-image. Recreation is a response to aesthetic experience, achievement of person's goals, or positive feedback from others. It is independent of activity, leisure or social acceptance.

It is what happens within a person that determines whether or not recreation occurs. The unity within oneself, the mood and the situational elements themselves all go to make up the recreational experience. Hence participating in an activity does not in and of itself provide recreation. The psychological response of the individual is what determines what is recreation for him or her.

There is an apparent drawback to the school of thought that defines recreation as any experience at all: it loses any connection to either leisure or activity. Graham and Klar sum up the practical difficulties [18]:

> Should all positive feelings be categorized as recreation? Is the scientist's moment of discovery recreation? Or the student's feeling of satisfaction with a term paper well done? If we assume that recreation is independent of either leisure or activity, virtually all satisfying experiences become labelled recreation which seems too far reaching and presents barriers to communication since that is not the context in which most people view recreation.

> Practically speaking, this definition will not be easily applied as it now stands since it incorporates so many types of experience. The psychological focus provided by Gray, however, is important and should be uppermost in the minds of leisure service practioners.

In their interim report the Recreation Management Training Committee [19] stated as their reference point: 'We take recreation to mean any life-enhancing experience which is the outcome of freely chosen activity.' Here experience is allied to activity. Graham and Klar [20] take the matter closer to 'recreation' activity. It is imperative, they believe, to put the experience into a recreation setting to achieve understanding: recreation experience occurs as a direct result of involvement in a recreation activity. It is an emotional condition providing inner satisfactions and feelings of well-being. They define a recreation experience as:

> positive emotional response to participation in a recreation activity, defined as such by the individual or by a sponsoring agency or organization. Responses associated with the recreation experience include feeling good about self and others, experiencing a sense of inner calm or personal satisfaction, or feeling an enriched sense of self-worth which results from motivators of either an intrinsic or extrinsic nature. There is a clear absence of stress and tension which produce anxiety; the joy of re-creative experience is achieved. The essence of the classical view of leisure is achieved.

The principal difference between such a definition and that of Gray is that it is not independent of recreation activity. It is related both to leisure and activity. It therefore avoids the broadness of definition that views all positive experiences as recreation, which is extremely difficult to put into any operational context. Graham and Klar perceive recreation in narrower terms, but they retain the psychological component.

3.4 Recreation – an institution and a process?

Confusion exists in our understanding of how we can translate individual recreation into community-sanctioned activity. We have seen that recreation can be viewed as an activity and as an experience. Extrapolating from the recreation activity focus, recreation is to do with promoting activities, providing facilities, programmes and opportunities. As such, recreation can be perceived as a structure, an institution. Following the experience focus, recreation is viewed as something which is personally motivated. In this sense, it can be perceived as a process of what happens to an individual. Thus on one hand recreation can be perceived as a directing social force, and on the other hand as an inner-directed experience.

3.4.1 Recreation as a social process

Recreation experience, according to Murphy [21], is a process whereby the human organism strives to reach optimal arousal levels, the primary ingredients of which are exploration, investigation, manipulation and learning behaviour. (Such a theory of recreation is akin to the play theory in chapter three put forward by Ellis.)

Murphy, like several writers before him, lists an impressive array of physical, psychological, social and educational values as the potential outcomes of recreation. He views recreation, for example, as a process towards self-realization, fostering interaction, novelty, challenge, diversity, adventure, identity and other qualities. It would appear that many of these needs are not being met through recreation programmes, and he believes that a shift of emphasis towards an enabling community catalyst role will come about as a reflection of changing social demands. He puts forward a humanistic perspective for recreation services and believes that basic needs can and should be satisfied through recreation participation. In these terms, recreation should be viewed from a process orientation, in order to see its role in the dynamics of change. Thus, to Murphy, recreation and leisure services are processes.

The process perspective includes aspects of psychological response rather similar to play – i.e. fulfilment, satisfaction in the doing. Recreation requires freedom and activity and seems to absorb the participant to the point of complete involvement. A related element appears to be creativity both in process and outcome and recreation may well culminate in peak experience.

3.4.2 Recreation as a social institution

Kraus [22] takes some important and differing views from many of the foregoing authors. Recreation is more than a conceptual framework, a kind of activity or a condition of existence. Instead it refers to all the social institutions which have been formed to meet the leisure needs of people. It includes activities and organizations which are sponsored by government at various levels, schools, churches, industries, voluntary agencies and the business world – all of which provide varied recreational opportunities [23].

Kraus challenges many of the theories put forward: voluntary participation is dependent on available choices; immediate gratification does not necessarily occur with many activities that take time to master before they become fully satisfying; and participating without extrinsic motivation is questioned – people engage in activities, often with goals in mind, and are motivated by external reasons. Community-based recreation is concerned with reinforcing the prevalent value system and must therefore provide a structured and manageable service which often precludes such aspects as voluntary, immediately satisfying and intrinsically based participation.

Avedon [24] supports the social institution argument. He points out that, as in the case of other social institutions, 'recreation has form, structure, traditions, patterns of operation and association, systems of communication, and a number of other fixed aspects'. Kraus [25], in the second edition of *Recreation and Leisure in Modern Society* concludes that recreation has emerged as a 'significant' social institution: 'Once chiefly the responsibility of the family, the church or other local social bodies, it has now become the responsibility of a number of major agencies in our modern industrial society.'

The *Dictionary of Social Sciences* defines an institution as 'an aspect of social life in which distinctive value-orientations and interests, centering upon large and important social concerns, generate or are accompanied by distinctive modes of interaction'. The term 'institution' is therefore different from the term 'association'. An association is essentially composed of people, while an institution is essentially composed of interactions and interrelationships. They are social patterns that have distinctive value orientations, they direct the behaviour of human beings and characteristically tend to be permanent and to resist change. They exist because they have been reasonably successful in meeting societal needs. Recreation in a collective social setting can thus be perceived as a social institution.

3.5 Recreation and its implications for leisure services

Recreation, as we have seen, can be described and defined in a number of ways. Two main ways of perceiving recreation are from an activity focus (the activities which we call recreation) and from an experience focus (the experience we enjoy from actively or passively taking part). From an activity base, recreation is seen to be an activity related to sports, games, art and other leisure-time pursuits. In this respect, recreation is product-orientated and concerned with facilities and programmes. The activity focus presents recreation as a structure, a framework and as a social institution in society.

The experience focus is process-orientated and the concern is on what an activity does for a person. Its concern is with well-being and self-fulfilment. The experience focus is perhaps more play-like in spirit. A recreation experience can occur in varying degrees depending on the level of satisfaction experienced, much the same as other feelings, which may be of stronger or weaker intensity. This is consistent with the theory of self-actualization advanced by Abraham Maslow. Hence recreation can be regarded as a means to an end, or as an end in itself.

Looking at recreation experience, it follows that whatever activity or situation renews, revises, refreshes and re-creates for the individual, is a recreation for him or her at that time. This has far-reaching implications for recreation services. Any activity implies no right or wrong, no good or bad; no moral issues are at stake. But society will not allow just any activity. Even while many liberal views are held in Western society, individuals are still constrained, and inevitably so, in what is and what is not acceptable behaviour.

Throughout its history, recreation has kept its moral tag and this has been part of its non-appeal for many people. Modern society, with its wide interpretation of what is moral and what is socially acceptable, casts doubt on to the value of identifying recreation with high ideals of morally sanctioned behaviour.

In recent times, greater attention has been given to the debate as to whether recreation is primarily determined by the nature of the activity, the attitude of the player towards the activity or the player's psychological state during the activity. Inherently there is a belief in the right of the individual to self-expression, the expanding of experiences and horizons, but within society's social ethic.

3.5.1 Recreation, well-being and leisure

A relatively new concept is that of well-being, permeating the public and private health and leisure sectors in many parts of the world, and spawning a commercial industry in the USA and beyond. What is the relationship between well-being and recreation?

The impact of recreation on well-being was studied by the Western Australian Government [26]. 'Recreation', as defined by the community, included 'any activity that was undertaken in discretionary time and about which the participant had a choice'. It included active and passive elements. Indeed, involvement in passive recreational activities was the most widespread among the sample of people surveyed. All these activities could equally come under the banner of 'leisure'. Respondents found it difficult to define well-being, but an almost perfect correlation was found between 'satisfaction with one's life' and well-being. Contributing factors included: health and self-esteem; interpersonal relationships; and participation in recreational activities. Increasing satisfaction with recreation activities directly affected well-being and this held true for all ages.

The research demonstrated that recreational activities are far more diverse than competitive sport and non-competitive fitness activities. Recreational activities include a wide variety of both active and passive pursuits. Providers of recreational facilities and services, such as local government authorities, must meet this wider agenda.

3.6 Recreation and management

The leisure professional has to live in a world of recreation traditions, systems, institutions and facilities, together with vociferous demands, employers, budgets and politicians. A Recreation Manager cannot therefore present a complex picture of what recreation is. The problem in viewing recreation solely as experience is that it is almost impossible to define operationally, and it is difficult to communicate with understanding. We therefore need to find tangible criteria on which to base planning, management and programmes. For the leisure professional to communicate with policy makers and public alike, it may be appropriate and beneficial to talk in terms of recreation experience arising out of recreation or leisure activity.

Although recreation can occur at any time, and almost any situation can function for it to occur, it is during free time for leisure that recreation is more likely to come about. Furthermore, recreation experience is more likely to be 'felt' if the following factors are incorporated into recreation programmes and activities.

1   Recreation is personal, therefore activities should be concerned with individual satisfactions.
2   Recreation is concerned with freedom, therefore programmes should offer a satisfactory choice.
3   Recreation is refreshing, therefore activities should have immediate value, be novel and stimulating.
4   Recreation can be found in any activity, physical, social, intellectual and spiritual, therefore programmes must be concerned with the whole person.
5   Recreation is creative, therefore programmes should have concern for the indirect benefits and creations which arise from the activities.
6   Recreation will often arise through play, therefore opportunities for participation in the spirit of play, with the players in control, need to be encouraged.
7   The fullest recreation experience is found in oneness and unity, therefore activities should be sought which give opportunity for 'peak' experiences.

Most people find no difficulty in identifying informal games of soccer, volleyball or netball as recreational, or in perceiving swimming, cycling, climbing and arts and crafts as recreation activities. These are the activities that have been offered by recreation administrators, clubs and organizations. Recreation has become institutionalized in so far as we have a common understanding of the services, activities and events offered as part of the recreation service.

3.7 Summary – recreation

'Recreation', like any other word, is an abstract symbol, having many meanings, depending on the context in which it is used. It has perhaps a ring of condescending moral, puritan authority: whether you like it or not, take it; it does you good. In this context, physical recreation is close to the outmoded concept of 'muscular Christianity'. The word 'recreation' suggests leisure activities, recuperation, relaxation, pleasure, satisfaction – but these do not reveal its nature. It is traditionally seen as an action performed. Its outward manifestation indeed is that, but it contains a more inclusive meaning as well. Recreation for the individual can be a matter of emotions rather than motions.

Recreation as a concept of activity is understood. Recreation as an inner personal experience is yet to be understood, but it is from an individual, as well as collective orientation, that community recreation planning, programming and management should be built if people's needs are to be met.

The term 'recreation' can be used in a variety of ways. One may look at it within its traditional, institutional framework of activities, programmes, facilities and in the context of *homo ludens*, 'man the player'. Recreation can also be considered as an activity performed, a set or cluster of activities or leisure-time expressions. It has also been defined as a social institution and as a professional service. This stance is understood and generally accepted by society. However, what the experience of recreation is, and what it does for people, is of the essence to purposeful planning and management of recreation.

From its re-creative centre, recreation can be seen as the new person, the 'aah feeling', the job well done, success, the top of the mountain – 'Eureka!'. The experience is the moment itself; recreation value is post-experience: a game of squash (under this definition), where the player feels let down with a poor performance or poor attitude, would not be recreation. A mother who normally is reinvigorated after a weekly relaxing sauna but has had to cut short her visit because the children are to be home early from school may lose the completeness of the recreative experience.

Why recreation? There is no accepted scientific explanation. It is generally accepted that while we need to maintain a state of biological equilibrium, psychologically too we need to restore a mental balance. However, we also seek some degree of stress or activity that provides meaning to existence. Stress in effort helps to provide a form of biological and psychological 'tone', analogous to muscle tone. Effort, however, must be recognized by the individual as worthwhile, whether 'work' or 'leisure'.

In terms of recreation management, recreation is not only individual, but also collective and deeply entrenched in systems of public recreation, sport, art and physical education. The complexity and the interrelationships make it almost impossible to construct a unified theory. One definition which meets many of the points put forward in this chapter relating to the multi-faceted phenomenon of recreation and which comes close to an all-round description is proposed by Kraus [25]:

Recreation consists of activities or experiences carried on within leisure, usually chosen voluntarily by the participant – either because of satisfaction, pleasure or creative enrichment derived, or because he perceives certain personal or social values to be gained from them. It may also be perceived as the process of participation, or as the emotional state derived from involvement. . . . When carried on as part of organized community or voluntary agency programmes, recreation must be designed to meet constructive and socially acceptable goals of the individual participant, the group and society at large. Finally, recreation must be recognized as a social institution with its own values and traditions, structures and organizations, and professional groups and skilled practioners.

Hence recreation can be viewed as personal experience (what it does to a person); as activities (the forms it takes); or as an institution (the structure in which it is made available to the community). Taken yet another way recreation can be viewed as a process (what happens to an individual), and as a structure (the framework in which recreation is practised).

Regardless of what we perceive the word to mean, in practical terms, recreation appears to be good both for individual people and collectively for the community. A balanced lifestyle is important to an individual's well-being. It follows that improving people's satisfaction with recreation will increase their well-being and their quality of life. All providers of such services – public, voluntary and private – have a role to play. It is local government, however, with its mandate to educate and serve its citizens, which has the responsibility to ensure opportunity for all. Providing for or enabling community recreation is money well spent. Clearly, participating in recreation activities can have a positive effect on our well-being, self-esteem and confidence.

Notes and references

1   Hutchinson, J. L. (1949), *Principles of Recreation*, A. S. Barnes, New York, p. 17.
2   Romney, G. O. (1945), *Off the Job Living*, A. S. Barnes, New York, p. 14.
3   Avedon, E. (1974), *Therapeutic Recreation Service*, Prentice-Hall, Englewood Cliffs, NJ.
4   Gray, D. E. and Greben, S. (1974), 'Future perspectives', *Parks and Recreation*, July, 27–33 and 47–56.
5   Gray, D. E. and Greben, S. (1979), 'Wanted: a new word for recreation', *Parks and Recreation*, March, 23.
6   Slavson, S. R. (1948), *Recreation and Total Personality*, Association Press, New York.
7   Jacks, L. O. (1932), *Education through Recreation*, Harper & Row, New York.
8   Nash, J. B. (1953), *Philosophy of Recreation and Leisure*, C. V. Mosby, St Louis, MO.
9   Neumeyer, M. and Neumeyer, E. (1958), *Leisure and Recreation*, Ronald Press, New York.
10 Sports Council (1969), *Professional Training for Recreation Management* (Chairman, D. D. Molyneux), Sports Council, London, p. 5.
11 Miller, N. P. and Robinson, D. M. (1963), *Leisure Age: Its Challenge to Recreation*, Wadsworth, Belmont, CA.
12 Meyer, H. D. and Brightbill, C. K. (1964), *Community Recreation*, Prentice-Hall, Englewood Cliffs, NJ.
13 Butler, G. (1968), *Introduction to Community Recreation*, McGraw-Hill, New York.

14 Shivers, J. S. (1967), *Principles and Practices of Recreational Services*, Macmillan, New York.
15 *ibid.*, p. 90.
16 Gray, D. (1980), *Parks and Recreation*, March 62–4, 94.
17 Gray, D. and Pelegrino, D. (1973), *Reflections on the Recreation and Park Movement*, William C. Brown, Dubuque, Iowa, p. 6.
18 Graham, P. J. and Klar, L. R., Jr (1979), *Planning and Delivering Leisure Services*, William C. Brown, Dubuque, Iowa, p. 7.
19 Department of the Environment (1978), *Recreation Management Training Committee: Interim Report*, Discussion Paper (Chairman, Anne Yates), HMSO, London, p. 5.
20 Graham, P. J. and Klar, L. R. Jr (1979), *Planning and Delivering Leisure Services*, William C. Brown, Dubuque, Iowa, p. 8.
21 Murphy, J. (1975), *Recreation and Leisure Service*, William C. Brown, Dubuque, Iowa.
22 Kraus, R. (1971), *Recreation and Leisure in Modern Society* (1st edition), Goodyear, Santa Monica, CA.
23 *ibid.*, p. 263.
24 Avedon, E. (1974), *Therapeutic Recreation Service*, Prentice-Hall, Englewood Cliffs, NJ. p. 47.
25 Kraus, R. (1978), *Recreation and Leisure in Modern Society* (2nd edition), Goodyear, Santa Monica, CA, 1971, p. 37.
26 The Marketing Centre (undated c. 1995–6), An Executive Summary of *The Community Value of Recreation and its Relationship to Well-Being*, Ministry of Sport and Recreation, Western Australian Government.

Chapter four

Leisure – towards a philosophy and understanding of its evolution

This chapter starts and ends with questions relating to a philosophy of life and leisure. It traces the evolution of leisure and its meaning and relevance today. First, leisure is seen in its historical perspective, from the Ancient Greek civilization to the Middle Ages, to the Renaissance, the Reformation and Industrial Revolution and on to the twentieth century. Second, a variety of descriptions and definitions are described. Third, the development of mass leisure and popular culture and the ensuing benefits and problems are considered. Fourth, leisure is viewed in the light of its relationship to the traditional concepts of work. Fifth, leisure is set in the changing times of today, the 'time squeeze', and the loss of traditional structures.

This chapter is enlarged to incorporate part of a former chapter in the third edition. New sections include: the similarities between play, recreation and leisure; the implications on leisure services; and a construct 'pleisure' is introduced as a core of a needs-based approach to provision and management.

Having studied this chapter, the reader will know more about how it is that leisure has become significant in the lives of people; about its nature; and about its potential role in providing opportunities for personal well-being and self-fulfilment. The chapter illustrates how the freedom of leisure requires us to make good choices for ourselves and the community. It causes us to ask the question: how can leisure live up to its ideals and fulfil its potential to help people to become all they are capable of becoming?

By keeping this theme as a recurring question throughout this book, readers will examine their own beliefs and discover ways to achieve leisure's potential.

4.1 A philosophy of life and leisure?

We may be unaware of it, but each one of us has a philosophy of life, no matter how vague and no matter how inarticulate we might be in defining it. It is our view of the world. What reality means for us is decided by our philosophy of life.

Now, to have 'leisure', to live the life we want to live, to do the things we want to do, freed from undue constraints, and to be all that we want to be, is a dream few achieve and some might not even want because with such freedom comes the responsibility to make 'good' choices. Yet, as we move into a new millennium, we have more knowledge, more resources and more opportunity than before, in which to have a fullness of living, undreamed of in time past. The question is: has leisure a central role in a way of life that harnesses opportunities for self-fulfilment, at harmony with both oneself and the world? Without an understanding of such leisure, albeit as an ideal – the 'good life' for one and all – we cannot have sound principles on which to formulate policies for leisure planning, provision and management.

The philosophy – love of wisdom – of which I speak is nothing new. The Ancient Greek philosopher, Aristotle, described a philosophy, of which leisure was a cornerstone, as being about free and exalted souls. It is a far cry from trying to acquire happiness by buying more and more material possessions, consuming more and more leisure goods and seeking endless, fleeting pleasurable experiences – a merry-go-round existence, where some of today's Western children, when not being entertained, describe their world as 'boring'.

Yet philosophy, like theory, is not just thinking, for it is concerned with reality. It is practical. Our philosophy of life and leisure must be born out of the reality of our culture and our circumstances. Ancient Greek philosophy was shaped by a political system based on an aristocracy of a privileged elite and an economic system based on slavery. That is not for us. Our philosophy of leisure must be based on our culture, social and economic systems, human rights, equal opportunities, personal dignity and a belief that what is good and elevating for the individual is also good and elevating for the community.

4.2 Leisure: historical perspective

The first thing to be said about leisure is that it is not new: 'That is the principal point, with what kind of activity, is man to occupy his leisure' (Aristotle). Leisure is an ancient idea. It has been identified with elitism and class privilege since the earliest civilizations. However, it is probable that leisure began with primitive cultures once the pressures for sustenance, security and basic needs were removed, or in celebration after a 'kill' or during inclement weather.

In simpler societies the line between work and leisure is not indelibly drawn. In times past, and even in many parts of the world today, there are still people who work so hard and long to sustain themselves and their families that their lives are devoid of what we might term 'leisure'. Peasant life often means working to survive, and playing when opportunity permits. In simple social systems leisure is part of the rhythms of life – night and day, the climate, the harvest. Margaret Mead's vivid descriptions of life in Samoa [1] illustrate the ebb and flow of life, as distinct from a separation of life into work and leisure. Opportunity for leisure came with the obligations towards festivals, celebrations, feasts, weddings, special days and with the sacred mythology of early cultures. Godbey [2] points out that there was no *deliberate* leisure, nothing that was the result of the exercise of individual choice. In such societies, leisure is structured around the life cycle of necessary daily tasks; it is integrated into the daily or seasonal life pattern rather than being separate from it. Cutten [3] states:

> It was from these days or hours of primitive leisure, when crude but very real beginnings were made, that the arts, the sciences, the games and all the products of civilization date. In fact, civilizations were the products of leisure, and yet they have not always admitted their origin.

In many parts of the world, the development of agriculture widened the gap between the ruling classes and the rest of the population. Early advanced cultures, with clearly differentiated work roles, developed elite classes and leisure became associated with 'high culture', social standing and political status. For example, the Egyptian civilization (prominent from about 2500 BC until well into the Roman era) and the Assyrian and Babylonian cultures included many 'leisure' activities but these were primarily activities of the upper strata in society – the nobility, the military and religious leaders. Their activities included horse racing, wrestling, boxing, archery, arts, dance, music, drama, hunting, warfare and lavish entertainment. Drinking and gambling were common. In ancient Assyria and Babylon there were royal estates and parks, zoological and botanical gardens and large formal gardens of geometric designs. The terraced Hanging Gardens of Babylon became one of the seven wonders of the world. Developments also occurred in the Indian subcontinent and in China, famous for its gardens [4].

In *Retail, Leisure and Tourism* [5], under the subheading, 'Nothing new under the sun', we read:

> The Sumerian and Mesopotamian caravanners of 4000 years ago originated the concept of combining retail with leisure. They knew well the importance of creating just the right atmosphere for selling. No unit would depart from Damascus on its journey to Jeddah without the support of a full complement of magicians, snakecharmers, story-tellers, dancers, sword swallowers and craftsmen who theatrically fashioned goods in situ and offered them for sale to the public. Showmanship and retailing read as one. The act of a simple purchase assumed the importance of an event. Advance men travelled from village to village to draw the crowd and the caravanner made sure that his customers were placed in the mood to purchase by supplying them with a good time in the process.

It is clear, we cannot understand present leisure without understanding something of the past. None appear to have thought more about leisure than the Ancient Greek philosophers, so that is where we start.

4.2.1 Leisure and the Ancient Greeks

The early Greek civilization has influenced current leisure thinking and this is primarily as a result of the writings of Plato and Aristotle [6,7]. At the height of Greek civilization (around 500 BC), the growing professionalization of sport, public entertainment and competitions, saw in contrast the birth of the 'leisure ethic' – the intelligent use of free time was the purpose of life. The natural life of man was collective, life in the community. The ideal was the perfection of civil life and political life. The 'proper life' was good citizenship and good citizens were created out of leisure and education [8].

Plato expressed a low regard for manual labour and a high regard for well-employed leisure, with the capable citizen performing music, drama, sport, citizenship and education during leisure time. Much of Plato's writings include reconstructions of the thoughts and dialogues of Socrates, his mentor. Time for thought, contemplation, philosophy and self-development are required for happiness. That time, for Plato, is leisure. A study of Ancient Greek words illustrates the philosophical juxtaposition of culture, education and leisure. The word *paideia* meant 'culture' and *paidos*, 'boy' or 'child', *peod* forms the root of our word 'pedagogy', the art and science of teaching. *Paideia* also referred to education and self-improvement. Education referred to the deliberate moulding of character and the ultimate justification of life.

Now the Greek word *schole* denoted both schooling and leisure; it led to the Latin *scola* and English 'school' and 'scholar'. Aristotle, in Book 1 of the *Politics*, defines leisure as time free from the necessity to work. Leisure is different from work (*ascholia*) and from children's play (*paideia*). Leisure leads to aesthetic, spiritual or intellectual enlightenment through a search for understanding. Manual workers were believed to be incapable of leisure. This was not simply a case of discriminating against those earning a living by the sweat of their brows; it was rather a belief that kinds of work performed in manual occupations made workers unfit for the duties of citizenship. Development of the concept of the natural slave was a solution to the problem of getting the necessary work done, so that the rest of the city could be free for the more worthwhile pursuits.

For the twentieth century two aspects of that Greek civilization endure: the work–leisure distinction and the Greek leisure ethic, together with the belief that people can make choices. The purpose of knowledge was to enable a person to make the right ones. Central to Aristotle's philosophy was how to attain happiness. Moderation in all things was in keeping with natural justice. Happiness is continuous: leisure is not a brief period but a lifetime [9].

The work–leisure distinction may well have begun with the Greek philosophers. Work was associated with the toil of manual labour and with providing the necessities of life, while leisure was valued as those moments of life in which one contemplated the eternal truths and participated in music and drama.

Aristotle placed business and war on one side and leisure and peace on the other; this view held that no occupation could be regarded as leisure, nor could leisure be anything related to an occupation. 'We are unleisurely in order to have leisure', he claimed, 'facts, as well as arguments, prove that the legislator should direct all his military and other measures to the provision of leisure and the establishment of peace.'

Plato did not share this understanding of the work–leisure divide. In the *Republic*, Plato employs the word *schole* with different meanings, i.e., spare time, freedom from other activities and self-possession or freedom. There is a further concept of leisure as idleness. When Plato referred to this, he used the word *agria* – i.e. a degenerate condition and not to be thought of as leisure. Hence leisure becomes the *quality* of the activity.

The Greek conception of leisure was central to a much wider view of the life and nature of a free man. However, the range of activities that qualified as leisure was severely restricted. To Plato, music, poetry and philosophy lead to beauty and eternal truths. To Aristotle, only music and contemplation were worthy of the name leisure. Moreover, as Godbey [2] points out, the style of life and leisure regarded as appropriate to free men was in fact that of the privileged elite. Thus the Greek ideal, even if it existed in the purest terms as set out in the writings, was obtainable for only a very small proportion of the population. The Greek ideal is therefore something of a myth. Indeed, it is not consistent with what actually occurred, in practice, in Ancient Greece. The early Olympic Games, the stadia, gymnasia, extensive gardens and the open-air amphitheatres for festivals all illustrate the range of leisure pursuits and the range of public provision of facilities. In addition, while in the early days all citizens were encouraged to participate and compete, this spirit of amateurism gave way to specialist performers, commercialization and mass spectatorship and led from the amateur to the professional.

Although founded on slave labour and elitism, the Greek leisure ethic shows that leisure can be an essential opportunity for the development of man and woman and the unity of body and mind. Moreover, whether myth or fact, the spirit of the Greek ideal is still a goal which many subscribe to and there exist, even today, small enclaves of esoteric minority pursuits devoted to the enlightenment of mankind.

Our inheritance from the Ancient Greek philosophers is immense in philosophy, education, government, science, art, drama and poetry – and the search for the good life in which wisdom, virtue and leisure were pursued. Many of their words and ideas survive in the English language – 'pedagogy', 'gymnasium', 'stadium', 'lyceum', 'academy', etc. As Goodale and Godbey [9] remind us, a symposium is a gathering of learned people to share ideas: 'to them it was a drinking party. The Greek *schole* became not only school but also *skole*, a drinking song. Ancient philosophers were full of life.' Alas, the leisure ideal died with the Ancient Greeks and little evidence of its resurrection is found until the birth of the university and the Renaissance.

4.2.2 The Romans

The empire of the ancient Romans established in 27 BC continued until AD 395, when it divided into Eastern and Western empires. Roman culture spread across the known world. In ancient Rome military success and conquests led to affluence, a powerful nation and a move from agricultural democracy to urban populations with a class structure. Masses of the new urban population had considerable free time and as many as two hundred holidays a year by AD 354. Leisure was important for the Romans, but its importance was different from that of the Greek leisure ethic. To the Romans leisure was important for fitness for work. Sports were practised for maintaining physical fitness and for war. Leisure was utilitarian rather than aesthetic. Baths, amphitheatres and arenas were constructed for the benefit of the mass of the population. In Rome itself there were over eight hundred public baths at little or no cost to the public.

Free time, however, became a problem. Emperors attempted to keep people content by providing free food and entertainment – 'bread and circuses'. Slaves not only toiled, but were also used for entertainment, which at first included music, drama and sports, but later included contests, simulated land and sea battles, chariot races and exhibitions of violence. Violent spectacles included animals and then humans; professional gladiators fought to the death. The Colosseum, built about AD 80, became the hub of life in Rome and large arenas, gymnasia, parks and baths were built in most large towns. The Circus Maximus could hold 385,000 spectators.

As Rome became more decadent it declined. Historians have suggested that the inability to cope with leisure was one cause of the fall of the empire [10]. Economically, and perhaps in other ways, the spectacles contributed to the financial ruin of the empire, as the aristocracy competed to outdo each other, often to the point of bankruptcy.

Ancient Rome shows that mass leisure is no new phenomenon. It illustrates leisure in a social context of urbanization and the political use of leisure to quieten the masses. It also shows the massive investment in public recreation facilities and services and, above all, the growth of leisure consumption rather than participation. Although, like the Greeks, the Romans built and planned for leisure, the stress was upon law and custom and consumption, a political instrument, as distinct from learning, discovering and enlightenment. Later cultures used the example of Rome to show the consequences of uncontrolled misuse of leisure.

4.2.3 The Middle Ages

The fall of the Roman Empire and the spread of Christianity had profound and lasting effects on leisure and recreation. The Catholic Church taught that the purpose of life was to prepare for the next life. The early part of the Middle Ages, from about 400 to 1000 is often called, aptly, the Dark Ages. For centuries it was for most people a time of relative drabness, and for many of doom and gloom.

The first of the monasteries in the Western world was founded by St Augustine in North Africa. The monasteries represented an early case of lives segmented into discrete parts. The Benedictines preached, 'Work, do not despair'. Work became a virtue, as it is today, a far cry from Ancient Greek philosophy.

The monasteries expanded, preaching hard labour, good works and self-deprivation. As a reaction to the extremes and debased activities of the Romans, the Church prohibited most kinds of leisure activity except those relating to worship and religious observance. Work was glorified; and idleness was evil. However, while music and morality plays flourished, social drinking, gambling and secular music were practised by the public often on 'holy'-day celebrations, and the aristocracy continued their leisure activities of hunting, falconry and holding tournaments. But life in the Dark Ages was harsh to the common man.

During the late Middle Ages, up to approximately AD 1500 there were some relaxations from those strictures of the Dark Ages, but life for the masses remained much the same with religious festivals, cock fighting and other such activities coming as breaks in the round of toil. However, throughout the Middle Ages leisure elitism, a modified Greek ideal for the landed gentry and political leaders, continued. Leisure activities included hunting, hawking, music and dance. Sports and jousting were a means of entertainment, but were primarily preparation for feuding noblemen and for war.

For the masses, leisure came through the church's 'holy'-days and from the trading markets – medieval leisure shopping! In the thirteenth and fourteenth centuries royal charters set up boundaries for the Great Fairs, attracting merchants from Europe and Asia. The Fairs attracted entertainers – singers, dancers, jugglers, magicians, fortune tellers, dancing bears and sports such as wrestling, archery, jousting, dog and cock fighting and gambling followed. Religious festivals and wakes, likewise, attracted entertainers and made for revelry. Gradually, the power of the Church declined, but Europe was still controlled by powerful monarchs.

4.2.4 *Renaissance and Reformation*

The two movements of the Renaissance and the Reformation, one a cultural revolution and the other a work ethic and a moral way of life, developed in historical parallel. Over the centuries the power of the Catholic Church declined, permitting a reawakening in humanity and the arts. The fifteenth century marks the transition from the Medieval world to modern Western civilization. This period of rebirth, developing in Italy and spreading across France and England is known as the Renaissance, the movement which helped to transform the Medieval world and gave birth to modern times.

The spread of knowledge and liberalism – the liberal arts liberated from ignorance – broke through religious dogma. Liberal thought, however, opened up opportunity for both enlightment and extravagance and a breakdown in order and discipline. The Italian Renaissance collapsed through greed and excess. Upon its decline came other philosophies such as that of Niccolo Machiavelli – to gain power by whatever means, fair or foul.

It was not until the time of the Renaissance that leisure ideals became more generalized and more opportunities were available to the masses. The populace continued to enjoy both religious and secular festivals. The development of printing enabled literature to become available to a wider public, since it had previously only been available to those who studied in monasteries, universities and aristocratic homes. Music, drama and dance were professionally performed in theatres and education became more readily available. Later, educators such as Rousseau and Locke extolled the benefits of play in the education of children. During these times, the nobility became the patrons of the arts and the works of many of the great artists of that time hang in galleries all over the world today.

During the Renaissance, the Protestant Reformation took hold in many parts of Europe and later moved on to America. The liberalism brought about by the Renaissance had also encouraged a pleasure-seeking aristocracy, a public more prone to drinking, gambling and practising cruel sports and a worldly, often corrupt, Church; these and other factors led to the Reformation. In the early sixteenth century, Martin Luther began a revolt against the established church in Germany, where marriages and divorces could be purchased and indulgences (monetary penance) could wipe clean the slate of sin, given sufficient payment. Calvin and Knox began similar reformed churches. A time of austerity followed, with emphasis on religious matters and a diminishing of many leisure activities. In some communities, even children's play was discouraged as it was said to foster 'idleness'.

A turning point in English history came with Henry VIII's divorce from Catherine of Aragon and marriage to Anne Boleyn. The Act of Appeals (1533) abolished the Pope's rights and the Act of Supremacy declared that the King of England was supreme head of the Church of England. The sale or destruction of all the religious houses and monasteries of the Catholic Church has had implications on the tourism industry in Britain today! By the turn of the century, England had rejected the authority of the papacy in Rome and the Anglican Church was established during the reign of Elizabeth I but, as now, rifts between warring religious factions continued. The Counter-Reformation of Ignatius Loyola, with the creation of the Jesuits, had a lasting legacy in Europe. The Tudor dynasty (1485–1603) ended with the death of Elizabeth I and England in turmoil. The Stuarts were one of England's least successful dynasties (though James I's reign brought some growth in political stability and a lessening of religious passions); Charles I was publicly beheaded and two decades of civil war and revolution again changed the course of history. To counteract the growing religious opposition to active leisure pursuits, James I of England issued the *Book of Sports* in 1618, making it legal for working people to play certain games outside church hours.

The Puritans, drawn from the poor and middle classes, were dissidents who sought to purify the church along the lines of Luther and Calvin and as a protest against the pleasures of the rich. They became entangled in the political struggle between Parliament and king, which was to lead to civil war, Cromwell's government and the Restoration, with the re-establishment of the monarchy under Charles II in 1660.

Early philosophy was based on subjective thought, ideas and religious precepts. The Renaissance had brought in its wake great discoveries in world exploration, science, medicine, astronomy, mathematics and philosophy. The greatest 'explosion' was in art and painting in northern Italy, with the works of Botticelli, Leonardo da Vinci, Michelangelo, and hundreds of others.

As the movement spread across northern Europe, there came also philosophers such as Francis Bacon, Hobbes, John Locke and Spinoza; poets such as Spenser, Dryden and later Voltaire, the French dramatist and historian; and also there came great writers, Shakespeare and Moliere, painters including Rembrandt, and landscape architects like André le Nôtre who designed gardens for Louis XIV at the Palace of Versailles, and later on Capability Brown.

René Descartes embodied the notion of the philosopher–scientist, as Leonardo da Vinci had done a century before. The world was becoming a smaller place, as a result of the adventures of explorers like the Spaniard Mendoza, the colonizer of South America; of Sir Francis Drake who voyaged around the world; and the growth of world trade with trading companies such as the East India Company.

There was a non-stop activity in the scientific world as well. Not surprisingly, there was reaction to such rationality, for example, with the 'Romantic movement' of Rousseau, the political philosopher and educator. His philosophy of the child of nature became one of the foundation stones of modern physical education. His ideas of a 'social contract' and political reform were significant in the lead up to the French Revolution against the monarchy and aristocracy, a revolution whose reverberations were to continue for over a century.

Despite being heavily suppressed by the Reformation, the cultural revolution of the Renaissance continued. In the seventeenth and eighteenth centuries parks and gardens were developed for the nobility, who went hunting and fishing and enjoyed the beauty of the gardens. Commons and plazas were developed for the public. Holidays were declared by the kings and lords. The Tuileries and Versailles gardens in Paris, the Tiergarten in Berlin, and Kensington Gardens in London were gradually opened to the public.

Although the Renaissance brought about more freedom for leisure, the Reformation has been shown to have had an even greater effect on Western attitudes. The Reformation was a period which idealized work and distrusted the evils of leisure – a work ethic which has persisted throughout the twentieth century. The Protestant ethic sought to condition leisure to behaviour fitting men and women for devotion and work. The humanism of the Renaissance sought the creativity and development of people through education and greater freedom in leisure. Regrettably, yet another revolution was to suppress still further the opportunities for leisure development for the mass of the people.

4.2.5 Effect of the Industrial Revolution

The Industrial Revolution of the eighteenth and nineteenth centuries led to profound changes. Factories brought about the growth of cities. Populations were uprooted from the land, and from small towns and villages, to the cities. The consequent rise in urban population, overcrowding, poor housing, poverty, crime and the increase in working hours and child labour, all militated against leisure. British industrial history records examples of the hardship caused by the Industrial Revolution and the exploitation of the workers, poor wages and conditions of the miners, the cotton-mill workers and many others.

From the villages where people lived amid nature, where children could play in the fields and families could walk in the countryside, people came to cramped conditions with little room to play and little time to enjoy leisure. Recreation areas were not planned. For children, often viewed as cheap labour, the consequences were devasting and many forms of play were condemned as evil.

From the mid-1800s to well into the 1900s a reform movement took shape. Reformers were deeply concerned about welfare, especially the welfare of children and they were deeply troubled by the conditions of an urban life bereft of opportunities for healthy exercise and play. The urban churches, in many cases, gradually began to recognize such problems and to come to terms with a new role in regard to recreation.

The reforms dealt more with the concept of recreation than leisure; 'wholesome' opportunities for activity after work which refreshed and renewed the worker for more work. The central element of the leisure philosophy of social reformers was that recreation served socially useful ends, a theme which has continued throughout the twentieth century. Even today, while there are undoubtedly generous motives based on human welfare, industrial and company recreation is still rationalized on the grounds of lower absenteeism, lower employee turnover, higher morale and higher productivity.

It was in response to appalling social conditions that the organized recreation movement began. At the turn of the century, an interest in leisure as it relates to industrial society was awakened. It was during this period also that several of the writings and theories of play and recreation began to emerge. The reformist movements were reactions to specific social situations. The Great Depression of the 1930s and world wars were to bring still further social emergencies.

Also re-emerging at this time was what Thorsten Veblen described as 'the leisure class'. Capitalism, urbanization and industrialization had brought about yet another division in society. In America, Veblen [11] began to identify weaknesses in the industrial system. He criticized the 'leisure class' and its 'conspicuous consumption'. With industrialism, the arbitrary division of labour and class continued to exist and to perpetuate itself. Status becomes symbolized by purchasing power and accumulation of wealth. To Veblen, writing at the turn of the century, leisure was perpetuated for the leisure classes.

It was out of times of hardship and social injustice that social pioneers influenced governments to act. In Britain public health and physical recreation, baths and parks and open spaces were gradually made available to the public. But leisure was never the right of the masses until it was recognized as a part of life *separate* from the excessively long working hours. The Saturday half-day was a significant turning point in Britain towards an acceptance of leisure for the mass of the people.

Gradually the working class began to demand leisure, not for any idealism or enlightenment, but for time off, because workers (and unions) were now selling their time. The demand for work and free time led to the organization of modern work and the world of public, voluntary and industrial recreation.

The twentieth century has seen the growth of recreation, but more important, the need for play as a process of learning for the young and leisure for the sake of enjoyment rather than just for social welfare. Throughout the century there have been provided public parks, 'baths', pubs in their thousands, music halls in the first part of the century and after the First World War, cinema and spectator sports and then the greatest hypnotic leisure attraction of them all – the television. Today technology has revolutionized leisure in its many forms. (Read chapters six and eleven on trends and the commercial leisure industry.)

4.3 Leisure – a variety of approaches, descriptions and definitions

The English word 'leisure' appears to be derived from the Latin *licere*, 'to be permitted' or 'to be free'. Hence the French word *loisir*, meaning 'free time', and the English word 'licence' – permission or freedom to act. Thus the word 'leisure' is associated with a complexity of meanings in our language. Generally it is defined in terms of 'freedom from constraint', 'opportunity to choose', 'time left over after work' or as 'free time after obligatory social duties have been met'. However, according to the Parrys, leisure as a social phenomenon itself, 'involves social constraint and social obligation and can best be thought of as being embodied in a whole way of life. Such an idea immediately invokes the concept of culture' [12].

The concept of leisure permits widely varying responses. Leisure is commonly thought of as the opposite of work, but one man's work can be another man's leisure, and several activities combine both leisure and work characteristics. Freedom from obligation is often regarded as a key attraction of leisure, but many non-work activities – e.g. domestic, social, voluntary and community activities – involve considerable obligation. Some regard leisure as being an opportunity for relaxation and pleasure but often people spend their leisure time in dedicated service, study, personal development, hard training, discipline, stress or writing a book. The problems of definition and understanding are considerable.

Most theories have been developed in the twentieth century. Many arose out of the troubles of the Industrial Revolution; hundreds of theories and descriptions of leisure have been written from then until now. From the mass of literature, five discernible, though overlapping, approaches are evident:

1   leisure as time
2   leisure as activity
3   leisure as a state of being
4   leisure as an all-pervading, 'holistic' concept
5   leisure as a way of life.

4.3.1 Leisure as time

Within the broad framework of leisure defined as time there are many interpretations. Some make a very broad distinction, defining leisure as the time when someone is not working primarily for money [13]. With such a definition, however, we are left with a large proportion of people's time which is filled in a multitude of ways. Such a definition of leisure is far too broad to be of use and is only perceived in the context of doing 'work'. *The Dictionary of Sociology* describes leisure as 'free time after the practical necessities of life have been attended to'. This gives 'surplus time' to do with as we please. Several other writers refer to leisure as free time or unoccupied time. The problem in viewing leisure as free time is that it is difficult to draw a line between necessities and spare time.

Parker [14] contrasts between 'residual' definitions and others. Residual time is the time left after taking out of total time everything that is not regarded as leisure. The Countryside Recreation Research Advisory Group defined leisure as 'the time available to the individual when the disciplines of work, sleep and other needs have been met'.

To Brightbill [15] and others, while leisure is concerned with time, it is only leisure if it falls into 'discretionary' time – i.e. time beyond existence and subsistence, 'the time to be used according to our own judgement or choice'. Hence three time-slots are identified: existence, subsistence and discretionary.

Yet the matter is complicated further: what is necessary for some will be discretionary for others and many necessary activities, for example, eating and sleeping may be chosen as discretionary activities. However, in general it appears that the word 'leisure' is correlated with positive or constructive behaviour. Free time appears to have some negatively charged characteristics. This aspect of leisure, as time, appears to establish leisure in a positive relationship to time. As Goodale and Godbey point out, in idealistic terms, 'we dis-locate leisure by consigning it to particular periods during days, weeks and years' [9].

4.3.2 *Leisure as activity*

A classical understanding of leisure is that it is made up of activities which enlighten and educate. Leisure therefore is made up of activities. Today we hear leisure described as a 'cluster of activities'. The Neumeyers [16] define leisure as 'an opportunity to engage in some kind of activity, whether vigorous or relatively passive, which is not required by daily necessities'. Kaplan [17], in describing leisure as activity, saw it as an end, distinct from work which was a means to an end. A definition of leisure by the International Group of the Social Sciences of Leisure [18] states that:

> Leisure consists of a number of occupations in which the individual may indulge of his own free will whether to rest, amuse himself, to add to this knowledge, or improve his skills disinterestedly or to increase his voluntary participation in the life of the community after discharging his professional, family and social duties.

Nash [19] viewed the use of leisure for specific activities on four levels: passive, emotional, active and creative involvement. His leisure model illustrates use of leisure time with a progression of leisure activities in similar vein to Maslow's need hierarchy [20,21]. Nash attaches a value to each level. Those at the apex of the pyramid are values to be regarded as worthy and those at the base are negative in value and undesirable.

Many look at leisure as activities freely chosen. However, in reality, absolute freedom is rarely achieved. Dumazedier [22] coined the term 'semi-leisure', to describe those activities which one was obliged to do but that brought about satisfactions in the doing. Such activities as domestic, do-it-yourself, family obligations, and the like, could be pleasurable or diversionary and could function as 'semi-leisure'.

4.3.3 Leisure as an end in itself, a state of being

The complexity of definition is illustrated by Kaplan [23]. From the sociological viewpoint, 'nothing is definable as leisure *per se* and almost anything is definable as leisure, given a synthesis of elements'. What is described as the 'humanistic' model views leisure as an end in itself, a state of being. Pieper [24] stressed this idea:

> Leisure it must be understood, is a mental and spiritual attitude – it is not simply the result of external factors, it is not the inevitable result of spare time, a holiday, a weekend or a vacation. It is, in the first place, an attitude of the mind, a condition of the soul.

Leisure, to Pieper, was not a means to an end but rather an end in itself. (This is a concept similar to Huizinga's understanding of play: chapter two.) Brightbill [25] also described leisure as 'a state of quiet contemplative dignity'. Larrabee and Meyersohn [26] saw it as a 'mood of contemplation'.

To de Grazia [27], leisure is a state of being free of everyday necessity. He denounces as a popular misconception the notion that free time is leisure. The mentality of 'clock-watching' produces synchronization, impersonal tempo, conformity and unthoughtful action. The free time produced by industrialization is typified by passivity, an uncritical spirit and craving for fun. We have not developed 'true' leisure for the masses; it may well be 'beyond the capacity of most people'. In de Grazia's opinion – closer than most to Aristotle's view – leisure perfects man and woman and holds the key to the future. It needs to break the grip of the machine and release human energy for free expression and exploration of truth, beauty and knowledge. He casts doubt on whether there is indeed any freedom in the quantitative framework called 'free time'. Marcuse [28], however, takes a totally opposing view, defining leisure as free time and questioning the freedom of leisure.

Parker [29] argues, setting the semantic problems aside, if free time and leisure are different conceptually, they cannot be measured by the same criteria. The distinction is not confined to the area of non-work: it applies also in the work sphere.

Nakhooda [30] suggests that the meaning of leisure to the layman could be defined as that part of the individual's daily life 'in which he finds himself free from the demands of his regular calling and able to enter upon any line of activity he may choose within his own interests – whether it be work or play or meditation'.

4.3.4 Leisure: an all-embracing, 'holistic' concept, or leisure as meaning

While many authors define leisure as time, activity and a state of being, most of them incorporate all three aspects, giving greater weight in one direction. Indeed, many of the prominent writers, such as Kaplan, Brightbill, Dumazedier and de Grazia, use different definitions at different times, depending on the point which is being made at the time. This can be seen in several of the all-embracing descriptions of leisure. The three primary functions of leisure, according to Dumazedier [31], are: relaxation, entertainment and personal development. Within these three aspects people find recovery from fatigue, deliverance from boredom and liberation from daily automatism: 'Leisure is the expression of a whole collection of man's aspirations on a search for a new happiness, related to a new duty, a new ethic, a new policy and a new culture. A humanistic mutation is beginning.'

Murphy [32] believes that there has been erosion of the effectiveness of work to serve the need of self-identity. In contrast, there has been an increase in the value of leisure in establishing one's status and personal identity. He sees this as a major factor in the trend towards the fusion of work and leisure. The holistic view of leisure is seen in the context of the wholeness of the individual. A full range of possible forms of self-expression may occur during work or leisure. According to the holistic concept: 'the meaning of work and leisure are inextricably related to each other.' However, as we will see later in this chapter, work and leisure may not be as interrelated as Murphy suggests when people do not have the means to enjoy leisure, nor the positive attitude towards it, nor the perception of what it might mean in terms of life satisfaction.

The more important questions are: what does leisure do for people; how do they perceive leisure and what does it mean to them? Neulinger [33], a psychologist, takes an attitudinal approach. Leisure is concerned with people's attitudes and perceptions. Leisure has three dimensions in his paradigm: it includes perceived freedom, it is intrinsic and it is non-instrumental. Leisure is the perception of free choice for the sake of doing or experiencing. Neulinger and Crandall [34] point out that we are no longer satisfied just to name the activities that people engage in; we now want to find out what they *mean* to people.

Pieper [24], a theologian–philosopher, links leisure to culture through divine worship, festival and celebration: 'Culture depends for its very existence on leisure, and leisure, in its turn, is not possible unless it has durable and living link with the cultus, with divine worship.' Leisure, to Pieper, is a mental or spiritual attitude which is not the result of external factors, not the result of spare time and not idleness. It is an 'attitude of mind, a condition of the soul'. It produces an inward calm; it means not being busy, but letting things happen.

Our notion of free time is almost exclusively that of 'time off' which we have earned by working. Goodale and Godbey [9] remind us that seldom do we equate the word 'free' with something that is given to us as a gift. Holidays are free time worked for; holy-days recognize what we receive as a gift: 'The idea that leisure and even free time is a gift is novel. But not new.'

John Kelly in *Leisure* [35] ranks, in order of importance, leisure activities of adults, relatively stable in socio-economic terms, in three communities in the

United States. Leisure, for them, appeared to be informal, readily available and, largely, inexpensive. Of the most highly stressed, six out of ten families, in the absence of organized recreation, partake in the following activities:

1   marital affection and intimacy
2   reading for pleasure
3   family conversation
4   activity as a couple: walking, shopping, etc.
5   family outings
6   visiting family and friends
7   playing with children
8   watching television
9   outdoor sport
10   eating out
11   religious worship
12   short auto trips
13   gardening
14   home decorating
15   arts and crafts.

Hence leisure means many things depending on the way we see leisure functioning for us, on different interpretations and on the orientation we have towards it. An understanding of the basic orientations gives individuals the opportunity to sort through these and accept, reject or modify them.

As we have seen, there appear to be four main orientations to leisure, namely time, activities, state of mind and a holistic approach, each having a variety of factors which colour and modify the basic approach. Parker points out that while the first three meanings – i.e. time, activities and state of mind – often overlap, the classification is useful in determining which aspect of the word has the greater emphasis within particular contexts.

4.3.5   Leisure – a way of living

Yet there remains a fifth orientation, mentioned earlier by the Parrys and the essence of the findings by Goodale and Godbey described in *The Evolution of Leisure* [9]. It is idealistic and bears resemblance to the philosophy of Aristotle. Leisure is not a commodity of time or a state of mind, but a way of living:

> Leisure is living in relative freedom from the external compulsive forces on one's culture and physical environment so as to be able to act from internally compelling love in ways which are personally pleasing, intuitively worthwhile, and provide a basis of faith.

In noting that leisure is living, we avoid the time and state of mind notions. We recognize that freedom is limited; we are not free to do anything we wish to do. So, then, leisure as a way of living can offer opportunities or times with which we can choose what to do. Aristotle, in Book 2 of the *Politics* in describing the need for 'freedom from the necessity of labour', is concerned as much about freedom for, as about freedom from. It is how we use time that matters. We need to be relatively free from those external compulsive forces so as to be able to act – i.e. it is a 'freedom to', rather than a 'freedom from' idea. And the motivation for those acts is intrinsic – i.e. not being motivated by some external force or pursuing some external reward. In life-enhancing terms, leisure appears to be the process of gaining freedom and finding meaning through self-understanding and self-improvement, it is a self-directed process. Idealistic, yes. But without ideals and goals we have a shallow philosophy of life, and leisure.

4.4   Leisure – a social problem?

So vast are the reaches of 'leisure' today that it appears to bestride the Western world like a colossus. At one extreme it is seen as a gigantic movement for great good, enhancing the quality of life for the mass of people, and at the other extreme it is seen as a major twentieth century problem, with people incapable of coping with leisure and where, for some, time hangs heavy or is consumed in greed and destruction. Clearly, leisure can lead to a personally fulfilling life and carry social benefits. But is it also a social problem? Industrial societies have created leisure as we know it today. Godbey [36] refers to the creation of 'leisure potential'. The increased potential for leisure, however, has also created factors that have negated the meaning of leisure in our society. They include: limitless materialism, increasing societal complexity and change, increasing demands of labour and carry-over of 'work values' into leisure. Thus, while our potential for leisure has increased, we are nowhere near the society of leisure about which so much has been written. What has increased, according to Godbey [37], is 'anti-leisure' – i.e. activity which is undertaken compulsively, as a means to an end, from a perception of necessity, with a high degree of externally imposed constraints, with considerable anxiety, time-consciousness, minimum personal autonomy and which avoids self-actualization: 'In regard to romance, the practice of taking a mistress has largely died out because it is too time consuming. It has been replaced by the "one nighter".'

In the same vein, Linder, a Swedish economist, in *The Harried Leisure Class* [38] believes that sexual promiscuity today is primarily due to the desire to speed up the courtship process and achieve what intimacy can be achieved in a very short period of time! He believes that life has become so demanding in time that consumption eliminates, for all practical purposes, the time necessary for leisure. This consumption production creates a 'leisure deficit'. Industrial society has set its face towards increasing economic growth by all possible means. Hence one of the problems is viewing time as a commodity. Research by the German sociologist Scheusch [39] illustrated that many people during a large part of the day do more than one thing at one time. The term 'time deepening' was coined to describe a person's ability to do several things simultaneously, and so crowd a greater number of activities into the same twenty-four hours.

Time experts in the United States found that if we did all the things that are expected of us, it would take at least thirty-six hours in a twenty-four-hour day. In business and at home we now spend money to save time. Goodale and Godbey believe that these changes have been so drastic that the notion of leisure among many today is almost in direct opposition to its ancient meanings. As de Grazia observed, humans rejected the tyranny of man, while submitting to the tyranny of the clock! Just as time spent in work became more carefully regulated, so too did leisure time. Leisure itself was slotted between periods of work, whose values washed over into it continuously.

Picture how we spend much of our 'leisure' time. Fast-food stops on the motorway encourage us to hurry. We park as close as possible to save walking and taking up time. We order in quick-coded language 'Big Mac'. We eat our meal in a few minutes or order American style 'to go', so we can eat and drive at the same time. Then we drive and speak on the telephone at the same time, saving valuable seconds! Fast foods will get us on our way faster. Why? If we rush through life, will we be more or less happy? Can happiness be tied to consumer goods? One wonders how much of our 'workaholic' lifestyle, harried leisure and pursuit to purchase happiness is in fact an escape from freedom. With freedom, you have to make difficult choices. Perhaps we are looking for an 'unfreedom', a pretend freedom?

The Frenchman de Toqueville [40], writing about American culture a century ago, but whose words ring true still, described the lack of leisure philosophy: 'Leisure, for us, is like jam for Alice in Wonderland to put on your bread. You shall have jam on your bread tomorrow, but tomorrow never comes. It is always today.'

Activities which take time, thought and care – family life, listening to the problems of others, visiting the sick – are often swept aside with the demands of more pressing things to get done by deadlines. But some, having lived through life in the fast lane amid the rat race, are turning back to simpler values where stewardship of the environment, the enjoyment of what nature, families and friends have to offer, become appealing.

Futurists and economists, however, tell a different story for the mass of people: 'Time starvation' and 'hurry sickness' were to become the hallmark of the 1990s, according to the Henley Centre [41], which predicted that some consumers would have money but no time to spend it. The prediction of time starvation was partly true and could well apply in the years ahead. The harried consumer will increasingly be looking for new ways to cope with the conflicting demands of work, love and family. While time for leisure can be used to enrich the lives of many people, for others it may be a curse upon them. For example, it can be a time for loneliness. For some, it is an opportunity for vandalism, warring factions and gangs looking for excitement and trouble. The extraordinary lengths taken by governments and the football fraternity to head off trouble erupting at the World Cup in France in 1998, were an indictment of the way in which we have failed to meet the social needs of some young people whose choice of leisure activity is gang warfare.

In some cases, leisure has taken on the mantle of business and work. The inability to relax, even for a moment, is a common complaint and evidence of neurotic disturbance; even leisure time is taken at a workrate pace. Some find it hard to take holidays, and suffer from after-work irritability and the 'Sunday neurosis'. Most suicides occur during weekends and vacations. The attraction of 'moonlighting' or the second job is not just the money. It indicates the relative importance given to work compared with leisure. Up to eight million Americans need psychiatric assistance every year, 125,000 are treated in hospital for depression and 50,000 commit suicide.

Time viewed as a commodity, rather than expanding life, can make our lives shorter. One is reminded of the passage from Ecclesiastes. To everything there is a season, a natural pattern: 'A time to weep, and a time to laugh; a time to mourn and a time to dance.' Hence many writers view leisure as a social problem. Cutten [42] saw aspects of the problem in restlessness and the need for excitement, the inability to be alone, lack of self-discipline, boredom, fatigue and lack of play experience. The heart of the leisure threat according to those who see it as such is its unwise use; an aspect of the problem is mass availability. Two aspects of leisure – mass leisure and popular culture – illustrate divergent opinions.

4.5 Mass leisure

The twentieth century has brought time for leisure not only for the few, but also for the many. Leaders of the world governments in the last years of the twentieth century have to ask the same question posed by Aristotle: with what activity is man and woman to occupy his or her time for leisure? To Aristotle, people must be capable of handling leisure: 'The provision of an external opportunity for leisure is not enough; it can only be fruitful if the man himself is capable of leisure, and can, as we say, occupy his leisure or work his leisure (as the Greeks say).'

De Grazia believes that even today there are many who are incapable of leisure: anyone can have free time, not everyone can have leisure. Others take a very different viewpoint. The emergence of mass leisure has reduced, if not eliminated, many of the previous social and class differences in leisure behaviour. Roberts [43] considers that leisure is now the great equalizer. He indicates that there are typical leisure-time occupations of people of all classes. Others, however, see the picture in another perspective. Despite the increases in time, affluence, travel and mass consumerism, there are differences between the classes, particularly at both poles of the social spectrum.

Kraus [44] believes that inequalities in leisure remain deep in modern society, particularly in the spheres of recreation, cultural taste and social contacts. Zuzanek [45] reported on a study of urban family expenditures in Canada. Respondents from the lowest family income quintile were spending five times less money on recreation than respondents from the highest quintile. Yet in view of those who advocate a 'holistic' approach to leisure, emphasizing self-development and fulfilment through freely chosen meaningful activities, leisure participation will be particularly valuable for those people in society who are less advantaged.

4.5.1 Popular culture

Within the framework of mass leisure has emerged the concept of 'popular culture'. It is important because it continually reaffirms common cultural values and identity of people in that culture. It also appears to embody or express the social and cultural change brought about in large measure through 'the new leisure'. Lewis [46] states:

> Popular culture, then is all culture not considered elite culture or serious art, or exclusively defined as the property of a minority subculture, and that is usually, but not necessarily, disseminated through some form of the mass media. It is culture consumed nearly entirely during the leisure time of the majority of members of a social system. Thus, my definition includes popular music, films, sports events, comic books, and even fast food dispensers such as McDonald's or Kentucky Fried Chicken.

Put simply, Gans [47] points out, some culture is popular because people want it. It encompasses the kinds of pursuits and behaviour that most people do in their leisure and the marketing and communications market makes the ideas of popular culture available. However, there is more to popular culture than just its popularity. It is popular not just because of its availability, but because it represents and is part of social development. The growth of a youth culture with its fashion, tastes, music and ways of life is symbolic of its identity. If culture is the way of life of a people, then popular culture is part of developing new types and new styles of culture – a new or different culture in the making. Some popular movements, however, will come and go – e.g. 'the mods', 'the rockers', the 'flower people' are far removed from today's youth culture. There will be changes as seen in the worlds of popular music and entertainment. Some things will be important at different times. Some new cultures will reject traditional cultures and mores, and some people may well experience little of their traditional culture and heritage. There will also be counter-culture movements, such as between a more liberalized and a less liberalized society. Counter-culture movements have been traced by Kando in *Leisure and Popular Culture in Transition* [48].

Lewis fears there is a real danger of 'cultural unemployment', as well as destruction of tradition. Kato's studies in Thailand show that the popular heroes are mostly Japanese television stars rather than local heroes [49]. Thai children see and hear very little about their 'national' popular heroes in the culture they consume. The fastest-growing restaurant chain in Hong Kong in the early 1980s was McDonald's! It was reported in the *Nation* [50]:

> Prosperous city dwellers and the rural poor in Thailand have one thing in common: poor dietary habits and the tendency to eat too much junkfood, according to a senior health official. . . . As a result, Thailand is now faced with diseases of the rich like hypertension, heart disease, diabetes as well as diseases of the poor like malnutrition.

Most industrialized popular culture is targeted at a middle-class, affluent urban audience, probably American, Japanese, British or French:

> As this material is beamed across the world, millions outside that target audience are exposed to it. To the extent they begin using it as a baseline against which to judge their own lives, one can predict an increase in feelings of dissatisfaction in such populations.

The impact of television is illustrated dramatically in the showing of the 1990 Association Football World Cup, viewed across the world by an estimated audience approaching one billion people, some of whom in poorer countries bought television sets for the first time. Lewis [46] sees a threefold outcome of popular Western culture beamed across the world: first, it will bring out feelings of personal inadequacy; second, a turning outward to forms of political unrest and dissensions; and third, developing countries will accept such popular culture as the goal towards which they should strive, at exactly the same point in history when the major economically developed countries are beginning to realize that the world does not have the energy, nor the resources, to support such life-styles of leisure.

Popular culture, however, has brought to the mass of people television, radio, popular music, fashion, sport and new life horizons. Mass leisure and popular culture are part and parcel of most civilizations today and must be fashioned to improve the quality of life for the great mass of people but, at the same time, must prevent the destruction of a nation's culture and heritage.

4.6 Leisure – its relationship to work

Other than the very essential, the ancient Athenians and Romans did not think much of work. Work was a curse: the Greek word for work, *ponos*, meant 'sorrow'. The philosophers agreed with the poets. The only solution, as most clearly expressed by Plato and Aristotle, was to have the vast majority, the slaves, provide the necessities and material goods for all, so that the minority – the citizens – could engage in leisure which produced the arts and sciences, politics, government and philosophy.

The relationship between the concepts of 'work' and 'leisure' has been well debated and documented, though there are no satisfactory universally accepted theses. We have noted that some societies, both ancient and modern, have made a clear distinction between work and leisure.

4.6.1 Work: a heritage of slavery, a tradition of paid employment

History has shown that the life of leisure could only be pursued by those who had sufficient free time and means to free themselves from the 'curse' of work. The blessing of leisure for some meant intensive work for many. The Greek aristocracy could not have pursued their leisure without widespread slavery; the English aristocracy could not have been the epitome of the cultured stock without suppression of the poor.

Bertrand Russell [51], in *In Praise of Idleness*, asserted that harm was caused by the belief that work was virtuous; the morality of work was the morality of slaves. Work was indeed slavery to the suppressed. The boys and girls who slaved in the coalmines and textile-mills in England just over a century ago had neither the time nor the energy to enjoy leisure.

The word 'work' covers a multitude of things. It is often used synonymously with words such as 'labour', 'occupation', 'employment', 'effort' and 'production'.

Work may also be a time for personal development, creativity and other personal satisfactions. Marx's [52] ideal model of work was 'a process in which man and Nature participate, and in which man of his own accord starts, regulates, and controls the material recreations between himself and Nature'. However, work in industry contradicts this ideal. Specialization, fragmentation, isolation, rigid time structuring, repetitiveness and depersonalization contribute to anonymity, a sense of helplessness and alienation for many workers.

To the public at large the question 'what is work?' is so obvious that definitions and understanding seem to be totally inappropriate. Work is paid employment. It is concerned with earning a wage, the money on which to live. In addition, work has been traditionally valued. It has been a means of self-identification. Traditionally too, work is what adults, particularly adult males, have to do. But in the United Kingdom today, traditions no longer apply, with the loss of a manufacturing base and growth in the service industries, there is more work available for females than males. Leisure is something you don't have to do; traditionally again, it is conceived as freedom from commitment. Yet for those involved, many leisure activities require considerable commitment. And those out of work – and not by choice – do not count their enforced free time as leisure. It is clear to see that these two realms of 'work' and 'leisure' need to be considered not as dichotomized entities, but in far more fluid and complex dimensions.

4.6.2 *The work–leisure dichotomy*

People's lives are segmented in a variety of ways. One person, close to my heart, is a mother, grandmother, homemaker, part-time teacher, church steward, school governor, volunteer worker and recreational 'player' – all wrapped up in the same person. Work and play are becoming more and more alike; in some lives they are becoming, in a sense, fused. Focus here, however, is on only the segmentation of life into leisure and non-leisure.

In modern Western civilization different approaches to the work–leisure dichotomy are evident. As Parker [53] outlined:

> One (clearly declining) [approach] is that work is the serious business of life and leisure is subsidiary or even non-existent. The second is that leisure is the aim and purpose of life and work merely a means to that end. The third is a more integrated approach: work and leisure as reconcilable parts of a whole life, such as that of the craftsman or artist. . . . An important clue to the relative importance attached to work and leisure is the choice that people make between having more income or more leisure. In non-industrial societies people tend not to seek additional work after they have achieved a comfortable margin of income over what they consider to be necessary. But among the economically advanced nations more people prefer additional work (overtime or a second job) to more leisure.

'Moonlighting' has become a familiar term. It was used in the British Parliament during the debate on the 1979 Budget, which was denounced as a 'moonlighter's charter'. Although moonlighting does not appear to be a major problem to employers, it could grow to significant proportions. The move away from standard hours for some and flexi-hours for others, and the tendency to trade leisure for extra income, could become an issue in years to come.

Some of the relevant factors in appreciating the juxtaposition of work and leisure in modern times are as follows.

1   Working hours determine how much time and money are available for leisure.
2   Work may determine the energies, enthusiasm and motivations left over for leisure.
3   Some work affords leisure opportunity during work hours or as part of work itself.
4   Some jobs are more akin to certain types of leisure occupation.

There are several arguments to suggest a fusion of work and leisure.

1   More people use free time for work purposes both for employment and for effort towards obligatory or non-obligatory actions.
2   Some work decisions are made with leisure in mind as one of the perks of the job.
3   Many leisure pursuits have become employment for some and extremely hard work for others.

Several sociologists and other academics have taken particular stances concerning the work–leisure issue including Berger [54], Wilensky [55] and Bacon [56]. Kelly [57] suggested three types of leisure activity: 'unconditional leisure' is independent of work and freely chosen; 'coordinated leisure' is similar to work such as undertaking a hobby; and 'complementary leisure' which is independent of work in form and content, but the need to take part is influenced by one's work such as being obliged to participate when it is expected of you.

Blauner [58] concludes that work remains the single most important activity for most people in terms of time and energy. Argyris [59] illustrates the difficulties of making leisure compensate for work: if people experience dependence, submission, frustration and conflict at work, and if they adapt to these conditions by psychological withdrawal, apathy and indifference, then these adaptive features will guide their leisure behaviour outside the workplace.

A case can be formulated to show work and leisure as opposites. However, this is a far from adequate formulation. Concepts such as play, recreation and leisure become relative terms. One man's play is another man's work: one man's leisure is another man's drudgery. In addition, the seriousness of work is seen in play and the play element is seen in some of our work.

4.6.3 Work, leisure and unemployment

Work has been traditionally valued. It has been a means of self-identification. A person's leisure appears to relate not only to individuality, but to whether one is working, how satisfying the work is, whether one is unemployed and the extent of dissatisfaction with the situation, and whether there is an overall feeling of being involved with society or alienated from it. The extent to which job dissatisfaction and unemployment foster feelings of alienation is an important issue for employers, and leisure providers. Can opportunities for recreation and re-creation counter life dissatisfactions?

Those people who are made to retire early, are made redundant or who simply do not want to retire can also find themselves feeling alienated, isolated and robbed of the purposefulness of life. We are moving into a period where the dependence on paid work as a means for organizing one's life and that of one's family is declining. The situation makes it a mistake to consider 'leisure' as 'time free from work'. Also it is becoming less appropriate to consider 'work' only as a job for which one is paid. Over half the population – i.e. dependent children, houseworkers, the retired, the unemployed, students and many of the handicapped – are not in paid employment and therefore are not included in the present conceptual boundaries of such a definition of leisure.

John Maynard Keynes [60] revolutionized economic thought after the First World War. In 1930 he envisaged a future society whose needs could be satisfied with no more than fifteen hours of work per week, *if* it chose to devote its energies to non-economic purposes. The problem was how to use freedom from economic worries and how to use leisure so as to live wisely. He mused on a future when:

> We shall once more value ends above means and prefer the good to the useful. We shall honour those who can teach us how to pluck the hour and the day virtuously and well, the delightful people who are capable of taking direct enjoyment in things, the lilies of the field who toil not, neither do they spin.

Today, higher education levels among workers, a shift in jobs from manufacturing to the service sector and the rise of professionalism, and other factors, have made work less like slavery for many and more like leisure for some. The leisure pattern of evenings, weekends and holidays is changing: the linear pattern is breaking up. Among the reasons are the changing role of women, the changing age composition of our society, expanding continuing education, changes in attitudes toward work, and so on. Also work is being removed from the workplace with computer links to home, portable word processors, and mobile and conference telephones. The times are changing!

4.7 Changing times from 1960s onwards

In the 1960s, Bob Dylan sang 'The times they are a-changing'. The song ushered in a new era for leisure in the United Kingdom – the first sport, leisure and arts centres; integrated local authority leisure services, and corporate management; joint use and dual provision in schools; the Beatles and the growth in a new kind of popular music; an age described by Harold Macmillan as 'you never had it so good'. There was an upbeat spirit of 'onwards and upwards'. In 1965 Michael Dower [61] wrote for the Civic Trust a watershed publication *Fourth Wave – The Challenge of Leisure*.

> Three great waves have broken across the face of Britain since 1800. First, the sudden growth of dark industrial towns. Second, the thrusting movement along far-flung railways. Third, the sprawl of car-based suburbs. Now we see, under the guise of a modest word, the surge of a fourth wave which could be more powerful than all the others. The modest word is leisure.

Today's changes are equally important and equally significant. There is an ever-increasing choice for consumers and increasing expectations; demographic changes call for improved programmes for growing market segments, such as the older age-groups. Yet modern society does not yet treat leisure seriously. The patterns and rhythms of life are determined by work and its demands, and any spare time, the residual, is labelled as a leisure period.

Echoing Bertrand Russell in 1932, who suggested that if workers worked four hours a day, there would be enough for everybody, Clive Jenkins and Barrie Sherman in 1979 wrote *The Collapse of Work* [62]. In *The Leisure Shock* [63] they predicted:

> What is work? Will there be enough of it to go round? Must there or should there be enough of it to go round? Will many of us suffer withdrawal symptoms if we cannot have our share of it? . . . Our approach is to have a reduced working week, month, year and lifetime, but with at least the same level of remuneration. This implies that some employers would have to take on extra labour, that both profits and returns to capital would fall – in other words a redistribution of monies towards labour.

However, twenty years later, a quite different picture has emerged. A quarter of all British male employees work more than 48 hours a week; 44 per cent of British workers come home exhausted. More than half suffer from stress; 7 out of 10 workers want to work a 40-hour week; only 3 out of 10 do so; and full-time working women have 32 hours a week free time, 14 hours less than men in full-time employment.

In Japan, 10,000 people are thought to die each year from overwork. More people are more pressured about time – or lack of it. The patterns of work, shopping, leisure – the building blocks of life are disappearing. We are moving to home shopping, video-on-demand, the internet, flexitime work, home banking. Life used to be lived on fixed timetables – a time to reap and a time to sow and a rhythm of life. This has given way to a post-industrial culture: metaphorically, we 'fast-forward life's video tape' to cram more into a reduced time slot. Today time is seen as a precious resource. We are time-conscious whether at work, shopping, cooking or at leisure – a contradiction of terms if ever there was one. We are in an age of technology which promises to increase personal autonomy and freedom, to cut waste and foster leisure. But we are in what *Demos* describes as 'the time squeeze' [64].

Right across society there is a sense of time being squeezed. And policy has lagged behind, as it always does, with a lengthening series of failures: the growing imbalance between overwork for some and zero work for others; poor management and public spaces and transport which has forced up the times taken to get to work, to care for (and transport) children, even to shop; and severe stress for millions – particularly women – trying to juggle competing responsibilities.

This new post-industrial culture offers, perhaps for the first time in history, the promise of people using time for their own needs. But far from ushering in a leisured utopia, its most immediate effect has been a growing divide between those with too much work and those without any. In top jobs long hours have become a mark of status and success. In the 1930s the phrase 'banking hours' referred to a leisurely working day that began at ten and ended at four, with a generous lunch hour. By contrast today's bankers may be having to cope with 24-hour capital markets. One in eight British managers works more than 60 hours a week and more than half take work home during the week.

Guardian, 6 June 1995

These pressures are not confined to top executives. One in six households has no jobs; others fear redundancy; some are working all hours to pay the bills. So we have work overload on the one hand, with high stress and anxiety levels (for white and blue collar workers) and the dangers that these bring, and no work for some on the other hand. The job market demands that women return to work, yet they still have to care for the home and the family.

A new government in the United Kingdom in 1997 – aptly called 'Labour' – set itself the task of getting people to work. Jobs would be found for 250,000 young people. Five hundred thousand single mothers would come off benefits. The Bishop of Liverpool, David Sheppard, campaigns in the belief that work is essential to give people a sense of worth. But many jobs do not add to the quality of life. As the French novelist, Albert Camus, commenting on work said: 'Without work, all life goes rotten. But when work is soulless, life stifles and dies.'

A problem exists in that large numbers of people cannot get any work and large numbers cannot get away from it. The answer, according to Natasha Walter, writing in *The Observer*, is not to see work as the ultimate good.

That ideal only widens the divide. It forces people in work to cling grimly on to their job – terrified of losing their grip on it, and uneasy about taking holidays and getting home in time for their children's bedtimes. And it encourages people out of work to believe that their lives are being wasted and that they will achieve nothing concrete until they have an employer and a pay packet. If we are really to see the beginning of a more equal society, the way forward must be to celebrate the other side of life, the delights of idleness.

We have come to a critical point where many people are searching for alternative lifestyles and a better balance between paid work and other aspects of life. Some fortunate academics are allowed 'sabbaticals' to re-charge, to travel and to learn new skills.

In the past, leisure was seen as an escape from work. But this misses the point. Many of us enjoy work and find it fulfilling; and also many people work harder at their chosen leisure time occupations. Many young people say that they would rather work at something worthwhile, for nothing, than to be unemployed. To be valued and to have self-worth is hugely motivating.

As we approach the year 2000, we have more knowledge, more resources and more opportunity than before, in which to have a fullness of living, undreamed of in times past. The question is: has leisure a central role in a way of life that harnesses opportunities for harmony with oneself and the world? Without an understanding of such leisure, albeit as an ideal, we cannot have sound principles on which to formulate policies for planning, provision and management.

4.8 Loss of structures and traditions – 'casual' and 'serious' leisure

Lifestyles and traditional ways have changed and so has leisure. Robert Stebbins [65] uses the term 'detraditionalization' to describe the rejection of certain major traditions and cultural staples of everyday life such as work, class, gender and nation. With the loss of some traditions emerges 'individualization', bringing a different relationship between individuals and their socio-cultural environment. A third process he describes as 'tribalization', a disintegration of mass culture, leaving a diversity of 'tribes'. These three 'post-traditional' processes are important in understanding leisure. Stebbins believes that they move us away from perceiving leisure within a single overarching definition or leisure as a list of activities representative of leisure. Post-traditional leisure varies widely according to the type of activity. He distinguishes 'serious leisure' from 'casual leisure'.

Casual leisure is immediately intrinsically rewarding, relatively short lived, pleasurable activity.

> Among its types are play (including dabbling), relaxation (e.g. sitting, napping, strolling), passive entertainment (e.g. TV, books, recorded music), active entertainment (e.g. games of chance, party games), social interaction (sociable conversation), and sensory stimulation (e.g. sex, eating, drinking).

Serious leisure, the substantial leisure of amateurs, hobbyists and career volunteers, has a decidedly different effect on lifestyle and identity.

> Individualisation occurs when participants enter specialised pursuits where they find powerful personal rewards special to each pursuit, including self-actualisation, self-expression, self-enrichment, self-gratification and psychological flow as well as an attractive, profound personal identity. At the same time, all these activities apart from the most recent are carried out within established (i.e. traditional) social worlds and associated lifestyles; they are pursued within the framework of, for example, shared norms, values,

practices, and traditions as developed and maintained through constellations of groups, networks, individuals and organizations. Still, today, individualization gives birth almost regularly to new serious leisure tribes (e.g. snowboarders, female body builders).

A 'profound' lifestyle awaits anyone who routinely pursues a serious leisure career. Stebbins asserts that lifestyles, new and old, constitute a main form of individualization and tribalization. Often, these lifestyles become 'central life interests'. Either work or serious leisure can become a central life interest. A workaholic lives and breathes an occupation or profession. Indeed, the reaction of many people to leisure is to work longer and harder or to turn leisure into work. 'The bicycle is not to be taken lightly. Bicycling is serious business. Do not go slowly in front of a serious cyclist' (Charles Gordon, *Ottawa Citizen* 21 June 1992, cited in Stebbins [65]). A dedicated sportsman or woman works through the pain barrier to gain peak performance.

> A committed gardener, stamp collector, opera buff, jet setter, cook, housewife, mountain climber, bird watcher, computer 'hacker', novel reader, fisherman, or gambler are all usually devoted to their activity as a central life interest. Give such individuals a chance to talk freely about themselves and they will quickly reveal their CLI through fixation on the subject and obvious emotional fervour with which they talk about it.

However, career volunteers also find a lively central life interest in their pursuits, whether in politics, religion, anti-poverty or civil rights campaigns. It appears that only some types of leisure – mostly the serious variety – are sufficiently profound to become central life interests. Moreover, they often need substantial support in the form of financial commitment and put pressure on families.

Leisure produces tribes of all social classes and age groups. Both casual and serious leisure tribes can engender feelings of belonging, but serious leisure tribes make significant contributions to the community. Casual leisure tribes fail to contribute in the same way nor 'engender individualization through distinctive contributions'. They do not contribute to societal organizations and integration. In a post-traditional age, many will fail to benefit from leisure opportunity. In this new age, leisure appears to have even greater significance in terms of a leisure identity which can arise with a person's leisure-based central life interest.

> The work, or more accurately, the non-work situation of many people in the Information Age will consist, in part, of being cast adrift from the key organisational moorings of their employment days, a clear sign of a post-traditional existence. More and more, these people will find themselves floating, without a rudder in an organisationless sea, a result of their unemployment, retirement, or marginal affiliation with a work organisation as a contractual worker [65].

In the future, for those without jobs or few hours of paid work, fashioning a leisure identity may be the remaining area of life in which personal qualities and aspirations can be realized. Membership of, and commitment to, a club, orchestra or society – Stebbin's serious leisure tribes – could serve as a better means towards this end than casual leisure tribes who are unable to fill the craving for organizational belonging, as they rarely become formally organized.

As Bertrand Russell said, 'To be able to fill leisure intelligently is the last product of civilization, and at present, very few people have reached that level.' Russell died in 1970. Clearly, his message rings true today.

However, is serious leisure a contradiction of the word leisure? In 'Preferences for work and leisure' [66] when people were asked what they enjoyed doing, people tended to place first various social activities – playing with their children, visiting friends. However, placed second were their working activities. Their 'leisure' activities – sports, DIY and watching television came third; (watching television was seventeenth in a list of twenty-eight activities.)

Therefore, like the quality of leisure, the quality of work also contributes to the quality of life, happiness and human development. If society makes work challenging and rewarding, will leisure choices also reflect those qualities? Kohn and Schooler [67] believe so, particularly where there are opportunities to exercise self-direction. Challenging work, they claim, actually encourages the selection of uses of leisure time that are also challenging. 'It seems that the road to better uses of leisure time is not through increasing leisure time, but improving the character of work time.'

Research carried out by the Henley Centre for Forecasting [68] showed that free time for full-time working adult men had declined over the past decade by 4 per cent. For full-time working women, the decline had been over 10 per cent. 'To be busy is to be needed, and staying at work all hours indicates how important we are – even if it means no time to give to family and friends.' By international standards, the British are veritable workaholics. Moreover, amongst the middle classes, time planning disciplines are almost as rigorous at weekends as they are during the week. We can now talk of people's 'productivity' in terms of leisure as well as work time.

In terms of leisure, however, the Henley Centre finds that the British are not an active and busy population, but one that is 'extraordinarily passive'. The activities that the majority of the British do at least once a week are watching TV, reading and listening to tapes and CDs. The average person spends over twenty hours a week watching TV. 'This means that TV accounts for nearly a third of our leisure time because the average available free time (after sleep, work, travel to work and essential activities are taken into account) is 65 hours per week.'

Robinson's findings [69] are at odds and portray a more jaundiced perspective. When released from work, increased time was spent in sleep, in resting, in personal care, and in automobile travel.

Asked about the 'meaning of leisure to them', samples in Kansas City and in New Zealand chose the following answers most frequently: 'just for the pleasure of it', 'a welcome change from work', 'gives a new experience', 'permits contact with friends', and 'makes time pass'. So far, there is little to gladden the heart of the apostles of the humanistic ideal of human development through leisure, but, finally, in fifth and seventh places one finds 'a chance to achieve something', and 'a chance to be creative'. A few, of course, use their leisure to develop their potentials.

4.9 Leisure – a search for identity?

4.9.1 Leisure opportunities

Opportunities afforded through leisure have awakened for many a spirit of self-development, adventure and creativity. Economists and sociologists may tell us that we have not reached the 'age of leisure', but it is clear to see that many people are in search of new leisure identities. The tenth London Marathon attracted 60,000 applications, of which 35,000 were accepted to run. Between them the runners raised millions of pounds for charity. Former Race organizer, Christopher Brasher, commented: 'Make no mistake, it is hard, desperately hard, to run 26 miles 385 yards and the only reward for the masses is that every single one of them is a winner.'

The increasing army of joggers, orienteers, climbers, hang-gliders, cavers, skin-divers, parachute jumpers, surfers, sailors, dancers, amateur historians and archaeologists, painters, writers, actors, fitness fanatics, tri-athletes and meditators shows that people are looking for new and innovative activities and experiences. But what are all these people searching for, while sometimes risking their lives, money and loved ones? Maslow described it as a 'peak experience', brought about by 'affirmation of our identity and confirmation of our existence'. Peak moments are some of those high moments in life when one is totally immersed in an activity, at one with the world and with oneself. Top-class skiers say they have the sensation of blending into the mountain; runners, having gone through the pain barrier, have described a feeling of 'floating'; and top gymnasts have achieved a moment of sheer 'perfection'.

Although such experiences cannot be made to happen, some conditions can create an enabling environment. Most people (drug free!) reporting 'highs' in, say, sport or music have achieved some mastery, a high level of skill. Often outdoor activities, battling with the elements, or being surrounded by natural beauty, may cause us to reach beyond our ordinary existence. Many peak experiences (e.g. mountaineering, parachute jumping, white-water canoeing) involve risk. It is clear that recreation and leisure activities have much to offer in helping people reach beyond themselves. Spectators and supporters can share in moments of achievement but it is the doers – those participants motivated by intrinsic rewards – who will gain greatest satisfaction and who are the ones more likely to achieve peak experiences or feelings of re-creation or oneness.

More than peak experiences, however, many people are looking for self-fulfilment, maybe to be or to become 'somebody' – all they are capable of becoming. The spirit is caught in the poem by Robert Browning: 'Ah, but a man's reach should exceed his grasp. Or what's a heaven for?' Is this not akin to the leisure ideal of the Ancient Greeks, but more useful because it widens the scope of their narrow choice?

The search for identity is important in understanding leisure behaviour. It is a search for the whole person, not a split person. This idea is exemplified in the growth of spiritual and meditative movements. Some Eastern disciplines and philosophies, for example, emphasize a unification of the body, mind and spirit, through movement, meditation and deep relaxation. These Eastern cults, which promise a unity with oneself and with the universe, have captured the imagination of the Western world, perhaps because of the vacuum created by our artificial splitting of the body from the mind and spirit.

It is clear, then, that leisure offers opportunities for enrichment. But the time for leisure potential can also bring problems because freedom not only allows us, but also forces us, to make choices.

While leisure opportunity contains a time element, leisure behaviour must not be time conscious, if people are to play and find satisfying preoccupations, interests and leisure in their lives.

4.10 Similarities between play, recreation and leisure

This section moves away from the word 'leisure' alone and attempts to bring together the findings from chapters two to four to link 'play', 'recreation' and 'leisure' together.

The characteristics of 'play' and ' recreation' have been highlighted in preceding chapters and 'leisure' has been covered in this chapter. However, in many instances the three phenomena overlap to different degrees. Several words, ideas or themes are used frequently in describing each concept, including the following:

1   *Freedom* This is the free expression of play; the free choice of recreation; the freedom of choice in leisure.
2   *Self-expression* Each emphasizes individual self-expression.
3   *Satisfaction* Play is characterized by satisfaction in the doing, manifest joy; recreation and leisure are both satisfying to various degrees.
4   *Quality* The quality of experiencing is important to all.
5   *Self-initiated* Play is usually self-initiated, and leisure and recreation also appear to be so in large measure; recreation, however, can also be directed by others.
6   *Absence of necessity* Play cannot be forced and remain play; leisure has the same connotations; in recreation too there is an absence of necessity, but a level of obligation may be attached to it in its institutional setting.
7   *Playfulness* Play, though often serious, is abundant in playfulness, in fun; recreation is often playful but many elements are so competitive that they appear to be more akin to work; leisure is freer and 'looser' and therefore exhibits more playfulness.
8   *Any activity* In its purest terms almost any activity can function as a play, recreation or leisure for someone; recreation, however, is more socially constrained in its institutional setting.

9   *Experiencing* Again, in its purest terms, each has an inner dimension; play is totally absorbing in the doing ('lost in play'); re-creation can be an inner-consuming experience of oneness; leisure can be the perception of freedom for the sake of doing or experiencing.

10 *Timelessness* In totally absorbing situations in play and recreation, time can stand still. While leisure has a time frame, leisure behaviour should not be time conscious.

It is tempting to dismiss this line of enquiry as mere semantics. However, there is more to it than just words because we often provide for these three aspects of life in different ways. We provide *play space*, *community recreation facilities* and *family leisure centres*. Moreover, these similarities emphasize that play, recreation and leisure are integrated and they appear, collectively, to have an inner core. We use the words, however, with different emphasis.

Play can be described as activity, freely chosen and indulged in for its own sake for the satisfaction it brings in the doing; it exhibits childlike characteristics of spontaneity, self-expression and a creation of its own special meaning in a play world.

Recreation, unlike play, appears to need to be justified, 'keeps youth off the streets', 'produces good citizens'. It carries greater social responsibilities than 'leisure'. It has concern for community well-being, which is epitomized in 'therapeutic recreation', 'industrial recreation', 'recreation counselling'. Recreation is thus a social institution, a structure for recreation organisations, services and activities.

Re-creation is another meaning. In its purest sense, it is characterized by an inner-consuming experience of oneness that leads to revival. Like all feelings, it can have different strengths. At its strongest, it can be a 'peak' experience. Recreation experience therefore renews, restores and 'recharges the batteries' – in our waking moments. Like sleep, it is a process of re-creating!

Leisure is perceived in different ways – time, activity, experience, state of being, a way of life, and so on. It is in a way multidimensional. It can encompass

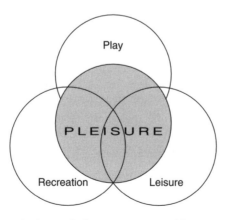

FIGURE 4.1 'Pleisure' at the heart of play, recreation and leisure experience

play and recreation activity. It can also function as the psychological perception of freedom to choose and to do and to experience. It also has the capacity to be perceived as a way of living – a 'leisure ideal'. Leisure, then, can be perceived as experiencing activities, chosen in relative freedom, that are personally satisfying and innately worthwhile and that can lead an individual towards self-actualization and, ultimately, a self-fulfilling life.

Hence play, recreation and leisure exhibit a sameness at their core. And at the core they can be interlocked into one meaning, which is greater than the sum of the three individual parts.

4.11 The inner core – the leisure experience – 'pleisure'

An inner-consuming experience may occur in the process of play, recreation or leisure. This experience I shall now call 'pleisure' (a derivation and an acronym for the words 'play', 'leisure' and 'recreation') as there is no word in the English language to describe it. Indeed, the experience goes beyond the description afforded by words – it is experience, wordless.

What implication does this 'discovery' have for the management of leisure? Put simply, the 'pleisure principle' implies that, in meeting the needs of people, the quality of the experience is more important than the activities themselves, the numbers attending or the income generated. Furthermore, managers must take into account that different people have different needs, which change according to their circumstances and stage in life. The quality of the experience is of greatest importance for 'pleisure' to occur. The activity itself may be secondary to what it does for a person, or what it means to him or her. People will 'purchase' satisfying experiences. Ask any successful commercial leisure manager!

If, as leisure professionals, we want to provide a choice of activities and opportunity for people to experience and develop leisure potential, then we must provide favourable environments: the right conditions; satisfaction; and positive outcomes.

1   *The right conditions* There need to be sufficient levels of some of the following ingredients: freedom; choice; absence of necessity; self-initiation and spontaneity.
2   *Satisfaction* To be satisfying, there need to be levels of some of the following experiences: self-expression; challenge; novelty; stimulation; playfulness; quality experiences (ideally, peak experiences) and re-creative moments.
3   *Positive outcomes* To be effective, there should be some positive outcomes, for example: physical, emotional, social and psychological well-being; level of achievement; and heightening of self-esteem.

Favourable experiences give satisfactions. Satisfactions lead to consuming interests. Consuming interests can lead to life-enhancing experiences, a goal of leisure.

4.12 Public services designed to meet needs – problems and possibilities

Were it all as simple as that! Regrettably, there are a number of individual and institutional barriers to providing integrated services based on the needs of people. The reasons are complex. Individual people are not free agents and are limited in their response to leisure services and programmes; some people have physical, mental and social limitations or their environments limit choice (e.g. family, peer group, culture, resources). Leisure for others is eroded through obligations, lack of time or through enforced free time without the means or motivation to use it. Then activities, such as sport, can be practised in such extremes that they can work not for the good, but for the bad, and where the spirit of goodwill and fair play are submerged and dominated by over-zealous competition and cheating – winning at all costs.

Do providers adequately consider people's needs in planning facilities and formulating programmes? It is apparent that there are not only personal and social barriers to integrated services, there also exist strong organizational and institutional barriers. Commercial organizations are concerned with financial profits; monetary results therefore are the goal. Many voluntary organizations and institutions are concerned with their own autonomy and their own programmes, in isolation from the needs of the larger community. Public authorities provide fragmented services between authorities, between tiers in the same authority and sometimes within the same department. It is not uncommon to find people going from one local authority department to the next, to find a satisfactory solution to a problem. Organizations, professions, voluntary bodies and public departments all have a tendency to isolate themselves and operate independently. The lack of cohesion and customer care may deprive people, whose needs may go unheeded.

Hence, while an integrated approach to leisure service is desirable, there are organizational and institutional barriers and increasing financial barriers to overcome. To provide appropriate services, principles must be founded on the best theoretical framework, the obstacles and limitations should be recognized and assumptions made about which services and programmes can be developed.

4.11.1 *Learning to choose*

Leisure implies freedom. Freedom implies choice. Choice enables people to be involved in activities which are either personally worthwhile and which lead to good citizenship or which are of doubtful value.

In the United Kingdom, in the 1990s, some new leisure provision increasingly panders to the apparent need for entertainment and diversion. 'Provide slides and rides; people will pay for the pleasure.' On balance, this is fine. We need amusement and fun. Yet consider, does the individual who flits from experience to experience, like an impulse buyer in a supermarket, have the opportunity to gain an appreciation of the activity which will make it, in Godbey's words, 'intuitively worthwhile'? For most people, enjoyment and satisfaction in an activity increase as knowledge and skill increase. Whether gardening, playing the violin, cooking, playing tennis or collecting antiques, all are enriched by an increase in knowledge and skill. 'Leisure involves sacrificing that which is potentially good for that which is potentially better. The lack of willingness to sacrifice one desirable activity in order to undertake another, however, suggests an inability to obtain leisure [70].'

As Jacob Bronowski [71] pointed out, appreciation is essentially an act of re-creation; a deep sense of appreciation envelops us and lifts us to a higher plane where we discover that there is peace, beauty and joy in this world. And that may carry over into increased appreciation of life itself. That is leisure's promise.

It seems hard for us to appreciate and accept the gift of leisure. Ideally, leisure can be a way of living the 'good life' for individuals and communities. But as Goodale and Godbey point out, only we can determine for ourselves what that will be. However, education and knowledge will help to give the opportunity and ability to make good choices. Education can help make us free, and freedom forces us to make choices because the world of opportunities opens up before us. But education should not be limited to finding jobs. Schools and colleges are not simply employment agencies. The more we learn about ourselves, how to choose to find fulfilment, the better society we create.

4.11.2 A needs-based Utopia?

People have diverse needs, and different people have different needs, which change according to their circumstances and stage in life. Old people have different needs from the young; disadvantaged people have different levels of need compared with those highly advantaged. People have a whole range of needs, some of which are basic to survival, some are essential to cope with living in an uncertain social world and some are at the apex of a complex human network bringing balance, harmony and self-worth to individual people. It is particularly in this latter category where leisure opportunity can help people to meet some of their needs. Leisure therefore is linked, inextricably, to other elements of life. For example, leisure for the vast majority of disadvantaged groups is likely to remain low while major life constraints persist such as lack of income, poor housing and the unrelieved pressures of parenting.

If, as a society, we want to provide integrated leisure services based on the needs of people, authorities must make a number of assumptions on which to base principles, aims and objectives; for example, that the services are open to all and meet individual needs, so that a person can choose activities, in relative freedom; that priorities should be balanced to serve the greatest number and those in greatest need, recognizing that those in greatest need may well be in the minority; and that services should not be pockets of competing interests.

The question is: can leisure, with emphasis on freedom, be organized, planned and managed? The activity can be but the experience cannot. However, opportunities can be enabling. What is the Manager's role?

1   Leisure Managers can market, involve people and then create an environment where personally worthwhile choices can be made and satisfying experiences are more likely to occur.

2   Leisure Managers can extend the range of activities to offer a wide and varied choice.

3   Groups can be enabled to participate through supportive services.

4   Other groups can be encouraged to fashion their own destiny.

On a wider scale:

5   Work conditions can be improved to give people a greater chance of self-expression, recreation activity and recuperation. Leisure Managers can advise employers.

6   Education can inculcate leisure skills (physical, social, cultural and intellectual) which can help people to realize their potential. Leisure managers can work in consulation and co-operation.

In these and other ways, management can help to extend opportunities. The assumptions provide principles on which to force a reorientation towards an enhanced 'people approach' to leisure services. The reorientation stems from the belief that each individual has worth and has a need to express himself or herself, and that society will benefit from citizens who have the ability, adaptability and resourcefulness to cope, create and find fulfilment.

Leisure time without the opportunity, the means and the ability to cope can be a two-edged sword. Along with a marked increase in leisure participation, there has been a marked increase in antisocial behaviour, particularly in those areas where leisure opportunity is low. Free time has not solved the social problems of loneliness, poverty or job satisfaction. Indeed, leisure time may have exacerbated those problems. Can leisure opportunity help to solve some of them? Opportunity for leisure has no value to people, of course, unless advantage is taken of it. This is where the leisure professional has a special role to play, that of enabling people to take up the opportunities by effective and sensitive marketing.

The job of the manager is to help people to take advantage of that leisure opportunity. That opportunity can be seen as a favourable or advantageous combination of circumstances; it can be a suitable activity, occasion or time, an opening, a chance, a break. It allows the time and access to behave in ways that we want to, and which we find satisfying – i.e. to play, to rest, to enjoy, to contemplate, to work, to serve and to be ourselves.

The study of leisure shows how important it is to deal with men and women as complete, whole persons. In addition, it is important to look at leisure and work not as two discrete, mutually exclusive components of life. The interrelationships and the overlap between the two are evident: 'Man was not born to work. Rather man was born with an innate capacity for effort, which can be dissipated in any activity be it sailing, cooking, sex, chess, Frisbee or art' [72].

The leisure we are talking about in this chapter can be for some a way of living, and for most a major sphere of life that brings innate satisfaction. To be able to grasp leisure opportunity, people must develop preoccupations and interests which can be expressed through leisure activities. These activities need resources, organization, planning and management.

4.13 Summary – leisure

Leisure is a historic idea. It has survived war, greed and revolution. During its evolution, it has been considered in varying degrees from a quality of life reflecting the highest ideals to being the worst evil – the devil incarnate. Leisure has been perceived as blocks of time when we are freest to be ourselves, as activities, as a state of being, as an all-embracing attitude to life merging the three dimensions of time, activity and state of mind, and as perceived freedom to choose. It is also described, ideally, as a way of life – a philosophy of living.

Leisure has become the right of most people in Western civilization in the twentieth century but time for leisure can be seen both as a blessing and a curse. Time, without the means, the motivation and the opportunity, or free time forced on to people, are not regarded as leisure. To function as leisure there appears to be a need for positive approaches to life and the activity. The idea of leisure potential stresses the need to offer opportunities for individuals to express themselves in ways of benefit to themselves and to society.

The history of leisure has shown that it has been difficult to hang on to the elevated concept of the Ancient Greeks. Wars, religious stringencies and intellectual bias have stood in its path. Christians put the stamp of ascetic teaching on labour and leisure. Leisure (idleness) was condemned. When leisure did become accepted, it was accepted conditionally – not as value in itself, but as a means of renewing for the work ahead. The word 'recreation' epitomizes the attitude of conditional joy; man works, wearies, takes recreation that he may work again. Take some free time, but not too much! Too much leisure is unearned time. As we approach the Millennium, even with millions of people unemployed in the United Kingdom, Europe and the United States, many people still regard social security payments as 'handouts' and as pandering to the idle. The Puritan work ethic is alive and well!

Leisure was thought to be totally opposite to work but increasingly leisure and work are considered to be on a continuum. Effort (work) is expended both at work and in many leisure activities. With high unemployment, early retirement, longer life and greater leisure potential, an understanding of the relationship between work and leisure is more important than before. Man is both *Homo ludens*, man the player, and *Homo faber*, man the worker. Worthwhile productive labour (effort) appears to be as essential to human self-fulfilment as positive, productive leisure. Both can lead to human satisfactions. It is leisure, however, free from compulsion and necessity, which gives greater potential for human self-fulfilment.

The study of leisure has revealed that while ideas such as pleasure, freedom, contemplation, activity, self-expression and creativity are predominant, considerable stress is being put on leisure not only as an opportunity framework, but also as an attitudinal framework. How do people perceive leisure? What does it mean to them? How do attitudes to choice and participation come about? These further questions are taken up in chapter five.

Our upbringing and history make it difficult for us to recognize and accept the gift of leisure. Ideally, it can become a way of living the 'good life'; however, only we can determine for ourselves what it will be. Yet education and knowledge will help to give opportunity and the skills and abilities to make good choices. Education can make us free, and freedom provides the necessity to make choices.

Leisure is important therefore in the rhythm of our lives. It is to do with activities, usually chosen for their own sake, and in relative freedom and which bring intrinsic satisfactions. Leisure is not time, but a 'leisure use' of time. The personal and social orientations of the use and satisfactions appear to be what make the activity 'leisure'.

Notes and references

1   Mead, M. (1928), *Coming of Age in Samoa*, William Morrow, New York.
2   Godbey, G. (1978), *Recreation, Park and Leisure Services*, W. B. Saunders, Philadelphia, PA, p. 8.
3   Cutten, G. B. (1929), *The Threat of Leisure*, Yale University Press, New Haven, CT, p. 2.
4   For a detailed history of leisure see Chubb, M. and Chubb, H. (1981), *One Third of Our Time*, Wiley, Chichester.
5   ETB and Jones Long Wootton (1989), *Retail, Leisure and Tourism*, ETB, London.
6   Plato (1952), *Complete Works*, Encyclopaedia Britannica, Chicago, IL.
7   Aristotle (1952) *Aristotle 2. Great Books of the Western World*, Encyclopaedia Britannica, Chicago, IL.
8   For a fuller discussion on leisure and the ancient Greeks: Kelly, J. (1982), *Leisure*, Prentice-Hall, Englewood Cliffs, NJ, and Goodale, T. and Godbey, G. (1988), *The Evolution of Leisure*, Venture Publishing, State College, PA.
9   Goodale, T. and Godbey, G. (1988), *The Evolution of Leisure*, Venture Publishing, State College, PA, pp. 28, 6, 62.
10   Miller, N. P. and Robinson, D. M. (1963), *Leisure Age: Its Challenge to Recreation*, Wadsworth, Belmont, CA.
11   Veblen, T. (1953), *Theory of the Leisure Class*, Mentor, New York (originally published 1899).
12   Parry, N. and Parry, J. (1977), 'Theories of culture and leisure', paper presented at Leisure Studies Association Conference, University of Manchester, September.
13   Soule, G. (1957), 'The economics of leisure', *Annals of the American Academy of Political and Social Science*, September.
14   Parker, S. (1971), *The Future of Work and Leisure*, MacGibbon and Kee, London, p. 20.
15   Brightbill, C. K. (1964), *Recreation, 57*, January, p. 10.
16   Neumeyer, M. and Neumeyer, E. (1958), *Leisure and Recreation*, Ronald Press, New York, p. 17.
17   Kaplan, M. (1960), *Leisure in America*, Wiley, New York, pp. 21–2.
18   Dumazedier, J. (1960), editorial, *International Social Science Journal, 1*, Winter, 526.
19   Nash, J. B. (1960), *Philosophy of Recreation and Leisure*, William Brown, Dubuque, IA.
20   Maslow, A. (1954), *Motivation and Personality*, Harper, New York.
21   Maslow, A. (1968), *Towards a Psychology of Being*, D. Van Nostrand, New York.

22 Dumazedier, J. (1967), *Toward a Society of Leisure*, W. W. Norton, New York.

23 Kaplan, M. (1975), *Leisure Theory and Policy*, Wiley, New York, chapter 1 and p. 19.

24 Pieper, J. (1952), *Leisure the Basis of Culture*, New American Library, New York, p. 40.

25 Brightbill, C. K. (1963), *The Challenge of Leisure*, Prentice-Hall, New York, p. 4.

26 Larrabee, E. and Meyersohn, R. (eds) (1958), *Mass Leisure*, The Free Press, Glencoe, IL. pp. 2, 252.

27 de Grazia, S. (1962), *Of Time, Work and Leisure*, Doubleday, New York.

28 Marcuse, H. (1964), *One-Dimensional Man*, Routledge, London, p. 49.

29 Parker, S. (1971), *The Future of Work and Leisure*, MacGibbon and Kee, London, pp. 24–5.

30 Nakhooda, J. (1961), *Leisure and Recreation in Society*, Kitab Mahal, Allahabad, India, p. 14.

31 Dumazedier, J. (1967), *Toward a Society of Leisure*, W. W. Norton, New York, pp. 16–17, 37, 236–7.

32 Murphy, J. (1975), *Recreation and Leisure Service*, William C. Brown, Dubuque, IA, pp. 6, 11, 15.

33 Neulinger, J. (1974), *The Psychology of Leisure*, Charles, C. Thomas, Springfield, IL.

34 Neulinger, J. and Crandall, R. (1976), 'The psychology of leisure', *Journal of Leisure Research, 3*, August, 181–4.

35 Kelly, J. (1982), *Leisure*, Prentice-Hall, Englewood Cliffs, NJ, p. 5.

36 Godbey, G. (1978), *Recreation, Park and Leisure Services*, W. B. Saunders, Philadelphia, PA, pp. 10–12.

37 Godbey, G. (1975), 'Anti-leisure and public recreation policy', in Parker, S. *et al.* (eds) *Sport and Leisure in Contemporary Society*, Leisure Studies Association, London.

38 Linder, S. (1970), *The Harried Leisure Class*, Columbia University Press, New York.

39 Scheusch, E. (1972), *The Time Budget Interview*, quoted in n.9, above, p. 127.

40 de Toqueville, A. (1899), *Democracy in America*, (translated by H. Reeve), Colonial Press, New York, Vol. 1 and 2.

41 Henley Centre (1989), in *Retail, Leisure and Tourism*, English Tourist Board/Jones Long Wootton, London, p. 9.

42 Cutten, G. B. (1929), *The Threat of Leisure*, Yale University Press, New Haven, Conn.

43 Roberts, K. (1970), *Leisure*, Longman, London, and Roberts, K. (1977), 'Leisure and life styles under welfare capitalism', in Smith, M. A. (ed.) *Leisure and Urban Society*, Leisure Studies Association, London.

44 Kraus, R. (1978), *Recreation and Leisure in Modern Society* (2nd edn), Goodyear, Santa Monica, CA.

45 Zuzanek, J. (1977), Leisure trends and the economics of the arts', in Smith, M. A. (ed.) *Leisure and Urban Society*, Leisure Studies Association, London.

46 Lewis, G. H. (1978), 'Popular culture and leisure', *Leisure Today* (Journal of Physical Education and Recreation), October, 3–5.

47   Gans, H. J. (1974), *Popular Culture and High Culture*, Basic Books, New York.

48   Kando, H. (1975), *Leisure and Popular Culture in Transition*, cited in Lewis, G. H. (1978), Popular culture and leisure. *Leisure Today* (JOPER), October, 3–5.

49   Kato, H. (1975), cited in Lewis, C. H. (1978), Popular culture and leisure. *Leisure Today* (JOPER), October, 3–5.

50   Reported in the *Nation*, 21 June 1990.

51   Russell, B. (1935), *In Praise of Idleness*, Allen & Unwin, London.

52   Marx, K. (1952), *Manifesto of the Communist Party*, Encyclopaedia Britannica, Chicago, IL.

53   Parker, S. (1971), *The Future of Work and Leisure*, MacGibbon and Kee, London, pp. 101–2.

54   Berger, B. (1963), Sociology of leisure, in Smigel, E. D. (ed.) *Work and Leisure: A Contemporary Social Problem*, College and University Press, New Haven, CT.

55   Wilensky, H. (1960), 'Work, careers and social integration', *International Social Science Journal, 12*, 543–60.

56   Bacon, A. W. (1972), 'The embarrassed self', *Society and Leisure*, 4, 23–39.

57   Kelly, J. R. (1972), 'Work and leisure: a simplified paradigm', *Journal of Leisure Research, 4*, 50–62.

58   Blauner, R. (1964), *Alienation and Freedom: The Factory Worker and his Industry*, University of Chicago Press, Chicago, IL.

59   Argyris, C. (1973), 'Personality and organisation theory revisited', *Administrative Society Quarterly, 18*, 141–67.

60   Keynes, J. M. (1963), 'Economic possibilities for our grandchildren', in *Essays in Persuasian*, W. W. Norton, New York.

61   Dower, M. (1965), *Fourth Wave – The Challenge of Leisure*, reprinted from *Architects' Journal*, 20 January 1965.

62   Jenkins, C. and Sherman, B. (1979), *The Collapse of Work*, Methuen, Fakenham.

63   Jenkins, C. and Sherman, B. (1981), *The Leisure Shock*, Methuen, Bungay.

64   Mulgan, G. (1995), 'The time squeeze', *Demos*, 5.

65   Stebbins, R., Casual and Serious Leisure and Post-Traditional Thought in the Information Age, WLRA Fourth World Congress, Cardiff, July 1996.

66   Juster, F. (1985) 'Preferences for work and leisure' in Juster, F. and Stafford, F. (eds), *Time, Goods and Well-Being*, Institution of Social Research, Ann Arbor, MI.

67   Kohn, M. and Schooler, C. (1983), *Work and Personality: An Inquiry into the Impact of Social Stratification*, Norwood, NJ.

68   Tyrrell, B. (1995) 'Time in our lives: facts and analysis on the 90s', *Demos*, 5, pp. 23–25.

69   Robinson, J. (1985), 'Changes in time use: an historical overview', in Juster, F. and Stafford, F. (eds), *Time, Goods and Well-Being*, Institution of Social Research, Ann Arbor, MI.

70   Goodale, T. and Goodbey, G. (1988), *The Evolution of Leisure*, Venture Publishing, State College, PA, pp.218–9.

71   Bronowski, J. (1965), *The Science and Human Values* (rev. edition), Harper Torchbooks, New York.
72   Levy, J. (1977), 'A recreation renaissance', *Parks and Recreation*, December, p.18.

Recommended additional reading

Argyle, M. (1996), *The Social Psychology of Leisure*, Penguin Books, London.

Chapter five

People's needs and factors that influence participation

In chapters two to four we have dealt with three separate yet overlapping concepts: play, recreation and leisure. However, these are of limited value unless they help to meet some of the needs of individual people and thereby the good of the wider community. This chapter consists of two main parts. The first is concerned with people's needs; the second considers factors which influence participation.

Community leisure and recreation services are said to be based on the needs of people. Yet policy makers, planners and managers have insufficient insights into people's needs. How can leisure, play and recreation meet such needs? In order to know this, we must know as much about the needs of people and what influences people to take part as we do about leisure. This chapter therefore attempts a brief overview of people's needs in relation to leisure.

First, some theories about human motivation are introduced and the question is posed: do leisure needs exist? Second, an identification is made of many of the social needs and the differences between needs and demand are discussed, together with their relevance to leisure services in the community. Third, factors which influence participation, personal, social and opportunity are considered.

Having read this chapter, readers will be able to distinguish needs from demands. They will be able to understand how leisure opportunity, sensitively managed, can help to meet some of the social and physical needs of people. They will understand the importance of offering different kinds of activity and experience to different people, at different stages in life. Readers will also be aware of the range of influences that are brought to bear on individual people in making choices of leisure activity. Leisure professionals will realize that they have no influence on some factors and little on others. However, they will be able to gauge what influences they do have, in terms of planning, providing opportunities, creating the right environments and managing services and facilities.

5.1 Human motivation and need

One simple view is that human need is something that is missing, a deficit. It has been defined as 'any lack or deficit within the individual either acquired or physiological' [1]. Needs here are distinguished from drives and are seen as preceding them; they are the cause of motivation, rather than the motivation itself. Others equate the need with the motivating force [2].

McDougal [3] attempted to explain behaviour by reducing it to a series of innate, but modifiable, instincts. Instinct theory has now been generally discarded, but McDougal's theory was in many ways a watershed in motivational theory. It led to the further efforts of behavioural scientists to discover why we behave as we do. It also led many psychologists to look for more widely extended, diffusive concepts which explain human motivation. One of the central ideas to be salvaged from McDougal's theory was that of the purposeful, goal-directed nature of the greater part of human behaviour.

Drive is goal-directed; it releases energy. It is generally considered to be the motivating factor within human personality. There appear to be different sorts of drive such as the drive for food, the drive for sex, the exploratory drive, and so on. Summarizing the concept, Young [4] says: 'Drive is a persisting motivation rather than brief stimulation. Drive is an activating energising process.'

Many psychologists who see the motivational aspect of human needs as drives do so in conjunction with the concept of homeostasis. People have a fundamental need to maintain a state of relative internal stability. Needs can therefore be perceived in terms of the elements that disturb homeostasis; drives are the forces which impel the individual to regain the equilibrium that has been lost.

Homeostasis is easiest to understand in terms of physiological needs, for example, the relief of cold or hunger. Needs which are social in nature, such as the needs for achievement, self-fulfilment and acceptance, are less easily accounted for in terms of homeostasis. However, as indicated in the discussion on recreation in chapter three, the principle of 'psychological homeostasis' was used by Shivers as the basis of 're-creation'.

All human behaviour is motivated, according to Freudian theory. Nothing happens by chance, not even behaviour which appears to be 'accidental'. Thus we often remark on the 'Freudian slip'; everyday errors, accidents and slips of the tongue, far from being just 'accidental', are caused by underlying and unconscious wishes or intentions [5].

In terms of motivation, Freud saw two fundamental driving forces in human beings: the sexual and the aggressive. The basic drives which motivate all behaviour operate unconsciously at a basic level of the psyche known as the id. They are not fixed patterns of behaviour, but function through 'external' demands and constraints – i.e. the 'realities' of the outside world. The two psychic structures which channel and modify the basic drives are the ego and superego. They direct the basic drives into socially acceptable channels.

Freud placed great emphasis on the developmental stages of early childhood, but little on the later life-cycle stages. Erikson [6], however, viewed development as a process which continues throughout life. His theory of development demonstrates that needs themselves are developmental, that needs change at different stages of the life-cycle right up to old age.

It appears to be a reasonable conclusion that need is concerned with motivation: 'In theories of motivation need is seen as a state or force within the individual. This can be either a deficit state leading to a search for satisfaction, or else a stage of psychological incompleteness leading to a movement towards completeness' [7]. In either case, need is a motivational concept referring to the processes – conscious or unconscious – involved in goal-orientated behaviour.

5.1.1 Do leisure needs exist?

In management and leisure discussion the most often cited theory pertaining to needs is that of Maslow [8,9]. He suggests that needs are hierarchically ordered. At the base of the hierarchy are the primary physiological needs of the human being (e.g. food, sleep, shelter), and at the apex of the hierarchy are those needs which are related to the psychological factors of self-actualization, such as creativity and sense of achievement. According to Maslow, the lower needs must be satisfied before any of the higher needs come into play .

There are a number of problems in the application of Maslow's hierarchy; for example, needs are not necessarily hierarchically ordered, nor divided into sectors, but are often overlapping and occur simultaneously. However, the theory emphasizes the developmental needs of the individual. Need is no longer seen by Maslow as the reduction of some state of tension or the return to homeostatic equilibrium. Instead people are seen as striving towards the fulfilment of more positive growth. Many others with a humanistic approach to psychology also emphasize the human need for self-actualization and growth [10]. Maslow's hierarchy is also a useful way of identifying and categorizing the different types of need that individuals have.

Tillman [11], building on this theme, examined needs and identified ten which he felt are important in determining the 'leisure needs' of people, namely:

1 new experiences like adventure
2 relaxation, escape and fantasy
3 recognition and identity
4 security – being free from thirst, hunger or pain
5 dominance – to direct others or control one's environment

6   response and social interaction, to relate and react to others
7   mental activity – to perceive and understand
8   creativity
9   service to others – the need to be needed
10 physical activity and fitness.

However, the concept of 'leisure needs' is misleading. People have needs, which can be satisfied in a variety of ways. One way of meeting some of them may be through leisure opportunity: leisure needs as such may not exist.

5.2   Social needs

Bradshaw's conceptualization of needs is concerned with the problems that arise in identifying different types of social need [12]. He suggests that social needs be classified into four categories: normative; felt; expressed; and comparative. He explores a system by which the overlapping considerations of the four approaches to 'need' can be utilized to form a model to assist in making objective assessments of 'real' need.

Mercer [13], and later McAvoy [14] and Godbey [15], have applied Bradshaw's concepts to recreation. Godbey and others have expanded the number of classifications in the social needs model by adding additional categories: created needs; changing needs; and false needs.

5.2.1   Normative needs and leisure

These represent value judgements that are made by professionals in the recreation and leisure field (such as criteria for open space standards). These normative needs, stated as standards, are usually expressed in quantitative terms.

The use of normative needs as the major determinant of leisure provision can be challenged on a number of points. The development of standards is often based on small-group value orientations, often arbitrary and biased. They cannot be valid for the population as a whole. (A full discussion of the problems and benefits of standards is presented in chapter eight.)

5.2.2   Felt needs and leisure

The problem is that people find difficulty in articulating their needs, which are influenced by one's aspirations and cultural environment. Felt needs can be defined as the desires that an individual has but has not yet actively expressed; they are based on what a person thinks he or she wants to do. According to Mercer [16], felt needs are largely learned patterns; we generally want what we have become used to having. In many cases, felt needs are limited by the individual's knowledge and perception of available recreation and leisure service opportunities. However, mass communication has expanded the individual's potential for knowledge and experiences ordinarily outside his or her realm of existence. Thus felt needs, on the one hand, are limited by an individual's perception of opportunities; but, on the other hand, they can be based on what a person imagines he or she would like to do.

The concept of felt needs can be of use to the recreation and leisure service for two reasons. First, it enables people to express desires of what they would like to do. Second, individuals are likely to be happier participating in what they perceive they want to do during their leisure than if leisure options are simply dictated to them.

5.2.3 Expressed needs and leisure

Those activities in which individuals actually participate are expressed needs. They provide the manager with knowledge about current leisure preferences, tastes and interests. Expressed needs are felt needs 'put into action'. However, if leisure resources, programmes and services are based solely on expressed needs (what people are doing), the practitioner may preclude the initiation of new services and programmes. In addition, participants' behaviour is limited by the specific programmes that are available. Expressed need itself does not give a total picture of involvement potential. Factors of cost, access, weather and fashion may induce number fluctuations. New and novel provision may create its own demand, where none existed previously. Yet programming based on expressed needs may tend to favour those who shout loudest!

5.2.4 Comparative needs and leisure

Often an individual or organization will compare itself with another individual or organization. This may be done purely out of interest, or it may serve to help to identify deficiencies. This approach can be applied to services, facilities, resources and programmes. Care must be practised when utilizing the comparative needs method in needs assessment and programme planning. One cannot assume that what works well in one situation will automatically be effective in another.

5.2.5 Created needs and leisure

Godbey [17] has expanded on Bradshaw's taxonomy of social needs by adding a fifth level: created needs. The concept implies that policy makers and professionals can create leisure interests and values independent of what people do, or what they want to do. Created needs refer to those recreation activities which organizations have 'introduced to individuals and in which they will subsequently participate at the expense of some activity in which they previously participated'. In other words, created needs refers to those programmes, services and activities solely determined by the organization and accepted by the participant without question, desire or prior knowledge.

According to Edginton *et al.* [18] the created needs approach can be useful to the participant and to the organization as a method of defining needs:

> Many individuals are grateful to organizations for helping them identify an area of interest that previously they had not considered. In a sense, the approach is a form of leisure education that is an important component of the philosophy of recreation and leisure service organizations. The organization also benefits by serving as an agency that creates opportunities for stimulation and enrichment. As a result, individuals may look to the organization as a vehicle for providing innovative experience.

Implicit in the created needs approach is the notion that the professional's knowledge is sacrosanct, but this is a wrong assumption. The participant also has the ability to diagnose his or her felt, expressed and comparative needs. As with the other approaches, the created needs method should be used in conjunction with all the available tools for defining and interpreting needs.

5.2.6 False needs and leisure

Needs may be created which are inessential, which are in fact false needs. Young [19] points to the distinctions between what an individual is aware of needing and what others may think is needed. This raises the issue of the value which is placed on need by the individual and by outsiders. These values may differ.

Marcuse [20] developed the concept that society encourages the individual to develop certain sorts of 'need', which are not in any sense essential but which serve the interests of society as a whole. Thus people acquire the 'need' for cars, television or videos which it is in the general interest of society to promote. Such needs Marcuse calls false needs for the reason that they are not strictly essential. In fact they are hard to prove different from other sorts of need but, for Marcuse, they represent undesirable values.

5.2.7 Changing needs in leisure

Rhona and Robert Rapoport in *Leisure and the Family Life Cycle* [21] claim that although every person has needs, these needs change as one progresses from one phase of life to another. The key concepts which reflect the developmental nature of the changes in the life-cycle are preoccupations – mental absorptions, interests and activities. Preoccupations arise at a deep level of motivation. Some preoccupations might be present throughout the life-cycle but tend to become particularly salient at a given phase. The preoccupations attributed to each stage in the life-cycle are worth considering since they are of fundamental importance if providers are to make the most appropriate provision for different segments of the population. The major stages reported in Kew and Rapoport [22] are outlined below:

Stage one – youth (school years)
- emergent personal identity
- tendency to fight against authority
- exploration – experimentation and sexual, physical, mental and emotional stimulation

Stage two – young adult (school-leaving to settling down)
- development of a social identity
- more intimate and committed relationships
- tendency to reintegrate with family previously rejected

Stage three – establishment (extended middle age)
- commitments to life investments of work and family
- importance to productivity and performance
- later tendency to question ideals and commitments, perhaps leading to disillusionment and depression

Stage four – final phase (between end of work and of life)
- emphasis on achieving social and personal integration
- attempts to achieve harmony with surroundings
- major reorganizations of attitudes and demands
- great variety of interests, dependent on very many factors

The Rapoports believe that recreational activities arise out of interests, and interests arise out of preoccupations. There is no one-to-one relationship between preoccupations and interests, and particular interests can be satisfied through different activities. However, it appears that specific 'clusters' of interests are clearly related to each major life-cycle phase. The Rapoports' thesis is that all people have a quest for personal identity. At the root of their search, people have fundamental preoccupations. Specific preoccupations can be experienced through a variety of interests, and expressions of interest may be facilitated through specific activities.

Each person is seen as having a 'career' consisting of separate but interrelated strands. Three major strands relate to family, work and leisure. Each life strand therefore produces changes in preoccupations, interests and activities at life crises such as at marriage and at the birth of children.

5.3 Needs, demands and leisure and recreation services

Leisure policy makers, researchers, planners and managers often equate 'needs' with demands. But there is a very real difference between the two. Lowry and Curtis [23] believe that a common error of regarding demand and need as synonymous should be avoided: they see 'need' as the more fundamental concept and 'demand' as perhaps generated by need.

Researchers have generally been concerned with establishing recreation demand, rather than understanding people's needs. Large-scale surveys in Britain, for example, have identified certain demands but have not discovered what motivates people to recreation, why people participate and what are the most important influences on participation: 'Whereas a "need" appears to be conceptually "woolly" and operationally elusive, "demand" appears tangible, measurable, even predictable' [24].

In recent years, however, there has been a growing dissatisfaction with macro-social demand studies, and a feeling that if researchers are to provide information of real value to policy makers and planners, they must look for approaches that are also of relevance to the people being researched. Knetsch [25] calls into question the concept of demand: 'The myth persists that somehow we are able to multiply population figures by recreation activity participation rates obtained from population surveys and call it demand.'

Effectiveness and efficiency are not the same thing. An effective leisure service could be described as one that ensures that the right opportunities are provided, at the right time and in the right place, based on the needs of the people it is intended to serve. This is, of course, impossible to achieve in the sense that any collective service cannot be all things to every person. Yet the approach which encourages ways for people to attain self-fulfilment can be stressed. If not, providers may provide an efficient service and ensure its smooth running but the service could be ineffective 'Of the two, the provision of an effective service is the more important, as it is better to provide an effective service that meets needs, however inefficiently, than to provide a super efficient service that meets nobody's needs' [26].

Although little direct research has been undertaken on the 'social' need of the individual being a prime motivating factor, Crandall [27] has reviewed relevant research. He concludes that the success of many leisure and recreation services may depend more on their ability to bring together compatible people than on their programmes and facilities. And although Maslow's hierarchy of needs has been criticized on the ground that the self-actualizing needs are largely culturally determined, it is generally accepted that people have a need for psychological growth and that a social need is a basic survival need. Maslow's basic survival needs, physiological, safety and social needs, correspond with the hygiene factors of Herzberg [28], who regards them as preventative, in that they do no more than prevent unhappiness, while the higher needs of Maslow may be equated to some extent with the motivator factors of Herzberg. (See chapter twelve for a fuller explanation of Herzberg and management.) Hence both Maslow and Herzberg see a person's ultimate need as being that of self-actualization, and Farina [29] sees this need as the 'goal of leisure'.

5.4 People's needs and leisure planning

Leisure planning and management exist, in large measure, to provide opportunities for individual satisfaction and development. Everyone has a quest for personal identity. Can this personal need be met, in part, by effective leisure planning and management? What stands in its way? Later in this chapter some of the many influences are identified.

Needs assessment should allow for a broad base of public involvement. It is suggested that such an approach will:

1   provide an increase in individual and community input and involvement in planning and decision making;
2   provide the planner with a better understanding of the community and individuals within it;
3   provide information as to the activities in which people are involved, the activities in which they would like to be involved and how these can be planned and provided for within an overall leisure delivery system;
4   provide supportive facts and ideas on which to base decisions in the planning process.

Two most important factors have emerged, which argue against the focus of current recreation planning policies on standards of provision. First, people have diverse needs. Second, these needs change or take on greater or lesser degrees of importance according to one's stage in the life cycle. The individual chooses on the basis of certain personal and social elements current in his or her life.

Needs assessment attempts understanding of individual and group behaviour as it relates to recreation and leisure. It accomplishes several things. Through such assessment, recreation planners and managers can become aware of people's underlying motivation, interests, opinions, habits, desires and knowledge regarding recreation and leisure. Practical ways of gathering such data include demographic characteristics, time use, leisure behaviour and opinions and attitudes. Hedges [30], for example, sought to develop a technique for more accurate charting of people's leisure patterns through their lives, namely their 'leisure histories'. It has become abundantly clear, however, that methods must include both quantitative and qualitative assessments.

In terms of need, people are three-dimensional. We are like everybody else, requiring the basic needs of security, belonging and shelter; we are like some other people sharing the same wants, the same groups and the same interests. We are like no other person, a unique individual – the only one. Leisure opportunity could enable us to become a three-phase person: to become all we think we are capable of becoming. In the sections to follow we consider factors which influence people in leisure choices.

5.5   Factors that influence participation

Many factors influence our choice of how we spend our time for leisure. The first group of factors relate to the individual: his or her stage in life, needs, interests, attitudes, abilities, upbringing and personality. The second group relates to the circumstances and situations in which individuals find themselves, the social setting of which they are a part, the time at their disposal, their job and their income. The third group relates to the opportunities and support services available

TABLE 5.1 Influences on leisure participation

Personal	Social and circumstantial	Opportunity factors
Age	Occupation	Resources available
Stage in life-cycle	Income	Facilities – type and quality
Gender	Disposable income	Awareness
Marital status	Material wealth and goods	Perception of opportunities
Dependants and ages	Car ownership and mobility	Recreation services
Will and purpose of life	Time available	Distribution of facilities
Personal obligations	Duties and obligations	Access and location
Resourcefulness	Home and social environment	Choice of activity
Leisure perception	Friends and peer groups	Transport
Attitudes and motivation	Social roles and contacts	Costs: before, during, after
Interests and preoccupation	Environment factors	Management: policy and support
Skills and ability – physical,	Mass leisure factors	Marketing
social and intellectual	Education and attainment	Programming
Personality and confidence	Population factors	Organization and leadership
Culture born into	Cultural factors	Social accessibility
Upbringing and background		Political policies

to the individual: resources, facilities, programmes, activities and their quality and attractiveness, and the management of them.

Recreation policy and planning are by no means simple. There is a complex mixture and interaction when thinking about the factors which affect participation. In Table 5.1 some of the discernible factors are outlined which individually, jointly or collectively affect participation. This listing is not comprehensive, nor is it a classification but an illustration of the complexity and variety of influences which bear on an individual. In addition, even if people have identical circumstances and opportunities, still one person may choose one activity and another something entirely different. Nevertheless, by understanding some of the correlations between personal circumstances and participation, Leisure Managers can foresee some of the constraints and difficulties encountered by some people, and management approaches can be modified accordingly.

5.6 Individual, personal and family influences on leisure participation

The personality of an individual, his or her needs, interests, physical and social ability, the culture into which one is born and a person's will and purpose in life, and a whole range of personal factors, could influence choice and participation. Three factors are further considered below: age and stage in family life-cycle, gender and education.

5.6.1 Age and stage in the family life-cycle

Age has an important influence on leisure participation but its effect will vary depending on the person and the type of activity. For children, there is a rapid change, in the space of a few years, from toddler to pre-school to junior to teenager – each calling for very different kinds of provision. Even for adults, there is a marked change with age, with participation in most active leisure pursuits declining sharply as people grow older.

The availability of time also has an influence on recreational participation and the greatest amount of free time appears to be concentrated at the ends of the age continuum with the adolescent and the retired having considerably more time at their disposal than the middle age-group who live under a greater degree of time pressure. Further, with the increased purchasing power of teenagers and the popularity of commercial entertainment amongst this age-group, there is a greater age segmentation in leisure choice. A sharp fall with age occurs, for example, in cinema-going, which is predominantly a young person's leisure pursuit.

The *General Household Surveys* [31] emphasize the general decline in active leisure participation with increasing age but also reveal that some home-based activities, such as gardening and do-it-yourself, are most popular with the middle-aged. Some activities are relatively 'inelastic' with the change of age. These are generally regarded as home-based activities, such as television watching and reading; other activities, such as membership of voluntary organizations, have a curvilinear trend, with a slight increase in participation rates in one's late pre-retirement and early post-retirement phase.

Age should not be considered in isolation, however. Age may be less restrictive than life-cycle changes, such as getting married and having children; for some, participation may increase with age as a result of the children leaving home or a person retiring from work. Although age may influence the level of fitness and energy, a reduction in family and work responsibilities may more than compensate for this. The type of leisure activity is also likely to be influenced by stage in the family life-cycle. For example, single people may be more likely to go to a dance or a club, while a family may be more likely to visit the seaside.

5.6.2 Gender and leisure participation

The leisure patterns of males and females show similarities and differences. However, two major obstacles have faced women: family commitments, particularly looking after children, prevent many women from participating outside the home, and for many older women, an upbringing that did not include pursuits like physical recreation within their compass.

In a study made over thirty years ago, *Leisure in the North West* [32] it was found that gender makes little difference in participation rates for either full-day or half-day trips and excursions, but that there is a marked contrast to the impact of gender on sport and physical recreation. The ratio of men to women was 61:39, even though women outnumbered men by a ratio of 54:46 in the sample. This finding is consistent with both Sillitoe [33] and the *General Household Surveys*, which show that of all the sporting activities, only keep fit/yoga had a higher participation rate among females.

Max Hanna [34] found that while gender has been of fundamental importance in differentiating leisure activities, the two sexes appeared increasingly to share activities as more opportunities for women are opened up. Extending Hanna's thesis would suggest that many of the social filters, which can operate against female participation, will diminish and disappear. The problem is compounded, in that many other life factors militate against leisure equality. For example, when a woman goes out to work, as well as maintaining a house and family, the extent of her leisure time is eroded since responsibilities for domestic work within the home are not normally abdicated.

Within the 'cultural' field of leisure, women are the predominant users. Thirty years ago Mann [35] found that for all theatre audiences in Leeds the highest proportion were women; at the ballet they comprised 73 per cent; drama had a female audience of 69 per cent; and opera 59 per cent. This was supported by Davey [36], in Hornchurch, and by the Mass Observation Study in Birmingham [37].

Women are without a car more often than men, and in view of the dependence of sports and arts participants on the motor car, this is probably one of the factors that inhibits female participation. Green et al. [38], in a thoughtful and forceful study of women's leisure experiences in Sheffield, illustrate the damaging influences upon the leisure potential for women: 'the constraints and social controls on women's freedom to spend their leisure time as they may choose can be seen as a direct result of the operation of economic, political, and cultural forces, which exemplify the oppression of women under capitalism.'

Clearly, women have had, and continue to have, greater constraints placed upon them than men. However, one of the misleading factors in looking for similarities and differences stems from the fact that most surveys have studied traditional recreation activities – i.e. sport, day trips and theatre – and organized activities like classes, clubs, team games and committed activities. Once a wider view of leisure is taken, encompassing the range of activities in and around the home, holidays, socializing, entertainment, excursions or walks in the park, a totally different picture starts to emerge.

Looking at the broader spectrum, it would appear that overall participation rates do not differ substantially between men and women; women take a greater part in 'cultural' activities, men take part substantially more than women in active sport and sports spectatorship. When taking all leisure pursuits into account, then the similarities in leisure participation between the sexes are more striking than the differences [39].

5.6.3 *Education, educational attainment and leisure*

The type of education, the length of education and the educational attainment of people are closely related to upbringing, class, occupation, income and other factors. In terms of leisure participation, the better qualified tend to be male, young, in non-manual occupations and enjoying higher incomes. All these factors are reflected in higher participation rates for those with qualifications than for those without and, in general, the higher the qualification, the greater the degree of participation [40].

Education influences to some extent the type of leisure choice. Considerable evidence is available to support this view, from national surveys such as the *General Household Survey* and from specific research into leisure facilities such as libraries, theatres and recreation centres. For example, there is a sharp differential between members and non-members of the public library when related to educational institution and level of educational attainment. Possibly the best illustration is within the arts. Mann [35], in Leeds, found that 57 per cent of the whole drama audience, 42 per cent of opera audiences and 33 per cent of ballet audiences were now at or had been at university or a college of education. In Birmingham, the Mass Observation Study found that the influence of education attainment was of greater significance than social class [37]. With the exception of the pantomime, all audiences had higher proportions of people who had completed their full-time education at 19 years of age and over. In the early days of sports and recreation centres, the bias was still significant although not to the same extent [41, 42]. However, by the late 1990s the balance has been more than struck with more women than men participating in swimming and in aerobics and dance-related activities.

5.7 Social and situational circumstances and leisure participation

The range of social and situational circumstances as they affect leisure participation include the home, school, work environment, income, mobility, time, social class, social roles and group belonging. Time availability is a major determinant of leisure behaviour. Working women have the least unobligated time of all groups, mainly because of home obligations. Retired people and unemployed men have the most time for leisure, but much of it may remain simply free time. In this brief section these aspects are further considered under three headings: income, social class and social climate.

5.7.1 Income and leisure participation

General Household Surveys have examined household income. They show that income levels are closely linked to participation rates, and for almost all the leisure activities they examined, the proportion participating rose with income. In only three activities (bingo, needlework and going to clubs) did participation not increase with income. Even where little or no financial outlay is incurred, such as walking, participation rates were also higher. With betting, bingo and doing the pools, participation rates fell among those with higher-than-average incomes.

Over an average working life, white-collar workers earn appreciably more than blue-collar workers and often attract hidden benefits (e.g. perks, pensions, less unemployment), all of which add to quality of life style. It is perhaps not surprising that since income correlates with both education and social class, the higher-income group has the higher participation rates in many recreational activities. Even with facilities and activities provided by the local authority, such as for arts and sports, more people with higher incomes are attracted.

If lower-income groups are to be attracted in larger numbers to community recreation, then greater social service approaches would need to be applied, for example, through differential subsidies, cheaper admissions, positive discrimination towards those who are disadvantaged, outreach programmes, the lending of equipment free of charge, taster courses at minimal costs, community programming application, community bus services to facilities, improved marketing such as 'passports for leisure', incentives and, above all, sensitive and appropriate management. Some 'passport' schemes involve the collection and completion of a detailed form, obtaining a photograph and processing these in person at the civic offices. The target market – those in greater need – has been hardly touched in some areas, despite good overall numbers joining the schemes. The difficulty of the process of joining appears to have produced the opposite effect to that intended.

The choice of activities and the amount of money that people can spend on entrance fees, equipment, travel, and so on, is dependent on the extent of people's disposable income. Those on unemployment benefits or state pensions may have little or no disposable income. Families with highest incomes tend to spend a smaller proportion of their income on essentials such as food and clothing and a greater proportion on non-essentials such as recreation. Manual workers, when presented with a choice between more income and more leisure, generally choose the former; consequently, they have to undertake overtime which, in turn, diminishes the time available for recreational participation.

Personal property has much to do with leisure. However, what were once luxuries and leisure items are now considered almost as necessities. 'Necessities' such as alcohol, tobacco and petrol are relatively insensitive to financial change; large, discrete items like holidays and house improvements are vulnerable. People who earn, or who have more money, have greater personal property and the wherewithal to permit a wider choice of leisure pursuits. Owning a large house with a garden, and driving a second car may immediately open the door to leisure activities which will be denied those living in a high-rise flat, without personal transport and with a low income.

5.7.2 Social 'class' and leisure participation

The nature and meaning of social class is generally regarded as being problematic. 'Social class' can be regarded as 'a grouping of people into categories on the basis of occupation' [43]. Because of the interrelationship between social class and income, education and mobility, it is generally considered that social class, as determined by occupation, is the most influential factor in determining recreational participation. Occupation is not therefore an independent characteristic, but is closely associated with other factors.

The *General Household Surveys* found that generally, it was professional workers who tended to have the highest participation rates in leisure activities and unskilled workers who had the lowest rates. Particularly striking are the differences in participation levels for outdoor sports (over half of professional workers, falling to under 20 per cent for unskilled workers). Even playing and watching football were more popular among professional and skilled manual workers, and the pattern is not confined to sport and the arts. Outings, sightseeing, entertainment, gardening and do-it-yourself showed similar bias. Even knitting and needlework were more popular among female professional workers. According to the *General Household Surveys*, only two activities are more popular among manual workers: betting/doing the football pools and playing bingo.

5.7.3 Social 'climate' and leisure participation

The IFER/DART researchers [44] refer to the concept of 'social climate', a complex of factors in addition to those which relate to age, gender, income, occupation and education. The attitudes and values of people in their social setting are seen as enabling or inhibiting factors concerned with leisure choice. Isobel Emmet's study, in 1970 [45], is pertinent today in our understanding of social climate. She argues, for example, that providers act both consciously and unconsciously as social filters, controlling who uses particular facilities and affecting the behaviour of those people. The social filters let through and channel different groups to different facilities. There appear to be both formal and informal social filters. The filters are influential in people's adopting of attitudes and behaviour appropriate to the situation. Behaviour patterns become habits. As Leigh [46] points out, 'The habits of leisure are habits of mind as well as habits of behaviour'.

Despite the cheapness of such activities as rambling, climbing, tennis and camping, these activities remain relatively 'middle-class' occupations. Free museums and subsidized theatre lack working-class patronage, as do evening institute classes. More manual workers may be playing golf but this is mainly on public golf courses, while some private clubs are becoming more expensive and more exclusive. Also the professional classes are finding an increasing number of esoteric and expensive ways of occupying their leisure time. Leisure between the classes differs not only in kind, but also in quantity. The recent *General Household Surveys* conclude that the middle classes are not only more active culturally, socially and intellectually, but they also play more sport and travel more widely.

5.8 Opportunity and leisure participation

It is no good providing opportunity unless good advantage is taken of it. Opportunity – making it possible for a person to participate or be involved – can be, in many instances, even more important to community participation than personal, social and circumstantial influences, despite current studies which show the strongest correlation between participation factors, already discussed. Opportunity can come in a variety of forms: available resources and services, political policies, management styles and systems, community leadership and support, accessibility, and so on. It is most likely that opportunity will entail various interrelated components.

From his study in Greenwich, Gwynne Griffiths [47] arrived at the conclusion that the key factor that influences recreation participation is accessibility in its various forms. By accessibility, Griffiths does not refer simply to access and mobility, rather accessibility is defined as the 'ability to participate' where the constraints to participation have been eliminated. He divides accessibility into four main divisions: perceptual accessibility; physical accessibility; financial accessibility; and social accessibility.

5.8.1 Perception and leisure participation

Perception refers to the world as it is experienced – as it is seen, heard, felt, smelt and tasted. Consequently, the way an individual perceives the world will largely determine his or her behaviour. The way people perceive leisure provision (facilities, activities, etc.) may influence their participation, more than the actual form of provision. Leisure provision is concerned with providing satisfying 'experiences' for people; facilities, programmes and activities are means of achieving this. People who do not feel properly identified (or feel ill at ease) with the style of management and organization, or with others using the facilities, will be deterred; indeed, preconceived ideas about a leisure facility will influence a person's decision whether or not to make even an initial visit to see it, let alone use it!

Perception has been used in recreational planning, especially in the field of countryside recreation. Burton [48], in her studies relating to perceptual capacity, found that one's perception of crowding in the countryside was related to one's level of educational attainment. Individuals of high educational attainment were more sensitive to crowding and thought of it as unpleasant; others actually preferred high levels of use. Like the countryside, people have varied perceptions about the city: 'Some people see the city as a place for having fun, for going out on the town; others feel oppressed by the tightly packed nature of its dwellings, excited by the hustle and bustle of city life or overwhelmed by its pressures' [49].

Perceptual capacity as such appeared to have little effect on recreational participation within Griffiths's study, but the perception of one's actual neighbourhood appeared to have a significant effect on inhibiting recreational participation. The vast majority of those interviewed perceived their neighbourhood as being violent, and the elderly were fearful of venturing out of the house at night. Even the close proximity of the police station to the library and the adult education institute had little influence on encouraging use of facilities at night. Consequently, how the public perceive their neighbourhood and the facilities can either encourage or inhibit recreational participation. As with attitudes, where a negative aspect is perceived, this perception may be difficult to eradicate. Positive perception of recreation opportunity will enhance the desire and motivation to participate, will attract people and make them more aware of opportunities available.

5.8.2 *Access and supply and leisure participation*

Recreation participation undertaken outside the home involves some travel – i.e. walking, cycling, bus, taxi, car, train or plane. The method of travel can affect the level of satisfaction: one method will take more time; it can determine distance and destination; apart from walking, all other means of travel incur financial cost; the method of transportation will lessen or heighten the experience. For example, travelling to a recreation centre during the rush hour, by public transport, for a prepaid 5.30 p.m. court booking, could be harrowing.

The *Fair Play for All* study [50] appears to confirm this: 'though low mobility can act as a deterrent, higher mobility is not necessarily a pre-requisite of greater participation: rather it can reduce some of the inconvenience associated with travel.' Families with cars have reported greater participation over almost the whole spectrum of activities than families without cars. The mobility conferred by the ownership of a car has revolutionized people's use of leisure time. According to the *General Household Survey 1996*, 70 per cent of households in Britain had use of a car. For almost every activity, with the striking exception of bingo, the chances of participating in leisure activities was increased for car users by between 50 per cent and 100 per cent.

Accessibility to recreation provision is influenced, however, by other important factors apart from transportation. The actual location of a facility is of the utmost importance and will affect use; the rate of use of the facility falls progressively as one moves further away from the facility. Veal [51] found with regard to post-war swimming pool users that people living within 1 km of the swimming pool were four times more likely to use it than those who live between 1 km and 2 km away, and sixteen times more likely than those living between 3 km and 4 km away from the pool. Distance decay, whereby usage falls as the distance grows between the user's home and the facility, shows up in many examples – e.g. the use of museums, urban parks and the use of water resources. Maw's study of swimming pools [52] showed not merely the effect of distance, but also the significance of public transport as a means of access, particularly for the young. Those who lived near to the main bus or tube routes to Swiss Cottage, London, came to the swimming pool there more frequently than those (within the same distance) who did not.

In terms of travelling time, the catchment area of even the largest recreational facility is comparatively small. Understandably, the catchment area of community centres and libraries, especially in the urban areas, is very local. Where local provision does not exist, facilities need to be located on bus routes, preferably at a nodal point of a bus network. Griffiths's study [47] illustrates the point:

> the location of the bus stop immediately outside the library is indeed an asset and the proximity of the zebra crossing also aids the accessibility especially for the children and the elderly, but unfortunately the bus services are not geared up for recreational use as their service deteriorates in the evenings and at weekends, when most people have their greater leisure time.

So, access and mobility are crucial elements relating to leisure opportunity. It is a sobering thought that, according to *Fair Play for All*, three-quarters of non-car-owning households in the country are among the poorer 50 per cent of households. In terms of facilities provided with public money, policies should exist which ensure the location of facilities on main transportation routes or within easy reach of the greatest number in the community . Where there is easy physical access, and where local residents can walk to a facility, the recreationally disadvantaged (i.e. the elderly, car-less, lower-income groups, women with small children) could have far greater potential use. In a study undertaken in Belfast [53], it was found that by 1988 many parts of the city had higher levels of sports participation than had been recorded in any other part of the United Kingdom. The reason was clear: between 1977 and 1984, Belfast had become the best-provided city in terms of indoor sport facilities per head of city population. Local opportunity had led to greater participation across a broader section of the community, despite the 'troubles' in Northern Ireland. All these aspects are important in the context of planning for leisure, discussed in chapter seven.

5.8.3 *Awareness and leisure participation*

One accessibility factor that is frequently ignored in considering the linkage of demand for and supply of leisure activities is awareness. If people do not know that something exists, then obviously they will not go to visit it, unless they stumble upon it. Because individual leisure facilities are not sought in the same way as a shopping centre or place of work, knowledge about them (particularly in urban areas) derives indirectly from seeing them, hearing about them or reading about them. It has been shown that people passing a leisure facility en route to work or the shops will be more likely to use that facility than a comparable one nearer home: they have become more aware of it. This factor has obvious implications with regard to the location of activities, as well as advertising and other marketing methods.

5.8.4 *Management and leisure participation*

People's use of leisure facilities is determined, as we have seen, by a number of discrete and interrelated factors. The management aspects of facility provision and leisure opportunity are no less important.

It is abundantly clear that the presence or absence of facilities and opportunities, and their accessibility, quality, pricing structures and policies, could have substantial influences on leisure participation. For example, the pricing, administrative and booking structures at a leisure centre could consciously or unconsciously establish a type of social filter.

The way in which a facility is managed can also have a profound effect on the extent that it is used, and by whom it is used. Not only is management attitude and policy shown in the atmosphere created, the 'image' and pricing policy, but also in the skill of programming for the people the facility is intended to serve:

programmes geared towards males (e.g. five-a-side football) are likely to result in male-dominated programmes. Programmes geared towards females (e.g. aerobics) result in female-dominated programmes.

The need to socialize with others is a major motivating factor in influencing one's leisure choice. The activity itself may well be of quite secondary importance compared with getting out of the house, having the children looked after for an hour and meeting and talking with people in the coffee bar. Management needs to be aware of these motivating factors in deciding management policy, programming and in providing an atmosphere of social warmth and welcome. At Harlow Sport-centre [54] where positive discrimination was made in favour of mothers with young children through 'ladies' activities', crèche and social activities, the proportion of mothers with children attending the centre was far above the national average.

5.9   Summary – people's needs and factors that influence participation in leisure

In summary, no single theory and no clear consensus exist relating to people's needs. In theories of motivation, need is seen as a force within the individual to gain satisfactions and completeness. There appear to be many levels and types of need, including the important needs of 'self-actualization' and psychological growth. 'Leisure needs' as such may not exist, rather there are human needs which can find satisfaction through leisure opportunity.

The concept of social need incorporating normative, felt, expressed and comparative needs has been enlarged to include created, false and changing needs. Needs appear to change in relation to one's life stage, and one's preoccupations, interests and activities at that stage. It has been hypothesized that needs can be created but, in so doing, can result in some 'false' needs being brought about, with both positive and negative results for the individual and society.

Many discrete and complex, and often interrelated factors, condition people's choice and participation in leisure activities. Furthermore, there are the strongest links between leisure and other elements of life. A person's age and stage in the family life-cycle, such as marriage, parenthood and retirement, affect opportunity and participation. Taking the widest view of leisure, the similarities in participation rates between men and women are more striking than the differences, though there are specific differences, and inequalities both within and between the sexes. The type and level of education people have undertaken has a profound effect on leisure participation. Education and recreation share in the same concern for the development of the 'whole' person – body, mind and spirit – through different approaches. The amount of income and property a person has influences leisure participation. Higher-income groups have higher participation rates in most active recreation activities.

Participation is closely and positively related to social status and the prestige of one's occupation. The 'middle classes' are not only more active culturally and intellectually, but also travel more and play more sport, compared with the 'working classes'. The way people perceive leisure provision influences participation.

Preconceived ideas, too, can have important positive or negative effects. Car ownership has revolutionized people's leisure opportunities. The accessibility of facilities and their location, and an awareness of opportunities, are important considerations. People's use of facilities and services is affected, to a considerable degree, by management policy and management activity. Facilities must be both accessible and acceptable. The attitudes of providers and managers, and the quality of management, will help more people to find satisfying experiences through leisure and recreation opportunity.

While there are many constraints to leisure choices (and, in practice, few people are free agents to choose whatever they will), leisure can offer significant opportunity for individual action and for personal decision, should opportunity permit and the individual wish to exercise such choice. As choice has to do with the individual, then two factors have to be stressed. First, there is a strong link between leisure and other elements of life; and second, because it 'matters' to the individual, the quality of the experience is of paramount importance.

In chapter four it became clear that the freedom to choose was an essential feature of leisure. But choice, as we have seen, is conditioned by myriad factors, many of which are interrelated. However, the amount of choice has increased for most people. Nevertheless, leisure activities compete with other activities, and for a share of disposable time and money.

Finally, from observation and working experience of people's use of leisure, it is clear that a great many people overcome the limitations of a poor education, family obligations and personal handicaps, and even overcome the obstacles of low income, insufficient facilities and resources, to find themselves preoccupying satisfying interests, self-fulfilling experiences and 'mountains to climb'. Leisure and recreation management has much to offer in the way of enabling people to discover themselves, to reach beyond their immediate grasp.

Notes and references

1   Morgan, C. and King, R. (1966), *Introduction to Psychology*, McGraw-Hill, New York, p. 776.
2   Murray, H. (1938) *Explorations in Personality*, Oxford University Press, New York, referred to in Institute of Family and Environmental Research and Dartington Amenity Research Trust (IFER/DART) (1976), *Leisure Provision and Human Need: Stage 1 Report* (for DoE), IFER/DART, London, Item 2.8.
3   McDougal, W. (1923) *Outline of Psychology*, Methuen, London, discussed in Institute of Family and Environmental Research and Dartington Amenity Research Trust (IFER/DART) (1976), *Leisure Provision and Human Need: Stage 1 Report* (for DoE), IFER/DART, London, Items 2.10 and 2.11.
4   Young, P. T. (1961), *Motivation and Emotion*, Wiley, New York.
5   Freud, S. (1974), *The Complete Works of Sigmund Freud*, Hogarth Press, London.
6   Erikson, E. H. (1959), 'Identity and the life cycle', *Psychological Issues, 1*, No. 1.
7   Institute of Family and Environmental Research and Dartington Amenity

Research Trust (IFER/DART) (1976), *Leisure Provision and Human Need: Stage 1 Report* (for DoE), IFER/DART, London, Item 2.46.

8   Maslow, A. (1954), *Motivation and Personality*, Harper, New York.

9   Maslow, A. (1968), *Towards a Psychology of Being*, Van Nostrand, New York.

10   H. Rogers (ed.) (1967) *Pilot National Recreation Survey, Report No. 1*, British Travel Association and University of Keele, London, referred to in Institute of Family and Environmental Research and Dartington Amenity Research Trust (IFER/DART) (1976), *Leisure Provision and Human Need: Stage 1 Report* (for DoE), IFER/DART, London, Item 2.22.

11   Tillman, A. (1974), *The Program Book for Recreation Professionals*, National Press Books, Palo Alto, CA, pp. 57–8.

12   Bradshaw, J. (1972), 'The concept of social need', *New Society*, 30, No. 3. pp.640–3.

13   Mercer, D. (1973), The concept of recreational need. *Journal of Leisure Research, 5,* No. 1, 37–41.

14   McAvoy, L.H. (1977), 'Needs and the elderly: an overview', *Parks and Recreation, 12*, No. 3, 31–4, 35.

15   Godbey, G. (1976), *Recreation and Park Planning: The Exercise of Values*, University of Waterloo, Ontario, p.2.

16   Mercer, D. (1973), 'The concept of recreational need', *Journal of Leisure Research, 5*, No. 1, 39–41.

17   Godbey, G. (1976), *Recreation and Park Planning: The Exercise of Values*, University of Waterloo, Ontario, p.13.

18   Edington, C. R., Cromton, D.M. and Hanson, C.J. (1980), *Recreation and Leisure Programming*, Saunders College, Philadelphia, PA, p.91.

19   Young, P.T. (1961), *Motivation and Emotion*, Wiley, New York.

20   Marcuse, H. (1964), *One Dimensional Man*, Sphere Books, London.

21   Rapoport, R. and Rapoport, R.N. (1975), *Leisure and the Family Life Cycle*, Routledge and Kegan Paul, London.

22   Kew, S. and Rapoport, R. (1975), Beyond Palpable Mass Demand, Leisure Provision and Human Needs – The Life Cycle Approach, paper presented to Planning and Transport Research and Computation (International) Company Ltd., Summer Annual Meeting.

23   Lowry, G. and Curtis, J. (1973), 'Satisfying leisure needs', in Lutzin, S. G. (ed.), *Managing Municipal Leisure Services*, Institute of Training in Municipal Administration (ITMA), International City Management Association, Washington, DC.

24   Institute of Family and Environmental Research and Dartington Amenity Research Trust (IFER/DART) (1976), *Leisure Provision and Human Need: Stage 1 Report* (for DoE), IFER/DART, London, Item 3.14.

25   Knetsch, J. L. (1969), 'Assessing the demand for outdoor recreation', *Journal of Leisure Research, 1*, No. 2, 85.

26   College, S. (1977), 'Recreation research in local authorities: a practitioner's view', in Veal, A.J. (ed.) *Recreation Research in Local Authorities*, CURS, University of Birmingham.

27   Crandall, R. (1977), Social Interaction, Effect and Leisure, Institute of Behavioural Research, Texas Christian University, unpublished.

28 Herzberg, F. (1968), *Work and the Nature of Man*, Stapes Press, London.

29 Farina, J. (1974), 'Toward a philosophy of leisure', in Murphy, J.F. (ed.) *Concepts of Leisure: Philosophical Implications*, Prentice-Hall, Englewood Cliffs, NJ.

30 Hedges, B. (1986), *Personal Leisure Histories – Social and Community Planning Research*, Sports Council/Economic Social Research Council, London.

31 Office of Population Censuses and Surveys, Social Survey Division, *General Household Survey, 1993, 1996*, HMSO, London.

32 Patmore, J. A. and Rodgers, H. B. (eds) (1972), *Leisure in the North West*, North West Sports Council, Salford.

33 Sillitoe, K. K. (1969), *Planning for Leisure*, HMSO, London.

34 Hanna, M. (1975), *Leisure*, IPC Sociological Monograph No. 12; see Institute of Family and Environmental Research and Dartington Amenity Research Trust (IFER/DART) (1976), *Leisure Provision and Human Need: Stage 1 Report* (for DoE), IFER/DART, London, Item 6.28, for fuller evaluation.

35 Mann, P. H. (1969), *The Provincial Audience for Drama, Ballet and Opera* (survey in Leeds), University of Sheffield.

36 Davey, J. (1976), Promoting a Regional Theatre: Queens Theatre, Hornchurch, Polytechnic of North London, Diploma in Management Studies (R.), unpublished.

37 Mass Observation (United Kingdom) Ltd (1974), *The Potential for the Arts in Birmingham*, Peter Cox Associates, Leamington Spa.

38 Green, E., Hebron, S. and Woodward, D. (1987), *Leisure and Gender – a Study of Leisure Constraints and Opportunities for Women*, Sports Council/ Economic Social Research Council, London.

39 Zuzanek, J. (1977), 'Leisure trends and the economics of the arts', in Smith, M. A. (ed.) *Leisure and Urban Society*, Leisure Studies Association, London.

40 Office of Population Censuses and Surveys, Social Survey Division (1979), and Office for National Statistics (1998) *General Households Surveys 1977 and 1996*, HMSO, London, p. 130.

41 Built Environment Research Group (BERG) (1978), *Sports Council Study 15. Sport for All in the Inner City, Sobell Sports Centre*, Sports Council, London.

42 Built Environment Research Group (BERG) (1978), *Sports Council Study 14. Sport in a Jointly Provided Centre, Medway Sports Centre, Reading*, Sports Council, London.

43 Reid, I. (1977), *Social Class Differences in Britain: A Source Book*, Open Books, London.

44 Institute of Family and Environmental Research/Dartington Amenity Research Trust (IFER/DART) (1976), *Leisure Provision and Human Need: Stage 1 Report* (for DoE), IFER/DART, London, Item 6.20.

45 Emmet, I. (1971), The social filter in the leisure field. *Recreation News Supplement*, No. 4, 7–8.

46 Leigh, J. (1971) *Young People and Leisure*, Routledge and Kegan Paul, London, p. 124.

47 Griffiths, G. T. (1981), Recreation Provision for Whom?, unpublished dissertation, Cranfield Institute of Technology.

48 Burton, R. C. J. (1973), 'A new approach to perceptual capacity: Cannock Chase research project', *Recreation News Supplement*, No. 10, December, 31–7,

49 Rapoport, R. (1977), 'Leisure and urban society', in *Leisure and Urban Society* (ed. M. A. Smith), Leisure Studies Association, London.

50 Hillman, M. and Whalley, A. (1977), *Fair Play for All. A Study of Access to Sport and Informal Recreation, 43*, Broadsheet No. 571, Political and Economic Planning (PEP), London.

51 Veal, A. J. (1973), *Ashton-under-Lyne Swimming Pool Study: First Interim Report*, Centre for Urban and Regional Studies, University of Birmingham; see also Veal, A. J. (1979), *Sports Council Study 18: New Swimming Pool for Old*, Sports Council, London.

52 Maw, R. and Cosgrove, D. (1972), *Assessment of Demand for Recreation: A Modelling Approach*, Working Paper 2.72, Polytechnic of Central London.

53 Roberts, K., Dench, S., Minten, J. and York, C. (1989), *Community Response to Sports Centre Provision in Belfast*, University of Liverpool.

54 Torkildsen, G. (for Harlow and District Sports Trust) (1984), Survey of Harlow Sportcentre, unpublished; and interview, *Leisure Management, 5*, No. 4, 8–11, April 1985.

Part two

Leisure trends, planning and government

Chapter six

Trends in the leisure industry

In recent years, in the United Kingdom, the pace of change not only in leisure, but in our quality of life generally, has been rapid. We are now enjoying higher standards of living filled with goods, services, activities and opportunities that in past years seemed unimaginable. Underlying this growth have been several major, and numerous other minor, trends related directly or indirectly to leisure and recreation.

This chapter starts by explaining the uses of trends in forecasting and planning and then highlights some of the more obvious trends in the leisure industry, including its growth; people's new expectations, the changing and unchanging markets and facilities and also the overall growth in participation.

Having read this chapter, readers will be in no doubt as to the rapid development and volatility of the leisure industry, and the need to use forecasting and marketing information to plan appropriately for today's and tomorrow's leisure. Leisure Managers will appreciate the need to adapt to changing situations. They will also be made aware of the demand for more individual and social leisure pursuits. Planners and providers of services and facilities, described in the chapters which follow, need to be able to use the knowledge of trends in leisure to help to read the signs for future growth in the industry.

6.1 Making use of information on trends in a growth industry

Exploring the past and predicting the future in terms of leisure provision and participation is itself a major growth area. 'Trends' ('to have a tendency or general direction'), as we have come to know them, have arrived as essential planning and management tools. Leisure commentators, forecasters, social scientists and researchers provide information on trends in areas such as leisure time, leisure participation, consumers' expenditure on leisure, leisure travel, government, commercial and voluntary sector involvement in leisure and the international aspects of leisure. Other commentators provide detailed economic, social and demographic trends which all impinge on leisure provision.

Trends are used in numerous ways in leisure management, including:

1   to predict the future behaviour of customers;
2   to reduce the element of risk in decision making on future policy;
3   to plan strategically;
4   to draw attention to specific problems or likely growth areas;
5   to monitor the reaction of customers to a service, facility or activity over several years;
6   to provide information for use in marketing of future facilities or programmes.

Trends are important indications of future needs and demands. However, they are normally indications of national movements. It is important for leisure planners and managers to remember that what is happening nationally may not be occurring locally. National trends need to be supplemented by local traits, and local situations, needs and demands, to ensure a substantial degree of success in interpretation. Moreover, many of the 'trends', so called, are short-lived, emphasizing the volatility of the leisure industry.

The following sections outline trends affecting leisure provision today and in the immediate future in the United Kingdom; they include:

*   leisure as a growth industry
*   population changes
*   changing social behaviour
*   changing markets
*   income, wealth and poverty
*   the National Lottery
*   use of time – leisure in the home
*   use of time – leisure away from home
*   other leisure-related activities
*   participation in sports and healthy lifestyles.

6.1.1   Leisure – a growth industry

Forecasting future trends can be dangerous! It was predicted that by now, we should have moved to the 'three 35s' – i.e. 35 years of working life, 35 working weeks per year and a 35-hour working week. This has not occurred. Indeed, many people in full-time employment are working longer hours now than a decade ago.

Over the past decade the volume of spending on leisure goods and services has grown at a faster rate than spending on non-leisure goods and is likely to continue to do so, particularly if the levels of service, facilities and customer care continue at the same pace as they have over the past several years.

In the United Kingdom, the 1980s was the decade of market forces, and the 'me first' culture, with the emergence of the 'yuppie' whose status depended on the amount of work, stress and money he or she could sustain. In the 1990s, 'time starvation' – insufficient time to do all the things we want to do – has become a trade mark for a proportion of those in full-time employment. They have money for leisure, but little time, in stark contrast to those with plenty of time, but little money.

People's expectations of leisure are rising rapidly. Attitudes to and perceptions of leisure and its relationship to work are shifting; customers are becoming more discerning and knowledgeable and, therefore, demand value for money. In terms of community leisure, therefore, residents expect to be provided with good facilities and a quality of service that would be expected from the private sector.

Leisure provision and choice of activity are increasingly affected by outside variables. They are increasingly influenced by health, fitness, fashion and concern about the environment. Those leisure activities that result in harming the environment, for example, motor sports, may suffer falls in participation unless active measures are seen to be taken to alleviate the problem of pollution. Developers applying for planning permission, particularly in the Green Belt, will face strong objections from local pressure groups and a less favourable attitude from local authorities. Leisure operators will have to consider how their provision of facilities and services fit in with prevailing attitudes.

6.2 Population changes

Population numbers, ages, profiles and lifestyles affect leisure provision. Leisure professionals have to respond to demographic changes and projections in order to plan strategically and deliver services effectively.

The population in the United Kingdom has grown steadily over the decades: from 55.9 million in 1971; 56.4 million in 1981; 57.8 million in 1991; to 58.8 million in 1996, according to the Office of National Statistics (Table 6.1). In 1996, 83 per cent of the people in the United Kingdom lived in England, 9 per cent in Scotland, 5 per cent in Wales and 3 per cent in Northern Ireland. *Social Trends 1998* records that increases in population are likely to continue to 2021, when there will be 62.2 million. After this, the population numbers will fall as a result of increased deaths of numbers of people born after the Second World War – the baby boomers reaching elderly ages.

Age is a key determinant of participation rates in various forms of leisure activity. The United Kingdom has an ageing population – the overall number of people aged 85 and over trebled between 1961 and 1996 to nearly 1.1 million. Children make up one-fifth of the population. The Office of National Statistics forecasts the population into the next century from a 1995 base shown in Table 6.2.

TABLE 6.1 Population of the United Kingdom

	Thousands					
	1971	*1981*	*1991*	*1996*	*2011*	*2021*
England	46,412	46,821	48,208	49,089	51,161	52,484
Wales	2,740	2,813	2,891	2,921	2,989	3,043
Scotland	5,236	5,180	5,107	5,128	5,059	4,993
Northern Ireland	1,540	1,538	1,601	1,663	1,720	1,724
United Kingdom	55,928	56,352	57,808	58,801	60,929	62,244

Source: Office for National Statistics (1998) *Social Trends 28*, HMSO, London

TABLE 6.2 Population by age in the United Kingdom

	Percentages			
Age	*1971*	*1996*	*2001*	*2011*
0–15 years	25	21	20	18
16–24 years	13	11	11	12
25–34 years	12	16	14	12
35–44 years	12	14	15	14
45–54 years	12	13	13	15
55–64 years	12	10	10	12
65–74 years	9	9	8	9
75 years and over	5	7	7	8

Source: Office for National Statistics (1998) *Social Trends 28*, HMSO, London

Overall, there were more females than males in the United Kingdom in 1996 and the ratio of women to men increases with age since, on average, women live longer than men. According to projected mortality rates for 1997, on average, boys can expect to live until 74 years while girls can expect to live to 80. For those aged 85 and over, there are three women to every man.

People over retirement age, combined with the population under working age, form the dependant population – a crude measure of the number of people supported economically by those of working age. The overall dependency ratio is expected to rise from 64 for every 100 working in 1994 to 68 in 2031 (Table 6.3).

The *Labour Force Survey* estimated that around 3.4 million people in Great Britain belonged to an ethnic minority group in 1996–7 – around 6 per cent of the population. The perception of large numbers of people from 'foreign' lands is greater than the reality. The ethnic minority population has a much younger age structure than the White population, reflecting past immigration and fertility patterns. About a third of the ethnic minority population was aged under 16 in

TABLE 6.3 Projected dependency ratios[1] in the United Kingdom

	Child dependency	Elderly dependency	Overall dependency
1994	34	30	64
2001	33	29	62
2011	30	31	60
2021	28	30	58
2031	29	39	68

Note 1 1994-based projections. Number of children and people over retirement age to every 100 people of working age. The ratios take account of the change in state pension age for women from 60 years to 65 years between 2010 and 2020.

Source: Government Actuary's Department

Spring 1996, compared with around a fifth of the White population. The Pakistani and Bangladeshi groups have particularly young age structures. The way the proportion of each ethnic group born in the United Kingdom varies with age reveals the pattern of earlier immigration: 85 per cent of all ethnic minority members aged under 25 were born in the United Kingdom compared with only 21 per cent of those aged over 25.

6.3 Changing social behaviour

One of the biggest changes in social behaviour over the past two decades has been the tendency for women to delay having their children. This tendency is linked to participation both in higher education and in the labour force. In addition, many women start a second family following breakdown of the former marriage or partnership.

In 1996, just over two-thirds (67 per cent) of households owned their own home, either outright or with a mortgage, compared with just under one half (49 per cent) in 1971. Most of the increase in owner-occupation occurred during the 1980s and was accompanied by a decrease in the proportion of households renting from councils or renting unfurnished accommodation in the private sector.

Another striking change in social behaviour is the increase in one-person households – 27 per cent in 1996–7 compared to 14 per cent in 1961, and expected to grow to 36 per cent by 2016. The reasons are three-fold: the growing number of 'never married' men and to a lesser extent, 'never married' women; the increase in separations and divorces (the highest rates in the European Union); and the increased number of elderly widowed women. There were 322,000 marriages in the United Kingdom in 1995, the lowest figure recorded since 1926. The *Divorce Reform Act 1969*, which came into force in 1971, introduced a new ground for divorce, that of irretrievable breakdown. This has contributed to the increase in both divorces and remarriages.

A household size of 3.1 in 1961 dropped to 2.4 in 1996, according to the *General Household Survey 1996* and is projected to drop still further. Most people live in families, but family structures have become more diverse. Married couples with children are not as prevalent as they were, while cohabiting couples and lone parents are now much more common. The *General Household Survey* in 1996 was the first year in which households consisting of married or cohabiting couples were shown separately. The most frequently occurring household types were: married couples with no dependent children (31 per cent); persons living alone (27 per cent); and married couples with dependent children (23 per cent). Cohabiting couples accounted for 7 per cent of all households, 3 per cent with dependent children and 4 per cent without.

There has been a substantial growth in lone parent families. Lone parents headed 21 per cent of all families with dependent children in Great Britain in 1996. A large part of the increase up to the mid 1980s was due to divorce, whilst after 1986, single lone mothers grew at a faster rate as the proportion of live births outside marriage accelerated. Most lone parent families are headed by a lone mother. In 1995–6, nearly two fifths of lone mothers were single and a slightly smaller proportion were divorced. In the early 1990s, on average, around 15 per cent of lone mothers per year ceased to be lone parents. If such a departure rate was maintained over time, half of all lone mothers would have a duration of lone parenthood of around four years or less.

6.4 Changing markets

The 'demographic time bomb' of a few years ago, when the teenage numbers started to drop significantly, now shows itself in forecasts for a sharp drop of 19 per cent in 25–34 year olds by 2005. Matching increases will show in the 35–44 and 55–65 year age groups, with a significant increase in the very old, calling for higher levels of health care and financial support.

Changes, particularly such dramatic changes, have implications for leisure. Different age groups have different fashions and tastes. Older groups have more time, greater affluence and higher expectations than ever before. Health care is a growing industry. Fitness Centres are now using the term 'Health and Fitness Centre'. Many local authority Leisure Centres are serving as GP Referral Centres and rehabilitation centres, with visiting doctors, physiotherapists, osteopaths, aromatherapists, and health care specialists. Soon, we may find qualified medical staff appointed to leisure centres. Commercial country clubs already have skilled medical teams associated with their leisure programmes. The advent of Healthy Living Centres advocated in the government's plans for a sixth good cause for National Lottery distribution, will add to this trend in health-related provision.

Provision for young people, notably in the lucrative commercial sector, used to be the key target market area. Now targets are more diverse. Sectors of the leisure market dominated by the preferences of teenagers have been competing for an increasingly smaller share of the United Kingdom population. With the youth market no longer culturally and commercially predominant, adjustments in leisure provision towards the older markets have needed to be made. For example, provision with a quieter, more sociable atmosphere, enabling people to carry out activities at their own pace are now considered. Leisure providers increasingly see themselves moving away from the standardized-only, mass-market provision, towards more flexible provision, for more segmented markets.

The leisure industry has increasingly had to cater also to the 25–34 year age group (family formers) and beyond, particularly the over 60s. The United Kingdom leisure market is ageing; the affluent 'empty nesters' or 'woopies' (well-off-older-persons) are an increasingly important market in both numerical and economic terms, indicating the 'greying' of our society. Many older people with small or repaid mortgages are becoming more affluent at a time of life when they have the freedom and time to enjoy leisure activities. Alas, too many remain or become poor on state pensions alone, and if ill-health strikes, leisure is no amelioration.

The presence of children in the family can be an important influence on both the extent and type of chosen leisure activity – swimming, for example, is particularly orientated towards young children accompanied by a parent. The family unit, however, is becoming more fragmented. Each member has a diverse range of opportunities and obligations, which means leisure time is often spent apart.

There are changes in household structures away from the traditional family markets. There is a greater need to consider couples as a prime market and to take into account the needs of single parent families, currently a growing, disadvantaged, market sector. Employment patterns have changed from predominantly men in full time employment to large numbers of women in part time employment.

Where people live can also affect the leisure pursuits that they engage in. Many rural populations can be as disadvantaged as inner urban areas. Around a fifth of the population of Great Britain lived in rural areas in 1995. Overall, the population of rural areas grew by 17 per cent between 1971 and 1995, faster than that of urban centres. In contrast, the population living in mining and industrial areas fell by 7 per cent over this period.

The number of people living in resort and retirement areas increased by 14 per cent to 2.5 million between 1971 and 1995, reflecting the general ageing of the population. Coastal retirement areas have the largest proportion of elderly people. In contrast, areas with new towns tend to have low proportions of elderly people.

6.5 Income – wealth and poverty

The leisure industry is a growth industry, with a value approaching £150 billion in the United Kingdom in the year 2000.

Income and wealth are important measures of the standard of living of individuals and the country as a whole. They also directly influence leisure behaviour. One of the most commonly used measures of living standards is disposable income: defined as the amount of money people have available to them to spend or invest (Table 6.4). Household disposable income per head in the United Kingdom rose by nearly 80 per cent between 1971 and 1990 – equivalent to an average growth of 3.1 per cent a year. Since 1990, it has levelled off. In parallel, the gap between high incomes and low incomes also grew rapidly in the 1980s, and remains at a high level.

Couples with non-dependent children have the highest gross income in the

TABLE 6.4 Disposable household income[1]: by household type in the United Kingdom

	£ per week per household			
	1993–4	1994–5	1995–6	1996–7
Retired households[2]				
One adult	109	117	121	124
Two or more adults	229	233	245	259
Non-retired households				
One adult	191	199	198	207
Two adults	357	367	383	415
Three or more adults	474	513	540	560
One adult with children	146	150	154	160
Two adults with one child	351	376	379	410
Two adults with two children	387	418	399	434
Two adults with three or more children	366	364	383	394
Three or more adults with children	454	486	532	534
All households	287	298	307	325

Notes 1 Including wages and salaries, self-employed income, occupational pensions and annuities, income from 'fringe benefits', etc.
2 Households where head of household is retired. All male heads of household are aged 65 or over, all female heads of household are aged 60 or over.

Source: *Family Expenditure Survey*, Office for National Statistics

TABLE 6.5 Socio-economic groups (all persons 16 and over)

	1981 percentage	1986 percentage
Professional	2	4
Employees and managers	9	15
Intermediate and junior non-manual	32	34
Skilled manual and own account non-professional	24	21
Semi-skilled manual and personal service	24	19
Unskilled manual	8	6

Source: The Labour Force Survey (1996) *General Household Survey*, Office of National Statistics

United Kingdom. Lone parents with dependent children receive nearly half their income in the form of non-contributory cash benefits. They are among the poorest. Retired households receive their income either from investment income, like personal pensions or from contributory cash benefits.

The growth in the leisure industry is, in large measure, a reflection of growing affluence generally.

Under the former Office of Population Censuses and Surveys, 'Classification of Occupations' categories, society is becoming more 'middle-class', with a growth in the number of people in the A, B and C1 socio-economic groups. More people are employed in white-collar jobs (Table 6.5). This changes attitudes to 'outside work' activities. 'Middle-class' lifestyles tend to lead to middle-class concerns in health and leisure.

6.5.1 Leisure spending

The Retail Prices Index (RPI) is the key indicator of inflation and a reflection of how much we actually pay for the goods we buy every month. It is very important to the leisure industry.

The fiftieth anniversary of the RPI was in 1997. Since it started in 1947, prices have changed dramatically, but not consistently. The National Statistics Office reveals that prices have risen overall by 2000 per cent, but Sunday newspapers by 10,000 per cent. Beer seems a better indicator of change, having increased by the average 2000 per cent.

An understanding of underlying price change patterns and the real changes in prices affecting leisure participation is essential for business and can be established from the wide range of price statistics available from National Statistics RPI business unit.

Clearly, one of the biggest influences on the level of expenditure for a particular individual or household is their level of income (Table 6.6). Not un-expectedly, the households with the lowest incomes spend a higher proportion of their income on essentials such as food, fuel, light and power than other house-holds. Conversely, those with the highest incomes spend a higher proportion of their income on leisure goods and services.

Recently, the *Family Expenditure Survey* (*FES*) has begun collecting information about children's expenditure patterns. Like the adults, children aged 7 to 15 are asked to keep diaries to record their spending over a two week period. In 1997, almost all children spent money on food with their spending money, averaging £9.30 (including fares) per week for children aged between 7 and 15 years. Food was the single largest item of expenditure by far; girls spent twice as much as boys on clothing and footwear; boys spent twice as much on leisure goods (including toys and CDs).

People are spending more on leisure. The *Family Expenditure Survey 1995–6* indicated that of average household expenditure of £290 per week, nearly £46 was spent on leisure goods and services (16 per cent). Retired households spent between 14 per cent and 20 per cent on leisure goods and services, depending on levels of disposable income. Those on state pensions alone spend a far higher proportion of their income on food, fuel and power. Children spent 31 per cent of their pocket money on leisure goods and services – a growing market. Disposable household income and personal disposable income in the United Kingdom more than doubled over the period 1985 to 1995.

Leisure itself, therefore, could become either the social equalizer or a social divider. Although an over-simplification, leisure may become dominated by two

TABLE 6.6 Household expenditure by income grouping, 1995–6

	United Kingdom percentages					
	Quintile groups of households					
	Bottom fifth	Next fifth	Middle fifth	Next fifth	Top fifth	All households
Food	24	22	20	18	15	18
Housing	15	16	16	16	18	17
Leisure goods and services	13	14	14	16	18	16
Motoring and fares	11	13	15	16	16	15
Household goods and services	13	13	13	13	14	13
Clothing and footwear	5	5	6	6	6	6
Fuel, light and power	7	6	5	4	3	4
Alcohol	3	4	4	4	4	4
Tobacco	4	3	2	2	1	2
Other goods and services	5	5	5	5	5	5
All household expenditure (=100 per cent) (£ per week)	158	191	273	351	477	290

Source: *Family Expenditure Survey*, Office for National Statistics

groups, those with the money, but not the time, and those with the time, but not the money! Poverty seems always to be with us. The Rowntree Inquiry into Income and Welfare depicted the United Kingdom as the second highest nation, behind New Zealand, in the 'rising inequality' league. Barry Hugill wrote of 'the underclass' (*The Observer*, 13 April 1997). Twenty-four per cent of the population in Britain live in poverty. Seventeen per cent receive income support; 19.1 per cent of households have no working adults; 7.5 per cent of all dwellings are 'unfit for human habitation'; and poor people are one and a half times as likely to have a long-standing illness and twice as likely to have a disability.

Poor people are caught in a vicious circle: bad housing, unemployment or low pay, poor diet, poor schools. One way out of the trap of poverty is to win on the football pools, the horses or the National Lottery!

6.6 The National Lottery

Gambling has long been a popular activity in the United Kingdom and with the launch of the National Lottery in November 1994, many households now participate in this particular form of gaming. The *FES* found that around 70 per cent of households participated (see Table 6.7). The most dramatic change in the provision

TABLE 6.7 Percentage of households participating in the National Lottery[1]: by social class[2] of head of household

	United Kingdom			
	Saturday draw			Wednesday draw
	1995	1996	1997	1997
Professional	63	55	54	21
Managerial and technical	70	70	62	33
Skilled non-manual	82	83	67	31
Skilled manual	89	80	80	47
Partly skilled	75	80	69	40
Unskilled	79	79	68	29
Economically inactive	62	62	52	29
All households	72	69	62	33

Notes 1 In the two-week diary-keeping period following interview between January and March each year for Saturday draw, and between February and March for Wednesday draw.
2 See Appendix, Part 13: Social class

Source: Family Expenditure Survey, Office for National Statistics

for sports, arts and heritage has been from the proceeds of the National Lottery, with an impact on the level of services and facilities and their management. During this time, some 27 per cent of the Lottery's proceeds were allocated to good causes divided between five separate funds administered by the Arts Council, Sports Council, Charities Board, the Millennium Commission, and the National Heritage Fund. By the end of 1996, more than 19,300 grants had been awarded, to the value of £3,153 million. London appears to have received a disproportionately high value of grants, but many of the largest grants were to institutions which have a national significance.

The proportion of households which participated in the Saturday night draw during the two-week diary-keeping period following interview between January and March declined from 72 per cent in 1995 to 62 per cent in 1997. A second, mid-week, draw was introduced on 5th February 1997; this is far less popular than the Saturday draw. Households headed by someone with a skilled manual occupation are the most likely to participate in the lottery.

According to the *FES*, households spent on average £2.10 a week on the National Lottery draws in 1996–7, representing less than 1 per cent of their total weekly expenditure. The amounts spent increase with the amount of disposable income available to households. Household expenditure on other forms of gambling has decreased, falling 15 per cent in real terms. Further information on the Lottery can be found in chapter eight.

6.7 The use of time – leisure at home

The amount of time people spend in work and on essential tasks impacts on the amount of time they have for leisure activities and upon their lifestyle. For most people, around a third of each day is spent sleeping. How people use their time for the rest of the day is related, among other things, to gender and economic status. Both men and women who are not working spend more time than their counterparts who are in work on domestic chores and on watching television, listening to the radio and socializing. It appears that the traditional gender division of labour is still strong. Overall, women from all social classes spend more than three times longer than men on average on cooking and routine housework and more than twice as long on caring for children and adults. However, men in the professional and intermediate social class spend longer than men in the other social classes on the care of children and adults.

The Home Office *Youth Lifestyles Survey* found that the traditional gender roles were filtering down to younger people, despite the apparent 'new man' sharing in the household. While only one in ten young men always did the household shopping, three in ten young women did so. The same was true for washing up. Also, nearly twice as many young women as young men usually, or always, made their own meals.

Women with children spend much more time on average doing household tasks than men. According to the *Value of a Mum* survey which was carried out for Legal and General in August 1996, mothers spent an average of 62 hours a week doing household chores compared with the 23 hours a week spent on such tasks by fathers.

Office for National Statistics (1997), *Social Trends 27*,
The Stationery Office, London

TABLE 6.8 Participation in home-based leisure activities

	Percentages		
	1980	*1990*	*1996*
Watching TV	98	99	99
Visiting/entertaining friends or relations	91	96	96
Listening to radio	88	89	88
Listening to records/tapes	64	76	78
Reading books	57	62	65
Gardening	43	48	48
DIY	37	43	42
Dressmaking/needlework/knitting	28	23	22

Source: *General Household Survey 1996*, Office for National Statistics

The *General Household Survey 1996* reported that almost all respondents had watched television (99 per cent) or visited or entertained friends or relations (96 per cent) during the four weeks prior to interview (Table 6.8). Listening to the radio (88 per cent) and records or tapes (78 per cent) were the next most popular activities. The popularity of television viewing is reflected in the fact that the most widely read monthly magazine was the *Sky TV Guide* in 1996–7. It was read by nearly 6 million adults while 5 million read *Take a Break*, the most popular women's weekly.

Even though it is less popular than television, people in the United Kingdom still spend an average of nearly 16 hours a week listening to the radio. In 1996, those in the 65 and over age group listened the most to the radio; at over 18 hours a week, this was over three times as much as 4 to 14 year olds, who were the age group who listened the least to the radio.

The greatest recent changes, between 1995 and 1996, were ownership of consumer durables: CD players (from 52 per cent to 58 per cent); microwave ovens (from 70 per cent to 74 per cent); video recorders (from 79 per cent to 82 per cent); home computers (from 25 per cent to 27 per cent).

For the first time, the *General Household Survey 1996* survey included a question about satellite television; 18 per cent of households had a receiver for satellite television. An increasing proportion of households have a video recorder, which means that programmes can be viewed later and viewers can also watch hired or bought pre-recorded videos. In 1996–7, at least eight in ten households in each socio-economic group had a video recorder. Video tapes are now more likely to be bought than rented, and this may be linked to the expansion of the distribution of pre-recorded videos in such places as supermarkets. Most video sales take place in the winter months. Whereas the all-time top 20 video sales are dominated by children's viewing, the top 20 video rentals are dominated by feature films. The most popular bought video in 1995 was *The Lion King*. Action/adventure was the most common type of feature film purchased, followed by comedy and drama/thrillers.

The dramatic rise in sales of CDs in recent years has been accompanied by a fall in cassette and LP sales. Indeed, LPs represent less than 2 per cent of all album sales. Nearly 160 million CDs were sold in the United Kingdom in 1996, representing over three quarters of all album sales in CD, cassette and LP format. Sales of singles rose for the fourth successive year, exceeding 78 million for the first time since 1982. People in the 25 to 34 age group were the most likely to be heavy purchasers in 1996; that is, those who bought 16 or more albums. This is perhaps an indication that they have greater disposable income available and are less likely to have financial commitments such as children and mortgages.

Some albums continue to be very popular long after their first release. Britain's best-selling album of all time list is the Beatles' *Sgt Pepper's Lonely Hearts Club Band*, which was released in 1967. The top-selling album in 1995 was *Robson and Jerome* by Robson Green and Jerome Flynn, with Oasis and Celine Dion in second and third places respectively. In 1996, the top-selling album was *Jagged Little Pill* by Alanis Morissette, with Oasis and the Spice Girls in second and third places.

The *National Readership Survey* reports that over half of people aged 15 and over read a national daily newspaper in Great Britain in the year to June 1997,

TABLE 6.9 Reading of national daily newspapers: by gender

	Males			Females		
	1981	*1991*	*1996¹*	*1981*	*1991*	*1996¹*
Sun	31	25	25	23	19	19
Daily Mirror	27	20	15	22	15	11
Daily Mail	13	10	11	11	9	12
Daily Star	13	8	7	8	4	3
Daily Express	16	8	6	13	8	6
Daily Telegraph	9	6	7	7	5	5
The Times	3	3	5	2	2	3
Guardian	4	3	3	2	2	2
Independent		3	2		2	1
Financial Times	2	2	2	1	1	1
Any national daily newspaper²	76	66	62	68	57	53

Great Britain percentages

Notes 1 July 1996 to June 1997; earlier years are calendar years
2 Includes the above newspapers plus the *Daily Record*, *Sporting Life* and *Racing Post*.

Source: National Readership Surveys Ltd

substantially lower than in 1981 (Table 6.9). Readership had declined particularly in the younger age groups. The *News of the World* is the most popular Sunday paper with over 11.5 million readers; the *Sun* has consistently been the most popular daily paper in recent years, with a readership of over 10 million. Men have been consistently more likely than women to read a national daily newspaper. A larger proportion of people read national Sunday newspapers than daily ones.

The library remains one of the most used out-of-home leisure facilities. According to the *General Household Survey 1996*, there were nearly 400 million visits made to the 24,000 public libraries in the United Kingdom in 1995–6, during which over 500 million books were issued. Generally, people borrow twice as many adult fiction books as non-fiction. However, since the mid 1980s, there has been a decline in the total number of public library books borrowed, mainly in adult fiction. Public libraries are increasingly extending their facilities beyond the borrowing of books. They also lend cassettes, CDs and videos, and photocopying and fax services have been available for some time now. Libraries are also becoming computerized and some offer a link to the internet. People who borrow books are likely to use other facilities within the library. For example, 10 per cent of borrowers said they also used the library for community information and 19 per cent of book borrowers also borrowed records, tapes or CDs.

TABLE 6.10 Borrowing of books from libraries: by gender and age, 1995

| | Percentages | | | |
| | Borrow at least monthly | | Borrow less than monthly | |
	Males	Females	Males	Females
15–24	24	33	35	39
25–34	14	20	24	39
35–44	13	34	36	38
45–54	16	35	28	24
55–64	33	42	22	18
65–74	22	48	27	21
75 and over	19	38	16	12
All aged 15 and over	19	34	28	29

Source: Book Marketing Ltd

Over half of people aged 15 and over held a library ticket in the United Kingdom in 1995, although not all ticket holders borrow books regularly (Table 6.10). Females were more likely than males to hold a library ticket. A third of females borrowed books at least monthly, compared with only a fifth of males. Women aged between 65 and 74 were the most likely to borrow at least monthly, whereas among men those aged between 55 and 64 were the most likely.

In the twelve months ending June 1995, authors whose books were most commonly borrowed from libraries by adults were Catherine Cookson, Danielle Steel, Dick Francis, Ruth Rendell and Agatha Christie. Janet and Allan Ahlberg and Roald Dahl were the most popular among children.

In summary, this section has illustrated the large amount of time and money spent in and around the home, in shopping and using the library. These factors have an effect on other leisure pursuits and hence on leisure management. We now turn to leisure away from home.

6.8 The use of time – leisure away from home

The most common leisure activity outside the home among adults in Great Britain in 1996 was visiting a public house, with 65 per cent of all adults, more men than women, saying that they had done so in the three months before being interviewed (Table 6.11). Seven in ten of those aged between 16 and 24 had gone to a nightclub or disco in the previous three months. Fast food was also more commonly eaten by those in the younger age groups.

Figures from the Henley Centre show that social grade affected participation in some leisure activities (Table 6.12). Among those in the non-manual social grades (AB and C1) a meal in a restaurant was more popular than a visit to the pub.

TABLE 6.11 Participation in leisure activities away from home: by age, 1995–6

	16–24	25–34	35–44	45–59	60 and over	All aged 15 and over
Visit a public house	78	81	72	62	42	65
Meal in a restaurant (not fast food)	57	66	65	65	56	61
Drive for pleasure	44	51	48	53	45	48
Meal in fast food restaurant	74	61	52	34	40	39
Library	42	37	42	34	40	39
Cinema	68	49	40	25	9	36
Short break holiday	33	32	26	31	28	30
Disco/nightclub	71	44	20	10	3	27
Historic building	23	24	28	27	19	24
Spectator sports event	28	26	27	17	12	21
Theatre	17	19	19	24	19	20

Source: The Henley Centre

People in social grade AB participated more frequently in most of the activities shown in Table 6.12 than those in the other social grades. The exceptions included visits to a disco or night club, betting shops and bingo. Activities which were much more popular with men than women included watching a sports event and going to a betting shop and a pub. Activities more popular with women than men were visiting a library or going to the theatre.

6.8.1 Entertainment and cultural events

Table 6.13 shows that the percentages of those aged 15 and over attending cultural events. When asked in 1995–6 whether they attend particular types of cultural events 'these days', nearly one in four of adults in Great Britain said that they attend plays, while fewer than one in ten said that they went to the ballet or opera. The proportion of adults that attend most types of cultural events has not changed much over the last decade or so. The exception is going to the cinema; whereas three in ten adults said in 1986–7 that they went to the cinema, five in ten said in 1995–6 that they did so.

From a high of 1.4 billion in 1951, cinema admissions declined sharply, particularly from the mid 1950s to the mid 1960s, and then continued to fall more slowly to reach a low of 53 million in 1984, caused by the arrival, first of television, and later of video. Cinema admissions rose over the last decade to 112 million in 1996. Most of the films are American 'blockbusters'. People in the non-manual social grades are the most likely to go to the cinema and younger people are more likely to go than older people. The massive investment in multiplex cinemas over

TABLE 6.12 Participation[1] in selected leisure activities away from home: by social grade, 1996

	Great Britain percentages					
	AB	C1	C2	D	E	All adults
Visit a public house	74	69	64	66	48	65
Meal in a restaurant (not fast food)	87	73	58	45	36	62
Drive for pleasure	54	47	48	46	38	47
Meal in a fast food restaurant	48	44	42	43	29	42
Library	59	43	31	30	31	39
Cinema	47	42	35	30	21	36
Short break holiday	41	33	28	22	18	29
Disco or night club	26	29	27	31	20	27
Historic building	41	31	17	15	10	24
Spectator sports event	30	25	23	18	7	22
Theatre	35	26	17	11	7	20
Museum or art gallery	36	24	14	11	12	20
Fun fair	14	13	19	16	10	15
Exhibition (other than museum/gallery)	24	18	13	7	4	14
Theme park	14	11	14	12	10	12
Visit a betting shop	5	6	11	12	12	9
Camping or caravanning	8	9	11	9	5	9
Bingo	2	5	8	10	14	7

Note 1 Percentage aged 16 and over participating in each activity in the three months prior to interview
Source: Leisure Tracking Survey, The Henley Centre

TABLE 6.13 Attendance[1] at cultural events

	Great Britain percentages		
	1986–7	1991–2	1995–6
Cinema	31	44	51
Plays	23	23	23
Art galleries/exhibitions	21	21	22
Classical music	12	12	12
Ballet	6	6	7
Opera	5	6	6
Contemporary dance	4	3	4

Note 1 Percentage of resident population aged 15 and over attending 'these days'
Source: Target Group Index, British Market Research Bureau International

the last decade has been largely responsible for the industry's sustained growth. There were only two such sites in 1986, offering between them 18 screens which represented only 1 per cent of the total number of screens in the United Kingdom. In 1996, these had grown to 98 sites, with a total of 875 screens, amounting to 40 per cent of all screens. Chapter eleven on the commercial sector contains a section specifically on the cinema.

6.8.2 Visits to tourist attractions

The most popular free tourist attraction in Great Britain continues to be Blackpool Pleasure Beach, which 7.5 million people visited in 1996. The second most popular free attraction is the British Museum. This attracted 6.2 million visitors (5.7 million in 1997), more than twice as many as in 1981. The most popular museums and galleries introduced admission charges in the late 1980s. This has had an impact on the number of visits. For example, visits to the Natural History Museum and the Science Museum more than halved between 1981 and 1991 though the numbers have remained broadly stable since then. Other attractions which charge admission have fared rather better. Visits to Madame Tussaud's increased by 35 per cent between 1981 and 1996 to 2.7 million (2.8 million by 1997), and visits to Alton Towers rose by 69 per cent, also to 2.7 million. Visits to the Tower of London fell initially over the period, but rose to 2.5 million in 1996 and 2.6 million in 1997. Data from the British Tourist Authority is in Table 6.14, and further information about tourism and the BTA can be found in chapter eight.

6.8.3 Day visits

The 1996 United Kingdom Day Visits Survey collected information on round trips made from home or work for leisure purposes (Table 6.15). These leisure day visits increased by 10 per cent between 1994 and 1996 to nearly 6 billion. Seventy-one per cent of day visits were to a town or city, 26 per cent were to the countryside and only 3 per cent were to the seaside or coast. The two most popular reasons for this all-year-round activity were visiting friends and relatives and going out for a meal or drink. People spent an average £9.10 per trip per person. Day visits which are not made on a regular basis and which last for three or more hours away from home are called tourism leisure day visits. In 1996, there were approximately 1.2 billion of these, over 20 per cent more than there were in 1991–2.

The car was the main form of transport used for leisure day visits, although travelling on foot accounted for around three in ten of all visits. Most visits involved total travelling of less than ten miles away from home.

6.8.4 Holidays

The *British National Travel Survey* found that 59 million holidays of four nights or more were taken by British residents in 1995, an increase of 43 per cent on the

TABLE 6.14 Visits to the most popular tourist attractions

	Great Britain millions		
	1981	*1991*	*1996*
Attractions with free admission			
Blackpool Pleasure Beach	7.5	6.5	7.5
British Museum	2.6	5.1	6.2
Strathclyde Country Park	—	4.2	5.5
National Gallery	2.7	4.3	5.0
Palace Pier, Brighton	—	3.5	4.3
Westminster Abbey	—	—	2.5
Eastbourne Pier	—	—	2.3
York Minster	—	—	2.2
Tate Gallery	0.9	1.8	2.0
Pleasureland, Southport	—	1.8	2.0
Attractions charging admission			
Alton Towers	1.6	2.0	2.7
Madame Tussaud's	2.0	2.2	2.7
Tower of London	2.1	1.9	2.5
Chessington World of Adventures	0.5	1.4	1.7
Canterbury Cathedral	—	—	1.7
Natural History Museum[1]	3.7	1.6	1.6
Science Museum[2]	3.8	1.3	1.5
Legoland	—	—	1.4
Windsor Castle	—	—	1.2
Blackpool Tower	—	1.3	1.2

Notes 1 Admission charges were introduced in 1987
2 Admission charges were introduced in 1989.

Source: British Tourist Authority

number taken in 1971. The number taken in Great Britain has been declining while the number taken abroad has grown strongly. However, there was a small drop in foreign holidays in 1995–6, and a rise in those taken in Great Britain. The *United Kingdom Tourism Survey* found that one in five holidays taken in the United Kingdom had an activity as their main purpose, with swimming and walking/hiking the most common activities. Nearly 60 per cent of people participated in an activity of some sort while on their holiday; visiting museums and heritage sites was also popular.

TABLE 6.15 Day visits from home: by main purpose, 1996

Great Britain	Percentage
Visit friends/relatives	18
Eat/drink out	18
Walk or ramble	15
Leisure shopping	11
For entertainment	6
Outdoor sport	3
Indoor sport	5
Pursue a hobby	6
Drive/picnic/sightseeing	3
Swimming	3

Source: United Kingdom Day Visits Survey, Countryside Recreation Network

For those people who stayed in Great Britain for their holidays in 1996, the West Country was the most popular destination, followed by Scotland and Wales. Greater London accounted for only 2 per cent. In contrast, the capital has a huge appeal for overseas visitors – 53 per cent stayed there in 1996. Spain was the most common destination for United Kingdom holidaymakers going abroad in 1996 (28 per cent), with around 24 per cent to France. France has become increasingly popular as a day trip destination in recent years, especially since the relaxation of customs regulations on duty paid goods and the opening of the Channel Tunnel which has reinforced France's position as a gateway to Europe. Europe is still more popular with British holidaymakers than other parts of the world, although the United States has been growing in popularity.

6.8.5 Other leisure-related activities

Leisure is not just about filling time for enjoyment alone, but includes a wide array of activities, some of which could be termed 'serious leisure', for example, hobbies, formal leisure learning, doing good works and religious activities. There appears to be an insatiable demand from a growing number of people to continue to learn through courses of instruction and attendance at leisure classes. Women predominate over men, though the gap lessens year by year as shown in Table 6.16.

The likelihood of attending classes varied with the economic status, socio-economic group and educational qualifications of men and women. Among men, those working part-time were most likely to be attending a class whereas, among women, the proportion was highest among those who worked full-time. Men and women in non-manual socio-economic groups were twice as likely as those in manual groups to be going to classes and the likelihood of attending a class also increased with the person's educational level.

TABLE 6.16 Attendance at leisure classes by sex and age: 1983 and 1993 (persons aged 16 and over)

Age	Men		Women		Total	
	1983	*1993*	*1983*	*1993*	*1983*	*1993*
16–24	5	8	10	12	7	10
25–34	3	6	11	12	7	9
35–44	3	4	10	11	7	8
45–64	2	4	7	11	5	8
65 and over	2	2	3	6	3	5
Total	3	5	8	10	5	8

Source: Office for National Statistics (1996), *General Household Survey*

Religious activities take up a good deal of 'free time' and form an important part of many people's lives. Whilst Trinitarian churches (Roman Catholic, Anglican, Methodist, Baptist, Presbyterian and Free Churches) have experienced a fall in membership from 9.1 million adults in 1970 to 6.4 million in 1995, other faiths have increased in membership. For example, the Muslim faith experienced a large increase in membership between 1970 and 1995, the numbers in the United Kingdom doubling to 1.2 million.

According to *Christian Research*, around 60 per cent of people active in their religion in Great Britain are female. Those people aged under 15 and over 45 are over-represented while those aged between 15 and 44 are under-represented. Only 11 per cent of adults questioned in 1996 in the *British Social Attitudes Survey* said they attended church once a week or more, a fall from 13 per cent in 1989.

6.9 Participation in sports

This section should be read in conjunction with chapter eight, which carries a section focussed on sport and the Sports Council.

The *General Household Survey* is an important national source of data on participation in sport and leisure activities. The information it provides shows how people spend their leisure time. The *General Household Survey* has included a section on sport and leisure activities at roughly three-year intervals since 1973. Surveys up to 1986 used an 'open-ended' style of questioning. A new set of questions was introduced in 1987 designed to improve the accuracy of the information. Since 1987, respondents have been prompted with a list of about forty types of sports or activities and asked about participation, both in the previous four weeks and in the twelve months before interview. Discussion of the change in methodology in 1987 and the difficulties of making comparison with earlier results is contained in a separate *General Household Survey* volume.

Sporting activity by children, which is important in assessing total demand for facilities, is not covered by the *General Household Survey*. The survey also excludes the use of facilities by people on holiday from outside Britain, although sports undertaken by respondents when abroad are included.

Two measures of participation are available from the *General Household Survey* questions:

- four-week participation rate – the percentage of people aged 16 or over who took part in an activity in the four weeks before interview
- twelve-month participation rate – the percentage of people aged 16 or over who took part in an activity in the twelve months before interview.

Twelve-month rates are likely to be higher than four-week rates because some of those who have participated during the year will be interviewed about a four-week period in which they did not participate. This is most likely to occur if the activity is highly seasonal or attracts infrequent participants.

The *General Household Survey* also asks participants about the number of occasions on which they took part in an activity. This provides two measures of frequency:

- frequency of participation per participant in four weeks: the average number of occasions on which participants took part in an activity
- frequency of participation per adult per year: the total number of occasions of participation in a sport per year averaged over the whole sample of people aged 16 or over.

In 1993 and again in 1996, 64 per cent of adults said that they had taken part in at least one of the sports covered by the survey during the four weeks before interview. Sports participation was dominated by walking: 45 per cent of adults said they had been for a walk of two or more miles in the previous four weeks. If walking is excluded, the proportion of adults who took part in at least one sport in the four week reference period was 47 per cent.

After walking, swimming was the most frequently mentioned activity: 15 per cent of adults said they had been swimming in the four weeks before interview. Only three other activities attracted more than 10 per cent of adults in a four week period on average through the year: these were cue sports (snooker/pool/billiards), keep fit/yoga and cycling. However, the statistics reveal a decline in the more traditional pub-based recreations of darts, snooker, pool and in the traditional sports-centre sports, such as badminton, squash and table tennis. The trends 1987–96 are shown in Table 6.17.

Participation rates for the twelve months before interview were higher than four-week rates: 81 per cent had taken part in at least one activity and 66 per cent in at least one activity other than walking. The frequency of participation in the four-week reference period was highest for cycling, weight lifting, gymnastics and horse riding. On average, participants had done each of these on eight separate occasions in four weeks.

Following a significant increase between 1987 and 1990, overall rates of participation in sport have stabilized. Four-week participation rates in most individual activities showed little change between 1993 and 1996, with the exception of

TABLE 6.17 Trends in participation in sports, games and physical activities: 1987, 1990, 1993 and 1996 (persons aged 16 and over in Great Britain)

Active sports, games and physical activities*	Percentage participating in the four weeks before interview			
	1987	1990	1993	1996
Walking	37.9	40.7	40.8	44.5
Swimming	13.1	14.8	15.4	14.8
Keep fit/yoga	8.6	11.6	12.1	12.3
Snooker/pool/billiards	15.1	13.6	12.2	11.3
Cycling	8.4	9.3	10.2	11.0
Weight lifting/training	4.5	4.8	5.5	6.9
Soccer	4.8	4.6	4.5	4.8
Golf	3.9	5.0	5.3	4.7
Running (jogging, etc.)	5.2	5.0	4.6	4.5
Tenpin bowling/skittles	1.8	3.8	4.0	3.4
Badminton	3.4	3.3	2.7	2.4
Tennis	1.8	2.0	2.1	2.0
Lawn/carpet bowls	1.7	2.1	2.0	1.9
Fishing	1.9	2.0	2.0	1.7
Table tennis	2.4	2.0	1.7	1.5
Squash	2.6	2.5	1.9	1.3
Horse riding	0.9	1.0	1.0	1.0
At least one activity (exc. walking)	44.7	47.8	47.3	45.6
At least one activity	60.7	64.5	63.7	63.7
Base = 100 per cent	19,529	17,574	17,552	15,697

*Includes only activities in which more than 1.0 per cent of all persons participated in four weeks before interview and sports for which results are available for all years

Source: Office for National Statistics (1996), *General Household Survey*

walking, the most popular activity, which increased from 40.8 per cent to 44.5 per cent and cycling from 8.4 per cent to 11 per cent.

In contrast, there has been a decline in the proportions of people playing cue sports, badminton or squash, and those running or jogging, in the four-week reference period.

Swimming has remained the most popular sport. Factors that contribute to this include the very strong attraction to water, its mass participation appeal, individual or family orientation; it is inexpensive, no equipment is required and it is easily available to the majority of the population. The traditional swimming market has, however, been segmented into those that wish to swim, dive, splash and have fun and those who want to improve health and fitness. The design of a proportion of swimming pools has, therefore, changed considerably in recent years from the standard rectangular shape to the modern free form with the addition of flumes, slides, 'tropical islands' and spas. However, the demand for conventional swimming pools is strong with 'lane swimming' on the increase.

While darts and snooker attribute reducing TV coverage as part of the reason for their relative decline, other sports have benefited from increasing coverage – basketball, for example, is now firmly established with youth culture (particularly with black youth culture). This factor is not yet shown in the national statistics, but has been recognized and acted upon in some local authorities with basketball in the parks initiative.

6.9.1 Social profiles and sporting activities

The *General Household Survey 1996* found that as in previous years, men were more likely than women to have participated in at least one sporting activity in either the four weeks or twelve months before interview, as shown in Table 6.18. However, the gap is narrowing. This table also illustrates the decline in sports and physical activities as people get older. There are dramatic changes in highly physical sports like football and even in more social sports like snooker. Walking remains the main activity and swimming and cycling the main sports.

TABLE 6.18 Participation[1] in the most popular sports, games and physical activities: by gender and age, 1996–7 (United Kingdom)

	Percentages							
	16–19	20–24	25–34	35–44	45–54	55–64	65 and over	All aged 16 and over
Males								
Walking	57	57	50	53	51	50	37	49
Snooker/pool/billiards	54	45	29	19	13	9	5	19
Cycling	36	24	19	18	12	8	5	15
Swimming	18	17	17	20	10	7	5	13
Soccer	47	28	17	10	2	1	—	10
Females								
Walking	45	43	44	45	49	43	25	41
Keep fit/yoga	29	28	24	20	14	12	6	17
Swimming	23	21	26	22	14	12	5	16
Cycling	14	11	10	12	7	4	2	8
Snooker/pool/billiards	24	17	6	3	1	—	—	4

Source: Office for National Statistics (1996), *General Household Survey*

Note 1 Percentage in each age group participating in each activity in the four weeks before interview

Table 6.18 shows that variation in participation by socio-economic group was not the same for all activities. Thus, there were relatively large differences in participation rates between the professional and unskilled manual groups for walking, swimming and running, but much smaller differences for cycling and soccer. In contrast, participation in cue sports and darts was higher in manual than non-manual groups.

The lowest participation rates were recorded for men and women who were economically inactive: 55 per cent for men and 44 per cent for women, compared with 72 per cent and 57 per cent respectively for all men or women.

When the effects of age are taken into account, men and women who were in paid employment still had relatively high participation rates, but the unemployed did not. There is also evidence that those in part-time work had the highest participation rates, which perhaps reflects the greater amount of leisure time available to them than to those in full-time work.

TABLE 6.19 Trends in participation in sports, games and physical activities in the four weeks before interview by socio-economic group: 1987, 1990, 1993 and 1996 (persons aged 16 and over in Great Britain)

Socio-economic group * Percentage participating in the four weeks before interview				
	1987	*1990*	*1993*	*1996*
At least one activity (exc. walking)				
Professional	65	65	64	63
Employers and managers	52	53	53	52
Intermediate and junior non manual	45	49	49	47
Skilled manual and own account non professional	48	49	46	45
Semi skilled manual and personal service	34	38	36	37
Unskilled manual	26	28	31	23
Total**	45	48	47	46

* Socio-economic group is based on the person's current or most recent job
** Total includes full-time students, members of the Armed Forces, those who have never worked, and those whose job was inadequately described

Source: Office for National Statistics (1996), *General Household Survey*

6.9.2 Healthy lifestyles

The Health of the Nation, a Green Paper published in June 1991, stimulated debate about the need for improved health. The White Paper, *The Health of the Nation*, published in July 1992 [1], provided a strategic approach to focus on health as much as health care, with the aims of 'adding years to life' and 'adding life to years'. The concepts are integral to the World Health Organisation's 'Health for all by the Year 2000' approach.

Health services are only one part of the strategy. Of importance are public policies (considering the health dimension in a number of public services), healthy surroundings, including physical environments and leisure, and healthy lifestyles through increasing knowledge, understanding and providing opportunities. Physical activity is a factor which may reduce early mortality and ill-health and contribute to healthy living. A lack of physical activity is accepted as a main risk factor for heart disease and stroke – a key area in the White Paper. With the decline in physical activity in everyday life and work, sport and physical recreation now account for most vigorous activity that a person engages in and they are central to the future health of the nation, as well as providing pleasure to millions of people of all ages and abilities.

Almost three-fifths of men and just under a half of women aged 16 and over in England were classed as overweight or obese in 1994, according to the *Health Survey of England*, Department of Health. Alcohol consumption above 'sensible' levels is associated with increased likelihood of various health problems. Smoking is also a recognized health risk. A Health of the Nation target has been set in England to reduce smoking to no more than 20 per cent by the year 2000. Alcohol abuse and smoking among children are of particular concern. The use of drugs is also widespread. The Youth Lifestyles Survey carried out by the Home Office in 1992–3 in England and Wales indicated that over a third of young adults aged 14–25 had, at some time, used controlled drugs. In 1998, the Labour Government brought out its own White Paper, *Our Healthier Nation – A Contract for Health* [2].

> Good health is treasured. It is the foundation of a good life. Better health for the nation is central to making a better country. We have major opportunities to improve people's health. Almost 90,000 people die every year before they reach their 65th birthday. Of these, nearly 32,000 die of cancer, and 25,000 die of heart disease, stroke and related illnesses. Many of these deaths could be prevented. Health inequalities are widening. The poorest in our society are hit harder than the well off by most of the major causes of death. In improving the health of the whole nation, a key priority will be better health for those who are worst off. There are sound economic reasons for improving our health. 187 million working days are estimated by industry to be lost every year because of sickness – a £12 billion tax on business.

The Allied Dunbar National Fitness Survey [3] was designed to measure the activity and fitness levels of the adult (over 16) English population. In terms of physical activity, 7 out of 10 men and 8 out of 10 women fell below their age-appropriate activity level necessary to achieve a health benefit; even among 16–24 year olds, 70 per cent of men and 91 per cent of women were below target. A growing number of the population were overweight.

However, 44 per cent of men and 40 per cent of women took part in sport or active recreation. Moreover, the Henley Centre reports that the most significant trend in the whole leisure field is the trend to more active leisure. The Centre predicts that this trend will continue and attributes it to concern with health and fitness, a growing interest in out-of-home sports and a developing keenness to improve sporting abilities and performance. Evidence from the *General Household*

Surveys indicates the growing popularity of sports associated with fitness and healthy lifestyles.

6.9.3 Participation by children and young people

The *General Household Survey* does not include children and young people under the age of 16 years. However, nearly all children 6–16 had participated in a sporting activity outside school lessons in 1994, according to the Sports Council's *Young People and Sport in England Survey*; only 2 per cent had done none at all [4]. However, the amount of time spent doing such activities ranged from less than one hour to over 15. Boys tended to participate in more sports outside lessons than girls and they also spent more time on sports than girls. Boys tended to participate in a wider range of sports than girls and were especially likely to take part in team games. Table 6.20 shows participation in the top ten sports with cycling/riding a bike and swimming as the most popular. Tables 6.21 and 6.22, the results of British Market Research Bureau surveys in 1993 show the sports children and young people play and which they liked best. Swimming, cycling and football consistently rate highly.

The concern expressed in such reports as *The Health of the Nation* White Paper is that inactive children are likely to become inactive adults, increasing the risks of obesity and heart disease. This report, coupled with *Raising the Game*, focussing on the decline in interest by the young in traditional team sports, has led to the launch of new initiatives aimed at children and young people. These are described in chapter eight and include the National Junior Sports Programme.

TABLE 6.20 Top ten sports participated in by children outside lessons[1] by age, 1994

England percentages

	6–9	9–11	11–14	14–16	All children aged 6–16
Cycling/riding a bike	67	66	48	44	57
Swimming	59	62	41	36	50
Football	38	44	33	35	37
Walking (over one hour)/hiking	29	26	18	19	23
Tennis	16	20	25	26	21
Cricket	14	20	20	13	17
Aerobics/keep fit	21	12	8	15	14
Rounders	12	19	13	7	13
Athletics	17	16	11	7	13
Gymnastics	22	15	7	5	13

Note 1 Those participating at least ten times in the twelve months leading up to the survey

Source: V. Mason (1995) *Young People and Sport in England 1994*, The Sports Council, London

TABLE 6.21 Sports participation rates, 11–19 year olds

Sport	Once a week (%)	Once a month (%)	Like best (%)
Aerobics	6.9	10.3	11.4
Athletics	10.4	13.4	15.4
Badminton	7.3	14.4	22.9
Basketball	9.2	16.1	22.4
Billiards/pool	10.5	17.5	17.4
Cycling	16.5	24.9	31.6
Football	21.1	26.1	39.7
Swimming	16.4	31.6	53.3
Tenpin bowling	1.4	8.9	28.0
Tennis	7.6	14.7	24.4

Source: Youth *Target Group Index* BMRB 1993

TABLE 6.22 Sports played and liked best by 7–10 year olds

Sport	% play	% like best
Athletics	25.6	9.7
Badminton	14.3	7.0
Basketball	19.5	9.1
Cycling	62.7	29.2
Dancing	31.8	16.3
Football	55.8	35.8
Rounders	53.2	20.7
Swimming	84.5	52.6
Tenpin bowling	29.0	17.6

Source: Youth *Target Group Index* BMRB 1993

6.10 Summary – trends in leisure

By the end of 1997, in the United Kingdom, main indicators of social change included: falling birth rates; middle-ageing population; longevity; single and smaller households; increasing disposable incomes for some market segments but growing differences between rich and poor; flexible work patterns; more women in the work place; and greater emphasis on personal independent lifestyles. Couples having families later and also having smaller families allows these relatively young people more time, freedom and money for leisure.

It is important for leisure managers to understand and be able to use information about trends in leisure. They need to know, not just what leisure activity people are engaged in at leisure centres, parks, swimming pools and theatres but also about people's time for leisure, their social situations and their disposable income. Leisure Managers need to know the market and the trends.

Notes and references

1   Department of Health (1992), White Paper, *The Health of the Nation: A Strategy for Health in England*, Cmnd 1986, HMSO, London.
2   Department of Health (1998), White Paper, *Our Healthier Nation – A Contract for Health*, Cmnd 3852, The Stationery Office, London.
3   Sports Council and Health Education Authority (1992), *The Allied Dunbar National Fitness Survey*, Sports Council, London.
4   Mason, V. (1995), for the Sports Council, *Young People and Sport in England 1994*, Sports Council, London.

A good deal of information in this chapter has come from the annual Office for National Statistics Social Trends and Household surveys which contain questions of people's leisure habits in every third survey. In particular the latest versions have been used:

Office for National Statistics (1998), *Social Trends 28*, HMSO, London.
Office for National Statistics (1998), *Living in Britain – Results from the 1996 General Household Survey*, HMSO, London.

Chapter seven

Planning
for leisure

The word 'planning' is used in a number of contexts. In management, it can be a set of processes in setting goals and objectives and developing courses of action. However, here the interpretation of planning – urban and regional planning, town and country planning, and city planning – incorporates specialized components, such as transport planning and leisure planning. The term leisure planning, then, refers to the physical development of areas and facilities for leisure activities and pursuits.

The various Acts of Parliament concerning leisure and recreation in England and Wales have placed statutory responsibility upon local authorities to provide only allotments, libraries, youth facilities and Adult Education facilities. However, no recommendations have been made with regard to the scale of provision required to fulfil this statutory obligation. This, coupled with the 'permissive powers' that relate to other forms of leisure provision, has resulted in considerable variation in the range and scale of provision made by different local authorities. The political philosophies of the respective councils have further exacerbated the situation, with traditional Labour councils generally perceiving provision for recreation, sport and the arts to have a greater social service orientation compared to traditional Conservative councils. However, the differences have narrowed with financial constraints on local government. Another influence is the advent of the National Lottery and the need to fit new facilities into a strategic plan. Indeed, the Chief Leisure Officers Association is urging the government to introduce statutory 'local leisure plans'. Leisure strategies and leisure plans need to fit into the formal planning process. This chapter provides a community and leisure management perspective.

This chapter has the following sequence. First, planning for leisure is seen in historical perspective. Second the differences between statutory plans and non-statutory local leisure plans are described. Third, the philosophical approaches adopted by local authorities, from which policies for leisure planning flow, are debated; they include equitable distribution, expressed demand and social control. Fourth, the complexity of assessing potential demand is illustrated by a critique of a wide range of approaches. These include standards of provision, spatial analysis, hierarchy of facilities, national participation rates and expressed demand; and also relatively less used, yet more sensitive methods, Grid and Need Index approaches and a wide variety of public consultation exercises. New to this edition of the book are case studies and recent demand modelling techniques – the 'playing pitch strategy' and 'facilities planning model'. The planning process model in the previous edition is extended into a ten-stage 'strategic planning process'.

Having read this chapter, readers will understand more about the complex nature of leisure planning, seen from the viewpoint of leisure professionals. They will appreciate that leisure planning differs from 'general' or conventional planning. They will understand why it is of fundamental importance to work from a sound philosophical base, together with an orientation towards a people-involved process. Readers will learn about the various methods which can be used in assessing needs and demands and discover that no one method or one system will be sufficient on which to plan.

7.1 Historical perspective – general planning and leisure planning

Planning has always been concerned, albeit often only peripherally, with the provision of facilities for recreation. The evolution of the planning movement was closely associated with the nineteenth-century fight for the retention of open spaces and commons which were threatened by unplanned urban development. The movement has evolved from a concern for public health, education and moral standards to problems of inner cities and countryside recreation and conservation. Since the *Public Health Act 1848*, which authorized local authorities to provide public walks and pleasure grounds, successive Acts of Parliament such as the *Physical Training and Recreation Act 1937*, the *National Parks and Access to the Countryside Act 1949* and the *Countryside Act 1968* were formulated to meet changing demands. In this evolution, the planner's role has been strengthened by the profession's wide powers over the control of land use.

The planner's objective is to provide the right facilities, in the best location and at the right time, for the people who need them and at acceptable cost. Dreams, however, seldom become reality. Planning is not a static process, but a dynamic and changing one. Planners should work with all the disciplines involved in creating amenities and opportunities for people in neighbourhoods, villages, towns, cities and in the countryside. Planners themselves are only part of the planning process. They do not directly acquire and manage land and amenities. They identify locations for facilities according to acceptable planning principles. They seek to minimize conflicts of interest, traffic, noise, pollution and congestion. Planners help to make towns functional, attractive and healthy places; they also have to safeguard public interest and help to conserve (and foster good use of) the countryside. Gold [1] defines recreation planning as

> a process that relates people's leisure time to space. It is both art and science, using the methods of many disciplines . . . into developing alternatives for using leisure time, space, energy and money to accommodate human needs. The process results in plans, studies and information that condition the public policy . . . to provide leisure opportunity.

7.1.2 Leisure planning

The social dimension of leisure planning emphasizes the difference between it and general planning. Leisure facilities, outside the home, in comparison to housing, retail outlets, roads, and so on, are non-essential facilities and have only a minority appeal to the community as a whole. Hence assessing the demand for a particular leisure facility is a complex and difficult process, particularly since there is a range of competing attractions for a person's leisure time.

Leisure planning as a discipline in its own right is not a new phenomenon. Indeed, leisure planning was to the forefront in the planning of the Garden Cities by Ebenezer Howard at the turn of the century and also he recognized the economic and social benefits associated with the dual use of school facilities. The first of many recreational standards of provision was established by the National Playing Fields Association in 1925. Leisure planning, however, is often a neglected area, despite the considerable advances made in recent years. Veal [2] states the problem:

> The problem with planning for leisure is that, generally speaking, the planning profession knows very little about leisure while the leisure professions know very little about planning. With some honourable exceptions, planners have tended to ignore leisure because they have had more pressing issues such as transport, housing or shopping to deal with. The leisure professions have ignored planning because they have been primarily concerned with management – the day to day operation of facilities and services. And yet the need for firmly based planning in the area of leisure is as great if not greater than in some other areas of public society. Leisure plans not only have to present politicians with proposals concerning the desirable quantity, types and distribution of facilities and services, they also very often have to present the case for any provision at all.

The word 'management' is used, in this quotation, only in an operational context. This book takes the position that management should be concerned not just with operational management, but also with inputs into policy and planning. Bereft of an input into policy, planning, outcomes and evaluation of services, the manager is rendered at best an efficient administrator, organizer and controller of users and personnel. The Leisure Manager should be involved in planning because an involvement at the earliest stage can ensure inclusion of the appropriate ingredients for leisure and elimination of factors not compatible with good management process and practice. An essential part of the planning process is to identify the needs of people and to provide products and services in response to those needs.

Unfortunately, however, there are far too many examples of poor planning. The most common failure is that leisure facilities are often placed in inappropriate locations, for example, on land which is owned by the local authority, but not necessarily in an appropriate location. In such circumstances, they are unlikely to achieve optimum levels of usage and hence require increased levels of subsidy. Facilities located on the periphery of centres of population or away from main transportation routes or alongside physical barriers, such as rivers, inaccessible motorways or difficult road systems, suffer from poor access and inevitably result in a restricted catchment area.

In recent years, planning for leisure and leisure strategies have become increasingly important. The *Town and Country Planning Act 1990* and *Planning and Compensation Act 1991* brought about sweeping changes in the planning system. It has led to a plan-led development system. The Department of the Environment (DOE) issues Planning Policy Guidance Notes (PPGs) and Circulars. For example, prior to 1991, national planning guidance for sport and recreation was provided in Circulars 33/70, 47/77 and 73/77. The most comprehensive guideline on policy and practice came with the publication of *Planning Policy Guidance: Sport and Recreation (PPG17, September 1991)*. This set out the formal planning process in England and Wales relating to sport and recreation. The system is referred to as 'plan-led' because decisions are taken in the context of plans drawn up by local councils in consultation with local communities and other organizations.

7.2 Statutory plans and leisure plans

Planners have a legal duty to conform to statutory planning regulations. In parallel, they have to try to meet local needs. The views of local councillors may well conflict with the planner's statutory role.

There are three main kinds of local authority plan: structure; district; and unitary.

1   *Structure plans* are drawn up by County Councils and set broad targets for development of housing, industry and transport in relation to predicted changes in the population and the economy of the area. For leisure, structure plans identify strategic land use policies for major initiatives (such as community forests) and projects affecting large areas or populations.

2   *District plans* are drawn up by Borough and District Councils (often called local plans) and designate the approved uses of different sites within the local area, such as including housing or industry. Local plans need to address local

needs for leisure and recreation. To do this, deficiencies have to be identified, sites found and policies adopted to balance the requirements of landowners, developers and residents. Local plans tend to deal with open space allocations and they tend to be site specific. One of the problems for local councils is that a structure plan may demand allocations for industry and housing, thereby utilizing space for local council's leisure plans.

3   *Unitary development plans* in London boroughs, Metropolitan districts and the new Unitary Authorities are formed by combining structure plans and district plans.

Whilst it is the statutory duty of County and District Councils to produce structure and local plans, the borough or district leisure strategies produced by Leisure Departments are discretionary. However, the most able and effective local authorities incorporate their leisure strategies in their local plans.

In *District Sport and Recreation Strategies: A Guide (1991)* [3], local authority leisure departments are encouraged to link with local organizations in drawing up district strategies in consultation with the planning authority. The purpose of the document is to 'encourage local authorities to take a strategic approach to the planning, provision and development of sport and recreation opportunities in their area'. The guide provides an approach to identify issues and stages in the process, but little practical help is given in determining what facilities to build.

7.2.1 Planning obligations

Local authorities have a statutory duty to implement a local plan which makes 'appropriate' community recreational provision. Local authorities may enter into planning obligations, under Section 106 of the *Town and Country Planning Act 1990*, 'to secure the provision of public open space and sporting, recreational, social, educational or other community facilities as part of larger mixed developments'.

Planning obligation is the process whereby a planning application may be granted provided certain obligations are fulfilled. *Planning Obligations for Sport and Recreation – A Guide for Negotiation and Action* [4] sets out ways in which councils can use the powerful tool of planning obligations (formerly referred to as planning gain) to improve the provision of sport and recreation facilities by agreements with developers, planning applicants and land owners.

The Sports Council encourages local authorities to use planning obligations to benefit sport and recreation in addition to locally developed district sport and recreation strategies and development plans. Developers can help when recreational land or open space is lost through development. They can provide facilities both on and off site and councils can demand a contribution to nearby sports and recreational open space or community provision. Thus, planning obligations give councils another means of securing facilities for the community.

7.2.2 Safeguarding land for leisure and recreation

These leisure opportunities are provided within the constraints imposed by central government (e.g. financial) and in accordance with local government policies at local level, for the common good of the community. Unfortunately, in practice, community needs can be overruled by central government. There are examples of playing fields, designated in local plans, being permitted, upon appeal, to be used for housing and commercial development. The action taken in the 1980s by the Department of Environment in such circumstances, led to a belief that there is presumption in favour of allowing applications for development. However, there has been mounting concern over many years to protect and provide recreational open space. Government guidance is embodied in Planning Policy Guidance Note 17 *Sport and Recreation* [5], the joint Sports Council/National Playing Fields Association/CCPR report, *The Playing Pitch Strategy* [6] and the decision to compile the *Register of Recreational Land*.

The Register grew out of a need for accurate and comparable data on playing fields at the local and national level, 'to improve decision making and monitor change'. The Register collected information on over 73,000 sports pitches in England across 24,500 sites, covering a total of 150,300 acres of land. Information on ownership, type of usage (for example, public, schools, private), ancillary facilities and threats from development are detailed.

PPG 17 establishes that it is the responsibility of local planning authorities (LPAs) to take account of the community's need for recreational space, to identify current levels of provision and deficiencies and to resist pressures for the development of open space which conflict with the wider public interest.

The Charter for Playing Pitches and the Pitch Sports adopted in April 1991 by the Sports Council, National Playing Fields Association and Central Council for Physical Recreation sets out to change planning policy radically. The strategy aims to make any loss of land subject to far more stringent safeguards. In other words, the former presumption to dispose of land is reversed in the proposal to keep land, except in very special circumstances. Once built on, open space is likely to be lost to the community for ever. Designation of land in local plans, therefore, is vital for long-term retention of land.

With the *Local Government Act 1972*, land could be disposed of at less than 'best consideration'. Now, when local authorities want to dispose of their land, they are under obligation to seek the 'best consideration'. In the case of green belts, for example, there is a general presumption against 'inappropriate' development, but outdoor sport is one of the uses which will often be appropriate.

7.3 Local government – philosophical basis for leisure provision

It is perhaps surprising that some local authorities which spend millions of pounds each year on the operation and maintenance of their leisure services do so with no stated philosophy for the allocation of such resources. In such circumstances, one is tempted to ask: 'why incur this expenditure?' It is acknowledged that much of the leisure provision is an historical inheritance, but this does not justify the continued expenditure without an explanation of its purpose.

Historically, a paternalistic concern for the health and welfare of the community was the major influence on recreation planning. The standard response was the provision of facilities such as parks, playing fields and swimming pools, and these remain today primary areas for local authority provision and finance. Former planning policies appear to have been based on three philosophies or a combination of two or more: equitable distribution, expressed demand and social control.

Equitable distribution

In this context, leisure participation is seen as being of intrinsic value to the participant, with the community also benefiting from the resulting spin-off. However, equity is by no means synonymous with equality; equal distribution of facilities does not necessarily provide either equal opportunity or equal participation. As we have seen in chapter five, the social inequality that exists in our society manifests itself with the more affluent sections predominantly represented as users of public sector facilities. Planners, therefore, should consider the leisure needs of the less affluent and less able members of society in providing appropriate facilities at locations that the non-mobile can reach; when people have most free time the public transport system is at its worst. Therefore, to provide an equitable distribution, there must be a policy of positive discrimination in favour of the disadvantaged in order to ensure equality of opportunity.

Expressed leisure demand

Planning policies based on the expressed demand of its residents are attractive to local government decision makers. If there is a perceived demand for a particular type of facility, then councils are more likely to say: 'we have provided what was demanded – we have therefore met community wishes.'

The use of petitions, staging public meetings or having media-inspired campaigns can influence planning decisions, particularly when a council election is imminent. Pressure groups, however, tend to be represented by the more articulate and vociferous, and their influence is far greater than the proportion of the electorate they represent. In contrast, those with the greatest leisure needs are unlikely to be heard, and without the advocacy of the professional leisure leaders, such expression of demand can be misleading.

Social control

There is a strong and instinctive belief that the provision of sports and leisure opportunities will alleviate anti-social behaviour and many ills of the world. This belief is well established in the minds of local authority members and at central government level. The government White Paper, *Sport and Recreation* [7], claimed that such provision was a means of 'reducing boredom and urban frustration' and stressed its contribution 'to the reduction of hooliganism and delinquency among young people'. This belief was also stressed in more recent reports and White Papers, such as *Policy for the Inner Cities* [8] and the Report of the Scarman Inquiry [9]. If this belief is true, then the issue is what kind of facilities and services are likely to attract those persons who are, or are likely to become, delinquents: is the present type of public sector provision perceived by this target market as attractive? Until answers to these questions are forthcoming, such a philosophy for the allocation of leisure resources could be a hit or miss affair and as such may be inappropriate and expensive.

Local authorities are faced with dilemmas. Who most needs leisure facilities? Which facilities should be provided? Where should they be located? Is there sufficient demand to make for a viable project? There are a range of methods to try to assess demand and these are debated in the section to follow.

7.4 Assessment of demand

Leisure behaviour is by no means fully predictable and there is no single correct method of assessing potential demand.

Provision should not therefore be based upon a simple set of measurements, criteria or rules. By using different approaches to the same problem, greater confidence can be attached to the solution. Eight methods are described in this chapter.

- standards of provision
- spatial or geographic analysis and hierarchy of provision
- national participation rates
- grid approach
- need index approach
- expressed demand and playing pitch strategy
- facilities planning model
- public consultation.

7.5 Standards of provision

Surprisingly, one of the most developed and widely accepted approaches to the 'equitable' distribution of recreational services is the use of scales of provision, standards and norms (Table 7.1). Many standards are not based on empirical research, but on long-accepted assumptions of what is 'needed'. For some unexplained reason, standards have a fascination for planners and politicians. They have the almost hypnotic effect of drawing attention to themselves. Veal [2] captures this paradox of leisure standards:

> Leisure planners love standards. This is one of the great paradoxes of our time. When government Ministers try to tell local authorities how to organize

their affairs they rise up as one and complain of threats to local democracy. And yet in the area of leisure provision, the one area where local authorities are virtually completely free from government interference, they frequently look nervously over their shoulders to ensure that they are sanctioning their activities.

With standards, you don't have to think. Someone else, 'in authority', has done the thinking for you. Standards are simple and efficient; they can lead to the same level of provision area to area; they act as an external authoritative source; and they can be measured, monitored and assessed. Standards are important and useful when they have been based on sound methodology and are used with flexibility and local knowledge. Tempered with wise judgement they have considerable advantages. They give yardsticks against which to measure existing provision, they are easy to understand and communicate and they cover many of the facilities provided by local authorities.

Gold and Mercer [10,11] criticize standards for not being supported by empirical research; beliefs or myths have become accepted and with time have become institutionalized. They believe that the people who develop the standards differ in their social background from the majority of the population and, by implication, impose their own standards upon the population. They also argue that standards across the board do not take into account areas of deprivation, factors of accessibility, and socio-economic or demographic differences. Hence, while standards have some advantages they have many disadvantages, including the six discussed briefly below.

First, they become institutionalized as if written on tablets of stone. Once entrenched, they become authoritative, unmovable and are given far greater strength and importance than they merit. The best known and most frequently applied recreation standards in Britain are those of the National Playing Fields Association. Founded in 1925, the National Playing Fields Association first established its minimum standard of 6 acres of outdoor recreational playing space per 1000 population in 1937. Reviews were undertaken in 1946, 1955, 1971 and 1986 to account for changing conditions. This target has remained intact and is a valuable target guideline for local authorities [12].

Other former standards and approaches to assessing requirements included the Sports Council's *Planning for Sport* (1968), and *Sport in the Community – The Next Ten Years* (1982). Previous methods have now been abandoned in favour of new techniques such as the facilities planning model and playing pitch strategy described later in this chapter.

Second, standards vary. Different authorities have different standards for the same leisure facility. Most major pursuits requiring public recreation facilities have standards – pitches, pools, indoor sports centres, libraries, and so on. Yet all have a variety of standards and sometimes the same activity has different standards. This prompts the questions, whose standards: who should make the standards? Should it be central government, local government, national agencies, governing bodies or the local community? At present, in many areas of leisure provision nobody has a mandate to dictate what the standards should be.

TABLE 7.1 Standards or guidelines of provision (many are undergoing change)

Category / Facility	Standards	Recommended by:
Outdoor recreation 'playing' space	6 acres (2.42 ha) per 1,000 population	National Playing Fields Association
Outdoor equipped playgrounds	0.5–0.7 acres (0.2–0.3 ha) per 1,000 population	National Playing Fields Association
Casual or informal play space within housing areas	1.0–1.25 acres (0.4–0.5 ha) per 1,000 population	National Playing Fields Association
Athletics and miscellaneous	0.5 acres (0.2 ha) per 1,000 population	National Playing Fields Association
Sports pitches	Playing Pitch Strategy	Sports Council/NPFA/CCPR
Golf courses	1 9 hole course per 18,000 population	Sports Council
Metropolitan parks	150 acres (61 ha minimum) within 2 miles (3.2km) of population	GDLP – Greater London Development Plan
District parks	50 acres (20 ha) within 0.75 mile (1,200m) of population	GDLP
Local parks	5 acres (2 ha) within 0.25 mile walking distance (400m)	GDLP
Small local parks	under 5 acres (2 ha)	GDLP
District indoor sports centres	1 per 40,000–90,000 population, plus 1 for each additional 50,000 population ($17m^2$ per 1,000 population) [Former guideline: now use Facilities Planning Model]	Regional Sports Councils
Indoor swimming pools	1 25-metre pool and 1 learner pool per 40,000–45,000 population ($5m^2$ per 1,000 population) Rural [Former guideline: now use Facilities Planning Model]	Regional Sports Councils
Squash courts	1 court per 5,000 population	Squash Rackets Association
Indoor bowling rinks	4, 6 and 8 rink centres to serve populations of up to 30,000, 44,000 and 59,000 respectively [Guideline]	Regional Sports Councils
Ice skating rinks	1 in conurbation if 250,000 within a 5 mile radius [Guideline]	National Ice Skating Association of the UK
Artificial turf pitches	1 per 60,000 within 20 minutes drivetime [40,000 long term]	English Sports Council
Libraries	1 service point within 20 minutes on foot or public transport. Mobile library at least 1 every 2 weeks. Housebound visits every 4 weeks, minimum	Library Association

Third, as Veal [2] rightly points out, it is the problem of validity that is the greatest difficulty with standards. The way they are derived is open to question and none more so than many of the major physical recreation standards of playing fields, swimming pools and indoor sports centres. Playing space standards, for example, are based on participation rates, but participation is largely dependent on the level of supply. The number of swimmers will depend on the number of pools, their location and accessibility, whether they are all open to the general public, the strength of swimming in the area, the type of pool, the marketing and quality of provision, whether instruction is good and cheap and whether the water is warm!

To make assumptions that only so many people will play sports and so many people will swim is not only misleading, it perpetuates the traditional system of planning based on artificial standards. The jogging movement and the 'fun runs', the growth of indoor bowls and fitness centres, the decline in squash and the decline and re-birth in tenpin bowling, all show how misleading fixed standards can be. Hence some standards of just a decade ago are no longer valid or appropriate. Alas, even those minimum standards have still to be met in many cases. Other standards such as those pertaining to public open space cannot be achieved in many of our inner cities. In London the initial standard of 7 acres of public open space per 1000 population has been substantially reduced to meet the specific circumstances of different boroughs and neighbourhoods.

Standards must always be tempered by local knowledge and circumstances. If they are unrealistic, they will be ignored. Applying so many acres per 1000 of population in a high-rise environment may be wholly unrealistic. If, for example, 50,000 people live within a half mile radius, applying a standard of 2.5 acres of park space per 1000 would result in the need for 125 acres!

Fourth, while standards are usually fairly easy to understand, they can be misinterpreted and used as a justification for taking no further action. Some authorities have been known to interpret standards to suit their own purposes, not those of the community; they do not wish to be seen as failing to provide. For example, some authorities may show that they have more than adequate indoor playing space but analysis might reveal that most of the total space is made up of small units quite unsuitable for activities in demand, or that access by the general public is restricted.

Fifth, standards are inanimate, inhuman. They assume a 'need' for a facility rather than a need which might be fulfilled in a variety of ways. They are concerned with quantitative and not qualitative aspects of provision. They take no account of the leisure potential of the specific areas – i.e. local needs, local priorities, local differences and local environments and conditions.

Sixth, while many leisure pursuits are amenable to standards of provision, many are not. Water recreation, tourism, heritage, entertainment and arts have no comprehensive basis for evaluation.

In summary, it is clear that standards of provision, whether local, regional or national, can be a very crude assessment of demand. As they are based on national information, they can often bear little relationship to local circumstances; they deal in quantities, thereby ignoring the quality of provision, aspects of distribution, use and management. The ready acceptance of artificial standards prevents planners from considering the unique qualities and possibilities of each situation. Ready acceptance may preclude more dynamic, flexible and responsive approaches to planning.

Standards of provision can be used as a starting point by providing a useful benchmark for measuring the adequacy of facilities in an area and for identifying sub-areas that may be under- or over-provided, while recognizing that most standards indicate minimum levels of provision. From this initial assessment, the need for further provision can be identified and more detailed standards of locally formulated criteria can then be used to test the feasibility of particular schemes. The National Playing Fields Association has gone to great lengths to overcome many of the difficulties in applying standards.

7.5.1 National Playing Fields Association six acre standard

The National Playing Fields Association's 6 acre standard per 1000 head of population does not apply to open space *per se*, but is concerned with public-availability *playing* space standards, i.e. 4–4.5 acres for outdoor sport and 1.5–2 acres for children's playing spaces per 1000 of the population. The breakdown of the standards is as follows:

A)   *Outdoor Sport: 1.6–1.8 hectares (4–4.5 acres)*
  1   facilities such as pitches, greens, courts, athletic tracks and miscellaneous sites such as croquet lawns and training areas owned by local authorities, whether at county, district or parish level;
  2   facilities described in 1 within the educational sector and which, as a matter of practice and policy, are available for public use;
  3   facilities described in 1 which are within the voluntary, private, industrial and commercial sectors, and serve the leisure needs for outdoor recreation of their members, or the public.

B)   *Children's playing space: 0.6–0.8 hectares (1.5–2 acres)*
  1   outdoor equipped playgrounds for children of whatever age;
  2   other designated play facilities for children which offer specific opportunities for outdoor play, such as adventure playgrounds;
  3   Casual or informal playing space within housing areas.

As a result of the combination of A and B, the minimum standard of playing space is 2.4 hectares (6.0 acres) per 1000 population. Included within the broad 2.4 hectares (6 acres) standard is a specific allocation of 1.2 hectares (3.0 acres) per 1000 population for pitch sports. The National Playing Fields Association recommends that the Outdoor Sports Standard and the Children's Playing Space Standard should be adopted by all planning authorities within statutory development and local plans and non-statutory policy documents, and should be met or exceeded in all new developments. Planners in most local authorities take cognizance of the National Playing Fields Association standards, often modifying or exceeding them to suit local circumstances.

7.5.2 *Applying standards to children's play areas*

All local authorities provide play areas for children. Before applying standards, it is important at the outset to have an appreciation of the different needs of children at different stages of life. Play provision needs to match the ages, abilities and motivations of children.

- Toddlers, aged one to about three years usually play alongside, but not with, other children; try out new abilities; enjoy fantasy and role play.
- Pre-school children show great curiosity about new things; try out new physical skills; are eager to learn; move a great deal – running, climbing, and digging, are keen on construction and building, enjoy unformed materials (sand, water, clay); continue with fantasy and role play; experiment with mimicry and imitation; become gradually more sociable.
- Children in primary school years take an interest in animals and plants; are able to go further from home; explore their environment; enjoy sand, water, clay; construction play; movement play – running, climbing, jumping, balancing, ball play; wheeled toys; are often noisy; the peer group is very important.
- Older school children (about 10–13 years) are more competitive in their play; sexes usually play apart; both sexes range further from home; enjoy rough and tumble games, but also music, conversation and social activity; construction, movement and fantasy play continue; playing games is important; more participation in organized activities.
- Adolescents' play becomes more focussed, may include music, dance and hobbies; informal street or neighbourhood groups; greater independence from home and parents; more rebellious and boisterous behaviour; the beginning of play in mixed groups again.

There is also a need for features, fixtures and equipment in stimulating built play areas. The range and type of equipment provided can influence the level of attraction, particularly if the opportunities provided contain elements of uncertainty, complexity and novelty. In the circumstances, it is hardly surprising that, to children, adventure playgrounds are perceived as being more attractive than the traditional static playground. The National Playing Fields Association identifies three main categories of unsupervised outdoor children's playing space:

- pre-school children's play space
- equipped play areas
- areas for casual and informal activities.

Historically, the National Playing Fields Association has recommended a global figure for the amount of outdoor playing space based on population. In 1992, the National Playing Fields Association introduced a new hierarchical system for providing a mixture of equipped and casual playing space for children in new and existing communities [12]. Three new categories for housing developments and re-developments were introduced:

173

- *Local area for play (LAP)* – a small area of open space suitable for young children up to five years old and sited within one minute's walking time of home.
- *Local equipped area for play (LEAP)* – a LEAP is a larger area with at least five types of play equipment for children, mainly aged from 4 to 8 and situated within five minutes' walking time of home.
- *Neighbourhood equipped area for play (NEAP)* – a NEAP is an area which should offer a minimum of eight types of play and recreation for children mainly between 8 and 14 and sited within fifteen minutes' walking time of home.

It should be emphasized that the deciding factor in locating the facilities is *time*. When using radii as straight line distances, the design of the footpath network and busy crossing points need to be taken into account. The new hierarchy is summarized in Table 7.2.

TABLE 7.2 Outdoor play areas

	LAP (Local Area for Play)	*LEAP* (Local Equipped Area for Play)	*NEAP* (Neighbourhood Equipped Area for Play)
Time	1 minute	5 minutes	15 minutes
Walking distance	100m	400m	600m
Straight line distance	60m	240m	600m
Minimum size activity zone	100m²	400m²	1,000m²
Total (inc. buffer)	400m² (0.04 ha)	3,200m² (0.36 ha)	8,500m² (0.85 ha)
Nearest house property boundary	5m from activity zone	20m from activity zone	30m from activity zone
Characteristics	Small, low-key games area (may include 'demonstrative' play features)	About 5 types of equipment. Small games area	About 8 types of equipment. Kickabout and cycle play opportunities

Source: National Playing Fields Association (1993), *The NPFA Six Acre Standard*, National Playing Fields Association, London

7.6 Spatial analysis

In recent years in the United Kingdom, extensive user surveys have been taken of many leisure facilities, and from these an indication of the size of a leisure facility's catchment area can be made. By using this approach, the geographical area covered by the facility's perceived catchment area can be identified, with areas beyond that, theoretically, not being served. The limitations associated with this include:

1   No consideration is taken of the quality of the existing facility or whether it currently has spare capacity, or if the demand for its use exceeds the supply available.
2   It assumes that the density of population is evenly distributed, while in reality (particularly in the inner-city areas) there are pockets of heavily populated areas and other areas, incorporating parks, where fewer people reside.
3   The catchment areas of leisure facilities are not necessarily circular in nature and are distorted due to many factors. Physical barriers which have to be crossed such as rivers, railway lines and busy motorways can restrict a catchment area, while access to a facility along a major road can extend the catchment area along its route [13].
4   The assumption that similar-sized facilities will have identical catchment areas is fraught with problems as the respective populations may differ in size, affluence (and hence mobility) and social composition. These factors will undoubtedly influence the perceived attraction of the facility to its potential users.

Much of the above criticism can be overcome if a user survey is conducted of the existing facilities and action taken dependent on its findings. Additionally, if the level of penetration and frequency of visit is determined in relation to distances travelled by the users to the facility concerned (by using enumeration districts or grid squares), this can be used to project the likely attendance should a new facility be developed.

An example of how this can be applied is shown in Figure 7.1, where in an imaginary situation a local authority is contemplating developing a further swimming pool in the southern part of the district. The user surveys conducted at the existing pools are revealed in Table 7.3, with Pools A and B being the existing pools. From the analysis of the survey results the percentage of users from the different catchment areas can be determined, together with the penetration/ weekly visits expressed in percentage terms, and the expected weekly visits can be calculated, given the population within the perceived catchments of the proposed pool. This can be calculated, based on the average performance of the existing facilities. It should be stressed, however, that this assumes that the population profile and accessibility is constant and no consideration has been given to the increased attraction effect of the new pool.

7.6.1   Location and attraction factor of leisure facilities

When asked what were the three most important factors in the development of hotels Conrad Hilton cited 'location, location, location'. This equally applies to most leisure facilities. Ideally, a public leisure facility should be located on or near a main

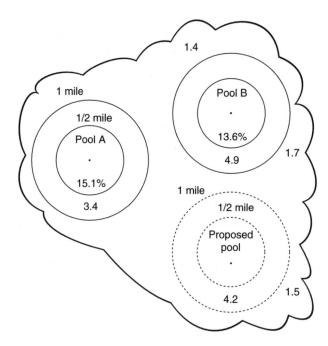

FIGURE 7.1 Penetration/visits per week (per cent) from perceived catchment of existing pools and proposed pool.

TABLE 7.3 Survey results – two imaginary swimming pools, visits within catchment area

Facility	per cent users from catchment			per cent penetration			
	½ mile	½ mile – 1 mile	1 mile +	½ mile	½ mile – 1 mile	1 mile +	Total weekly visits
Pool A	71	20	9	15.1	3.4	1.4	3,900
Pool B	67	23	10	13.6	4.9	1.7	3,500
Proposed pool	69	21	9.5	14.3	4.2	1.6	?

road that is well served by a public transport system, in close proximity to other leisure facilities, with good direct access to and off the site. In this way, the accessibility of the facility is improved and the catchment area is extended along the main road. The main road location will ensure that the people travelling along the route will have a high level of awareness of the facility, and this can be exploited in terms of promotion.

Locating a facility alongside other facilities will benefit from a degree of spin off that will not be available for 'stand alone' facilities. Also, a cluster of facilities is likely to appeal more to family groups because their divergent interests and preferences are more likely to be fulfilled. In order that the main road does not act as a physical barrier to the potential users of the facility, pedestrian access in the form of traffic lights should be provided in close proximity to the facility. This will improve access to the walking user and increase the level of awareness to motorists that use the route for work or leisure.

The more attractive a facility is perceived to be by the users and potential users, the greater distances people are prepared to travel and the more frequently they are likely to use it. The perceptual capacity of a facility can be both an attraction and a distraction depending on the type of facility involved and the individual concerned. In a country park setting, for example, a large number of people within a person's eyesight can be a distraction.

7.6.2 Large facility versus distribution of smaller facilities

In an ideal world, both centralized and localized facilities are required. However, with scarce resources, often a choice has to be made. This is a debate that is of primary importance to any strategy: whether to provide a large centrally located facility or numerous smaller facilities strategically placed throughout the district. There will probably be savings in the capital costs if only one large centre is provided as the economies of scale would apply.

Research, however, has shown clearly that the closer a person resides to a leisure facility such as a swimming pool, community centre, library or sports centre, the more likely the person concerned is to use the facility as compared to a person who resides some distance away – distance decay curve [2]. Further, the person living closer is also more likely to use the facility on a more frequent basis. Hence, in terms of a strategy, the greater the distribution of facilities, the more accessible they become to local people.

A large centre has a larger catchment area because of the 'attraction factor' and the range of opportunities on offer. This will necessitate a large percentage of users having to travel to the facility by private car, which in town manifests itself as a more mobile class clientele. From a political perspective, it appears to be much more difficult to get a local authority to sanction the development of, say, five small centres as opposed to one large centre, and this could possibly be the reason why in the 1970s, so many local authorities chose the centralist strategy.

7.6.3 Travel time

New ways of purchasing in recent years, for example, out of town shopping and family entertainment centres, have had a profound effect on traditional buying. As a result of many factors, geography has become a key determining factor of consumer behaviour, including leisure. Travel time is a key factor. People make longer journeys to specialist facilities such as theatres, ice rinks, leisure pools and indoor tennis centres, than to conventional swimming pools and sports halls. The greater the number of competing facilities in an areas, the smaller the catchment becomes for a specific facility. Moreover, the nearer people live to a facility, the more likely they are to use it. Eighty per cent of users of conventional swimming pools and sports halls, for example, travel within journey times of 20 minutes or less. Once the time and effort of travel exceeds the satisfaction to be gained from the activity, motivation is diminished.

7.7 Hierarchy of facilities

A modified version of the standards approach is the hierarchy of facilities approach, normally applied to a range of facilities for a given population size. It has been used in the development of new towns where the planning of leisure facilities is seen as a prerequisite of attracting people to the towns. However, the approach is of value also in small communities. An example of a hierarchy of facilities is given in Table 7.4 which was developed specifically for use in the small communities along the Lambourn Valley in Berkshire [14]. Such an approach used for small-scale community facilities has more validity than most other approaches. However, if it is used for large-scale projects, then the limitations associated with the use of standards equally applies to this planning approach. An example of the hierarchy approach that has merit is the Hierarchy of Parks developed by the Greater London Council over thirty years ago [15]. This was established as a result of extensive user surveys of London parks that identified the catchment area of different-sized parks and led to the development of a strategy for parks by the GLC and most of the London boroughs.

7.8 National participative rates

Large-scale national or regional participative surveys such as the *General Household Surveys* and British Market Research Bureau surveys can be used to help determine what the potential demand may be for a given community. However, the level of participation is largely dependent upon the level of provision and does not take into consideration potential or deferred demand. Additionally, such surveys do not normally indicate the participation rates within different types of neighbourhood.

The *General Household Survey* is undertaken by the government's Office for National Statistics. Every three years, the survey asks questions relating to leisure activities, which cover active participation in sports, games and physical activities, watching spectator sports and participation in other leisure activities, including entertainment and day visits. The survey also determines the frequency of participation. The sample size is in the region of 25,000 and is confined to those aged 16 years and over.

Another national survey that can be used in this approach is the *Target Group Index*, which is a national consumption survey funded by the British Market Research Bureau. It is an annual survey with a 24,000 adult sample taken in 200 parliamentary constituencies. The advantage of using the *Target Group Index* is that it is linked with ACORN (which is the acronym for *A Classification of Residential*

TABLE 7.4 Suggested hierarchy of leisure provision for rural communities based on a specific location in Berkshire [14]

Community size	Recommended facilities that could be offered	Examples of activities relating to location	Additional comments
1. Hamlet/small village, 100–500 population	1. Village hall – suitable for social functions. Kitchen, snooker table depending on demand and local tradition	1. Meetings, dances/discos, concerts, table tennis, youth club, voluntary organizations, e.g. scouts, adult education classes	1. Centrally located – preferably linked to community open space
	2. Community open space, 2–3 acres, with children's play area with equipment	2. Children's play, football and cricket, informal recreation, village festivals, carnival, etc.	2. Location – central avoiding the necessity for children to cross main roads. Possibly linked to primary school
	3. Mobile library service – van	3. Books, records, tapes, etc.	3. Preferably linked to form focal point of village
2. Medium-sized village, 500–1,500 population	1. Community hall (15–20m × 10m × 6.7m) with kitchen, toilets, temporary stage, changing facilities, storage areas. Bar facilities depending on demand, car parking	1. Recreation, badminton, keep-fit, yoga, aerobics, meetings, drama, concerts, dances/discos, youth clubs	
	2. Community open space, 3–7 acres, including football pitch with pavilion, (or linked to community hall), children's play area with equipment, seats, floral beds. Space for tennis and/or bowls, depending on local demand	2. Children's play, football club level, informal cricket, informal recreation, village festivals, carnival, pony club	
	3. Mobile library service – trailer library	3. Books, records, tapes, etc.	
	4. Community mini-bus – availability for hire – provision dependent on public transport service and facilities available within village	4. Organized visits in connection with sporting, art, entertainment and social events	4. Hire costs and maintenance schedules important

continued

179

TABLE 7.4 continued

Community size	Recommended facilities that could be offered	Examples of activities relating to location	Additional comments
	5. Mobile recreation service	5. Offering sports and arts activities, particularly for the very young, females, etc. unemployed and the elderly.	5. Depending on the range of opportunities available and the degree of initiative and leadership within the village. One half-day visit per week
3. Large village, 1,500–2,500 population	1. Community hall (20m × 10m × 6.7m), marginally larger than that required for a medium-sized community, plus bar facilities	1. A range of sports (including gymnastics, martial arts, badminton, possibly 4-a-side soccer, etc.), arts and social recreation	1. Location – central, focal point of public transport
	2. Community open space, 9–14 acres, 2 or more football pitches, 1 cricket square, bowling green, 2 hard/tarmacadam surfaced tennis courts/ netball courts. Pavilions for changing, plus bar refreshments facilities. Children's play area with kick about and equipment	2. Activities to include club football/rugby, cricket, bowls, tennis, netball	2. Depending on the availability of open space, it might be necessary to have the facilities at more than one location. Each site should have pavilion with changing facilities
	3. Library – fixed accommodation	3. Books, records, tapes, etc.	3. Opening times staggered throughout week to meet different people's needs
	4. Mobile recreation service – depending on the facilities within the village and whether they are professionally managed	4. Sport and recreation activities	4. Visit restricted to half-day a week
4. Small country town, 2,500–6,000 population	1. Sports hall (26m × 16.5m × 7.6m), depending on the size of community, consideration to be given to ancillary facilities such as weight training area, 2 squash courts	1. Increased range of sporting activities including 5-a-side football, cricket, indoor bowls, basketball, volleyball, weight training, squash, archery, tennis	1. For economic reasons dual use with a secondary school or a large sports club/ voluntary organization should be explored
	2. Swimming pool (25m)	2. Swimming, life saving	2. As above; provision only if dual-use arrangement can be achieved

TABLE 7.4 continued

Community size	Recommended facilities that could be offered	Examples of activities relating to location	Additional comments
	3. Community hall/arts centre – to include stage and projection facilities, plus meeting rooms, kitchens, bar, toilets, craft workshop	3. Meetings, drama, concerts, cinema, whist drives, bingo, table tennis, adult education classes, displays	3. Linked to other community provision – improve spin-off and awareness
	4. Community open space (15–40 acres), including park area, children's play areas with equipment, 4 football/ rugby, hockey pitches, 2–4 tennis courts, bowling green and pavilions with refreshments, 1 cricket square, multi-purpose floodlit hard all-weather area	4. Children's play, town show, carnival, soccer, rugby, cricket, bowls, tennis, netball, 5-a-side football, training purposes	4. Children's play areas, easy access to housing estates. Playing pitches best located near sports hall – economies of scale and spin-off
	5. Library facilities – branch library	5. Books, cassettes, records, video, pictures	5. Permanent accommodation – spread opening hours
	6. Mobile recreation service	6. Sports/recreation activities	6. Programmed to meet specific market segments, e.g. unemployed – off peak times/one day per week

Neighbourhoods), and is available from CACI Information Services, a company authorized to use the census data. By using the activity index for each ACORN type of household, the potential demand for a particular activity can be determined.

Unfortunately, the *Target Group Index* survey has disadvantages. In addition to those associated with the *General Household Survey*, the main disadvantages of the *Target Group Index* relate to the actual wording of the self-completing questionnaires and the lack of precision in the data collected. While the *General Household Survey* determines what activities the respondents participate in, in the four weeks prior to being interviewed, the *Target Group Index* is more open ended such as: 'Do you attend these days'. The consequences in the different approaches are reflected in the results, with some of the participation rates in the *Target Group Index* sample being substantially higher than those found by the *General Household Survey*. Also the reliability of some of the data is in question, as the results relating to some of the minority activities are not consistent.

7.9 Grid approach

The grid approach is more of a management technique than a planning approach, but it has an important function in specific situations. A situation where it is frequently used is where planning criteria have been established for a range of possible developments on a particular site. A further application is where the facilities within a park or geographical zone have to meet the demands of all sections of the community. By dividing the community into different categories, e.g. pre-school, young children 5–12, teenagers, etc., listing their needs and matching these against facilities available, deficiencies can be determined. A further application of this technique within the overall planning approach is that it can be used to place a list of facility/service deficiencies into a priority ranking list or to select the most appropriate site from a range of possibilities. The following list suggests a range of questions that could be asked to achieve a priority–criterion ranking system for new public sector developments based on a policy of community recreation effectiveness.

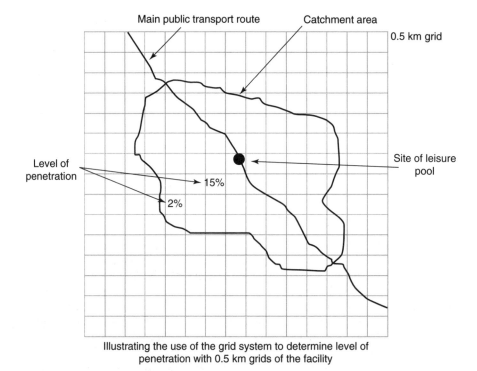

Illustrating the use of the grid system to determine level of penetration with 0.5 km grids of the facility

FIGURE 7.2 Example of a grid system

- Does the proposed facility meet a previously unfulfilled leisure need within the locality?
- Has there been a high level of expressed demand for the facility?

- Does the facility replace and/or renew an existing facility with a high value to the community?
- Does the facility specifically benefit persons from a leisure deprived area?
- Does the facility substantially benefit specific target groups such as children, the elderly, disabled?
- Will the proposed facility be regarded as a district facility – i.e. to meet the needs of the whole district?
- Does the facility meet the needs of different age groups?
- Is the facility likely to attract a high level of usage?
- Will the facility involve the council in nil or minimal capital investment?
- Will the facility involve the council in nil or minimal revenue expenditure?
- Will the facility attract substantial grant aid and/or sponsorship?
- Is the facility likely to make a contribution to reducing the level of vandalism and delinquency within the district?

This system helps to eliminate bias; it can incorporate the importance that the Council places on a specific element by giving it an additional weighting.

Figure 7.2 illustrates how a grid system can be used to measure the level of penetration from different parts of the catchment area. A simple questionnaire at a facility will determine the neighbourhood from which people have travelled.

7.10 Need index approach

The need index approach not only determines whether a deficiency exists, but simultaneously places the different deficiency areas into a priority ranking. The basic concept behind this approach is simple and can be illustrated as in Figure 7.3.

At present, most of the methods of assessing demand concentrate upon the relationship between resources available and potential users and little emphasis is attached to the concept of need. It is logical to assume that those areas with a low resource level, as well as a high level of need, should have a higher priority than areas with a high level of resources and a low level of need. These can be identified by using this approach which is well illustrated when applied to children's

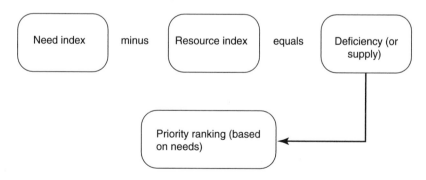

FIGURE 7.3 Need index approach

playgrounds, particularly to small study areas. In an urban environment, a cluster of census enumeration districts can be used as units of small study areas. Within these designated areas it is necessary to develop a resource index and a need index.

To develop the need index, it is necessary to identify factors that affect children's opportunity to play, together with indicators of social deprivation. These include, for example: number of children; incidence of high-rise flats; lack of gardens; dwellings lacking basic amenities; number of unemployed; working mothers; and lone parenthood.

In developing the resource index, there are factors that are of significance, including: location of the play area; size of the playground; range and nature of the equipment; and whether the playground is supervised.

Although this method has limitations, largely relating to subjective nature of determining the resource play index values, it is a method that does concern itself with the concept of need and has the potential for refinement and improvement. A case study using the need index approach in Basingstoke and Deane [16] is described below.

Case study: Applying the need index

Basingstoke and Deane Borough Council commissioned consultants Leisure Management George Torkildsen (LMGT) to design a system for awarding funding for children's play areas by Ward, equitably. LMGT devised a system based on the need index approach.

First, the social needs of children were considered, based upon the Department of Environment's 'Index of Local Conditions'. This provided a need index for children in the borough by ward. Second, play provision in each ward was examined in terms of distribution, age suitability, safety and play area value. This provided a play resource index. Third, the two indices were combined to produce a hierarchy of needs, i.e. wards were placed in priority order, those with greatest needs and least resources were highest on the list.

The basic concept behind the approach was a 'needs' minus 'resources' model which provides an index to establish gaps in provision and priorities.

The need index

In 1994, the Department of the Environment produced a new set of indicators to measure the relative degree of deprivation to be found in the 366 local authority areas of England, using various sources, but largely based on the 1991 census. In all, there are 13 indicators, 7 of which apply to ward level:

1   unemployment
2   overcrowded housing
3   lacking or sharing basic amenities
4   children in low income households
5   no car within a household

6   children living in 'unsuitable accommodation', e.g. flats
7   17 year olds not in full-time education

These indicators create a heavy bias towards children and young people. Not only do three indicators specifically refer to them, a fourth, overcrowding, rarely occurs without children. In households where the head of the household is unemployed, or is in receipt of a low income, the level of disposable income is likely to be minimal and the amount of play equipment and opportunities within the home may also be few. Likewise, limiting factors include the amount of space for children to play within the home and in the garden (should one exist) of dwellings that are lacking in basic amenities, or are considered to be unsuitable for children, or are considered to be overcrowded.

Households without cars can also give a general indication of lack of affluence, but more importantly, can restrict access to play opportunities that are located beyond a child's walking distance.

The closer focus through small enumeration districts (EDs) is more useful in deciding priorities, as it is possible to identify levels of need in a few streets or an estate. The problem is that there are 25 wards in Basingstoke and Deane and over 300 enumeration districts. Therefore, the formula was based primarily on Wards and is supplemented by ED information, for example, where the distribution of play areas is skewed away from the main ward populations. Where EDs are used, numbers (as distinct from percentages) will be needed, as percentages of low numbers can be unreliable.

The theory is simple; the practice is more complex. To make for a relatively easy transfer from theory to practice, the model is built up on a broad step-by-step approach. Four key aspects were identified:

1   the number of children under the age of 16 years within each ward
2   the social deprivation indicators within each ward, giving weighting to two key factors 3 and 4
3   children in 'unsuitable accommodation' in each ward
4   children in low-earning households in each ward.

The number of children in each ward is of critical importance as it is logical to assume that the areas with the greatest number of children will have the greatest demand for the use of playgrounds provided, all other variables being the same. Various social factors can influence or inhibit a child's ability to participate in play activities and where the social deprivation is high, it is safe to assume that the need for the provision of play facilities will also be high.

Resource index

Giving a score value to playgrounds is a difficult exercise, as there is a wide range of factors to consider, many requiring subjective analysis, best carried out by experts. LMGT used specialist consultants to the National Playing Fields Association to carry out inspection of around 180 sites. (The National Playing

Fields Association's play value assessment form, for example, mentions over 20 site features and over 20 equipment features).

To make the formula work, the variables needed to be contained within reasonable units. LMGT identified three key factors to be taken into consideration when developing the resource index:

1   the scale of play provision within each ward
2   the quality of provision, facilities and equipment
3   the distribution of playgrounds within each ward.

Playgrounds differ in size and facilities and are provided to meet the needs of different age groups. Unsupervised playgrounds fall within four broad Basingstoke and Deane Council categories and their contributions to the overall resource index differ. Hence, it was suggested that the different sized play areas be given a range of points:

1   small playgrounds   10 units per site
2   medium playgrounds   20 units per site
3   large playgrounds   40 units per site
4   extra large playgrounds   60 units per site

The range of equipment, the capacity and attraction of the playgrounds and the quality of the provision can influence the number of children attracted to the facility, the frequency of their visits, the length of their stay and the physical and cognitive benefits. The factors that need to be taken into consideration are:

1   maintenance and condition of the playgrounds and their equipment
2   the safety factors, taking into consideration whether the playgrounds have impact absorbing surfaces, are enclosed by a fence, and are safe from passing traffic
3   the play value of the play area – an assessment of the overall physical, social, creative, educational and motivating features to be found.

Up to five units per play area were allocated to these factors. Play areas need to be distributed and located where they best match the populations they are to serve. Are the play areas spread across the ward appropriately? Are they located to match housing and sited for informal supervision? Up to five units per play area were allocated to these factors.

Combining the indicators

Statistical steps are used to combine the indicators into an index. One key step is that of 'standardization'. If indicators are to be combined, account has to be taken of the fact that, for example, 15 per cent is a high proportion for 'unemployment' but a low proportion for 'no car'. Standardization alters values to make them of equal worth. In order to be able to make worthwhile comparisons between different wards, it was necessary to convert all the collected data and points allocated to a comparable form. A statistical tool known as the 'C' Scale has proved to be valid as a descriptive and comparative tool. To convert a range of data to a 'C' Scale is comparatively simple. Each range is set against a scale of 0–100. As an example, consider the following range of hypothetical data – 50, 200, 225 and 500. This range is 0–500 (500 units) and, therefore, each unit on the 'C' Scale (0–100) or 100 units, represents 5 units on the range data. Thus, the figures are converted as follows by dividing the base data by 5.

Data	50	200	225	500
'C' Scale	10	40	45	100

For the other ranges of data, it is a case of determining the conversion factor and applying it as appropriate. The key is to reduce every range of data to the 0–100 of the 'C' Scale. The best way of converting data to a 'C' Scale is by using a range of numbers rather than percentages.

Applying the model

The resulting index has been used to place the wards in order of priority. The Council initially allocated funding to the top twelve wards on the basis of areas in greatest need, to improve the play areas up to the year 2000. All these play areas are monitored to see what effect the improvements have on the needs within the ward. It will mean that wards lower down the priority scale will move up as their needs become greater in relation to those areas already refurbished. By using this method, areas (wards) with a high level of need and a low level of resources will be given a higher priority than areas with a high level of resources and a low level of need.

Refining the formula

The formula is a broad, and hence crude, method of placing wards into priority order. It has limitations. This approach involves interpreting need, a difficult concept. However, the DoE *Index of Local Conditions* offers the most appropriate basis of interpretation, making adjustments to focus the data onto children within each ward.

The resource index is limited in that some elements require a subjective judgement, e.g. quality. However, subjectivity was minimized by awarding the most 'units' to factual information, i.e. actual provision. In terms of play area distribution, enumeration district numbers can be used to supplement ward analysis.

Priority ranking

The formula of 'Need – Resource = Deficiency = Priority' also provides a need ranking by ward and resource ranking by ward. In determining ward priority, it will be useful to also bear in mind the relative ranking in the two indices. A ward with low ranking in both indices could achieve higher priority although it may have a similar overall index score to other wards.

In summary, the formula results in a Play Area Index, giving a ranking by ward. This ranking, in computer spreadsheet form, will change as ward demographic data change or resources change for better or worse. Information needs updating regularly and the formula should be reviewed on at least an annual basis.

Source: The index for Basingstoke and Deane was devised by George Torkildsen, Gwynne Griffiths and Pat Kendall; the play area inspection was carried out by consultant to the NPFA, Tony Chilton.

7.11 Expressed demand and the Playing Pitch Strategy

The level of demand for existing facilities can provide a useful guide as to whether additional facilities are required in an area. The analysis of a sports centre's booking sheets, for example, can reveal the amount of spare capacity available, or whether the demand for specific facilities exceeds the supply available. This section describes an approach which assesses the demand for outdoor playing pitches

There is wide variation across the country in the level of provision of adult-sized pitches (including secondary schools) for all sports (Table 7.5). Football accounts for about half of the provision and cricket a quarter, with rugby and hockey sharing a balance.

The Playing Pitch Strategy [6] published in 1991, is a guidance document written by The Sports Council, The National Playing Fields Association and the Central Council for Physical Recreation. *The Playing Pitch Strategy* recommends a model approach for assessing the demand for playing pitches based on the expressed demand as indicated by the number of teams requiring pitches within the study area.

Local authorities have been slow in adopting this approach to the provision of playing pitches, perhaps because it is time consuming, may be perceived as complex, and it adds to the workload and constrained budgets. Indeed, the tendency has been to delegate responsibility for playing pitches in many cases to local clubs in exchange for cheap or even peppercorn rentals.

TABLE 7.5 Population per pitch

	Average	*Range*
Football	1840	1274–8640
Cricket	4243	2216–6750
Hockey	8271	3683–31963
Rugby	8968	3320–24000

Source: Sports Council *et al.* (1991) *The Playing Pitch Strategy*

The Playing Pitch Strategy takes a different line from the standard approach, starting with actual participation; it is, therefore, sensitive to local situations. *The Playing Pitch Strategy* provides a process of calculating the demand for pitches based on current and latent demand. It recommends:

1   the undertaking of a detailed local assessment of facility requirements using the Playing Pitch Methodology. The methodology is designed to cater for voluntary participation in competitive activity by adults and young people in the pitch sports – principally football, rugby union, rugby league, hockey and cricket. It excludes: participation within school (but not outside it or the outside use of school playing fields) and informal kickabouts; and athletics, tennis and bowls (which are included in the National Playing Fields Association's standards);
2   the formulation of local standards of facility supply per 1,000 population;
3   if impracticable, the adoption of the National Playing Fields Association standard as an interim minimum general standard or global measure of land available for a given population – 3 acres (1.21 ha) per 1,000 population.

The difference between the Playing Pitch Methodology and previous approaches is that, instead of using land area per head of population as the basic unit, it measures demand (at peak times) in terms of teams requiring pitches and then compares this with the pitches available. Basic information required to employ the methodology comprises:

Demand
  • number of teams in an area
  • whether adult or junior team, male or female
  • each team's home ground
  • day and time of week when home games are played
  • number and type of home games played in a season
  • number of weeks of the playing season
  • demographic data for study area (actual and projected)

Supply
  • size and surface (grass/artificial) of each pitch
  • sports for which it is used
  • ownership of the pitch: public, private or educational
  • availability at different days and different times.

In addition to these quantitative elements, other qualitative information and trends in demand can be gathered.

The Playing Pitch Strategy

Stages of the methodology

Stage 1: Identifying teams for each sport, whether league, friendly or casual, senior or junior; using surveys and secondary sources

The methodology introduces a new concept, Team Generation Rates (TGR) as an alternative to gathering original data. TGRs are a measure of the number of people in the specified age group required to generate one team and are derived by dividing the appropriate population age band in an area by the number of teams in the area in that age band:

TGR = Population in age group ÷ Number of teams

A TGR is not a participation rate (as defined in the *General Household Survey*), but provides an indication of levels of participation in a given sport.

Stage 2: Calculating home games per team per week

This can be identified exactly or a value of 0.5 for winter sports and between 0.6 and 0.8 for cricket can be used. This variable is calculated as follows:

Total number of games played
in a season by all teams
÷
Number of weeks in a season
} = average number of home games per week

Average number of home
games per week
÷
Total number of teams
} = average number of home games per team per week

Stage 3: Assessing total home games per week (stage 1 × stage 2)

This indicates how many games have to be accommodated in the study area in an average week.

Stage 4: Establishing temporal demand for games

This stage identifies which day of the week and at what time of day games are played.

Stage 5: Defining pitches required on each day (stage 3 × stage 4)

This indicates how many pitches are required on each day, and time, of the week.

Stage 6: Establishing pitches available

Data on all known pitches, their availability and use. An inventory of the existing provision of pitches is produced distinguished between: different sports; type of surface (grass/artificial); whether public, private or educational sectors; availability on different days and at different times. Type of ownership as categorized by the Register of Recreational Land provides a useful framework. Additional information on location, size, capacity, quality and floodlighting will be needed.

Stage 7: Identifying problems and issues

This compares the number of pitches required on each day (stage 5) with the number of pitches available (stage 6). This will reveal whether there is excess demand or supply or if supply matches demand.

Stage 8: Exploring policy options and solutions

Stages 1–5 are closely linked and can be completed at more or less the same time. Stage 3 is optional, depending on whether or not stage 2 is derived from actual survey data or from applying an assumed value.

It is essential that the methodology is used as a means of understanding the relationship between the demand for pitches and their supply and not as an end in itself; its outputs should always be related to the particular circumstances of the area, tempered by detailed local knowledge and common sense. However, as it will be firmly rooted in the local circumstances of the study, its calculations and the resultant findings will be unique, and should enable policy makers to deal confidently with the issues raised. The relevant costs and benefits of pursuing different options can be assessed, and decisions made as to the optimum solution. Decisions on options for one sport should not be undertaken until the work on all the sports has been completed. Solutions for one sport are likely to have repercussions for the others since there may be competing demands for scarce capital resources.

7.12 Facilities planning model

The Sports Council's *Facilities Planning Model* [17] is a method of assessing the demand for sports facilities at the community level of provision. The basic structure of the model is to compare demand for facilities with supply using the same unit of measurement: this being number of visits per week at peak times.' The approach has three components: demand; supply; and catchment areas.

1   The demand is measured by the rate and frequency of participation using local and national data, e.g. from surveys.
2   The supply side is measured by working out the number of attendances a facility can accommodate in a specified peak period.
3   In terms of catchment, calculations are based on identifying the distance the regular participants (70–80 per cent of users) travelled from. Guidelines from data collected in the 1980s illustrated the need to take into account urban and rural situations.

Former guideline from The Sports Council: catchment areas (miles)

	Urban	Rural
Community sports hall (4 badminton court size)	3	6–8
Swimming pool	2	8–10
Golf courses	5	8
Squash	5	8
Ice skating	6	N/A

These guidelines were based on a limited geographical spread. New data collated from all regions is likely to change or add to these conclusions. Thus, the model is based on comparing demand and supply, applying that to a specific geographical area and thereby:

• identifying where demand is located;
• whether, and to what extent, demand exceeds supply;
• whether, and where, spare capacity exists.

In order to achieve this the local demand is measured on the basis of the number of visits per week in peak period for any particular sports facility, determined by:

• the total number of people resident within the study area;
• the demand rate – the proportion of residents who want to use the facility type for particular sports;
• the desired frequency of visits – how often they want to visit;
• the proportion of visits which arise in the normal peak periods per week.

At the time of writing this fourth edition, the Sports Council had embarked on launching the *Facilities Planning Model* on a regional basis.

The current model has benefits and some limitations. Benefits include: actual participation; local population; discrete geographical area; different facilities can be assessed using the same approach; and the model can be used in urban and rural settings. The model, therefore, is a substantial improvement on standards *per se*. The model, however, deals only with known demand and not with latent demand, nor visitor demand, nor demand created by innovative management. The model relies on consistent information about existing facilities and is a technique (the Sports Council's description) not a policy making instrument.

7.13 Public consultation

Public consultation, after expressed demand, is arguably, the most important indicator of public demand. The weakness is that the more articulate and organized individuals or leisure groups become the most vocal. Nevertheless, public consultation remains invaluable in gauging local feeling and opinion. Not only is it politically desirable to consult the people the provision of leisure facilities is intended to serve, but more important, the planning process itself is incomplete unless people are consulted about their leisure needs and demands, their perception of existing facilities and services and their expectations of future provision. Without such consultation, the planning process is one of providing *for* the people, as opposed to planning *with* the people. Planning for the people presupposes that those concerned with leisure planning know more about the requirements of people than the people themselves.

As with other methods, public consultations are not without their shortcomings. These are normally associated with the expressions of demand not being representative of the community, as a whole, and with the subjective nature of many of the responses made. The major methods of consulting with the public are described briefly below and consist of

1   community demand surveys
2   user surveys
3   organization surveys
4   public meetings
5   working parties
6   interviews
7   focus groups.

1. Community demand surveys

All too often, local authorities demand very large surveys to be undertaken, while from a statistical point of view, comparatively small surveys can provide the necessary information at a relatively high level of confidence. Four surveys used regularly are: household interviews; street surveys; postal surveys; and telephone surveys.

• The face-to-face household interview is a sound approach, but can be both time-consuming and expensive to administer. In order to avoid unnecessarily alarming residents, particularly the elderly, household interviews are best undertaken following an introduction from a friend or an associate. This, of course, requires even more time.

- A face-to-face alternative is the street survey. This requires achieving randomized quota sampling, e.g. a reasonable cross-section of males and females, different age groups, etc. It also calls for trained, sensitive interviewers.

- The postal survey is much easier and cheaper to administer, although it too is not without its limitations. The response rate can be in the region of only 5–15 per cent (or even less), unless some interest has been created in the local media or an incentive is associated with a return of the questionnaire; even so, response rates tend to be low.

- A telephone survey is comparatively easy to undertake, provided the questionnaire is short and simple. The problems associated with this method of research are those of contacting the selected people and getting accepted. Many sales personnel use the telephone in an attempt to sell products such as double glazing and kitchen refurbishments, hence there will be some resentment by residents to this form of consultation. Telephone surveys require skilful and sensitive research staff.

2. Leisure facility user surveys

User surveys conducted in a face-to-face approach or by self-completing questionnaires can be informative, providing information on the user profile, the facility's catchment area (and also the areas not being served), participation data (e.g. activities, frequency), perceptions of the facility and how it is managed and expectations for the future. Such surveys can be useful in improving the efficiency and effectiveness of the existing service, as well as obtaining the opinions and attitudes of users and residents regarding future provision. User surveys, where the questionnaires are self-administered, tend to be less representative and the response rate is reduced, though this method is easier and far cheaper to undertake.

3. Survey of clubs, societies and organizations

The voluntary organizations for sports and arts are the backbone of leisure groupings in the United Kingdom. Hence, in any leisure planning process, knowledge of their collective contribution is required, so that the full spectrum of the leisure provision in a particular area can be determined. A survey of local clubs and societies can provide valuable information regarding the leisure opportunities programmed for their members, their membership levels, their resources and their current and future requirements. Additionally, clubs provide an insight into the attitudes and opinions of a section of the community.

The drawbacks with undertaking this form of research are that the local council's data base of clubs and societies is often inadequate and changes in club officials go unrecorded. Additionally, there is normally a delay in the responses because of the seasonal nature of the clubs and, in some cases, the need to discuss the questionnaire at a committee meeting. Further, too many clubs are inward looking and are not prepared to look at aspects beyond those that directly affect their members. Responses tend to be low.

4. Public meetings

Although opinions given at public meetings are not necessarily those representing all the community, they do give an indication of the strength of the support or opposition to a particular proposal. Good promotion is necessary to ensure that adequate attendances are achieved at the meetings and that those who 'shout loudest' or have vested interests do not hold sway.

5. Working party approach

A much under-used approach is that of a working party, whereby members of local clubs, residents associations, etc., together with officers and members from the local council are formed into a working party that has delegated authority to propose recommendations. Examples of where such an approach has been used include the designing of a new park and the conversion of an old school into a community centre. It is important, however, that such working parties have authority to influence decisions, or they simply become talking shops!

The advantages associated with this approach are considerable. It is democracy at work and, hopefully, the realistic expectations of the local community can be fulfilled. Unfortunately, in such a situation, decision making can be slow and the commitment of its members will wane if progress is not seen to be made. But the greatest problem may be associated with many members making unrealistic demands that require excessive amounts of space and finance to fulfil.

6. Interviews

Interviews with community leaders, including politicians, teachers, youth leaders, social workers, police, ethnic minority, disadvantaged and disabled groups and the business community, can be an invaluable source of information. Likewise, informal interviews with shopkeepers, publicans, postal workers – all those who come into contact with a wide range of residents – helps to build a picture of how different people perceive the current provision and how it is managed and what deficiencies they think exist. A 'living-in' approach for some of the research time will assist in identifying issues and deficiencies from a resident's viewpoint.

7. Focus groups

Focussed interviews originated in America in the evaluation of audience response to radio programmes. They were adapted into focussed group interviews after the

Second World War. The pioneer was Robert Morton [18]. The 'focussed interview' differs from others in four ways: a) all those interviewed have been involved in a practical 'concrete' situation; b) the 'content' has been previously analysed and hypotheses have been arrived at; c) an interview guide has been fashioned; and d) the interview itself is focussed on the subjective experience of the persons exposed to the pre-analysed situation.

The focus group interview generally involves eight to twelve individuals who discuss a particular topic under the direction of a moderator who promotes interaction and assures that the discussion remains on the topic of interest. Smaller groups may be dominated by one or two members, while larger groups are difficult to manage. A typical focus group session will last for one and a half to two and a half hours.

Depending on the intent of the research, the moderator may be more or less directive with respect to the discussion, but more often is non-directive. The moderator might begin with a series of general questions but direct the discussion to more specific issues as the group proceeds.

7.13.1 Putting people into plans - getting below the surface

It is clear that, at present, there is no one way of determining the level of potential leisure demand for a particular activity. All the approaches described in this section have different degrees of limitation, and in order to be able to make a fairly accurate projection of the likely demand for a specific activity, it is necessary at present to use a range of different leisure planning techniques. Planning for people means putting people into the planning process. To make future leisure provision more appropriate and meaningful, a greater understanding is required of people's needs and demands, what leisure means to people and the role it plays in their lives. The government's new policy under 'Best Value' calls for greater public consultation – a step in this direction.

In *Leisure and the Family Life Cycle* [19], the Rapoports and Strelitz look beneath the surface of leisure planning and reveal underlying predispositions towards leisure: planning for people's leisure should not be undertaken simply by 'feasible' extensions of what already exists and is known to be workable and on hunches about what people's needs are; social research must look beyond mass demand and begin from the 'people's side of the equation'. They suggest that by building up knowledge and information about people in leisure, by learning about their motivations, preoccupations, interests and activities and injecting their knowledge into the planning process of large-scale fact finding, small-scale local findings and community projects, decision makers will have a broader platform on which to plan policies.

More recently, Brandenburg *et al.* [20] have developed this model further towards an understanding of why a person adopts a particular activity.

The process commences with preoccupations and interests. Four conditions, opportunity, knowledge, favourable social milieu and receptiveness, are deemed necessary and sufficient to enable an interest to be expressed through adoption of a specific activity. These conditions are focussed upon a specific activity by one or more key event(s), which may at the same time modify the conditions themselves. The decision to actually adopt that activity finally rests on the extent to which the individual anticipates satisfaction through participation. Participation, in its turn, may lead to clarification, development or change of preoccupations and interests.

While various research projects have revealed much about the conditions (opportunity, knowledge, favourable social milieu and receptiveness) that influence actual participation, further research is required for a greater understanding of the impact of the 'key events'.

7.14 The leisure planning process

The leisure planning process, in conceptual terms, is a very simple model based on a four-stage cycle approach, whereby first, the leisure needs and demands of a community are identified; second, from the resources available, facilities and/or services are selected to meet this requirement; third, these are subsequently implemented; and fourth, the outcome is monitored. In reality, however, the process is far more complex. Set out below is a ten-stage leisure planning process 'model' based on leisure theory and current practical application from a leisure management perspective (Figure 7.4). This runs parallel to, and in collaboration with, the formal planning process and Local Plans.

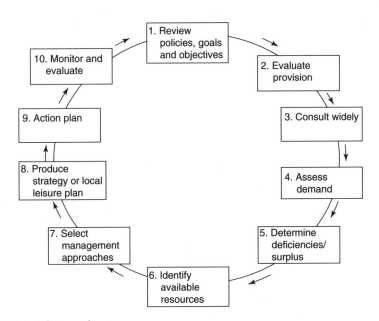

FIGURE 7.4 A leisure planning process

Stage 1: determine council policies, goals and objectives

This concerns the philosophical basis of providing for the community and the roles of the council (e.g. as provider, enabler, etc.). The council's policy towards the allocation of leisure resources (i.e. the reasons behind its investment in leisure provision) is important, as it can influence the type and range of facilities provided (i.e. their location and the way they are financed and managed). Additionally, it is necessary to determine what the council's policy is in respect of partnership developments with other local authorities (e.g. local education authority) or with the voluntary and/or commercial sectors.

Stage 2: evaluate current leisure provision and services

This stage identifies the type, range and ownership of facilities, whether public, voluntary or commercial. It also evaluates effectiveness and efficiency, usage and management. It determines levels of demand and spare capacity. A population study will identify resident concentrations and specific sections of the community that require special consideration, while a transportation analysis will highlight the accessibility of existing and potential leisure sites.

It is important that existing facilities are used to the optimum level and wasteful duplication of facilities is avoided. Hence it is necessary to evaluate the current service and, where possible, determine areas of spare capacity and where demand exceeds the available supply. This evaluation should also involve making a performance appraisal of each element within the service and, in particular, examine its efficiency and effectiveness. Although a comparison of a specific facility with national norms is fraught with difficulty, because no two facilities are identical (they differ in design, philosophy of use, quality of management and staff and the environment in which the facility is located), valuable indications of the performance level can be obtained.

Stage 3: consult widely

This stage provides the opportunity to find out whether what is to be provided and how it is delivered are appropriate for those it is intended to serve. Consultation is needed with local residents, workers and organizations. A range of techniques include surveys, public meetings, focus groups and community working groups. Consultation is also needed with agencies such as arts and sports governing bodies, with education authorities and schools, and with neighbouring authorities to avoid overlap and duplication.

Stage 4: assess known and potential demand

Although there is no single leisure planning technique that can accurately indicate what the potential demand may be for a particular activity or facility, a good indication can be obtained by using an array of leisure planning techniques, including demand modelling. These include national and, more specifically, local data; population profiling; and importantly, the results of consultation, identifying known and latent demands.

Stage 5: determine deficiencies and surpluses

This stage analyses the supply–demand relationship. Comparing the level of potential demand with the actual provision should, theoretically, produce a list of deficiencies. Such a list is likely to be extensive and it would be unrealistic for any authority to contemplate redressing all the perceived inadequacies across the whole leisure spectrum. It will, therefore, be necessary to place the deficiencies in rank order of importance, determined by establishing criteria based on council policies and the needs of the community. Facilities that are regarded as inappropriate for a specific area would be omitted from the list, together with those having a low level of priority.

Stage 6: identify and assess resources available

It will be necessary to examine all potential sites for leisure development and these should be assessed in terms of their suitability (e.g. size, terrain, accessibility, environmental considerations). A feasibility study should be undertaken of priority developments in order to be able to estimate the capital cost involved for each facility and its likely outcome in terms of attendance and net operating cost. Sources of capital funding will need to be investigated, including possible grants from government agencies, the National Lottery, European Community funds, planning obligation opportunities or partial funding arising from a partnership development. Upon completion of this exercise, it may be necessary to review the priority order.

Stage 7: select management approaches

There now exists a range of management approaches and it is incumbent on local authorities to provide 'Best Value'. Options include: Competitive Tendering; Not for Profit Organizations; Trusts; Buy-Outs; Buy-Ins; Concessions; Partnerships; and hybrids. Different facilities and services may well require different management approaches.

Stage 8: produce leisure strategy or local leisure plan

Arising out of the decisions made in the previous stages, it should be possible to produce a leisure strategy or local leisure plan or series of specific plans (e.g. Arts; Sport and Recreation), incorporating short, medium and long-term development plans for the area, with the council's role in these developments being clearly defined. The strategy will set out the roles of the council, the policies, the development and management objectives, and a plan of actions.

Stage 9: action plan

To implement the leisure strategy, it will be necessary to produce an action plan with clear objectives, targets, methods of measurement and areas of responsibility will need to be assigned to key committees and officers with delegated areas of responsibility. In order to ensure that the tasks are completed on time, it is advisable that a detailed critical path analysis network be drawn up.

Stage 10: monitor and evaluate

The progress made will need to be monitored and results measured. This should include the effect of the actions upon the community. The leisure strategy will need periodic review in the light of economic, social and environmental changes.

7.14.1 Towards leisure strategies or local leisure plans

At the time of writing the previous edition of this book in 1991, local authorities were being encouraged to write leisure strategies, i.e. to take a strategic view of provision for sports, arts, recreation and leisure. Some authorities acted positively; most were very slow to react. Since that time, the National Lottery has had a dramatic impact; in order to secure funds, there is a need to show that any new provision can be fully justified in terms of need, use, management and funding and, moreover, fits into a strategic local and regional plan.

Regardless of Lottery funding, the case for a leisure strategy or local leisure plan is well made. Some local authorities have produced corporate leisure strategies; others have written specific activity plans to incorporate into a leisure plan (Figure 7.5).

Why a strategic local leisure plan?

1   To plan, set out and communicate what an authority wants to achieve for its residents, workers and visitors
2   To influence and improve opportunities for participation and recreation – active and passive – and performance in leisure, arts, sports for all sectors of the community
3   To co-ordinate the contributions from a number of providers and avoid duplication
4   To provide clear guidance for all agencies and organizations in the public,

voluntary and commercial sectors on what the needs of the community are and to identify where the authority can work in partnership with others to meet the needs

5   To think long-term and overcome short-termism and parochialism.
6   To enable the principles enshrined in Local Agenda 21, the UN Charter on the rights to leisure, and to fulfil the government policies and direction contained, for example, in *The Health of the Nation*, the *Children Act* and in the concept of 'Best Value'.

But what is a strategy? It is a 'mission' or statement of intent which identifies issues, outlines policies and provides a framework for action. It is an agreed policy agenda, a plan to which, ideally, all are committed and 'signed up', regardless of party policies. The strategy must also identify the means and resources to achieve the goals, objects and targets. The strategy has to be built upon a number of foundation stones:

1   the policies of an authority or organization
2   geographic and environmental issues
3   demographic characteristics of the perceived catchment area
4   leisure priorities
5   needs and known and latent demands
6   resources – physical and financial
7   the statutory planning process
8   good management.

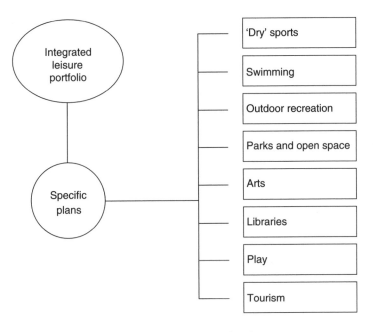

FIGURE 7.5 Corporate leisure strategy and specific plans

An authority needs to ask and provide answers to fundamental questions:

1   What are we trying to achieve in providing leisure services? What is our mission?
2   What policies and priorities must we adopt to enable us to get there, given finite cash limits and resources?
3   What internal opportunities and problems enhance or limit our goals?
4   What external, legal and financial constraints must we overcome?
5   What resources and opportunities already exist within reach of our communities and beyond our borders?

7.15   Summary – planning for leisure

Until recently, leisure planning has been a neglected discipline and there are numerous examples of poor leisure planning in the United Kingdom and elsewhere. Leisure planning differs fundamentally from general planning, as leisure outside the home is made up of a wide variety of minority activities, and the potential participant has to choose between a range of opportunities.

The suggested leisure planning process that can be implemented in a local authority setting is illustrated in Figure 7.3 and involves ten distinct stages. An integral, but often ignored, stage is the evaluation of current provision and services which can identify areas of spare capacity and where the demand exceeds the supply available.

The nature and scale of leisure provision by many local authorities is the result of inheritance and possibly this may be the reason why many councils have no philosophy for the allocation of leisure resources (i.e. no stated purpose for the expenditure on leisure services), which in most large councils represents many millions of pounds each year. Where such philosophies exist, these fall into policies based on equitable distribution and/or expressed leisure demand and/or social control. Although the bases of these philosophies are sound, they often appear to have been forgotten or neglected in their practical implementation.

With the assessment of demand, there is no one method of accurately determining the potential demand for a particular activity or facility. In this chapter we have examined different methods of assessing demand: standards of provision; spatial demand; hierarchy of facilities; national participative rates; the grid approach; the need index approach; expressed demand; and public consultation. Although these approaches have their limitations, used collectively, they can provide a good indication of the level of deficiency. To develop a more accurate method of assessment, greater research is needed into why people choose a particular activity.

Planning the facilities themselves, in urban and rural settings, and designing them to meet the physical, social and environmental needs of a catchment area, are important areas not covered in this book. In this chapter the planning process and methods have been debated. The following chapters deal with leisure provision and management.

Notes and references

1 Gold, S. M. (1981), 'Meeting the new recreation planning approach', *Parks and Recreation, 53*, No. 6, 74–80.

2 Veal, A. J. (1981), *Planning for Leisure: Alternative Approaches*, Papers in Leisure Studies No. 5, Polytechnic of North London.

3 Sports Council (1991), *District Sport and Recreation Strategies: A Guide*, Sports Council, London.

4 Sports Council (1993), *Planning Obligations for Sport and Recreation – A Guide for Negotiation and Action*, Sports Council, London.

5 Department of the Environment/Welsh Office (1991), *Planning Policy Guidance Note 17: Sport and Recreation*, HMSO, London.

6 Sports Council, National Playing Fields Association and Central Council for Physical Recreation (1991), *The Playing Pitch Strategy*, Sports Council, London.

7 Department of the Environment (1975), *Sport and Recreation*, Cmnd 6200, HMSO, London.

8 Department of the Environment (1977), *Policy for the Inner Cities*, Cmnd 6845, HMSO, London.

9 Lord Scarman (1981), *The Brixton Disorders, 10–12th April 1981*, Report of the Right Honourable Lord Scarman, HMSO, London.

10 Gold, S. M. (1973), *Urban Recreation Planning*, Lea and Febiger, Philadelphia, PA.

11 Mercer, D. (1973), 'The concept of recreational need', *Journal of Leisure Research, 5*, Winter, 37–50.

12 National Playing Fields Association (1993), *The National Playing Fields Association Six Acre Standard, National Playing Fields Association Minimum Standards for Outdoor Recreational Playing Space*, National Playing Fields Association, London.

13 Maw, R. and Cosgrove, D. (1972), *Working Paper 2172; Assessment of Demand for Recreation – A Modelling Approach*, Polytechnic of Central London.

14 Torkildsen, G. and Griffiths, G. (1987), *Lambourn Valley Recreation Study* (commissioned by Newbury District Council), LMGT, Harlow.

15 Greater London Council Planning Department (1968), *Surveys of the Use of Open Space*, GLC, London, Vol. 1.

16 Torkildsen, G. (1996), for Basingstoke and Deane Borough Council, *Play Area Need Index*, unpublished. The index was devised by George Torkildsen, Gwynne Griffiths and Pat Kendall; the play area inspection was carried out by consultant to the National Playing Fields Association, Tony Chilton.

17 Sports Council (1998), *Facilities Planning Model, a Planning Tool for Developing Sports Facilities*, Sports Council, London.

18 Stewart, D. and Shamdasani, P. (1990), *Focus Groups – Theory and Practice*, Applied Social Research Methods Series, Vol. 20, Sage, London

19 Rapoport, R. and Rapoport, R. N. (1975), *Leisure and the Family Life Cycle*, Routledge & Kegan Paul, London.

20 Brandenburg, J., Greiner, W., Hamilton-Smith, H., Schotton, H., Senior, R.

and Webb, J. (1982), A conceptual model of how people adopt recreation activities. *Leisure Studies, 1*, No. 3, September.

Recommended further reading

Department for Culture Media and Sport (1999), *Guidance for Local Authorities on Local Cultural Strategies*, DCMS, London.

English Sports Council (1999), *Land Use Planning Policy Statement*, (Consultation Draft), ESC, London.

Veal, A.J. (1997), *Research Methods for Leisure and Tourism: A Practical Guide*, second edition, Pitman, London.

SPORT ENGLAND

ENGLISH HERITAGE

Chapter eight

The government and leisure agencies in the United Kingdom

8.1 Introduction

In the last edition of this book, national agencies and institutions were identified and grouped together within a chapter on voluntary providers, not being within either the local government sector, nor commercial sector. In this edition, the national agencies warrant a chapter in their own right. The main reason for this is the establishment of the Department of National Heritage by the Conservative government in 1992, re-named the Department for Culture, Media and Sport by the Labour government in 1997, providing leisure for the first time with its own government department and, with it, a seat in the cabinet.

National agencies assist government at all levels and provide help at local level in planning, provision and management. Countryside recreation, for example, is fraught with conflicts of interest between planning, agriculture, forestry, tourism, water resources, sport, recreation and conservation. Leisure management has an important part to play in the network of voluntary bodies and agencies; the Leisure Manager is part of a multi-disciplinary framework for leisure planning and management. (Chapter ten deals with the voluntary sector.)

Central government is not a single entity, but a federation of separate ministries, each with its own policy and ministers. In the area of leisure, prior to 1992, there were six government departments with a role to play; the position with local government was more comprehensive, though still fragmented. In providing for recreation, central and local government work with and through a number of quasi-statutory institutions, quangos and agencies. Some have been

207

established by Royal Charter, some by legislation and others by ministerial direction. Central government, therefore carries considerable weight and influence on national agencies.

There are a whole range of national, regional and local agencies which assist in providing for public leisure and recreation. They are often hybrids of public authorities and private organizations, and while it is not their primary function to provide facilities, some of them do, and all of them influence provision through grants, loans, technical advice or support of some kind. The major agencies form a regional network of services.

This chapter takes a brief look at some of the major national agencies and their main activities, including: the Arts Council; the Sports Council; the Central Council for Physical Recreation; the National Playing Fields Association; the Countryside Commission; and the Tourist Boards. Before this, a synopsis of the role and some of the work of the Department for Culture, Media and Sport (formerly the Department of National Heritage) is given, including the National Lottery and its effect on the provision of leisure facilities.

8.2 Department for Culture, Media and Sport

The Department of National Heritage (DNH) was formed in April 1992 with responsibility for the arts, museums and galleries, libraries, the heritage, film, sport, tourism, broadcasting, the press and the National Lottery. The areas covered by the DNH were formerly the responsibility of other departments: the arts, museums and galleries, libraries, and some aspects of film were dealt with by the Office of Arts and Libraries; heritage by the Department of the Environment; film and export licensing of art, antiques and collectors' items by the Department of Trade and Industry; tourism by the Department of Employment; broadcasting, press and the safety of sports grounds by the Home Office; and sport by the Department of Education and Science (now Department for Education and Employment).

Following the general election, with a change of government, in July 1997 the department was re-named the Department for Culture, Media and Sport (DCMS). The reason for the change appeared in *The Times* on 15 July 1997 in a letter from the new Secretary of State: 'The name of Department of National Heritage was as inadequate and as partial as its unofficial alternative, the Ministry of Fun. Worse, it was inaccurate. Heritage looks to the past. We look to the future.' However, the word 'culture' conjures up an image of arts-related and intellectual pursuits, rendering other pursuits, therefore, non-cultural and in a way inferior. This is a long way from the concept of culture as the way of life of a people. In the first Annual Report, Secretary of State Chris Smith, concludes:

> I want to see the Department for Culture, Media and Sport as a dynamic force at the centre of Government, making a significant addition to the quality of life in every community in Britain, providing jobs, generating wealth, contributing to the perception of our country, at home and abroad, as a nation which recognises and celebrates creativity and talent in all its people. The work of this Department contributes to the Government's determination to

deliver on its manifesto commitments, and to build a modern Britain built on a stable economy with a fair society, with everyone playing a full part, and opportunities for all. Our four aims: promoting access, ensuring excellence, nurturing education throughout life, fostering creativity in our economy; these four provide a sound basis for carrying out the commitments we have made to the British people.

The DCMS is responsible for government policy on the arts, sport, the National Lottery, libraries, museums and galleries, broadcasting, film, press freedom and regulation, the historic environment and tourism. It is also responsible for the listing of buildings and scheduling of ancient monuments, for the export licensing of cultural goods, for the management of the British Library St Pancras project and the Government Art Collection, and for two agencies – the Historic Royal Palaces Agency and the Royal Parks Agency.

The DCMS provides funding, mainly through grant-in-aid, to a large number of executive and advisory Non-Departmental Public Bodies (NDPBs). These bodies play a role in the process of national government, but are not government departments. They operate to some extent at 'arm's length' from ministers as regards decision making, although they are expected to account for their decisions to government. Executive NDPBs have executive, administrative, regulatory or commercial functions. They usually carry out a variety of prescribed functions within government guidelines, but the degree of their operational independence varies. The department provides funding to and is responsible for thirty-eight executive NDPBs, including: Arts Council of England; British Film Institute; Crafts Council; Museums and Galleries Commission; Sports Council; British Tourist Authority; English Heritage.

The organizational structure of the DCMS is outlined in Figure 8.1, and Table 8.1 shows the cash plans of the department [1].

8.3 The National Lottery

The National Lottery was set up by the government to raise extra money for good causes. The draw attracts huge TV audiences to 'Lottery Live' on Saturday evenings. Well over two hundred millionaires were created within the Lottery's first two years.

The Lottery is the responsibility of the Department for Culture, Media and Sport. The Office of the National Lottery (OFLOT) is responsible for regulating the conduct of the operator – Camelot plc, who pay 28 per cent of their income into the National Lottery Distribution Fund (NLDF). The Director General of OFLOT is independent of government, but answerable to Parliament. Camelot is a private company, wholly independent of the operations of the Lottery Distributing Bodies.

The aim of the National Lottery is

To provide a major new source of funding for projects in the arts, sport, heritage and charitable sectors and for projects to celebrate the third Millennium, with a view to improving the quality of life for everyone in the UK and leaving a lasting legacy for future generations.

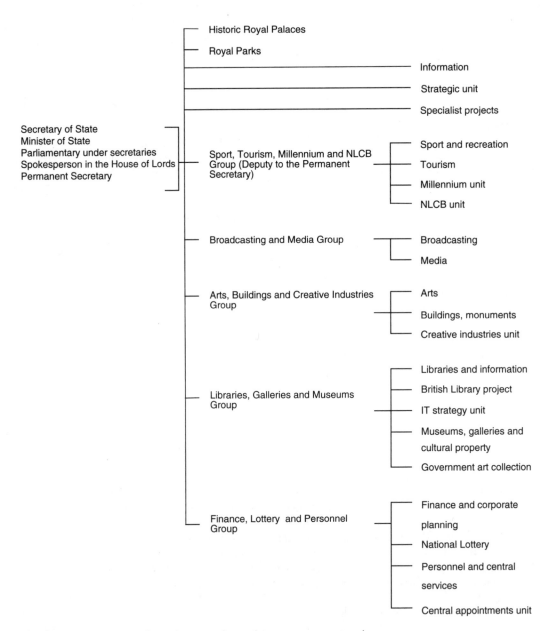

FIGURE 8.1 Department for Culture, Media and Sport: organizational structure
Source: Adapted from DCMS (1998) *Annual Report*, Cmnd 3991, HMSO, London

TABLE 8.1 Cash plans – Department for Culture, Media and Sport, Central Government expenditure voted in estimates

	1995–6 outturn (£m)	1996–7 outturn (£m)	1997–8 estimated outturn (£m)	1998–9 plans (£m)
Museums and galleries	228	214	227	208
Libraries	171	114	107	90
Arts	200	195	196	193
Sport	54	52	50	49
Historic buildings, monuments and sites	174	172	160	146
The Royal Parks	25	23	22	21
Tourism	45	46	45	45
Broadcasting and media	98	97	43	99
Administration, research and other services	20	21	23	28
Commemorative services and Royal funerals	3		4	
European Regional Development Fund	6	16	6	6
Total voted in estimates	1024	950	882	885

Source: DCMS (1998), *Annual Report*, HMSO, London

Setting up a National Lottery was the main new mission of the DNH when it was created in 1992, along with establishing the Lottery distribution mechanism under the *National Lottery Act 1993*. The National Lottery was launched on 14 November 1994. It is already an established part of Britain's national culture and is said to be the most successful national lottery in the world. Over 90 per cent of people over 16 have bought a Lottery ticket since its launch. By 31 December 1997, over £4.7 billion had been awarded by the five Lottery Distributing Bodies (LDBs). A sixth 'good cause' was to be launched by the end of 1998 under the title of the New Opportunities Fund. The National Lottery Distributing Bodies are: Arts Lottery Fund, Lottery Sports Fund, National Heritage Memorial Fund, Millennium Commission Fund, National Lottery Charities Board, and the New Opportunities Fund.

Each of the Lottery Distributing Bodies (LDBs) operates on a different basis for partnership funding, i.e. most organizations receiving grants contribute towards the overall costs of the project. The reason for a requirement for partnership funding is that it provides evidence of community support and it allows Lottery proceeds to be spread more widely. As at September 1998, the following rules applied.

- The National Lottery Charities Board has no requirement for partnership funding.
- The Arts Lottery Fund requires partnership funding. Applications for £100,000 or more need to be supported by partnership funding of 25 per cent.

Applications of less than £100,000 need only 10 per cent. Partnership funding can take the form of a financial contribution, in kind support, an agreement to support the project's running costs, or money raised prior to the Lottery application being made.

- The Lottery Sports Fund requires that, with exceptions, applicants for capital awards contribute at least 35 per cent of the total cost of the project and preferably more, with 50 per cent now expected for many projects. There is scope for non-cash support such as donations of property, buildings, labour, materials. There are, however, exceptions: the School Community Sport Initiative (SCSI); the Priority Areas Initiative (PAI); and the development of talented individuals.

- The Heritage Lottery Fund terms are similar to those of the Arts Lottery Fund. For grants over £100,000 at least 25 per cent partnership funding would be required, for those under £100,000, 10 per cent is expected.

- The Millennium Commission projects are expected to be of significant size and of value to the community so allowing Lottery funding to be used more widely. Each application is considered on an individual basis.

The importance of the Lottery to local authorities is very significant and concerns both direct and indirect provision. Local authorities can apply for direct financial assistance for projects at council-owned facilities and also enable organizations within the district to obtain funding for projects which complement existing provision and fit into local strategies. To harness these opportunities effectively requires a co-ordinated and focussed approach by local authorities. The creation of a leisure strategy is crucial to ensure effective use of total resources.

8.3.1 The share for the arts

The National Lottery has created unparallelled new funding opportunities in the arts. At the end of December 1997, the Arts Council of England had made 7,334 awards, totalling £936 million. In its early stages, Lottery distribution focussed on capital projects. Revenue programmes started in 1997, with £50 million awarded under the Arts for Everyone (A4E) and Arts for Everyone Express schemes. The A4E Express scheme was a pilot programme. The aim of A4E is to develop new audiences, increase participation and encourage new work and young talent.

During 1997, the first awards were made under a pilot Lottery 'stabilization' programme, designed to allow a small number of arts organizations that provide substantial public benefit to review their artistic and managerial operations and to place them on a basis that is sustainable in the longer term.

8.3.2 The share for sport

Sport is a good cause because it enriches the lives of millions of people of all ages in this country. It provides people with the opportunity to participate for simple pleasure and, for those with talent and ambitions in sport, the chance to reach their full potential in international competition. It improves the health and well-being of the nation and opens the doors to many new friendships. Above all, it produces pure enjoyment for those who play and those who watch. Not everybody is able to achieve levels of excellence in sport, but everybody can be inspired by the achievement of champions.

Department of National Heritage (1995), *Annual Report 1995*,
Cmnd 2811, HMSO, London, p. 7

The English Sports Council (ESC) distributes the Lottery Sports Fund in England; the Scottish Sports Council and the Sports Councils for Wales and for Northern Ireland are responsible for the funds in their own countries. The United Kingdom Sports Council (UKSC) has been added to the list of LDBs to allocate Lottery grants to projects with a United Kingdom-wide dimension, for example, in supporting British teams.

The government lays down rules for how funds should be used. Originally, the Fund could be used solely for capital schemes such as new buildings, construction projects and upgrading or modernizing existing facilities. Hence, for the first three years, funding was used for capital facilities projects. Since 1 April 1996 the Lottery Sports Fund (LSF) could be used to: provide support to individual talented sportsmen and women and teams; develop sports coaching and talent-identification projects; and fund one-off major international sporting events. The 'World Class Performance Programme' is designed to enable national governing bodies of sport to apply for revenue funding towards long-term training and preparation programmes to develop individuals who are members of a national junior or senior squad, and have the potential to achieve success at international level.

The purpose of the Lottery Capital Programme is to make important and long-lasting differences to the quality of people's lives. Preference is given to projects that cater for the widest possible cross-section of people. Particular priority is given to projects which will encourage people who do not usually have much opportunity for sport and recreation. Two key initiatives are the School Community Sport Initiative (SCSI) and the Priority Areas Initiative (PAI). The Lottery Sports Fund can assist schools to develop a range of sporting facilities that will be used by young people and the whole community. Strict rules apply concerning finance, planning, design, partnership funding, sports development, management and business planning. Schools that provide clear evidence against the SCSI guidelines may receive up to 80 per cent funding towards capital costs.

The PAI was launched in January 1996 to ensure that the benefits of the Lottery Sports Fund are available to all. Schemes within the Priority Areas can apply for up to 90 per cent award. Areas of sporting deprivation tend to coincide with areas of social and economic deprivation. The areas were designated using the DoE 'Index of Local Conditions', a measure of deprivation generally accepted as the best available analysis of urban deprivation, and 'Rural Development Areas' as designated by the Rural Development Commission. Ninety-nine local authority areas have been designated 'high priority' by the English Sports Council. In every case the whole district is included in the scheme but there are particular parts (the identified wards) which are of the highest priority. To qualify for above 65 per cent funding the applicants must demonstrate that: people affected by recreational deprivation will be attracted; partnership funding has been applied for; there is a clear facility deficiency of the type; and that they have an appropriate sports development plan.

8.3.3 The People's Lottery

In July 1997, the government set out its proposals for reform in a White Paper, *The People's Lottery* with the focus shifting from buildings to people: a new good cause, supporting initiatives in health, education and the environment; and a new Lottery distributor, the New Opportunities Fund (NOF). The NOF's first initiatives cover training and support in the use of information and communications technology for serving teachers and librarians; out of school hours activities, including child-care and healthy living centres. The White Paper also proposed the establishment of NESTA – the National Endowment for Science, Technology and the Arts – a national trust for talent and creativity endowed from the Lottery but operating independently of government.

8.3.4 National Lottery Distribution Fund

Money raised for the good causes is kept in the National Lottery Distribution Fund (NLDF) where it earns interest for the good causes until it is drawn down by the distributing bodies. From its launch in November 1994 until 31 December 1997 the distributing bodies made 26,157 awards in support of 38,360 projects, for a total value of £4.64 billion (see Table 8.2).

TABLE 8.2 National Lottery Distribution Fund: November 1994 – December 1997

Distributing body	Amount awarded (£m)	Number of projects
Arts Council – England	936.85	7,334
Arts Council – Scotland	56.22	333
Arts Council – Wales	26.66	346
Arts Council – Northern Ireland	17.07	315
Sports Council – England	685.65	2,496
Sports Council – Scotland	53.0	464
Sports Council – Wales	39.10	409
Sports Council – Northern Ireland	21.43	393
National Heritage Memorial Fund	874.77	1,385
Millennium Commission	1,274.26	1,957*
National Lottery Charities Board	794.32	12,991
	4,779.33	28,423

* supporting almost 18,000 schemes
Source: DCMS (1998), *Annual Report*, HMSO, London

TABLE 8.3 National Lottery sales

National Lottery Game	Start to 31 December 97	Average weekly sales for the financial year 96/97
Saturday	£10,868.63m	£62.63m
Midweek*	£1,360.94m	£28.96m
Instants (Scratchcards)	£3,0037.31m	£15.46m
	£15,266.88m	

* Launched February 1997

In the same period the NLDF had received more than £4.5 billion from the proceeds of the on-line game and instants, unclaimed prizes, underpayment of the prize fund and interest gains.

The National Lottery game consists of two on-line games (on Saturdays and Wednesdays) and various scratch card games ('instants'). The total ticket sales figures for each game to the end of 1997 are set out in Table 8.3.

The Government now forecasts that the Lottery will generate at least £10 billion for the good causes over the lifetime of the current licence.

8.4 The arts and the Arts Council

According to the DCMS, the annual turnover of the arts and creative industries is of the order of £50 billion a year, directly contributing 4 per cent to United Kingdom GDP. Tourists spend £40 billion a year in the United Kingdom, giving employment to 1.7 million people; a high proportion of visitors come to the United Kingdom for this sector of the leisure industry.

The 'arts' cover a wide and diverse range of pursuits. The public, voluntary and commercial sectors are all involved in the provision of facilities and in arts related activities and events. *Towards a National Arts and Media Strategy* [2] called for a strong partnership between the public and private sectors: 'The arts and culture are at the core of citizenship; they are central to the individual and in society and to community and national life.' *A Creative Future*, published by the Arts Council [3] promotes a clear message: the arts do not exist in isolation; to be involved with the arts is to be involved with society. The 1982 Select Committee report on *Public and Private Funding of the Arts* [4] uses the definition provided by the Congress of the USA:

The term 'the arts' includes, but is not limited to, music (instrumental and vocal), dance and drama, folk arts, creative writing, architecture and allied fields, painting, sculpture, photography, graphic and craft arts, industrial design, costume and fashion design, motion pictures, television and radio, tape and sound recording, the arts related to the presentation, performance, execution, and exhibition of such major forms, and the study and application of the arts to the human environment.

TABLE 8.4 Participation* in selected leisure activities away from home in Great Britain in 1996

	Percentage
Library	39
Cinema	36
Disco/night club	27
Theatre	20
Museum/art gallery	20

* Percentage aged 16 and over participating in the three
   months prior to interview

Source: Leisure Tracking Survey, The Henley Centre

TABLE 8.5 Attendance* at cultural events in Great Britain (percentages)

	1986–7	1991–2	1995–6
Cinema	31	44	51
Plays	23	23	23
Art galleries/exhibitions	21	21	22
Classical music	12	12	12
Ballet	6	6	7
Opera	5	6	6
Contemporary dance	4	3	4
Pop/rock			22

*Percentage of resident population aged 15 and over attending 'these days'

Source: Target Group Index, BMRB International

How many people are involved in the Arts? It is impossible to tell because the range is too vast. However, indications of the attendance at 'art-related' venues can be obtained and two examples are shown in Tables 8.4 and 8.5.

Popular music and rock concerts are the most popular forms of music events for all ages up to the mid-40s and across all socio-economic groups.

8.4.1 The national structure for the arts

The Arts Council of Great Britain (ACGB) was established by Royal Charter in 1946. The impetus for its creation was the success of the Council for the Encouragement of Music and Arts which had been established during the Second World War. It had threefold aims: to develop and improve the knowledge, understanding and practice of the arts; to increase accessibility; and to co-operate with government and local authorities to achieve the objectives. Regional Arts Associations (now Regional Arts Boards) were established in 1950 to work closely with the Arts Council but independent of it. A working party set up in 1978 recommended a more efficient and economic organization structure with a reduction in the size and number of committees and delegation of more executive powers to the council officers. The recommendations of the more recent Wilding report [5] aim to shift the emphasis, particularly in terms of funding and organization to the Regional Arts Boards. The changes will dramatically increase the influence of the Regional Arts Boards.

On 1 April 1994, the ACGB's responsibilities and functions were transferred to the Arts Council of England (ACE), the Scottish Arts Council (SAC) and the Arts Council of Wales (ACW). The Arts Council of Northern Ireland (ACNI) was already established as a separate body. Each of the Arts Councils is responsible for the development and funding of the arts in their respective countries. They are independent, non-political organizations, operating at 'arm's length' from central government, although they account for their decisions to government, the arts community and the general public.

The Arts Councils receive revenue from central government. The ACE receives its grant-in-aid from the DCMS and is accountable to the Secretary of State. The ACNI, SAC and ACW receive their funding from, and are accountable to, the Northern Ireland, the Scottish and Welsh Offices respectively.

8.4.2 The Arts Council of England

The ACE operates under a Royal Charter which sets out its constitution, describes its membership and gives the organization three objects:

1   to develop and improve the knowledge, understanding and practice of the arts;
2   to increase the accessibility of the arts to the public;
3   to advise and co-operate with departments of government, local authorities, the Arts Councils of Scotland, Wales and Northern Ireland and other bodies on any matters concerned, whether directly or indirectly, with the foregoing objects.

In addition to the Charter, the ACE has a mission statement, which develops the ideas in the Charter:

> The mission of the Arts Council of England is to enable everyone to enjoy and derive inspiration from the arts. It will do so by nurturing creativity, responding to innovation, promoting excellence, sustaining our living traditions, supporting multi-cultural interests, fostering new audiences and helping more people to encounter the work of artists throughout England.

The ACE works with England's Regional Arts Boards and together they make up the integrated system for arts funding and development in England. For the financial year 1997/98, the grant-in-aid for the ACE was £186.1 million. In addition, the ACE is responsible for distributing National Lottery money to the arts in England. Lottery funds currently total around £250 million a year.

The ACE supports a number of art forms – artists' film and video; dance; drama, mime and puppetry; interdisciplinary arts; literature; live art; music; and visual arts (including architecture and photography). The ACE distributes some of the grant-in-aid directly and some through the Regional Arts Boards. The majority of the funds are given to a number of regularly funded arts organizations.

There are ten Regional Arts Boards (RABs) covering between them the whole of England. In 1998, about 30 per cent of the Arts Council's funding was awarded to the RABs to be spent on arts organizations that have a predominantly regional remit, and arts projects and initiatives that are based in a particular region. Although the Arts Council and the RABs are all constitutionally independent from one another, their successful operation relies on close working relationships and their roles are complementary and interdependent.

The RABs receive their core funding from a number of sources: in addition to the Arts Council of England; other funders within the region, in particular local authorities; the British Film Institute; and the Crafts Council. The RABs in turn provide funding to arts organizations and artists working in the performing and visual arts, literature, film and video, and crafts in their region, through regular grants and one-off Development Funds.

8.4.3 Local authorities and the arts

Local government plays a vital role in supporting the arts. For local authorities in England and Wales, funding of the arts is discretionary; that is, although authorities are empowered to support the arts, they are not mandated to do so. There are a number of motivations for local government funding of the arts, for example, a wish to enhance the quality of life for residents, attract visitors and tourists and the contribution of the arts to the local economy.

Support for the arts is provided by local authorities in a number of ways, including, for example:

- providing and operating arts venues
- funding of independent arts organizations, artists, performers and venues
- funding 'in kind' – reduced rent and rates
- funding of their local Regional Arts Board
- providing venues for other events – community centres, town halls, and often the organization or promotion of such events
- promoting festivals and other arts events
- funding of Percent for Art schemes – a percentage of the cost of new building or environment schemes is allocated to commission artists and craftspeople
- public art projects – art works that are in public places.

As local authorities do not have a statutory obligation to provide arts funding, new developments have tended to be *ad hoc* and opportunity-led. Lottery funding has been on a demand-led basis, thereby compounding sporadic development, rather than the strategic allocation of resources. Local authorities are encouraged to link voluntary organizations with VAN – the Voluntary Arts Network – which assists voluntary and amateur organizations.

There are large numbers of artists, crafts people and art-involved enthusiasts, but provision and opportunity are in a variety of pockets. However, small specialisms may well thrive by being separate. The performing arts, on the other hand, need to be co-ordinated because each cannot have its own performing venue.

The ACE reports that over half the local authorities in England have arts policies. *Evaluation of Local Authority Arts Policies* [6] is a report that studied the different types of arts policies and processes which have been developed in England. It concluded that an arts policy can have an impact on the level of resources applied to the arts, but usually only when supported by other measures. Local authorities which had pursued cultural policies linked to economic regeneration had increased funding for the arts. The research found that individuals – committed officers or members – have often been more effective than a weak policy. In only one-quarter of councils were the arts understood and valued by members, according to the ACE. More effective advocacy is required. Changes in council member attitudes are a strong indication that an arts policy (or programme) is beginning to have a real impact.

The arts are included in Key Stages 3 and 4 in the National Curriculum for schools, and arts for young people has been given added impetus by government and through the National Lottery in recent years. *Setting the Scene: The Arts and Young People* [7] was published by the DNH in July 1996, committing public funding to the arts and to widening choice, engaging communities and tapping the skills and interests of young people. Meeting children's needs must now take account, not just of the National Curriculum, but also of the delegation of budgets to schools. Museums also have educational value and should support the needs of the National Curriculum.

Rural areas suffer more than urban areas in terms of provision for the arts, not just in terms of isolation, but from people's low incomes, high unemployment, poor transport and higher costs to local authorities, with most funds targeted towards urban centres. European grants in small communities tend to be at a low level of funding.

8.4.4 The arts and business

The Business Sponsorship Incentive Scheme promotes growth in sponsorship on the basis of matching funds from Government. It has succeeded in bringing over £82 million of new money into the arts (including a Government contribution of £27 million) and has attracted nearly four thousand first-time arts sponsors.

The Pairing Scheme for the Arts is a competitive scheme which provides an incentive to businesses to sponsor the arts. Managed on behalf of the DCMS by ABSA, the Association for Business Sponsorship of the Arts, the scheme matches business sponsorship with cash awards to sponsored arts organizations. The scheme is designed to encourage businesses to sponsor the arts for the first time, and existing business sponsors to increase their support, by offering matching funds, at different ratios, for new sponsorship money. Additional incentives are in place to encourage long-term commitment by sponsors, and for those sponsorships which generate easier access to the arts. Since the scheme's inception in 1984, it has succeeded in bringing in over £130 million in new money to the arts.

Visiting Arts is a joint venture of the Arts Council of England, the Scottish Arts Council, the Arts Council of Wales, the Arts Council of Northern Ireland, the Crafts Council, the Foreign and Commonwealth Office and the British Council. It promotes and facilitates the inward flow of foreign arts into England, Scotland, Wales and Northern Ireland in the context of the contribution they can make to international arts contacts and activities at all levels. Visiting Arts work includes: consultancy; advisory services; publications; information and training.

8.5   Crafts Council

The Crafts Council, a registered charity which receives an annual grant from government, is the national organization for promoting contemporary craft in Great Britain with priority given to innovative work. The object of the Crafts Council is to advance and encourage the creation of works of fine craftsmanship and to increase the interest of the public in the works of craftspeople.

The Crafts Council receives most of its funding from the DCMS. The Council distributes funds to the Regional Arts Boards for allocation to crafts projects in their regions. It also offers financial support by means of grants to individuals and organizations. The Council exercises most of its relevant powers through the RABs.

In 1994, the Council published the report of a major socio-economic study of the crafts in Britain which demonstrated a significant increase in the size of the sector in the previous ten years. Twenty-five thousand people are now said to be involved in crafts professionally; those engaged in crafts in an amateur capacity is, of course, hugely greater.

The Crafts Council publishes the monthly magazine *Crafts*, which covers all crafts disciplines at a 'serious' level.

8.6   British Film Institute

The British Film Institute (BFI) works to promote and develop the country's major art form, the moving image. The BFI's concerns range across all aspects of film, television and video – production, distribution, exhibition, preservation, education and research. In some cases, the BFI undertakes these activities directly, in others it provides funds and support to enable others to undertake activities similar to its own. Approximately half of the BFI's funding comes from the DCMS. The rest is raised from the subscriptions of its members, provision of services, sponsorship and donations.

The BFI publishes a comprehensive annual, *BFI Film and Television Handbook* providing further details on the work of the BFI as well as information on the sector as a whole.

8.7 Museums and galleries

The United Kingdom has some of the finest museums and galleries in the world. There are in the region of 2,500. Around 40,000 people are employed in United Kingdom museums. According to the DCMS, over 76.6 million visits were made to museums and galleries in 1996. Of these, about 23 per cent were made by overseas visitors. Hundreds of thousands of school children visit museums every year for study which supports the National Curriculum.

The Museums and Galleries Commission (MGC) is the Government's principal advisory body on museum matters; and it provides grant support to the seven English Area Museums Councils and to a number of other bodies. Local authorities provide and manage about 650 museums, about 40 per cent of the total listed in the *Museums Yearbook*. The relevant legislation concerned with museums is discretionary.

Two major reports are shaping current and future policy for local authority museums: a report by the MGC, *Local Authorities and Museums* and *The Road to Wigan Pier?* [8], a report by the Audit Commission. Other initiatives include the establishment of Area Museums Councils and the introduction of the Registration Scheme for Museums, prescribing minimum standards.

The Secretary of State announced in June 1997 the first list of thirty-two museums and galleries through England designated as a mark of quality. Designation gives formal recognition to non-national museums and galleries with pre-eminent collections of more than local or regional significance. The list is to be increased to a maximum of fifty institutions.

Public support and visitor numbers have been increasing over the past decade and visitors expect high quality display and presentations and good public facilities. The threat to museums – exemplified in many boroughs – is financial. Short term economies, and inadequate maintenance create longer term problems.

Through the Conservation Unit, the MGC aims to set, promote and raise standards of care of heritage items and collections in both the private and public sectors. The MGC administers on behalf of the government the Acceptance-in-Lieu scheme, which enables inheritance tax liabilities to be satisfied by the acceptance of works of art and heritage items into the nation's care. The MGC also administers the Government Indemnity Scheme, which provides insurance cover for loans to non-national museums and other bodies.

The MGC receives its grant-in-aid from the DCMS. Approximately 80 per cent of this is distributed in grant form to museums. The MGC works closely with and provides revenue funding to the seven Area Museum Councils (AMCs) in England; those in Scotland, Wales and Northern Ireland are funded by the Education Departments of the Scottish, Welsh and Northern Ireland Office respectively.

The National Lottery has led to unprecedented levels of capital investment in the nation's museums and galleries: by December 1997, over 390 awards, totalling over £590 million. The *National Heritage Act 1997* has provided the Heritage Lottery Fund with new powers with which to assist a wider range of museum projects. The HLF is now able to support projects relating to access, education and IT, as well as heritage.

Museums Week, organized by the Campaign for Museums, is held each May, and aims to raise the profile of museums and stimulate public interest. In 1997, a record 869 museums participated from all over the United Kingdom and between them, organized an estimated two thousand special events.

8.8 The library sector

The library sector is one of the most important to people's leisure. Indeed, most community leisure surveys all over the country show that visits to the library are more frequent than nearly all out-of-home venues. There are a range of libraries: public libraries, academic, educational and specialist libraries and the largest, the British Library. Libraries play a key role in underpinning education in its broadest sense and are focal points for communities.

There are 131 library authorities in England: 3,700 central, branch and mobile libraries and 16,300 small outlets in homes, hospitals, community centres and clinics. About 60 per cent of adults are members of their local library, and half of these borrow at least once a month. The number of books borrowed has remained at a high level: 423 million books and 30 million audio visual items were loaned by English public libraries in 1996–7.

Public libraries are eligible to bid for Lottery funds where projects meet the criteria set by the distributing bodies, although the library element may form a minor part of the total project. One of the New Opportunities Fund's first priorities will be to equip all 27,000 library staff in the United Kingdom with the skills to help learners make the best use of information technology. The NOF will also support an initiative to develop homework clubs for which public libraries will be eligible to apply.

In October 1997, the LIC, the Library and Information Commission, published *New Library: The People's Network* which recommends the establishment of a national public library IT network.

8.8.1 Local library authorities

The Secretary of State has a statutory obligation under the *Public Libraries and Museums Act 1964* to ensure that local library authorities in England provide a comprehensive and efficient public library service. All library authorities are now (since 1998) required to produce Annual Library Plans in a common format to help the DCMS to carry out the statutory obligation. Public libraries fall within the remit of County Councils and Unitary Authorities. However, borough and district councils need to work in close collaboration because libraries, potentially, can be the hub of communication, in addition to being one of the major leisure facilities.

Public libraries attract a wide audience – shoppers dropping in to exchange a book, retired people spending time browsing the daily newspapers, business people using resources, students studying, children at story telling. Libraries, often, are also the first point of contact for information and with IT. However, too often public libraries are closed when many people most want to use them. (The introduction of Sunday opening at Sutton Library has increased visits to the library significantly, and visits at weekends are now greater than during the week.)

About 39 per cent of the population aged 16 and over visited a public library in the three months prior to interview in 1996 [9], though the most popular method of getting a book these days is to buy one. Public libraries need to respond to this and other changes. Commercial book-selling, for example, may be an appropriate means of providing the back-catalogue. With Local Management of Schools (LMS), many schools are now buying direct from suppliers, rather than through centralized purchasing schemes. As Ken Worpole of Comedia comments: 'The worlds of the bookshop and public library are drawing closer together.'

The use of new technology in libraries will ultimately change the way libraries are run. The library can be the nerve centre of the community, providing information, knowledge and service. The Government's 'IT for All' programme, a four year scheme launched in December 1996, set out to raise public awareness, in collaboration with a number of participating libraries.

Links with the higher and further education sectors are essential using applications such as the Joint Academic Network (JANET). The concept of 'a library without walls' is based on any member of the public being able in a public library to call up on a screen, and have printed, information held in the British Library or any other internationally important reference collection. It could also encompass library resources accessed from computers and digital TV equipment in the home.

8.9 Sport and the Sports Councils

It is claimed by the Sports Council that some 36 million people – around two-thirds of the British population – take part in sport or physical recreation at least once a month. Participation continues to grow as more people become aware of the health benefits of an active lifestyle and this is epitomized in the phenomenal growth in the health and fitness market in recent years.

> Sport and physical recreation have a vital role to play in today's society by giving a sense of pride, by helping to alleviate the consequences of social and economic disadvantage and by having a positive effect on the mental and physical well-being of individuals and the nation. Sport also enables people to participate in activities which can bring together those of different races, gender, social class, age, ability or religious belief.
>
> The Sports Council (u.d.) *Factsheet: what is the Sports Council?*,
> Belmont Press, Northampton

Sport is also good for business and the British economy. The Sports Council estimates that 400,000 jobs are related to sport, and consumers spent over £10 billion on sports goods and activities in 1995 [10]. Even with the Lottery Sports Fund, sport gives back to the tax payer nearly £5 for every £1 it receives in grant. Above all, however, sport and physical recreation give pleasure to a large number of people.

8.9.1 Establishing the Sports Council

The Sports Council has gone through a number of changes and at the time of writing this edition of the book, further changes are anticipated.

The Wolfenden Report of 1960 [11] commissioned by the Central Council for Physical Recreation (CCPR) identified the need for a Sports Development Council. In order to satisfy this need, the Sports Council was eventually established in 1965. Originally, it was simply an advisory body, closely linked to the government through the civil service, with a government minister as its chairman. However, in 1972, it was granted independent status by Royal Charter, taking over both the staff and the assets of the CCPR and assuming responsibility for the Technical Unit for Sport (TUS) which prior to this had come under the auspices of the Department of Education and Science.

In addition to the Sports Council, there were three national councils. The Scottish Sports Council and the Sports Council for Wales were set up as independent executive organizations by Royal Charter in 1972. They received annual grant-in-aid direct from central government and performed similar general functions to those of the Sports Council. The Sports Council for Northern Ireland was established by statute in 1974 to advise government on capital expenditure and financially to assist voluntary sports organizations. The members of all three councils were appointed by their respective secretaries of state. In parallel with the setting up of the Sports Council, the second report from the Select Committee of the House of Lords on Sport and Leisure called for action to remedy deficiencies in sport provision. Then in 1974 the government produced a White Paper on sport and recreation [12].

In 1976, regional councils took on extended remits. Regional Councils for Sport and Recreation, for England, were set up by the Minister of State for Sport and Recreation. These councils supplied a forum for consultation among local authorities, local sports councils, various regional bodies of sport and recreation and other interested parties. They were concerned with the planning of facilities and the promotion of opportunities for participation in organized sport and recreation, as well as with informal countryside recreation and the conservation problems inherent in its development. They were independent, autonomous bodies with representatives from organizations which had a major role to play in the development of sport and recreation. Following the DoE Circular 73/77, *Guidelines for Regional Recreational Strategies July 1977*, the regional councils were also responsible for the production of strategy plans for the development of recreation within their regions.

In the 1980s, several initiatives were undertaken: Action Sport, a project to recruit over 1,100 sports leaders; the Standardized Approach to Sports Hall – SASH schemes; the ITI (Indoor Tennis Initiative); the Small Pool Development project; and the establishment of the National Coaching Foundation (NCF) followed later with a network of fourteen National Coaching Centres.

In 1990/91 changes in Sports Council policy increased the emphasis on sport for school-aged children and 'Champion Coaching' pilot schemes were launched to provide high quality after-school sport for the 11–14 age-group. The Allied Dunbar National Fitness Survey illustrated the need for increased fitness levels for children, young people and adults throughout the country.

The direct link between the GB Sports Council and the Regional Councils for Sport and Recreation came to an end on 1 January 1996. The regional offices of the Council have now been identified with the implementation of national sports policy, bearing in mind regional circumstances. In this way, the English Sports Council will be at arm's length from local authorities and other local agencies who may apply for grants from the National Lottery. Regional representatives will act as advisers and ambassadors for the English Sports Council in the regions and help to present policy to schools, clubs and voluntary organizations, feeding back information and building relationships between sporting interests in the region.

Facilities for sport have increased substantially over the past two decades. In England, there are now 1,300 public pools (excluding school pools); 1,500 indoor sports halls; 500 indoor tennis courts; 300 indoor bowls clubs; 40 ice rinks; 100 dry ski slopes; 412 athletic tracks (40 per cent synthetic); 1,270 eighteen-hole (or equivalent) golf courses and 282 artificial grass pitches [13].

Besides the professional sports clubs there are 150,000 voluntary sports clubs affiliated to the national governing bodies of sport in the United Kingdom. The clubs are predominantly run by leaders and coaches who freely give of their time. It is estimated by the Central Council for Physical Recreation that 6.5 million people play sport in such clubs, many run by professional staff funded by the club members.

The Second Report of the House of Lords Select Committee on Sport and Leisure (1973) stated: 'The state should not opt out of caring for people's leisure when it accepts the responsibility of caring for most of their other needs. The provision of opportunities for the enjoyment of leisure is part of the general fabric of the social services' [14]. Central government is also of the belief that the provision of sports and leisure opportunities will alleviate anti-social behaviour and many ills of the world. This belief was stressed in *Policy for the Inner Cities* and *The Report of the Scarman Inquiry* [15].

8.9.2 Reorganizing the Sports Council

In July 1994, the then Minister of Sport announced a major reorganization of the Sports Council. A new UK Sports Council and English Sports Council would be established in place of the GB Sports Council. The UK Sports Council would oversee those areas where there is a need for a United Kingdom-wide policy; and represent the United Kingdom on the international stage and co-ordinate policy for bringing major international sporting events to the United Kingdom.

The Sports Council for England would concentrate its resources on an increased programme of support to the governing bodies to help 'grass-roots' sports, with particular emphasis on young people, and to develop services for sporting excellence. It would take responsibility for the distribution of National Lottery funds for sport in England. Since that time the changes have been affected – and more are to come.

The Great Britain Sports Council's Royal Charter has been revised by the Secretary of State to bring about the separate UK and ESCs. The Government's future responsibility for sport is based upon five autonomous councils:

- the United Kingdom Sports Council
- the English Sports Council
- the Sports Council for Wales
- the Scottish Sports Council
- the Northern Ireland Sports Council.

The DNH published a sports policy document, *Sport: Raising the Game* [13], in July 1995. It set out the government's proposals to provide the 'highest standards' of sporting provision and facilities from grass-roots to international level. Sports participation in schools had declined and *Raising the Game* aimed at reversing the trend, promoting closer links between schools and sports clubs and establishing a new British Academy of Sport (now the United Kingdom Sports Institute) that would serve as a pinnacle of a national network of centres of excellence.

All five Sports Councils (UK and the four home countries) are accountable to a Secretary of State and to Parliament. The UKSC and the ESC work is monitored by the House of Commons through a Select Committee and the Public Accounts Committee.

8.9.3 The United Kingdom Sports Council

The United Kingdom Sports Council was established on 1 January 1997 and receives annual grant-in-aid from the DCMS. It is an independent body with the objects of fostering, supporting and encouraging the development of sport and physical recreation and the achievement of excellence in the United Kingdom. Its functions are:

- 'to identify sporting policies that should have a UK-wide application;
- to identify areas of unnecessary duplication, overlap and waste in the way sport is administered in the UK;
- to consider with the Sports Councils of England, Scotland, Wales and Northern Ireland how grant programmes for sports bodies with a United Kingdom or Great Britain remit could best be administered;
- to oversee policy on sports science, sports medicine, drug control and coaching and other areas where there may be a need for the Home Country Sports Councils for England, Scotland, Wales and Northern Ireland to deliver a consistent UK-wide policy;
- to co-ordinate policy for bringing major international sporting events to the UK; and
- to represent the UK internationally and to increase the influence of the UK at international level.'

These aims are a major challenge and resources will need to be found to accomplish them. The task is one of negotiation and diplomacy also. For example, deciding which major international sporting events should be attracted to the United Kingdom, and where to hold them involves a wide range of agencies, including government, other Sports Councils and, critically, governing bodies. Generally, the national governing bodies bid to stage events, but they will require the support and enabling from the UKSC. The Council will also promote the United Kingdom as a venue for international sporting events.

An anomaly existed concerning the UKSC and Lottery funding. The four home country Sports Councils were the distributors of the Lottery Sports Fund, the UKSC was not. However, changes were announced in the summer of 1998, with a transfer of the chairman of the ESC to head up the UKSC. This change was accompanied by additional resources, including making the UKSC a Lottery distributor.

8.9.4 The English Sports Council

The English Sports Council (ESC), established in January 1997, is an independent body which fosters, supports and encourages the development of sport and physical recreation and the achievement of excellence in England. The aim of the ESC is 'to see more people involved in sport, more places to play sport and higher standards of performance in sport.' Sports Councils in Scotland, Wales and Northern Ireland have similar remits in their countries.

In September 1997, the ESC published *England the Sporting Nation* – a strategy 'bringing together of vision, framework and targeted action'.

We want England to be the sporting nation providing equal opportunities:

- for everyone to develop the skills and competence to enable sport to be enjoyed;
- for all to follow a lifestyle which includes active participation in sport and recreation;
- for people to achieve their personal goals at whatever their chosen level of involvement in sport;
- for developing excellence and for achieving success in sport at the highest level.

English Sports Council (1997), *England the Sporting Nation –
A Strategy*, English Sports Council, London.

To promote excellence in sport, the Sports Council undertakes a number of activities, for example, running six National Centres of Excellence with the primary objective of meeting the top-level requirements of select sports. The centres are: Crystal Palace (athletics, swimming and other major sports); Holme Pierrepont, the National Water Sports Centre; Lilleshall (soccer, gymnastics, cricket, etc.); Bisham Abbey (tennis, hockey, rugby, etc.); Plas y Brenin, the National Centre for Mountain Activities; and the National Cycling Centre, Manchester .

The Sports Council has grant-aided the development of national facilities: £3 million for the National Indoor Arena, Birmingham; £2 million for the National Cycling Centre, Manchester; and £1.5 million for the National Hockey Stadium, Milton Keynes.

In 1983, the Sports Council established the National Coaching Foundation (NCF) to help meet the demand for trained coaches. The NCF provides a range of educational, training and advisory services and works with United Kingdom governing bodies and locally with coaches through its network of National Coaching Centres. The NCF 'Champion Coaching' scheme (in partnership with local authorities and the Council's regional offices) provided more than 7500 young people with access to coaching opportunities in 1997–8, with 696 coaches employed on 'Champion Coaching' programmes. The partnerships have been used as a catalyst to strengthen youth sports and coaching structures within 136 local authorities and national governing bodies in England, Wales and Northern Ireland.

The Sports Council has also been heavily involved in an extensive anti-doping campaign, sports science initiatives, research and information dissemination.

Sports science is vital to the success of sportsmen and sportswomen. The Sports Council provides sports science support to over thirty governing bodies of sport, in conjunction with the British Olympic Association, the NCF and the British Association of Sport and Exercise Sciences. There are now accredited psychologists, biomechanics and physiology laboratories. The Council also provides a co-ordinated approach to the development of sports medicine through the National Sports Medicine Institute, which brings together representatives from all Sports Councils, the BOA, the British Association of Sports Medicine, and others.

A research programme evaluates innovative projects such as: the National Fitness Survey, the largest ever survey of the nation's patterns of physical activity and fitness levels, sponsored by Allied Dunbar, in conjunction with the Health Education Authority; National Demonstration Projects; review of sports science research; the National Survey of Injuries in Sport and Exercise; and study of participation by young people.

A focal point exists for the collection, exchange and dissemination of information – both nationally and internationally and running a National Information Centre.

The ESC has a clear mandate in several key areas including: young people and sport; the development of excellence; and regional organization.

The ESC has placed greater emphasis on the preparation by governing bodies of sport of clear plans with specific targets for the development of their sports at all levels. The plans are expected to specify effective links with schools and youth organizations to realize the talent of young people. Less emphasis is now placed on the promotion of mass participation, informal recreation leisure pursuits or health promotion. The main responsibility for encouraging and providing opportunities for mass participation and informal recreation will rest primarily with local authorities, but also with the private sector.

8.9.5 Sports development

A key focus of the Sports Council of late is sports development. It is based upon two key principles: the Sports Development Continuum; and Sports Equity.

The Sports Development Continuum provides a framework for sports development. This identifies four levels of involvement in sport with an emphasis on pathways of progression from one area to the next:

1 *Foundation* – among young people, particularly school age, the acquisition of basic movement and sports skills to provide a foundation for personal development and future participation
2 *Participation* – among all levels of community; the opportunity to take part in a wide range of activities, whether for reasons of enjoyment, fitness, social contact or simple desire to get involved in sport
3 *Performance* – among those already participating; where the desire to improve is a key factor for involvement and the full realization of improved performance is the attainment of personal excellence
4 *Excellence* – among those with the interest and ability; the opportunity to achieve publicly recognized levels of excellence.

There is not yet equality of opportunity in sport in England. Sports Equity is about fairness in sport, equality of access, recognizing inequalities and taking steps to redress them. It is about changing the culture and structure of sport to ensure that it becomes equally accessible to everyone in society, whatever their age, race, gender, disability or level of ability.

The Sports Council works with national agencies to develop sporting excellence. They include the British Olympic Association, the British Association of Sport and Exercise Sciences, the National Sports Medicine Institute, the Sports Aid Foundation and the National Coaching Foundation. Through the last, its coaching arm, the Council has been able to raise and maintain high standards of coaching across the country. In 1995–6 over 1,000 courses were held, which attracted approximately 15,000 coaches.

The Sports Council is also heavily involved in advising on sports planning, design, development and management. These areas of work have become even more crucial with Lottery funding and the need to provide value for money and sustainable facilities. The Council has a role as a statutory planning consultee. Particular attention is being focussed upon the Facilities Planning Model, the Register of Recreational Land and encouraging the development of sports facilities on education sites.

8.9.6 Involving young people in sport and the National Junior Sport Programme

In 1993, the Sports Council published its policy for young people and sport and frameworks for action. Its aim is to provide opportunities for all young people to become involved in sport and physical recreation and to realize their full potential. The Sports Council is working with a number of other organizations, including the Youth Sports Trust, local authorities and the voluntary sector, to develop and deliver a national multi-sport programme – the National Junior Sport Programme (NJSP) – for young people aged 5–18 years.

Other new initiatives formally announced by the Sports Council in October 1996 included: the £1 million Challenge Fund to promote links between schools, clubs and governing bodies; Coaching For Teachers; and Sportsmark awards to recognize schools which have especially good policies for sport. These initiatives allow the DCMS and the Sports Council to take a wider strategic view, working, for example, with the Department for Education and Employment (DfEE) to involve more people in sport.

The emphasis placed on sports development has increased the need for qualified personnel in the field, with a significant growth in the market for coaches, leaders, and particularly, Sports Development Officers and Youth Sports Development Officers.

The National Junior Sport Programme was launched by the Sports Council in March 1996. It provides a framework within which schools, local authorities, governing bodies of sport, sports clubs and youth organizations can work together to provide quality sporting opportunities for 4–18 year olds in a planned and co-ordinated way. Developments within the programme include the production of curriculum resources and in-service training for teachers and a series of nationally produced resources to be delivered locally. Included within the NJSP are several key projects.

1   TOP Play (a programme of core skills for 4–9 year olds) and BT TOP Sport (introducing games to 7–11 year olds) were introduced into 2,000 primary schools in April 1996. 19,000 primary schools and 33,000 community sites are the targets by April 1999, reaching over 4 million children.
2   Champion Coaching (a coaching programme for 11–14 year olds in 16 sports) has been developed by the NCF and ESC. Local authorities are assured a five-year commitment.
3   TOP Club is being developed by the ESC and the Youth Sports Trust, in conjunction with the governing bodies of sport. Clubs are asked, initially, to produce an action plan for new opportunities for young people.
4   Sports Fair is a programme to promote sporting activity with youth groups. It has been jointly developed by the Sports Council and Youth Clubs UK, and includes Sports Train education and training materials for youth workers.

The Central Council for Physical Recreation's Junior Sports Leaders Award, which also forms part of the National Junior Sport Programme, provides for young people aged between 14 and 16 wishing to develop sports leadership skills.

Priority areas for development of the infrastructure to deliver the National Junior Sports Programme were identified as:

• support for Local Education Authorities in the delivery of TOP Play and BT TOP Sport within the National Curriculum
• the establishment of Youth Sports Development Officer posts within local authorities
• the establishment of posts for Sports Specific Development Officers.

8.9.7 The Sports Council, government and the economy

The Leisure Industries Research Centre estimates that 400,000 jobs relate to sport, and consumers spent over £10 billion on sports goods and activities in 1995.

To 31 March 1998, £670 million of Lottery monies had been awarded by the ESC to around 2,600 sports-related capital projects in England, contributing to total project costs of over £1 billion. The ESC had also awarded revenue grants of over £23 million to top athletes under the World Class Performance Programme, and £4.3 million under the new World Class Events Programme to help governing bodies attract and stage international events.

The government-funded Sportsmatch scheme – the business sponsorship incentive scheme for sport – continues to attract new business sponsors to grass-roots schemes designed to increase participation in sport [16]. It is designed to improve the quality of business sponsorship of grass-roots sports by: introducing new business to sponsorship and encouraging sponsors of major events to extend their involvement and existing sponsors of grass-roots sports to increase their support. The scheme is funded in England by the DCMS and managed by the Institute of Sport Sponsorship (ISS), a national non profit-making organization representing business sponsors of sport. In Scotland and Wales the scheme is funded by the Scottish and Welsh Offices respectively and managed by the Scottish and Welsh Sports Councils. Since its inception in November 1992, the scheme has made over £16 million of awards, attracting at least an equivalent amount of private sector sponsorship. The average Sportsmatch award is £8,000, with the majority going to small projects, including a new category of school schemes costing £1,000 or less.

The Football Task Force was launched in July 1997, chaired by David Mellor, to consider and advise ministers on issues facing football. A funding package of £55 million for the Football Trust was announced by the Minister for Sport in June 1997 to help League clubs complete the safety work required by the government in response to the Taylor Report into the Hillsborough disaster. Funding is being provided by the Lottery, the Football Association and the FA Premier League.

During 1997, the project for a centre of excellence in British sport – the British Academy of Sport – was redefined, following consultation with athletes and sports organizations. Redesigned as the United Kingdom Sports Institute, it will provide support services throughout the country through a network of regional and sport specific facilities. The HQ training facilities will focus primarily on Olympic and minority sports. The competition for the HQ site concluded in December 1997 when Sheffield was selected. The Home Countries' Sports Councils are working with the government to identify sites for the regional centres.

8.9.8 The Sports Councils for Wales, Scotland and Northern Ireland

The Sports Council for Wales

The Sports Council for Wales has overall guiding principles akin to all the home country Sports Councils, with local development work focussed on creating opportunities for school-age children to take part in sport, while nationally concentrating on raising standards of performance and excellence. SPORTLOT, the Lottery Sports Fund for Wales, manages the money coming in from the National Lottery.

'Sport and Young People in Wales' [17] provides impetus for the Council to work with its partners in achieving targets to be met by the year 2000. In 1997, participation among children had increased significantly: for example, 44 per cent of children were active within sports clubs, compared with 38 per cent two years ago. Like the English Sports Council, a number of targeted initiatives, particularly with children are being piloted with the Youth Sports Trust.

A major difference in Wales is reorganization of local government, resulting in 22 unitary authorities replacing entirely the two-tier local government system. The proposed establishment of a Welsh Assembly will undoubtedly affect the way public money is spent and prioritized.

For each year 1997–2000, the corporate plan of the Sports Council for Wales includes a projected level of grant to the Council from the Welsh Office of £6.624 million, which includes £284,000 for Sportsmatch. Impacting on the work of the Council will be SPORTLOT as the Fund has been expanded to include certain categories of revenue grants.

The Scottish Sports Council

The Scottish Sports Council also has strategies for Youth Sport and Excellence. To enhance sports development in Scotland, a Scottish Coaching Unit and a Governing Body Sports Development Unit have been established. The Scottish Sports Council Lottery Sports Fund has made a substantial improvement in the country's facility infrastructure.

More than £250 million is invested each year by Scotland's local authorities. Like its Welsh counterpart, the Scottish Sports Council has a priority in forging new partnerships with the new local authorities.

With the establishment of the United Kingdom Sports Council, the home country Sports Councils must build bridges and overcome problems relating to their international and United Kingdom roles, now that the UKSC has an overall United Kingdom remit to bring together the many elements and national 'preserves' for the future benefit of British sport. The relationship with the UK Sports Institute will also be crucial. A devolved government for Scotland will add to the complexity of the DCMS and UKSC vis-à-vis Scottish sport.

The Sports Council for Northern Ireland

In its 1996 Annual Report [18] the Sports Council for Northern Ireland reflects all other home country Councils, focussing 'more sharply than ever before on our young people and the development of excellence' and on the best possible use of Lottery funds. *The Future of Young People in Sport* [19] complements the United Kingdom policy document, *Raising the Game*, and reflects the circumstances in Northern Ireland.

In terms of the UK Sports Institute, Northern Ireland will have its own satellite centre, supported by existing Centres of Excellence.

8.10   The Central Council for Physical Recreation

The CCPR was formed in 1935. After the transference of the CCPR's staff and property assets to the Sports Council in 1972, the member bodies of the CCPR voted to retain the CCPR's independence as a forum for the national and governing bodies of sport and recreation. In addition, the Royal Charter setting up the Sports Council specified the need for a 'consultative body' to the Council, and the CCPR has been accorded this role.

The CCPR is thus an independent voluntary body with the following objectives:

1   to constitute a standing forum where all national governing and representative bodies of sport and physical recreation may be represented and may collectively or through special groups, where appropriate, formulate and promote measures to improve and develop sport and physical recreation;
2   to support the work of specialist sports bodies and to bring them together with other interested organizations;
3   to act as a consultative body to the Sports Council and other representative or public bodies concerned with sport and physical recreation.

The CCPR also provides a number of services to its member bodies, including a press service, help with sponsorship, legal advice and assistance with fund raising. For example, 'Kick Rates into Touch' outlined an action plan to bring 'pressure and persuasion' on all local authorities, for non-profit-making clubs and associations who are not granted relief from rates under section 47 of the *Local Government Finance Act 1988*. It also spearheaded a campaign to introduce an internationally accepted code of ethics on standards of sporting behaviour.

To fulfil its role of representing the interest of sports governing bodies and clubs, the CCPR has a wide network of key contacts. In Europe, the CCPR has links with the European Parliament Sports Intergroup and the European Non-Governmental Sports Organization. The Institute of Sports Sponsorship (ISS) (set up in 1985 following the Howell Report), in conjunction with the CCPR, drafted a model sponsorship agreement, *A Model Contract*, to the benefit of all parties. The Institute of Professional Sport (IPS) was launched in 1992 demonstrating the influence professional sports players have on the public at large and the need to enhance the reputation of the players and the sport.

The British Sports Trust was established in 1988 by the CCPR as a charitable trust with the primary function of administering the Community Sports Leaders Award Scheme. Hanson plc has sponsored the scheme to 1998, contributing £1 million in total. In 1995/96, a landmark was reached with the 10,000th student successfully completing a Hanson Leadership Award course. The Junior Sports Leader Award (JSLA) for 14–16 year old pupils has been introduced in the final two years of their physical education in school at National Curriculum Key Stage 4.

The CCPR's directional and policy formulation is achieved through a framework of six divisions, each chaired by a member of the executive committee: major spectator sports; games and sports; movement and dance; outdoor pursuits; water recreation; and interested organizations.

The CCPR's income in 1996 of about £1 million was primarily from a contribution of nearly £900K from the Sports Council. The British Sports Trust had an income of about £0.5 million, including a contribution of £200,000 from the Sports Council.

The CCPR, as a national association of governing bodies of sport, acts as a pressure group to challenge central government, political parties and local authorities to promote sport and treat sport with greater priority. To this end, *A Manifesto for Sport* [20] sets out the CCPR's driving principles. These include: co-ordination across government departments; funding for sport additional to the National Lottery; appropriate tax and Uniform Business Rate exemptions; recognition of volunteers, particularly in relation to local sports strategies; increased physical education in schools; greater consultation with governing bodies of sport over European Directives; safeguarding playing fields; and promoting co-operation between those who live, work and play in the countryside.

8.11 The National Playing Fields Association

Prior to 1925, the supply of public recreational facilities was a local matter with provision being spasmodic and held back by lack of central direction. The National Playing Fields Association, a voluntary body, was founded in 1925 to offer such direction by encouraging the provision of adequate playing fields and recreation facilities throughout the country. The association was incorporated by Royal Charter in 1933, and in 1963, it was registered as a national charity. There are affiliated Playing Fields Associations and a branch in Scotland.

The NPFA is responsible for the protection of over 2,000 playing fields, including 374 King George's Fields presented to the nation in memory of King George V. The Association campaigns for the protection of recreation grounds and keeps a register of fields known to be under threat of development.

Since its inception in 1925, the National Playing Fields Association has established minimum standards for outdoor playing space. In 1986, the association reconsidered its own target, set in 1938, for a minimum of six acres per 1,000 population of outdoor playing space. This target was reaffirmed for use by local authorities and others, but for the assessing of actual pitch requirements, they were referred to Sports Council guidelines.

The NPFA runs the National Play Information Centre, the world's largest collection of books, magazines, journals and videos dedicated to this subject.

Reference to the National Playing Fields Association is made in a number of parts of this book, including chapter two on children and play and chapter seven on planning. In particular, the association is noted for *The National Playing Fields Association Six Acre Standard*. National Playing Fields Association is the adviser to the DCMS on Playwork Education and Training, Information Dissemination and Playground Safety. New European Standards were brought into operation in 1998 and the National Playing Fields Association is the body that will be advising on its implementation.

The NPFA is building ten Millennium Centres – village halls for the inner city – managed by the local community and funded by the Millennium Commission.

8.12 The Countryside Commission

The *National Parks and Access to the Countryside Act 1949* created the National Parks Commission and gave it the power to establish national parks. To date, eleven of these parks have been created. Concern soon began to grow, however, about the conflicting claims of conservation and recreation within the national parks and a need was seen to ease the pressure on the parks by developing countryside recreation and conservation in general. To this end, the *Countryside Act 1968* abolished the National Parks Commission and set up the Countryside Commission, with the purpose of keeping under review: 'matters relating to the conservation and enhancement of landscape beauty in England and Wales, and to the provision and improvement of facilities of the countryside for enjoyment, including the need to secure access for open-air recreation.'

Independence from the Department of the Environment was granted by the *Wildlife and Countryside Act 1981*, when the Countryside Commission became a grant-in-aid body.

Scotland has a separate Countryside Commission, set up under the *Countryside (Scotland) Act 1967*. In 1991, as a result of the Nature Conservancy Council being split, responsibility for countryside issues in Wales passed to the Countryside Council for Wales.

The role of the commission in relation to the countryside is very similar to that of the Sports Council in relation to sport. It does not itself provide facilities, but provides finance and expertise for providing bodies, particularly local authorities. It has the power to aid financially countryside projects, to designate national parks, areas of outstanding natural beauty and heritage coasts, and to advise on countryside planning and management. It undertakes research into all aspects of countryside management and usage and produces educational and informative literature about the countryside in general, and specific areas such as national parks and long-distance footpaths.

Statutory agencies funded by government include: the Countryside Commission; English Nature; English Heritage; Scottish Natural Heritage and Countryside Council for Wales. The new Environmental Agency also has a powerful influence on countryside matters.

English Nature is the statutory body which achieves, enables and promotes nature conservation in England. It works in partnership with a wide range of organizations including government, representative bodies, agencies and voluntary organizations. English Nature is responsible for protecting and conserving wildlife, habitats and natural features.

Scottish Natural Heritage and the Countryside Council for Wales each have the combined responsibilities of the Countryside Commission and English Nature in Scotland and Wales respectively.

English Heritage protects and conserves historical and archaeological features and the built environment. The Forestry Commission is the government's agency promoting woodland and forestry.

Funded mainly by government, the Countryside Commission is the government's statutory adviser on rural issues and seeks to influence the EU on Common Agricultural Policy. One main innovation of the Commission is the introduction of Millennium Greens. In April 1995, a bid was submitted to the Millennium Commission for the creation of Millennium Greens throughout England. A grant of £10 million was awarded which will create 250 Millennium Greens. A Millennium Green is a new area of open space within easy walking distance of people's homes, which is owned and managed by the community through the establishment of a local Millennium Green Charitable Trust.

In March 1996, the Countryside Commission set out its strategy for the next ten years in *A Living Countryside* [21] in which a number of important issues were addressed:

- encouraging local pride
- promoting sustainable leisure activities
- achieving long-term benefits from farms and woodlands
- planning for sustainable development
- providing better information
- protecting and promoting the areas of finest landscape
- improving the countryside around towns.

The commission has five national programmes division units, with leisure and recreation integral to the work. The programmes run by divisional units cover:

- sustainable leisure – recreation and access issues, including national trails, cycling and a network of 120,000 miles of rights of way
- local identity – encouraging local pride, including community and voluntary activity, village design; protecting landscapes and countryside around towns, including community forests
- sustainable development – planning, housing and transport issues
- farms and woodlands – agriculture and forestry issues
- National Heritage – protecting and promoting areas of finest landscapes – national parks, areas of outstanding natural beauty (AONB) and heritage coasts.

The commission works closely with a number of agencies, including the Forestry Commission, the Nature Conservancy Council and the new government Environment Agency.

The Forestry Commission

The Forestry Commission is the largest landowner in Britain, with 3 million acres. It was constituted in 1919 by an Act of Parliament, being charged with the responsibility for the interests of forestry. Its primary role is that of timber production. In 1935, the commission recognized the public's need for greater opportunities of access to its forests for recreational purposes and opened the first of its forest parks in Argyll.

In 1970, the commission set up a conservation and recreation branch at its headquarters and established eleven recreation planning officers in each of its conservancy regions. Recreation plans for each of these regions have been written.

The problems resulting from the primary forest needs, tree planting and felling, and the secondary recreation requirements, need policy sensitivity and diplomatic management. In addition to the user problems, the commission must make a return on investment. The greater the provision for public recreation, the more difficult it becomes to show the level of profit required.

The Nature Conservancy Council (NCC)

The NCC was established by Act of Parliament in 1973. It has responsibility for 'the conservation of flora, fauna and geological and physiographical features throughout Great Britain'. The council is an agency, financed by the Department of the Environment, which controls and manages large areas of national nature reserves. In April 1991 the NCC split into three separate bodies, namely the Countryside Council for Wales, English Nature and the Nature Conservancy Council for Scotland, each responsible for nature conservation in its own area.

8.13 The Environment Agency

Created on 1 April 1996, the EA merged the National Rivers Authority, Her Majesty's Inspectorate of Pollution, the Waste Regulation Authorities and other smaller units from the Department of the Environment.

The National Rivers Authority was established by the *Water Act 1989*. The authority operates through ten regions based upon the ten river catchment areas of England and Wales. In addition to its responsibilities for environmental protection, pollution control, water resources and flood defence, it was also responsible for the promotion of recreational activities such as boating, fishing and walking by rivers.

England and Wales are now divided into eight EA regions. The Thames Region, for example, is responsible for the protection of a 13,000 square km area from Cirencester in the west to Southend in the east and from Luton in the north to the Surrey Downs in the south – an area containing one-fifth of the population.

The agency is now one of the most powerful environmental regulators in the world with the aim of protecting and enhancing the whole environment. As such, the EA has a strong influence upon leisure and recreation, particularly in areas such as water recreation, fishing, camping, canoeing and enjoyment of the countryside. As an example, 21,000 boats are registered with the agency's Thames Region. Two-thirds of them are motorized craft and there are 8,000 visiting craft. Every pleasure boat, including inflatables and tenders must be registered and every boat with an engine must have a licence to navigate. 'Without control, there would be conflict and danger. Just think – 30,000 pleasure boats on 217 kilometres of navigable river – about 7 metres per boat, but fortunately not all at the same time!' (EA Thames Region publicity leaflet).

8.14 Tourism and the tourist boards

The World Travel and Tourism Council (WTTC) estimates that one in nine jobs globally is generated either directly or indirectly by tourism and that by the year 2005 an additional 125 million jobs will be created worldwide in this field. In the United Kingdom, 1.7 million people (about 7 per cent of the working population) are directly employed in tourism, and tourism contributed £40 billion to the economy in 1997 – equivalent to 5 per cent of GDP (DCMS) – earning more from exports than North Sea oil, financial services or civil aviation. Taking indirect benefits into account, estimates of the total economic impact are as high as 12 per cent of GDP (DNH 1997). Tourism supports and is sustained by much of the hospitality, travel and leisure industries.

Tourism was defined by the former Department of National Heritage as signifying 'all aspects of the visitor experience, whether the visitor is on a day trip, a short break or a long holiday, visiting for leisure or business from this country or overseas'. This broad description remains today.

Core ingredients of the 'product' include accommodation, meals and visitor attractions, and substantial spending is on shopping, but the totality of tourism encompasses a wide range of services and facilities, including countryside, built heritage, pubs, restaurants, sport and leisure, theatres, museums and galleries, conferences and all the elements of travel by road, rail, water and air.

Innovation and new ideas of what constitutes a tourist attraction are helping to open up new markets and with them, economic growth, particularly in areas unable to support traditional tourism. Television series such as *Coronation Street* and *Heartbeat*, period dramas such as *Wuthering Heights* and films like *Braveheart* have created demand for visiting studios in Manchester, and villages in Yorkshire and the Highlands of Scotland. Hotels offer activity holidays, murder mystery weekends, wine tasting, musical appreciation. New themed attractions, such as the highly successful Legoland at Windsor, expand visitor markets.

According to the United Kingdom Tourism Survey, domestic trips in England rose by 10 per cent to 99.6 million, accounting for 82 per cent of all trips within the United Kingdom in 1995. The increase in spending on holidays of 4–7 nights' length (+13 per cent), raised total holiday tourism spending in England to record levels of £6.8 billion. More business travel and shorter break holidays, stimulated an 8 per cent increase in trips by United Kingdom residents. However, overall tourism expenditure in England fell by 6 per cent to £10 billion, mainly due to a lower spend per head on trips to visit friends and relatives and on business and work trips.

Seaside holidays make up nearly 4 in 10 of all holiday trips in England, generating over £3 billion in 1995. Northumbria (+25 per cent) and London (+22 per cent) experienced the greatest growth in holiday trips, with the West Country remaining the most popular destination.

Madame Tussaud's in London topped the list of English attractions charging admission in 1997, with 2.8 million visitors, slightly more than Alton Towers in Staffordshire (2.7 million) and the Tower of London (2.6 million). The British Tourist Authority reports that United Kingdom residents made 133.6 million trips in the United Kingdom in 1997, spending £15,075 million; overseas visitors made 25.5 million trips, spending £12,244 million as shown in Table 8.6. Overseas visits to

TABLE 8.6 Distribution of United Kingdom tourism 1997

Destination	United Kingdom residents		Overseas visitors	
	Trips (m)	Spending (£m)	Trips (m)	Spending (£m)
Cumbria	3.1	405	0.31	63
Northumbria	3.8	380	0.51	205
North West	9.7	1000	1.26	490
Yorkshire and Humberside	10.1	965	1.04	327
Heart of England	17.0	1300	2.18	689
East of England	14.8	1565	1.65	571
London	14.6	1040	13.46	6449
West Country	16.7	2755	1.66	513
Southern	11.9	1250	2.11	755
South East	11.6	1000	2.44	712
England	111.5	11,665	21.49	10,788
Northern Ireland	1.1	290	0.14	55
Scotland	11.1	1690	2.09	860
Wales	10.0	1125	0.92	226
United Kingdom (including Channel Islands and Isle of Man)	133.6	15,075	25.5	12,244

Source: British Tourism Authority (1998), *Tourism Facts and Figures*, British Tourism Authority, London.

the United Kingdom have increased from 15.6 million in 1987. Blackpool Pleasure Beach, with an estimated 7.3 million (7.5 million in 1996) was by far the most popular attraction. The British Museum remains the most popular museum with 5.7 million visitors and Hampton Court gardens attracted more than 1.2 million people.

8.14.1 The government and tourism

Tourism is the job of national and local government in collaboration with the private and voluntary sectors. Central government provides grant-in-aid to statutory tourist boards. Local authorities spend about £66 million on tourism promotion alone. Within central government, DCMS has lead responsibility, working through the statutory tourist boards – the British Tourist Authority (BTA) and English Tourist Board (ETB) – and the non-statutory Regional Tourist Boards.

In 1995 a government action plan, *Tourism: Competing With the Best* [22], resulted in advice to over 40,000 accommodation operators on standards and customer expectations. The English, Scottish and Wales Tourist Boards and the AA and RAC sought to harmonize ratings on serviced accommodation. London, as the main gateway for visitors to the United Kingdom and the most powerful 'brand', is being given special attention in Focus London Initiative in 1995–8.

Building on *Competing With the Best*, the DNH launched a strategy for tourism in 1997 entitled *Success Through Partnership* [23], a joint strategy shared with the BTA and ETB. The DNH issued guidance to local authorities in October 1996, aimed mainly at 'successor' authorities emerging from the Local Government Review in England. The DNH report *People Working in Tourism and Hospitality* [24] set out an agenda to spread good management practice, collaboration, understanding of consumer needs, improvement of image and extension of supply of skilled tourism staff.

The English Tourist Board published *Action 2000* in January 1998 focussing on quality assurance, market intelligence, the provision of visitor information, marketing co-ordination, customer care and communication. Also, the ETB, AA and RAC jointly announced details of the new harmonized rating schemes for serviced accommodation which are designed to raise standards. Inspections under the new criteria have begun, and the schemes will be launched to the public in the summer of 1999.

The government's role is to provide a framework within which tourism can best develop. In November 1997, the Secretary of State announced plans for the development of a new strategy for tourism, to be launched in 1998, though changes had not been announced at the time of writing this edition.

Central to the new plans is the creation of a new, expanded Tourism Forum with fifty-seven members from all sectors – tourism, hospitality, leisure and also consumer groups, employee representatives and local authorities.

The government's New Deal programme to enable long-term unemployed people to find jobs (see chapter eighteen on training) relies heavily on the tourism, hospitality and leisure industries, which are well placed to provide jobs in the New Deal programme.

8.14.2 English Tourist Board

The English Tourist Board was established under the *Development of Tourism Act 1969* to provide the industry in England with a cohesive strategy as a national co-ordinator. Pragmatically, the ETB's primary purpose is to assist the tourism industry increase the overall tourism expenditure in England, working with the British Tourist Authority; it acts as a strategic body providing leadership, encouraging the industry to raise quality standards and acting as a catalyst for change. The board advises the government and others on tourism matters affecting England, encourages the provision and improvement of tourist facilities and amenities in England and promotes England as a destination to United Kingdom residents. It therefore has a central role in taking forward the work outlined in *Competing With the Best*.

A major review of the 'crown' accommodation classification and grading scheme has taken place in order to provide the consumer with an easily understandable system to identify quality accommodation. The hotel crown scheme was strengthened in 1996 by endorsing only four categories: approved; commended;

highly commended; and de luxe. The basic 'classified' option ceased. The ETB Annual Report 1996 recorded that 11,500 hotels were in the scheme. Another 11,000 properties fall within the Key scheme for approved self-catering accommodation.

Tourism For All is a national scheme to improve the accessibility of accommodation for disabled people. Disability awareness within the tourist industry is a growing feature. Under the terms of *The Disability Discrimination Act 1995*, it will be unlawful to provide a lower standard of service or offer less favourable terms to those who are disabled.

The ETB works in partnership with regional tourist boards: Cumbria; Northumbria; Yorkshire; North West; Heart of England; East Midlands; East Anglia; Southern; South East; East Midlands; East Anglia; Southern; West Country; and London. About half the ETB's grant-in-aid is distributed to regional boards. In addition, each has access to the Tourism Development Fund, managed by the ETB and BTA. Regional Tourist Board income of over £27m in 1995/96 accrued from:

Commercial membership	£ 2,003 m
Local authorities	£ 1,978 m
ETB funding	£ 5,575 m
Other commercial	£17,680 m

Over one-third of the total was raised from the Southern Board and from London.

There is a strong relationship between heritage, visitor attractions, art, sport, events and tourism. Activity holidays, for example, are now the focus of hotel developments.

In terms of its Citizen's Charter, the ETB has adopted a minimum service standards agreement for all tourist information centres (TICs). Although these are run mainly by local authorities, they follow ETB guidelines. The Tourism and Environment Task Force in 1991 identified the need to achieve a balance between the needs of local people, visitors and the environment. The results of jointly funded partnerships are contained in *Sustainable Rural Tourism – Opportunities For Local Action* (ETB Annual Report 1996) [25].

Training to improve management and customer service is a key factor in meeting the growing shortage of people skilled in tourism, identified by the ETB. Courses include 'Welcome host', concerned with making the right impression and making every visit a special occasion. 'Welcome management' shows how to create a culture of customer care. 'Welcome host international' tackles the needs of a worldwide audience – more than 21 million visitors came to England in 1995, according to the ETB.

The English Tourist Board provides a collective voice for over 200,000 businesses which depend on tourism. The government's relaxation of rules concerning white on brown tourist road signs has led to wider communication of tourism locations. The liberalization of English licensing laws has enabled pubs to stay open on Sunday afternoons. The campaign Daylight Extra seeks to bring the United Kingdom in line with Western Europe and extend the tourist season.

Co-operative marketing is a growing feature of cost effective tourism promotion – day trips packaged with household goods; colour film processing deals to visitor attractions; pizzas and 'child goes free' vouchers to pantomimes. Successful advertising campaigns have generated substantial new business. The ETB estimates that, for every £1 it spends, an additional £13 is created for the industry.

The ETB produces a wide range of publications, with *Where to Stay* a best seller. The main titles, *Hotels and Guesthouses*, *Bed and Breakfast* and *Self Catering*, are in their 21st edition. *Families Welcome* was a new guide in 1996 listing accommodation catering especially for children and young people. *Somewhere Special* lists highly commended or de luxe quality accommodation.

The extent of the economic impact upon a community from tourism will vary according to the type of visitor attracted and their length of stay. Generally, hotel guests spend the most and have the greater 'multiplier' effect – with conference delegates amongst the high spenders. The development of tourist facilities tends to be 'supply-led' with local authorities investing public money as a 'pump priming' exercise, which in turn attracts investment from the private sector. The development of the Brighton Conference Centre is an example where this has been most successful.

8.14.3 *British Tourist Authority*

The British Tourist Authority's main purpose is to maximize tourism earnings from overseas visitors to Britain. It promotes Great Britain as a tourist destination overseas and advises the Government and others on tourism matters affecting Great Britain. It operates 40 overseas offices in 34 countries world-wide.

In 1995, the number of overseas visitors to the United Kingdom increased by 13 per cent to 23.7 million and tourism revenue increased by 20 per cent to £11.9 billion [20]. According to the BTA, £949 million can be attributed to its activities – a return of £27 for every £1 of public money.

The BTA received £34.5 million in grant-in-aid and focussed on market segments in countries that offered the greatest business opportunity. The affluent young were such a customer group. According to the BTA, 18–34 year olds make 80 million trips a year world-wide; a quarter are from Asia. Nearly 24 million visitors came to the United Kingdom in 1995, with the largest numbers from Europe (see Table 8.7).

TABLE 8.7 Visitors to the United Kingdom in 1995

	Visits	*Expenditure (£)*
Europe	15,990,000	5,847,000
USA/Canada	3,884,000	2,370,000
Central/South America	358,000	305,000
Asia/Pacific	2,505,000	2,134,000
Middle East	391,000	618,000
Africa	618,000	611,000
Total	*23,746,000*	*11,885,000*

Source: International Passenger Survey, Central Statistical Office

Overseas visitors spend most of their money in England (89 per cent) and over half the total expenditure is in London. In the United Kingdom, 36 per cent is spent on accommodation, 24.5 per cent on shopping and 22 per cent on meals. The BTA reports that the inbound 'incentive market' is worth £142 million a year, with American visitors spending £2,320 per trip and Europeans £880 per visit. People on incentive trips inject £300 per day into the economy, twice as much compared to conferences, trade fairs and exhibitions. With London as the main destination in the United Kingdom, the BTA supports plans to build a fifth terminal at Heathrow Airport.

The European Union could have a substantial effect on Europe's share of the global tourism market, which has declined over the past few years. The BTA responded to the European Commission's Green Paper on *The Role of the Union in the Field of Tourism*, particularly concerning policies affecting transport, consumer affairs and taxation.

Ken Robinson of the Tourism Society is quoted in the BTA 1996 Annual Report, *Designs on Tourism*: 'Thousands of small businesses would find it very hard to understand or comply with the increasingly complex regulations governing tourism – let alone make their views heard – without the invaluable services of the BTA's policy department.'

8.15 English Heritage

Britain's built heritage is a prime national asset. And it is not just buildings and monuments from the past; it includes historic parks, gardens, battlefields and other sites.

Conservation contributes to economic regeneration, and an attractive environment draws more economic activity to an area, underpins sustainable development strategies and helps maintain a sense of community. English Heritage gives advice and grants for conservation; it is the Government's principal expert advisor on the historic environment and is responsible for the maintenance, repair and presentation of 406 properties in public ownership or guardianship.

In preserving the past, every year hundreds of buildings are added to a statutory preservation list – 1,400 buildings were added in 1997 alone. This represents more than just old buildings: the listing process increasingly includes modern architecture, for example, the National Sports Centre at Crystal Palace opened in 1964 was added to the list in 1997. Anyone can ask the DCMS to consider a building for listing and this could have a huge impact on those seeking to knock down leisure buildings of the recent past – pre- and post-war swimming 'baths' and more recent 1960s sports centres.

The DCMS is also engaged on a review, with English Heritage, of all archaeological remains in England, to identify which of some 600,000 sites are of outstanding national importance.

The Treasure Act 1996, the first ever reform of the medieval law of treasure trove, came into force on 24 September 1997. Forty finds were reported as treasure within the first three months of the Act's operation, compared with thirty during the whole of the previous year! The DCMS and the British Museum are also funding pilot schemes in six areas of England to promote the voluntary recording of all archaeological finds for two years from September 1997.

The Heritage Lottery Fund (HLF) is having an increasing impact on the heritage sector. As at the end of January 1998, £892 million had been awarded to heritage projects. Notable recent awards which have made a particular impact include £6 million towards Conservation Area Partnerships. These schemes are operated in conjunction with English Heritage and local authorities.

On 4 March 1998, the provisions of *The National Heritage Act 1997* came into force, offering scope for the HLF to use the Lottery for new initiative supporting access, education and youth projects and to work more with the private sector to achieve its objectives.

Notes and references

1   Department of Culture Media and Sport (1998), *Annual Report 1998*, Cmnd 3991, HMSO, London.

2   National Arts and Media Monitoring Group (1992), *Towards a National Arts and Media Strategy*, Arts Council, London.

3   Arts Council (1993), *A Creative Future*, Arts Council, London.

4   Department of Education and Science (1982), *Public and Private Funding of the Arts*, Eighth Report from Education, Science and Arts Committee, HMSO, London. [This definition was originally contained in Public Law 209 of the 89th United States Congress in setting up the National Foundation for the Arts and Humanities, Section 3(b).]

5   Wilding, R. (1989), *Supporting the Arts. A Review of the Structure of Arts Funding, 1989*, HMSO, London.

6   Bond, A. and Roberts, S. (1998) *Evaluation of Local Authority Arts Policies*, Arts Council of England, London.

7   Department of National Heritage (1986), *Setting the Scene, The Arts and Young People*, Department of National Heritage, London.

8   Museums and Galleries Commission (1991), *Local Authorities and Museums*, MGC, London; and Audit Commission (1991), *The Road to Wigan Pier? Managing Local Authority Museums and Art Galleries*, Audit Commission, London.

9   National Office of Statistics (1998), *Social Trends 28*, The Stationery Office, London.

10 English Sports Council (1997), *Policy Briefing*, English Sports Council, London.

11 Wolfenden Committee (1960), *Sport and the Community*, CCPR, London.

12 Department of the Environment (1975), *Sports and Recreation*, Cmnd 6200, HMSO, London.

13 Department of National Heritage (1995), *Sport: Raising the Game*, Department of National Heritage, London.

14 House of Lords (1973), *Second Report from the Select Committee of the House of Lords on Sport and Leisure*, HMSO, London.

15 Department of the Environment (1977), *Policy for the Inner Cities*, Cmnd

6845, HMSO, London and Scarman, L. (1981), for the Home Office, *The Brixton Disorders: First Report of an Inquiry*, 25 November, Cmnd 8427, HMSO, London.

16   Institute of Sports Sponsorship (undated), *Sportsmatch Rules*, ISS, London.

17   Sports Council for Wales (1996), *Annual Report 95/96 and Corporate Plan Summary 97/98–99/2000*, Sports Council for Wales, Cardiff.

18   Sports Council for Northern Ireland (1996), *Annual Report 1996*, Sports Council for Northern Ireland, Belfast.

19   Sports Council for Northern Ireland, *The Future of Young People in Sport*, Sports Council for Northern Ireland, Belfast.

20   Central Council for Physical Recreation (undated), *A Manifesto for Sport*, Central Council for Physical Recreation, London.

21   The Countryside Commission (1996), *A Living Countryside – Strategy for the Next Ten Years*, Countryside Commission, Cheltenham.

22   Department of National Heritage (1995), *Competing with the Best*, Department of National Heritage, London.

23   Department of National Heritage (1997), *Success Through Partnership, A Strategy for Tourism, February 1997*, London.

24   Department of National Heritage (1996), *People Working in Tourism and Hospitality*, Department of National Heritage, London.

25   English Tourist Board (1996), *Annual Report 1996*, ETB, London.

Recommended further reading

Department of Culture, Media and Sport (1998), *A New Cultural Framework*, DCMS, London.

Note to readers

Since this edition was submitted to the publisher, the English Sports Council has become Sport England and the Countryside Commission has become the Countryside Agency. The Countryside Agency came into being in April 1999 and set out its mission and role in *Tomorrow's Countryside – 2020 Vision*.

Part three

The leisure
providers

Chapter nine

Leisure provision in the public sector

This chapter is concerned with public sector provision of leisure services and facilities; the following two chapters deal with the voluntary and commercial sectors respectively.

At the end of 1998, the public sector was facing a period of further change with the introduction of 'Best Value', which was being piloted in selected local authorities. Legislation over much of the 1980s and 1990s had the effect of tightening councils' budgets and diminishing management control. Compulsory competitive tendering (CCT), in particular, had a dramatic effect on the role of local government in relation to the management of facilities and services, and *The Education Reform Act 1988* and *The Children Act 1989* have compounded the situation. On top of these has come a reorganization of local government in Great Britain, bringing unitary authorities into Scotland and Wales and some parts of England. There was also a change of government to Labour after eighteen years of Conservative rule. All these changes make both complications and opportunities for leisure and recreation management.

This chapter is written in the following sequence. First, the range of public sector services and facilities are described. Second, development of local authority services, with some Acts of Parliament going back well over a hundred years are placed in historical context, with greater concentration on the years following the Second World War; included is the watershed period in the 1960s which set the course for new wide-ranging provision such as sport and recreation centres and dual-use and joint-provision facilities in schools. Third, and arguably the most dramatic for local government, the effects are shown of compulsory competitive tendering legislation. Fourth, other recent key Acts concerned with the local management of schools and with the duties and powers to provide for children, are considered. Fifth, the framework and management in local government, the constraints under which local councils have to operate and options for the management of services are described. Sixth, a hint is provided as to the future with the introduction pending of legislation to 'modernize local government' which was anticipated at the time of writing this fourth edition.

This chapter will assist readers' understanding of the essential characteristics of the public sector, the range of provision and its development from early nineteenth century legislation, successive enabling Acts of Parliament and the reorganization of local government through to the current issues.

Students will be made aware of the opportunities and traditional constraints on leisure through mandatory and permissive powers – the few 'must do's' and the many 'may do's'. The role of local authorities in leisure is essential, but it is changing with consulting, enabling and co-ordinating functions taking on greater importance in the new millennium.

9.1 Providers of leisure services and facilities

People's leisure and recreation is made possible in part through a wide range of resources, services, facilities and management. A range of facilities is needed, both indoors and outdoors, in and around the home, in the urban environment, in rural areas, in the countryside and on dry land and on water. A range of services and programmes is needed to meet the diverse needs and demands of individuals, families, groups, clubs and societies.

The providers of services and facilities for leisure and recreation come from within the public, voluntary, institutional and commercial sectors. The pressure on land, and on financial capital, in the United Kingdom, has encouraged some providers to combine efforts and pool resources. However, with some notable exceptions, habits die hard and changes come about very slowly. Even within the public sector, co-operative ventures between county councils and district councils, with exceptions, have progressed little since the relative euphoria of the early joint provision leisure centres in the 1970s.

It is recognized from the outset that there is overlap between the public, voluntary and commercial sectors and that, in many cases, the three will be involved in the same kinds of provision and services. They are also increasingly dependent on one another. However, there are distinct differences in philosophy, objectivity and approach, between the public, voluntary and commercial sectors which need to be understood in order to provide appropriate recreation services. Here we deal with the public sector.

9.2 Public sector services and facilities

In the United Kingdom, public services and facilities for leisure can be provided by a public authority, or by legislation, for the general use of the public. Some facilities are provided by public funds for a restricted use, such as educational establishments, facilities for Her Majesty's Services and restricted forestry areas. Commercial operators have veered naturally towards those facilities and activities that give a good return on their investment. The increasing costs of land and construction have left the local authorities the task of providing more of the land-extensive facilities such as water recreation and parks, and more of the expensive buildings such as swimming pools, theatres, sports centres and concert halls.

Local authorities provide a wide range of facilities and services for leisure. They also provide – often indirectly – through financial and other support, through planning decisions and generally by acting as an 'enabling authority'. Local authorities thus play a major role in the provision of facilities and opportunities for public recreation.

Government agencies, such as new town corporations, regional water authorities and national park boards, also have major roles in recreation provision. All these bodies have powers or duties to assist in or to initiate provision.

The scope of recreation and leisure services within local authorities is very wide. However, there are a number of identifiable elements and spheres of influence; different authorities will have some or all of these elements depending on the location and the size of the authority, its policies and its responsibilities. These spheres and elements are shown in Figure 9.1. Many of the elements are combined or overlap; no two authorities are exactly alike either in provision or management. There are general similarities but specific differences.

Local authorities provide their range of facilities in a variety of ways. The public has access to a large number of facilities, for which no direct payment is made, such as urban parks, playgrounds, libraries, picnic areas, nature trails, beaches and country parks. While the public does not pay directly for these amenities, it does so indirectly through rates and taxes. Local authorities also provide facilities such as swimming pools, playing fields, golf courses, marinas, arts centres, theatres and sports centres, where there is a direct payment by the user, albeit often at highly subsidized charges.

Local authorities are important providers of leisure, education, arts and cultural activities, sport and recreation centres, art galleries, museums, concert halls and libraries. They have statutory duties to provide public libraries, though there are widely varying standards of provision. Youth and community services are provided usually through education, but the totality of services is a mixture of local authority provision and services provided by voluntary bodies.

While local authorities often look to voluntary and commercial sectors to provide for social activity and entertainment, they nevertheless do provide for entertainment, both directly and indirectly. They provide directly, for example, through village and community halls; community centres are particularly widespread in new town developments. They also directly provide through the provision of civic halls which are used for entertainment, and urban parks with their bandstands and entertainment facilities. Many new leisure centres are also prime venues for public entertainment.

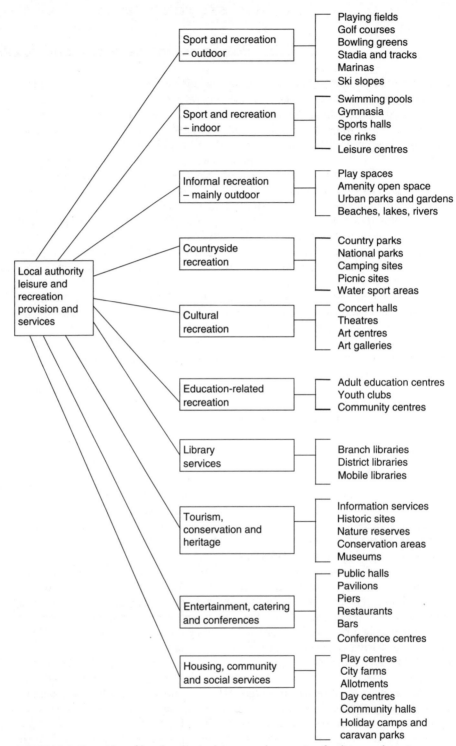

FIGURE 9.1 Examples of local authority leisure and recreation facilities and services

The vast majority of services, manpower and finance is used for the traditional, existing facilities. Despite the emergence of new facilities, such as indoor recreation centres and country parks, it is clear that it is the staffing and management of existing provision which call for the largest part of local authority recreation services expenditure. When education-related services and libraries are included in the comprehensive recreation coverage, then the picture becomes even clearer, with all the new areas of leisure expenditure taking up a small proportion of the total. In terms of expenditure on recreation, local authorities allocate large proportions to libraries, parks, pitches and swimming pools.

9.2.1 Support and indirect provision

Local authorities are not simply providers of facilities. They have a support service to perform. They support organizations of all kinds, private institutions, voluntary organizations and even commercial bodies, when it is shown that greater service will be given to the public by so doing. The support given is basically of two kinds. The first is to make 'its own' facilities and equipment available for use, with or without charge. The second is to make financial grants.

The local education authorities are usually involved in support to youth and community services and organizations, for example, by making schools available for youth and adult classes, and by making capital and annual grants to community associations and other social groups. They may pay the salaries of wardens, leaders, teachers and managers of purpose-built community centres.

Local authorities have discretionary powers to assist in all manner of ways. They can assist trust bodies to provide theatres and sports centres, sports clubs to provide bowling greens and tennis courts and community groups to provide facilities for children's play, community arts or facilities which help the aged. The authorities also provide considerable support, indirectly, by sponsoring arts, sports and entertainment festivals and major events, by meeting deficits or by funding community events and activities.

Often, small services or small grants given to organizations to help to provide for themselves can benefit the community enormously. The redistribution of local authority funds for recreation based on individual, group and social need could enhance, particularly, recreation opportunity for the disadvantaged in the community.

The local authority planning function is crucial to recreation. As planning authorities, they can assist with the availability of land and resources. As housing authorities, they can assist with leisure in and around the home, in gardens and walkways, in play areas associated with high-rise dwellings and in access to community provision.

Local authorities give planning consent. They make decisions on development proposals and give consent for recreational facilities provided by other agencies. Planning authorities have to consider proposals in the context of broad overall and long-term policy. To consider leisure and recreation planning only in local terms would not take account of increased mobility, greater affluence and the movement across local authority boundaries. Countryside and regional facilities are particular areas of vulnerability for poor planning. Urban fringe leisure and recreation is gaining greater importance not only because of higher expectations, but also because of the cost of travel. Another aspect of movement into recreational areas is holidaymaking, tourism and sightseeing. Since local government re-organization, many local authorities have taken up their greater powers relating to the enhancement of tourism.

This brief résumé is sufficient to show that local authorities are major providers of leisure and recreation opportunities through planning, facilities, services, budgets and support. They have a duty to provide recreation opportunities through education and libraries. They have very wide discretionary powers in England and Wales (unlike those in Scotland and Northern Ireland, which have a duty to provide) to assist the arts, sports, informal recreation, countryside recreation, entertainment, conservation, tourism and youth and community services. In addition to these direct services, local authorities can assist leisure and recreation through many indirect ways, such as planning and housing and through social services that help the disadvantaged, who may need recreation services more than most, but who may make the least demand.

9.3 Government and recreation – the development of local authority services

Leisure and recreation services and facilities are subject, like all other services, to the laws of the land; while there is no comprehensive leisure or recreation Act, recreation is made possible and is guided and constrained by a whole variety of Acts, laws, statutes, government circulars and reports and regulations, both national and local.

Acts of Parliament impose duties or confer authority or powers to provide for recreation. Acts cover such diverse areas as allotments, swimming pools, parks, catering, clubs and associations, betting and gaming, public entertainment, libraries, licensing, preservation, waterways, employment, local authorities, institutions, charities and companies.

What is immediately evident in studying the public provision for recreation is that it is historical, traditional, institutional and facility orientated. Progress must be made within and through the system; changes will come about slowly. Despite the surge of new facilities in the 1960s and 1970s, the bulk of local government expenditure on recreation is still reserved for parks, pitches and pools, which is clearly a result of what exists, what is tradition, what local government is geared up to handle and what is known and understood.

9.3.1 The origins of recreation services

The origins of local authority recreation services as we know them today go back to the nineteenth century. To understand the rationale behind early legislation, it is necessary to comprehend the poverty and the unhealthy and debilitating social conditions that prevailed at the time of the Industrial Revolution and the era of the puritanical work-ethic (chapter three). In such an era, there was a need for a fit, healthy nation.

The *Baths and Wash-Houses Act 1846*, from which many of our present-day recreation departments originated, was concerned primarily with personal cleansing and hygiene. However, swimming pools were built alongside these, mainly for instructional purposes, but also for recreation. Today the recreation role is paramount and the 'baths' service in many cities embraces other indoor provision in the form of sports halls, squash courts, entertainment facilities and, of late, fitness centres.

Many parks departments also originated in the second half of the nineteenth century. Again, the movement was partly philanthropic and partly provided by the local authorities. Many bequests of land were received and acquisitions made. Parks departments, like the baths departments, expanded their sphere of authority and took over areas for organized outdoor sports and facilities for tennis, athletics, golf, boating, bowls and the range of outdoor entertainments and festivals.

The *Public Health Act 1875* was the first major statutory provision enabling urban authorities to purchase, lease, lay out, plant, improve and maintain land for use as public walks or pleasure grounds. Later statutes had to be passed to empower local authorities to set aside parts of such lands for the playing of games. In the *Public Health Act 1936* authority was given to provide public baths and wash-houses, swimming baths and bathing places, open or covered, and the right to close them to the public for use by school or club and to charge admission. The *Physical Training and Recreation Act 1937* was introduced as a result of unrest in Europe. There was a need for a strong, fit nation. The Act was thus very much a movement towards national fitness, away from the Victorian idea of 'public walks and pleasure grounds'. Local authorities could acquire land for facilities and clubs, with or without charge for their use. The 1937 Act was the first major Act to use the word 'recreation', but support from government had come not because recreation was fun and enjoyable, but on the grounds of social and physical health and welfare, character training and improvement.

9.3.2 Postwar improvements to recreation services

The recreation lobby continued promoting its arguments during and after the Second World War. Organizations such as the Central Council for Physical Recreation and the National Playing Fields Association played an effective, persuasive role.

The *Town and Country Planning Act 1947* made it possible for the development plans of local planning authorities to define the sites of proposed public buildings, parks, pleasure grounds, nature reserves and other open spaces or to allocate areas of land for such use. Powers were extended in the *Town and Country Planning Acts* of 1971 and 1974. The *National Parks and Access to the Countryside Act 1949* gave local planning authorities, whose areas include a national park, opportunity to provide accommodation and camping sites and to provide for recreation. The scope of countryside recreation was greatly enhanced with the passing of the *Countryside Act 1968*. The Act permits local authorities to provide recreation facilities; the 1949 Act placed a duty to manage national parks, along with other permissive powers. Importance has been given to the debate relating to use and abuse of the countryside, the preservation of heritage and the needs of conservation.

Local authorities have considerable powers to provide for recreation through education facilities, personnel and services. The major *Education Acts* of 1918 and 1944, coming after two world wars, gave education authorities permissive powers (in 1918) to create facilities for social and physical training and then in 1944 made it mandatory on all education authorities to provide adequate facilities for 'recreation and social and physical training' for primary, secondary and further education. This resulted in the growth not only of the Youth Service, adult education and physical education (and hence sport), but also of facilities such as sports grounds, swimming pools, larger gymnasia and some sports halls. However, it was not until many years later that additional finance through other local authority sources made it possible to increase greatly the standards of provision. Only by joint planning and provision between different tiers of authorities or between different departments were the larger, community-based facilities made possible. Despite the progress throughout the twentieth century up to this point, and despite the statutory and enabling Acts of Parliament, governments consistently viewed recreation as a beneficial means towards some other ends. The report of the Wolfenden Committee [1], published in 1960, led to the eventual recognition by Parliament of recreation in its own right.

9.3.3 The transition: an awakening to recreation

An acceptance of the benefits of recreation in its own right did not come until the 1960s. But the initiative did not come from the government. The Wolfenden Committee was appointed in October 1957 by the Central Council for Physical Recreation (CCPR) and produced its report, *Sport and the Community*, in 1960 [1], to examine the factors affecting the development of games, sports and outdoor activities in the United Kingdom and to make recommendations to the CCPR as to any practical measures which should be taken by statutory or voluntary bodies in order that these activities might play their full part in promoting the general welfare of the community.

The committee recommended the establishment of a Sports Development Council. Although the Sports Council was to be formed many years later, the recommendations were never implemented. The report, however, was a watershed in the eventual acceptance of recreation by Parliament.

The Wolfenden Report, and the Albermarle Report on the Youth and Community Service [2], stressed the need for more and better facilities for indoor sport and recreation. Even before the Wolfenden Report was published, the first community sports centre had been planned, had opened its first facilities and appointed its first manager. The centre was developed by a charitable trust, the Harlow and District Sports Trust. The Crystal Palace National Sports Centre was also under construction and was eventually opened in 1964. Again, the spearhead was a voluntary organization, the CCPR, in collaboration with statutory authorities and government.

During the 1960s, in addition to new proposals for sport and recreation and for youth and community services, the expansion of education services, library services and the arts was also proposed. The Plowden Report, *Children and their Primary Schools* (1967) [3], advocated the development of community schools to encourage interaction between home and school and proposed that a policy of 'positive discrimination' should favour schools in neighbourhoods of social and home disadvantage.

The *Public Libraries and Museums Act 1964* repealed all other legislation, some going back to before the turn of the century. It placed a duty on every library authority to provide a comprehensive and efficient library service, to promote and improve the service. From April 1974 non-metropolitan counties, metropolitan districts and the London boroughs became library authorities. The Department of Education and Science's *Circular 5/73, Local Government Reorganization and the Public Library Service* [4], stressed greater links between the major services for education, health and social services in encouraging activities for the whole community.

The arts have been the subject of numerous reports since the mid 1960s, for example, the 1965 White Paper, *Support for the Arts: The First Steps* [5]. The 1977 Maud Report [6], sponsored by the Calouste Gulbenkian Foundation, has been greatly influential. Redcliffe-Maud recommended that counties and districts should have a duty to ensure a 'reasonable range' of opportunity for arts enjoyment and that there should be a development plan for the arts with linkages to the education, libraries, museums and sport and recreation services.

Despite the acceptance of recreation and the enabling Acts of Parliament, many of the major proposals for sport, the arts, and the youth and community service were never introduced. In addition, in practical terms, local authorities and other providers had still to operate through a maze of Acts or sections of old statutes. They also had to operate through a proliferation of departments and, as Molyneux pointed out [7], the system allows and almost encourages separate policies, separate budgets and different attitudes and changing policies towards recreationists, particularly the clubs.

In 1968, with the establishment of a new county borough merging five former authorities, Teesside County Borough established a major committee and matching department for the arts and recreation. The new department, headed by a chief officer, spanned former services covering the arts, libraries, museums and art galleries, entertainments, sport and physical recreation, baths, parks and catering. Similar restructuring followed in a number of other authorities and in London boroughs.

One of the major influences which led to these developments was the inquiry headed by the then John Redcliffe-Maud into the machinery of local government administration and this was reported in 1967 [8]; it recommended the streamlining of committees and departments. Recreation services were ready to begin to rationalize the total sphere of leisure and recreation.

9.3.4 Dual use and joint provision

The 1960s and 1970s witnessed not only the advent of new purpose built facilities for recreation and the restructuring of local government administration, but also the recognition that thousands of schools and education facilities throughout the country were in essence embryo community leisure and recreation centres. The Department of Education and Science and the Ministry of Housing Local Government *Joint Circular 11/64:49/64, Provision of Facilities for Sport* [9], advanced a new policy guideline:

> In assessing local needs and the resources to match them, it is appropriate to consider how far facilities for sport and physical education already provided or in the course of provision at schools and other educational establishments can be shared with other users or can be economically expanded to meet those needs. Consultation with other authorities will be necessary, not only because facilities in one area may serve neighbouring areas; but also there will normally be more than one authority with powers to provide them.

The Ministry of Housing and Local Government *Circular 31/66, Public Expenditure: Miscellaneous Schemes* [10], drew attention again to the savings which could be achieved by joint provision and the need for consultation with the new regional sports councils on new projects. The Department of Education and Science's *Circular 2/70, The Chance to Share* [11], gave more control to local authorities over their own local expenditure, free of government control, for locally determined schemes including almost all sport and recreation schemes. Local authorities could now go ahead in providing facilities, provided they stayed within their overall block allocation of capital investment.

9.3.5 Local government reorganization and its effect on recreation

A Royal Commission under Lord Redcliffe-Maud was established in 1966 to consider the structure of local government in England, outside Greater London [12]. The commission proposed that the greater part of England should be divided into fifty-eight unitary authorities. Public reaction to the unitary concept was, in general, unfavourable and three of the four local authority associations preferred a two-tier system. A government White Paper in 1970 [13] proposed a new structure based on fifty-one unitary areas and five metropolitan areas. In 1971 the new Conservative government's alternative proposals emerged in two White Papers – one for England and the other for Scotland – and a consultative document for Wales [14]. A compromise solution of a two-tier structure and a radical reorganization of boroughs and urban and rural districts was proposed.

The *Local Government Act 1972* gave effect to the proposals contained in the 1971 White Paper. The Act conferred no new powers, but transferred the previous powers to the new local authorities. The *Local Government (Miscellaneous Provisions) Act 1976* brought together the various powers relating to the provision of leisure and recreation facilities. The Act consolidated most of the powers for leisure services other than those relating to 'cultural' and 'educational' services. The Act permits local authorities to provide such recreational facilities as it thinks fit, unlike the *Libraries Act 1964*, which placed a duty on library authorities to provide services.

In 1974 six new metropolitan county councils were established and the 1,400 existing district councils were reduced to 333. As far as recreation services were concerned, the greatest impact was felt in the 296 non-metropolitan district councils. These councils were now larger and more powerful and had, in many cases, inherited a range of facilities. Reorganization also encouraged the creation of new facilities, particularly indoor leisure centres, before reorgnization actually took place.

Prior to local government reorganization in 1974, most local authorities were structured on the basis of a number of departments operating under the control of committees. The committees competed for their share of the available financial resources. The Bains Report [15] placed emphasis on the corporate approach to management. It was felt that, in this way, an authority could formulate more realistically its long-term objectives covering all services, and make forward planning projections. With increased facilities, increased awareness towards community recreation and the emergence of new, larger departments, jobs were created for managers within recreation services and rapid promotions and movements of staff were prevalent throughout the United Kingdom.

The *Local Government Act 1972* and the *Local Government (Miscellaneous Provisions) Act 1976* provided the framework for local authorities with respect to the provision and administration of facilities for sport and recreation with the emergence of leisure services in their own right. Local authorities are the largest providers of leisure facilities for sport and outdoor physical recreation and have traditionally been so. Central government has placed an obligation on local authorities, in England and Wales only, to provide leisure services in three specific areas: library services, the youth and adult education facilities and allotments, but no indications of the scale of provision are given. In Scotland and Northern Ireland local authorities also have a duty to make provisions in other areas of sport and recreation. Local authorities therefore have 'duties' and 'powers'; however, they are allowed to interpret the needs and demands of the community in different ways and, consequently, the level of provision varies considerably from one local authority to the next.

9.4 Compulsory competitive tendering

The *Local Government Housing and Finance Act 1988* (containing provisions for the uniform business rate and compulsory competitive tendering (CCT)) had the most dramatic effects on the role of local government. The *Local Government Act 1988* (Competition in Sport and Leisure Facilities Order 1989) imposed upon local authorities the necessity to offer the management of their sports and leisure facilities to competitive tendering; there were certain exceptions, such as dual use centres, which combine education and public recreation provision. This was compulsory but not out-and-out privatization; local authorities still had control over aspects such as pricing, programming and opening hours. Undoubtedly, this resulted in some economic savings with most leisure and recreation facilities being operated by local authority direct service organizations, who had to improve their performance to provide more efficient services. CCT also spawned a new breed of private leisure facility management companies which were established to run public facilities. Many of these companies, for example, Relaxion, CCL, Circa and DC Leisure, were formed by former local authority leisure officers. They have been highly successful; others have failed. In addition, CCT has led to a range of non profit distributing organizations (NPDOs) in the form of charitable trusts, industrial provident societies, management buy-outs and other hybrids. The face of local authority leisure services is now very different from what it was when previous editions of this book were written. Currently in vogue under the new government, better known as 'New Labour', is the concept of 'Best Value'.

When one takes into account the whole spectrum of leisure services, the scene is far from uniform – it is diverse and fragmented, although greater standardization of service requirements has come about in recent years. A plethora of recent legislation is having a profound influence on the management of community leisure in its many forms. New Acts of Parliament include the *Children Act 1989*, the *Local Government Act 1988*, the *Education (No. 2) Act 1986* and the *Education Reform Act 1988*. These, while putting local authorities under severe pressures, change and uncertainty, have brought about a semblance of structure, rules and broad framework to which all are subject. There is no getting away from the fact that the systems and delivery of leisure and recreation services have been changed dramatically and in some areas possibly changed for all time. The greatest shake-up in local authority leisure service came as a result of compulsory competitive tendering (CCT) aimed at tightening budgets and improving efficiency, through competition.

CCT, soon to be abolished, currently operates under a range of regulations contained in Acts of Parliament, Circulars and Guidance documents: *Local Government, Planning and Land Act 1980*: *Local Government Act 1988*; *Local Government Act 1992*; *Local Government (Direct Service Organizations) (Competition)*; *Regulations SI 1995/1336*; DoE *Circular 10/93*; DoE *Circular 5/96*.

The *Local Government, Planning and Land Act 1980* introduced a wide range of local authority services which must be subject to compulsory competitive tendering. A local authority could only undertake certain 'defined activities' in-house, through its own direct labour organization (DLO) or direct service organization (DSO) *if* the work has been advertised, tendered out and won in open competition. The defined activities, initially, were few and revolved around construction and related activities. These were extended to include a wide range of a local authority's function. Indeed, nearly all of the services it is called upon to deliver became subject to competition as the list of 'defined' activities illustrates:

- *Local Government, Planning and Land Act 1980* – new building (including renewal); building repair and maintenance; highways construction and maintenance
- *Local Government Act 1988* – refuse collection; building, street cleaning; school, welfare and other catering; grounds and vehicle maintenance.

Added in 1989 were management of sport and leisure services. Added in 1994 were a range of services, including on-street parking; security; legal; housing management. Added in 1995 were information technology; finance; personnel.

These new regulations and guidance endeavoured to ensure that the process was fair and above board and did not have the effect of restricting, distorting or preventing competition – a 'level playing field'. The sweeping changes brought about through CCT have also encompassed a number of associated functions, including: procurement policy; financial accountability; and companies in which local authorities have an interest.

Client organizations – direct service organizations (DSOs) or direct labour organizations (DLOs) – are required to keep separate accounts for each of the defined activities and to meet the financial objective to break even, having first allowed for a 6 per cent rate of return on any capital employed – a capital financing charge. The purpose of the financial objective is to ensure that client organizations prepare realistic bids, comply with these if successful and offer value for money.

European procurement rules require all prospective contractors to be treated equally and are implemented in British law by secondary legislation which sets down transparent criteria for selecting tenderers and awarding contracts. These regulations and guidance also deal with the *Transfer of Undertakings (Protection of Employment) Regulations 1981* (TUPE) and the European Union *Acquired Rights Directive*. For the past twenty years, the European court has been dealing with matters relating to company take overs. In a sense, a contractor is 'taking over' a business and much uncertainty exists as to what constitutes a 'transfer of undertaking'. In effect, TUPE now applies – staff are taken over on their existing terms and conditions – unless there is significant reason why they should not be.

Regulations came into force in 1995 relating to the length of CCT contracts with new minimum and maximum periods. For example, the maintenance of grounds, formerly 4–6 years, was extended to 5–7 years and managing sports and leisure facilities extended from 4–6 years to a minimum of 5 years and a maximum of 10 years. The leisure extension made it far more attractive to potential contractors contemplating investment.

9.4.1 *Anti-competitive behaviour*

The 1988 Act introduced the concept of anti-competitive behaviour; the 1992 Act helps to define it in law and the 1993 Regulations assist local authorities in conducting competitive tendering and avoiding anti-competitive behaviour. *Circular 10/93* gave further guidance and this was superseded by DoE *Circular 5/96*. These Regulations and guidance apply to work tendered under the 1980 and 1988 Acts. Under the 1993 Act and the 1996 Circular, the rules and guidance given by central government to local government are spelled out unequivocally in the following areas.

1   There should be clear separation of client and contractor responsibilities – those involved in the process should have no direct interest in the outcome.
2   Prospective contractors must have sufficient time to prepare bids.
3   What costs can be taken into account in the bids?

4   Packaging of contracts should be within the scope of as many contractors as is practicable.
5   The content of contract documentation should not be so onerous and complex that it discourages or prevents contractors from tendering.
6   The use of performance bonds only to cover the extra costs involved in remedying defects and procuring the service from another contractor in the event of failure.
7   Model contract documentation should be used.
8   Quality should be treated in the evaluation of tenders.

The thrust of the rules was to ensure that no anti-competitive practice entered into the process. The DoE *Circular 5/96, Guidance on the Conduct of Compulsory Competitive Tendering* focussed on five key principles of good tendering practice:

1. Transparency

Authorities have to ensure that the competition process is conducted, and is seen to be conducted, in a fair and transparent manner. A transparently fair approach 'is to provide to the appropriate committee a full report on the appropriate stages in the competition process whenever significant contracts are let, beginning with a report which explains how particular services have been selected for competitive tender'. An authority should require the same standards of performance from a successful in-house team as from an external contractor, and monitor the performance of the work on that basis.

2. Removing obstacles for good market response

The government was looking for a good market response in the belief that value for money is more likely to result if there are contractors willing and able to compete for the work. Authorities need to demonstrate that they have considered the market and consulted 'a reasonable range of prospective tenderers'.

3. Focus on outputs

In the specification of services, authorities should specify the output to be achieved, rather than the way the service is to be performed, so that evaluation of bids and monitoring performance can concentrate on the contractor's ability to deliver the required service.

4. Evaluating quality and price

Authorities should adopt clear procedures for evaluating tenders to ensure that the quality which is being sought, can be achieved. Aspects such as equal opportunities and environmental standards should be 'explicitly stated in the specification' for the service or work in question. Details of the quality required should be given to the tenderer as to how the evaluation will be carried out. In this way 'it should not be necessary to look beyond the lowest tenderer'. Where a quality bid outweighs price advantage, authorities should be able to explain where lower price tenders fall short.

5. Fairness between in-house and external bids

Authorities must act fairly to ensure that the conduct of tendering does not put any provider at a disadvantage. Authorities are expected to make available to all the tendering conditions, including the specification; conditions of contract; pricing schedules; the evaluation criteria in descending order of importance; the terms and conditions on which assets will be made available; and workforce information to assess the possible transfer of an undertaking. Authorities should bear in mind that unduly or unreasonably onerous requirements may deter potential contractors. For example, performance bonds and guarantees should be based on perceived 'significant risk', not as a matter of course.

At the time of writing this edition, pilot 'Best Value' schemes were being monitored to set up a replacement for CCT. Nonetheless, the influence of CCT, bringing in competition has changed council services profoundly and perhaps for all time.

9.5   The Education Reform Act

The leisure and recreation resources to be found in educational institutions in the United Kingdom make up the largest volume of built facilities available to the public. Indeed, half of the newly-built leisure complexes of the past three decades are linked in some way with education. Moreover, schools are often the birthplace of our love or hate of music, art, crafts and sport – our future leisure time interests. In the United Kingdom, relatively few young people play a musical instrument, draw and paint for pleasure and although most play sport, a large proportion are unfit and take insufficient exercise outside school. Anything that affects the provision and management of education, therefore, affects the scope and delivery of leisure and recreation to the community.

Major Education Acts this century have each had substantial effects, not only on schools and compulsory education, but on leisure – community education in its widest sense. The Education Acts of 1918 and 1944, arising out of world wars and looking to new horizons and better deals for all citizens, changed community sport and recreation. The Education Acts of 1986 and 1988 likewise, made changes of substance.

In common with Conservative government policy, the Education Acts aimed to make the education service 'more responsive to consumer needs', devolve responsibility to local levels and reduce bureaucracy. Local Education Authorities (LEAs), schools and teachers ploughing through reams of paperwork, Standard

Assessment Tasks (SATS) and involved in Attainment Targets (ATs) and constant new directives, may well question the latter.

While many schools currently have good community use of premises, the 1986 Act encourages greater use. The market-forces approach, however, poses problems which can restrict wide-ranging opportunity and a co-ordinated policy, resulting in different arrangements and standards from district to district, and from school to school. A policy, agreed and understood, between district schools and district leisure departments can do much to assist local organizations and clubs. One-off 'wheeling and dealing' may make for an individual school winning out in the marketplace, but is likely to be a short term measure, lacking continuity and making it difficult to inculcate an integrated, comprehensive approach to the management of community recreation

9.5.1 Local management of schools

In terms of leisure and recreation management, the impact of the 1988 Act is felt under two main headings: the National Curriculum and local management of schools (LMS). In addition, there are further, far reaching implications, including:

1   the option for schools to 'opt out' and become a 'grant maintained school – GMS';
2   'open enrolment', whereby parents can choose the school they wish their children to attend;
3   providing each school with a devolved budget based upon the number of pupils in the school under a system called 'formula funding';
4   the requirements for schools to publish performance indicators such as examination results;
5   school governing bodies now have greater powers, with the LEA no longer having a majority or casting vote;
6   legislation is introduced on charging for school activities.

Some schools have already become far more 'commercial' in their approach, seeking to maximize income from community leisure uses and limit costs. However, if schools are seen to be excluding what parents perceive as important physical and social aspects of the education of their children, numbers in some schools could reduce. Yet, school income from the LEA is dependent on its number of pupils, which is dependent in some measure on how parents perceive the school. School 'organization', therefore, is fast becoming school 'management'.

Adding to the difficulties, activities requiring travel – field visits, outdoor pursuits, sports centres, theatres – have been restricted. The problem is exacerbated in that schools are prohibited from charging children for activities which take place off the school site, during the school day, to fulfil the requirements of the National Curriculum. Schools, particularly those with inadequate resources and staff, which have been making use of the local swimming pool, sports centre and theatre, now have to convince the Borough or County Council of the need and therefore gain a subsidy, pay for the facilities out of their allocated budgets or simply cut out the activity. In a climate of limited budgets, the latter route becomes expedient. The activity is dispensable. An example, one of many, is use made of a sports centre by schools and colleges in Essex as one of the key mainstays of Physical Education programmes for twenty-five years. The LEA cancelled the whole arrangement, leaving schools to cope and the sports centre to go into deficit funding.

If school governors are to fund use of community sports halls, swimming pools, outdoor pursuit centres, visits to museums and so on from their delegated budgets, then it is likely that activities beneficial to pupils will be excluded on purely financial grounds. Leaving school governors and head teachers to balance curriculum requirements against financial requirements is something of a 'tall order'. Business obligations call for a pragmatic, cost-centred, market approach. Therefore, physical education, art and music need to build up a very strong case and compete vigorously for a share of the curriculum time and resources. Only then can these subjects become foundation stones necessary for an effective balanced education and post-school involvement.

The new role of teachers in curriculum 'musts', attainment 'musts' and increased involvement in testing and assessment of pupils, inevitably results in less time and motivation for extra-curricular activities – the means by which the leisure and recreation skills and interest of children and young people are fashioned for now and the future.

Most people will agree that children and young people need a balanced education – mental, spiritual, physical and social – in order to become balanced, positive citizens. Healthy individuals, who also have skills for leisure activities and life skills, make for more fulfilled people. Reducing the range and depth of activities and skills, which lead to leisure interests and life skills, can only diminish a balanced education. Inactive children are likely to become inactive adults. Therefore, the leisure manager in a local authority now has an even more important role to play in positive links with schools both in school time and after school.

9.5.2 School and community funded facilities

One of the problems with jointly funded leisure facilities is the extent to which the facilities are 'school' facilities or 'community' facilities. Who owns and has management responsibility for sports halls, swimming pools, ice rinks and theatres on school campuses, when these have been partly or wholly paid for by district councils?

The facilities, which will have been provided solely under local education authority powers, form part of the school and can be used for a variety of activities, e.g. sport, drama, music, adult education, youth club, drop-in centre, etc. The government body is empowered to control such use and it is also responsible for establishing the scale of charges. Under the Act, community use of school facilities must not be subsidized from the delegated budget which can only be used for school purposes and curricular activities. Such community use has to be seen to be self-financed.

Joint provision, as distinct from dual use, is where the facility, whilst forming part of, or adjacent to, the school and used by the students, has been provided to

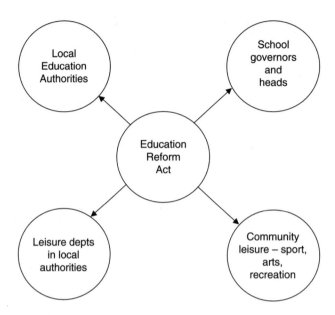

FIGURE 9.2 Community leisure – a part of the education network

standards appropriate for general public use and has been part financed from other agencies. Under the legislation, the opportunity exists to allow these other agencies to become involved in the day-to-day running of the facilities. If the facility is totally managed and maintained by another department of the local authority, e.g. a sports hall managed by the recreation department, and the school pays the recreation department for its use of the facility during school hours, the governing body will not have management control over the facility. If the school manages and maintains the premises, the governing body will have the power to control its use by the community.

The Community School is a school which engages in non-school activities and in which the governing body has control as well as the responsibility for those members of staff who are wholly or partly engaged in non-school activities. Each LEA, under the Act, has the 'right to insist' on school facilities being used by the community, and LEAs can provide specifications and guidance.

Leisure services departments can play an important role in achieving the best from the new legislation. For example they can:

1   provide help and advice on community recreation, sharing with schools ideas and systems relating to programming, pricing, management, business planning, etc.;

2   achieve levels of parity between different agencies; for example, some school premises are being let at 100 per cent higher charges than some agencies and this militates against a corporate strategic approach;

3   offer an advisory service to school governing bodies on the management of

leisure facilities or offer to manage the non-educational use on a contract basis;

4   organize courses in recreation management, and courses for leaders and coaches;

5   in collaboration with the LEA, Sports Council or Arts Council and the local authority, appoint Development Officers to work with schools – a corporate approach to community recreation (see the TOPS programme, chapter eight);

6   promote links between school and clubs;

7   provide collaborative promotion, awareness and publicity of the facilities and activities offered at the school;

8   advise on applications to the National Lottery;

9   include the school resources in leisure strategies and local leisure plans.

9.6 The Children Act

The *Children Act 1989* came into force on 14 October 1991. It is the most significant legislative change on behalf of children this century. The Act can be perceived as a unifying Act, replacing in part or whole fifty-five other Acts of Parliament, one going back a hundred years. How does this new Act, providing a common legal frame-work, affect the management of leisure, play and recreation? Leisure managers will be involved as: providers of services for children; providers of facilities; employers of paid staff and volunteers; providers of information; a body of expertise.

Leisure Managers, therefore, have to work with other departments, particularly Social Services and take a co-ordinated viewpoint. They need to be 'pro-active' in making the Act work for all concerned. The *Children Act* contains new regulations, duties and powers that affect everyone who is responsible for planning, managing and delivering services to children, particularly those to children under the age of eight. The clear direction and commitment behind the legislation is to put children at the heart and give priority to their needs in all those processes which affect their lives.

The Act lays down four duties:

1   to provide services
2   to publish information
3   to review
4   to register.

The Act also provides powers: to provide for all children; to provide training; to provide advisory services; to have concern with children's racial, religious, cultural backgrounds.

The key principles include: the recognition of the child as having an important place in the community; the right of the child to be cared for in the context of the family; and the responsibility of local authorities to ensure this whenever possible. The Act recognizes the right of the family to have roots and stability. A resort to care proceedings should only be made if this has failed. The

Act directs local authorities to consider preventative services and calls for the provision of a range of day care facilities which must be provided for children in need, but may also be provided for all children.

The Act, therefore, encompasses a number of wider issues:

1   the needs of different age groups, not just those up to the age of eight;
2   the needs of all children, including those with disabilities, as well as those from different ethnic and cultural backgrounds;
3   the need for adequate procedures to be developed between tiers of local government and different departments;
4   the need for clearly defined standards of good practice so that children have a good, safe and creative experience;
5   the application to statutory, voluntary and private sector provision.

Considered in this wider perspective, one could say that almost by accident the Act encompasses the role of leisure services in its work with children and their families. Of greatest significance is that a duty is placed on all those involved with 'children in need'. Clearly, leisure departments deal with many children in need. For the first time in the sphere of play and recreation, the local authority has a statutory duty to provide in this respect. The role of the leisure department can be significant in this process of co-operating and making progress. The main implications of all these matters are that local governments should positively plan for children rather than taking a narrow departmental and traditional perspective. One of the practical outcomes of the Act is the requirement for registration. Any person or organization providing services for children under eight years old, whether in public, voluntary or commercial sectors, must register, if those services are provided for more than two hours a day. Registration applies to the service that is open for two or more hours, whether or not the children stay for a shorter period. Playgroups, child minding and crèches in shopping centres, churches or leisure centres, for example, fall into this category. The temptation, unfortunately, is for some services to last just one hour and fifty minutes! The process takes into account four main factors:

1   the body or organization applying for registration;
2   the people who are being proposed to look after children under eight: the local lauthority has to satisfy itself that people who are working (whether paid staff or volunteers) are 'fit', i.e. suitable to do this work;
3   premises: the local authority will need to satisfy itself as to the 'fitness', i.e. suitability and physical condition of the premises;
4   inspection: local authorities have a statutory duty to inspect premises.

The *Children Act*, itself, unfortunately, does not mention play, recreation and leisure, as such, which is a major difficulty in understanding the Act and discovering where leisure and recreation fit into it! Guidance notes to the Act, however, give an indication of where play and recreation play a part. The Act, by implication, does affect leisure and recreation providers in all sectors in view of their services and provision for children and also in view of their expertise in areas in which Social Services are likely to have limited knowledge and little expertise.

Leisure services for children under eight in out-of-school hours will assist the authority in providing for 'children in need' as a duty. The local authority also has the power to provide for all other children. Leisure managers provide services for children, which include:

- crèches
- playschemes
- activities in leisure centres: 'Tumble Tots', 'Mini Movers', ballet, trampolining and swimming classes
- activities in museums, art galleries
- adventure playgrounds
- commercial 'Kids Play' centres
- city farms
- theme parks
- play spaces in shops and supermarkets
- holiday schemes in libraries, theatres and sport centres
- after-school 'clubs'.

These 'persons' (people and organizations) may need to be reviewed, inspected and registered. In very many cases, staffing, volunteers, programmes, equipment and facilities will need increase or improvement.

9.7 The framework under central control

Local government is required by law to conduct its business under the constraints and guidelines provided by Parliament. It must be, and must be seen to be, accountable to the public. The overall management hinges around three main structures: the committee structure, the officer structure and the departmental structure.

Local authorities have to provide certain services and therefore need certain departments. They have a duty to appoint certain officers and they have permissive powers to appoint others. Hence the structures in local government are made up with a mixture of 'have tos' and 'may dos'. This renders all local authorities similar; it also renders all local authorities dissimilar.

The work of a local authority cannot be undertaken without money and it is the financial considerations which loom largest at the end of the day. The local authority budget is the single most important function, the mainspring of its activities. The local authority is a business organization. Finance is needed for recreation services and can be classified under two main headings: capital finance and revenue finance. Capital funding is accessible to local government from several sources, though capital expenditure is principally financed through borrowing sanctioned by central government. As from April 1990, the capital control system has altered. Local authority capital receipts are taken into account when the borrowing limit is fixed. A percentage of such receipts are earmarked to pay outstanding debts. Where sports facilities are provided by private developers in return for land, the notional value of the land is taken into account and treated as a capital receipt.

Capital projects may be of local, regional or national importance. Depending on the amount of capital a local authority can borrow, certain projects may be controlled by the central government departments concerned; others may fall within the jurisdiction of the local authority. For these projects, each authority or group of authorities is given a block allocation for each year. This allocation has fallen sharply since the mid-1970s and recreation services have had to compete against many other even more pressing services. However, there are sources other than borrowing from which to finance capital expenditure. Some of the ways are outlined below, along with the main sources of capital funding:

1   direct grant from central government
2   loans from central government
3   rate support grant
4   revenue contributions
5   capital receipts through the sale of land and other assets (greatly reduced under the new capital spending regulations)
6   capital internal funds (e.g. community amenity funds)
7   loans from commercial concerns and a variety of joint arrangements with development companies and funding institutions
8   user finances (e.g. lotteries)
9   rates
10 and, not least, the National Lottery (see Section 8.3).

Finance from these sources is used to develop and construct amenities for use by members of the public, whether through clubs and organizations or by direct local government management. Like capital expenditure, revenue expenditure has also been strictly limited in recent years. Revenue finance is needed to support the ongoing running costs of the service and facilities. The finance is generated from: income from fees and charges; library fines; hire of facilities; catering etc; grant aid; and rates.

Restrictions in powers of borrowing and spending, the decrease in financial allocations from central government and in the rate support grants limit severely the expansion of local authority leisure and recreation services. In times of economic restraint, it is this sector in which the most severe cuts are made. Other services receive greater priority. This state of affairs has prompted some local authorities to explore a variety of ways of funding new capital leisure projects including:

1   capital sales
2   lease and lease-back schemes
3   deferred purchase methods
4   partnership projects
5   commercial development where a developer purchases, develops and manages leisure projects and the council benefits from 'planning gain'
6   arrangement with private operating companies who invest and manage.

9.8 Management in local government – the policy-makers

Management of local authority services is a highly complicated process [16]. It revolves around the local authority structural framework and involves a large number of people: elected members; departmental staff; facility managers and staff; and all the organizations and programmes through which recreation is made available to the public. Elected members, however, are of utmost importance to the management of public leisure and recreation services: they decide policy; they decide what is to be built and made available; they budget; and they control.

Councillors are citizens who devote part of their time to the service of local authorities. They are not salaried, but can be paid allowances and expenses. The business of local authorities takes time and is often arduous and complex. A councillor is a representative of his or her area. He or she is essentially a man or woman of the people, and should represent the community and involve the community. A councillor should be seen as making decisions not just *for* the community, but *with* the community. Current government policy – 'Best Value' – is calling for consultation and dialogue with the general public as an essential part of open local government.

A councillor's job involves using the local authority framework, departments and staff to determine needs and demands, establish policies, priorities and objectives, make decisions, implement measures to achieve them, monitor progress and make evaluations. In providing for recreation demand and need, councillors must work with and through officers, with recreation-involved people in the community and with the public – the users of the services being provided.

In order to undertake those responsibilities, councillors need the ability, the professional guidance and the motivation to achieve results. Their decisions are based on intuition, 'feel', experience, party policy and gut reaction. Their decisions are based, too, on some knowledge and information acquired from their officers but rarely, if ever, from training. Councillors have the authority and the power. They are 'trained' on operational experience. Leisure professionals must therefore inform, educate and influence councillors in the execution of their important task in the field of leisure and recreation.

Corporate management aims to provide a framework for local government business, whereby the needs of a community are viewed comprehensively; the activities of the local authority are planned and directed in a unified manner to satisfy those needs within available resources. Corporate management requires a masterplan combining policy making, corporate planning and collective management. The committee structure envisaged in the Bains Report [16] is used as a guideline by many authorities, but by no means all, and in recent years many comprehensive, corporate leisure departments have been abolished, despite the fact that leisure and recreation services can be greatly enhanced where corporate management includes a chief leisure officer within the corporate management team. The current situation is that in some authorities, leisure services is a major directorate with principal officers, planners, researchers and managers. In most other authorities, it remains a fragmented service and is often splintered into several sectional responsibilities. In yet other authorities, recreation is seen as a unit, but is swallowed up within a general service department such as community services, technical services or housing. In the larger authorities and the metropolitan districts, in particular, large departments exist, but there is often a traditional split between 'sports' and 'arts' departments. Hence recreation and leisure services are by no means standardized. Different areas have different needs and what is appropriate for one area may be inappropriate for another.

Local authorities, while they have an extremely important role to play in the provision and management of leisure and recreation, are constrained in what they can do and the way in which they can go about it. There are several reasons.

First, administration at all governmental levels is complex, often confusing and peculiar to the traditional institution of British government. Organized recreation was originally a matter for private and voluntary effort. By the time 'statutory' provision began to supplement this, numerous agencies were already established and working in the field. They were unco-ordinated and autonomous. When we look at facilities alone, even within the same authority, it appears that we have somehow managed to keep the left hand in ignorance of what the right hand is doing. One major consequence of CCT was that it forced a unified local authority into the position of splitting itself in two – client and contractor. In many authorities this had a damaging effect, causing rifts in the same department and the resultant lowering of morale. Today it is clear that for generations we have wasted many of our resources and facilities by keeping strict divisions between school, youth, community, young and old, public and private and then created further divisions with the client–contractor split. Often the problem has been not a shortage of facilities, but rather administrative weakness and an inability to coordinate functions of separate departments within different tiers of local government. Local authorities have in the past concentrated too much on facilities and not enough on services and opportunities. The National Lottery, after initial years of being facility-driven, now recognizes the value in being people- and process-driven. If local authorities are to serve all sections of the community, then supplying facilities alone is not enough. Community developments, partnerships, 'outreach' programmes, neighbourhood schemes, community leaders and 'animateurs' must be encouraged.

Second, recreation administration is fragmented. Different Acts of Parliament and regulations govern separate services such as social, health, community, education and leisure. Before the creation of the Department of National Heritage (now the Department for Culture, Media and Sport), different elements of leisure were the responsibility of different arms of government. Tourism was a function of the Department of Employment; sport, physical education and the arts came within the remit of the Department of Education and Science, then the Department of the Environment; local government leisure and recreation provision fell under the Department of the Environment. Other departments too, such as the Home Office, the Department of Health and Social Security and the Ministry of Agriculture, Fisheries and Food, are also involved in leisure provision and many of the functions are devolved to agencies such as the Tourist Boards, the Arts Council, Sports Council and Countryside Commission (now the Countryside Agency).

The multi-sector and multi-department approach of central government and the resulting complexity and overlap, constituted inherent problems between the 'fit' between central government and local government. Furthermore, most local authority functions, for example, libraries and adult education, have central government controls, guidance and sources for grant aid. However, this is not universally applied: for example, children's play, entertainment, catering and urban parks fall into several sectors and no one department takes overall responsibility.

Third, the *Local Government Act 1972* invests in all the county councils and district councils equal powers to provide recreation and leisure facilities for the community. Thus county councils and district councils have concurrent powers which leads to overlapping and duplication. The exceptions to this general provision are education, libraries and national parks.

Fourth, in Scotland and Northern Ireland a duty has been laid on local authorities to provide recreation facilities, but in England and Wales local authorities are under no obligation to provide for recreation other than through education, libraries, allotments, some national parks and of late, opportunities for children under *The Children Act*. The 'duty to provide' was specifically rejected by the government in its 1975 White Paper, *Sport and Recreation*. Local authorities thus have permissive powers.

Fifth, at local level, leisure services can be combined through corporate management and comprehensive departments, or partially combined or remain separated into autonomous departments. Since the advent of CCT some former leisure departments have been dissolved or drastically reduced in size and influence.

Sixth, it is not surprising that, given obligatory and permissive powers, we find problems over policy and priorities and a patchwork development of services. Local government departments have often been unclear about their rationale, aims and objectives for leisure. Aims are often all-embracing – 'to serve the whole community' – and can mean all things to all people. They are difficult to translate into operational objectives. Fundamentally the status of leisure is still problematic and planning for leisure is not a main priority for local government. However, all local authorities are being advised by agencies such as the Sports Council to think strategically and produce leisure strategies or local leisure plans. This new situation comes as a result, not of local governments' 'seeing the light' but the pragmatic action to attract Lottery monies!

Seventh, several management problems exist at an officer–manager level, and these have an effect on the face-to-face work with the community, for example, officer and staff behaviour is often controlled and guided by formal, organizational structures. This system of 'working to rules' can inculcate formal attitudes and responses to informal and flexible situations. The formal approaches tend to make it difficult for local government to attract or to articulate with the socially disadvantaged, who find little identification with the services. The Department of the Environment (DoE) Report *Recreation and Deprivation in Inner Urban Areas* [17] describes the problems which arise when simple approaches to providing recreation facilities 'for the whole community', without considering the special needs of particular groups, are adopted. A similar lesson is drawn from the report *Fair Play for All* by Hillman and Whalley [18]. The 'apparent' constraints of public accountability, allied to local government 'standards' tend to make local authorities wary and uneasy concerning commercial investment. However, greater co-operation is now becoming essential in times of local government spending constraints and the need for external sources of funding.

Another fundamental problem is the inevitable bureaucracy which comes through public accountability, public service, institutionalized systems and approaches, which render the whole machinery a slow moving animal, one which cannot readily respond to the needs of a fast-moving, changeable and flexible society.

9.9 Management and financial options

Local authorities have powers to provide leisure and recreation. There is a range of options. With the introduction of CCT came a need for local authorities to decide not only what they were in business for in relation to leisure and recreation, but what strategy they would adopt in achieving their aims and what management and financial option they would adopt. Options were appraised by the Audit Commission and summarized, as shown in Table 9.1.

TABLE 9.1 Financial Options

Option	Client	Contractor
Franchise	Meets debt charges and external maintenance of buildings	Meets other costs. Retains income from users. Pays a fee to the client.
Deficit guarantee	Meets debt charges and the external maintenance of buildings. Pays fee to the contractor.	Meets other costs. Retains income from users and uses this and the fee to meet costs and provide profit.
Profit sharing and deficit guarantee	Meets debt charges and external maintenance of buildings. Pays fee to the contractor.	Meets other costs. Retains income from users and uses this and the fee to meet costs and provide profit. Pays a proportion of any profit to the client.
Income sharing deficit guarantee	Meets debt charges and external maintenance of buildings. Pays fee to the contractor.	Meets other costs. Retains income from users and uses this and the fee to meet costs and provide profit. Pays a proportion of income to the client irrespective of whether or not the operation is profitable.
Risk sharing	Meets debt charges and external maintenance of buildings. Meets a proportion of any operating loss.	Meets other costs. Retains income from users. Shares any profit with the client.
Open book management fee	Meets debt charges and external maintenance of buildings. Meets contractor's costs. Pays contractor a fee.	Passes all income to the client.

Source: Audit Commission Review *Local Authority Support For Sport – A Management Handbook*

The Audit Commission favours approaches in which the maximum possible cost to the authority is set out in the contract, such as the income sharing 'deficit guarantee' approach.

The Department of Environment Consultation Paper 'Local authorities' interests in companies' and the *Local Government and Housing Act 1989* provide a statutory framework to govern local authorities' interest in companies. The government considered that it was an anomaly that local authorities had influence or control of companies outside the rules governing the conduct of local authority business. Three types of company were identified in Part V of the 1989 Act: Local authority-controlled companies; Arms' length companies; and Local authority-influenced companies. (Chapter ten deals with local authorities and companies in relation to trusts and other not-for-profit organizations.)

9.10 'Best Value'

The Labour Party's manifesto in 1997, *Because Britain Deserves Better*, contained a commitment to introduce a duty of best value into local government. Its objectives [19] were: efficiency; competition; partnership; quality; and public first. To achieve these objectives 'Best Value' would be linked to three of the party's commitments: local performance plans; new powers for the Audit Commission; and action to deal with failing councils. In July 1998 the government launched its White Paper *Modern Local Government – In Touch with the People* [20], which sets out how it intends to improve local services through Best Value.

> Best value will be a duty to deliver services to clear standards – covering both cost and quality – by the most effective, economic and efficient means available. In carrying out this duty local authorities will be accountable to local people and have a responsibility to central government in its role as representative of the broader national interest. Local authorities will set those standards – covering both cost and quality – for all the services for which they are responsible.

Councils will have to deliver best value for local people through four main channels:

1   clear standards
2   targets for continuous improvement
3   more say for service users
4   independent audit and inspection.

Thus under 'Best Value', it is hoped that local people will be clear about the standards of services which they can expect to receive and they will be better able to hold their councils to account for their record. The government proposed a legislative framework which will require authorities to undertake a number of key steps:

1   establish authority-wide objectives and performance measures
2   agree programme of fundamental performance reviews and set out in local performance plan

3   undertake fundamental performance reviews of selected areas of expenditure
4   set and publish performance and efficiency targets in local performance plan
5   independent audit/inspection and certification
6   areas requiring intervention referred to Secretary of State.

'Best Value' will replace CCT, which had made the cost of services more transparent and tightened budgets but which had been so definitively subscribed within tight time limits that the competition led to unimaginative tendering; ways were sought to circumvent the rules; splits were formed in the councils between clients and contractors; and the process did not enhance real competition. The government's intention now is an approach based on partnership rather than on confrontation. After all, well-motivated, competent, staff will be the best people to deliver 'Best Value'.

The government intends to apply the *duty* to obtain best value to all authorities except smaller town and parish councils. A *de minimis* level linked to the limit on financial reporting – c. £500,000 per annum budgeted income – has been proposed.

Best Value will have a number of key components.

1. Performance indicators

Some local authorities have developed their own key performance indicators and made use of those specified each year by the Audit Commission. Building on these, a new set of national performance indicators will be developed. Each authority will be expected to set targets in respect of these indicators and to publish both their targets and performance against them in annual local performance plans. 'As far as possible, the indicators will be designed to focus attention on what services have delivered (outcomes), rather than what resources have been devoted to them (inputs)' [20].

2. Performance standards

The government intends to provide a clear lead in relation to performance standards where it judges the national interest requires it.

3. Performance targets

Locally set performance targets in respect of strategic objectives, efficiency, effectiveness, quality and fair access in respect of all key services 'should be underpinned by a minimum requirement for improvement'. Initially, the government will require that as a minimum local authorities set:

*   quality targets over five years that, as a minimum, are consistent with the performance of the top 25 per cent of all authorities at the time the targets are set;

- cost and efficiency targets over five years that, as a minimum, are consistent with the performance of the top 25 per cent of authorities in the region at the time the target are set;
- annual targets that are demonstrably consistent with the five-year targets.

This framework of targets will put most pressure on those authorities who are currently performing poorly on both the quality and the efficiency with which they deliver services. However, it is likely to exert pressure on nearly all authorities because very few authorities score very highly on both aspects of performance at the same time [20].

4. Fundamental performance reviews

Authorities will be required at an early stage to assess their priorities and draw up a programme of fundamental performance reviews of all their services over a five year period, making 'early inroads into areas of significant weakness'. The purpose of the reviews is to ensure that continuous improvements to all services are made. The principal outcome of each review will therefore be performance targets. Key elements are the four Cs – to *challenge, compare, consult* and *compete*. Local authorities will be challenged to find best ways. 'Best Value' opens up the possibility of meeting community needs in entirely new ways. 'New technology or best practice may mean that traditional ways of providing a service are no longer viable or acceptable.' Authorities will be expected to compare their performance with the best using the national performance indicators and any other means which have been developed locally, for example through benchmarking. Local authorities will need to consult with their local communities in carrying out their reviews.

5. Competition

There will be a requirement to use and develop competition as an essential management tool. A number of ways that an authority might meet the test of competitiveness are set out in the White Paper:

- 'commission an independent benchmarking report so that it could restructure the in-house service to match the performance of the best private and public sector providers;
- provide a core service in-house and buy in top-up support from the private sector. This would enable comparisons to be made that could help improve in-house performance or result in more of the service being bought-in externally;
- contract out a service to the private sector after a competition between external bidders only;
- form a joint venture or partnership following a competition for an external partner;
- tender part of a service with an in-house team bidding against private sector and other local authority bidders, before deciding whether to provide the bulk of a service internally or externally;
- dispose or sell-off competitively a service and its assets to another provider.'

6. Audit and inspection

New audit and inspection arrangements with 'a rigorous external check on the information provided' in local performance plans will be needed to ensure best value. The Local Government Association's proposal is to develop a model of self-assessment, based on the business excellence model. (See chapter seventeen on training, Figure 17.1). This, and other quality schemes such as Investors in People, ISO 9000 and the recently re-launched Charter Mark will also have important roles to play in achieving best value.

These then are the principles behind 'Best Value', which had not been started at the time of writing this edition. Time will be needed to tell to what extent the new laws have been successful.

9.11 Modernizing local government

This edition of the book is being published at a time when 'Best Value' is being piloted and local government is being modernized. The Deputy Prime Minister in his foreword and introduction to the White Paper said:

> People need councils which serve them well. Councils need to listen to, lead and build up their local communities. We want to see councils working in partnership with others, making their contribution to the achievement of our aims for improving people's quality of life. To do this councils need to break free from old fashioned practices and attitudes. There is a long and proud tradition of councils serving their communities. But the world and how we live today is very different from when our current systems of local government were established. There is no future in the old model of councils trying to plan and run most services. It does not provide the services which people want, and cannot do so in today's world. Equally, there is no future for councils which are inward looking – more concerned to maintain their structures and protect their vested interests than listening to their local people and leading their communities.
>
> *Modern Local Government – In Touch with the People*
> (July 1998)

Every council will need to respond at local level and embrace the changed agenda. The framework will make it possible to separate the executive from councillors' other roles and to appoint executive mayors, including those directly elected. Universal capping is to be abolished and local financial accountability will be strengthened. Councils will have a duty to promote the economic, social and environmental well-being of their areas. There will be new rules to encourage capital investment. The government intends to set up a scheme of 'beacon councils' as best councils examples. There will be a duty on councils to obtain best value in the delivery of local services linked with a 'rigorous regime of performance indicators and efficiency measures'.

The main points outlined in the White Paper are listed here:

1   Councils should be 'in touch' with the people, provide high quality services and give vision and leadership.
2   The old culture of paternalism and inwardness needs to be abolished.
3   The government will legislate to provide opportunities and incentives for councils to modernize.
4   'Beacon councils' will serve as pace-setters and centres of excellence.
5   Current committee systems are confusing and inefficient, with significant decisions usually taken elsewhere.
6   New models of political management for councils will include
    • a directly elected executive mayor with a cabinet
    • a cabinet with a leader elected by the council
    • a directly elected mayor with a council manager
    • Councils wanting a directly elected mayor will need endorsement through a local referendum.
7   'Crude and universal' council tax capping will be ended: to provide greater stability, the aggregate grant provision for councils for the next three years will be formulated.
8   There will be a new ethical framework – a code of conduct for councils and employees through standards committees.
9   Councils will have a duty to secure best value in the provision of services: the current compulsory competitive tendering (CCT) regime will be abolished and there will be new national performance indicators for efficiency, cost and quality. Some standards and targets will be set nationally, others locally. Fundamental performance reviews of all services will be taken over a five-year period, starting with the worst performing. The reviews will challenge the way a service is being provided; compare the service with others; consult with local taxpayers, users and the business community and 'embrace' fair competition. Councils will prepare annual performance plans and there will be new audit and inspection arrangements.
10 Councils will have a duty to promote the economic, social and environmental well-being of their area. They will work with other public, private and voluntary organizations and with local people. A new legal framework will enable new approaches to public service.
11 New investment will be made available for modernization and there will be incentives for councils to make better use of capital resources; assets (other than council houses) will be abolished.
12 In terms of business rates, within limits, councils will be able to set a supplementary local rate, or to give a rebate on the national business rate.

At the time of writing this edition, 'Best Value' was being piloted in selected local authorities.

9.12 Summary – the public sector and leisure

Successive legislation over the past few years has had (and will continue to have) a dramatic effect on the way local governments manage their affairs and how they provide for leisure and recreation. Capital controls have constrained local government capital and revenue expenditure in tandem with compulsory competitive tendering. The advent of 'Best Value' is unlikely to 'take the brakes off'.

Local government in the past, by its nature of public accountability and bureaucratic systems, has been slow to adapt to new demands. But changes brought about by legislation and new ways of managing have witnessed a 'sea change' in approach and practice for most authorities.

The measures have already changed the face of local government from that of mainly provider, to enabler, partner, and importantly, co-ordinator. Partnerships with the private and voluntary sectors will lead to more facilities for the market targets that can afford to use commercial facilities and the voluntary organizations will be enabled to cater for their activities and be 'masters of their own destiny'. There will still be a great deal for local authorities to do. Their role in planning and providing a range of services and facilities will continue.

Local authorities have considerable permissive powers. They can act independently or in partnership; they can enable, support and encourage self-help and initiative. They equally have the power to help those who are unable to help themselves and to provide various opportunities which would be denied the community without local authority assistance.

One role which local authorities can take upon themselves is that of co-ordination. In all districts there is a range of providers. There is a need for co-ordination, support and enabling functions to be performed to make the best possible use of the immense voluntary, commercial, institutional and governmental services. This should be a key role for local government.

Notes and references

1   Report of the Wolfenden Committee on Sport (1960), *Sport and the Community*, Central Council for Physical Recreation, London.
2   Ministry of Education (1960), *The Youth Service in England and Wales: Report of the Committee November 1958* (Albermarle Report), Cmnd 929, HMSO, London; Department of Education and Science (1969), *Youth and Community Work in the 70s*, HMSO, London.
3   Central Advisory Council for Education (England) (1967), *Children and their Primary Schools. Volume 2, Research and Surveys*, for Department of Education and Science (Plowden Report), HMSO, London.
4   Department of Education and Science (1973), *Circular 5/73: Local Government Reorganization and the Public Library Service*, HMSO, London.
5   Department of Education and Science (1965), *Support for the Arts: The First Steps*, Cmnd 2601, HMSO, London.
6   Lord Redcliffe-Maud (1977), *Local Authority Support for the Arts*, Calouste Gulbenkian Foundation, London. See also Lord Redcliffe-Maud (1976), *Support for the Arts in England and Wales*, Calouste Gulbenkian Foundation, London.
7   Molyneux, D. D. (1968), 'Working for recreation', *Journal of Town Planning Institute, 54*, No. 4, April, 149–56.

8   Ministry of Housing and Local Government (1967), *Management of Local Government. Volume I, Report of the Committee*, and *Volume V, Local Government Administration in England and in Wales*, HMSO, London.

9   Department of Education and Science and Ministry of Housing and Local Government (1964), *Joint Circular 11/64 and 49/64: Provision of Facilities for Sport*, DES, London.

10 Ministry of Housing and Local Government (1966), *Circular 31/66: Public Expenditure: Miscellaneous Schemes*, MHLG, London.

11 Department of Education and Science (1970), *Circular 2/70: The Chance to Share*, DES, London.

12 Lord Redcliffe-Maud (1969), *Report of the Royal Commission on Local Government in England 1966–1969*, HMSO, London.

13 Department of the Environment (1970), *Reform of Local Government in England*, Cmnd 4276, HMSO, London.

14 Department of the Environment (1971), *Local Government in England: Government Proposals for Reorganization*, Cmnd 4584, HMSO, London; Department of the Environment (1971) *Reform of Local Government in Scotland*, Cmnd 4583, HMSO, London; Welsh Office (1971), *The Reform of Local Government in Wales*, HMSO, London.

15 Study Group on Local Authority Management Structures (1972), *The New Local Authorities: Management and Structure* (Bains Report), HMSO, London.

16 See Seeley, I. H. (1978), *London Government Explained*, Macmillan, London.

17 Department of the Environment (1977), *Recreation and Deprivation in Inner Urban Areas*, HMSO, London.

18 Hillman, M. and Whalley, A. (1977), *Fair Play for All. A Study of Access to Sport and Informal Recreation*, Broadsheet No. 571, Political and Economic Planning, London.

19 Filkin, G. (1997), *Best Value for the Public*, a joint project by Municipal Journal, Barony Consulting and SOLACE, MJ, London.

20 Department for the Environment, Transport and the Regions (1998), *Modern Local Government – In Touch with the People*, Cmnd 4014, HMSO, London.

Recommended further reading

Audit Commission (1998), *Better by Far: Preparing for Best Value*, Audit Commission, London.

Chapter ten

Leisure provision in the voluntary sector

In chapter nine we have been concerned with the public sector. We now turn to aspects within the non-public sector, which is large, complex and diversified. It exists in collaboration with the public sector and is often interlocked with it.

This chapter deals with the voluntary sector. First, a brief outline of the range of recreation provision in the voluntary sector is given. Second, voluntary organizations are seen in the context of their historical background. Third, the role of voluntary groups in society is examined. Fourth, the concept of volunteerism is debated, illustrating the differences in structured and unstructured voluntary work. Formal volunteering encouraged by government and its agencies is shown to have both economic and social benefits.

In addition, two types of provider – charitable trusts, and industrial and company recreation clubs – are studied, to understand their function and relevance to the community, but more important, to understand their approach to leisure and recreation management. Company clubs are invariably managed as non profit-making organizations, hence in terms of management they are included here and not with the commercial sector.

Readers will learn that the voluntary sector has a substantial role to play in enabling like-minded people to fashion their own 'destiny', to choose to behave in ways which are worthwhile and satisfying to them; this is one of the hallmarks of leisure. Leisure

Managers will appreciate the value in supporting and enabling voluntary groups to prosper and to relinquish the notion that the job of providers is to provide leisure 'on a plate'. For public sector Leisure Managers, the enabling and co-ordinating roles and links with the national and local agencies become important functions.

10.1 Leisure and recreation in the voluntary sector

The resources, facilities and opportunities offered to people through the vast range of many thousands of voluntary bodies in the United Kingdom represent collectively a significant contribution to the field of recreation and leisure. Voluntary bodies vary greatly, from neighbourhood groups to national organizations. The voluntary sector is dominated by a vast array of leisure and recreation clubs and associations.

Sport is managed, in large measure, by local voluntary sporting clubs and associations, which are the backbone of sport in the United Kingdom. Governing bodies of sport are linked nationally by organizations such as the Central Council for Physical Recreation (CCPR). The role of the Sports Council is to support sport and physical recreation groups at all levels, the vast majority being voluntary amateur groups. Arts, community arts and cultural activities in their variety are largely catered for through local voluntary societies, associations and groups of many kinds. The Regional Arts Boards themselves, while dependent on grant sources, are nevertheless voluntary bodies, supported by the Arts Council.

Informal outdoor recreation is encouraged through organizations such as the National Trust, the Ramblers' Association, and local walking and cycling and other clubs. Tourism is encouraged through voluntary organizations like the Youth Hostels Association.

Social recreation and leisure are catered for by a large number of social, entertainment or multi-activity organizations. Consumer organizations protect interests, including leisure products. Women's Institutes, community associations, religious organizations, youth organizations and hundreds of others all go to make up the array of resources and opportunities for recreation and leisure participation. In nearly all cases, other than the conservation of buildings and lands, all these voluntary organizations are concerned with the interests of their members and users. They help to provide and manage leisure opportunity.

Although not part of the voluntary sector as such, a number of bodies provide for the voluntary sector. Private and institutional bodies, such as landowners, employers, universities, schools, colleges and institutes, make an important contribution to provision and services for recreation. Many firms provide social and sporting facilities. University extramural departments provide adult education classes. Many universities and colleges provide holiday residential courses, partly as a means of keeping residential accommodation and services open throughout the long vacations. The growth of the 'activity holiday' has been rapid in recent years. Private schools, such as Millfield, have become famous for their 'schools of sport'. Private landowners also play a significant part in the provision for informal recreation. They own much of the rural land in the United Kingdom which is the setting for outdoor informal leisure and recreation. They also own and manage facilities for public leisure through historic houses, country parks and many of the great tourist attractions.

In many cases, voluntary bodies are inextricably linked to public providers and public money. Charitable trusts are often partly sponsored by local authorities and, in some cases, wholly subsidized. Advisory and counselling services such as the Citizens Advice Bureaux, while volunteer based, are funded largely by local authorities. Local councils support and initiate many thousands of voluntary groups and projects and, in many cases, fund and staff them. The interdependence between many voluntary bodies and public authorities is part and parcel of the wide framework of public community services, including leisure and recreation.

Some voluntary organizations are also dependent upon commercial bodies. Some 'art' and sporting institutions might perish without the financial backing and marketing skills of major commercial companies. At local level, many clubs rely on the brewer's contribution or the room at the back of the pub.

Further complicating the issue is the problem of demarcation between what is commercial and what is voluntary. Some private institutions and voluntary organizations adopt a style of management which, in certain elements, is wholly commercial. With some private landowners, the earning of income is a major objective and therefore in terms of management they can be considered similar to commercial bodies.

10.2   Voluntary clubs and organizations in historical context in the United Kingdom

Voluntary recreation and leisure groups have existed for centuries but not in the number and variety of recent times. In the eighteenth century the coffee-house was, for the 'gentlemen of leisure', a social group – a club in embryo. Coffee-houses were in theory open to all, but often developed into clubs for specified groups, with restricted membership. Today in the United Kingdom we still find that many private and institutional bodies confine the use of their facilities to certain groups of people.

In early-industrial Britain, recreations were often communal affairs based on seasons, festivals and commemorative events. The sports, dances, processions and ceremonies were within the context of the whole community, as they are in underdeveloped, simple societies today. It was the rationalization of work that led to a separate and identifiable sphere of social life [1]. Simultaneously, the first half of the nineteenth century saw the disappearance of 'old playgrounds' which were not replaced by anything new until the growth of clubs and provision for recreation by voluntary bodies later in the century. Unions, factories and schools established their own football clubs; YMCAs and the Sunday School movement created clubs for recreation.

Most national governing bodies for sport were also formed from the creation of interest groups of like-minded people such as the MCC (Marylebone Cricket Club), the founders of the game of cricket as it is played today. Leisure interest groups like the Royal Horticultural Society date back to 1804 and animal societies, such as the Royal Society for the Protection of Animals, to 1824. The Cyclists' Touring Club was formed in 1878.

Clubs featured in the eighteenth and nineteenth centuries as important organizations in the recreative and social life of the community. The great expansion of clubs took place in the last quarter of the nineteenth century but this was not a long-term trend. Working men's clubs developed through several stages from the last quarter of the nineteenth century. The most significant development was the move towards professionally based entertainment. The switch produced a change in the membership participation from producer to consumer patterns. Despite these changes, activities such as snooker and darts have continued and have increased with television exposure.

Many voluntary movements and associations arose out of the Great Depression as responses to social injustice. For example, the National Association of Women's Clubs arose in that way. Many were post Second World War outlets for wives of the unemployed, and for unemployed women themselves.

Today the voluntary sector national organization groups and clubs are as strong as ever. In 1998 there were 570,000 Scouts and 700,000 Guides, over 250,000 members of the National Federation of Women's Institutes, just over 1 million members of the Royal Society for the Protection of Birds and a huge rise to 2.5 million in membership of the National Trust. Membership of most environmental organizations has dramatically increased in recent years. For example Friends of the Earth's membership grew 65-fold from 1971 to 1988 [2].

Suffice it to say, then, that the voluntary groups have a substantial part in providing opportunities for people's leisure, whether as participants, supporters or service-givers.

10.3 Leisure participation and the role of voluntary groups

People go to extraordinary lengths and exhibit wide variations of behaviour in order to express their individual and collective needs in their leisure. People express themselves in all manner of participation groups, for example there are religious, community and welfare groups, men's, women's, old people's and young people's groups, advisory and counselling groups or para-medical and military groups. Some people join clubs and associations that are culturally uplifting or educational. Some join acting, ballroom, jazz, line dancing, keep-fit, slimming, singing, operatic or pop groups; others play sport in groups, sail the seas with yachting clubs and climb with mountaineering groups. Many groups identify themselves by wearing badges or special clothing; others have a uniform to create a new identity – a leisure identity, or even a way of living identity.

The range of groups is wide and diversified and no adequate classification has yet been made to cover all groups that exist. Several different types of grouping can, however, be identified; some of these are listed in Table 10.1 but the overlaps are many. For example, many uniform groups are youth groups, many women's groups are welfare groups, and so on. The list is by no means an attempt at classification or taxonomy; it is simply a means of showing the range and diversity of voluntary leisure groupings.

TABLE 10.1 Range of voluntary organizations

Community organizations	Community associations, community councils
Community action groups	National Council for Voluntary Organizations, Inner City Unit, Inter-Action Trust Limited, Gingerbread
Children's groups	Pre-School Playgroups Association, Toy Library Association
Youth organizations	Scout Association, Girl Guides' Association, National Council for YMCAs, National Association of Youth Clubs
Women's organizations	National Federation of Women's Institutes, National Union of Townswomen's Guilds, Mother's Union, Women's Voluntary Service (WVS)
Men's groups	Working men's clubs, servicemen's clubs
Old people's groups	Darby and Joan Clubs, Senior Citizens
Disabled groups	Gardens for the Disabled, Disabled Drivers' Motor Club
Adventure organizations	Outward Bound Trust, Duke of Edinburgh's Award, National Caving Association
Outdoor activity organizations and touring groups	Camping Club of Great Britain and Ireland, Youth Hostels Association, Central Council of British Naturism, Ramblers' Association, British Caravanners' Club
Sport and physical recreation organizations	Keep Fit Association, British Octopush Association, National Skating Association of Great Britain, Cycle Speedway Council, GB Wheelchair Basketball League
'Cultural' and entertainment organizations	British Theatre Association, Museums Association, English Folk Dance and Song Society, British Federation of Music Festivals
Educational organizations	National Institute of Adult Education, Workers Educational Association, National Listening Library
Hobbies and interest groups	National Association of Flower Arranging Societies, Citizens Band Association, Antique Collectors Club, Handicrafts Advisory Association for the Disabled, British Beer Mat Collectors' Society
Animals and pet groups	Pony Club, Cats Protection League
Environmental, conservation and heritage groups	National Trust, Friends of the Earth, Royal Society for the Protection of Birds, Keep Britain Tidy Group, Save the Village Pond Campaign, Rare Breed Society
Consumer groups	Consumers' Association, Campaign for Real Ale (CAMRA)
Counselling organizations	British Association for Counselling, Citizens Advice Bureau, Alcoholics Anonymous, Marriage Guidance Councils, Samaritans Incorporated

continued

TABLE 10.1 continued

Philanthropic groups	Rotary International in Great Britain and Ireland, Inner Wheel, Variety Club of Great Britain, Golddiggers
Paramedical organizations	British Red Cross Society, St John Ambulance Brigade
Uniform groups	Voluntary Reserves, Territorial Army, Sea and Army Cadets, Air Training Corps
Religious groups	Methodist Church Division of Social Responsibility, Church Army, Church of England Children's Society
Political groups	Political parties, trade unions

The English Tourist Board [3] identified the membership of 211 national voluntary leisure groups with over 8 million members collectively, of which 29 per cent belong to youth groups, 27 per cent to sports groups, 13 per cent to conservation and heritage groups, 8 per cent to touring groups, 7 per cent to women's groups and 7 per cent to animal or wildlife conservation groups. The National Trust is by far the largest national organization, with a membership rise of over 700 per cent in 20 years. Well over 40 per cent of the groups identified have memberships of over 5000. Over the long term (with exceptions such as some church, cycling, para-medical and women's groups), very few national groups have had a fall in membership.

The Leisure Manager has an important role in helping groups of people to negotiate with public bodies, planners, architects and other organizations. Supporting groups, by helping them to run their own projects, may be more important than providing projects 'on a plate'. With the advent of the National Lottery in the United Kingdom, the National Funding Bodies ensure that voluntary bodies part-fund their own projects; this helps to spread funds more widely and, importantly, encourages self-help and volunteerism.

10.3.1 The role of voluntary groups in society

It is clear from the range and growing variety of leisure groups that such participative behaviour is important to people. What is the role of the voluntary group? Modern life in Western civilization is more complex than life in under-developed societies. Voluntary groups have therefore to play a far greater role in modern society [4]. In simple societies there can be no real voluntary association or club-life, whereas in advanced society there exist numerous small-scale associations catering for varying numbers of individuals. In modern society people can behave both as individuals and collectively within groups. Leisure has importance, in that it has potential for both individual and group expression. Individuals can choose their group identity.

One of the motivations for corporate action in the recreation and leisure field is often that individuals and groups of people find themselves isolated and cut off from opportunity and support. Voluntary groupings are initiated at a grass-roots level. They usually start with people's felt needs, demands, wishes or inclinations. They are voluntary. They might become non-voluntary, according to Tomlinson [5], in either of two ways: by becoming commercialized and turning into entrepreneurial bodies, or by turning inwards and becoming secret societies.

In terms of the management of community recreation, the primary interest groups should feature strongly in any comprehensive community programme. People want to retain their individuality, yet many people too want to belong to groups. The Leisure Manager has the dilemma in planning and programming as to the extent to which provision should be made for group interests. Understanding group belonging and group behaviour will assist the manager in coming to terms with the problem (see Section 12.8 on group behaviour).

At first glance, each club appears to be decidedly different from another. A ladies' darts club meeting in the local pub, for example, might appear very dissimilar to the ladies' choral society meeting in the church hall. Hutson [4] has shown, however, that there are many basic similarities between all forms of clubs and voluntary associations: there are similarities in patterns of activity and the ways in which clubs develop and decline. She has shown how organizers tend to form a distinct, closely connected, elite within a town or region. Social class, life-cycle, physical mobility, kinship and sex roles affect both patterns of attendance and leadership. Voluntary associations tend to reflect 'the economic and social milieu' and tend to be dominated by a group of people of similar type. This leads to a proliferation of many small groups.

Like-minded people tend to gather together and form associations. Recruitment is normally along lines of friendship or kinship. Most clubs are social clubs, whether the primary activity is social or not. People who are felt 'not to belong' to the predominant group are often kept out through formal procedures. In the areas in Swansea studied by Hutson, there were often internal political pressures and several examples of cliques leaving a club as another clique took over. These may be some of the reasons why newcomers, if they are in any numbers, tend to set up their own associations rather than join existing groups. While youth clubs were more socially mixed, and some associations claimed to draw members from all social categories, most clubs did not.

Study of the differences and similarities of clubs and associations reveals four important factors for the Leisure Manager to consider.

1   All the clubs tend to be, at least partially, exclusive. Many clubs, theoretically open to all in principle, have been able to 'guarantee' their exclusiveness with high enrolment fees, membership systems, etc.
2   Clubs are not static, but changing, organizations. The Wolfenden Committee Report (1978) on voluntary associations [6] found that, 'New organizations are formed to meet newly discerned needs, others die. Yet others change their emphasis or venture into fresh fields. . . . There is nothing static about the scene.' The Leisure Manager should bear in mind therefore that new clubs, in particular, are likely to change in membership and will have different leadership patterns within the first few years. Shorter-term initial bookings of facilities and flexible and supporting management roles may need to be given.

3   Clubs display similarities in behaviour: they are social groupings. Sports clubs can be seen, in some sense, as less exclusive than some other clubs, but just like other leisure groupings, sport generates separate groups and activities for different social categories. Managers must not therefore neglect the important social aspects of group leisure participation.

4   Clubs are dependent on support services such as premises. Local authorities, commercial bodies and all the institutions who have premises and administrations can be important enablers in providing support services and premises. The local authority's co-ordinating role plays an important part in this respect.

One of the characteristics of leisure-time participation is that a considerable proportion of people take on new roles i.e. new leisure roles; indeed, they are no longer factory workers, bank clerks or housewives. They become instead leader, coach, club chairperson, golfer, sailor, official, youth worker, lay preacher or sergeant-major. In some cases, the adoption of new identities is intensified by the wearing of a uniform: the uniform is the symbol of the organization; it gives identity, and 'image' – it stands for something, a faith, a belief in what one is doing.

The taking on of new roles in leisure time is an interesting phenomenon and may be significant. There is commitment, purposefulness and responsibility. Are these meaningful roles absent from other aspects of everyday life? What does it tell us about having clearly defined group norms and cultures?

In summary, the voluntary sector is and remains the backbone of leisure and recreation organization and participation. The sector is vast, diversified and linked with the public, institutional and commercial sectors. Voluntary organizations give people both the chance to participate and the opportunity to become involved in all levels of organization and management. They also give the opportunity to serve. In terms of community recreation, in its widest sense, managers must be aware that the voluntary sector, more than other sectors, holds many of the keys to individual self-fulfilment, one of the main goals of effective leisure and recreation management.

10.4 Volunteerism

There has been an increasing interest from sociologists and researchers in leisure, from government and from agencies, such as the Sports Council, Arts Council and Countryside Commission (now the Countryside Agency), in fostering volunteerism.

Is voluntary activity work or is it leisure? Although they like to think they are, volunteers are not always altruistic! Consider volunteers on committees of governing bodies or local government councillors wielding power, or coaches (particularly parents) looking for glory from the achievement of their protégées, and think of the status conferred upon presidents and chairmen and women in clubs and societies.

Volunteering is undertaken with different motives and in pursuit of different purposes. Stanley Parker [7] identifies four types of volunteer, each sharing certain elements with one or more of the others: altruistic volunteering as giving of time and effort unselfishly to help others; market volunteering as giving something 'freely', but expecting (later) something in return; cause-serving volunteering as promoting a cause in which one believes; and leisure volunteering as 'primarily' seeking a leisure experience. 'I say "primarily" because motives are often mixed. Who is to say a particular act of apparently altruistic volunteering does not also provide a leisure experience for the volunteer? Some leisure activities enable people to feel they are doing something worthwhile and serving a cause, while at the same time enjoying themselves.' Motives are seldom pure, as Parker muses: 'Perhaps there is sometimes an element of self-delusion, as when giving something apparently without thought of return, but secretly expecting some quid pro quo.' I am reminded of the adage 'there is no such thing as a free lunch'!

A good deal of volunteering in the leisure field encompasses elements of 'leisure' – doing something we like to do, accomplishing something. In volunteering, we feel we are contributing, for example, in community action, civic responsibility or environmental concern. In the arts and sports, we experience the satisfaction of bringing out the talents of other people, enabling the orchestra or choir to perform at the music festival, to coach the sports team to success. Volunteers tend to give their service in the field of 'organized' leisure, as distinct from 'casual' leisure. Robert Stebbins [8] identifies on-going involvement with a voluntary organization as serious leisure. Others label it as 'formal volunteering' and 'constructive leisure'. Stebbins presents the idea of what he terms 'serious leisure' which acknowledges the presence of a serious orientation to leisure. Since many volunteer roles offer 'special careers and a distinctive set of rewards to the individual', these roles can be viewed as serious leisure, falling between work and casual leisure. With the rise in the number of people out of paid work, volunteering offers benefits such as personal fulfilment, identity enhancement and self-expression.

The work of volunteers in society and citizen participation is undergoing change. Susan Arai [9] believes that empowerment theory can help in understanding this change. She explores the relationship between empowerment, volunteering and serious leisure. She concludes that while volunteering is often in the form of serious leisure, it can have both desirable benefits and undesirable elements such as tensions and power relationships at a personal level and at a community level. Among the benefits volunteers described under the heading of the development of community were opportunities for shared learning, opportunities to contribute to community, development of camaraderie, feeling connected to community, and enhancement of individual knowledge about the community. Thus volunteering is connected not only to psychological empowerment (self-conception, self-efficacy, locus of control), but also to social empowerment (increased access to information, knowledge, skills and resources; increased social connections) and political empowerment (access to decision making processes, power of voice and collective action).

Cnaan, Handy and Wadsworth [10] considered four key dimensions and categories in defining the volunteer (see Table 10.2).

Nigel Jarvis and Lindsay King [11] point to the traditional meaning of volunteering which is composed of three elements: the gift of time; the element of free choice; and the lack of payment. Although this definition is undermined by the spread of paid volunteer schemes in recent years, the core premise remains that volunteering involves spending time, unpaid, doing something which benefits others.

TABLE 10.2 Key dimensions and categories in definitions of the volunteer

Dimensions	Categories
Free choice	1. free will (to choose voluntarily)
	2. relatively uncoerced
	3. obligation to volunteer
Remuneration	1. none at all
	2. none expected
	3. expenses reimbursed
	4. stipend/low pay
Structure	1. formal
	2. informal
Intended beneficiaries	1. benefit/help others/strangers
	2. benefit/help friends or relatives
	3. benefit oneself (as well)

Source: Cnaan, R., Handy, F. and Wadsworth, M. (1996), 'Defining who is a volunteer: conceptual and empirical considerations', *Non-profit and Volunteer Sector Quarterly, 25*, 371

General household surveys have shown that, generally, women are more likely to volunteer than men, yet with more women now in full or part-time work, in addition to looking after homes and families, volunteer commitment may be eroding. Jarvis and King's study of the Guide and Scout Associations in Sheffield reports that there appears to be a general disillusionment among volunteers.

In this regard, the loyalty of leaders is a strength of the Associations, and the degree to which they are involved in 'serious leisure' commitment appears higher than in other voluntary organizations (Stebbins, 1997). However, the fact that a few people do everything has implications for the recruitment and retention of volunteers. Leaders complained there were not enough people to volunteer. Still, those who do may be perpetuating this problem leading to their own disillusionment. Those who might volunteer may be put off by the image that these 'super-humans' project. In some cases, current and potential volunteers believe that an open-ended commitment is expected of them, which clashes with family and job responsibilities.

Most of us have been in the position where we have felt obliged to volunteer; we have not been able or willing to say 'No'. 'Obliged' volunteers can be found in almost all branches of leisure activity and organizations. However, Stebbins [8] warns that too much coercion can at times 'obliterate' for some people the leisure and volunteer components that other people find there.

10.5 The government and volunteersim

Government, increasingly, is recognizing the massive role played by the voluntary sector, particularly in community and 'caring' organizations. The work of volunteers in the leisure sector is also receiving some attention from government, though to not the same extent. The main 'official' help comes via national agencies such as the Arts and Sports Councils and English Heritage. For example, the Department for Culture, Media and Sport (DCMS) administers grants in support of national, generalist voluntary organizations which increase the effectiveness of the United Kingdom voluntary sector by providing services and support to other voluntary organizations, or the voluntary sector as a whole. However, the national scheme does not go as far as it might, and grants are restricted to the 'top' end of the scale, i.e. organizations operating across England, Wales, Northern Ireland and Scotland or any combination of these countries. The object is to promote volunteering, community development and self-help. However, this top-heavy and top-down approach appears to have minimal effect at the local level, where most volunteer community work occurs.

The DCMS is also engaged in encouraging the involvement of young people in volunteering. In its booklet, *Young People Make a Difference* [12], the government's plan of action is set out to provide grants to volunteer bureaux and to local youth volunteer facilitators and funding for the National Volunteering Helpline.

The statutory services rely heavily on volunteers to enhance the work of their paid professionals and national and local voluntary organizations offer opportunities to volunteer in the activities they manage. The business community also recognizes the value of unpaid as well as paid work.

The 1997 National Survey of Volunteering [13] compared volunteering in 1981, 1991 and 1997. Between 1991 and 1997, the number of volunteers decreased, but was still at a higher level than in 1981, but the amount of time given by volunteers 'in formal organizations' increased from 2.7 hours per week in 1991 to 4.05 hours in 1997. Volunteers were critical of the time volunteering took. This factor may be one of the reasons for the substantial decrease in volunteering in the 18–35 age groups, with 18–24 year olds averaging 0.7 hours per week in 1997 from 2.7 hours in 1991.

10.6 Volunteers in sport

There are claimed to be over five million volunteers in United Kingdom sport, providing nearly £6 billion of value to the sector [14]. The English Sports Council in *England, The Sporting Nation: A Strategy* [15] recognizes the contributions made to sport by volunteers. In *Sport, Raising the Game* [16], the Department of National Heritage (DNH), now Department for Culture, Media and Sport (DCMS) stressed how the mobilization of competent volunteers provides scope for enhancing the support given to coaching and sports development.

Volunteers at all levels have been described as 'the backbone' of sport in the United Kingdom and in many parts of the world. The Sports Council defines a volunteer as 'An individual who helps others in sport through formal organizations such as clubs or governing bodies whilst receiving no remuneration except expenses.' 'For every champion, there will be hundreds of unpaid enthusiasts who make that success possible.'

Research undertaken by the Leisure Industries Research Centre (LIRC), *Valuing Volunteers in United Kingdom Sport* [17], commissioned by the Sports Council and sponsored by Barclaycard, revealed a number of findings.

1 In 1995, there were just under 1.5 million volunteers in United Kingdom sport.
2 Volunteers invest on average 125 hours per year or 2.5 hours per week for 48 weeks of the year.
3 This equates to the equivalent of 108,000 full-time workers added to the existing sports labour market. [LIRC made a comparison with the public sector: in 1990, the *Employment Gazette* reported that there were 81,000 full-time and 36,000 part-time local authority employees in Recreation, Parks, and Baths departments in England and Wales.]
4 Volunteers outweigh paid personnel working in the sports market by a factor of three.
5 Sports clubs are the foundation of voluntary effort in the United Kingdom, accounting for 80 per cent of the total estimated sports volunteers in the United Kingdom.
6 The total annual value of the United Kingdom sports volunteer market is estimated at over £1.5 billion.

Volunteers are the lifeblood for the organization and running of minor and major events. For example, the European Swimming Championships held in Sheffield in 1993 involved 700 volunteers working an average of 8 hours a day for up to 17 days – a total commitment of approximately 95,000 hours.

Volunteers also provide essential assistance in schools (particularly primary schools) and youth and community organizations and play an indispensable role in the support of disabled sport. Generally, there is a low ratio of participants to volunteers in disabled sport – typically less than 5:1. Riding for the Disabled is supported by volunteers with an average of one helper for less than two riders. The British Paralympic Association has a high concentration of volunteer support with a small volunteer workforce donating high levels of hourly support.

Volunteers are highly motivated people. They are more likely to be motivated by the benefits accruing to their family, friends or their own needs. The Sports Council/LIRC identified a number of issues.

1 The biggest problem faced by volunteers (cited by 74 per cent) is that there are not enough people to help.
2 The second highest concern was work being increasingly left to other people.
3 Coaching training is needed, with courses viewed as too expensive in terms of cost and travel.
4 Increasing professionalism within clubs places an additional burden on administrators.
5 Legislative changes such as *The Children Act 1989* and Health and Safety

requirements continue to demand stringent standards of procedure and operation. *The Activity Centres (Young Persons Safety) Act 1995* has implications for a number of adventure and outdoor pursuits clubs.

6   Junior development was viewed as a problem area, with transport cited as a key deterrent.

7   Attracting sponsorship and funding is a major task; many clubs require help and advice in making application for Lottery funding.

The key LIRC findings were: volunteers have a key role to play in United Kingdom sport; they need assistance to help motivation, retention and recruitment; and they need ongoing support at local, regional and national levels. Volunteers need opportunities for training and development.

> The most common perception was of a dedicated few doing a large proportion of the work – leading to multiple roles in the club – though the dependency on key individuals was also seen as normal practice within clubs, providing a more effective and stronger nucleus for the club. . . . The widespread feeling is that it is harder to attract volunteers to take on roles in clubs. This had led to problems in recruitment and retention which has deterred others from becoming involved as volunteers.

Nicholas *et al.* [18] comment that pressures on volunteers may leave a hole in the English Sports Council strategy.

> Those who have been most likely to volunteer in the past may be feeling increased pressures from time at work; more two-income families means less time to give to volunteering; the propensity to volunteer may be reduced among young people for whatever reason; (and voluntary coaches were more likely to be younger volunteers); there may be more retired people to volunteer, but have they got the aptitude, empathy and energy to promote opportunities for young people? Even if sufficient volunteers can be found, their contributions need to be co-ordinated in a way that facilitates a young person's progress through the sports development continuum. . . . This important role is made more difficult by the small and fragmented nature of sports clubs in Britain: an officer may set up a good relationship with a club which then collapses within three years or key people leave the committee. The small size of British sports clubs, in contrast to much larger multi-sports clubs on the continent, makes it harder for them to support junior sections.

10.7 Volunteers in the arts

Without volunteers, some of the most beneficial work carried out in leisure and recreation, arts and sports would not be possible. As in sports, volunteers are a substantial support network for active and passive participation in 'cultural' pursuits, such as arts, crafts and heritage. National voluntary organizations, with tens of thousands of members, covering the fields of music, choral, dance, drama and crafts collectively come under the umbrella of the Voluntary Arts Network (VAN), which provides a means of encouraging wider participation, promoting standards and supporting initiatives.

Local libraries use volunteers to deliver library materials to the housebound. Local historians undertake research for local libraries. Hospital and student radio stations operate almost exclusively through volunteers. The Royal Commission on the Historical Monuments of England uses volunteers to help carry out some of the survey work involved in recording the heritage. The Historic Royal Palaces agency uses volunteers on conservation work, and the Royal Parks benefit from the work of community service groups such as the British Trust for Conservation Volunteers. The Museums and Galleries Commission has published *Museums Among Friends* [19] to raise awareness of volunteer groups. Twenty-five thousand volunteers work in museums and art galleries across the country.

English Heritage is increasingly making use of volunteers at its properties and, through its local management initiative, has delegated management of some of its sites to local managers, including volunteer groups, in order to make its sites more relevant to local communities.

10.8 Recreation charitable trusts and non-profit sector

A number of management systems exist in the 'delivery' of leisure services. One system has become known as the 'trust' system. The term usually applies to charities, or more widely to non-profit-making organizations, which can be charitable or not.

The origins of charities go back centuries. The church encouraged people to give money or property to benefit the poor. With the 'nationalization' of church property by Henry VIII, there followed *The Act of Charitable Uses 1601* to protect property given to charity, an Act which still has an influence (though no power) even today. The abuse of charities led eventually to the *Charitable Trusts Act 1853*, which set up the Charity Commissioners. Its work culminated after the Second World War, following the ideas of Lord Beaverbrook and the subsequent Nathan Committee, in the *Charities Act 1960*, which applies to England and Wales and extended Charity Commissioners' powers, including the provision for the registration of charities. The register, which is primarily intended to inform the public about charities, provides conclusive evidence that the registered institution is a charity in law.

The *Charities Act 1960* gave local authorities power to carry out reviews. The 1985 Act places a stricter duty on trustees and enables small charities to be wound up. It is also concerned with the transfer of property to another charity. In 1989, a government White Paper proposed strengthening the Commission's ability to deal with charity abuse and amend the law relating to appeals and collections, among other things. The *Charities Act 1992* increased the powers of the Commissioners to investigate mismanagement.

Before starting down the road to a charity, organizations need to think very carefully about reasons and motives behind the proposal – is it just because it is cheaper, or circumvents legislation or keeps the local authority at bay? These are not good reasons, morally, if not legally. It must be asked, why do we need a charity? Is there a similar charity already doing the job? Are the objectives charitable in law? Are there calibre trustees to carry out the business?

10.8.1 What is charitable and where does recreation fit in?

There is no legal definition of the word 'charity'. Yet, an organization must be considered 'charitable' by law if it is to be registered with the Charity Commissioners. To become a charity, the Charity Commission must be satisfied that the purposes or objects of the organization fall entirely under one or more of the four 'heads of charity'. These are:

1   the relief of poverty
2   the advancement of education
3   the advancement of religion
4   other purposes beneficial to the community.

It is important to emphasize that a purpose cannot be charitable unless it is for the *public* benefit. In the 'other purposes' category, a decision has to be made whether there is a benefit to the community within the spirit and intent of the 1601 Act – an Act long since repealed.

Leisure and recreation, generally, fall into the 'other purposes' category, though some elements, particularly in the arts, can fall into the advancement of education. Sport has difficulties in falling into any category other than 'other purposes'. Even here, the registration of sports groups is problematic, e.g. sport for entertainment is certainly not charitable; it must fall into the 'interests of social welfare'. These aspects are addressed in the *Recreational Charities Act 1958*. Under this Act, it is charitable: 'to provide or help to provide facilities for recreation or other leisure-time occupation', but the facilities must be provided 'in the interests of social welfare'.

It is clear that bodies which exist to promote individual sport or art or for excellence or professionalism, or which exist to only benefit their members, are not charitable. In this context, most clubs are set up to benefit their members and so are not charitable. These are more likely to fall within the non-charitable 'not for profit' group.

There are many advantages in being registered as a charity – social, managerial and financial. However, the law also limits what a charity can do [20]. Let us first consider the advantages in becoming a registered charity and forming a Trust Management System.

1   *Choice of organizational structure* The trust system is flexible. The governing body can be built up on a widely representative basis to include all appropriate authorities, industry, commerce and local community.
2   *Tailor-made governing instrument and constitution* The purpose of the

business can be written to suit its primary aims and objectives within its legal framework.

3   *Management autonomy, independence, influence, control and stability* The organization can be master of its own destiny, rather than have decisions imposed upon it. Being a non-political body, the trust can establish a system of key member stability and can build upon the experience gained over years of development.

4   *Fiscal benefits* Registered charities can take advantage of financial benefits – tax exemptions, covenant opportunities, savings on rates – charities have mandatory relief from 80 per cent of national non-domestic rates – and non profit-making bodies operating sporting facilities are exempt from VAT.

5   *Financial and forward planning* Monies can be borrowed and invested with greater flexibility, provided the governing instrument permits it. Furthermore, trust management encourages good commercial business acumen because it cannot rely on the state.

6   *Fund raising* Charities can plan fund raising to support both capital and revenue. With tax relief on charitable donations, they are able to attract sponsorship. They are looked on favourably by National Lottery funding agencies.

7   *Voluntary endeavour and community commitment* As a voluntary enterprise, it can encourage a strong spirit of community endeavour. Members of trusts feel that they belong and they have to pay for and look after resources. Many paid staff, too, can feel a greater sense of personal commitment. Voluntary endeavour can produce economies in operation. As self-governing projects, trusts encourage leaders in commerce, industry, the professions and the community to want to be associated with them. Charities tend to be single-focus bodies in which people can rally behind a cause.

8   *Low level bureaucracy* There can be direct access by management to executive control, cutting down levels of bureaucracy and streamlining decision making.

9   *Lack of competition* Trust management systems with legal autonomy are not subject to competition faced by local authorities.

10   *Pioneering* Being flexible and free from too many ties with authorities, the system lends itself to experimentation, new ideas and pioneer projects.

While there are advantages in adopting a trust system, the advantages pre-suppose that the organization has the resources, finances and capability for funding and managing capital and revenue budgets in the short and long term. In reality, most trusts experience financial and other problems and the need for partnership with local authorities or others becomes vital. Hence, trusts also carry difficulties and some disadvantages.

1   *Non-charitable activities* Charities cannot undertake certain political, campaigning and pressure group activities. They cannot trade 'permanently' and persons running the organization cannot benefit personally. These non-charitable activities open up a number of grey areas which need careful consideration. An excellent solicitor is essential.

2   *Insufficient capital resources* There are usually insufficient capital resources. Often, many savings have to be made, particularly in ancillary accommodation. Successful Lottery bids have improved the situation, but there has been a need in most cases to raise substantial sums of money, thereby limiting applications from many worthy causes.

3   *Insufficient operational resources* Often, there are insufficient operational resources. A voluntary body can be at the mercy of local councils, needing to approach them 'cap in hand' for assistance every year.

4   *Constant fund raising* Trusts constantly need to raise money and some are having to sell/lease land to help fund projects.

5   *Staff over-commitment* Often, there are either too few staff or low paid staff, many giving service beyond the 'call of duty'.

6   *Public misconception* The public have expectations of good recreation facilities. People may not know, or even care, that a theatre or sports centre is being run by a trust. To the public, it is a public facility.

7   *Ultimate heavy trustee commitment* Trustees – all involved in the management committees – carry a heavy burden of responsibility. Key 'players' are usually busy people, already engaged in many causes in the community.

10.8.2 Different types of legal structure

The term 'trust management' is used here as a system of the control and management by a registered charity for the purposes of community welfare, as distinct from the management of facilities by a local authority, commercial organization or institution. However, in charity legal documents, the word 'trusts' carries a more specific understanding. The most common types of legal structure include the following:

Type of organization	*Governing instrument*
• Trusts	• Trust, deed or will
• Unincorporated associations	• Constitution or rules
• Incorporated organizations – companies	• Memorandum and articles of association
• Non-charitable industrial and provident society	• Registered rules approved by registrar
• Charitable industrial and provident society	• Registered rules approved by registrar
• Royal Charters	• Charter

These types of organization are described briefly.

1. Declaration of trust

Charities can be created by a 'declaration of trust'. Property can be given for charitable purposes by trust deed or by will. The trust document should set out the purposes of the trust and include provisions for managing it, including a power to vary any of the administrative provisions. However, trustees' liability is not limited.

2. Unincorporated associations

There are many kinds of unincorporated organization, including associations, friendly societies and trusts. These are free of the statutory controls to which companies are subject, and, therefore, can be less expensive to run. The group adopts a constitution or rules which sets out, for example:

- the purposes or objects of the association and how it is to be managed;
- the constitution of the committee of management;
- the rules for governing the membership;
- for what other charitable purposes the assets should be used if the association is wound up;
- rules for altering the constitution.

Many charities are established as unincorporated trusts or associations. Their main disadvantage is that their trustees have unlimited personal liability. Therefore, in terms of running leisure and recreation services and facilities for the benefit of the community at large, being an incorporated organization would appear to be essential.

3. Incorporated organizations – companies

A legal difference between unincorporated and incorporated organizations is that an incorporated organization has a corporate legal existence independent of the individuals that are its members. It acts through its members, but has rights and duties in its own right.

Charities may be incorporated under the *Companies Act 1985* as companies limited by guarantee without a share capital. There are two main forms of limited company. The most usual in the field of commercial activity is the company limited by shares. This is an unsuitable format for a charity 'for social welfare' to adopt. The appropriate form is a company limited by guarantee. In a limited company, there are no shareholders, but the members agree to guarantee to pay any debts of the company, up to a limit of normally £1 each. These members elect the directors to run the company. Company governing instruments consist of:

- a memorandum of association; and
- articles of association.

The directors of a corporate charity are in broadly the same position as the trustees of a charitable trust in that both act as trustees of the charity. Directors of charitable companies are, therefore, subject to the provisions of the Companies Acts and also to the laws controlling trustees.

4. Industrial and provident society

An industrial and provident society, through the Registrar of Friendly Societies, is an accepted method of creating a new charity. It is currently an 'exempt' charity, by the Charity Commissioners, as are companies.

Non-charitable industrial and provident societies are being used in the creation of new housing associations and have been used for an employee-controlled transfer of leisure facilities from local authorities, for example, in Greenwich and in Bristol. The business world, however, is more familiar with companies limited by guarantee, than with exempt charities.

Under the *Industrial and Provident Societies Act 1965*, societies can be registered with the Registry of Friendly Societies. A society qualifies for registration under the Act if:

a. it is a society for carrying on an industry, business or trade; and
b. it satisfies the Registrar that either:
    *   it is a *bona fide* co-operative society; or
    *   in view of the fact that its business is being or is intended to be conducted for the benefit of the community, there are special reasons why it should be registered under the Act rather than a company under the Companies Act.

There is no statutory definition of a bona fide co-operative society, but such a society will normally be expected to satisfy conditions relating to: the business of the society conducted for the mutual benefit of its members; control of the society vested in the members equally; and matters relating to shares, profits and non-restriction of membership. To qualify for registration, otherwise than as a *bona fide* co-operative society, a society must satisfy two principal conditions:

a. that its business will be conducted for the benefit of the community; and
b. that there are special reasons why it should be registered under the Act rather than as a company under the Companies Act.

A society claiming that it will be conducted for the benefit of the community must be able to show, amongst other things, that it will benefit persons other than its own members and that its business will be in the interests of the community. Every society seeking registration under the Act, unless the society consists of two or more registered societies, must have at least seven members.

5. Royal Charters

Royal Charters, considered by the Privy Council, are only granted to large 'significant' bodies such as Sports Councils and Arts Councils. A Charter, however, does not confer charitable status. The English Sports Council is not charitable; it has a separate charitable trust established by means of a Company Limited by Guarantee.

10.8.3 Financial benefits to registered charities

Charities can benefit in the context of their own tax and in the tax paid by their supporters. Subject to certain qualifications, charities are entitled to relief from: income tax; corporation tax; and capital gains tax. A charity is exempt from tax on monies used only for charitable purposes and have actually been spent or saved up for such purposes, including: rents from land and property; interest and dividends; covenanted donations; and single gifts by companies paid after tax has been deducted. In addition:

1   payroll giving schemes are not counted as taxable income;
2   stamp duty is not normally payable in respect of gifts to, and purchases of, property;
3   inheritance tax is not payable if the gain accruing is applied for charitable purposes;
4   development land tax no longer applies to charities;
5   national insurance surcharge: charities are exempt;
6   borrowing money: borrowings automatically qualify as charitable expenditure when they are actually spent for charitable purposes;
7   trading assets: if a trade is charitable, the expenditure qualifies for exemption.

Four main financial attractions are rate relief, non-taxable trading profits, reclaiming tax from covenanted donations and subscriptions and some VAT exemptions.

- *Rate relief* – charities are entitled to receive mandatory relief of 80 per cent of the rates on premises occupied by them and used wholly or mainly for charitable purposes. The rating authorities, in addition, have the discretion to allow relief on such part of the remaining 20 per cent as they think fit under Sections 43 and 45 of the *Local Government Finance Act 1988*.
- *Trading profits* – profits are exempt from tax so long as the trade carries out a primary purpose of the charity or the work is done by beneficiaries of the charity.
- *VAT* – charities, generally, are liable to VAT, although there are a number of specific reliefs by way of zero rating or exemption. In addition, there are two areas where the transfer of local authority activities to a not-for-profit body has positive VAT advantages.

There are some supplies on which VAT must not be charged. A list of such 'exempt supplies' is set out in Schedule 9 of the *Value Added Tax Act 1994*. That list includes 'the supply by a non profit-making body to an individual of services closely linked with and essential to sport or physical education'. A charity, as a 'non profit-making body', making an exempt supply to its customers, e.g. at a sports centre, *must not* charge VAT. In contrast, a local authority is not covered by the exemption and, therefore, a local authority which operates a sports centre, *is obliged* to charge VAT to its customers.

Charities which run sports centres have to charge VAT for catering, bar and social functions, but do not charge VAT in respect of entrance fees to a sports hall, swimming pool or squash court, whereas a local authority would. One consequence of being exempt is that input tax on major expenses such as refurbishment, building costs or replacement of equipment, will not be recoverable, so each case would have to be considered on its own merits.

In the public sector, VAT exemption may also apply for admission to museums, art galleries or theatrical and musical performances, provided there is no 'distortion of competition to place commercial enterprises at a disadvantage'. There is no such proviso for not-for-profit bodies or those managed on a voluntary basis by persons having no direct or indirect financial interest.

Trading, charging and making profits are increasingly having to be debated in light of charitable status. A charity can charge reasonable prices, but they should not be so high that the charity endangers its status by ceasing to benefit a sufficient section of the public. A local charity, like a recreation trust, will find that even though there may be an apparent profit, it is not making a true net profit. If a true profit were to be made, doubt may be cast upon the 'public benefit' of what the charity is doing. The Inland Revenue might interpret it as a trading profit, on which corporation tax should be levied.

Trade as such is not a charitable object. However, increasingly, charities need to trade in order to provide the funds for the charity to do its work. Some trade, therefore, is allowable by charity law, and exempt under tax law. One is where the trade is a direct and necessary implementation of the very object of the charity – this applies in part to community leisure and recreation projects. However, many recreation trusts run their facilities in such a way that it is difficult to distinguish them from other businesses. This throws into question whether their activities can be construed as exclusively charitable purposes in law. One potential way out of this dilemma is to set up a separate trading company – usually a company with limited liability. This new company, not subject to the laws of charity, is free to trade like any commercial company. The trading company can covenant its profits to the charity. No corporation tax will be paid if all the profits are passed to the charity. If the trading company retains some of the profit, it will be subject to corporation tax.

Trading through a separate limited company in this way has the advantage that it will insulate the funds of the charity against the risks of something going wrong with the trade. It is important that the activities of the two companies are kept separate otherwise the charitable status of the charity could be put into jeopardy. As the two organizations may well share premises and facilities, rents and wages and other costs involved, these should be fairly divided between the charity and the trading company. In this way, no hidden subsidy of the trading company takes place at the expense of the charity. It will be a breach of its constitution for its funds to be used to subsidize the trading company.

10.9 The role of local authorities

Local authorities may be involved in the work of charities in a number of ways: trusteeship; land and property; rates; grants; fund raising; and changes to charities.

In some cases, local authorities can be trustees – as holders of property for the benefit of the people it is to serve. In some cases, the governing instrument of a charity may give a local authority power to appoint or nominate some, or indeed most, of the trustees of the charity.

A good deal of land for recreation is owned by charities. In some cases, such as rural parishes, the property can be transferred to the parish or community council or an alternative group, provided the Charity Commissioners and councils consent. Where a local authority has given money, goods or services to, say, a charitable recreation ground, the authority has power to make bye-laws for the land.

The permission of a local authority may be needed for fund raising. A good deal of legislation, strengthened by the *Charities Act 1992*, exists concerning a wide number of activities carried out by charities such as: house-to-house collections; street collections; competitions; and gaming and lotteries, including bingo, tombola and 'race nights'. A licence is needed, not just for house collections, but to go collecting in pubs, factories and offices and to sell things on behalf of a charity. Most local authorities also have regulations for street selling on behalf of charity.

Setting political differences aside, what is clear and what is most helpful to management of leisure and recreation is that it is possible for charities and local authorities to work together. Both have legal powers to co-ordinate their activities in the interests of the people who benefit from their services. Hence, there are benefits to both charity and local authority. For the local authority, there can be: direct and indirect cost savings; less use of central resources; enterprise to involve new capable people with fresh ideas for provision and funding; and opportunity to promote a successful recreation facility and safeguard community provision.

10.9.1 Management options

In addition to direct council management, there are a number of options by which local public leisure services and facilities can be owned and managed. They include:

- joint provision, e.g. between tiers of authority
- dual use, e.g. sports hall at a school managed by a local council
- local authority participation in companies
- facilities management contract
- management/employee buy-out/buy-in
- sale
- sale/joint venture
- independent NPDO (non profit distributing organization) with local authority involvement
- independent NPDO without local authority involvement
- private sector NPDO.

10.9.2 Local authorities, trusts and companies

It is possible for a council to form a joint-venture company with a private sector partner. The partner would provide leisure management expertise, capital investment and (potentially) operating economies through access to bulk-purchase contracts. However, the *Local Government and Housing Act 1989* and the Local Authorities' Interests in Companies Order 1995, and Amendment Order 1996 create a regulatory code setting out the legal consequences and implications of local authority participation in companies. The rules are extremely complex: for example, councils cannot participate at a higher level than 20 per cent of its financing powers.

Forming a trust involving local authorities is now limited by regulations relating to companies 'influenced by' local authorities. The Department of the Environment Consultation Paper *Local Authorities' Interests in Companies* and the *Local Government and Housing Act 1989* provide a statutory framework to govern local authorities' interest in companies. The government considered that it was an anomaly that local authorities had influence or control of companies outside the rules governing the conduct of local authority business. Three types of company were identified.

1   *Local authority controlled companies* These form part of the public sector and their expenditure must, therefore, be treated, for the purposes of controlling public expenditure, as part of the public sector.
2   *Arms' length companies* These companies
    a.   have directors whose status protects them from undue influence
    b.   the relationship between the authority and company is clearly regulated to avoid deficit funding and
    c.   the company is in competition with a market.
         Such companies do not need to conform to many local authority regulations, e.g. CCT, access to information.
3   *Local authority influenced companies* Action was deemed to be necessary to control companies over which a local authority has a dominant influence, either in 'personnel relationships' or 'financial relationships'. As an example, a recreation trust came within the Act as being influenced because more than 20 per cent of the members of the board were associated with the council and the grants made by the council exceed half of the company's net assets.

Several 'creative' ways have been fashioned to overcome similar difficulties, such as a leisure trust, with two companies – an investment company and a management company (operational) and from these formed also a limited partnership to carry on the commercial business. All three businesses covenant any net profits to the leisure trust.

In summary, in setting up a charitable recreation trust, key aspects have to be considered and satisfied.

1   The Charity Commissioners have to be convinced of the need for and the *bona fides* of the organization and its 'governing document'.

2   The Inland Revenue needs to be persuaded that tax exemptions are justified.
3   The Acts governing companies need to be adhered to.
4   The Acts governing local authorities and their influence on companies need to be satisfied to show that no undue subsidies or benefits accrue to companies.

10.10 Industrial and company recreation provision

Industrial and company recreation, by and large, is the provision of private facilities, ostensibly not provided for commercial gain, but for the workforce as private individuals. It is conceded at the outset that a happy workforce may achieve greater efficiency and output and thereby greater profits, but in terms of management, industrial provision is more akin to the private members' club than to the commercial enterprise.

The development of the industrial sports and social club in the latter part of the nineteenth century has often been attributed to the philanthropic motives of benevolent and paternalistic employers, influenced by religious and humanitarian ideals. However, underlying this, more practically orientated motives may have been at work, and certainly the development of industrial recreation into the twentieth century is unlikely to be attributable solely to the altruistic behaviour of the employer.

A number of factors have been put forward as being influential in or motivating the decision by an employer to contribute large capital and recurrent expenditure towards the provision, maintenance and management of facilities for the recreational benefit of the employees. Six influencing factors can be identified:

1   philanthropy
2   fitness for work
3   reduction in staff turnover
4   company image
5   company prestige
6   employee pressure.

The provision of company services and facilities is likely to have been influenced by a combination of these and other specific factors, not all of which will have been relevant at any one time.

10.10.1 Historical perspective

Whatever the motivation, the beginnings of industrial recreation provision in the United Kingdom started in the nineteenth century, probably with the founding of Pilkington's Recreation Club in 1847. The growth of company clubs in the latter part of the nineteenth and the early part of the twentieth centuries was evident with the early days being dominated by such pioneers as Pilkington, Cadbury and Rowntree. The government-initiated Clarendon Report, going back to 1864, extolled the virtues of sport participation as a means of developing comradeship, team spirit and loyalty to an organization.

Following the First World War, many industrial clubs sprang up, often associated with religious and welfare organizations. However, the Great Depression caused a decline in the number of clubs owing to the closure of companies and impetus was only once again regained after the Second World War. In general terms, there was a boom in industrial recreation provision in the 1950s, when profits were high and a spirit of altruism led to a spate of companies 'investing' in sports and social clubs. In the 1960s responsibility for the organization and management of many of these clubs changed from employer to employee, under the guidance of a sports and social secretary and/or committee structures. Finance remained a joint effort with the employers often providing for capital expenditure and/or an annual block grant. The employees contributed by membership subscriptions, lotteries, and bar and vending profits.

Cullen [21], and Parker [22], reported a decline in the movement in the 1960s with some of the smaller companies being unable to sustain an acceptable level of interest among their employees, and consequently selling or using the facility's land for building development, and this is still partly the case. But the picture is a far from clear one. Cullen's 1979–80 industrial recreation survey [23] revealed that twice as many clubs were formed in the 1970s as disbanded, and these new clubs were 'by no means' connected solely with large companies (more than 1000 employees); few companies had disposed of recreation sites, and relatively few clubs reported a decrease in interest. In Cullen's survey practically all respondents either wholly or partly agreed with the statement:

> Almost irrespective of the level of employee interest in company sports and social clubs, these clubs and their facilities are now looked upon by company employees as a normal 'fringe/welfare benefit' – a sort of background benefit which is always available to the employee, whether or not he or she actively uses the club and its facilities.

Nevertheless, changes in the British economy, allied to changes in employee recreation and where they reside in relation to the sports grounds, has led to the closure of many sports and social clubs. For example, with the advent of Saturday closure of the banks and the escalating house prices in the suburbs and in the areas where many of the sports clubs are located, the demand by employees to use the sports facilities provided by the banks has declined. This has been due largely to the increased travelling inconvenience and the cost involved. The declining number of participating members has coincided with the increasing cost of maintaining the grounds and the indoor facilities.

It is difficult to make an accurate estimate of the number of industrial sports and social clubs in the United Kingdom, let alone guess the numbers in Europe and elsewhere. In addition, the types of clubs vary enormously from industrial 'giants' to small local manufacturers; the programmes vary from a few activity sections to as many as thirty in a club and there are considerable differences in funding. The type and size of the company appear to have a bearing on provision; for example, with its greater financial and physical resources, a firm with two thousand or more employees can offer a wider range of activities and opportunities one of the largest in the United Kingdom, the Shell Lensbury Club, is such an example.

10.10.2 *Industrial clubs and community recreation*

The goals of industrial clubs may vary, but in general clubs appear to aim at providing recreation opportunities for their company workforce. It is strange therefore, bearing in mind the preponderance of working-class employees in manufacturing industries, that some of the finest facilities and programmes are clearly directed towards 'middle-class' tastes, and that while more working-class people join company clubs than other clubs, nevertheless, professional and semi-professional employees predominate [24]. It would also appear that, in general, the majority of industrial workers do not participate in company-organized sport or recreation, and often less than 10 per cent of employees use company facilities [25]. This raises the contentious issue of under-use of industrial recreation facilities, and the possibility of shared use with the community in order to maximize facility potential.

A Regional Sports Council Survey [26] identified a willingness among the majority of industrial firms to make their sports facilities available to outsiders, but because the majority of sports facilities are maintained with the help of weekly contributions from employees, they were jealously guarded by the company club members themselves. Many club members are reluctant to share.

The practical problems of preservation of standards, employee safeguards, cost of additional use, bar and excise licences, security, staffing costs and legal and insurance problems are also put forward as reasons against involvement with the community, as is the problem of community clashing with company use, particularly in those industries where shiftwork is prevalent.

Another, perhaps major, but underestimated reason for 'keeping themselves to themselves' may be that the industrial sector provision offers recreational experiences which are different in kind from those offered in the public sector – 'identification', 'small units', 'belonging', 'minority groups' (e.g. 'aero modelling catered for') and 'getting together with work colleagues' [23].

Most companies with their own leisure facilities provide access of some kind to individuals and groups other than their own employees, but this is usually carefully limited. Families, retired employees, members' guests and associate members are the main beneficiaries and large companies make available high-standard facilities for county matches, national sports coaching, sports festivals, and the like. The Bank of England Sports Club at Roehampton is a prime example, providing for the pre-Wimbledon Qualifying Tournament and training for the England Rugby Union Squad, and others. Shared use, however, is quite another matter and is the exception rather than the rule.

Managers or sports and social secretaries of the larger clubs have wider responsibilities than the counterparts of earlier years. As well as a knowledge of management techniques, licensing laws and financial control, the industrial Leisure Manager should also be providing a programme relevant to the needs of the company's workforce. The extent to which the manager simply performs a care-taker role, letting out the facilities to worker-organized clubs, or the extent to which he or she performs the role of enabler, actively promoting and encouraging participation through coaching schemes, special events and leagues, and for the unattached as well as the club user, is not clear and, again, is likely to differ from organization to organization. With exceptions, however, most programmes revolve around the traditional games and social activities.

10.10.3 Employee health and fitness

In recent years, the concept of 'corporate fitness' has slowly been gaining momentum in the United Kingdom as statistics become more widely publicized regarding the poor health of British workers and executives. For example, the World Health Organisation shows British workers at the top of the table when it comes to heart disease and lung cancer. British industry loses over 27 million days per annum due to heart-related problems and a further 13 million days per annum are lost due to back-related problems.

A significant number of large corporations in the United Kingdom, including BP, Shell, Nortel, SmithKline Beecham, Marks & Spencer, British Airways, British Telecom and most of the major banks offer employees extensive and often luxuri-ous sports and social facilities in recognition of the considerable mutual benefits of corporate fitness to the employer and the employee. The Burton Group has established its own 'staff only' fitness club and many other city firms in London and elsewhere include corporate health club memberships within their remuneration packages. Exclusive London sports clubs, such as Cannons, Lambs and Cottons, have a very high proportion of corporate memberships.

10.10.4 Joint provision involving industry

Industry is involved in sport and recreation in a number of ways other than making provision solely for its own workforce. Essentially this involvement can be split up into two areas: promotion and sponsorship, and joint provision. Joint provision of recreation facilities by industry and local authorities for use by both employees and the community was advocated by B. Seebohm Rowntree, in 1921, when in *The Human Factor in Business* he wrote:

> That adequate opportunity for wholesome recreation is desirable for all workers, especially in view of the shortening of the working week will not be disputed. The question is whether an employer has any responsibility in connection with the matter. I think the right answer is that if many of his workers live near the factory he should satisfy himself that adequate recreational facilities exist for them. He may do this in two ways: either he may provide adequate recreational facilities for his own employees only, or, by his influence and possibly also his financial help, he may assist communal effort to provide such facilities for the community as a whole. Strong

arguments can be brought forward in favour of either course. In the case of a town where voluntary committees or local councils are seeking to provide playing fields, clubs and similar amenities for the general public, it is certainly a disadvantage if large employers refuse to co-operate in the public effort because they are concerned merely with their own employees.

This view was endorsed in *The Pilkington Report* [27]:

the Study Group was firmly of the opinion that, in the logical development of sociological planning following all the improvements in the overall standard of living, it is no longer the function of private or public industry to provide recreational facilities for the exclusive use of their own work people but that they might well combine their resources with those of the local authorities in order to provide facilities which could be used and enjoyed by all.

There have been a few successful collaborative projects – though too few to mention. One is left to ponder whether companies could apply the same drive and imagination in discharging responsibilities to employees and the community, as they do in meeting responsibilities to shareholders. If so, there could be a brighter future, but all the signs show a move away from the traditional company sports and social provision and use by their premises by outside players and teams.

10.10.5 Industrial sports and social club of the 1990s

Philanthropy, a major early influence on the development of individual sports and social clubs, is no longer a common motive for provision of employee facilities. Fitness for work is increasingly perceived as the major justification. Economic realism has become the hallmark of the 1980s and 1990s. Corporate fitness concepts are slowly infiltrating into the boardrooms of the larger British companies from the United States and Japan. The arguments for corporate fitness are strong; the economic benefits can be substantial and company image and prestige can be enhanced at no real cost.

Large companies with or without established 'traditional" sports and social clubs, which tend to be centred on extensive bars and playing pitches, are increasingly looking to the health and fitness type of facilities. Some are providing their own facilities. Still more are arranging for corporate memberships of commercial clubs. Yet the corporate fitness market remains small relative to American and Japanese experiences.

The traditional sports and social clubs are, in many cases, going through a transitional stage. The days of liberal financial support from their sponsoring companies are over for many and clubs are increasingly being required to adopt more commercial approaches to management. Common trends include greater use of volunteer staff, higher subscription and activity participation charges, more and better quality catering, more hires to outside organizations and a broadening of associate membership qualifications, section membership rules and guest allowances to increase revenue and reduce costs. A few have opened their entire facilities to their local communities, while large numbers have begun to permit a proportion of community memberships within certain activity sections. Others now hire pitches and changing rooms to local clubs who are dissatisfied with local authority provision.

Many of these measures are becoming necessary not just through reductions in company support, but also due to the influence of some of the general trends in leisure. Drink–drive legislation and the trend, particularly in the south-east, for more people to live some distance from their workplace, has exacerbated these trends.

People's tastes are changing – more sophisticated leisure experiences are now in demand, boosted by television advertising and the fashion industry. The commercial leisure industry is growing and filling gaps in the market. Just as many of Britain's manufacturing industries have declined, industrial sports and social clubs in the traditional sense belong to a fast-fading age. In general terms, many of the more traditional clubs are only used regularly by the older or retired employees for whom the style of facilities remains appropriate and attractive. The younger, more affluent and mobile employees have tended to forsake the sports and social clubs for alternative, more dynamic venues such as the nightclubs, the wine bars, the private health or sports clubs and the restaurants. Clearly, sports and social club committees and their sponsoring companies need to be addressing these trends and defining the future role and nature of recreation facilities for their employees and memberships.

10.11 Summary – the voluntary sector and leisure

The voluntary sector is extremely large and diversified and is linked with the public, institutional and commercial sectors. It is dominated by clubs, societies and associations. As a result of the sheer volume of organizations and numbers of people, there are more people involved in the 'management' of leisure and recreation in the voluntary sector than in the other sectors. Voluntary organizations give people both the chance to participate and the opportunity to become involved in all levels of organization and management. They also give the opportunity to serve. The range and diversity of voluntary leisure groupings, the motivations of people and the apparent need to belong and to participate with others, are significant factors and as such should be studied by leisure professionals. Clubs offer individuals a group identity. Inter-club competition and rivalries reinforce the identity and sense of belonging. Membership can confer status, and offer purposeful activity and a sense of importance.

Voluntary organizations hold one of the keys to personal self-fulfilment; leisure and recreation professionals need to harness their assets and public authorities should enable and encourage their development.

Not-for-profit organizations linked to local authorities have been a feature of recent years. A charitable trust has considerable advantages. It can forge ahead through its own enthusiasm and initiative. It encourages community and commercial support and can save public money. But it needs support from authorities in the way of subsidy, grants, technical advice and help towards capital development costs. The days of community service having to beg for financial assistance should end and can do so if local authorities and voluntary organizations collaborate. The trust system can be the bridge between voluntary bodies and statutory authorities; it represents partnership. There are precious little land, money or resources available for organizations and authorities to continue to pay and develop facilities themselves without the widest consultation, co-operation and co-ordination. Projects are often well managed where authority lies in a small, strong, high calibre, independent committee, with wide terms of reference and complete control of day-to-day management. This may be easier to achieve in a recreation trust. However, it is important that the committee is independent, has strong powers and is not constantly blown off course by undue political pressure.

Industrial companies provide a large share of the nation's sport facilities. They offer considerable perks to employees and their families and contribute to company cohesion. If these facilities could be more widely available, they would contribute greatly to community recreation. Companies possessing good sports facilities with spare capacity have a ready-made opportunity to demonstrate their goodwill. There are some examples of dual use and extension of club membership to the general community. However, these remain exceptions.

Leisure management has an important part to play in the network of voluntary bodies and agencies; the Leisure Manager is part of a multi-disciplinary framework for leisure planning and management. The growth area for the profession in the new millennium could be the management of voluntary leisure and recreation resources.

Notes and references

1   Thompson, E. P. (1967), quoted in Tomlinson, A. *Sports Council/Social Science Research Council Review: Leisure and the Role of Clubs and Voluntary Groups*, Sports Council/SSRC, London, 1979.
2   Central Statistical Office (1990), *Social Trends 20*, HMSO, London.
3   English Tourist Board (1981), *Aspects of Leisure and Holiday Tourism*, ETB, London.
4   Hutson, S. (n.d.), *Sports Council, Social Science Research Council: A Review of the Role of Clubs and Voluntary Associations based on a Study of Two Areas in Swansea*, Sports Council/SSRC, London.
5   Tomlinson, A. (1979), *Sports Council/Social Science Research Council Review: Leisure and the Role of Clubs and Voluntary Groups*, Sports Council/SSRC, London.
6   Wolfenden Committee (1978), *The Future of Voluntary Organizations*, Croom Helm, London.
7   Parker, S. (1997), 'Volunteering – altruism, markets, causes and leisure', *World Leisure and Recreation, 39* (3), 4–5.
8   Stebbins, R. (1996), 'Volunteering: a serious leisure perspective', *Non-Profit and Voluntary Sector Quarterly, 25* (2), 211–24.
9   Arai, S. (1997), 'Volunteers within a changing society: the use of empowerment theory in understanding serious leisure', *World Leisure and Recreation, 39* (3), 19–22.

10   Cnaan, R., Handy, F. and Wadsworth, M. (1996) 'Defining who is a volunteer: conceptual and empirical considerations', *Non-profit and Volunteer Sector Quarterly, 25*, 364–83.

11   Jarvis, N., and King, L. (1997), Volunteers in Uniformed Youth Organizations, *World Leisure and Recreation, 39* (3), 6–10.

12   Department of National Heritage (1997), *Young People Make a Difference*, Department of National Heritage, London.

13   Davis Smith, J. (1998), *The 1997 National Survey of Volunteering*, National Centre for Volunteering, London.

14   Gratton, C. and Kokolakakis, T. (1997), 'Show of hands', *Leisure Management*, October, supplement, p. 11.

15   English Sports Council (1997), *England, the Sporting Nation: A Strategy*, English Sports Council, London.

16   Department of National Heritage (1995), *Sport, Raising the Game*, Department of National Heritage, London.

17   Gratton, C., Nichols, G., Shiblis, R. and Taylor, P. (1997), *Valuing Volunteers in UK Sport*, Sports Council, London.

18   Nichols, G., Taylor, P., Shiblis, R., and Gratton, C. (1998) 'Can the Sports Council rely on volunteers?', *Recreation*, June, 14–16.

19   Heaton, D. (1991), *Museums Among Friends*, Museums and Galleries Commission, London.

20   Read, for example: Charity Commissioners for England and Wales (1997), *A Guide to the Charities Acts 1992 and 1993*, Charities Commission, London; Lawrence Graham, (undated), *Charitable Trusts for Local Authorities*, (3rd edition) Lawrence Graham, London; Sports Council, National Playing Fields Association, Central Council for Physical Recreation (1993), *Sport and Charitable Status*, Sports Council, London; Evers, S. (1992), *Managing a Voluntary Organization – Guidelines for Trustees and Committees*, Burston Distribution Services, Bristol.

21   Cullen, P. (1966–7), 'Whither industrial recreation now?' *Sport and Recreation, 7* and *8*, Central Council of Physical Recreation, London.

22   Parker, S. (1971), *The Future of Work and Leisure*, MacGibbon and Kee, London.

23   Cullen, P. (1979–80) Industrial recreation survey, unpublished data and notes on findings.

24   Ministry of Housing and Local Government Urban Planning Directorate (1967), *Provision of Playing Pitches in New Towns*, Ministry of Housing and Local Government, London.

25   Sillitoe, K. K. (1969), *Government Social Survey. Planning for Leisure*, HMSO, London.

26   Greater London and South East Council for Sport and Recreation (1971), *Industry and Community Recreation: Report of a Working Party*, GL and SESR, London.

27   Sports Council Study Group (1968), *The Pilkington Report*, Sports Council, London.

Chapter eleven

Leisure provision in the commercial sector

In chapters nine and ten we have focussed attention on the public and voluntary providers, and it was shown that there is a level of integration and overlap between them. This chapter is concerned with the commercial sector. This chapter needs to be read in conjunction with chapter six, 'trends in the leisure industry', particularly because many trends over recent years have taken place in the commercial sector.

The major difference between a commercial organization and a public or voluntary organization is that the primary objective of the commercial operator is financial profit or an adequate return on investment. The other sectors may also make profits, but they are established primarily for other reasons.

This chapter first provides an overview of the commercial leisure sector. Each of the main constituent elements making up the 'commercial package' is described, relating to the home, and then in large measure to activities away from home:

- pubs and eating out
- gambling
- entertainment centres
- tenpin bowling
- cinemas
- indoor play centres
- hotels
- health and fitness centres

- arts and sports
- tourism
- sponsorship.

Having read this chapter, readers will learn that while the motive for commercial leisure provision is different from the other sectors, there is still overlap, inter-sectorial involvement and collaboration, so that the strict demarcation lines are not indelibly drawn. An appreciation will be gained of the power of the commercial leisure sector to attract mass markets and also the public's attraction to its products.

People's residual income is taken up in large proportion with commercial products and services. Students will learn that commercial operators, while meeting demands and needs by providing what the public wants and is willing to pay for, also create demands, which hitherto people were unaware of wanting. Lessons can be learned from the revitalized cinema and tenpin bowling chains and from the synergy of putting different facilities on the one site making up a night out 'package'. Managers need to learn some of the skills shown by the commercial sector in developing, marketing and delivering leisure services. Both commercial and non-profit organizations must attract customers or fail.

11.1 Commercial providers of leisure services inside and outside the home

Commercial organizations do not have an intrinsic interest in leisure and recreation, in and of itself, but in leisure as a source of profit. This is not to say that many organizations and managers are not deeply involved in leisure and recreation, nor is it to say that there is no altruism on the part of the providers. Indeed, patronage has long been an element in recreation provision, and commercial support has kept alive many activities which would not otherwise have survived. In addition, the mass media have been responsible for increasing interest and participation in a whole range of leisure pursuits, such as snooker, darts, bowls, golf, gardening, DIY and even collecting antiques. However, while there is a desire to increase the popularity of a number of leisure pursuits, commercial operations (outside the realm of patronage) will only maintain their interest if there is direct or indirect benefit to the organization.

In terms of numbers, millions of people buy sports equipment and cinema tickets, eat out socially, drink, smoke, gamble, watch television and are entertained in their leisure time through services and products provided commercially. The objective of the commercial provider is to make money by serving the public; the public provider is also concerned with serving the public. Hence the enterprise, whether public or commercial, must attract the public or fail.

However, does the commercial provider provide the products and services that the public actually needs or wants, or is the public persuaded to want them? Is the public obliged to take what is on offer? Product choice is often limited in order to streamline production. For example, a few large breweries control the majority of Britain's public houses. Without voluntary consumer organizations such as CAMRA (Campaign for Real Ale) the specific wishes of people could become secondary to products and distribution efficiency.

The commercial provider is therefore in essence, different from other providers – being, literally, in it for the money. Yet many private businesses are not always 'commercial'; they do not make profits; 40 per cent of American commercial ventures apparently never make a profit, but break even or go under, and 50 per cent of the rest of the companies make only marginal profits. In such a climate, many private/commercial leisure organizations find it hard to stay in business and, compared to public sector business, competition is fierce and many companies and services go under. Changing trends in leisure and leisure spending add to this uncertainty.

In recent years, we have seen a significant increase in the British commercial leisure market and currently this includes sports clubs, squash clubs, indoor tennis, indoor bowls, hotel swimming pools, sports villages and sporting holidays, country clubs, themed restaurants, tenpin bowling, bingo, and so on. Hence the commercial leisure industry is made up of many thousands of businesses, from the neighbourhood sports or hobbies shops to the giant multinationals.

While the industry is widely diversified and contains many retailers with only a few full-time staff and Saturday part-timers, the large companies predominate. The commercial sector is dominant in the provision of hotels, amusement parks, theme parks, holiday camps, cinemas, theatres, bowling alleys, ice skating, horse racing, greyhound and speedway tracks, bingo halls, restaurants, public houses, ballrooms and others. Despite major developments by relatively large companies, however, these providers are dwarfed by the expanding leisure giants – the multinational companies.

The most significant change over the past two decades has been the increase in the size of the multinational companies through mergers, takeovers and diversification of interests. They dominate the commercial leisure industry. At the time of this publication, Manchester United Football Club was in negotiation with Rupert Murdoch's media empire for the sale of the club to BSkyB for £625 million!

The major players in the United Kingdom include the following commercial leisure companies: Allied Leisure plc, Bass plc, Brent Walker plc, Camelot Group plc, First Leisure Corporation plc, Granada Group plc, Ladbroke Group plc, Littlewoods Organization plc, Pearson plc, Rank Leisure Ltd, Scottish and Newcastle plc, Stanley Leisure plc, The Tussauds Group Ltd, Vardon plc and Whitbread plc.

11.1.1 Home-based leisure

Commercial providers have enormous influence in home leisure pursuits. The nature of home-based activities and their enjoyment will be affected by factors such as housing conditions, availability of a garden and standard of living. Leisure-time use will vary according to the home itself, home improvements, family interests and hobbies, and material possessions of the household, which may be leisure 'instruments' in themselves (television, video, radio, computer) or may be time-saving appliances (dishwashers) which release members of the household from various tasks, so creating greater leisure time. Another often underrated factor pertaining to leisure at home is the keeping of pets, including many millions of domestic cats and dogs. A dog, in particular, is often the main reason for regular walking and taking time away from the home.

Research commissioned by the Sports Council/ESRC [1] into leisure and the home found that four-fifths of all activities and three-quarters of all leisure activities took place there. Activity in the home dominated life in all social groups, especially women, single parents, retirement and pre-retirement age groups, the professional classes and the unemployed. Their research showed little linkage between life-styles, social profiles, housing or household characteristics. However, they concluded

> Though basic use patterns varied little, different types of homes offered contrasting potential as centres for leisure. People's satisfaction with their homes related to some extent to what they were able to do there and to how well the home accommodated their equipment and activities.

The media have the most influential effect on leisure in terms of what people do with their time. Media in the home revolves around not only television viewing, but also radio, records, tapes, video, hi-fi, newspapers, books and magazines. The motivations for watching television are likely to include a mixture of needs for entertainment, information, education, social cohesion (e.g. watching television may become a 'family activity') or simply because there is, through either lack of opportunity or apathy, nothing else to do. Furthermore, television is cheap. Viewing appears to be the most frequent among children and the elderly, although overall there has been an increase in the time spent watching television over the past fifteen years.

The commercial sector's direct involvement with television revolves around the commercial stations which make the programmes and the manufacture of the television sets themselves. The biggest influence is, of course, that of advertising. A second is the expansion of the video recorder market. A third is the use of the television for active participation (i.e. video games). A fourth growth area is the use of the television as an information service, for example, Ceefax, Oracle and TeleText.

Projections for the future use of television indicate that leisure behaviour could be markedly affected by technological advances. Mechanisms such as Ceefax are the forerunners of more sophisticated systems, where not only will information about leisure pursuits such as concerts, sporting events, theatre and entertainment, and even clubs and organizations specializing in particular activities or hobbies, be more readily accessible, but it will also be possible to book and pay for tickets, via the same system. Some have suggested that the growth of home-based leisure could be the embryo of an introverted society. Even twenty years ago in 1979, a Finnish social psychologist wrote 'The family is alive but not well!' [2].

In relation to listening to the radio, it is interesting to query how much time spent in so doing is purely for leisure, and in fact how much is actually home-based.

Often the radio is listened to in conjunction with the pursuit of markedly non-leisure activities, such as doing the housework, cooking and driving to work. Listening to records and tapes is another booming home-based leisure pursuit.

The written word is another source of home recreation although, as with the radio, it is not solely a home-based pursuit. Publication of newspapers, magazines and books is primarily the prerogative of commercial organizations, although private, voluntary and government organizations publish technical and research material that could conceivably be read for pleasure. Direct commercial involvement can also be found with the organization of book clubs, while indirectly leisure behaviour may be influenced by the content of magazines, both in terms of their advertising and the values they promote.

The house and garden can in themselves offer opportunities for leisure activity, depending on whether home improvement and gardening are viewed by the individual as leisure or as an unwelcome commitment. Whatever the motivation, there appears to be an increase in activity in this area. Home improvements together with normal house maintenance entail considerable expenditure on do-it-yourself tools and equipment. Gardening and the provision of gardening implements is the other area of 'home improvement' in which the commercial sector is involved. The popularity of the garden (either as a place for cultivation or for other leisure activity) is reflected in the growth in the number of gardening programmes on television and garden centres, and in the associated increase in the range of products sold.

As well as accommodating the various leisure media, the home can be used as a base for recreation and social activity, for the playing of indoor games, for informal gatherings, parties, hobbies and other activities. The commercial sector's involvement here is with the provision of the necessary accoutrements and equipment for the pursuit of such activities. Alcohol is one such provision. The increasing popularity of home drinking is indicated by the increase in supermarket sales, and the rise in the number of off-licences.

Home-based leisure in terms of playing indoor games has been a developing market. The developing 'technology' games and the insatiable demand for more updated board games stimulate commercial investment. The latest and most powerful addition to home-based leisure is the computer, with computer games and its uses as a new-found interest and hobby. The 'game' of surfing the internet is potentially the most powerful and equally the most dangerously anti-social of all home leisure interests.

11.1.2 Leisure outside the home

Moving away from home as an area for and object of leisure activity, provision in terms of social recreation can be divided up in a number of ways – e.g. visiting a pub and eating out, gambling, cinema going, 'clubbing', window shopping and many more. The most common free-time activity outside the home among adults in Great Britain in 1995–6 was visiting a public house. The Henley Centre reported that 65 per cent of adults had visited a pub in the three months prior to being interviewed.

Age is an important factor, with young people far more likely than older people to visit a night club, disco, cinema or fast food restaurant. There is a steep decline with age for cinema going, with an even steeper drop for discos! Gender also leads to different levels of participation with men more likely to visit a pub than women, 73 per cent to 57 per cent, and sports events, 30 per cent to only 13 per cent (Henley Centre). Women, however, are more likely to visit a library or attend the theatre [3,4].

The sections which follow concern specific commercial leisure activities. In 1997, Leisure Week, supported by Whitbread produced *The Leisure Industry Report* [5] focussing on commercial providers.

11.2 Pubs, bars and restaurants

One institution which performs a unique and distinctive function is the public house. As a focal point for social activity, the selling of alcohol, and often staging live music events, the pub caters for a variety of needs. The breweries not only cater directly for leisure activity via their own outlets, but also give financial aid to private clubs in the form of grants and loans for the improvement or expansion of premises, usually in return for use of their products. Sales of alcoholic drink associated with eating out are also high.

The alcohol industry is dominated by the few major breweries, although consumer demand, focussed through consumer organizations, has led to the growth of some small, independent breweries. In 1989 the Monopolies Commission released its report into the brewery 'tie'. The report examined a system which permitted six breweries virtually to dictate the habits and tastes of the British pubgoing public. The original recommendation stated that breweries should sell all of their pubs over a 2000 limit. After a watering down of the recommendation, it was decided that breweries with over 2000 pubs would be forced to cut the tie with half of their outlets over the limit and be allowed the right to sell 50 per cent of the excess pubs which they cut free from the tie. The smaller, unprofitable pubs were sold and the number of pubs decreased. A decade on, the pub market is again going through upheaval. The traditional pub has changed for all time. Today there are pub restaurants, micro-breweries, theme pubs, sports bars and a proliferation of brands.

Market researchers Keynote [6] report that there were 55,500 pubs in the United Kingdom in 1988 which fell to about 49,500 pubs in 1997 (Table 11.1). Mergers and acquisition have witnessed the market becoming dominated by just three national breweries: Whitbread; Bass; and Scottish and Newcastle. There are also non-brewing operating companies such as Allied Domecq.

The public house market has seen a growing diversification of products and segmentation of the market brought about by the growth of pub food. Market research company Mintel, in its 1997 *Eating Out Review* [7], reported that the contribution to total pub turnover from sales of alcoholic drinks had fallen from 57 per cent to 53 per cent, with catering increasing from 22 per cent to 26 per cent during the years 1992 to 1996. Some businesses reported food sales of up to 55 per cent. Food expands the market to a wider public and profit margins on food are

TABLE 11.1 Public houses in the United Kingdom

Pubs	Number of sites	
	1997[1]	1998[2]
Whitbread	4,100	3,963
Bass	4,000	2,500
Allied Domecq	3,800	3,735
Phoenix Inns	2,900	–
Intrepreneur	2,900	1,400
Scottish and Newcastle	2,750	2,624
Greenalls Group	2,500	2,194
Pubmaster	1,900	1,400
Green King	1,140	1,100

Source: [1] Keynote, 1997; [2] Mintel, 1998

greater than on drinks. Pub brands of catering such as Harvester (Bass) and Brewer's Fayre and Beefeater (Whitbread) are highly attractive to the family market. Family pubs are increasingly characterized by the provision of indoor and outdoor play areas and children's soft play facilities. Whitbread has 'Charlie Chalk's Fun Factory', and Scottish and Newcastle have 'Jungle Gym's'.

Pubs have had to adapt to these new markets. The days of the pub as the preserve of men has changed with more women customers. Design, decor and image have been changed so that the buildings meet the expectations of women and families as well as men. Along with these changes has also come the nostalgia for the traditional pub, with real-ale brands providing a wider choice.

Pubs have been under severe pressure in recent years, from the range of alternative leisure products, the increase in home sales from supermarkets, cheap purchases from across the Channel, and from the drink–driving laws. Operators have had to adapt and innovate. They will need to develop new brands, new themes and new ways of attracting customers in order to keep market share. The major players have the 'clout' to expand the range of products and manipulate the marketing mix to meet changing demands. For example, Mintel reported that in 1997, the estimated market value of eating out in pubs was nearly double that of restaurant meals.

Mintel's *Eating Out Review* estimates that pub catering has 38 per cent of market share; the fast food sector has 29 per cent with McDonald's (691 outlets), Burger King (420) and Kentucky Fried Chicken (390) the major fast food chains. Mintel estimates that in 1997 there were about 9,300 fish and chip shops in the United Kingdom; 9,000 Chinese take-aways and 7,500 Indian take-aways. Unlike the major chains, these tend to be single outlets, and many are family-run businesses.

The branded restaurants account for 24 per cent of market share. Restaurant theming and brand development are areas of growth. Planet Hollywood, for example, has led to a range of themes emanating from the USA. Capital Radio's Capital Café is themed on the radio station. The Rainforest Café is based on 'natural' products from around the world. The 'eating out experience' is becoming entertainment and the English language has fashioned a new word 'eatertainment'!

11.3 Betting and gambling

Another favourite area of social recreation is that of gambling. This includes amusement arcades, the football pools, bingo, on- and off-course betting, casinos, lotteries, and even Stock Exchange dealings on the outcome of the World Cup football finals. Gambling turnover – consumer expenditure minus winnings – has increased by approximately 10 per cent over the past few years. It is estimated that over the next few years, with the onset of satellite information service systems, improved facilities including corporate hospitality boxes, restaurants, etc., attendances and spending will continue to rise.

It would appear from all the data available that four out of every five people in Britain gamble in one form or another, despite the drop in the number of betting shops and the drop in spectator attendances. Betting has been encouraged by new government legislation, new technologies and greater commercial marketing. For example, bingo, having been in decline for over a decade, has experienced a formidable turnaround and reaped the benefits of refurbishment, rationalization and the national game link-up. Bingo is even altering its 'older generation' image with a new breed of young players entering the game.

Throughout the twentieth century (and possible for all time), gambling has been a popular activity, from gaming with 'serious money' in Monte Carlo to a 'flutter' on the Grand National, playing bingo and the tradition of filling out the pools.

The launch of the National Lottery in the United Kingdom in November 1994 has witnessed an unprecedented increase in this form of gaming. The Family Expenditure Survey (FES) found that around 70 per cent of households participated in their two-week diary-keeping period in 1995–6. On average, households spent £2.12 a week on the National Lottery Saturday night draw between October 1995 and March 1996. However, the FES indicates that household expenditure on other forms of gambling has decreased, falling 15 per cent in real terms since 1994–5 to £1.53 per week in 1995–6.

The *Gaming Act 1968* imposed strict controls on the amusement industry – casinos, betting shops, bingo and amusement machines. The sector has been hit hard by the National Lottery Saturday and mid-week draws and by the Lottery scratch cards. However, the industry has massive earning power and is adapting to the new environment. This is being helped by an easing of the Gaming Act sanctions, with less constraining rules and elements of deregulation. The amusement industry is lobbying for a wholesale review of the 1968 Act so that it can compete on an equal footing with the Lottery. Four areas of the gaming industry are: betting shops; casinos; bingo; and amusements.

1. Betting shops

There are 8,500 betting shops in the United Kingdom [5] and three companies own half of them – Ladbroke, Coral (Bass) and William Hill (Brent Walker). There has been little change in the annual turnover (around £6.6 billion) since the advent of the National Lottery, which means there has been no growth; indeed, the Betting Office Licensees Association (BOLA) estimates a loss of over 3,000 jobs and the Henley Centre reported a loss of 32 per cent in profits. However, a number of changes to the law have enabled betting shops to keep customers and attract new ones, for example, a daily draw which is televised to betting shops. Betting shops can now also install up to two amusement machines, with some reporting at least £80 profit per week, per machine.

2. Casinos

There are about 116 casinos in England, Scotland and Wales. Casinos are not permitted in Northern Ireland. During 1995–6, nearly 11 million people visited them. *The Leisure Industry Report* claims that the annual drop – the amount of money exchanged for chips at a casino – was £2.55 billion; the casinos took 18 per cent. Over 70 per cent of all licensed casinos are owned by six public limited companies: Rank (31 Grosvenor casinos); Stakis (21); London Clubs International (7); Ladbroke (4) and Capital Corporation (2). Changes in the law have benefited casinos through, for example, longer licensed drinking times; a shorter 'cooling off' period, i.e. the time between joining a club and being allowed to gamble reduced from 48 hours to 24 hours; and payment for chips with debit cards. However, the rise in the top rate of gaming duty from 33 per cent to 40 per cent in 1998, and the growth in competition, has led to a down turn for some operators such as London Clubs.

3. Bingo

It is estimated that two million people play bingo in Britain on a weekly basis and that they staked £906 million in 1995–6 [5]. There are 855 clubs, but the market is dominated by two major companies. Gala, owned by Bass, runs 138 clubs. Top Rank runs 135 clubs. Carlton, First Leisure, Vardon, Walker and Noble run nearly 100 clubs between them.

As with other sections of the commercial entertainment industry, the National Lottery had an immediate effect, with 70 bingo clubs closing down in the eighteen months following the introduction of the Lottery. However, advertising restrictions were lifted on bingo operators in 1997 and the major companies are investing heavily to increase market share. Gala immediately invested in a national poster campaign, direct mailing and local radio promotion. Top Rank is also investing with plans for television advertising of its Mecca bingo sites.

4. Amusements

Bacta is the trade association of the amusement sector. Amusement machines are the dominant, highly lucrative, products of the sector – in manufacturing, distributing and operating. Prize machines earn substantial sums of money for their owners and operators. Bacta estimates that they can generate up to 30 per cent of public house income.

There are about 220,000 prize amusement machines in various venues: 38 per cent in public houses; 17 per cent in inland arcades; 14 per cent in seaside arcades; 14 per cent in bingo clubs; and they are also in places such as betting shops, restaurants, roadside service stations, leisure complexes and other venues. Bacta estimates that these machines generate about £9 billion per year, paying between £360 million and £700 million to owners and operators.

There is also a range of other machines – skill machines, pinball machines, video games and an increasing variety of challenges. Skill machines with prizes, however, slumped in business when a £250 amusement licence duty was imposed in 1994. With the introduction of the National Lottery, followed soon after by the scratch card Lottery, the amusement sector turnover reduced substantially. However, with so much money at stake, changes to the Gaming Act and deregulation, the sector is recovering losses. Crown Leisure, one of the major companies, announced a substantial increase in profits in 1998. Changes to the law have included: increases in cash payouts; amusement machines in betting shops; increase in the number of machines on one site for casinos, bingo clubs and members' clubs. In members' clubs and bingo halls, the maximum jackpot is £250, but within pubs and other outlets, the maximum payout is only £10.

New ways of winning back market share are also being developed. Video games, with advanced technologies, are being created which can compete with the home video market. Highly sophisticated motion machines such as Sega's flight simulator and Namco's ski simulator are being sited at key entrances to amusement locations.

11.4 Family entertainment centres and multi-leisure parks

Themed commercial complexes known as Family Entertainment Centres (FECs), urban entertainment centres and youth entertainment centres are currently in vogue. The traditional amusement arcades were not attractive to the family market and had an image sometimes described as 'sleazy'. FECs created a new, attractive image. The first major company into the market was Sega, the Japanese computer games leader, when it opened a centre in the toy store, Hamleys, in London in 1992. Sega now has a dozen United Kingdom venues with its flagship Sega World, described as an 'urban indoor electronic theme park', in the Trocadero Centre in London's West End. Namco opened its first centre in the Meadowhall shopping centre on the edge-of-town site in Sheffield and its second in Soho in London targeted to the youth market. Allied Kunick's Smilin' Sam's entertainment centres focusses on the adult market with amusements, food and bars.

Two growth areas are multi-leisure parks and night clubs.

1. Multi-leisure parks

Despite the rise of leisure activities in or around the home, i.e. television, DIY, and gardening and the growing acquisition of leisure equipment such as videos, music centres, etc., activities outside the home are expanding. A significant development in the United Kingdom during the 1990s that will influence leisure habits is a move away from the stand-alone facilities of the past to the integrated centre, offering a range of leisure activities.

Developers and operators have realized the economies of scale in the form of central services and car parking, associated with putting a number of leisure attractions together. There has been a growth in multi-leisure complexes with a synergy between the cinema, tenpin bowling and nightclubs. It is a facility mix that currently makes for commercial success, given the right location. Collectively, the three activities expand the leisure experience, widen the base and add to the 'night out' market. Of particular interest is that each activity has improved its products to meet new public expectations. Cinemas and tenpin bowling centres both suffered slumps in the recent past, but by improving facilities, re-development, re-packaging and image-making, they have re-built these flagging leisure activities.

2. Night clubs

The movement towards a leisure-experience package – a night out, is also to be seen in the redevelopment of the conventional night club. Admissions in Britain rose from 137 million in 1991 to 173 million in 1996, according to Mintel's 1996 *Nightclubs and Discotheques* report. However, the 'downside' of the business has been the negative images of 'clubbing' – drink and drugs. Drug-related deaths among teenagers led to the passing of a private members bill, the *Public Entertainment (Drugs Misuse) Act*, which contains powers to close a club immediately if it is considered to have a 'serious' drug problem. The nightclub sector's trade body, the British Entertainment and Discotheque Association (BEDA), however, is campaigning to have introduced a nationwide register of door supervisors (formerly called 'bouncers'). BEDA is also attempting to have Sunday dancing legalized. In night clubs it is still illegal to dance on a Sunday night outside London – a law that dates back to 1780. The association is also lobbying for a wholesale reform of the licensing procedure. If, for example, pubs are allowed to stay open on Friday and Saturday nights to midnight, the nightclub trade will suffer.

Like other sectors of the commercial leisure industry, nightclub ownership has major players and a wide range of independents, some 1,800. In 1997, there were six major companies (Table 11.2).

A recent innovation has been to have two clubs at the one venue, for example, one for under 25s and one for over 25s. Getting the mix of activities right for more discerning markets has seen leisure companies updating old concepts; finding new combinations and being innovative.

Independently owned clubs are generally smaller than the major clubs and tend to be conventional in terms of disco nights. The major clubs need large regular throughputs and run a number of special events and promotions to increase business on quiet nights, i.e. early in the week.

TABLE 11.2 Nightclub ownership in the United Kingdom

Night clubs	Number of clubs
Rank Leisure	43
European Leisure	40
First Leisure	37
Northern Leisure	17
Luminar Leisure	16
Scottish Inns	14

Source: Mintel, 1997 [7]

Life Restaurants combine club and bar activities and offer a range of styles, from café bar, to live venue, to party nights, each drawing different target markets. Chorion plc is developing a new bar business which uses a late nightclub licence to trade as nightclub/bars. Even the former indoor tennis chain owner David Lloyd and his son Scott Lloyd's New Generation clubs, linked with brewer Scottish and Newcastle, plan to bring the pub operation closer to their new chain of health clubs. Many health clubs are now owned by brewers, which makes this kind of merger relatively easy. However, one has to ask how an ethos of healthy living and the drive for lucrative alcohol profits sit together when it comes to boardroom decisions about shareholder investments!

Another example is Luminar Leisure, the theme bar and nightclub operator. The firm plans to invest £16 million to open twelve Chicago Rock Cafés, three nightclubs and one Rhythm Room, increasing the size of its estate by one-third; it is also branching out into the health and fitness market.

11.5 Tenpin bowling

Games of bowling balls against pins date back thousands of years. Modern tenpin bowling was developed in the United States during the nineteenth century. The first indoor centre in Britain opened in 1960. Tenpin bowling became popular in Great Britain during the 1960s, but declined during the 1970s. The 1980s witnessed a resurgence, especially as a recreational activity. The game received recognition by the International Olympic Committee and was included as a demonstration sport in the 1988 Seoul Olympics. Tenpin bowling is especially suited to people with disabilities and many centres have facilities available for disabled people. The sport was included in the 1990 European Summer Special Olympics.

The British Tenpin Bowling Association (BTBA), founded in 1961, is the governing body responsible for the game in the United Kingdom. The National Association of Youth Bowling Clubs (for those aged 5 to 18) is also part of the BTBA and in 1984, the BTBA formed the Young Adults' Club to cater for the needs of participants aged between 17 and 23 years. The Tenpin Bowling Proprietors Association (TBPA) consists of owners and operators of tenpin bowling facilities and equipment. In 1990, Themes International, First Leisure and Granada Enter-tainments linked up with the BTBA to form the Tenpin Connection, in an effort to boost the profile of the sport.

There are now around 250 tenpin bowling centres in Britain. There are five major companies – Allied Leisure, Bass Leisure Entertainments, First Leisure, Rank Leisure and AMF. Apart from a few other firms with a handful of sites, such as Wessex and Quattroleisure, the rest of the market is made up of single-site operators. Like the brewing industry, tenpin bowling is dominated in terms of market share by the major chains. However, it is not the number of centres, *per se*, but the number of lanes which dictate the position in the market.

The number of bowling centres more than halved between 1960 and 1973. The image of bowling centres has changed radically from the 1960s as a result of substantial investment in refurbishment and new buildings. Improved design and advanced technology combined with improved bar and catering facilities have contributed to the increasing popularity. An industry marketing body, Go Tenpin, was launched in 1997 with the aim of uniting those involved in the sport under the British Tenpin Bowling Association and operators, most of whom belong to the Tenpin Bowling Proprietors' Association.

Tenpin bowling centres are increasingly being developed as part of wider family entertainment centres with supporting features such as amusement machines, video games, American pool and even soft play, to encourage use by family groups. In the Mintel survey 1993, nearly one-third of adults described tenpin bowling as 'a good outing for the family', 'an evening out' rather than a sport. Only 2 per cent of respondents to the survey went regularly, one-quarter went occasionally and nearly one-third went as part of a group. The development of social facilities is significant – bar and catering, amusement machines, snooker tables, laser adventure games, satellite television and at some centres, a crèche. The key target group revealed in the Mintel survey were 15–35 year olds. The managing director of Allied Leisure apparently coined the phrase 'third-generation bowls' in 1995 to describe the new centres, predicting income from bowls at 25 per cent, with 75 per cent from catering and other activities [8].

So tenpin bowling is another leisure pursuit that has been transformed over the past few years, largely as a result of computer technology with visual scoring displays and through a change of image from the structured, dull facilities

TABLE 11.3 Tenpin bowling sites in the United Kingdom in 1997

Tenpin bowling	Number of sites
Allied Leisure	35
First Leisure	24
AMF	22
Bass	16
Rank Leisure	8

Source: Leisure Week (1997) *The Leisure Industry Report*, Leisure Week, London

dominated by league and club events, to an activity that presents itself as a family-based pursuit in facilities that are bright, relaxing, with associated services such as restaurants and cafeterias. The game itself has changed little over the years. One of the most innovative additions has been glow-in-the-dark coatings for lanes and balls, coupled with good sound systems for 'disco bowling'. Popular centres attract over 1,000 people per day. It is predicted that this activity will continue to grow in popularity as its development becomes more and more 'bankable' with facility planners and financiers.

Allied became the largest operator in November 1995 through its £20 million acquisition of Granada's nineteen-strong GX Superbowl chain. It now has thirty-five sites, having converted some of the GX sites to its own MegaBowl brand. The firm has developed sub-brands such as the McCluski's bar concept, Gameworld machine areas and is adding branded foods such as Burger King to its tenpin bowling centres. The Minnesota Fats tenpin sports bar piloted in Gloucester at the end of 1996 is now being added to other centres.

First Leisure is the next largest tenpin operator with twenty-five sites, mainly under the Superbowl brand name. Cardiff Arena One site includes an indoor fairground and 'animatronic' displays. Bass Leisure's tenpin brand is Hollywood which also features sub-brands, including Wendy's fast food outlets and its own micro-brewery. Rank, a relatively new entrant to the tenpin market, has eight Hotshots sports bar/tenpin centres and has opened another as part of a Leisure World multi-facility development in Southampton. AMF centres focus on those who play tenpin as a sport. Its expansion has been through acquisitions.

Riva! bingo club at the heart of Surrey Quays Leisure Park is part of a £20 million Morrison Developments scheme and is accompanied by a nine-screen UCI (United Cinemas International (United Kingdom)) multiplex, Hollywood Bowl tenpin centre from Bass, and restaurants including Fatty Arbuckles, Pizza Hut and a Greenalls' Quinceys outlet. The club is one of the first to open since the management buy-out from First Leisure in 1998.

The new Brighton Marina twenty-six lane tenpin bowls centre, Brighton Bowlplex, owned by Wessex Leisure Group, includes the Video World amusements area, Pool Pit American pool facility and Stadium Sports Bar and Grill. Included in the complex is a large dance floor with decor, lighting and sound rig to turn it into a nightclub with a 2am licence.

11.6 Cinema

The hundredth anniversary of the cinema was celebrated in 1997. In 1897, the moving picture was one of the earliest forms of packaged entertainment for the masses. Then came the talkies. Cinemas were built all over the world – one screen in one building – and this continued until the creation of the multiplex, and we are now moving into the era of the megaplex. Cinema-going is now classed within a commercial leisure category called the cinema exhibition market.

Cinema attendances fell dramatically from a peak of 1,635 million in 1946 to 156.6 million in 1972 and then to an all time low of 54 million in 1984. Yet, cinemas like tenpin bowling and bingo, experienced an upturn in their fortunes. Admissions to cinemas in 1989 were 88 million, and by 1997, admissions had reached 139 million, with 180 million predicted by the year 2000.

Although there had been a decline in the number of cinema sites, there was a corresponding increase in the number of screens; this was brought about by the division of many of the existing cinemas into multi-screen units. However, the decline in the number of cinema sites has left many towns without cinemas and commercial organizations now consider 30,000 as the minimum population to support a cinema. This policy can cause problems when new districts are built with a population less than 30,000, but have a high proportion of young people.

The cinema revival began in 1985 when AMC opened the United Kingdom's first multiplex at The Point in Milton Keynes with ten screens. The advent of multi-screen complexes with six to twelve or more screens, many at out-of-town sites, added further to the accessibility for the mobile populations. The development of multiplex cinemas, with well designed comfortable surroundings, car parking, and computerized booking, and which offer food and choice has contributed to maintaining and increasing admissions in the United Kingdom.

Every major provider of cinema sites and screens currently has an expansion programme. Over a hundred new cinemas are planned for the next two to three years, 1998–2001. Odeon, with a large stock of city centre sites, has the most sites and screens. New government legislation and the 'sequential' test, focussing on town centres provides the company with considerable advantages. Odeon planned to open six new multiplexes in 1998 and eight in 1999. However, UCI has the largest number of multiplex sites in the United Kingdom, with twenty-nine cinemas with expansion plans including two twenty-screen cinemas in Greater Manchester . The city centre site opening in 1999 includes a 3D IMAX screen.

Virgin Cinemas was created from the acquisition of the MGM chain of 114 cinemas in 1995. Subsequently, 90 conventional cinemas were sold to ABC Cinemas, leaving Virgin to focus on its prime London sites. With a substantial rise in profit from its 26 multiplex sites, Virgin increased investment from £11.7 million in 1996 to £34.5 million in 1997; 20 new cinemas will open over the next three years with 11–20 screens in each.

TABLE 11.4 Cinemas in the United Kingdom*

	Number of sites[1]	Number of screens[1]	Planned sites[2]
Rank (Odeon)	74	361	30
ABC Cinemas	52	200	
UCI	29	256	50 % more screens
Virgin Cinemas	26	182	10
Warner Village	17	152	14
Apollo (Hollywood Parks)	16	64	
National Amusements (Showcase)	15	183	
Cine-UK (Cineworld)	3	38	17

Source: 1 Leisure Week (1997) *The Leisure Industry Report*, Leisure Week, London
2 Cinema chains' press releases
*Numbers are constantly changing. See *The Leisure Industry Report 1998*.

In 1996, Warner Brothers Theatres entered into a joint venture with the Australian corporation, Village Roadshow. The Warner Village company, with cinemas in Germany and Italy, hope to have 40 United Kingdom multiplexes with about 470 screens by the year 2000. Cine-UK was formed in 1996 out of a plan to buy the MGM chain – the focus of most of the major companies. Cine-UK opened its first multiplex in Stevenage with the aim of having 20 sites by the year 2000. The Stevenage Leisure Park is an example of the unabated development of the multi-leisure commercial development offering: a Cineworld multiplex cinema; a David Lloyd Leisure Club; Allied Kunick's Smilin' Sam's; a Hollywood Bowls; an Academy Bar; McDonalds; and an Exchange Diner. Apollo has a chain of 16 cinemas, most of them traditional, but has plans to build 20 multiplexes.

The number of screens per site is increasing. AMC is set to join the United Kingdom market with a 24-screen development in Hounslow. Virgin is to open a 20-screen site in Sheffield. The advent of 20–30 screen 'megaplexes' – Warner Village plans a 30-screen cinema near Birmingham – has fuelled debate as to the merits of such a vast complex. Clearly, cinema-going is developing into a night-out experience with bars, wine bars, 'cappuccino cafés', amusements and merchandising – videos, CDs and T-shirts. However, they need substantial populations to draw on and could challenge other multiplexes for business. To build such structures requires large amounts of space and huge car parks.

Virgin Cinema's multiplex, which opened in April 1998, is in Birmingham Great Park. The site is near the M5/M42 junction and one million people live within a twenty-minute drive. The 4645m^2 facility has 13 screens and 2,975 seats. The largest screen has 540 seats and the smallest 90. All screens use stadium seating, feature wall-to-wall screens and have air-conditioning. The 90-seat auditorium houses Virgin's Premier Screen concept with its own bar and waiter service until the film begins. Complimentary bowls of dips and popcorn are available and the 'armchair-style' seats recline to take full advantage of the extra leg room. The multiplex attracted 31,000 people in its first week following a successful two-for-one offer. Other facilities on the site include restaurants and an hotel. Bass has signed up to develop a Hollywood Bowl tenpin centre, and there is also an opportunity for a health and fitness club. Safeway has opened a supermarket on the site. The Great Park facility features a Café Bar, Movie Store and Screen Snacks self-serve area. There is also a Scoop 'n' Go confectionery area and Milk Bar. The Party Room is also the children's play area.

According to *The Leisure Industry Report*, despite the growth of multiplexes, the United Kingdom is still under-screened compared to many other countries, with less than 40 screens per million people compared to 50 per million in Ireland, 77 per million in France and nearly 100 per million in the US. Annual visits per head are also lower, about 2.1 in the United Kingdom in 1996 compared to about 4.82 per head in the USA. 'Currently, new multiplexes do not take much business away from existing cinemas, they simply create a new audience. Basically, as more multiplexes open, admissions figures rise.'

11.6.1 Growth potential for large and small companies?

Like the brewing industry, the top six cinema operators have the major share of the business and they are likely to increase their share of the business. Admission to cinemas estimates suggest that there will be 180 million by the year 2000 (Dodona) [9]. During this time, 600 multiplex screens could be added to the 900 operating in 1997. However, the industry faces fierce competition, rising rents and planning problems at out-of-town sites. John Carroll [10] warns:

> A whole variety of players are now jumping on the leisure bandwagon, yet many don't have much knowledge of the product. The result is high prices for sites and unrealistic rents. There are dangers ahead in the leisure boom, but if we steer round them and create total leisure experiences, the future looks bright.

Leisure property agents indicate that the present 'standard' being used in Britain is 1 screen per 25,000 people, or 40 screens per million population. This would appear to be based on current provision rather than potential demand. Some providers require a minimum catchment of 100,000 people within a twenty-minute drive time for a new multiplex, with no other multiplex competition in the catchment.

The growth of the large 3D format theatre network, dominated by IMAX, is fast outstripping the number of films available for exhibition, according to Euromax. If operators open huge megacentres, then smaller units stand little chance in the face of such dominating competition. Given the choice of different film centres within their catchments, customers will decide which to go to, not on the basis of which film is showing, but on other features and factors – accessibility, ambience, ancillary attractions.

Figures from the British Film Industry (BFI) show that multiplex cinema operators own 10 per cent of United Kingdom cinemas, but 30 per cent of the screens. This indicates that smaller sites continue to operate successfully. Indeed, smaller independent companies are redeveloping and adding new sites. City Screen, for example, runs nine sites. Its latest development is the £3.5 million Stratford Picture House in Newham, East London. Sited next to the Theatre Royal, it is part of a coherent regeneration programme within the plans for an Arts Quarter in the borough.

11.6.2 Out-of-town test case – the sequential test

Progress in the development of multi-leisure parks has been slowed in recent times due to changes to the government *Planning Policy Guidance 6*. PPG 6 favours town centre and edge-of-town sites, rather than out-of-town sites; but many commercial operators favour the out-of-town sites because of ease of development and car parking. Multiplexes demand a lot of car parking space, so they have usually been built on out-of-town or edge-of-town sites.

The proposal to build a ten-screen Virgin multiplex cinema out of town at Eastleigh became a test case. Referred to the Secretary of State, Department of the Environment, the application was turned down on the grounds that smaller sites were available in the town centre – it failed the 'sequential test'. The test means that there is a presumption in favour of town centre sites. But what happens, if, at a later date, planning permission is given to another operator for an out-of-town site with larger space for car parking and other facilities? The sequential test applies to town centre development, primarily retail. Are the needs of the retail market the same as the commercial leisure industry? The Eastleigh decision was overturned by the incoming Labour government but only on narrow legal grounds. The sequential test is still in place.

Planning committees have huge responsibilities and powers when it comes to granting or refusing planning permission. In 1997, UCI built an in-town multiplex in Wakefield, fulfilling demands of current planning policy. Two days before the opening, the Council granted planning permission for another multiplex on an out-of-town leisure park. Similar problems are occurring in the large cities.

11.6.3 IMAX and Iwerks

IMAX and Iwerks are two rival producers of a similar product. The literature on the products can sometimes be confusing as IMAX, who are the market leaders, are increasingly having their name used in a generic sense, e.g. as Hoover is used to describe vacuum cleaners and Jacuzzi to describe spas.

The IMAX product is relatively new. It uses a completely different cinematic technology with a 15 perf/70mm film format and a film some ten times the size of a traditional 35mm movie. The films can be either in 2D or 3D. There are essentially three levels of product:

1   the large screen/large theatre format which normally seats 400–500 people: there is now also the technology to provide for a number of smaller theatres, i.e. approximately 280 seats (the IMAX at the Trocadero has 300 seats);
2   the IMAX Dome which provides 360-degree projection;
3   smaller, 80–100 seat, motion-based theatres which provide seat movement co-ordinated with the film. This is not the same as the smaller, capsule based simulators which can be found at theme parks and fairgrounds throughout the country.

There are currently 150 IMAX cinemas worldwide with an expected growth to 200 by the year 2000. The films for IMAX theatres are extremely costly to produce and there is a limited range of product available, which seems to be one of the major concerns for the industry at present. The duration of the films is generally no more than forty minutes, and for the smaller, motion-based theatres from five to fifteen minutes. It is expected that by the year 2000 the catalogue of 15 perf/70 mm films will reach 160 (only 10 per cent of which will be 3D).

The location of IMAX theatres tends to be in areas which either: a) have a high throughput of people/tourists, e.g. the new IMAX at the Trocadero which has an annual passing footfall of 45 million people, half of whom are tourists; or b) are part of a larger heritage/theme park attraction, e.g. IMAX at Bradford at the National Museum of Photography, Film and Television.

There are other IMAX/Iwerks being developed, the British Film Institute having recently received a Lottery grant for the IMAX in London, and there is the smaller motion-based Iwerks in Manchester, which is part of the Granada studios. The development of the IMAX product is still in its relatively early stages with a limited range of products that requires a large throughput of new (as opposed to repeat) visits to make it sustainable. It is certainly an exciting concept and the smaller movement-based theatres may well have a long-term future.

11.7 Children's indoor play centres

The ideas for safe adventure play were pioneered by the Adventure Playground movement and by those play specialists in the voluntary sector designing equipment for disabled and handicapped children to play in safety, without risk of injury.

The concept of children's indoor adventure play centres is relatively new on a mass scale. Adventure Play centres can be found in places such as large shopping centres or where large numbers of children are likely to be attracted. However, they are also to be found in smaller towns, attached to leisure centres and also constructed in warehouses and converted buildings and most recently at family eating out spots, supermarkets and pubs. Their long-term viability is yet to be determined. However, at present, they are proving to be very attractive for young children and for groups for special treats.

The needs of children and the family market have stimulated demand: indoor facilities to counter the inclement weather or the cold of the winter; the concerns as to the safety of young children; the need for healthy physical and adventurous activities; family 'entertainment'; and the social dimension to leisure and play activities, e.g. birthday parties.

These play centres go by many different names – 'Playworld', 'Adventure World', 'Pirates', etc. Different areas can be developed for different ages, such as soft play adventure for under 5s and for 6–12s a large area with sufficient height for 'jungle gym' activities, on different levels, is fitted out with slides, rope ladders, soft landings, ball pools, etc; lighting and sound effects can be included.

The success of such centres will depend on many factors:

- the range of activities and equipment;
- the setting and attractiveness of the play centre;
- the location and accessibility for regular usage, particularly places such as town centres, and leisure centres, that are busy day and evening, all year round;
- the catchment area and the market competition (not just from play centres but also other opportunities for children and families);
- operational management, pricing and customer service;
- catering and social elements and party opportunities;

- facilities and services for parents and adults accompanying children;
- adjacent or nearby car parking.

The range of venues for children's play centres varies enormously from converted squash courts to old school gymnasia and from converted warehouses and barns to purpose-built centres. A range of capital costs from about £50,000 to £650,000 can be found throughout the United Kingdom.

11.8 Hotels

Long before there was any thought of 'leisure management', services were being provided and managed for people's leisure. Hotels have been market leaders in a number of aspects of leisure management and are very much a part of the hospitality sector of commercial leisure. Hotels, as well as being essential for business, are also essential for holidays and leisure travel. There is hardly a new hotel built or extended which does not have leisure elements including, in many cases swimming pools and fitness facilities.

The hotel industry is greatly affected by the economy and the tourist industry. At the time of writing, the strength of the pound is such that it is very expensive for overseas tourists to Britain, particularly to London and a drop in the number of visitors occurs at times like these. The corollary to this is that Britons going to overseas destinations is at its highest level. The British Incoming Tour Operators Association report that there was a fall in passenger numbers coming into the United Kingdom during the first quarter of 1997 compared to the same period in 1996. A further drop was experienced in the first quarter of 1998.

Like other sectors in the commercial leisure industry, a few major players dominate the hotel market at the top end with chains of hotels. At the other end of the scale is a vast number of independent establishments, particularly at seaside and inland holiday destinations. There are three major hotel chains in the United Kingdom: Granada, which became the market leader after acquiring Forte in January 1996; Whitbread; and Thistle Hotels.

The Leisure Industry Report provides information concerning the leading hotels in 1997 (Table 11.5). Granada has 326 hotels and 28,298 rooms. These hotels include the Travelodge properties, Forte Posthouse and Forte Heritage Hotels. The Whitbread Hotel Company, with Travel Inns and Mariott hotels, has 190 hotels and 11,727 rooms in the United Kingdom. Thistle Hotels, formerly Mount Charlotte Thistle, has 101 hotels and 13,595 rooms. Other key players include Queens Moat Houses, Ladbroke-owned Hilton hotels, Stakis, Holiday Inns, Macdonald Hotels, Friendly Hotels, Jarvis Hotels, Scottish and Newcastle and Regal Hotels.

Each hotel group is building up its own brand or brands and positioning itself in the market for instant recognition. With Holiday Inns, for example, once inside an hotel one could be almost anywhere in the world. Stakis sold its three-star hotels to focus its business at the four-star level. Thistle is consolidating its four-star hotels; the relatively new and fast developing Regal group is concentrating on three-star accommodation. The Whitbread Hotel Company, formed in 1996, has

TABLE 11.5 Hotels in the United Kingdom

Chain	Number of hotels*
Granada Forte	326
Whitbread Hotel Company	190
Thistle Hotels	101
Regal Hotels	95
Jarvis Hotels	68
Macdonald Hotels	67
Scottish & Newcastle Hotels	54
Stakis	52
Queens Moat Houses	51
Friendly Hotels	46

Source: Leisure Week (1997) *The Leisure Industry Report*, Leisure Week, London
*Numbers are constantly changing. See *The Leisure Industry Report* 1998

developed the top range Marriot brand but is also focussing on its Travel Inns to reach the 200 mark.

The budget, lodge-style of hotels in the United Kingdom, were developed when Forte and Granada, learning from their success in continental Europe, opened up accommodation for those on the move as extensions to their roadside service stations. These budget hotels focus on the core of the business to provide quality bedrooms at a cheap price, without the frills of service and ancillary facilities. Economies of scale are realized, with hotel guests eating and purchasing goods at the service stations which have increased in both range and quality of products and services.

11.9 Holiday centres

The number of holidays taken by British holidaymakers has increased in the long term for both holidays in Britain and holidays abroad. Approximately 60 per cent of British residents in the United Kingdom now take a holiday, although the number and length of stay are affected by personal characteristics. Short breaks, including family activity holidays are becoming very popular as second/seasonal holidays. Considered in this very brief section is only the growth and development of the major family holiday centres.

The Butlin's Holiday Worlds of today are a far cry from the Butlin's Holiday Camps of post-war Britain and the era of 'Good morning campers', portrayed in television comedies. The British Holiday and Home Parks Association values the holiday parks market at over £600 million, which would appear to be an underestimation considering the cost of £100 million for the latest Oasis Forest Holiday Village in Cumbria.

Over the years, standards of provision have risen with improved accommodation, leisure facilities and services. The first Center Parcs holiday village, opened in 1987 in a secluded, wooded, countryside location in Nottinghamshire with lakes, quality outdoor and indoor leisure facilities and good-quality chalet-style lodge accommodation, revolutionized the holiday centre market in the United Kingdom.

Center Parcs in Sherwood Forest, Elveden Forest in Suffolk and Longleat Forest Village in Wiltshire, owned by Scottish and Newcastle, are examples of a commercial holiday and short-break village which has at its hub a very large domed leisure water facility that appeals to a wide age group. This type of facility is becoming extremely popular particularly with family groups. The Center Parcs concept, founded in the Netherlands, has been, arguably, the most significant leisure development in recent times. It is a development that gives participants the opportunity to experience not only indoor tropical water facilities but also the opportunity to participate in a number of sporting and non-sporting pursuits, in a clean, friendly, informal atmosphere. These centres are open all the year with around 90 per cent occupancy. Furthermore, a majority of holidays taken there are additional to the United Kingdom domestic tourism market.

Major holiday sites are owned by five companies [5]: Rank has 60 sites; British Holidays, the largest independent owner, has 20 sites; Scottish and Newcastle has 19 sites including three market-leader Center Parcs and 16 Pontin's holiday villages in Britain and 1 in Ireland; Queensborough Holdings has 14 caravan parks; and Parkdean Leisure, acquired in 1995 by Vardon – better known as a company involved in attractions, bingo and health and fitness centres – has 10 caravan parks, 5 in Scotland and 5 in England.

Rank has four market brands: Butlin's, Warner, Haven and Oasis. Oasis, in Cumbria, is the Rank Group's flagship centre and its answer to Center Parcs. The village is set in 400 acres of woodlands and can cater for up to 3,500 self-catering guests in 700 lodges and 78 apartments. Like Center Parcs, the central indoor space is a 'World of Water' centre and there are extensive indoor and outdoor leisure facilities and a choice of restaurants.

Haven has 49 sites on a smaller scale than the Butlin's Holiday Worlds, some with an emphasis on entertainment, some known as Family Parks and others set in countryside locations known as Family Villages. Almost all have swimming pools as a main feature.

In part, the holiday centre market has followed the classic commercial route of major players coming into the market, investing in it and acquiring facilities or going concerns. However, some unique characteristics are evident. The first is building on the tradition of the 'working-class' holiday camps, particularly Butlin's and Pontin's, which have been acquired and developed, thereby widening the market. The second is the advent of the holiday village concept of Center Parcs, a major landmark in market positioning in a very short space of time. The third is the diverse field of large numbers of holiday 'parks' and caravan sites. What they all have in common in the late 1990s is a buoyancy in the market and the potential for growth and development.

11.10 Health and fitness centres

The increase in positive awareness of health and fitness has meant a boom in the market and considerable interest from all sectors – public, voluntary, institutional and commercial. In the public sector, nearly all large leisure centres now provide fitness centres, aerobics studios and health suites; to provide space, squash courts all over the United Kingdom have been converted into fitness facilities. In the voluntary sector, sports clubs are installing fitness machines and new tennis facilities rely on the fitness centres to ensure their financial stability. In the commercial sector, as public demand continues to increase and operators expand their businesses often through acquisition, the health and fitness market seems set to thrive for the foreseeable future. Indeed, the market is so buoyant it has spawned its own fashion wear industry. No new hotel operator would think of building an hotel without a fitness centre and most large established hotels, country clubs and holiday centres have added facilities. The sale of home health and fitness equipment has also soared.

What has brought about this level of interest? Vanity and health are prime reasons for individuals; money-making is the major business driving force! People want to look good and feel good. There is an increasing awareness of the benefits of exercise which have been promoted by agencies such as The Sports Council and the Health Education Authority. The drive for fitness, however, has not been based in sport but in health and lifestyle. In the commercial sector, the Fitness Industry Association (FIA) has been active in spreading the 'gospel of fitness for life'. BUPA has joined forces with the FIA to form the BUPA-approved Health and Fitness Club Network. Successful GP referral schemes, pioneered at leisure centres, illustrate that when the doctor tells you to exercise, you are far more likely to do so, than when exactly the same message comes from elsewhere!

Income-generation is the main reason for business interest in the fitness market. However, it is also one of the primary reasons in both the public and voluntary sectors. The first community multi-sport centre, Harlow Sportcentre, run by a charity, is an example of how an ageing centre (where all local authority financial support has been withdrawn) can cover the cost of its other, non-profitable community activities from its Technogym, which runs at a substantial profit. It also delivers one of the most successful GP referral schemes in the county, using the health and fitness facilities as its base.

The £25 million Doncaster Dome which was opened in 1989, in 1998 turned its indoor bowls centre into 'The Fitness Village' to provide a large income stream from an estimated 11,500 attendances a month. The Village features 170 fitness machines and the old gym has been converted to a free weights area. There is also a women's conditioning gym, circuit training gym and a 90-metre indoor warm-up track.

These are just two of many examples throughout the United Kingdom and illustrate the volume of demand, the income streams flowing from the fitness industry and the use of commercial techniques, e.g. direct debit payments. However, while the activities and their operation are identical in many ways to the commercial sector, their *raison d'être* is different. One objective of the Harlow and District Sport Trust is to use Technogym surpluses to make the Sportcentre financially viable. The Dome Fitness Village income will help to reduce local authority subsidy to the trust. The private sector fitness sector however is part of the business portfolio intended to make returns to investors. An example is one of the new breed of stand-alone health and fitness centres, akin to the David Lloyd Centres – the Racquets and Healthtrack Group, with the following range of facilities at their Ealing club:

- 'ultimate gymnasium'
- 25m training pool
- leisure pool
- outdoor tennis courts
- squash/racketball courts
- large aerobic studios and beauty retreat, Miami suntanning centre and hair studio

- three saunas, spa, steam room
- sun terrace and barbecue area
- croquet lawn
- crèche and junior club
- restaurant and bar
- 300 free parking spaces

So explosive has been the fitness centre market that it is difficult to be precise as to the extent of the industry. The Online Information Company publish a list of around 1300 health and fitness centres with over 500 members and they estimate that there are in the region of another 2000 private clubs with less than 500 members. The Mintel report, *Health and Fitness – Fit For Future Growth* estimated that the 23 largest operators accounted for only 21 per cent of the United Kingdom clubs, illustrating that the overall market is dispersed and mainly in the hands of relatively small operators. The value of the industry is also difficult to measure and a figure of around one billion pounds of income is estimated broadly. Part of the difficulty in measurement is the fragmented nature of the market, its expansion and its volatility, with acquisitions at the top end of the market. In addition, some commercial operators work in both the public and the private sector, for example, Archer Leisure which was taken over by Vardon and Harpers; public sector contract managers (part of the Relaxion Group) was taken over by Kunick. The two leading commercial companies Living Well and David Lloyd Leisure (both recently acquired by larger companies), between them have a major share in the commercial fitness industry with an estimated 50,000 members each.

There are many varieties of health and fitness private clubs but they fall into three broad types. First, there are large clubs (over 2320m^2) with swimming pools, fitness and aerobics suites, beauty and treatment rooms and bars and catering; and some clubs offer squash and indoor and outdoor tennis. Second, smaller, stand-alone, clubs offer some additions to the core business of fitness and aerobics rooms but on a smaller scale. Then, third, there are a whole host of private clubs that are part of hotels, leisure centres, squash clubs, tennis centres and add-ons to a number of establishments such as residential and office blocks. *The Leisure Industry Report* listed the private sector leading players in 1997 (Table 11.6).

The fitness industry is so widespread that it may not show the classic product growth life-cycle (Figure 11.1), nor the typical business progression from discovery to maturation, though this may well be the case at the top end of the commercial market as the larger players take hold.

Some of the signs are there. First Leisure entered the market in 1994 with a £2.7 million acquisition of the Berkshire Racquets and Health Club in Bracknell. In

TABLE 11.6 Leading health and fitness clubs in the commercial sector*

Club owners	Number of clubs
Livingwell	59
Fitness For Industry	49
Swallow Hotels	29
Greenhalls	25
David Lloyd Leisure	23
Holiday Inns	20
Sebastian Coe	17
First Leisure	13
Fitness First	12
Archer Leisure	9
Mike Corby Group	9
Dragons	9
Fitness Express	9
Village Leisure	9
Wates Leisure	9

Source: Leisure Week (1997), *The Leisure Industry Report*, Leisure Week, London
*Numbers are constantly changing. See *The Leisure Industry Report* 1998

1997 it acquired Riverside plc for £61 million, with Riverside clubs in Chiswick and Northwood and City-based Espree Clubs and has also been developing its own Esporta Club brand. Whitbread acquired David Lloyd Leisure (market leaders in tennis and fitness clubs) in 1995 for £201 million and the Curzon Fitness Clubs in 1997. Starkis plc took over Living Well Health and Leisure in 1996. Other corporate expansion has included Greenalls' takeover of Boddington's, with its Village Leisure Clubs and Jarvis Hotel's substantial investment in its Sebastian Coe brand. Independent operators such as Wates Leisure, Holmes Place, Dragons Health Clubs and Fitness First have all been raising funds for major expansion. At the time of writing, new entries into health and fitness are taking place, Sally Gunnell branded clubs having a high profile.

Clearly, the fitness industry is still relatively young in terms of its development. It has entered the phase where the major players have fuelled a rapid expansion, and every month there are announcements of new club openings and site acquisitions. Despite a developing market, the signs of establishing a mix of facilities as 'bankers' in a successful fitness business are apparent and include the following.

1. A fitness gym with cardio-vascular and resistance machines

The size of the gym has a direct bearing on the number of members that a club can accommodate. In general it must be able to comfortably manage usage during peak

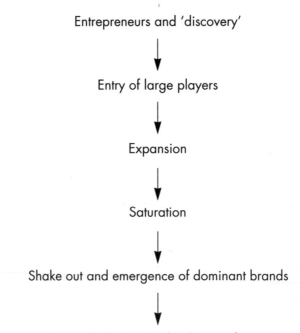

Entrepreneurs and 'discovery'

↓

Entry of large players

↓

Expansion

↓

Saturation

↓

Shake out and emergence of dominant brands

↓

Market maturation and domination by three or four major operators

FIGURE 11.1 Fitness industry growth life-cycle

times, so that club members are not having to wait around to use the equipment. The number of 'stations' in medium to large clubs is from 50 to well in excess of 100. Some free weights need to be included. Provision of 'women only' gyms is also increasing as part of a mixed club, particularly for those new members who are self-conscious about their shape and 'working out' for what may be the first time.

2. Dance/aerobics studio

All clubs have at least one dance/aerobic studio. Most cater for 25 to 35 people doing step classes and have a class programme of 40 to 60 step/aerobic/yoga classes a week. These activities are an important element in attracting female members.

3. A swimming pool with lanes

Although a gym and aerobics studio are core elements, evidence from the market shows that a swimming pool is the single most attractive facility a health and fitness club can offer. Few major new developments being built are without a wet area incorporating a pool and spa bath. Pools are likely to become a standard feature of any large credible health and fitness club.

4. Health and beauty salon

Areas for health and beauty treatments – facials, massage, aromatherapy, hairdressing etc. – are an essential adjunct to clubs with an holistic approach to health. Once again this appeals particularly to the female market. A number of clubs franchise out this service.

5. Squash

Squash courts tend to be provided when they are part of a major 2790m^2 plus development or were part of a sports club that had been converted into a new health and fitness facility.

6. Crèche

Whilst it is the view of many that a crèche is an essential prerequisite to attract the family market, facilities are poorly used. Nevertheless, for those aspiring to attract the daytime family market, a crèche of some description would seem to be an important element.

7. Health 'spas'

Most commercial health clubs have some form of sauna/steam room/spa/sun bed area. A relaxation element can be important in attracting those members who are not under severe time constraints, and those that enjoy the more passive elements of a health club, e.g. those most likely to be able to use the club at off-peak times.

8. Catering

Larger clubs have a range of provision, including bars, bistro and restaurant. This ranges from an upmarket restaurant to informal, health food catering. Catering is likely to be viewed as a service to club members rather than as a prime profit centre.

An example of the facility mix in five types of club ranging from under 930m^2 to 11,150m^2 is shown in Table 11.7.

11.11 Arts and sport

This section needs to be read in conjunction with chapters six on trends and eight on agencies for arts and sports. There has been a blurring of demarcation lines of what are profit-making and non-profit-making organizations, between public, voluntary and commercial.

TABLE 11.7 Core facilities and criteria for a commercial health and fitness centre

Type of club	Typical size	Facility mix	Typical development cost	Average number of members	Average monthly adult membership (£)	Location/catchment	Examples
Indoor tennis plus health and fitness	11,150m² 4 hectare site	Indoor tennis and badminton 8–12 tennis courts; fitness; aerobics; indoor pools; health suite; children's area; catering	£6m+	5,000	62+	Good access to large conurbations, typically 400,000 in 20-minute drivetime	David Lloyd, Riverside, Racquet and Health Club
Large city centre club	2 320m²	Gym, fitness, dance, beauty, catering, squash, some have pools		3,000–5,000: 50% upwards corporate members	64–107	Generally city centre; particularly companies close to wide range of businesses	Espree, Broadgate
Large stand-alone health and fitness	2790m²–5575m² 1.2–2 hectare site	Gym, fitness, dance, beauty, pool, health suite, crèche, catering, some squash	£3m–5m	3,000–5,000	50–60	Edge of town or town centre, min 90,000 ABCs in 15-minute drivetime; some, such as Holmes Places in shopping centres	Esporta, Holmes Place, Pinnacles
Mid range health and fitness	930m²–1860m²	Gym, fitness, dance, beauty, pool (most), crèche, health suite, varied catering, some squash	£1m+	1,500–2,000	30–45 depending on positioning and catchment	Converted sports clubs (typically ex squash facilities), retail units on margins of shopping centres, close to residential areas	LA Fitness, Dragons, Fitness First
Smaller units	up to 930m²	Gym, fitness, dance, some with catering or crèche		500–1,500	30–35	Wide range of locations	

Source: Torkildsen Barclay Leisure Management (1998)

Commercial leisure provision for entertainment and the arts outside the home covers a number of areas, although these can be divided into two basic categories: those which encourage active participation (e.g. ballrooms, discos, dance schools) and those in which provision is generally geared towards audience and spectators. This section deals primarily with the latter. This section needs to be read in conjunction with chapter eight which has specific sections on arts and the Arts Council and sport and the Sports Council.

Attending the cinema and theatre, going to popular and classical concerts, visiting art galleries or going to shows and cabarets are all part of the audience and spectator activities provided by the commercial sector. Going to the theatre is not as popular as going to the cinema. Only a small percentage of the population attend the theatre, opera or ballet. One-half of the professional theatres in Britain are owned or rented by commercial companies. Of these, nearly one-third are found in London; but West End theatres are finding it difficult to make a profit, owing to competition from subsidized national theatres and civic suburban theatres, and there is a declining number of commercial theatres in the provinces to accommodate touring plays and musicals.

Sport is an expanding market. More people are playing sport, more sports are being played and consumer spending on goods and services is likely to keep rising. Commercial providers are concerned in sport and physical recreation in a number of key areas, for example, spectator sport, sports sponsorship and leisure and sports goods and equipment. However, the commercial sector is involved in the provision of facilities for participants in only a limited number of sports. Of the outdoor sports, only golf, tennis and water sports are provided in any great numbers, and in the case of golf and tennis, these are sometimes provided as part of a leisure complex which also provides squash, health and fitness and other ancillary facilities. The growth in golf throughout many parts of the world has largely been commercially led. Of the indoor sports, snooker, tenpin bowling, ice skating, indoor tennis and, most recently, sport and health clubs are being provided by commercial organizations.

Commercial enterprise tends to deal with only a few sports in terms of spectatorship. Association Football is still the most popular spectator sport in the United Kingdom (here 'spectator sport' refers to actual attendance, rather than watching via the television set – a leisure activity which is forecast to increase dramatically with digital TV). Soccer spectatorship has declined since the postwar years, when spectators amounted to 41 million attendances in the 1948/9 season dropping to 16.5 million by the end of the 1985/6 season in the English Football League matches. Since then, there has been a small increase in attendances. Analysis of Premier League football in England and Wales in the 1997/8 season showed average attendances of around 29,000 and a total for the season of just over 11.1 million. By far the biggest gate (over 55,000) and season's total (over 1 million) was at Manchester United, followed by around three-quarters of a million at Arsenal and Liverpool. The bid to buy Manchester United by the television company BSkyB appears to have set in train the potential purchase of clubs in the United Kingdom, as in the USA, with the aim of attracting huge television audiences. Football remains the most popular spectator sport on television, well ahead of cricket, rugby union, horse racing and motor racing.

Spectator sports, apart from some Premier League football, rugby and cricket internationals and events such as Wimbledon, are generally not lucrative in terms of receipts from attendance, although many popular indoor spectator sports such as indoor tennis, indoor show-jumping and boxing lend themselves to viewing by comparatively large audiences. There are, however, some indoor sports such as snooker and darts which cannot accommodate large audiences on-site, but which become popular spectator sports through the medium of television – however, coverage has declined in recent years. Indoor bowls is another sport which has gained popularity through television.

Hence, although there has been a decline in the traditional spectator sports, others have increased in following, many as a direct or indirect result of television coverage and commercial sponsorship. Tennis and golf are examples and basketball seems set to follow.

A substantial industry to supply leisure goods, clothing and equipment has developed. The manufacture, distribution and retailing of a vast range of goods exist, from yachts, canoes, tents, bicycles and hang-gliders, to tracksuits and special footwear, rackets, balls, snooker tables, dartboards, trampolines and goalposts; to hi-fi, records, video, electronic devices and games of many kinds.

11.12 Tourism and holidays

The commercial sector is closely involved with, indeed part and parcel of, the tourist industry. This industry might be seen very broadly as providing for three markets in the United Kingdom:

1   foreign visitors to the United Kingdom
2   Britons holidaying (including visiting tourist attractions, day trips, etc.) in the United Kingdom
3   Britons holidaying abroad.

Inevitably, the provision for all three markets is interlinked with facilities and services provided by the commercial sector used by both foreigners and Britons alike, and with British travel agents organizing holidays both at home and abroad. There is also a close interrelationship between the commercial sector, other sectors and government-funded bodies such as the British Tourist Authority (BTA) and the English Tourist Board (ETB) – which also provide for and influence tourist development. (Chapter eight contains a section on tourism.)

11.12.1 Accommodation

Historically, London has been the premier tourist destination within the United Kingdom, attracting consistently high levels of visitors due to its position as the capital city and the seat of government, and the centre for business, culture and entertainment.

The overflow in demand for London bedspace has resulted in a shift to the provinces. This has proved beneficial to traditional tourist centres such as the south coast resorts, Stratford-upon-Avon, York and Edinburgh. The English Tourist Board surveys have illustrated that approximately 60 per cent of overseas visitors now travel outside London during their British visit. However, popular 'attractions' are at saturation point and methods of dispersing tourists to other venues are being actively encouraged.

Both foreign and British tourists require accommodation and this involves a wide range of options, from hotels to camping and caravanning sites and holiday homes. The types of accommodation may be simply a base from which to tour or visit the surrounding area, or it may provide leisure activity in its own right such as holiday camps or hotels that provide sporting and entertainment facilities. At the Aviemore Centre, for example, in the Spey Valley, leisure facilities include swimming, squash, ice skating and curling. A number of first-class hotels are clustered around the centre and caravan parks extend the variety of services and self-service accommodation.

Many prestige hotels, particularly in holiday resorts, have sporting facilities such as swimming pools, squash courts and tennis courts within the hotel precinct. A good example is the Gleneagles Hotel's world famous golf course, which has an indoor pool, saunas and spas, tennis and squash courts, in addition to bowls, shooting, equestrian and fishing facilities. Leisure facilities at hotels offer an additional lure to customers, even though relatively few residents may actually use the facilities. Leisure facilities are, however, becoming particularly important in the short break and business markets.

11.12.2 *Theme parks*

As well as organizing tours, the commercial sector is also involved with the provision and maintenance of tourist attractions such as historic buildings, zoos, wildlife and amusement parks and theme parks.

Over the past several years, there has been considerable growth in the British theme park industry. Theme parks have become very popular since Disneyland resurrected the amusement park industry, in 1955, in the United States. Their philosophy has been one of excellence, cleanliness, courtesy and safety. They create an atmosphere of fantasy, glamour, escapism, prestige and excitement. These parks have been successful in other countries such as Summerland, in Tokyo, and Tivoli, in Copenhagen. Theme parks are privately operated concerns with attractions built around one or more historical or fantasy themes.

Britain's first theme park was Thorpe Water Park at Chertsey, the concept and development of Leisure Sport Ltd, with a theme of maritime history. The predominant theme is water, with activities such as water skiing and tourist attractions such as 'Bluebird' and Viking Longships. Its development encouraged the provision of other 'theme' facilities elsewhere in the United Kingdom. However, many of the theme parks have not been resounding success stories. Britain's only world-rated theme park is Alton Towers, in Staffordshire. It offers a combination of magnificent surroundings and heritage with fun and fantasy. Alton Towers has been transformed from a stately home and gardens into one of the finest leisure parks in the world. Other British examples include American Adventure, Pleasurewood Hills, Camelot,

Gulliver's Kingdom, Chessington World of Adventures, and Lightwater Valley, with, reputedly, the longest roller-coaster ride in the world.

The United Kingdom theme market is extremely competitive. Every month several developments are proposed. Britain's history provides numerous ready-made themes, it has a day-trip tradition and it is densely populated; there must, however, be a limit to development. Projection 2000 estimate that admissions could double from approximately 8 million to 16 million between 1990 and the year 2000. Even though all social classes visit theme parks, the skilled C1/2 family is the prime target.

The effects of the Single European Market and the opening of the Channel Tunnel on the theme park industry have yet to be fully determined. However, the opening of EuroDisney near Paris indicates the level of competition that the market in the United Kingdom is having to face.

11.12.3 Tourism and transport

This very brief sketch of tourism and the commercial provider's role would be incomplete without some reference to leisure transport. Travel and the mode of transport can be a leisure activity in itself, whether by car, coach, boat, barge, train or plane. The importance of the commercial sector and leisure travel is summed up by Roberts [11]:

> Transport as a leisure activity in itself (pleasure motoring, from home, canal boat tours, sea cruises etc.) as a linkage between home and leisure destinations, or a means of enlarging their destination's attractions (coach tours, car trips, boat trips, fishing excursions etc.), forms a high proportion of leisure expenditure. The commercial sector is directly or indirectly involved in all leisure transport modes in addition to the private car. The sector owns and operates shipping lines, aircraft, coaches, some railways in continental Europe, taxis, pleasure boats and others. It supplies cars and bicycles for hire; provides catering services; provides the boots for hikers, and the shoes for less ambitious walkers. The supply of equipment generally (for example bicycles) is the prerogative of the commercial sector. Finally, it provides marinas and often owns seaside piers which provide landing stages for shipping.

The tourism and holiday market is a major commercial leisure industry. It is another expanding area in which the profession of leisure management has an important role to play and important lessons to learn. Two aspects are worth noting. First, there are a number of personal and social reasons for travel which may be as important as the destination itself. Second, travel is normally expensive and those who can afford it can go further and in greater comfort. Poorer people travel less. Even a simple journey across a large city with a young family could be formidable. More than most forms of leisure, travel is shaped by cost, both direct and indirect.

11.13 Sponsorship

Sponsorship has been defined as 'the provision of financial or material support for some independent activity which is not intrinsic to the furtherances of commercial aims, but from which the supporting company might reasonably hope to gain financial benefits' [12]. It differs from patronage where the financial, material or professional expertise is given by a commercial company to an activity for philanthropic reasons, without looking for any material reward or benefit.

Sponsorship can benefit the company in a number of ways:

1   by increasing publicity
2   by helping to reinforce or change its corporate image
3   by improving public relations, improving trade relations or providing a vehicle for the promotion of company products
4   by increasing market share.

The scale of sponsorship can vary enormously, from contributions of millions of pounds from a multinational company for national sports to the donation of a cup or prize from a small sports shop to a locally run competition. Sponsorship is now a high profile form of collaborative marketing between organizations which usually involves investment by the sponsor, in an event, team, competition, or facility in return for exploitable benefits, particularly favourable promotion and publicity.

Sponsorship growth, worldwide, can be attributed in large measure to increased television converage of major events both sports and arts, though sport predominates.

Favourable images are key, often diverting attention from less favourable products. With restrictions on tobacco and alcohol advertising, sponsorship offers an alternative. In some cases, the survival of professional sports is dependent on sponsorship. Spectators will only come to watch star players and performers, so events need sponsorship to help pay for appearances. Sponsors want television coverage which will only be attracted to events with large audience ratings and star players. Without sponsorship, many events would be uneconomic even with large audiences and ticket sales.

Sponsorship has the potential to promote greater awareness than advertising and can be more effective in changing perceptions and positioning an image. Sponsorship is being used not just to sell goods and services but to project a company and all it has to offer; international events can position a company on to a world stage.

11.13.1 *Sponsorship in sports and the arts*

Sports sponsorship began to develop in the United Kingdom in the early 1960s and dramatically expanded with the ban placed on television cigarette advertising. The cigarette companies had budgeted for television advertising, a large part of which was consequently redirected into sponsorship of sport, since sport had a wide appeal and helped promote a 'healthy image', thus attempting to counteract anti-smoking propaganda, and probably, most important, lending itself to surrogate advertising through the press and television. However, in 1977 the Minister for Sport placed a ceiling on the amount of sponsorship that cigarette companies could give to sport, and there has been a consequent withdrawal of some companies from this area of sponsorship.

Sponsorship has helped some sports to survive and others to flourish. Snooker and darts are cases in point, but other, once minority, spectator sports are now thriving. For example, basketball has turned from being an insignificant British spectator sport into an expanding one and a deal worth £1.3 million was arranged with Carlsberg in 1990, and involved amalgamation of the top teams from the two main leagues. Ice hockey and indoor bowls have experienced a similar growth pattern.

The exact amount of sports sponsorship is difficult to ascertain, many companies and governing bodies being reluctant to reveal information. Spending on sports sponsorship events in the United Kingdom is much greater than that for the arts, the latter accounting for approximately 10 per cent. However, there are signs that some sponsors are shifting their ground in favour of the arts. Until recent years, the arts were more usually the subject of private and company patronage.

Although the majority of sponsorships are a success story, there are some financial disasters, or companies do not achieve expected targets; or the company's name no longer has benefits in one or another direction. The brief history of sponsorship has shown it to be a rapidly changing and fluctuating 'industry'. Among the problems are that the larger the sponsorship investment, the greater the implications on the activity and the greater the harmful effects if sponsorship is withdrawn. With many sport and art events, or leagues or clubs, the need for continuity is essential.

A number of sponsorship ideas emanate from the USA. The 1997 Sports Sponsorship Survey targeted at US corporate sports sponsors and marketing agencies revealed that more than a quarter of sponsors (27.5 per cent) have no pre-defined goals for their sponsorship. The president of Sports Media Challenge adds:

> this lends more credence to the widely held opinion that companies often get involved in sports marketing primarily because of an intense interest in a particular sport by the senior most decision maker or the person who allocates how marketing dollars are spent [13].

Sponsors' primary concerns when selecting an endorser were: image; good representation; positive outcome; return on investment; and mutual respect. Not surprisingly, image was a common denominator for all concerned.

11.13.2 *The major sponsoring companies*

It is apparent that although there are many hundreds of commercial companies sponsoring all manner of leisure pursuits and events, national and international sport and art events gain the most from sponsorship. It is also clear that it is the major companies investing heavily in sponsorship that dominate the market financially.

As might be expected, the major sports services and equipment companies have a considerable stake in sports sponsorship. However, in cash terms the major sponsors tend to be the national banks, the oil companies, tobacco manufacturers, brewers and of late international computing companies; new multinationals have entered the field. The Whitbread Round the World yacht race and the Virginia Slims Tennis Tournaments were typical.

Why do the 'big four' – banks, oil, tobacco and alcohol – need sponsorship? Although commercially powerful, they are vulnerable to a tarnished public image. Banking and oil are connected with huge profits, drinking is linked with alcoholism and crime, and smoking with lung cancer. Sponsorship helps to buy respectability. Respectability means a good public image. Good images create favourable impressions to buy products and services. The major sponsor's main motive is not to aid sport and the arts, *per se*, but to achieve maximum publicity. Maximum publicity means exposure on television. By far the greatest sponsorship of sport is seen on the two BBC television channels. The BBC's charter, however, explicitly forbids paid advertising. Commercial television cannot sponsor. However, the line between advertising and sponsorship is somewhat fragile. There appears to be a qualitative difference between the two. The publication of a company brand name constitutes advertising; the company's name does not. The company nevertheless can obtain more exposure per hour for its name than would be permissible on the independent television network.

Sports and arts sponsorship is big business. Detailed computer compilations are available from companies such as Sportscan which give detailed information about who sponsors sport in the United Kingdom, for how much and why. Since the mid-1980s more and more companies have become involved in the sponsorship of sport and the arts. There has also been a much wider spread of activity across not only traditional events and new events, but in coaching, training, award schemes, youth, women's activities, facilities and equipment, as well as teams and individuals. With the increased popularity of sponsorship, the fifth television channel, breakfast television and cable and satellite television, sponsorship via the media will increase, and the prospect of digital television will spread sponsorship further still. However, sponsorship is no longer of national significance only, it is international – world-wide. Indeed, sponsorship is of such immense importance to sports companies and events that in some cases the sponsor for an event is itself seeking sponsorship from another company. Rothman is known worldwide as a major sponsor of sport including Grand Prix motor racing. In September 1997, 3Com Corporation (a leader in computer networking) announced its sponsorship of the Rothmans Williams Renault team the Austrian and Luxembourg Formula One Grand Prix. Such enormous deals illustrate giant commercial interest in what sport has to offer, both as a product and as a means for projecting a company and hence a company's products.

From a leisure management viewpoint, whether companies are advertising or sponsoring events and projects, they are all marketing to draw customers to their services and products by creating favourable impressions, so that people will buy what the company has to offer rather than a competitor's product.

11.14 Summary – commercial providers of leisure

The major difference between the commercial operator and the public or voluntary operator is the *raison d'être* of the business, the primary objective of the commercial operator being that of financial profit or adequate return on investment. Other sectors may make profits but are established and in being for other primary purposes.

Commercial providers of facilities, services and products for leisure consumption have by far the greatest influence on people's use of leisure time. This is seen particularly in leisure in and around the home and in social recreation. The holiday and tourist industry is an expanding commercial market and the continuing rise in active recreation has expanded the leisure and sports goods markets. Sponsorship has made it possible to promote many sports and arts events and has helped to bring major sporting and entertainment attractions of the highest calibre into the homes of millions of people through television.

Commercial businesses have to make profits or in the end they go out of business. In order to reap the best profits and returns on investment, management policies, approaches and techniques are often different from those employed in the public sector, though the gap is closing. The Leisure Manager should be aware of the differences and learn which approaches and techniques are best applied to specific situations. Many general management principles will apply to all leisure, whether in the public, private or commercial sectors. However, many specific differences will apply to different management situations and to meet different objectives. Leisure management is thus both general and specific.

Commercial leisure is a massive industry. It is limited, however, in what is likely to be provided through its market. Capital investment must produce an adequate return on investment and this therefore excludes many costly land-based resources such as parks and opens spaces (apart from 'resort' attractions inland and on the coast) and community and social service elements. At a local level particularly, the need for co-ordination between the public, commercial and voluntary sectors is of immense importance. Such co-ordination should fall upon local government in general, and upon leisure professionals in particular. Local leisure plans, for example, need to take account of all resources and all providers.

Notes and references

1   Glyptis, S., McInnes, H. and Patmore, J. A. (1987), *Leisure and the Home*, Sports Council/ESRC, London.
2   Tolkki-Nikkonen, M. (1979), *Adult Educators in Finland*, No. 3.
3   Office for National Statistics (1998), *Social Trends 28*, The Stationery Office, London.
4   Office for National Statistics (1998), *Living in Britain – Results from the 1996 General Household Survey*, HMSO, London.
5   Leisure Week (1997), *The Leisure Industry Report*, Leisure Week, London.
6   Keynote, cited *ibid*, p.47.
7   Mintel, cited *ibid*, p.23.

8   Allied Leisure, cited *ibid*, p.25.
9   Dodona, cited *ibid*, p.24.
10   Carroll, J. (1997), All wrapped up in a box, *Leisure Management, 17* (3) 12–14.
11   Roberts, J. (TEST) (1979), *Sports Council/Social Science Research Council Review: The Commercial Sector in Leisure*, Sports Council/SSCR, London, p.12
12   English Tourist Board (1978), *The Give and Take of Sponsorship*, ETB, London.
13   Sports Media Challenge (1998), *The 1997 Sports Sponsorship Survey*.

Recommended further reading

Leisure Week (1998), *The Leisure Industry Report*, Leisure Week, London.

The management of leisure

Chapter 12

Management

The first part of the book dealt with leisure and the needs of people; the second part focussed on the trends in leisure, planning and government, the third part considered the leisure providers, public, voluntary and commercial. The fourth part introduces the principles and practices of management.

Management is a word that can be applied to most situations of life – it is the act or art of managing. It tends to be used most often in business, industry and commerce, with 'managers' and 'staff' or 'workers' being juxtapositioned, yet often breeds apart in some industries. A number of institutions claim management as their *raison d'être*, for example, British Institute of Management, Institute of Leisure and Amenity Management and Institute of Sport and Recreation Management. Many of these kinds of organizations also focus on specialist technical knowledge. Is this the same as management?

The management of leisure requires the effectiveness and efficiency which is needed in all good management; the core elements of management will be the core elements of leisure management. Managing leisure will also have its own specialisms. This chapter deals with the general core elements of management, though these are discussed in the context of leisure situations; later chapters deal with the specialisms in greater detail.

This chapter first introduces the concept of general management to show that there are core elements which apply to all branches of management, including leisure. It sets the scene to encompass the range of situations from the commercial to the social. Second, management is viewed in an historical setting going back over this century and includes the management gurus of today. Third, general management functions and systems are introduced. Fourth, a large part of the chapter is devoted to key components of management – leadership, decision making, communication, and group behaviour. Relatively new concepts of managerial coaching, mentoring and the qualities of the 'servant leader' are introduced, adding elements to the third edition of this book.

Having read this chapter, readers will know that in order to manage leisure resources, services and facilities, managers need to understand and practise good management and hone the skills and techniques of management to achieve organizational goals and objectives. This chapter focusses on the movement towards 'quality' services and towards participative – employee involved – styles of management. The chapter also points in the direction of a theory–practice orientation to leisure management, an essential to grasping the theoretical framework for leisure management presented in the final chapter.

12.1 The management process – what it is and what it does

This section provides a setting for thinking about management before looking at lessons from the past and from current practice. Management is both an active human occupation and a process by which people and organizations achieve results. Management is a distinct type of work. The ability to do a job is not enough. The good physical education teacher, swimming coach, librarian, park ranger or sports or arts administrator does not automatically make a good manager. While technical 'know-how' is important, management is more – it concerns the work of people, effectiveness and accountability for end results.

What is the distinct type of work which relates to the manager? Management is not a science, with precise laws and predictable behaviour. No foolproof rules exist which can replace the need for judgement, common-sense and related experience. Management is not an art, if by that we imply only intuition and individual judgement, on the thesis that 'managers are born and not made'. Management is not a profession, even though a code of ethics, standards and ideals has been established, for example by the British Institute of Management. Management appears to be a bit of each: 'It is the sum of art and science that makes a manager.'

While management is fundamentally concerned with human behaviour, behaviour is not constant. Management situations vary. Management is concerned with change; it is continually flowing and interacting and few areas of life change as much as the world of leisure – a volatile profession if ever there was one. Peter Drucker [1] emphasized this aspect of management:

The job of management is never to be concerned with restoring or maintaining normality because normality is the condition of yesterday. The major concern of management, if they are to make their business effective, must be in the direction of systematically trying to understand the condition of the future so that they can decide on the changes that can take their business from today into tomorrow.

Discussions on management often start with a search for the best definition of the word. A cursory look at dictionary definitions illustrates the problem. The verb 'to manage' can mean 'to direct', 'to handle', 'to influence', 'to exert control', 'to make submissive', 'to contrive', 'to use economically and with forethought' and 'to cope with'. One can 'manage to make a muddle', 'succeed in one's aim', 'make proper use of' and 'manage on one's own'. Managing therefore has diverse meanings and differing interpretations. It also has varied interpreters. Its functions are changing, fluid and subtle.

Management has been defined in a variety of ways; some explain its purpose at great length, others more directly. Drucker [2], for example, states that management is a 'multi-purpose organ that manages a business *and* manages managers *and* manages workers and work'. If one of these is omitted, we would not have management or a business enterprise, according to Drucker. Here management is seen as a structure with functions. Later we will see management described more in terms of a process.

Management thus depends on a variety of factors, for example: the situation; the information available; the people involved; the organization; and the people doing the managing. In significant measure, management depends on the person, or persons, doing the managing. Management relates to people's behaviour. This conditions any definition of management. The qualities found in the good manager are therefore important in any definition of management.

What appears to be abundantly clear is that there is no one way, no one 'instant brew' for instant management and no one management principle that is right every time. Management is malleable, amenable to change and flexible in organization. It has many functions. The manager is not just a creator, but he or she is also a planner and forecaster, setting objectives, motivating, leading, deciding, checking and monitoring performance. Management – in the simple idiom of today – is getting things done with and through people, and as such management is a *social process*.

12.1.1 *Management is 'profit' orientated*

Management is usually considered in terms of economic efficiency; it can only justify its existence by the economic results it produces. There may be greater non-economic results, such as the contribution to community welfare, but management has failed, according to Drucker [2], if it fails to produce economic results. It must supply goods and services which the public wants, at a price the consumer is willing to pay. 'People service' programmes, including many aspects of leisure management, differ in some fundamental respects from a commercial profit-orientated company. Increasingly, however, local authorities, trusts and other not-for-profit organizations have to be concerned with economic viability as a factor but not as an end goal. In human service programmes, 'profit' needs to be defined in terms not just of money but in terms of a whole range of other additional criteria, for example: the physical, social and psychological benefits offered by the programme; the range of users attracted; the meeting of targets for, say, the socially deprived or the handicapped; improving performance; and the numbers attracted from the locality it serves. Here targets are of many kinds, including the level of financial viability aimed for. Extending this idea, some have tried to place an actual financial value on recreation participation. David Gray [3] says:

> We desperately need a method of planning that permits social cost benefit analysis. Lacking such a system we are turning control of our social enterprises over to the accounting mind. The accounting mind reaches decisions by a method in which short-range fiscal consequences are the only criterion of value. Recreation and park services will not survive in that kind of environment. Most of the great social problems that disfigure our national life cannot be addressed in a climate dominated by that kind of value system.

Similarly, Robert Wilder [4] states: 'The modern day name of the game seems to be quantification, justification, competition and cost-benefit analysis.' In search of a management tool by which to measure recreational benefits in terms of 'profit', Wilder presented his 'economic equivalency index' (EEI), which attempts to quantify recreation value in financial terms.

Good management, therefore, is needed to achieve objectives – financial and social. Leisure managers need above all else to be good managers, with both generalist and specialist skills. In whatever branch of management, they need to be 'profit' orientated.

12.2 The principles of management in historical perspective

Contemporary management practices have been influenced by many schools of management thought. Management understanding has progressed from the 'scientific movement' instigated by Frederick Taylor [5] and others at the turn of the century, through the 'human relations movement' influenced by Elton Mayo [6] and the now legendary Hawthorne studies, through the 'classical movement' stressing organization and administration and influenced by Henri Fayol [7] and Max Weber to the behaviourist view of management put forward by Douglas McGregor [9] and Frederick Herzberg [10], who built on the inspiration of Abraham Maslow [11,12].

The management of business organizations has been the subject of considerable interest over this century and 'leisure management' can benefit from the experience and knowledge of eminent thinkers. Hence, this part of the chapter explores the ideas of the past and the view of current experts in the field of management.

The management of people, organizations, societies and nations has been part of history over thousands of years. The management of the state, economics, property and social cohesion go back beyond Greek civilizations. Some power struggles and take-over bids of today exhibit the kind of thinking set out in Machiavelli's *The Prince*, written at the time of the Renaissance in Florence. However, management strategies, systems and structures found in business today owe much to ideas developed early this century.

12.2.1 Beginning of modern management

Management as we know it today has its beginnings at the start of this century. Four examples from the first half of the twentieth century are: the 'scientific' movement; 'classical' theory; bureaucracy; and human relations. We then look at the 'behaviourist' view of management.

1. The 'scientific movement

Frederick Taylor, an American engineer, dominated the beginning of what has become to be known as the 'scientific movement' from the turn of the century until the 1920s. Taylor's ideas are management foundation stones for many organizations and enterprises that sprang up in the first decades of this century. The term 'time and motion study' emanates from Taylor. His was a system of reward: the higher the productivity, the higher the pay. The belief was born that optimum work environments would enhance productivity. In *Principles of Scientific Management* (1911) [13], he set out four foundations of his principles: a) the development of a science of work and meeting goals, with pay linked to productivity – a fair day's work, for a fair day's pay; b) the scientific selection and training of each employee to fit the task; c) bringing together the science of work and the selection of the workers for the best results; and d) equal division of work and responsibilities.

2. 'Classical' management theory

Classical management theory is concerned with the efficient design and structure of organizations – the administration of the business. Building on Taylor's theories, the French mining engineer, Henri Fayol, had an important influence on management thinking, although his work was not published in English until 1949 (he died in 1925) in *General and Industrial Management* [14]. He emphasized five management processes which were applicable to any field of endeavour which required management: planning; organizing; commanding; co-ordinating and controlling. In addition to these five foundations, he developed fourteen general principles of management, including 'unity of command' in which each employee should have only one boss, without conflicting lines of command and the 'scalar' or hierarchical chain of command.

Classical theory is thus concerned with structures and hierarchy. Its fundamental principles have had profound effects on government and industry.

Local government, and hence public recreation services, conform to formal structures, organizational charts, hierarchical structures. Considerable support is given to these structures: people know exactly where they stand and what is expected of them; they know their station, their role and their influence; their jobs are defined.

Classical management structuring, however, appears to neglect the people-orientation. It is mechanistic, bureaucratic and red taped. Formal structures tend to put work into tight categories; departments tend to be sub-divided into units; labour is divided into specialisms; inflexibility is instilled and top-to-bottom chains of control – chains of command – become sacrosanct. In public recreation services we find that comprehensive departments, so called, may well be a series of tightly closed administrative boxes and specialisms, e.g. administration, finance, programming, catering and maintenance, without lateral linking, or they are divided into parks, pools, youth, aged, disabled – all acting out separate roles in separate units.

3. Bureaucracy

German sociologist and political economist Max Weber studied the role of the leader in an organization and how individuals respond to authority. Today we talk about charismatic management, yet it was Weber who recognized this quality in an individual's personality. Despite this finding, Weber believed that the bureaucratic organization, from a purely technical point of view, was the most efficient to run a business. However, as Wren [8] points out: 'Bureaucracy was conceived as a blueprint for efficiency which would emphasise rules rather than men.'

In terms of leisure and recreation management, the bureaucratic model has been the norm through Europe, including the United Kingdom.

4. The 'human relations movement'

The long-held theories of 'scientific' management and bureaucracy were challenged by writers such as Chester Barnard and Elton Mayo. Chester Barnard recognized that large organizations were made up of smaller groups, which were made up of individuals with personal motivations. Ahead of his time (*The Functions of the Executive*, 1938) [15], he saw the distinction between efficiency and effectiveness. To be effective, the aims of an organization must be accepted by those contributing to its success; in other words, authority in an organization only exists while employees are willing to accept it. He perceived the Chief Executive in an organization as a 'value sharpener' as distinct from the former authoritarian styles of management.

One of the founders of industrial sociology is Australian-born Elton Mayo, who studied in Australia and in Britain. He emigrated to the USA in 1923 and spent much of his career at Harvard. Mayo is best remembered for the Hawthorne Experiments which were conducted in Western Electric's Hawthorne Works in Chicago from 1927 to 1932. The tests were conducted following earlier experiments with two work groups.

An experimental group of women worked in one room; a control group of women worked in another room. Lighting conditions were varied in the experimental group. It was discovered that not only did improved illumination result in improved productivity, but that *all* changes to illumination resulted in improvements, including levels of illumination which were highly unfavourable. In addition, it was discovered that as well as increased production in the experimental group the same improvements occurred in the control group. Researchers from Harvard led by Elton Mayo were called in to continue the studies [6]. After the illumination experiments, other variables were also manipulated. For example, the experimental group were given scheduled work breaks, shorter working weeks and other benefits. Again, productivity increased both in the experimental group *and* the control. Mayo's researchers then removed all the benefits from the experimental group. Yet again, production increased in *both* groups!

What were the reasons for these effects? With the power of the trade unions and the need for fair treatment for all employees, we might not expect to find such results. Why had attitudes to work changed in this situation? Each group was found to be reacting to being an 'object of study' – the consequence of the presence of researchers. Mayo's methodology was to spend considerable time in interviewing both the experimental group and the control group. Employees were made to feel that the company *genuinely cared* for them, cared about their problems and their feelings. Management was seen to be concerned about employees as people. The improved social conditions appeared to be more important than improved physical and environmental conditions. Hence came the dawn of the 'human relations movement' and the discovery that the informal organization and the quality of supervision had a significant effect on morale and productivity. This realization was one of the pivots in the human relations school of management: inter-personal relationships are important; management is a people-orientated business.

The paternalistic concern of management in relation to industrial recreation may well be one of the products of this management movement. Many businesses try to provide a good working environment, offer fringe benefits, social benefits and appear to show genuine concern for workers at work and away from work. (See chapter ten on company provision for leisure.)

Employees' dissatisfaction with businesses in the United Kingdom today, which may be seen on the surface as wanting better conditions, tea-breaks, etc., may have more to do with lack of sensitivity and involvement of employees emotionally. Hence, the Taylorist philosophy of self-interest was disapproved of by Mayo. While the experiments had scientific flaws, they have shown the importance of the peer group in the work place and that within each formal organization there are many informal ones, which, far from being discouraged, should be welcomed. These discoveries make it possible to work towards motivating and encouraging employees or fellow colleagues to achieve corporate goals. For the leisure industry, it illustrates the need for both staff and customers to develop understandings and communications within and between them.

12.2.2 *The 'behaviourist' view of management*

One of the post-Second World War management movements is that towards a 'behaviourist' approach, which has been in vogue since the early 1950s. It arose, in part, in opposition to the rigid structuring and organizational character of classical methods. It was felt that organization structures should be tempered with flexibility and a greater concern for employee involvement. The inherent discord within closed systems needed to be eliminated; harmony would lead to improved work and work relationships. McGregor [9], Herzberg [10], Argyris [16], Likert [17] and others have enlarged management thinking within the behavioural approach, inspired by the work of psychologists such as Erich Fromm and Abraham Maslow and the human relations work of Elton Mayo. Probably the best known mangement theorist in the area of human psychology is Abraham Maslow, famous for his theory of the hierarchy of needs in motivating people, set out in his classic *Motivation and Personality* (1954) [11]. People have needs, some are basic to survival, some are social and some are self-fulfilling. Basic, lower levels, must be satisfied first. Maslow believed that once needs are satisfied, they no longer motivate. In those parts of the modern western world free from warfare, most people are fed, sheltered and have security. These things are no longer motivators. It is the social and ego needs which are dominant. But in war-torn countries, survival is an immensely strong motivator.

In an affluent society, most physical and safety needs have been consistently satisfied; consequently, it is the social and ego needs which are dominant. Maslow's concern that people should be 'self-actualized', whether at work or play, led to the kind of thinking which stressed working patterns that encouraged people to express themselves in work and in leisure. Leisure Managers, like most other people, want to be recognized as individuals, to have some measure of control over the decisions in their working environment and their own jobs, to accomplish something worthwhile – in other words, to see themselves in something that is successful and meaningful.

The value system of managers has changed and is changing constantly. Conventional management with rigid structuring, hierarchies and closed systems was challenged by the 'behaviourists' who believe that understanding and involving people leads to harmony, which leads to improved work and working relationships. Douglas McGregor, an American social psychologist, is in the annals of management history for his famous 'Theory X' and 'Theory Y' – authoritarian and participative management approaches set out in *The Human Side of Enterprise* (1960) [9]. He was a friend of Abraham Maslow and Rensis Likert and, like them, he provides a human, participative face for management. McGregor added support to the work of Maslow and influenced by the Hawthorne studies makes two basic approaches to management – 'Theory X' and 'Theory Y'.

Theory X is the traditional view of direction and control. Most people have to be coerced, controlled, directed and even threatened before effort is made towards the achievement of organizational objectives. The theory also suggests that people prefer to be directed, respond when disciplined, wish to avoid responsibility, have relatively little ambition and want security above all else. In essence, Theory X is the 'stick and carrot' approach, the carrot being money or reward and the stick being the threat of financial insecurity. McGregor believes that this must be replaced by Theory Y.

Theory Y is the theory of the integration of individual and organizational goals. Effort in work is as natural as play or rest. External controls are not the only means for bringing about effort towards objectives. People can exercise self-direction and self-control when commitment is high. They respond to honest praise and resent punishment. Moreover, people learn, under proper conditions, not only to accept but also to seek responsibility; the capacity to exercise a relatively high degree of imagination, ingenuity and creativity in the solution of organizational problems is widely, not narrowly, distributed in the population, as the old-style management of 'leaders' and 'followers' suggests.

Theory X managers will tend to push people to achieve a task. Theory Y managers will tend to lead people to achieve a task. McGregor claimed that those managers operating predominantly towards the principles of Theory Y were generally more successful in the following ways: their departments had higher outputs; staff showed greater motivation; and there were fewer labour problems, lower labour turnovers, less waste and greater profits.

McGregor's work has been enlarged by Rensis Likert, an American social psychologist [17], whose concepts are presented in four management systems: System 1, 'exploitative authoritative'; System 2, 'benevolent authoritative'; System 3, 'consultative'; and System 4, 'participative'. The nearer the management system is to System 4, the more productive the organization. It produces lower costs, higher earnings, better union relations, more positive worker attitudes and higher morale. Conversely, the nearer the management is to System 1, the more it results in lower productivity, higher costs, poorer union relations and lower morale.

The findings of McGregor and Likert confirm that more effective results can be obtained by a people-orientated approach to management. That being the case, the implications for leisure service management are considerable. If humanistic approaches to management can prove more effective in product-orientated industries, they should also produce more effective results in service-orientated organizations, such as those found in the leisure industry.

Frederick Herzberg, an American psychologist coined the term 'job enrichment'. His theory of motivation [10] relates to two main job satisfaction parameters: hygiene factors and motivators. Hertzberg's study of satisfaction and dissatisfaction at work was first published in *The Motivation to Work* (1959). He found that those aspects leading to feelings of satisfaction included achievement, recognition and personal growth and called these 'motivators'. Dissatisfaction mostly related to what he termed 'hygiene' factors, such as working conditions, salary, status and job security. These things in a modern context of, say, conditions of service, company car, car parking space, luncheon vouchers, incremental rise in pay and so on, keep us from being unhappy, they do not necessarily provide happiness – job satisfaction. Herzberg believes that as jobs become enriched, the need for job supervision lessens. Hence, today, employees in many organizations can be trusted to work at times and places more suited to their needs – flexi-time; home-based work.

Hygiene factors then are not part of the actual job, but relate to the work environment – policies, conditions, fringe benefits, and so on. These factors may affect job performance but are not part of the job itself. Motivators, on the other hand, are concerned with the job. Is the job challenging? Does it carry responsibility, recognition for achievement, give prestige and esteem? Herzberg is concerned with job enrichment but his theory is limited by being preoccupied with two strands of employment conditions.

Other 'behaviourists' have taken the ideas forward. Reg Revans, at one time a United Kingdom local government officer in the education field, is thought to be the 'inventor' of Action Learning – managers educating each other through shared working experiences. Action Learning is a method well suited to leisure management. E. F. Schumacher, the German economist who worked for the Coal Board in Britain, coined the phrase 'small is beautiful'. People need to be involved in the decision-making process in small units. Later, management theorists were to extend this idea to include delegating authority to far wider groups within an organization and to dub this approach 'empowerment'. Leisure, with its vast range of choice, offers great opportunity for work in small units, with high levels of delegated authority, for example, decentralized service units on a geographical or neighbourhood basis.

Argyris, building on Maslow's self-actualization theme, believes that job enrichment will increase employee initiatives and self-direction. There would appear to be much in common between Maslow's theory, the ideas of Argyris, McGregor's 'Theory Y' and Likert's 'System 4'. They are all concerned with job enlargement, job enrichment and self-fulfilment.

It is important that we learn the lessons of the past. They affect the present and can point to the future. However, we now turn to more contemporary thinking by learning from the management gurus – the 'pop stars' of management.

12.3 The management gurus

In recent times management experts have been feted with the equivalent of management 'pop idol' status. A thumb-nail sketch of some of their insights is provided in this section and owes much to the highly informative book by Carol Kennedy *Guide to the Management Gurus* [18].

1. Peter Drucker

The first to achieve fame was Peter Drucker. He was born in Vienna, came to Britain in the 1920s, worked as an economist in London in the 1930s and emigrated to the USA in 1937. Working as a consultant with General Motors, he wrote his first book in 1942, became a prolific writer and has had profound influence in the spread of management thinking for the past five decades.

Drucker's basic principles of management have been sustained over time: setting objectives; organizing; motivating and communicating; measuring performance; and developing staff. One of his most influential books is *Concept of the*

Corporation (1946) [19], in which he sought to discover what made large companies successful. He believed that these companies knew what businesses they were in, what their competencies were, and how to keep focussed on their goals. In *The Practice of Management* (1954) [2], which remains a classic, Drucker identified management by objectives as the first of seven primary tasks. In the United Kingdom, John Humble turned the principle of management by objectives into a system of management – MBO. Regarded by some as somewhat 'old hat' these days, MBO remains a key to the involvement of a workforce in setting and achieving an organization's goals.

Drucker's broad view of management is cited by Kennedy: to Drucker, management is central to life, not just to business. The chief executive in any walk of life is like a conductor of an orchestra:

> We are beginning to realize that management itself is the central institution of our present society, and that there are very few differences between managing a business, a hospital, managing a labour union or managing a government agency. All along, this has been the main thrust of my work, and the one that distinguishes it from practically all my contemporaries working in the field.
>
> Peter Drucker cited in Kennedy [18] p.47

Currently, local authorities in the United Kingdom are asking themselves whether they should be providers, organizers or enablers. Drucker advocates that government should govern, not 'do'.

2. Henry Mintzberg

The Canadian professor of management Henry Mintzberg [20] takes a different viewpoint from Drucker. He suggests that chief executives, far from planning, organizing, controlling and being an orchestral conductor, jump from topic to topic, thrive on interruptions, meet a steady stream of callers, read few reports fully and spend as much time dealing with people outside the organization as within it. He believes that chief executives favour intuitive thinking, creative strategies – 'right brain thinking'.

3. Chris Argyris

An American psychologist, Argyris is best known for his work in developing individual potential within organizations. Each individual has potential which can be enhanced or stunted depending on the way in which an organization is managed. Managers have to deal with conflicts. Chris Argyris and Donald Schon examined these kinds of conflicts and provide potential solutions in *Organizational Learning: A Theory of Action Perspective* (1978) [21].

4. John Adair

A pioneering British thinker on leadership, Adair is a strong advocate of training; he believes that leadership is a learned skill, rather than an inborn aptitude. Leadership is about a sense of direction; it is about achieving a task with a team. Leaders inspire others with their own enthusiasm and commitment. Adair is best known for his concept of action-centred leadership, and the overlap between the task, the team and the individual. In *Understanding Motivation* (1990) [22], Adair lists the functions of leadership as planning, initiating, controlling, supporting, informing and evaluating. In *Effective Teambuilding* (1986), he suggests that 50 per cent of success depends on the team and 50 per cent on the individual – 'the ultimate cure of the "us" and "them"'.

5. Laurence Peter

In *The Peter Pyramid* [23], the author demonstrates the ways bureaucracies sap human resources; major organizations are constructed upside down, with the point of the operation all but invisible beneath the bulk of a top-heavy administration. The bureaucrat is so busy keeping his job that he has no time to do it! Peter suggests that we simplify meaningless complexity and stop the procession of the 'blind leading the blind'.

6. Charles Handy

The world of management has changed in very recent times as a number of current management thinkers have sought to revolutionize management practice. Charles Handy has a concern with how companies reach goals far beyond financial profit levels. He believes that organizations are more than structures and systems. He sees the need to move from the 'status quo' to meet radical changes in business – a process of 'upside-down thinking', a process similar to the psychologist Edward de Bono's 'lateral thinking', which he described as generating new ideas and escaping from old ones.

According to Handy, in *Inside Organizations* [24], increasingly, companies are taking on a shamrock shape. The Irish clover, the national emblem, was originally used by St Patrick who demonstrated that the three leaves were still part of one leaf, so the three aspects of God were still the same God. Handy uses the symbol to postulate that in today's business there are three different types of workforce: the core workforce; the contractual fringe; and the flexible labour force. Each is a part of a larger whole.

The core workforce is made up of those people who are essential and give the organization its uniqueness; they are vital – they are the organization. They are increasingly precious. There are fewer of them; each is responsible for more; they are not easily replaced and they carry a large slice of the organization's know-how with them.

The contractual fringe are specialist organizations. They have the resources and they are geared to undertake specialist tasks in their fields. However in leisure management, what to contract out and what to keep in the core, as one's uniqueness, is not an easy decision. For example, in a private health club, is it good business to contract out the cleaning, catering and beauty treatment? Core workers and specialists are expensive. Can leisure make better use of a flexible labour force, e.g. for events and holiday programmes?

7. Warren Bennis

Clichés now abound in management literature and current jargon. Warren Bennis, an industrial psychologist, is remembered for his: 'Managers do things right. Leaders do the right thing.' Strongly influenced by the motivational theories, he sees the need to move from 'bureaucracy' to 'adhocracy', the opposite of bureaucracy, describing small, flexible groups that operate freely across departmental boundaries. He sees the leader as the bridge-maker between the now and the future – a person who can transform an organization.

A prolific writer, Bennis identifies 'vision' that provides a focus to guide personal and organizational activities [25]. He perceives effective leadership in four areas of management: attention (drawing others into his/her vision through a supreme focus); measuring (communicating meaning, directing and aligning staff to work in harmony); trust (conveying the leader's integrity and reliability); and self (the leader's ability to understand and accept his/her and staff personal limitations and thus exploit their strengths).

8. Tom Peters and Robert Waterman

Vision and mission have now become business trade marks. Three powerful books to hit the management scene in the 1980s were Tom Peters and Robert Waterman's *In Search of Excellence* (1982) [26], Tom Peters and Nancy Austin's *A Passion for Excellence* (1985) [27] and Peters' *Thriving on Chaos* (1987) [28], which Peters calls a 'handbook for a management revolution'. Peters' previous books were written against a background of stability and predictability. That no longer exists: we are in a time of accelerating change. Aspiring only to be excellent is not enough says Peters. Businesses must continually create new market niches and add new value – quality to their products. Leisure is an expanding industry also. It too, in my judgement, needs constantly to look for new quality niches.

9. Richard Pascale and Anthony Athos

In *The Art of Japanese Management* [29] the authors identified the reasons for Japanese post-war success. From this they invented the acclaimed 'Seven S Model'. This is made up of three 'hard' S factors (strategy, structure and systems) and four 'soft' S factors (style, shared values, skills and staff) in which the Japanese excelled. It was the soft S factors that made the difference and the best firms linked their purposes to human values as well as to economic measures.

10. Rosabeth Moss Kanter

In the changing management scene, 'empowerment' is also becoming a by-word. Empowerment goes beyond delegation. Moss Kanter, an American sociologist and a professor of Harvard, has become an authority on managing change. She sets out future organizations as 'post entrepreneurial', empowering individuals as a force for change. She sees new corporations, for example, as leaner and fitter, with fewer management levels and able to do more with less.

Moss Kanter's vision is to make fundamental changes within organizations, providing greater power to a wider range of employees, including clerical staff, and creating intermediate jobs to bridge the gap to top management. Hence, she calls for 'empowering' strategies leading to flatter hierarchies, decentralized authority and autonomous working groups. Her essential skills for future managers are set out in *When Giants Learn to Dance* (1989) [30].

Given opportunities and resources, decentralization and empowerment could work well in a number of leisure settings – library business units, sports development units, arts groups and so on.

11. W. Edwards Deming and Joseph Juran

Every few years, new sounding themes and new ways of managing come into vogue. The early 1990s resounded to the word 'quality' and abbreviations like 'TQM' – Total Quality Management, the symbol of the ideal organization and its management. There were also BS5750/ISO 9000, testimony that the organization has reached a certain standard of management, and 'Kite Marks' to denote quality.

Yet, the 'quality movement' had been instilled into Japanese management thinking in the post-war years by management consultants such as Americans W. Edwards Deming and Joseph Juran. Later, the Americans were anxious to copy the successes of Japanese industry. Deming's management philosophy was perceiving the customer as 'the most important part of the production line'. Profit in business comes from repeat customers. Hence, management must stay ahead of the customers, anticipating needs in the years to come [31].

12. Kenneth Blanchard

A leading American management consultant and author, Blanchard has become best known for a series of 'one minute' texts including: *The One Minute Manager*, *Putting the One Minute Manager to Work*; *Leadership and the One Minute Manager*, and *The One Minute Sales Person* [32]. These easy to read texts are noted for their 'strap lines', for example 'Help People Reach Their Full Potential – Catch Them Doing Something Right'; 'Situational Leadership Is Not Something You Do To People But Something You Do With People'. Blanchard, with his co-authors (Spencer Johnson with the first book and then Patricia and Drea Zigarmi), dismisses the idea that a person's age and service are the best qualification of management; they demonstrate that the ability to manage one's own behaviour and attitudes is an essential prerequisite to managing other people. This is a huge lesson for leisure managers and is a theme taken up later in this chapter.

Up to this point, we have looked at lessons from the past and also what the management gurus of today have to say. We now turn more prosaically to the traditional functions and systems which are still of value in general and leisure management.

12.4 Management functions and systems

Most businesses and public leisure services appear to be based on classical management theory. Many writers have revised Fayol's original model but generally the framework and logic have remained intact: planning (policies, forecasting, objectives); execution (systematic implementation of policies, co-ordination); and control (monitoring performance). More recent writers have added to Fayol's model with additional functions such as motivation, communication, budgeting, creating and staff development.

The functions of management are seen as important because they are the constituents of every management job. The emphasis they receive, however, will vary according to the type of job, the level of the manager, the nature of the environment and many other factors. It would appear that the classical principles of management theory, adapted and modified to meet the needs of different organizations, can be used as a basic framework for the management of leisure services, facilities and programmes, namely:

1   conceptualizing, having a mission, direction and marketing strategy;
2   establishing measurable objectives;
3   organizing, establishing a structure and system;
4   recruiting, training and developing staff;
5   carrying out the plan (programme) and obtaining results through people;
6   assisting subordinates and inspiring and motivating them;
7   seeking improvements and appraising results.

There appear to be a core of knowledge and skills that are needed for management at all levels; MacKenzie's classic 3-D management process illustrates his 'ideas–people–things' model [33]. These core management tasks are basically of three types: conceptual, human and technical.

The conceptual skills are developed on an understanding of the overall situations, the nature of the problems and complexities, and the ability to think clearly, analyse problems and plan carefully. These skills in formulating ideas and concepts determine the policies, orientation and objectivity of the organization, enterprise or programme being developed.

The human skills are concerned with people. They include the ability to select, develop, motivate, lead, decide, control and monitor performance. Managers must have good judgement and be able to work with and through people to meet objectives.

The technical skills are needed to incorporate experience and knowledge of

369

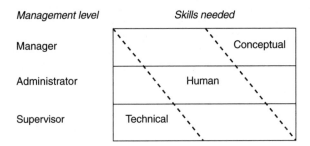

FIGURE 12.1 Management skills

Source: adapted from Hershey, P. and Blanchard, K.H., *Management of Organizational Behaviour: Utilising Human Resources* (2nd edition), p. 9.

the subject area, a sympathy with and understanding of the management environment and the methods and techniques which are needed to perform the tasks. In the leisure facility environment, for example, technical skills are needed for operating and maintaining parks, pitches, swimming pools, theatres, leisure centres, plant and equipment.

All managers, supervisors and group leaders need all three skills, but they are needed in different quantities, depending on their level of authority and the tasks in hand. Generally, the higher up the managerial ladder, the greater the need for conceptual skills, while the more 'sharp end' workers will need to have greater technical skills. The pools supervisor, for example, will have greater concern for the number of staff on poolside, the quality of the water, health and safety and the correct procedures and standards, and less on the demographic profile of those using the swimming pool – essential to the work of the manager.

While top managers need more conceptual skills to do their job and supervisors need more technical skills to do their job, all need human skills and it is these skills of dealing with other people that are critical to effective management practice. In identifying these three areas, Robert Katz confirms that individual management styles vary according to the management position one holds. This is illustrated in Figure 12.1, showing that whatever the management level, all managers need excellent human relations skills.

However, of critical importance is the appreciation that whilst management is concerned with planning, execution and control and is concerned also with ideas and people, management in and of itself is nothing: it needs a situation, a context. Management therefore is situational – i.e. it needs something to manage. In this context, that 'something' is leisure and recreation, which need both general and specialist management.

12.4.1 Management systems

While much current management practice appears to be based on the classical movement, many additional management systems and techniques have been added to it or have been introduced in recent years and many have been influenced by the behavioural scientists.

Management by Objectives (MBO) has become a popular management system over the past three decades. So well known has the term 'MBO' become that there are now a range of definitions of what it actually is. In addition, several systems have been built upon the MBO technique of setting and achieving objectives. Some look to the system being a philosophy of management, others take a more pragmatic view. George Odiorne [34], thought to be one of the founding fathers of the movement, defined MBO as:

> a process whereby the superior and subordinate managers of an organization jointly identify its common goals, define each individual's major areas of responsibility in terms of the results expected of him, and use these measures as guides for operating the unit and assessing the contribution of each of its members.

Whatever the differences of definition, two main strands of MBO are linked as the cornerstones of the system: the setting of objectives, and the participation by managers from all levels in an organization.

PPBS (Planning–Programming–Budgeting Systems) is a specific method of applying systems theory, developed in the early 1960s by the US Department of Defense. Another method, PERT (Programme Evaluation Review Technique), is a system of planning and control that identifies key activities needed to accomplish a given project successfully. It is frequently used on large projects in the management of resources by identifying when, where and the extent of the resources required. PERT incorporates a system known as CPM (Critical Path Method), which is a technique based on a network analysis that highlights the activities requiring completion in a particular sequence within a given space of time. A system currently in vogue is TQM (Total Quality Management).

12.4.2 Total Quality Management

Two movements in modern business appear to have gained ground during recent years: the computer-technology revolution worldwide, and the quality–customer care momentum, in which the North Americans have been ahead in the field. Markets, including the commercial leisure and tourism markets, have become increasingly competitive. Pricing, quality and delivery have been key determinants in satisfying customers and thereby increasing market share.

Whether managing in the commercial, public or voluntary sectors people have to be attracted to the services and facilities and these should be managed with excellence, that is with quality. But quality does not just happen. It has to be worked for. It has to be managed.

Total Quality Management (TQM) is an approach to improving the effectiveness and flexibility of a business as a whole – i.e. a process from top to bottom, which involves every person in an organization – to ensure customer satisfaction at every stage. TQM thus focusses on customer needs and builds a logical linkage between these needs and the business objectives.

The British Quality Association provides a definition of TQM:

Total Quality (TQM) is a corporate business management philosophy which recognizes that customer needs and business goals are inseparable. It is applicable within both industry and commerce. It ensures maximum effectiveness and efficiency within a business and secures commercial leadership by putting in place processes and systems which will promote excellence, prevent errors and ensure that every aspect of the business is aligned to customer needs and the advancement of business goals without duplication or waste of effort. The commitment to TQM originates at the chief executive level in a business and is promoted in all human activities. The accomplishment of quality is thus achieved by personal involvement and accountability, devoted to a continuous improvement process, with measurable levels of performance by all concerned. It involves every department, function and process in a business and the active commitment of all employees to meeting customer needs. In this regard the 'customers' of each employee are separately and individually identified.

If quality is synonymous with meeting customer requirements, then this has fundamental implications for leisure management. The first item on the agenda will be to find out who are the customers and potential customers and what are their requirements.

TQM is then a way of organizing and involving the whole business: every department, every activity and every person. It must establish an 'organization for quality'. The principles behind such total quality are identified by Pip Mosscrop and Adrian Stores [35]:

1. excellence as the objective and getting it right first time;
2. everyone is a customer or a supplier in every transaction – every transaction in the business, every link in the chain, has a supplier and a customer;
3. absolute clarity about customers' needs, the perceptions of customers are paramount;
4. commitment from the top;
5. measurement of all key outputs: 'We are convinced that control through measurement of key outputs in terms of ratios against past trends, standards and/or targets must become a way of life for all those employed in the leisure sector';
6. prevention not blame; sharing responsibility, preventing future occurrences;
7. training and education from top down;
8. integration of total quality into the business – a core business activity which permeates every aspect of leisure operations.

In other words, excellence is called for and is worked for by every person in all aspects of the operation. All activity throughout all operations is continuously directed at satisfying customer requirements: 'Total Quality Management in the leisure sector is about securing fundamental changes in attitudes towards colleagues, customers, products, services and quality.'

John Oakland [36] believes that Total Quality Management is concerned with moving control from outside the individual to within, the objective being to make everyone accountable for their own performance, and to get each person committed to attaining quality in a highly motivated fashion:

> While an intellectual understanding of quality provides a basis for TQM, it is clearly only the planting of the seed. The understanding must be translated into commitment, policies, plans and actions for TQM to germinate. Making this happen requires not only commitment, but a competence in the mechanics of quality management, and in making changes.

All the theories set out in this section ultimately point to the need for a manager to have motivational and leadership skills as key components in their management armoury. We now turn to leadership.

12.5 Leadership

Good leadership requires an understanding of people – ourselves, colleagues and customers – people's motivations. The handling of people and communications are probably the most important ingredients for harmony in management. Thus of the three core elements of skill needed by the manager – conceptual, human and technical – this chapter concentrates on the human factors. The concepts have been debated at length earlier in the book and the technical aspects are to be covered in later chapters.

Leadership cannot be separated from management, though management is not leadership *per se*. An unorganized group can have a leader, but managers only exist in an organized structure where specific roles have been created. Leadership is an important aspect of management – the ability to lead effectively is one of the factors that produces an effective manager. Leadership has been described as a mixture of art, craft and humanity. It is an essential part of a manager's job. A good leader is concerned both with people and results. Leadership is a word with positive connotations. We look to leaders to inspire, direct and pave the way. In leisure management, there is a need for excellent leaders at all levels.

The Chinese philosopher Lao-Tsu is reputed to have said: 'To lead the people, walk behind them.' The suggestion here is that not all leadership is waving a flag up at the front. Henry Miller, in *Wisdom of the Heart* [37], captures the same spirit: 'The real leader has no need to lead – he is content to point the way.'

Good leaders create a vision and define a strategy to get there; they provide:

1   direction – pointing the way, setting objectives and eliminating uncertainty;
2   support – listening, encouraging, facilitating and involving in problem-solving and decision making;
3   drive – giving motivation, inspiring confidence and building team cohesion;
4   communication and representation – to the outside world and from outside to the team.

But not everybody wants to be a leader. Moreover, some managers at all levels, including the top level, are poor leaders. Some so-called 'leaders' really need to be called 'administrators'. As the biblical saying goes, 'If the blind lead the blind, both shall fall into the ditch'. A number of managers can be good at some functions of management, but may not be good leaders. Generally, in leisure, a highly visible 'profession', managers without good leadership qualities cannot be said to be good managers. 'As a leader, you are visible; incredibly visible. And you have expectations to fulfil' (Peter Drucker).

One of the arts of leadership is to instil in staff the desire to want to do what the leader wants to do. Most people involved in leisure need very little motivation. Leisure directors, managers, supervisors, trainees, sports and arts teachers and coaches, countryside rangers, music directors, museum curators, play leaders, tourism managers and holiday activity organizers, in the main, are highly motivated to begin with. This gives leisure leadership a head start over selling used cars and double glazing.

A strong perception of leadership, handed down through the ages, is that of the generals leading the troops into battle. Whether it is a Winston Churchill, defending an island nation in war, or a Robin Hood, assembling an undisciplined and ragged mob into an effective force to defeat the Sheriff, leadership is seen as an ability to galvanize support and commitment to a cause and to direct and lead from the front, handing orders down the chain of command. In much the same way, we talk about the leaders or 'captains' of industry, like Henry Ford.

Leadership, fortunately, covers far wider territories than leading upfront into battle, waving a flag and beating a drum. There are other angles to leadership. Sometimes, managerial leadership skills are from within the team or exercised so subtly that they are not always overtly discernible. We can see evidence of this with some conductors of an orchestra or with captains in sport, who quietly get the best out of their players without shouting from the rooftops.

In earlier decades there appeared to be a clear demarcation between 'leaders' and 'followers', based on tradition, class and upbringing, which divided 'boss' and 'workers'. In business management the leader was portrayed as a person, normally male, who was endowed with initiative and the authority to lead men. The Military Academy of Sandhurst joke is of the commanding officer who says of one of his recruits: 'This young officer is not yet a born leader', illustrating a myth that has been perpetuated. Leadership can be a learned skill.

In distinguishing leadership from other management functions, it has been suggested that most management functions can be taught, whereas leadership skills must be learned. We learn through doing. Leadership stems largely from a manager's personal dealings and personal influence over others. Leaders then need to direct, support, inspire and communicate.

Leadership is closely associated with directing – clearly informing people what, when and how to do a job and then supervising performance. In the management situation, leadership could be said to be 'people power' – the power-house of most organizations. Leadership moves the organization along the chosen route towards its goals. Leadership provides the drive and the direction.

Good leaders must also have the ability to inspire followers through the use of appeal and persuasion. Some inspirational leaders have taken on apparently hopeless causes and have succeeded through the strength of loyalty and devotion that they have been able to instil in their followers. Martin Luther King was an example of such a leader.

Unlike good leadership, which may be difficult to define, poor leadership exhibits a wide range of easily recognizable traits in a person: aloofness, insensitivity to others, intimidating manner, abrasiveness, overbearing, over-supervising, failing to delegate, seeking praise first instead of giving praise to colleagues, blaming, finding scapegoats, indecision and so on.

12.5.1 Different styles of leadership

In *Leadership and the One Minute Manager* [32], four leadership styles are described: directing, coaching, supporting and delegating (Figure 12.2). Different styles of leadership will be appropriate to different situations. If you are going to bark every time you stand up, people will soon fail to listen. How can a manager be 'democratic' in dealings with subordinates and yet maintain the necessary authority and control in the organization to which he or she is responsible?

Over the past few decades has emerged the concept of group dynamics. Social scientists revealed the importance of employee involvement and participation in decision making. Democratic leadership began to be thought of as solutions coming from the ground floor and autocratic leadership attributed to the boss who makes most decisions himself or herself. Generalizations, lacking research evidence, spoke in simplistic terms of leadership being either 'democratic' or 'autocratic', and even more misleading, these terms became for some, synonymous with 'right' and 'wrong' styles of leadership and for others, 'strong' leadership and 'permissive' leadership. In this context, a leader should not be confused with the role of the 'head', who is imposed upon a group or organization from above.

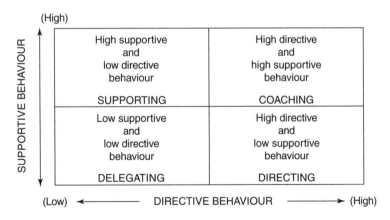

FIGURE 12.2   Leadership styles

Source: adapted from Blanchard, Zigarmi and Zigarmi (1986), *Leadership and the One Minute Manager*, Willow Collins, London

375

In answer to the question: 'what is leadership?', there appear to be three main schools of thought: first, leadership is a matter of personal traits (such as initiative, courage and intelligence). These traits must be possessed by individuals and then they are able to lead in most if not all situations. Second, who becomes the leader of a group, and what the leadership characteristics are in the given case, are a function of the specific situation but one person emerges as the leader. Third, leadership is a function. Any or all of the members of the group may perform, at various times, specific leadership acts or functions which are necessary if the group's objectives are to be obtained. These functions include, for example, initiating, regulating, informing, and decision making. This third view of leadership appears to be currently accepted by most management educators as realistic and appropriate to a successful group in terms of achieving targets. However, all three views are relevant in given situations.

In informal groups, which will apply more in voluntary sector management, the emergence of a leader is needed to satisfy the needs of the group. A leader is needed as a focal point for concerted action as often many groups are pulling in different directions. In these groups, representation, the voice of the organization, is also of importance. With special tasks of leadership, such as in running an event or the maintenance of premises, certain people will emerge as leaders. Different leaders for different situations is a concept worth pursuing in all diverse organizations.

Leadership, one of the core functions of management, is essentially a matter of human behaviour. The modern manager has to ask: 'what is the most appropriate leadership in this situation?' This brings us to leadership behaviour.

12.5.2 Leadership behaviour model

There are many leadership models. First, we look at the classic leadership continuum, then two other models – a managerial grid and the Five 'C' Model.

1. Continuum of leadership

Robert Tannenbaum and Warren H. Schmidt [38] studied the range of behaviour adopted by leaders and presented a continuum or range of possible leadership behaviour available to a manager. In their model (Figure 12.3) each type of action is related to the degree of authority used by the manager and to the amount of freedom available to the subordinates in reaching decisions. Actions on the extreme left characterize the manager who maintains a high degree of control, while those on the extreme right characterize the manager who releases a high degree of control.

The continuum is important, particularly in three main ways. First, it demonstrates that there are a number of ways in which a manager can relate to the group. In any situation, however, the manager must expect to be held responsible for the quality of the decisions made, even though operationally they may have been made on a group basis. Delegation is not a way of 'passing the buck'. Second, it is important for the group to recognize what kind of leadership is being adopted. For example, if the manager has already decided what to do and wishes to inform them, it is right that this is done. To adopt a façade of involving the group in

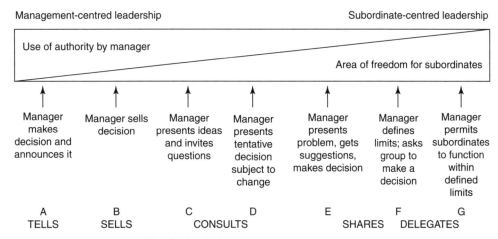

Management-centred leadership   Subordinate-centred leadership

FIGURE 12.3 Continuum of leadership behaviour

Note: under F and G, although the manager delegates, he or she must still accept full responsibility

Source: adapted from Tannenbaum and Schmidt (1958), 'How to choose a leadership pattern', Harvard Business Review, March–April, 95–101

the decision making process would be misleading, and lead to antagonism and frustration. Third, the democratic manager is not one who gives his or her subordinates the most decisions to make. That may be entirely inappropriate. There may be other more important priorities for them. The quality of involvement and decision making is important. Involvement only in low levels of decision making may simply prove to be patronizing to some members of staff.

2. The managerial grid

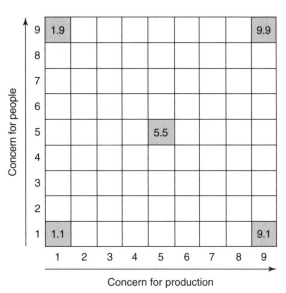

FIGURE 12.4 Concept of the managerial grid developed by R. Blake and J. Mouton

Another theory suggests that managers combine two styles simultaneously, but in differing proportions. One style is job- or task-centred. The other style is employee-centred. The managerial grid developed by Blake and Mouton [39] plots the two dimensions on a chart on scales 1 to 9 (Figure 12.4). The vertical axis represents increasing concern for people, and the horizontal axis, an increasing concern for production.

A manager rated at 1.1 is wholly ineffective. A manager at 1.9 has great concern for people, but is ineffective in achieving the task. A manager at 9.1 is task-driven with little concern for people. Managers at the midpoints (5.5) show balance. The ideal is 9.9, high regard for people, combined with optimum focus on results.

3. Five 'C' Model

James Weese of the University of Windsor in Canada has developed what he calls the Five 'C' Model of Leadership [40]. His synthesis of leadership identifies 'trait', 'behavioural' and 'situational' theories: personal traits and characteristics separating leaders from others; behaviour measuring the leader's orientation to the task and to the relationships with subordinates; and situational theories where time, place and circumstance had been overlooked in the trait and behavioural theories.

The work of several academics underpinned Weese's model, in particular Bernard Bass [41] who identified four characteristics of 'transformational' leaders: individualized consideration (for each person's situation and genuine concern for staff); intellectual stimulation (appealing to the intellectual capacities of followers and challenging them); inspirational motivation (charismatically inspiring ownership); and idealized influence (showing respect and influencing by example). Warren Bennis uses the term 'visionary leadership' rather than 'transformational leadership'.

The Five 'C' Model incorporates:

C1 – credible character: leaders must have the respect of those they lead and be perceived as trustworthy and reliable;

C2 – compelling vision: Followers need to believe in the leader and in the vision and know that they are doing a worthwhile job and their efforts are appreciated; these leaders provide support and extend the horizons of their followers;

C3 – charismatic communicator: charisma is linked to communication, emphasizing effective speech patterns and non-verbal actions which heighten a leader's standing in the eyes of followers;

C4 – contagious enthusiasm: leaders excite and inspire others to go above and beyond the call of duty; they challenge intellectually and emotionally;

C5 – culture builder: beliefs, values and attitudes shape and help interpret the behaviour of a group or organization.

12.5.3 Deciding how to lead

A leader's style should be flexible enough to change to suit the situation. Leaders have to balance the big picture – the vision – with the details. What they find is that little things matter – sensitivity, care, attention to detail. The ability to span the divide between the big picture and the small screen and to build bridges, often across difficult territory, is one of the hallmarks of a good leader. What factors should a manager consider in deciding how to lead? A false assumption is made in the belief that leaders are born, not made, or that one is either an autocratic, a democratic or 'free-rein' leader. Most leaders tend to use many styles but with a leaning towards one. Much will depend on the circumstances.

In emergencies, authoritative, autocratic leadership is eminently suitable. The authoritarian style can also be very effective when toughness is needed under certain conditions, even at some personal emotional cost to the leader. Leadership is not an easy option. It requires commitment. As one guru said: 'Leadership is a foul-weather job.' There is another American saying that 'nice guys don't win ball games' and there is a germ of truth in this, in tough situations. However, in longer-term organizational situations where leadership is an ongoing 'craft', and where the manager is working with and through other staff, then there are four major factors which help to determine the style of leadership which is most appropriate: the manager; subordinates; organization; and the problem.

1. The manager

The manager's behaviour occurs as a result of his or her personality, background, knowledge and experience. Among the significant internal forces are the manager's value system and the trust and confidence shown in the subordinates. External forces are also exerted upon the leader, and in order to retain the confidence and allegiance of his or her staff, the person concerned has to conform more to the norms and rules of the 'group' than do its normal members.

2. The subordinates

Assistant managers and staff will have expectations of the manager. Each member of staff has his or her own personality and ability factors: the better the manager understands these forces within the group, the better he or she can determine the role to play in achieving the best for subordinates and the organization. Generally speaking, under the leadership continuum, the manager can permit subordinates greater freedom if the following conditions exist:

1   assistant staff have high needs for independence;
2   there is a readiness to assume responsibility;
3   they prefer a wide area of freedom rather than simply clear-cut directives;
4   they have considerable interest in the problem and feel it is of importance;
5   they appreciate the goals of the organization;

6   they have sufficient knowledge;

7   they have been 'educated' to expect to share in decision making; there is a climate of mutual confidence and respect.

3. The organization

Management situations vary enormously. Much will depend on the organization itself, its aims and objectives and the efficiency of the group in given situations.

Organizations such as a local government district council will have traditional kinds of behaviour which are approved of and other kinds which are not. Its leisure services department may have dispersed sections and sites which preclude effective participatory decision making. In contrast, a commercial leisure club manager may have to decide prices and controls and meet tight financial targets.

4. The nature of the problem

The most important consideration is the problem itself, which will determine the kind of leadership. The problem may need specialist information or be of a complex nature involving many disciplines. The manager will need to be sure all the necessary knowledge is acquired within a given time. The pressure of time is often said to be the biggest headache, even though such pressures are sometimes self-imposed. With 'crisis' decisions, a high degree of authority is likely. When time pressure is less intense, it becomes easier to bring others into a situation where group dynamics – skilfully handled – will become one of the tools to good management.

Day-to-day problems in the leisure field, such as the upkeep and maintenance of the buildings and grounds, the staff systems, the programme, the handling of stock and the accounting for cash, will be more routine and administrative. A leadership pattern has been set and leadership choices are limited; changes are inappropriate. However, long-term decisions, strategies and solutions to new long-range problems give opportunity to involve others in achieving goals more effectively. For example, a leisure centre's programme and system may have been fixed for the coming twelve months, but a survey has indicated that only 25 per cent utilization is being made by females and that the daytime use by shift workers, the unemployed and the retired is negligible. The manager, anxious to increase the proportions of these customers to meet the aims of the organization, should confer with the assistant managers, initially, and discuss with them the scope of the problem, the constraints to time and money and the need to acquaint the staff and user groups with the problem and the opportunities.

It is in the strategy and the tactics of handling the problem where the manager's leadership skills are put to the test: can he or she raise the level of employee motivation? Can staff and key user groups be persuaded to accept change readily? Can the quality and effectiveness of managerial decisions be improved? Can teamwork and morale be developed? Can the manager improve individual development, enhance the quality of the organization, and improve the satisfactions of the customers?

12.5.4 Team building

While leisure managers should be leaders, leaders are not necessarily organizational managers. Leadership is needed at all levels. Leadership should not depend on the hierarchy of the organization and the status network. Leisure leaders are often community leaders, sports coaches, department representatives – those who are responsible for the essential face-to-face work. The leader is usually employed to get a job accomplished working through a group of people. The leader should: achieve the task; develop the individuals in the team; and maintain and motivate the team.

To achieve the task, the team must work together. The leader must develop the individual and maintain the team. A breakdown in one area will affect the others, will hamper progress and prevent the effective accomplishment of the task.

FIGURE 12.5 Effective leadership skills to achieve results

A lighter weight tug-of-war team, trained and well led can beat heavyweight teams who lack the knack of working together. The precision team works in concert and pulls only when it has to. The leader directs operations like the conductor of an orchestra.

Effective leadership in leisure management has much to do with team building. Good team leaders are likely to exhibit the following traits:

1   enthusiastically accept responsibility for leading the team
2   accept responsibility for achieving objectives
3   ensure that each team member knows his or her job and what is expected of him/her
4   ensure that the team understands and accepts its role in achieving objectives
5   have concern for individual welfare and the inner goals of members of the team and will face up to individual problems at the earliest opportunity
6   listen to members of the team and understand both the overt and underlying messages being given
7   be open with the team, showing loyalty to them and to the organization

8 instil confidence into the team and the individuals within it; highly motivated staff can put up with a good deal of upheaval, show resilience and come through crises more quickly than less motivated staff

9 have a job training plan for each person, each job and for the team

10 walk the job – everyday; in this way, leaders are less remote, they are close to the team and, hence, close to customers; they show they care.

Teams fashioned in these ways are more likely to be both efficient and effective – functionally and psychologically. All teams need good coaches.

Meredith Belbin (1991) [42] identified nine team roles: problem-solver, resources, co-ordinator, shaper, evaluator, team worker, implementer, finisher and specialist. He found the teams that are likely to perform best are the ones that have the best blend of team roles to play off against each other. The team is built up on the strengths we bring to the collective. No individual is perfect, but by putting together and developing different, yet competent, people, you can build the perfect team for the right job.

People, unlike machines, are flexible, and leisure management calls for stepping into other roles when the need arises. Then staff look upon it as 'our job'. When flexibility is needed, the team can stretch. (Bamboo scaffolding around Hong Kong tower blocks bends with typhoons; the rigid metal poles cannot cope when the pressure is on!)

12.5.5 Entrepreneurial leadership

Entrepreneurial leadership, usually seen as a domain of the private sector, is gaining momentum in the public sector as never before, in part due to success experienced in the private sector and the policy requiring local authorities to optimize income and decrease net expenditure. Commercial managers have primarily to be accountable for financial performance – or go out of business – and hence use entrepreneurial skills to increase income. This form of leadership is almost diametrically opposed to operating say, in government agencies. Public agencies have relied on the system, rather than the managers and staff, to provide services. The current climate calls for entrepreneurial, creative managers who are prepared – within budgets – to be bold and take action and lead, rather than simply react to what happens.

Leisure professionals and managers must be able to teach the skills of leadership to supervisory managers and community leaders. They will need to learn to accept responsibility for leading their teams, have loyalty to the organization and to the team, ensure that each team member knows his or her job, face up to individual and situational problems and 'walk the job' every day. The results of good leadership then, permeate throughout the organization. This ethos is much easier to inculcate through a sense of 'mission' and vision from the top. Hence leisure managers need more than entrepreneurial skills. They need vision.

Visionary leaders have principles and values. Their principles of personal leadership stem from inner convictions. These convictions, enthusiastically projected, influence others positively. The ability comes from the personal vision that is large and clear enough to be shared. Harry Alder in *The Right Brain Manager* [43] believes that such a person is a leader, not because he or she leads, but because people tend to follow. And, as Henry Mintzberg suggests, the processes 'seem to be more relational and holistic than ordered and sequential, and more intuitive than intellectual'. In the recent *On Becoming a Leader* [44] Warren Bennis's ingredients for a leader today include: a guiding vision; passion; integrity; trust; and curiosity and daring. 'What lies behind us and what lies before us are tiny matters compared to what lies within us' (Oliver Wendell Holmes).

In summary, the manager must be a successful leader in order to be effective. The manager must understand himself or herself and the staff and the customers. The manager recognizes that a high degree of subordinate-centred behaviour in helping to run an organization raises employee teamwork and morale. But this does not mean that a manager leaves all decisions to the staff. Situations vary and staff vary. Staff readiness and ability are important. The successful leader will behave appropriately in the light of his or her perceptions of the people and the situations, and cannot therefore be categorized as 'strong' or 'permissive'. He or she must have the insight and ability to act appropriately, remaining firm on cardinal principles, yet being flexible to permit degrees of freedom to the greatest advantage. In addition to leading personally, the manager must recognize that many subordinates fill important leadership roles themselves. They too need training in the 'art' of effective leadership. Leadership may result in the successful completion of a task, but effective leadership occurs when the team of staff not only complete the task, but do so willingly and find its accomplishment rewarding.

Good leadership is required for effective management. It is concerned with both results and relationships. Good management is largely the result of good managers! They are individuals who have the responsibility for providing leadership of the organization and the ability to move it towards its goals.

12.6 Decision making

One of the functions of management is decision making and a significant proportion of a manager's time is spent in handling problems and making decisions. How decisions are made is of importance. Hence the process of decision making, as well as the content of the decision, are important for success. The manager and his or her group, or groups, should have an awareness of alternative decision making procedures and processes.

Management has moved, and continues to move, from an intuitive 'art' with its 'rule-of-thumb' approach, to decision making on a more scientific basis. Science, however, is not solely the science of economics, physics or mathematics, but the sciences of people – the psychological processes which affect decision making.

Traditionally, decision making has been seen as being undertaken by only those 'at the top'. This has been shown to be wholly undesirable and inadequate. Decisions should be made at all levels of management. Robert Townsend, in *Up the Organization* [45], goes further still: 'All decisions should be made as low as possible in the organization. The Charge of the Light Brigade was ordered by an officer who wasn't there looking at the territory.'

12.6.1 Types of decision

There are three main types of decision identified by Video Arts [46], namely emergency decisions, routine decisions and debatable decisions.

1 Emergency decisions are needed under crisis. They require clear, quick and precise decisions, for example, to prevent destruction of the sports hall by a bomb, a possible drowning in the swimming pool or a fight at the discotheque or to make the call for ambulance, fire service or police.
2 The running of an organization and the ticking over of the service revolve around routine decisions. Changes to the duty supervisor rota, the change of menu, or giving the blessing for additional staff for the forthcoming major events, are all within an organization's policy framework. Many of these routine decisions simply require a 'yes'/'no' to maintain the status quo and staff are delegated to make such decisions, without involving wider deliberation.
3 Debatable decisions are debatable because they change the status quo. They mean changes for people and their work. They are debatable because the chances are that they will be improved through consultations, given effective leadership. They are debatable, too, because there may be a number of different ways of handling the particular situation.

Routine problems – maintenance of buildings and grounds, supervisory rotas, stock replenishment, inevitable programme changes – can be delegated by managers to other staff. However, long-term problems or changes, new programming initiatives, ways of substantially increasing income or reducing expenditure, call for skills in developing a strategy, building staff morale and cohesion and solving the problem with commitment by all. It is these debatable decisions which should occupy a manager's time more than others. It is these decisions which generally lead to harmony or disharmony; and it is these decisions with which the following section is concerned.

12.6.2 The decision making process

Decision making of a complex nature can be perceived as having phases: causes; potential decision options; their consequences; evaluation; and making a choice. The technique of perceiving decision making in this way helps to highlight the need for information and factual data and the relevance of it to the problem. It helps to analyse logically and so assist in effective decision making. Decision making is therefore a process which can be divided into a number of stages. A variety of texts suggest a different number of stages [46,47], though much the same logic is apparent. For the purposes of this chapter, nine simple stages are identified.

1. Defining the problem

Defining the problem is so obvious that it is often overlooked! It can be one of the hardest things to do (as many students writing theses will vouch for), but having defined the specific problem, we are a long way forward in finding solutions. We have to be clear: what is *really* the matter – the symptoms must not be confused with the problem itself. What is the decision supposed to achieve?

2. Gathering and examining information and identifying possible causes

What facts and information are needed? When are they needed by? What are the constraints and limiting factors? Are there cash limits, time pressures or staff shortages? Only valid and useful information should be used.

3. Consulting with people and considering their views

Others may think of ideas which you have not thought of. People need to be identified in the decisions that are reached. The leisure manager needs to identify who will be affected by the decision and to discuss with the group the facts and their implications.

4. Considering choices or alternatives

Consider all possible courses of action. A brainstorming session would help, in this respect, for we often stumble on important ways of achieving results by keeping our minds open to all the possibilities.

5. Considering the implications

The implications of certain decisions may solve the problem but cause even greater problems. (Recently a leisure organization was advised that fewer staff, redeployed would make for financial savings. The organization decided, however, to keep staff and morale at a cost.)

6. Making the decision and deciding a course of action

These decisions need to be clear and unambiguous.

7. Communicating the decision

In communicating the decision, the manager must be prepared to persuade people of its 'rightness'. This is made all the easier if staff (and clients) have been involved in the decision making or if the decision has been made by the representative group. Communicating decisions must be undertaken sensitively. For example, receptionists at leisure centres, often working part-time, are rarely part of the decision making team (and wrongly so in my opinion); they may learn about forthcoming events from the local newspapers!

Communicating the decision needs care, timing, sensitivity and, above all, the reasons why the decision has been made. Some Recreation Managers are careful to inform the staff of the reasons but fail to tell the customers why. How often have we seen 'No entry' and 'Cafeteria closed'? People tend to be more understanding and co-operative when they know why, and more so when they have been consulted. In communicating decisions, enthusiasm is important. You only generate enthusiasm in others if you give decisions and reasons with conviction. How it is done is important. When briefing the staff team, it is often best to undertake it collectively in order to show an open and frank situation and avoid the grapevine, contrived gossip and the subsequent miscommunications and misunderstandings.

Managers often hide behind memos in communicating decisions. They feel, in this way, that everybody knows, because the written word is clear. However, the written word is sometimes most unclear. It is conceived differently by different people; hidden messages might be imagined; and there may be an air of mistrust. Communication is a two-way process: 'no one can ask questions of the memo'. When preparing the brief – spoken first, then written – the manager needs to envisage how people will feel on the receiving end of the decision. Managers have to place themselves in the position of the receiver, into the shoes of the other person. This important component of management is considered further below.

8. Implementing and following up the decision

This requires briefing people together, whenever possible, being ready and willing to sell the decision with enthusiasm and belief and then confirming the decision in writing. Many 'debatable' decisions need a framework on which an evaluation can be made, such as timing, targets and implementation. It is important that the manager follows up and monitors progress and sees that areas implementing changes, and which create new problems, are alleviated, particularly where people's feelings are concerned.

9. Evaluation, feedback and modification

Most debatable decisions need time to see whether they have been successful or unsuccessful, and to what extent. Even the best preparation may result in the wrong decision being made. Once proof of its 'wrongness' is substantiated, managers need the courage to admit the fact and try again.

12.7   Communication

In understanding the process of decision making, we see how important it is to communicate on a wavelength understandable to all. This is a key component in successful management. It is through the function of communication that an organization's activities are focussed on common objectives. Good communication is essential for the internal functioning of an organization, because it co-ordinates its managerial functions. A leisure leader has also to communicate with external organizations: with clients, customers, the community, government agencies and many others. George Eliot once wrote: 'The people of the world are islands shouting at each other across a sea of misunderstanding.'

As we have seen, communicating is far more important than just transmitting a message. The way it is done can affect the attitudes and performance of staff and the relationship with customers. The purpose of communication is to ensure that whoever receives the message understands what is in the mind of the sender. This is not easy; what is obvious to the sender may be obscure to the receiver. One-way communication is fraught with difficulties. 'A' does not know if he or she is getting through to 'B'. Many problems of management, in industry and in leisure services, stem from the misunderstanding, misconception, mistrust and underlying feelings of not being put clearly in the picture which arise from one-way communications. If the goals of communication are to be understood by others, to get clear reception or perception, to get understanding, to get acceptance in order to get effective action, then two-way communication is essential.

12.7.1   One-way and Two-way communications

In both public and commercial leisure management, a substantial level of communication – and mis-communication – is of the one-way kind. One-way communication is quick and satisfying for the sender, but often frustrating for the receiver and it can lead to misunderstanding. Managers must beware the dangers of one-way communication and use it only for emergencies and when autocratic communication is essential. They should cultivate two-way communication whenever it is possible.

Staff should be trained to handle work through greater levels of two-way communication for more effective achievement of the task and greater harmony within the team. While two-way communication takes longer and may be frustrating for the sender, it is essentially more sensitive and more accurate. To communicate, we must understand others. Each one of us is different from everyone else. We are different psychologically; we vary in intelligence, education, political and religious beliefs, social background and experience. These experiences create different frames of reference with the result that people look at the world around them in a particular and unique way. Our physical and mental make-up and our environment have a direct effect on our perception and judgement. All too often, when interpreting information, we see or hear what we are taught 'ought' to be there and/or what we want to see or hear. Thus there are barriers to communication in ourselves, and these barriers also exist in our subordinates, our peers and our bosses.

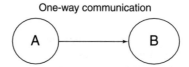

One-way communication

Has B picked up the right message. Or has he sensed, and believed, rightly or wrongly a hidden message?

While two-way communication takes longer, it is more sensitive and more accurate. To communicate, we must understand others. Each one of us is different from everyone else.

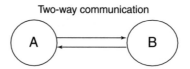

Two-way communication

A is able to answer, respond, reinforce and encourage acceptance.

B asks, clarifies, understands what is being conveyed.

B is more likely then to accept and support.

FIGURE 12.6 One-way and two-way communication

The argument for two-way communication is not only a moral one, it is also a practical one because the manager will become more effective by encouraging the group members to make full use of their abilities. Peter Drucker put the argument against the purely persuasive approach to communication in the following way:

> In many cases human relations has been used to manipulate, to adjust people to what the boss thinks is reality; to make them conform to a pattern that seems logical from the top down, to make them accept unquestionably what we tell them. Frankly, sometimes, I think it is better not to tell employees anything rather than to say 'We tell them everything, but they must accept it, and it is our job to make them accept it'.

In this instance, Drucker highlights the problems of forcing one-way communication on to people without their understanding and without understanding them. As Samuel Butler, the seventeenth-century poet observed: 'He that complies against his will is of his own opinion still.' One-way communication situations can frequently arise if the sender and receiver are not on the same emotional level. For example, if the sender takes a superior attitude, the receiver will react with some resentment, concentration will decline and the level of interference and distraction is likely to increase. The advantages of two-way communications are considerable. In small groups, such as those which apply in leisure settings (community arts centres, sports centres, recreation offices or community associations), the advantages can be summarized as follows.

1   Although one-way communication is faster, two-way communication is more accurate, particularly in complex situations.

2   Two-way communication will help both the sender and the listener to measure their standard of achievement, and when they both see that they are making progress, their joint commitment to the task will be greater.

3   The sender may feel under attack as the listener will pick up any mistakes and mention them. This is helpful rather than dangerous because a frank interchange of views will lead to a higher level of understanding and acceptance.

12.7.2   Communication 'models' and networks

All communication 'models' are simple illustrations of different basic theoretical concepts, the reality of which is far more complex and diffuse! Nevertheless, they serve to demonstrate that some methods of managerial communication serve particular circumstances better than others. The illustrations, however, do not show up the informal communications network which, far from being pushed underground, should be seen as essential for the gelling together in informal as well as formal processes.

Personal communications are usually one-to-one and face-to-face. Managerial communications, on an organizational basis, call for a variety of communication channels: downwards, upwards, sideways, crossways and informal communications. All have merit in different situations. However, most organizations keep strictly to the formal downward communications through hierarchical channels. This can lead to misunderstandings and also activate 'grapevine' communications. It is far better to have these essential cross-communications 'upfront' as necessary, open and informal communications where merited.

If leaders have to deal primarily with face-to-face communication with a single subordinate, this is not only time consuming, but more importantly, can impede effective management, reduce the span of control and could cause management overload which, in turn, can result in communication blockage.

There are different channels of communication and each has merit in different situations, but closed systems are more restrictive and centralized (Figure 12.7). Kent [48] identified: the chain – the straight line, with the manager at the top; the Y formation – simple gatekeeping, with the manager controlling at the centre; and the wheel – large control span, gatekeeping, with the manager at the centre 'calling the shots'.

These restricted networks can work fast and efficiently in tasks requiring simple mechanical processes, tightly controlled specifications and routine procedures. It is so much easier to carry out instructions! Alternatively, where there is a free range of ideas, such as in organic structures (growing and evolving) and where decentralized and horizontal structures are to be found, then open networks are to be encouraged (Figure 12.8). They include the circle – the manager is one member of the decision-making team and the web – the manager is central for strategic work, delegates operational functions to groups and is a team member where appropriate.

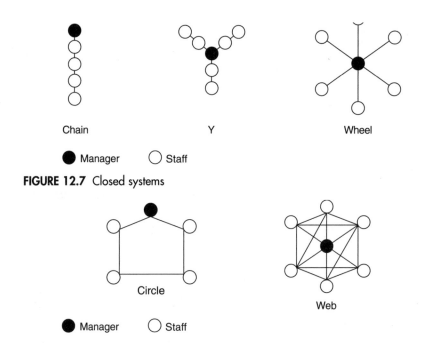

Chain   Y   Wheel

● Manager   ○ Staff

FIGURE 12.7 Closed systems

Circle

Web

● Manager   ○ Staff

FIGURE 12.8 Open systems

Given simple tasks, the wheel was a consistently quicker and more accurate means of communication than the other two; the chain was the slowest and least effective. However, in terms of job satisfaction, the circle was more effective than the other two. The circle was also more adaptable in complicated and ambiguous tasks. The wheel with its central 'gatekeeper' inhibited adaptability to changing situations.

Kent concludes that people never transmit information as well as they believe they do. He outlined commonly identified problems which restrict communication, for example, perceptual bias by the receiver, the distortion of information by the sender, the lack of trust on the part of both sender and receiver, too much information and power used to secrete rather than share information. The answer is to use more than one communication network. The formal and informal systems of communication Kent groups under four headings: 'hierarchical', 'expert', 'status' and 'friendship'. Further, it is important to encourage the two-way flow of communications and to improve the coordination within organizations: 'A lateral rather than a vertical direction of communications in an organization will avoid the problem of one person becoming the "gatekeeper" of all information, a gatekeeper being a person who can withold or pass on information as he sees fit.'

In both public and commercial leisure management, a substantial level of communication is of the one-way kind. Orders come down from the civic centre, town hall or head office, sometimes by word of mouth through the chain of command and often via the written memo – a system subject to all the misunderstandings and misinterpretations imaginable.

Managers and staff should be trained to handle work through greater levels of two-way communications for more effective achievement of the task and greater harmony within the team. Moreover, written and verbal communication are not the sole methods of communicating; physical gestures such as facial expressions, through the movement of eyes, or sitting positions, whether made consciously or unconsciously, can convey much to the receiver of the sender's attitude and understanding – and vice versa.

12.8 Group behaviour in the leisure management setting

In business, including the management of leisure programmes and services, it is likely that the important decisions are taken in consultation with others. Managers must therefore develop skills in understanding the behaviour processes at work when people are involved in the group decision-making process. It is clear that some behaviour assists in this work, and some behaviour hinders progress. Two main management parameters are the task and the relationships. The task is the job that has to be done and the targets that have to be achieved. If these are achieved, as most important ones are, through people, then the relationships of people working together becomes very important. The relationship aspects are referred to by some management researchers as 'maintenance'. What types of behaviour are relevant to the group's cohesion, working together and making the best use of the group's collective resources and strengths? What types of behaviour detract from group cohesion and are self-orientated rather than group/task-orientated?

Two main types of group can be classified as primary and secondary. Primary groups are made up of a relatively small number of people in a common task. Secondary groups are made up of a larger number and no one member has a clear picture of all the others. These groups can be further classified by their development – i.e. formal groups (those deliberately created), and informal groups (created by accident).

Primary groups are made up of individuals engaged in a common task who have regular face-to-face contact with one another – e.g. the family, the play group, the mother-and-toddler group, the work group, the club, the church and the youth group. The primary group is an instrument of society through which individuals acquire many of their attitudes, opinions and ideals and one of the sources of control and discipline. The primary group can be one of the main satisfiers of an individual's need for status and emotional security. In the leisure context, the club leader, the society secretary and the sports coach fulfil status and emotional needs. (See Section 4.8 on 'serious leisure'.)

Primary groups tend to 'appoint' or have a natural leader. Generally speaking, the more harmonious the group becomes, the more efficient will be its performance in most respects. The experience of team spirit, of belonging and sharing defeats and successes, make for extremely strong bonds. Disharmonious groups tend to be less effective.

Leisure Managers dealing with groups need to understand primary group behaviour and respect their standards, ceremonies and collective needs. Harmonious groups working together, helping the newcomer and maintaining good relationships are the groups likely to aid, not inhibit, the fulfilment of managerial goals.

12.8.1 Group behaviour

The modes of behaviour within groups have been termed task-orientated; maintenance-orientated; and self-orientated. Both 'task' and 'maintenance' are important in varying situations, depending on the needs of management and staff, whereas the behaviour within self-orientated groups hinders or obstructs the achievement of common goals. This behaviour can arise because the individual is faced with certain problems in the group, problems of identity, personal goals and needs versus the group goals and needs, and so on. These undercurrents cannot be ignored; they should be recognized and attempts made to integrate the individual needs with the group's goals.

The more commitment to a decision that is gained in the group, the higher the likelihood that the group will act in accordance with what has been decided. The process, the procedure and the way in which a decision is taken will affect the effectiveness of the decision.

As a guide, Argyris and others [49,50] have put forward ten criteria, based on empirical research, that they see as necessary for group competence and effectiveness.

1   Contributions made within the group are additive.
2   The group moves forwards as a unit, is team-spirited and there is high involvement.
3   Decisions are mainly made by consensus.
4   Commitment to a decision is strong.
5   The group continually evaluates itself.
6   The group is clear about goals.
7   It generates alternative ways of thinking about things.
8   It brings conflict into the open and deals with it.
9   It deals openly with feelings.
10 Leadership tends to go (or move) to the person most qualified.

Leaders have to deal with conflict and co-operation within and between groups. Conflict is not in itself undesirable; only through expression of differences can good problem solving take place. For everyone to agree is as unrealistic as expecting that no agreement is possible. But conflict so severe as to disable the participants and prevent the continuation of problem solving is undesirable and unacceptable.

What happens when two (or more) groups are faced with a problem of some kind involving their interest? The problem may be unsatisfactorily 'solved' by maintaining isolation between the groups, or by enforcing unification of the two groups, or by allowing one group to take over or destroy the other. However, assuming that a real solution is wanted which satisfies both groups, then some kind of joint problem-solving process must take place. The more the inter-group situation is defined as win/lose, the more likely we are to see certain effects leading to confrontation. The more it is defined as problem solving, the less likely the adverse effects. The effects, however, never wholly disappear.

The interaction between groups reveals a tendency for members of one group to become hostile towards the other group; there is a reduction in communication between the groups, and a lack of willingness on behalf of the group to listen to the views of the other; and there is mistrust by one group of the other. On the 'resolution' of the conflict, the winning group tends to retain its cohesion or become more cohesive. It becomes complacent ('fat and happy') and there is a release of tension with a reduction in fighting spirit and greater playfulness. There is a high element of co-operation but little work is actually done. On the other hand, the losing group splinters, fights, and reorganizes. There is an increase in tension, and the group ('lean and hungry') seeks scapegoats among its leaders and organization. If it sees future 'wins' as impossible, it becomes introspective, self-blaming and depressed. But the group can learn a lot about itself.

Effects like those described above are familiar enough in recreation services, political parties, committees, clubs and departmental sections and are exhibited in inter-departmental problems. The attempted English Football League club mergers like Queens Park Rangers and Fulham in England, and Glasgow Celtic and Motherwell in Scotland, vividly illustrate the point.

How can these negative effects be reduced, so that good problem solving can be maintained at a desirable level of conflict? The answer is to find an overriding goal – one which both (or all) groups accept as essential to reach and which all can reach – thus 'win/lose' changes to 'win/win' and both groups can be satisfied with their achievement.

In recent years, the use of groups such as Quality Circles, has become an accepted procedure for problem solving within an organization. In this way, a group that has a range of abilities and knowledge is more likely to identify all the possible options available, provided that the group environment is receptive to suggestions from all its members and that the size of the group is manageable.

12.9 Managerial coaching, mentoring and delegating

Like sports teams, leisure management teams need coaching. Why? Because learning takes place through practical experience and when learning experiences are guided by managerial leaders, then staff become more effective, more quickly. Coaching provides confidence in the job, as individuals and as valuable members of the team. Leisure managers have an abundance of practical situations and opportunities for inculcating in their staff fine leadership qualities. Leisure management coaches have two key tasks: to ensure that staff know what and how to undertake the work; and to motivate and instil confidence in staff so that they carry out the work willingly and effectively.

Staff can also be enabled to undertake new tasks, improve performance, develop new skills, learn how to solve problems and become even more valuable members of the team. No matter how good people are at their jobs, there is always need for improvement and often a need for confidence boosting. Some of the world's finest sportsmen and women, musicians and artists are still looking to improve. Wimbledon tennis stars have coaches and psychological motivators to keep them going. Good leaders will challenge staff to realize their potential, praise them when it is deserved, and show concern for their individual needs and welfare.

Staff need to work at their potential – for themselves, for the team, and for the organization. If they do not, they can be an expensive liability to the organization and they weaken the team. A motivated workforce is more likely to be successful than a de-motivated team. Pulling together is better than pulling apart. When people work as a team, they motivate each other – no-one wants to let the side down – and as a result, the team is more productive. Staff will feel, think and work like a team.

A leisure management 'coach' can also be a 'mentor'. In Homer's *Odyssey*, Mentor was the friend whom Ulysses (the Greek King of Ithaca) put in charge of his household when he left on his epic voyage to Troy. In particular, he was responsible for advising and overseeing development of Ulysses' son, Telemachus. Visionary leaders make good mentors because they have principles and values which stem from inner convictions. These convictions, enthusiastically projected, influence others positively. They have trodden the path before; they can empathize. The ability comes from the personal vision that is large and clear enough to be shared.

A mentor is an experienced guide – a believer, an understander, promoting the cause and showing the way – a teacher and coach who can make a lasting impression on an individual's life. College students will know the value of a good, sensitive and inspiring personal tutor. Mentors provide a helping hand, inspire mutual trust, loyalty and friendship. The bond between mentor and protégé is an emotional one. Professions such as law and accountancy include 'apprenticeship' periods, a time when recent graduates must work with qualified professionals to 'learn the ropes'. In this process, the apprentice absorbs an approach, a style, a life view, which can shape their future.

12.9.1 *Delegating*

A saying goes: 'Don't put off until tomorrow that which you can get someone else to do today.' A delegate is a person authorized to act as a representative for another or others. A manager can delegate authority, but not ultimate responsibility.

Delegation requires a leadership style combining directive and supportive behaviours. In *One Minute Manager* [32], four styles are identified: directing; coaching; supporting; and delegating. Delegating is the only style which is both low in supportive and low in directive behaviours. Delegation is not simply assigning work and off-loading tasks; it is assigning the delegator's work to others, and giving them the authority and the resources to get the job done. Some jobs, however, should not normally be delegated. They are likely to include: confidential matters; disciplining; buck-passing of unpleasant tasks; and key areas in which only the delegator has the power.

Thus, delegation for a leisure manager can free up time for key priorities and build up competences of staff and enhance their professional growth and development. It also allows decisions to be taken at the most appropriate level and increases the effectiveness of the organization. However, there is need for delegation clarity: focus attention on the results and standards; allow staff the freedom to decide and be concise about the power being handed on.

In *The Seven Habits of Highly Effective People* [51], Stephen Covey differentiates between 'gofer delegation' and 'stewardship delegation'. Gofer delegation means, 'Go for this, go for that, do this, do that, and tell me when it's done'. It spawns a creed which says: 'Tell me what you want me to do, and I'll do it.' This is inefficient and ineffective.

Stewardship delegation is focussed on results instead of methods. It involves mutual commitment to expectations – what, not how; results, not methods. It provides guidelines, identifying parameters, as few as possible to avoid 'methods delegation'. Delegation also requires resources – personnel, financial, technical; and organizational – accountability, performance standards and evaluation.

12.10 Quality management calls for quality managers and leaders

As we have seen, good management is largely the result of good managers, individuals who have the responsibility for providing leadership of the organization and the ability to move it towards its goals. In a study of successful facility managers in the public and private sectors [52], five essential criteria were found to be almost universal: sound leadership; objectivity; staff motivation; care of customers; and operational excellence.

In addition to these 'bankers' within the 'effective operational model', management to be effective needs to be flexible to accommodate changing circumstances and to meet the needs of different people. In addition, different managers have different styles of management. The same manager may also have a number of different styles, depending on the different situations. What is becoming clear is

FIGURE 12.9 A model for the effective operational management of leisure facilities
Source: based on observation and interviews by the author, reported in (1986) *Leisure Management*, February, 6, 2

that a manager armed with only one style of management may be ill-equipped for the variety of different tasks and people to be handled – just like a golfer with only one club.

The business of leisure, where people choose what to do and where staff have to be flexible and work unsocial hours, calls for styles of management in keeping with providing good customer service and care of staff. In these circumstances, the 'democratic' manager with a professional 'executive style' is more likely to succeed. He or she will see the job as effectively maximizing the efforts of others. This manager's commitment to both task and relationships will be evident to all. He or she is not afraid of conflicts and recognizes them as important in understanding the task and the people; such behaviour is seen as normal and sometimes appropriate: these managers often work with a team; ideas can come from any quarter; and the greater number of possibilities explored, the better the understanding of the problem. They still have to lead: they cannot hide behind the team; and they still have to make the ultimate decision but both manager and staff feel involved in the failures and successes. This style of management is an 'objective' art gained with experience and learning, allied to personal flair. Other styles of management will be far easier but it is this quality of management which is essential to the successful and harmonious leisure and recreation service.

12.10.1 *Servant leadership*

For people to benefit from leisure, other people paid and voluntary have to give service. The concept of the 'servant-leader' – caring leadership – fits well into many aspects of the profession of leisure management. The founder of what has today become a movement in leadership circles in the USA is Robert Greenleaf. The servant-leader is servant first – he or she has the desire to serve; then the aspiration to lead. It is based on the needs of people. The object is that the service given to them enables them to grow into healthier, wiser and more fulfilled people and contributing citizens.

> There is a revolution underway. In corporate boardrooms, university classes, community leadership groups, not-for-profit organizations and elsewhere, change is occurring around the ways in which we, as a society, approach the subject of work and leadership. Many people are seeking new and better ways of integrating work with their own personal and spiritual growth. They are seeking to combine the best elements of leadership based upon service to others, as part of an exciting concept called 'servant-leadership'. It has been, to be sure, a slow-growing revolution – but one which is now sending deep roots throughout society.
> Spears, L. (1994), *Inner Quest, 2*, p.1 (The Greenleaf Center for Servant-Leadership).

A great deal depends on what we want too accomplish. As Stephen Covey [51] says: 'Begin with the end in mind'.

12.11 Summary – management

In this chapter we have considered lessons from history and we have looked at the management processes, leadership, decision making, communications and group behaviour and systems such as Total Quality Management. Management must be appropriate to different situations, and the manager must adapt his or her style of management to be appropriate to changing situations. It is suggested that the principles of good management apply to any field of collective human endeavour and leisure and recreation is no exception. The management principles and process apply, whether in the public, the private or the commercial sector.

There are many differences between the public, voluntary and commercial sectors but the similarities – in terms of management – are fundamental. Managers in all sectors are managing people and situations in such a way as to provide opportunities for people's leisure. The operation of facilities and the specific technical tasks are secondary to the management of people to achieve results and meet objectives and targets.

The study of management has shown that there are two main management parameters – the task (the job), and relationships (the people). There needs to be a balance between the two. Other chapters which follow deal with aspects of task. This chapter has concentrated on the manager's need to understand people and the relationships between them, whether as individuals or in groups. Without this understanding, and without the ability to communicate, motivate and lead, the manager's chance of successfully and effectively undertaking a task or meeting the needs of his or her customers is considerably reduced. Moreover, management and leadership must be situational and adaptable to change. Wess Roberts [53], in *Leadership Secrets of Attila the Hun*, believes that it is a privilege to direct the actions of others. Leadership flexibility is crucial; no model can anticipate circumstances. The relatively new concept of the 'servant-leader' has much to commend it to professionals in leisure. Quality management requires quality managers and leaders.

Notes and references

1   Notes taken from a lecture tour by Peter Drucker c. 1965.
2   Drucker, P. F. (1955), *The Practice of Management*, Pan Books, London, p. 19. and p. 30.
3   Wilder, R. L. (1977), 'EEI: a survival tool', *Parks and Recreation*, August, 23.
4   *ibid*.
5   The work of Taylor is fully considered in Wren, D. (1972), *The Evolution of Management Thought*, Ronald Press, New York, 1972.
6   Mayo, E. (1933), *The Human Problems of an Industrial Civilisation*, Macmillan, New York.
7   Fayol, H. (1930), 'Administration industrielle et generale' (trans. J. A. Coubrough), *Industrial and General Administration*, International Management Institute, Geneva, pp. 40–107.

8   The work of Weber is fully considered in Wren, D. (1972), *The Evolution of Management Thought*, Ronald Press, New York.

9   McGregor, D. (1966), *The Human Side of Enterprise*, McGraw-Hill, New York.

10   Herzberg, F., Mausner, B. and Synderman, B. (1959), *The Motivation to Work*, Wiley, New York.

11   Maslow, A. H. (1954), *Motivation and Personality*, Harper and Row, New York.

12   Maslow, A. H. (1968), *Towards a Psychology of Being*, D. Van Nostrand, New York.

13   Taylor, F. W. (1947), *Scientific Management*, Harper and Row, New York.

14   Fayol, H., trans. C. Storrs (1949), *General and Industrial Management*, Pitman, London.

15   Barnard, C. (1938), *The Functions of the Executive*, Harvard University Press, Cambridge MA.

16   Argyris, C. (1957), *Personality and Organization*, Harper and Row, New York.

17   Likert, R. (1967), *The Human Organization: Its Management and Value*, McGraw-Hill, New York.

18   Kennedy, C. (1991), *Guide to the Management Gurus*, Business Books, London.

19   Drucker, P. (1946), *Concept of the Corporation*, John Day, New York

20   Mintzberg, H. (1983), *Structures in Fives: Designing Effective Organizations*, Prentice Hall, New York.

21   Argyris, C. and Schon, D. (1978), *Organizational Learning: A Theory of Action Perspective*, Addison Wesley, Wokingham.

22   Adair, J. (1990), *Understanding Motivation*, Talbot Adair, Guildford.

23   Peter, L. (1986), *The Peter Pyramid*, Allen and Unwin, London.

24   Handy, C. (1990), *Inside Organizations: 21 Ideas for Managers*, BBC, London.

25   Bennis, W. (1984) Good managers and good leaders, *Across the Board, 21* (10) 7–11 and read Bennis, W. (1989), *Why Leaders Can't Lead: The Unconscious Conspiracy Continues*, Jossey-Bass, San Francisco, CA; Bennis, W. and Nanus, B. (1985), *Leaders*, Harper and Row, New York.

26   Peters, T. and Waterman, R. (1982), *In Search of Excellence*, Harper and Row, London.

27   Peters, T. and Austin, N. (1985), *A Passion for Excellence*, Collins, London.

28   Peters, T. (1987), *Thriving on Chaos*, Macmillan, London.

29   Pascale, R. and Athos, A. (1981), *The Art of Japanese Management*, Simon and Schuster, London.

30   Kanter, R. M. (1989), *When Giants Learn to Dance*, Simon and Shuster, London.

31   Deming, W. (1986), *Out of Crisis*, Cambridge University Press, Cambridge.

32   Read, for example, Blanchard, K. and Johnson, S. (1983), *The One Minute Manager* and Blanchard, K., Zigarmi, P. and Zigarni, D. (1986), *Leadership and the One Minute Manager*, both Willow Collins, London.

33   MacKenzie, R. (1969), 'The management process in 3-D', *Harvard Business Review*, November–December.

34   Odiorne, G. (1965), *Management by Objectives: A System of Managerial Leadership*, Pitman, New York, p. 55.

35   Mosscrop, P. and Stores, A. in association with the Institute of Leisure and Amenity Management (1990), *Total Quality Management in Leisure. A Guide for Directors and Managers*, Collinson Grant Consultants, Manchester.

36   Oakland, J. S. (1989), *Total Quality Management*, Heinemann Professional, Oxford.

37   Miller, H. (1942) *Wisdom of the Heart*, New Direction, USA.

38   Tannenbaum, R. and Schmidt, W. H. (1958), 'How to choose a leadership pattern', *Harvard Business Review*, March–April, 95–101.

39   Blake, R. and Moulton, J. (1981), *The Managerial Grid*, Gulf.

40   Weese, W (1996), 'Follow the leader', *Recreation*, December, 26–30.

41   Bass, B. (1985), *Leadership and Performance: Beyond Expectations*, Free Press, New York; and Bass, B.M. (1990), *Bass and Stogdill's Handbook of Leadership: Theory, Research and Managerial Applications*, Free Press, New York.

42   Belbin, M. (1981), *Management Teams: Why They Succeed or Fail*, Butterworth-Heinemann, Oxford.

43   Alder, H. (1993), *The Right Brain Manager*, Piatkus, London.

44   Bennis, W. (1989), *On Becoming a Leader*, Business Books, London.

45   Townsend, R. (1970), *Up the Organization*, Coronet Books, London.

46   Video Arts Booklet, *Decisions, Decisions*, to accompany the film, *Decisions, Decisions*.

47   Welsh, A. N. (1980), *The Skills of Management*, Gower, Farnborough.

48   Kent, S. (1981), 'Good communications', *Parks and Recreation*, September, 27–30.

49   Argyris, C. (1976), *Increasing Leadership Effectiveness*, Wiley, New York.

50   Argyris, C. (1966), 'Interpersonal barriers to decision making', *Harvard Business Review, 44* (2) 84–97.

51   Covey, S. (1992) *The Seven Habits of Highly Effective People*, Simon and Shuster, London.

52   Torkildsen, G. (1986), 'Managers as they see themselves and as we see them', *Leisure Management, 6* February, (2), 26–7, 31.

53   Roberts, W. (1989), *Leadership Secrets of Attila the Hun*, Bantam Books, London.

Recommended additional reading

A very useful and comprehensive general management manual is: Elliott G. (ed.) (1990), *The Manager's Guidebook*, Longman, Harlow.

School Term Time Programme

Main pool

	7am	8am	9am	10am	11am	12noon	1pm	2pm	3pm	4pm	5pm	6pm	7pm	8pm	9pm	10pm

Time markers: 1.30, 3.30, 9.30

Monday — 3 lane swimming | 1 lane swimming / schools | 3 lane swimming | 1 lane swimming / schools | casual use | lessons | 3 lane swimming

Tuesday — 3 lane swimming | 1 lane swimming / schools | 3 lane swimming | 1 lane swimming / schools | casual use | lessons | ♀ 3 lane swimming | deep end swim ♀ water aerobics

Wednesday — 3 lane swimming | 1 lane swimming / schools | 3 lane swimming | 1 lane swimming / schools | casual use | lessons | 2 lane swimming

Thursday — 3 lane swimming | 1 lane swimming / schools | 3 lane swimming | 1 lane swimming / schools | casual use | lessons | 3 lane swimming | deep end swim water aerobics

Friday — 3 lane swimming | 1 lane swimming / schools | 3 lane swimming | 1 lane swimming / schools | casual use | lessons | 2 lane swimming

Saturday — 3 lane swimming | 1 lane swimming | lessons | casual use | 1 lane swimming | ✱ floats & toys | casual use | ★ private party hire

Sunday — 3 lane swimming | 1 lane swimming / casual use | 3 lane swimming

Shallow pool

	7am	8am	9am	10am	11am	12noon	1pm	2pm	3pm	4pm	5pm	6pm	7pm	8pm	9pm	10pm

Monday — casual use | schools | casual use | schools | casual use | lessons

Tuesday — casual use | lessons | schools | casual use | schools | lessons | casual use | lessons | ♀ casual use

Wednesday — casual use | schools | casual use | schools | casual use | lessons | casual use

Thursday — casual use | schools | casual use | schools | lessons | casual use

Friday — casual use | schools | casual use | schools | lessons | casual use

Saturday — casual use | lessons | casual use | ★ private party hire

Sunday — casual use

7am	8am	9am	10am	11am	12noon	1pm	2pm	3pm	4pm	5pm	6pm	7pm	8pm	9pm	10pm

School holidays are as follows

Monday 16 February - Friday 20 February '98

Monday 6 April - Friday 17 April '98

Monday 25 May - Friday 29 May '98

There may be variations to this programme on bank holidays and over Christmas. Any changes will be advertised at the pool two weeks in advance.

Chapter thirteen

Programming leisure and recreation services and facilities

Programming and marketing go hand in hand in the process of managing leisure. Programming is the key element in the delivery of services. It is the means by which opportunities are provided for people to enjoy their leisure time. It is also the mechanism by which the aims and objectives of an organization are realized. Programming is undertaken by Leisure Managers in the public, commercial and voluntary sectors.

Preceding chapters have shown that the Leisure Manager, particularly in the public sector, must have sufficient knowledge to assist policy makers, faced by complex political, economic and social conditions, in establishing guidelines for effective community recreation. The Leisure Manager must also have sufficient knowledge of programming strategies, approaches and methods in order to direct staff in achieving the aims and objectives of the organization.

While social conditions and economic problems must be faced, this chapter concentrates on the programming process and the manager's role in that process. The leisure field is so varied and complex that in giving practical examples to support ideas, there has been a need for selection. Greater emphasis has been given to public recreation services and facility programmes.

First, the question is raised: what is programming? Second, two main directional strategies are debated. Third, a number of specific programming approaches and methods which fall within the two main strategies are summarized. Fourth, the problems and the lessons to be learned from current practices are noted. Fifth, the case for greater caring and sensitivity in programming for disadvantaged groups is made. Sixth, examples of programmes at multi-leisure centres are described. Seventh, a leisure facility programme planning process – Programming by Objectives – is proposed together with a Programming Planning Guide.

Having read this chapter, readers will understand something of the complexity of programming and its crucial role in providing leisure and recreation opportunity for more people. It is the means by which objectives are met.

Readers will learn that programming is an ongoing process, that needs a framework and objectivity; it is not a series of activities strung together, but an integrated and planned process. They will learn how to establish aims and objectives, how to set strategies, approaches and methods, how to choose activities and balance a programme and how to measure results. In so doing, recreation activity programmers will be able logically to assign a continuous programming sequence to their services and facilities.

13.1 Why leisure and recreation programming?

Programming is important. It is a highly underrated factor in leisure management. It is a complex process requiring excellent management. Programming must achieve optimal use of existing resources – facilities, personnel and finance – to meet the goals of the organization and the needs of people.

Why programming? Two overriding reasons concern the need to deliver a service and to meet an organization's objectives. The programming process is the 'delivery' of leisure and recreation services and activities. There are other reasons for excellent programming.

1   There is a need to make the best use of resources – time, space, staff, money.
2   There is a need to resolve conflicting claims of time and space.
3   Most leisure facilities have potential permutations in which to exploit and provide opportunities.
4   Space not programmed and sold today is lost for ever.
5   There is a need for balance and for fairness between a wide range of potential customers.
6   Good programming is a means of achieving best results – optimum numbers, a range of different people and a choice of activities.
7   The programme provides order and structure; people know where they stand – they know when to come, what they can expect.
8   Without programming, there could be chaos, no order, no structure, no balance and unfairness, and resources will not be used to best advantage.

13.2 What is programming?

Leisure programming consists of planning, scheduling, timetabling and implementing action which uses resources, facilities and staff to offer a wide range of services and activities – passive, active, routine, guided, graded, varied and special – within the reach of the community to be served. Programming is a process of leisure management planning, that uses resources and organizes activities to meet the diverse wants and needs of different people and different groups. The programme is the essence of leisure and recreation services; it is their *raison d'être*. Programming requires skilful management. It results in an integrated plan. Programming provides the leisure products and should be linked to the marketing process.

Programmes will differ depending on the facilities and on the aims of the organization. A leisure facility may be run by different kinds of organization: a community recreation centre; an arts or sports association; a private sports company; or under local government contract management. Whether a public authority, a voluntary organization or a sports and leisure business, all have to attract the public, or they fail! Moreover, it is important to remember that it is people and their needs which are the reasons for a leisure organization's existence and therefore people's needs must be the focal point of services. Programmes are the tools of the Leisure Manager; they are the vehicles through which leisure opportunity is made available to the community.

The programme is the single most important function of a leisure and recreation organization. Everything that a service or department is concerned with – facilities, supplies, personnel, budgets, marketing, public relations, activities, timetabling and administration – is solely to ensure that opportunities exist for people to enjoy or experience leisure in ways satisfying to them. The opportunity is made available through the programme.

One of the hallmarks of good programming is the extent to which individual satisfaction, individual welfare and the values of the participant are important aspects of the programme. While numbers are important, the individual rather than the aggregate must be the core of the service. Programmes are often judged on how many have attended; qualitative aspects are rarely brought into any evaluation. In order to programme for people, we should bring people into programme planning. It is important not just to dictate, but to work towards participant planning. Within the broad range of leisure programming, a fundamental aspect, for public sector services, is community recreation.

13.2.1 Community recreation programming

Community recreation programming incorporates many social objectives, but local authorities, faced with economic difficulties, have now to programme within far greater financial constraints than in the 1960s to 1980s, the growth years in public leisure provision. The Leisure Manager should strive to offer a balanced programme. This makes good financial sense in addition to meeting social objectives. A balanced programme at a local authority leisure complex would have some of the following features:

1   opportunities to participate in a range of leisure activities
2   opportunities to participate actively or passively, or creatively
3   opportunities to be involved as an individual or with a club or group
4   opportunities for people to participate on a formal basis and on an informal basis
5   time set aside for a core programme of activities as well as time set aside for a variable programme.

The programme is also the principal mechanism for ensuring that objectives are achieved. Whether organizations are orientated primarily towards ends which are social, educational or financial or a combination, it is the programme, allied to its pricing and management, that determine whether the objectives are met. Organizations, such as public authorities and voluntary organizations, are concerned, in part, with social objectives. The programme, therefore, should provide for the able and less able, the advantaged and the disadvantaged.

Those organizations concerned primarily with financial objectives, such as a private health and fitness club, are also concerned with people and their needs. These organizations use the programme as a means of attracting customers at a price that provides a profit level to the company. The exception is the highly exclusive and costly club where numbers are limited and staff numbers are high in order to give exclusive service; but, here, too, programming is very important.

Many organizations, including local authorities in the new climate of competitive tendering, hope to achieve a mix of social and financial objectives. Such balanced programming requires great skill of management programming, negotiation and diplomacy. In all sectors, programming continues in some measure, to be founded in tradition, convention and guesswork – on hit or miss, 'common-sense' approaches. These are inadequate substitutes for good programme planning. Leisure Managers, therefore, need to be leisure programmers, interpreting policy and having the organization skills to deliver the programme.

13.2.2 Which main agencies programme leisure and recreation?

There are many sponsoring agencies involved in recreation programming: for example, education authorities, local government, commercial organizations, industry, HM Forces, religious organizations and private institutions, associations and clubs. There are, however, four broad categories: the commercial sector; institutional sector; voluntary sector; and the local government sector.

The commercial sector with its cinemas, bingo halls, night clubs, fitness centres, golf driving ranges, tenpin bowling centres, tennis centres, country clubs and holiday centres, has specified, defined activities, and segmented targets and user categories.

The institutional sector, such as universities, colleges and community schools, needs skilful programming, but, generally, there is a discrete main market – that of the institution first. In the industrial sector, a variety of leisure and sport facilities have to be programmed, but here, again, high levels of exclusivity and club-based organization makes for ease of programming.

In the voluntary sector, programming is largely for interest groups such as sports clubs or multi-activity groups, such as Girl Guides and Boy Scouts. Institutions like the YMCA/YWCA, with a range of facilities, however, find themselves in similar situations to leisure managers at public leisure centres in terms of programming.

It is in the diversified local government public sector, where broad-based programming skills are most needed, not only because of the range of facilities, the range of activities and the range of customers, but because Leisure Managers have to effect a balance between providing a 'social' service and, increasingly, a more economic one. Widespread leisure programming needs to be carried out because facilities are made available with public money to meet the needs and demands of communities, on the principle of equality of opportunity. Facilities such as swimming pools, leisure centres, playing pitches, theatres, community halls and dual use centres at schools need 'programming' to produce appropriate 'balances' of opportunity. One of the main problems that public providers have is that balanced programmes giving equal opportunity to all is extremely difficult to fashion. One of the problems is encapsulated in the truism 'There is nothing more unequal than the equal treatment of unequals'.

13.2.3 What constitutes a programme?

What makes a programme? Does it have to be a class, a timetable of bookings, a league or a list of events? Or can it be the planned availability of a playground, a park, a school or venture trail? Or can it exist through the organized distribution of services such as a recreation and leisure information service which collates all that is going on? A programme is all these things and a good deal more. It can take almost any form in the framework of one's definition of what constitutes a recreation experience. However, in terms of practicality, programmes revolve around activities, facilities, services, staff and money.

1   Activities can range from the completely spontaneous variety to the highly structured and all stages in between. Informal activities can be anticipated within a community programme by creating opportunities, encouraging spontaneity, having resources available such as space, time and equipment – e.g. a ball to kick about, a wall to scribble on or deck chairs to sunbathe on. Structured activities, for programming purposes, fall into several major categories such as: arts, crafts, dance, drama, entertainment, games, sport and health and fitness, hobbies, music, nature, social recreation, travel and tourism, and voluntary service to the community.

2   Facilities cover all areas, buildings, supplies and equipment within recreation. These can be designed and constructed for special purposes such as public arts centres or swimming pools; designed for self-directed or spontaneous activity like a park; or simply the natural resources available to the public such as riverside walks, forests and beaches.

3   Services cover all methods and means through which people are enabled to enjoy leisure and recreation, for example, information services, promotion and publicity, transport, passport schemes in local authorities, member credit card or direct debit schemes in private clubs, crèches and holiday services for parents with young children.

4   Staff are the enablers, connectors and controllers: duty managers, supervisors, coaches, countryside rangers, teachers, technicians, cleaners, stage hands, librarians, museum curators, sports development officers, youth and community workers and receptionists.

5   Money is needed for the investment to achieve financial profits or to break-even or to run services, facilities and programmes at an agreed subsidy level.

The Leisure Manager/programmer must use the available resources efficiently to deliver programmes that meet the aims and objectives of the organization. The recreation programme, however, is not a series of individual activities strung together. It is a carefully integrated and planned combination of many activities selected on the basis of individual and group interest, related ideas and themes, organized to achieve particular aims. Among these are the realization of personal fulfilment, satisfaction, enjoyment, physical and mental health and the development of positive social relationships. Essentially, programming is the balanced correlation of leadership, required space, facility, equipment and activity, for a client or customer at an appropriate time and place.

13.3   Programme classification

How a programme is classified is not of major importance. However, the type of programme needs to be known in order to communicate with the public and avoid preconceived misconceptions. Programme classification should describe and communicate the different activities in the programme. Classification is more than communicating what is on offer. It helps in providing programme balance through analysis of each category. The commercial sector is particularly adept at 'segmenting' market sectors for profitable outcome.

Simple classifications can aid communication and administration. Programmes can be classified in a number of ways and four, in particular are commonly used

1   by function – the most usual classification, normally by listing a number of activities or groups of activities; such as sports, arts, crafts, social; often, the functional classification is linked to special groups of people: children, youth, disabled, aged, beginners, advanced and so on;

2   by facilities – pitches available, pool opening times, halls to be let;

3   by people – who the programme is intended for: casual users, members, family days, over 50s, parents and toddlers;

4   by outcomes – 'Learn to swim', improver courses, 'Keep fit', 'Slim and trim' sessions.

Sociologists and psychologists tend to group people for classification into life stages. In chapter five stages in the life-cycle and their importance on leisure was discussed. Erikson [1] identified eight stages; six stages up to young adulthood and two stages beyond. Meyer [2] presented four adult stages. Farrell and Lundegren [3] identified a range of activities through eleven life-cycle changes: pre-school, early childhood, late elementary, youth, teenage, young adults, early adulthood, maturity, later middle age, old age and senescence. However, these can be merged for many programmes (e.g. youth, teenager and young adults can be grouped together), or the groups can be further broken down (e.g. pre-school into toddlers, infants and pre-school). Further classification can be made regarding the activities themselves: passive/active, structured/unstructured, planned/self-directed, high risk/low risk, etc.

In summary, the community recreation programme is both the end product and the means of attaining the aims and objectives of an agency or organization. It has been defined as 'the total experiences of individuals and groups resulting from community action in providing areas, facilities, leadership and funds. These experiences represent a wide range of activities, planned and spontaneous, organized and informal, supervised and undirected' [4]. Essential elements that influence the success or failure of the programme to meet its stated objectives are planning and management. Without these elements, programmes would be inefficient and ineffective. First, we consider the planning strategies.

13.4 Directional planning strategies for community recreation programming

Two major directions for public sector planning of community recreation programmes, put simply, are:

1   planned programmes directed professionally by officers or authorities
2   programmes which emanate from the community itself.

They could be termed 'other directed' and 'community initiated'. Recreation texts describe the directions as social planning and community development [5].

The social planning approach is the most common. The basic assumption underlying this process is that use of professional expertise and knowledge is the most effective way of meeting needs and solving community problems.

Community development, on the other hand, is a method of organization in which the role of the professional is one of assisting individuals in the programming process, rather than intervening with services to bring about the desired changes. The locus of control is the important factor. Change occurs as a result of community intervention and involvement, not as a result of the diagnosis of a professional or the authority. The process itself and the participation is part of the experiencing; participants assume initiatives for their own development.

The social planning method is participant dependent and professional and authority controlled. The community development approach fosters participant independence. The distinction between the differing approaches is put cogently by Edginton *et al.* [6]:

> It is important to draw a distinction between the work of a *community developer* and the work of a *social planner*. Perhaps the most important difference concerns the view that each has of the participant. The social planner views the participant as a consumer of his services. The role is to isolate individuals with needs and then intervene directly with services. The community developer, on the other hand, views participants as citizens with whom he or she engages in an interactive process of problem solving. The social planner is primarily involved in fact gathering in an effort to determine the needs of the individuals being served. Once the appropriate information has been gathered, it is used in the decision making process to develop a rational plan for the distribution of available or acquired resources. The community developer, however, maintains a basic strategy of change in which the role is to help individuals identify and bring about change through their collaborative efforts. The community developer works with individuals and small groups, whereas the work of the social planner is primarily carried out in large bureaucratic organizations. The skills needed by the social planner are primarily those of management and administration; the community developer's skills should be particularly strong in the areas of communications and small group behaviour.

The adoption of a community development approach needs capable, trained men and women 'out in the field'. Community developers have become known by many names: 'encourager', 'enabler', 'catalyst', 'friend', 'adviser', 'activator', etc. The French use the words *'animateur'* or *'animateur sociale'*. *Animateurs* are well trained, capable and sensitive people who work towards stimulating individuals to think about their own development and also the development of other people in the community, through community programming. They work to develop the leadership capabilities of others. They assist by supplying information about methods and procedures; they enable others to act for themselves.

The relationship between the *'animateur'* and the group changes as the group matures. Initially, the *'animateur'* fulfils the role of the 'benevolent authoritarian' leader and undertakes the necessary tasks associated with the activities of the group and its maintenance. With continued contact, the role of the *animateur* changes to that of a democratic leader; and as leaders emerge from the group, his or her role diminishes and the groups largely become autonomous but with support available, should it be necessary. This support is normally required if the natural leaders of the group leave and there are no immediate replacements.

The experience in the United Kingdom has shown that outreach programmes are only successful as long as the support is available over a sustained period of time. When the programmes cease, through lack of funding for example, the majority of the newly formed groups flounder after a period of time due partly to the lack of physical and/or psychological support. In the United Kingdom, the current expansion of Arts and Sports Development Officers is creating new opportunities. The systems which are being put in place are also providing pathways and networks to maintain and sustain new programme developments.

Traditionally, local authorities have undertaken the social planning approach to programming, with much of the work being administered centrally, away from the facilities. Such an approach has considerable disadvantages.

1   The decision makers are remote from the potential users of the facilities.
2   There is generally a lack of consultation and sensitivity concerning the needs and demands of the community.
3   The facility staff are not involved in the decision-making process and there is generally a lack of accountability and commitment at facility level; this can manifest itself in poor staff motivation and low job satisfaction.
4   Decision making is slow and programming tends to be repetitive and unimaginative.

In recent years, the tendency has been to decentralize the programming and there has also been a change in emphasis. Initially, the focus was on the facility but this has now moved towards specific activities and groups, while the most enlightened Leisure Managers have progressed further and a few are are now focussing on the community development approach [7].

Looking across the broad spectrum of recreation programming, it seems clear that to adopt one direction – social planning or community development – to the exclusion of the other would be inappropriate. Both strategies have merit. A blend of the two is not only possible, but also essential. In addition to the directional mixture, the actual specific approaches and methods can be selected to meet particular segments of the market or to suit particular requirements. To achieve a blend and balance of direction and of approach calls for high skills of management and for programme planning objectivity.

13.5 Specific methods and approaches

Within the broad framework of the two main directional strategies lies a range of specific approaches and methods of programming. Providing leisure opportunity is so diverse and complex that there is no one approach, system or method which is suitable for all organizations, all situations or all people. The different methods are known by a variety of names; most of them have no agreed formal titles. Most methods appear to evolve as a result of the nature and the aims of the organizations themselves. From around thirty approaches which have been identified, including those of Farrell and Lundegren [3], Edginton [6] and Kraus and Curtis [8], this section groups some of these together into twelve broad approaches or methods.

The programming methods employed depend on the organization, the aims, the community to be served, the directional strategy, staff skills, money, facilities and a wide variety of other factors. Most recreation programmers do not use a single method. Most use a number of methods, but if they are poorly planned, they can be an untidy mix, a 'hotch-potch', overlapping and un-coordinated. Specific methods include the following dozen, in no order of priority. They each have benefits if used along with other methods.

- *Lettings 'policy' or laissez-faire approach* – commonly found in the management of community 'centres'; the facility is provided and bookings and usage are awaited. Optimal usage and balance are seldom achieved.

- *The traditional approach* – this has been described as a 'rehash of the same old thing'. The approach, however, suggests that what has gone on in the past and is generally successful is likely to be repeated. It relies on the same format for future programme planning. It is not necessarily based on needs, but on what has worked before. As a single approach, it is ineffective. It can be a far more useful in terms of learning from the past and making modifications for the future.

- *The comparative current trends approach* – this approach relies on reacting to recent trends or activities in vogue. This has benefits in meeting some new demands. However, the approach is totally experimental. It is likely to serve only a segment of the market, and what may work in one area may be a total failure in others. Fads are important to provide for but must be seen in context.

- *The expressed desires approach* – by asking people, through questionnaires and surveys, and then programming for people's wishes, we assume we are providing what they want. But will this result in actual participation? And which activities will meet which desires? Such an approach is difficult to administer, but it is a valuable tool for the programme planner; it gives information about people's desires and wishes. This approach has its limitations, however, as many respondents may not really know what they want until they try it and cannot predict with any degree of accuracy what their future leisure behaviour is likely to be.

- *The authoritarian approach* – reliance is placed on the judgement of the controller, head of department or manager. The assumption is that he or she understands what the needs are and what the community wants. This is a quick and tidy approach at its design and planning stage. However, participants are denied any involvement in the programme process. Such an approach makes it difficult to adapt to a more community-orientated strategy. The 'prescriptive' approach [9], and 'perceived need' approach [8], are very similar to the authoritarian approach. They too require a diagnosis of needs. Programming by the manager's perceived needs of what a community wants, is a tempting approach to adopt because it appears to be based on needs. However, without community involvement, it relies on professional expertise to diagnose other people's needs.

- *The political/social approach* – Edginton *et al.* [6], and Kraus and Curtis [8], both use the term 'sociopolitical'. In this case, pressure from groups, often linked to social causes, is used as a basis for a community programme. Such causes are invariably grist to the political mill – they carry councillor support. For example, crime, poverty, deprivation, discrimination and social disorder may call for particular kinds of recreation planning and programming. Leisure Managers do not operate in a vacuum, but have to respond to political and social pressure and to changing conditions. The approach, however, needs careful handling and within the context of the overall goals of the organization.

SPECIFIC METHODS AND APPROACHES

- *Action–investigation–creation plan approach* – Tillman [10] suggests that a three-phase plan to programming is the most effective. The action plan is reaction to the demands generated by the community. The investigation plan is concerned with fact-finding. The creation plan is the interactive relationship between participants and professionals. The professionals use their own expertise and actively seek the views and involvement of participants. Such a three-phase plan, allied to aims and objectives, could form a logical basis for programming.

- *External requirements approach* – here the programme is basically dictated by an authority, an institution or a governing body. It tends to have uniform standards, leadership and resources and there is an external assessment for measuring. A Scout or Girl Guide troop, for example, will satisfy the association's requirements. Such organizations normally have vertical management structures, a hierarchical leadership pattern, similar resources, administration and an external reward system. Uniformed groups like British Red Cross, St John Ambulance Brigade and Girls' Brigade and Boys' Brigade, and newer groups like the Majorettes, are clear examples.

- *Cafeteria-style approach* – James Murphy is reported to have termed this approach the 'cafeteria' style [9]. In this 'smorgasbord' approach, a variety of diverse choices are assembled, giving many opportunities. People can make their own selection. This is a useful approach, in that there is a variety of choice; people may not know what they want and can try things out, or 'suck it and see'. Additionally, such an approach can help to meet the diverse needs of clients, such as family groups. It is a safe approach but tends to be expensive. While appearing to be the answer to the manager's dilemma, it is ineffective in the use of resources, in that it can create and provide services which are unused because they have not been chosen. And in addition, it is very difficult to set objectives and measure success – some activities will be winners and others losers, but the reasons may not be known. For example, poor marketing, rather than the activity, may be the cause. Nevertheless, any comprehensive programming will need to indulge in a cafeteria approach for some of its recreation programmes.

- *The demand approach: offer what people want* – this is the most usual form of programming in the public sector. Clubs, associations and interest groups make known their demands. Managers are faced with scores of applications requesting specific facilities. However, the most vocal, the most aware and the socially articulate will make their demands known most readily. The approach is not concerned with equitable distribution and may result in narrow segmental programming. Many people and groups will not be aware of the recreation options and benefits. Most comprehensive programmes, however, will and should include this approach within the overall plan.

- *The community orientation approach* – this is a process based on using people's talents and capabilities. Here individuals are involved in the planning process. The approach is only possible by using professionals or capable amateurs to meet people on their own patch, for example, through outreach programmes, associations and community counsellors.

  The discovery approach is an extension and continuation of community orientation. It assumes that people can work together, there being no superior or subordinate relationships. One's knowledge, skills, abilities and interests are used to meet another's needs without necessarily imposing value systems or external expectations. The approach is a people-to-people approach of interactive discovery requiring community face-to-face leadership.

- *Community leadership approach* – Here consumer input is made possible through advisory boards, user committees, tenants' groups and other action groups. They represent concerns of the community. This approach assumes that individual interests are represented by their group. This, of course, is not wholly possible, but it does indicate community interaction and a level of democracy. As Edginton *et al.* emphasize, it opens channels of communication between providers and consumers [6]. It is a valuable tool for the recreation programmer.

Few community recreation service programmes emanate from the community itself or from consumer input; this kind of programming is difficult, time consuming and expensive, usually requiring subsidy or managed by volunteers – hence, it is increasingly out of fashion with a growing commercial realism in local authorities.

Because there are problems and lack of understanding of the importance and complexity of programming, community programmes are often educated guess-work and built up on hunches. This results in a hit or miss approach. They are certainly not based on people's needs. And it is important to meet people's needs whether in public or private organizations. A carefully selected mix of programming methods needs to be chosen to best suit the situation.

In summary, this section has described, albeit briefly some specific approaches to community recreation programming. Which approach or method is the most appropriate? Which direction should Leisure Managers take? The review has brought to light several important factors to be borne in mind when programming; it has unveiled many problems and it offers some solutions. The next section considers the problems, the lessons to be learned and suggests a solution to some of the problem areas – a logical approach to community recreation programming.

13.6 The need for a co-ordinated, objective approach

Leisure and recreation organizations are faced with a twin dilemma: which strategic programming direction should be taken? Which methods should be adopted to meet objectives? The manager is the key person in finding solutions. This is where the manager should come into his or her own. He or she will be trained and experienced to 'read' the situation. One of the guiding principles will be that programming must be situationally and culturally specific. There are different communities, different problems, different aims and therefore different objectives. The good manager must be a realist and use whatever approaches and options are open to meet needs and demands effectively and to be efficient in planning and operating the programme.

Needs assessment is complex. Part of the solution is gradually to make it possible for people to interpret their own needs and plan their own programmes. Managers must therefore learn how to involve people in programme planning. The Leisure Manager must:

1   understand the lessons to be learned from the various strategies and approaches;
2   understand the problems within current community recreation programming;
3   devise a logical and objective approach to the situation, bearing in mind the goals of the organization and the resources available.

13.6.1   The lessons to be learned

One of the hallmarks of good programming, whatever the organization, is the extent to which objectives have been met *and* client satisfaction has been paramount. While numbers are important, the customers and clients, rather than the aggregate, should be at the core of customer service.

Managers should learn from the successes and the problems of many of the programmes currently practised. Outlined below are a number of problem areas which have been found over the past decade at community leisure and recreation centres. They are in no order of significance.

*   Demands and needs are not being assessed.
*   Objectives, so called, are not measurable.
*   Programmes tend to be too traditional, static and much 'the same old thing' – the same activities, same methods and same people.
*   Programmes lack variety and novelty.
*   Often a 'take it or leave it' approach is adopted, regardless of whether the programme is appropriate to the target groups in the community.
*   The advantages and disadvantages of different user systems (e.g. casual user memberships) are not evaluated fully.
*   The need to balance casual use with club use and events is not based on policy, but expediency.
*   The need to analyse the benefits and problems of different activities is rarely considered.
*   Client life-flow patterns such as regular, habit-forming activities (e.g. weekly sessions) are broken into by insensitive one-off programming.
*   Programme patterns, such as seasonality, are not given due consideration.
*   Incompatible activities are sometimes programmed together.
*   Insufficient programme flexibility to be able to adapt to given situations with sensitivity.
*   Ways of expanding an already busy programme are insufficiently explored (e.g. early/late bookings).
*   IT and computer systems are not being put to best advantage to aid efficiency; bureaucracy and cumbersome administration systems still abound.

- Many programmes which are claimed to be comprehensive contain imbalance; there is a myopic view to a programme (e.g. 50 per cent of time and space to badminton and football in a sports hall).
- Programme worth is increasingly judged on numbers allied to financial viability; qualitative programming gives way under such strain.
- Risk avoidance leads to a lack-lustre approach, with a lack of creativity, stifled programmes, lack of adventure and non-appeal for young people.
- Some community facilities are used for single purposes which occupy only a proportion of time and attract a narrow market segment.
- Many potential satellite resources remain unused for the community: schools, church buildings, factory canteens and industrial recreation facilities.
- Programme monitoring and evaluation are rarely carried out to change and improve programme content and presentation.

Not all poor programmes can be changed overnight. It may well take several cycles of the programme, for example, due to established patterns and 'sitting tenants'. However, most problems can be ironed out by making changes in easy stages.

13.7 Community recreation management and disadvantaged groups

It has been shown unequivocally that the public sector leisure facilities are used disproportionately by those who are more affluent and mobile than those who have social, economic and other hardships. Such social hardships, in relation to leisure participation, have been highlighted from a number of sources, including Gwynne Griffiths's survey in Greenwich [11], the author's survey of lone parents in Harlow [12] and in the work of a number of leisure researchers. Haywood and Henry's study [7] offers insights into non-traditional ways of developing services for communities and targeting disadvantaged groups. Effective community recreation management can be measured in part by the degree to which a reasonable balance of the various population market segments within a community have been attracted across the range of services. The Harlow study found that those least likely to use leisure facilities are characterized by having low incomes, poor mobility and dependent young children. The problems are exacerbated if children are being cared for by a lone parent. Recreation and leisure do not appear to be of much relevance to the lot of disadvantaged people due to a combination of factors, including constant responsibility for children, lack of money, no use of a car, loss of confidence and lack of a partner.

It is the continuing theme of this book that leisure participation can lead to building up of self-image and self-confidence. Management flexibility, to cope with the different needs of different customers, deserves far greater attention. Clearly, Leisure Managers need to make contact, to communicate effectively with disadvantaged groups.

13.7.1 How can providers and managers help?

Providers can assist greatly by lightening the social and financial burdens that some members of their community face. This will also help managers to give a better service. Authorities need to provide, and make known, concessions and opportunities on a far wider front. They need to support voluntary groups. They need to assist in a variety of ways – a helping hand, even in small ways, may be the catalyst that many people may need. Others will need more substantial help; as one professional worker put it: 'the disadvantaged need to be met more than half-way.'

Concessions and benefits to disadvantaged people will enable them to exercise greater choice and enjoy the relative freedoms which are open to people enjoying greater advantages. For lone parents, for example, these could include financial and programme benefits, outreach initiatives and marketing strategies (Table 13.1).

The single most limiting factor for many disadvantaged groups, such as lone parents, is said by them to be the cost of taking part [12]. Yet, even when providing facilities free of charge, the manager will still need sensitively to market and provide support and backup services such as more crèche facilities, taster sessions and mother and child activities, and far more sessions and attractions for women generally, and women with children in particular.

Attracting people through marketing and incentives, however, is not enough. Sensitive handling is essential, also. Many lone parent users felt that managers and staff could be far more helpful and sensitive to individual needs. There was a

TABLE 13.1 Positive programming to encourage wider community use

Financial	*Outreach*
• Cost subsidies • Reduced/free memberships • 'Passports', 'Leisure Cards' or free passes (not just for children) • Avoidance of lump sum payments • Bus passes	• Assistance to self-help groups • Baby sitting services • Neighbourhood contacts • Neighbourhood facilities • Mobile facilities
Programmes	*Marketing*
• Play schemes and family holiday programmes • Women's programmes • Transport, e.g. minibus shuttle • Crèches at minimal or no cost • Leisure skill learning – arts, crafts, sports • Taster courses • Family events • Open days and days out • Social and community programmes	• Leisure counselling • Advertising benefits • Help-line services • Leisure information service • Links with other community services and voluntary groups

greater need for a 'community' approach [12]. The style of management, and the in-house operational services also, are important. Customers lacking in confidence are the most vulnerable to 'take-it-or-leave-it' services and will be easily put off. First impressions count. The approach of leisure centre staff to some users was described as 'intimidating', particularly at receptions [12]. Procedures, regulations, membership cards and having to ask for information about concessions, for example, are daunting for some potential customers. An abrupt voice at reception can ruin a person's leisure experience. Disadvantaged people, who outwardly look perfectly capable, may need welcoming and encouraging. Managers and staff must be both sensitive and reactive to the needs. People market leisure and the benefits of leisure are most successfully promoted by face-to-face communication. Therefore, staff training in customer service is of vital importance.

13.8 Programming multi-leisure centres

Leisure centres provide the most challenging grounds for leisure programmers. In the United Kingdom, there are in the region of 2,400 'leisure centres' – a centre comprising at least a multi-purpose sports hall that is open to the community, whether provided by public, voluntary or private sectors. There are thousands of other pools, halls and outdoor leisure facilities that also need programming.

Of the centres listed in *The British Leisure Centre Guide 1993* [13], 72 per cent have fitness centres, 62 per cent squash courts, 51 per cent pools and 35 per cent outdoor all-weather pitches.

Two hundred of the leisure centres claim to attract between 400,000 and 2,000,000 attendances in a year. The vast majority of those attending participate in the centre programme of activities. Seventy centres have between 50 and 177 members of staff, averaging one member of staff per 9–10 attendances.

Sixty centres have seating accommodation for events of over 1,500 seats and altogether 276 centres have capacities of 550 or more seats. A high proportion have ancillary spaces to programme, such as fitness centres, health suites and squash courts; some have ice rinks; some have indoor bowls centres. Half the United Kingdom leisure centres have swimming pools, some of which are leisure pools.

At the large end of the scale, there are leisure centres with a range of sub-stantial facilities: indoor arenas in London, Birmingham, Sheffield and Manchester; the Ponds Forge International Centre in Sheffield; the Crowtree Leisure Centre in Sunderland; The Dome in Doncaster; and Fort Regent in Jersey – a leisure centre within a twenty-three acre eighteenth-century Napoleonic fort, with three acres under cover.

Harlow Sportcentre, run by a charitable trust, provided the first multi-purpose indoor community sports centre in the United Kingdom. Its versatile programming to meet the needs, from community recreation to sporting excellence, created a mechanism of dividing up playing spaces and producing programme permutations, that have survived, changed with time, and been used as blueprints for hundreds of other centres.

The Dome in the Doncaster Leisure Park comprises 'The Lagoons' – a six pool leisure complex; Ice Caps, the leisure ice rink; the Health and Fitness Centre (formerly the Bowls hall); the 'Events Hall' for sport participation, drama, concerts and shows. Other facilities include: a health hydro, aerobics and dance studio; fitness centre, squash courts and a range of social facilities. Programming is a mechanism for getting the best out of the resources for the benefit of customers. In this leisure centre, programming is needed within the separate spaces, with combined spaces, with packages and with fixed and flexible programmes. Joint tickets for water and ice are examples.

Fort Regent Leisure Centre attracts 900,000 visitors annually with a budget of over £4 million. It is a tourist attraction, a sports centre, a conference venue and a stage for entertainments and the performing arts. Each market or 'product' has needs, and priorities have to be set against conflicting claims. For example, do you suspend the sports programme for a show, when sport provides greater income generation than entertainment? In this example, clarity of objectives and priorities is essential in order to focus on programming requirements and deal more easily with potential conflicts.

Ponds Forge International Sports Centre in Sheffield is one of the most technically advanced centres in the world. It has three pools – a 52.6m × 25m × 2.3m pool, an international diving pool and a leisure pool, and a sports hall large enough for ten badminton courts and international volleyball and has seating for up to 1,800. Programming the range of water activities highlights the need to have firm general policies, which include a balance between local and international, community and club, casual and group, training and recreation. Programming problems for the management to overcome include: competition demands versus participation; club squad and structured activity versus casual use; and income versus development of excellence and social needs criteria.

Multi-purpose leisure centres require programmes which use the same space in a variety of ways. Swimming pools, for example, can be programmed for 'lane swimming', 'water fun', 'water aerobics', 'water therapy', galas, canoeing and even sailing, using a wind machine at one end of the pool! Sports halls are used for concerts, antique fairs, dances, fashion shows and Christmas parties, in addition to their main sports function. Many redundant squash courts are being used for activities such as aerobics, fitness and snooker and can also be used as sports shops, classrooms or information centres.

It is not just the large centres that need good programming. Small centres with limited space and resources need even greater skill at times. For example, in a one-court sports hall, (four badminton courts) programming may include sport (for schools, clubs, coaching, recreation), concerts, dances, exhibitions and antique fairs. In the early part of this century, swimming pools were covered over to programme sports events, dances and dinners. Leisure programming is not new.

13.8.1 Indoor arenas and large halls

The success of arenas is dependent on skilful programming. Indoor arenas are event orientated, but the range of events can be extremely diverse. The United Kingdom is developing its own kind of indoor arena, that is smaller than US counterparts and more diverse in programmes compared to many American or European arenas [14].

An arena programme depends on a range of factors including:

1. the philosophy of use (aims and objectives) – the National Indoor Arena (NIA) in Birmingham, for example, is committed annually to a substantial quota of events arranged by United Kingdom Governing Bodies of Sport;
2. The balance to be achieved between sport and non-sport, between entertainment, exhibitions and conventions/launches;
3. The extent of home-based teams – most US arenas depend on tenant teams for economic survival (the Sheffield Arena has attracted growing numbers to support the City's Ice Hockey Team);
4. Contracts, for example, between the arena and governing bodies of sport, entertainment promoters, local authorities and commercial developers;
5. Promotions – the extent of a) 'dry' hire, in which the premises are rented to a promoter at an agreed 'fixed price' with or without profit sharing; b) joint promotions; and c) own promotions. Other than the NIA, the most popular events are: rock and pop concerts; exhibitions; conventions and rallies; and then sport (unless there is a home-based team);
6. The flexibility of the arena design, e.g. the ability to change from a hard floor to a resilient surface or artificial turf, or ice, and changing from entertainment to sports participation.
7. Support services – the effectiveness of ancillary facilities and attractions to retain customers, maximize income potential – secondary spend – and stagger arrival and departure times;
8. Set-up and break-down times.

Programme versatility must be coupled with management flexibility and sensitivity. For example, the ambience and security issues for a rock concert or for a symphony concert, call for quite different management solutions. At the opening event in the London Arena, Luciano Pavarotti was disturbed by the constant sound of footsteps on a hard non-carpeted floor, as latecomers arrived throughout the first half of the concert!

Programming is affected greatly by design. A large space with a hard floor and strong walls and ceiling is often more flexible for programming large events of different kinds, compared with a purpose-designed building. All arenas need seating configuration permutations, good acoustic and lighting capability, ceiling catwalks, platforms and strong fixing beams, large staging capability, truck loading bays, etc. These factors emphasize the need for programming and management to influence design and not vice versa!

Income variables are affected by seating layouts, floor layouts, exhibition and sports layouts, changeover times, lettable space per event, and in large measure, dependent on the type of booking, whether 'dry' hire, joint hire or own promotion.

The simplest and most used form of hire is dry hire (or some variation on it). Wembley Arena and the National Exhibition Centre in Birmingham hire much of their programme time on this basis. Joint promotions are becoming more fashionable and there is considerable 'horse trading', particularly with pop concerts and sponsored events and especially over the extremely thorny problem of television rights.

13.9 Programming by objectives and leisure facility programmes

The basic assumption was made at the start of this chapter that programming is a process. It is logical therefore to make programming a systematic process, a system which takes a wide and open view of the variety of possibilities. First, the approach at public facilities must be capable of incorporating both major strategies: social planning and community development. Second, the approach must be capable of handling any of the options, from the wholly authoritarian-directed service at one extreme to the participant-controlled programme at the other.

Different approaches will suit different situations at different times. The 'Programming by Objectives' method builds on the principles of 'Management by Objectives'. It is a planning approach to achieve measurable targets, which lead to ultimate aims. It co-ordinates the network of several specific approaches; it sets targets, plans, implements, controls and monitors. It is a practical, objective approach which gets things done. Of all the approaches, it embraces several styles, yet avoids needless duplication because there is a co-ordinated network plan. It is businesslike; it is a professional approach.

Essentially, programming deals with people taking part in leisure activities which have been enabled or provided by leisure 'managers'. One thing we know about leisure behaviour is that, if the experience is satisfying, it becomes habitual – given opportunity. Programmes, therefore, need to offer levels of continuity.

Once established, programmes are difficult to change in a hurry. Moreover, programmes need time to set up and they need resources and finances to promote and organize. Hence, community participation programmes need at least a few months to run, unless, for example, they are short-term holiday or one-off weekend programmes.

Leisure programming, therefore, in most cases is an on-going cyclical process. Once a programme has been set in motion, it can go on in repeated cycles like a long-running saga. While it may be easier to just let matters take their cyclical course with the same content, good programmers will constantly review the programme, re-plan, implement afresh, run the programme, evaluate and then review again, and so the cycle goes on. This is because in spite of individuals' continuity of attendance, demands change, markets change and leisure managers have to match their products to the market.

The process outlined below is concerned with setting up the programme in the first place. But, most programming is concerned with dealing with on-going programmes with regular cycles of review, forward planning, implementation and evaluation.

A continuous programme must be offered to the public; hence, these stages in the process overlap and elements within an overall programme continue to be implemented and evaluated whilst review and planning for other elements or the next programme period is under consideration.

Set out below are seven stages for programming based on operational experience and founded upon workable programming theory. In leisure planning and management, the separate service elements such as marketing, programming and financing all stem from the same initial phases of the management process; it is inevitable, therefore, that overlap occurs when trying to explain these aspects in isolation. Marketing, for example, is covered at length in chapter fifteen and events in chapter sixteen.

The seven-stage programming model is described below.

1. Review policy and establish goals

A programme needs to be based on a sound directional philosophy. It needs principles on which to guide its course, and policies on which to plan and establish effective strategies. The philosophy is based on the general purposes and beliefs of the organization. It gives the organization a rationale – a justification for its existence, when it is asked 'What business are we in? Who are we here to serve? What do we want to achieve?' The purpose is synonymous with the rationale, the basic reason for an organization and its programme. The principles are the fundamental beliefs. The principles lead to policy guidelines. These guidelines give direction and, for local authority services, can be summarized into statements which are the consensus of the community. These statements become the aims of the organization. Many local authorities have no stated aims and, in such circumstances, the council policy has to be interpreted from previous actions.

Local authorities may wish to provide a social service or a balanced social, yet economic service; voluntary organizations will wish to meet the purposes for which they were established; commercial enterprises will wish to attract customers through good programmes and service, with a promotional and pricing policy to enable profits to be achieved.

Consider the programme in the light of marketing and financial strategies: identify market targets; turn policies into directional strategies, i.e. whether client-directed, contractor-directed, or community-directed; turn the organization's 'mission statement' or 'statement of intent' into the goals of the programme.

The aims of a community recreation service (which will need to be converted into measurable objectives and targets) could include, for example:

1   to serve and give substantial leisure opportunity to all people in the community regardless of race, colour, creed, age, sex, ability or disability
2   to meet significant social needs
3   to involve people in the community in recreation programming
4   to provide the most appropriate service to serve the greatest number of people in the community and also serve those in greatest need, recognizing the need for balance between majority and minority interests
5   to market community recreation effectively to discover need, to supply appropriate services and to attract participants
6   to give range, diversity and balance to programmes

7   to provide programmes which are flexible enough to cope with changing demands
8   to make the fullest use and most imaginative use of all resources
9   to give a large measure of choice through which variety, novelty and depth of programming is possible
10   to stimulate community initiatives and spontaneous activity
11   to manage services and facilities with capable and suitably qualified and trained personnel
12   to evaluate progress regularly and systematically.

2. Assess demand and resources

The Leisure Manager collates all the marketing information and discovers as much as possible about the community and the range of interests. This will include determining the user profile for the community and identifying gaps in the range of opportunities currently on offer. Next the manager evaluates what resources are available – the areas, facilities, organizations, agencies, personnel and finance. The process will cover the following areas.

- The likely client base: to what extent will the facilities and activities attract individuals, casual users, recreational groups, clubs, leagues, classes, courses and events? Will schools, industries and other institutions be hiring for their own communities?
- For new programmes, a profile of the current and prospective customers and the type of services and activities to meet their needs and expressed demands will need to be ascertained. This is part of a 'market assessment'.
- For existing programmes, review the customer profile and compare with the market profile and the catchment population. Also review the current performance and determine level of spare capacity or overloading.
- Assess the contribution made by other agencies, and the success and failures of other programmes.
- Identify market gaps.
- In terms of information, new programmes will need more general information compared to established programmes, which may need to concentrate on particular segments of the programme.
- Consider current leisure trends and the experience of other leisure providers; this can lead to injecting experimental and 'taster' activities.
- Set up programme review meetings, e.g. in local authorities between client officers and contractors.

3. Set objectives and targets

Objectives are different from aims. Aims are long-term, ultimate goals, which reflect the purposes of an organization. Objectives are short range, attainable ends, leading towards fulfilling the aims. They must be measurable. Objectives should be written as statements that are quantifiable with some dimension of time. Objectives answer questions such as: what? how? when by? how measured? Objectives describe the way in which action is to be carried out and how results are to be measured. Objectives can also be broken down into several shorter term targets.

In addition to objectives which are measured quantitatively, some objectives are needed which can be measured by more qualitative criteria. Objectives, so called, such as 'to maximize use', 'to serve as many people as possible' or 'to provide activities for the whole community' are meaningless unless they have some yardstick with which to evaluate the results. In short, they must be measurable. For example, take a hypothetical case of an indoor recreation centre where the programming aim is: to provide a balanced and broad-based programme of opportunities that meets the leisure and sporting needs and demands of the different sections of the community. First, understand the market. The community may consist of players of high and low standards of ability, young and old, male and female, able and disabled, sports persons and non-sports persons, highly competitive players and socially orientated players, etc., the programme will have to cater to some extent for their diverse requirements. Then, set programme objectives and make each objective measurable and within a time span. In local authority facilities, these could include:

- Short range targets for each objective, in each area, within a precise time period – weeks (e.g. holiday programmes), months (e.g. leisure courses), years (e.g. programme financial targets, social objectives, etc.)
- in terms of social objectives at community facilities, an appropriate balance between community-orientated and officer-directed approaches (e.g. a free taster session or free crèche);
- in terms of economic objectives, appropriate balances based on priorities, e.g. surplus financing in specific activities (e.g. squash; fitness) sufficient to balance social subsidy (e.g. beginners' badminton);
- in comprehensive services with wide ranging goals, balances between passive and active leisure, between sport, recreation, arts, social entertainments and educational activities (e.g. 30 per cent of time on average at weekends to events);
- pricing levels, including, where appropriate, subsidized levels, surplus levels for some activities such as courses, and commercial levels, or what the markets will bear, for entertainment;
- budgets and performance ratios – financial, numerical, social.

In a sports hall programme, for example, the following might be considered:

1   the range of opportunities (sporting and non-sporting activities) to be offered (e.g. 80 per cent sporting, 20 per cent non-sporting);
2   the range of leagues, competitions, ladders, etc., to be provided in specific sports;
3   the range of courses to be offered in specific sports for adults and juniors at different levels of ability;

4   the sports development programmes in specified focus sports;

5   the specific opportunities to be provided to identified market targets, such as disabled; mothers with young children; 50 plus; the unemployed;

6   the range and type of non-sporting events to be staged;

7   the balance of the programme with specific elements being restricted in terms of time and space, e.g. clubs not to exceed 30 per cent of the week-day evening programme.

Additionally, where objectives are likely to be in conflict, there is a need to establish priorities, particularly with regard to the programming of, say, a leisure centre's main hall, where at peak times the demand is likely to exceed the supply.

4. Plan the programme

The programme offered represents the practical application of the purpose of the facility or service and the fulfilment of the set objectives. To ensure that the proposed programme is well balanced, there is a need to analyse the activities offered, the space allocated and the anticipated profile of different users. It is also necessary to ensure that no sections are ignored and that the incompatibility of activities and users is avoided. The extent of the programme will be affected by the resources available (e.g. facilities, personnel and finance) and the activities offered will, of necessity, have to be provided within the allocated budget.

Every programmer should have a checklist of essential aspects that must be considered in planning the programme. Some of these are included below.

- *Time* The basis on which the programme operates. Establish hourly, daily, weekly and seasonal patterns of use. Consider both fixed (e.g. schools) and flexible (e.g. casual bookings) timetables.
- *Types and forms* Determine programme types and classification (arts, sports, social, etc.) and forms of organization (clubs, courses, events, etc.) and recognize the different needs of different people (e.g. recreational, young, older, beginner, improver, high standard competitor).
- *Activities and balances* Choose activities and methods which collectively are most likely to meet objectives and sustain interest. Build flexibility and novelty into each programme cycle. Plan appropriate balances.
- *Budget* Set budgets for each main programming stream and ways of achieving targets.
- *Priorities* Because of conflicting claims, establish priorities. In public settings, avoid totally exclusive use – it narrows the field. Avoid totally casual use – it also narrows the field.
- *Compatibility* Programme activities which go well together, that don't clash! Avoid incompatible activities in terms of health and safety, noise, age, level of play, ambience, etc.
- *Expand* Expand the programme with new activities, new methods (e.g. self-bookings) and new people (bring a friend for free taster session). Sell 'packages' not just single items. Try experiments.

- *Resources* Consider the resource implications and staffing, particularly staffing ratios in vulnerable areas, for example, swimming and children's activities, being cognisant of health and safety matters, *The Children Act* and other guidelines.
- *Safety* Undertake equipment and maintenance safety checks.
- *Training* Train staff to undertake programming functions.
- *Contract* With contract management, ensure that the contractor complies with the specification not just in the letter of the contract, but importantly, the spirit also.
- *Systems* Establish easily handled and easily understood administration systems and methods. Anticipate the likely problems (potential for double booking; potential clashes between regular users and new customers with different requirements). Try new technologies to programming – giant screens for information and entertainment, visuals to show court spaces available; self-service/DIY bookings.
- *Promote* Produce excellent promotional and publicity materials. Ensure weekly story in the local press and that all events are given media space. Advertise the programme and monitor the usefulness of different promotional methods.
- *Critical path* Programme planning needs to be undertaken methodically. Use a bespoke 'Critical Path Network'. Be guided by Murphy's Law: 'Nothing is as simple as it seems. Everything takes longer than you think. If anything can go wrong, it will!' Or adopt the P's motto: 'Prior Proper Planning Prevents Poor Performance!'

5. Implement the programme

To ensure that the potential participants are aware of the opportunities offered, it will be necessary to promote both the centre and what it offers. Programmed time within a facility is a most perishable product (space not used today is lost for ever) hence the general and specific awareness of a facility is of the utmost importance.

In order to be able to manage the programme efficiently, a range of systems needs to be developed that deal with specific aspects associated with programming. These include, for example, the booking system, the administrative system relating to internal leagues and competitions, the payment of coaches and tutors, the collection of entry fees, issue of invoices, etc. In order that the programme runs smoothly, it is advisable to anticipate any problems that might arise. By so doing, an alternative strategy can be planned – in advance – and introduced, should the need arise. In this way, crisis management and panic reaction can be avoided.

Programme control is a management function; it helps if one manager has overall responsibility. He or she must have the necessary ability and authority and be part of the policy making team. Ensure that the way the programme is being delivered meets the highest customer service and that staff are carrying out their own jobs efficiently. Programming success is often dependent on seemingly small items, administrative or technical. Double-bookings cause problems far in excess of the minor mistake. Practical operational knowledge might show a need to:

- adjust staffing levels in light of changes in occupancy levels;
- anticipate operational problems, e.g. staff sickness;
- obtain daily feedback – walk the floor, check that the resources, facilities and equipment are up to scratch;
- use a specially designed, comprehensive management information system that can be used on a day-to-day basis; today's computer technology such as smart cards, used well, can be a boon to effective management;
- deal with complaints immediately and turn them into opportunities for getting things right.

6. Evaluate and monitor progress

In the United States considerable work has been undertaken on recreation programme evaluation [15]. In the United Kingdom comparatively little has been achieved in this area, particularly in terms of community recreation. It is crucially important to evaluate the programme. How else can a manager know whether the objectives have been met, the goals reached? Evaluation is often thought of only in terms of the end-result of a programme – the 'bums on seats' approach. However, this is merely part of the evaluation picture. Evaluation is methodically appraising a programme's worth, taking into consideration:

1   the input – how much has gone into the programme planning and organization;
2   The process – what has actually occurred during the programme;
3   The outcomes – what were the end-results and how these compared with the target objectives and performance objectives.

The input is the planning stage. What were the total costs of the exercise? How many resources were used? How many staff and how much time and effort were put into the operation? What promotion was undertaken? In other words, what was involved in putting the programme together?

The process is concerned with the running of the operation. What actually went on? This gives clues as to why a programme was successful or unsuccessful. It refreshes one's memory. It lets others know about the running of the programme and what methods were employed, what management style was predominant, what leadership techniques were successful.

The outcome involves comparing programme objectives with actual performance. Why have objectives if you do not gauge them with what has been achieved? Outcomes are often too heavily weighted on financial performance. While this is paramount in the budget target setting, financial yardsticks are but one measure. The question is: did the programme fulfil its purpose? That is, were the objectives met? How did performance match the targets etc? Were customers, as individual and groups, generally satisfied?

How should evaluation be undertaken and who should do it? Evaluation can be undertaken in three main ways.

1   Inside evaluation can be more sensitive to staff feelings, but is more likely to be biased and less objective and more likely to justify failures, or to exonerate from blame.
2   Outside evaluation is likely to be more objective, but can be hampered by staff suspicion or worry about the outcome. External evaluations sometimes misinterpret the complex relationships and common-sense know-how.
3   A combination of inside and outside evaluation makes better sense. Involvement from all sources is better still – from the policy makers, the officers, the clients, the contractors, the staff and the customers.

The process should seek answers to a number of questions, including:

1   By what criteria is success to be measured?
2   To what extent has the programme been successful in meeting objectives?
3   How well has the programme been delivered and received?
4   How well have the staff performed?
5   What 'profits' have been made – quantitative and qualitative?
6   What proportion of complaints have been turned into opportunities for better service?
7   Have markets expanded – wider customer base, catchment areas?
8   How effective have the promotional methods been?
9   How adaptable has the organization been to the changes? Have systems (and staff) been able to adapt?
10   Have resources been adequate – facilities, equipment, staff, space, time, budget?
11   Have all statutory and other regulations been met?
12   What lessons have been learned?

When, how and who should evaluate are further questions to be considered by the Leisure Manager. Both inside and outside evaluation make good sense as the evaluation can be both situational and objective. Feedback from as many as possible – policy makers, officers, staff and customers – makes for greater understanding, validity, and improvement to the existing programme.

We have seen (in chapter twelve) how employee motivation improves performance when they are involved in the decision-making process. Staff and leaders are closest to people; they and the participants are first-hand observers. Therefore, managers should endeavour to collect information from everyone. What was good? What went wrong? Why? How can the programme be improved? This style of evaluation needs skilful and sensitive handling.

13.10 Summary – programming

Programming provides the leisure products that we are in business to sell. It is the mechanism for meeting objectives. It is the single most important function of Leisure Managers. Programming is an on-going process characterized by repeated cycles of evaluation and review, planning and implementation.

Good programming results in achieving objectives. It offers choice, provides balance, attracts the markets being aimed at, and is responsive to the needs and wants of customers. Conversely, poor programming results in confusion. Programmes do not meet organization objectives, choice is limited and too many customers become dissatisfied.

Community recreation programming is a process. The programme is the means to achieve the aims and objectives of the organization. There are many agencies, authorities and organizations whose function it is to provide recreation. The local authority, however, has a special enabling and co-ordinating function in addition to supplying its own services and facilities.

Programming hinges around five main factors: the policies; the people; the activities; the facilities; and the management. There are many ways in which programmes can be classified, including by function, by areas and facilities, by people and social interaction and by the expected outcomes of the recreation programme. The classification into functional activities is the most common.

There are different approaches to programming. Two major directions can be loosely termed 'social planning', where the locus of control is with the authority and professionals, and 'community development', which is a more people-orientated direction. There are a great variety of specific methods of approach. In practice, a mix of approaches is tried but in many without a sound co-ordinating network.

'Programming by Objectives' is an approach which overcomes many of the inherent problems in other, more subjective methods. In this approach, the Leisure Manager undertakes several actions, including working with policy makers to establish aims, setting objectives, choosing activities, and promoting and presenting the programme. This will include sectors of the programme where community initiatives are given full rein, enabled by organization resources. It will also include several approaches: meeting demands, giving choice and trying experiments. The programme will be constantly monitored: it is important to keep in touch with the programme and the people. Finally, the programme is evaluated; the evaluation is concerned with the input (what has gone into the planning), the process (what has occurred) and the actual outcome.

Programming is perceived as an ongoing continuous process, and while there are steps in the procedure, different sections will be at different stages – the whole programme will be changing and evolving. This is why high-quality management is needed to co-ordinate and control the entire operation. Recreation programming needs quality managers. As way of a summary, and a checklist, a 'seven-step' guide to successful community leisure and recreation programming is outlined below.

Planning by objectives – seven-step community programming planning guide

1. Interpret policy, establish aims and objectives

Understand the purpose of your organization, its philosophy and its fundamental beliefs.

1.1 Produce a 'mission statement' or 'statement of purpose' – i.e. the aims and goals of the organization.
1.2 Produce programme policy guidelines and directional strategies.
1.3 Where no written philosophy/policy exists, top managers should interpret the organization's purpose, communicate with others, produce a written policy statement and obtain endorsement.

2. Assess resources and current and potential demand

Produce a profile of the current and prospective consumers and the type of services and activities to meet their needs and demands.

2.1 Evaluate current resources, facilities, organizations, services, programmes and opportunities.
2.2 Evaluate the current performance of facilities and services; determine the level of spare capacity, etc.
2.3 Collate all marketing information. Use surveys, suggestions, community councils and recreation organizations.
2.4 Evaluate the contribution made by other agencies – e.g. voluntary sector, commercial enterprise, education and industrial clubs.
2.5 Establish a profile of potential users – i.e. the individuals and groups likely to participate.
2.6 Assess forthcoming year's new opportunities – e.g. historic celebrations, sponsorship and campaigns.
2.7 Identify market gaps and determine areas of deficiency in terms of services and programmes.

3. Set objectives

Translate policies and market demands into action, first by setting objectives and make each objective measurable and within a time span.

3.1 Involve policy makers, staff and community in the setting of objectives.
3.2 Set short-range targets in each area within a precise time period: weeks (e.g. holiday programmes); months (e.g. leisure courses); and years (e.g. financial targets, social objectives, etc.).
3.3 Set an appropriate balance between community-orientated and professionally-directed approaches.
3.4 Set balances between passive and active leisure, between sport, recreation, art, social, entertainment, etc. to meet the aims.
3.5 Agree performance indicators, financial income/expenditure ratios, subsidies and targets.
3.6 Establish priorities with regard to objectives: because there will be conflicting objectives, and no programme can meet all potential demand.

4. Plan the programme

Adopt the programmer's motto: 'Proper Prior Planning Prevents Poor Performance.'

4.1 Time is the basis on which the programme operates. Establish hourly, daily, weekly and seasonal patterns of use.
4.2 Consider both fixed and flexible timetables.
4.3 Determine programme areas (arts, sports, social, etc.).
4.4 Determine programme forms (clubs, courses, events, etc.).
4.5 Recognize the different needs of different people: recreational, competitive, beginners, high standard, older, younger, etc.
4.6 Balance the programme providing width and depth – balance implies diversity. Because of conflicting claims, it is necessary to establish priorities.
4.7 Choose and analyse activities and methods which collectively are most likely, within resources, to meet objectives.
4.8 Avoid totally exclusive use, it narrows the field.
4.9 Avoid totally casual use, it also narrows the field.
4.10 Build flexibility into the programme. It will lead to variety, wider use and greater balance.
4.11 Consider how the programme fits into the marketing strategy, e.g. corporate approach to marketing, specific promotions.
4.12 Consider the staffing implications and management style, division of labour, responsibilities, etc.
4.13 Train staff to undertake responsibility and gain job satisfaction and professional skills. Train staff for a customer-orientated approach.
4.14 Avoid administration problems by establishing easily handled and easily understood systems and methods – i.e. easy for the user and easy for the organization.
4.15 Make full use of information technology and modern computerized systems.

5. Implement the programme

Construct, promote and implement the programme with vitality, enthusiasm and charisma.

5.1 Implement the agreed marketing strategy, using the most appropriate promotional methods. Spend time on promotion.
5.2 The flexible approach needs skilful management to enable individuals to participate in the way they want to. Flexibility is needed to meet changing situations.
5.3 Give sensitive care to staffing aspects, especially with regard to community development. Staff/helpers are needed to support newly formed groups until they become self-supporting. Consider some outreach approach.
5.4 Try new technologies for programming – e.g. video, computers, giant screen for information, visuals to show court availability, self-service, do-it-yourself bookings, etc. Use information technology to advantage.

5.5 Control the programme through appropriate staffing and delegation of authority, financial and operational systems.

5.6 Develop monitoring systems to provide management with information relating to current level of usage, profile of users, changing trends.

5.7 Anticipate the likely problems; be ready with alternatives.

5.8 Avoid incompatible activities in terms of health and safety, noise, age, level of play, etc.

5.9 Expand the programme with new activities, new methods and new people.

5.10 Sell 'packages', not just single items.

5.11 Try some experiments; try out regional and national activity trends, yet always enhance local success.

5.12 Extend product life-cycles through changes, variety and new ways of selling.

5.13 Use pricing flexibility as a marketing tool; consider the benefits of differential pricing.

5.14 Keep all informed of what is going on. Use a variety of communication systems.

6. Evaluate the programme

Evaluate – or how else will you know whether you are doing a good job?
To what extent has the programme been successful or unsuccessful? Measure its effectiveness – i.e. to what extent have objectives been met?

6.1 Evaluate inputs – what has gone into planning the programme.

6.2 Evaluate the process – what has occurred in carrying out the programme from start to finish.

6.3 Evaluate the outcome – the results.

6.4 Measure the efficiency of the operation: how well has the job been carried out? How adequate has the staffing been; how well have staff performed?

6.5 Use several criteria, not just financial, to measure 'profits', both quantitative and qualitative: throughput; social mix; use by less advantaged; age mix; income generation; subsidy per user; levels of sponsorship achieved; etc. Measure cost-effectiveness.

6.6 Determine any changes in user profiles, catchment areas.

6.7 How effective have the marketing methods been?

6.8 How adaptable has the organization been to the changes in the programme?

7. Obtain feedback and modify programme

Think of programming as an ongoing process. Therefore, every cycle should see some change or modification.

7.1 How can the programme be improved? Modify the objectives and targets accordingly.

7.2 Obtain feedback from users (duty manager daily records; surveys; focus groups, user forums) and through the community network and community leader resources.

7.3 If the programme or elements of it have been unsuccessful, first, determine the causes for failure to meet targets; second, consider staff training or retraining; third, consider changes in staff areas of responsibility; fourth, consider the effectiveness of the management style.

Notes and references

1 Erikson, E. (1963), *Eight Ages of Man in Childhood and Society* (2nd edition), Norton, New York.

2 Meyer, H. D. (1957), 'The adult cycle', *Annals of the American Academy of Political Science and Society, 33*, 58–67.

3 Farrell, P. and Lundegren, H. M. (1978), *The Process of Recreation Programming*, Wiley, New York.

4 Butler, G. D. (1976), *Introduction to Community Recreation*, McGraw-Hill, New York, p. 231.

5 Edginton, C. R., Crompton, D. M. and Hanson, C. J. (1980), *Recreation and Leisure Programming: A Guide for the Professional*, Saunders College, Philadelphia, PA, pp. 28–43.

6 *ibid.*, p. 38.

7 Haywood, L. and Henry, I. (1986) 'Policy developments in community leisure and recreation, part one', *Leisure Management*, July 6(7), 25–9.

8 Kraus, R. G. and Curtis, J. E. (1977), *Creative Administration in Recreation and Parks*, C. V. Mosby, Saint Louis, MO.

9 Edington *et al.*, *Recreation and Leisure Programming*, chapter 2.

10 Tillman, A. (1974), *The Program Book for Recreation Professionals*, National Press Books, Palo Alto, CA, pp. 57–8.

11 Griffiths, G. (1981), *Recreation Provision for Whom?* unpublished.

12 Torkildsen, G. (1987), *Recreation Management: A Framework for the Effective Management of Community Recreation Facilities*, unpublished.

13 Richardson, J. (ed.) (1993), *British Leisure Centre Guide*, John S. Turner/Longman, Harlow.

14 See Shields, A. and Wright, M. (eds) (1989), *Arenas: A Planning, Design and Management Guide*, Sports Council, London.

15 See Theobald, W. F. (1979), *Evaluation of Recreation and Park Programs*, Wiley, New York.

Marketing of leisure and recreation

Marketing was developed for selling products profitably. The marketing of leisure, particularly public service leisure, is relatively new. However, marketing (of some kind) is undertaken by all those involved in providing services, resources and goods for recreation and leisure, whether in the public, private or commercial sectors. Public knowledge, or lack of knowledge, about services and facilities and the image they portray are essential components of marketing. It could be argued therefore that every organization in the leisure business is already 'marketing'. The question is whether they are marketing well or badly. The concept of marketing is relatively simple. It is about understanding the needs of the potential customers and responding to them. It is also about understanding your organization and ensuring that your customers and your organization get what they need and want.

Marketing, promotion and customer service have received a good deal of attention of late in training courses and literature within the field of leisure management. This chapter deals with the concept, moving flexibly between theory and practice, with examples and anecdotes from working experience; it provides approaches, messages and clues to providing attractive public leisure services to customers at a social 'profit'.

This chapter is structured around four main themes. First, the concepts of commercial marketing, social marketing and public service marketing are described and distinguished one from another. Second, as the *raison d'être* of marketing is selling to

433

customers, the motivations to buy and the demotivators are described. Third, the constituents of the 'marketing mix' – i.e. product, price, place and promotion – are considered in a leisure context. Fourth, approaches towards achieving a marketing plan are proposed.

Having read this chapter, readers will be made aware of the substantial influence of marketing on the buying habits of the public and what motivates and demotivates customers. They will also be aware that marketing starts with customers and their needs, not with products and organizations.

Students will learn what comprises the 'marketing mix' and that commercial marketing will need to be adapted to suit the social, political and institutional structure within the local government setting. They will learn about market segmentation and positioning.

Leisure Managers will be reminded of the need for customer care training for all levels of staff and that the face-to-face employees need particular motivation. They will learn how to set up a marketing strategy and the process to be followed, to set objectives and to achieve them.

14.1 Introduction

Marketing is an essential part of good management practice, an integral part of the management process. Marketing is a process of identifying customer needs, wants and wishes and satisfying them. Leisure services and facilities depend on satisfied customers or they go out of business.

Marketing is not selling, as such. It was developed for selling. It is concerned with the needs and demands of potential customers. Selling is one of its ingredients, but that comes late in the marketing process.

> Selling focusses on the seller
> Marketing on the needs of the buyer

In simple terms, what we are trying to do is to discover what our potential customers need, and are prepared to buy, then to create products and services to suit the needs and to sell these 'profitably'. Therefore, marketing, far from being the end activity of a business – selling the goods – is at the beginning and goes on as part and parcel of the business itself. The key is to match leisure services and products to the people – the marketplace. Indeed, Leisure Management itself is essentially a marketing process – meeting the needs and demands of people through leisure opportunities.

The historical development of marketing is encapsulated in the growth of the car industry: first, no competition, then competitive selling, then marketing. Henry Ford, in the early days of the industry, is believed to have said, 'You can have any colour of car you like, as long as it's black'! The growth in competition increased the need for promotion and selling. Later, the products (the cars) had to be adapted to the needs of the market (the buyers), hence, a number of different models were produced – a variety of choice to suit different tastes. Japanese business captured the car and motor cycle markets by providing what customers were looking for – style, colour, speed, comfort and fuel economy, and at a lower price.

This industrial and commercial marketing base has expanded into not-for-profit institutions and into leisure – private and public. For example in the public sector, when the conventional local 'baths' were the only swimming facility in town and few people had cars to travel far, there was little choice. But today many of those same towns have better traditional and leisure pools within easy travel distance and customers also have a wider variety of leisure choices, including more 'private' pools in health clubs.

We are all influenced by marketing. In Western civilization marketing is part of the fabric by which we go about our daily business. 'It is part of the modern survival kit – because we depend on it' [1]. Marketing is simple. There is no mystique about it. Some treat it with reverence, as a formal, academic subject. Others take a more liberal and relaxed view. Robert Townsend [2], in *Up the Organization*, captures the latter spirit: 'If you can't do it excellently, don't do it at all. Because if it's not excellent it won't be profitable or fun and if you're not in business for fun or profit, what the hell are you doing here?'

14.2   Marketing – what is it and who does it?

In the commercial world marketing has proved to be an effective means of staying in business and making greater profits. For leisure services in the public and voluntary sectors, it can also bring greater success.

The purpose of marketing is to earn profit by 'adding maximum value at minimum cost' [1]. Put simply, marketing is concerned with satisfying customers – profitably. However, 'profit' should be measured not just in terms of money, but also by satisfactions, the quality of the services, the turnover, the range of people, the choice and scope of the programme, the improvements made and other relevant criteria.

Marketing is a process and co-ordination network that analyses, creates, develops products and services, packages, prices, promotes, distributes and sells. It is a beginning-to-end process. This process is usually aimed at a segment of the public or a target market.

The marketing process is co-ordinating the activities of the business in the pursuit of adding maximum value at minimum cost. Its point of origin is consumer demand.

In essence, marketing is that essential part of the management process that matches markets with the leisure 'products' and services. It

- assesses the needs and wants of potential customers
- analyses the situation and the market profile
- creates and develops tailor-made products and services
- packages the products and services to increase sales and avoid price resistance
- promotes in ways to best get to the target markets
- distributes the products

- sells the products and services at a 'profit'
- analyses, evaluates and adjusts.

Hence, marketing is concerned with consumer need and demand. The process is often aimed at a segment of the public or a 'target market'. One feature of the concept of marketing is that of voluntary exchange: 'It calls for offering something of value to someone in exchange for something else of value' [3]. For example, public recreation is provided for the community in exchange for people's money, time and level of community charge.

Commercial 'product' marketing and public 'service' marketing have some aspects in common but there are conceptual differences. In the commercial field the product is the means of achieving a different end product – the making of financial profits. In the services field the quality of the service should be paramount.
Many people treat marketing with suspicion:

> It's an unfortunate fact that marketing – the profession, trade, way of life or what you will – is held in pretty low esteem by the public at large. It's probable, of course, that the public at large doesn't actually understand what marketing's about, but for many, the term has too close an association with the street trader, who would sell his sister if the price were right.
>
> The whole panoply of consumer persuasion, from advertising and PR, through sales promotion, packaging, point-of-sale display and salesmanship itself, is bundled together in many minds as prima facie proof that marketing is immoral, in practice if not in theory.
>
> (*Marketing*, April, 1984)

14.2.1 *The marketing approach*

Marketing is not a single function in a business or service organization. It is a business philosophy, a business way of life. It starts in the marketplace with customers. It is about selling satisfactions.

Traditionally, many companies are process-led and product-orientated; they have a pre-determined product or service. They find customers and convince them they want the product. The approach is, 'This is what we've got – now sell it'. Local government services often work in this way. For example, facilities are built, equipment is installed, markings are put on to the floors, programmes are devised, times are decided, charges are determined, systems are established, and the council will proudly announce that the facility is open. Many councillors will then say of the facility, 'It is there for them to use; if they don't use it that is their lookout. We provide plenty of opportunity in our town'. This approach is concerned with providing pre-determined products.

The marketing way reverses the process and starts with the customer. It is market-led. It says, 'This is what the customer wants – now make it'. It then designs, produces and delivers the satisfactions for the customer, at a profit. Using the findings of a market research programme – i.e. information received – management organizes its business to ensure that the product is tailor-made for the market. By knowing who your customers are and about their wishes and wants, it is possible to produce appropriate products. When wants have been ascertained, sales resistance is apt to evaporate. The Japanese perfection in mass production, efficiency and knowledge of what the public wants in design, looks, performance and price has reaped a harvest in the motor cycle, motor car, home-based leisure and other industries. And indeed, the Leisure Manager's greatest competitor is leisure in and around the home. The question for Leisure Managers is: what does the public want from leisure services? Management trainer Ted Blake [4] said: 'Sports centres, pools, theatres, art galleries, libraries, museums, gymnasia, are merely warehouses holding tangible and intangible products that have no value except that brought to them by customers.'

Potential customers need to know therefore about the 'products' and be attracted to them. Local authorities have to compete for a share of the market. The financial profit motive, however, is not normally an issue, although greater stress on viability and commercial approaches is being employed. Viable services are important but service to the public at large should be pre-eminent. But is it? Marketing could be used to enhance social and community programmes. However, local government constraints in the United Kingdom could make for difficulties in this direction.

An emerging marketing myth is that local authorities can market public recreation in exactly the same way as one can market breakfast cereals, cameras or holidays. While local authorities have elements within their services which could be commercially orientated, and while marketing techniques can be used to promote recreation programmes, the overall purpose of the authority is not to make financial profit, but to meet need and demand. Moreover, the recreation product is extremely difficult to define and quantify, and quality of the service is difficult to measure, though the development of processes such as ISO 9000, Total Quality Management and Quest help towards this measurement. The aims and objectives, too, are decidedly different from many commercial undertakings: financial yard-sticks are only one measurement and should normally be quite secondary to other criteria. Local councils have political, governmental, traditional and institutional constraints, in addition to social and moral obligations. Marketing is needed but the way in which it is processed should also be different because the commercial product and the local authority service 'product' are not identical. Public sector marketing is a hybrid of approaches which have evolved historically and are now caught up with commercial approaches, primarily to limit subsidy or to help make the facilities pay for themselves. With the advent of compulsory competitive tendering in respect of public services (including leisure and recreation services), leisure managers are under far greater pressure to 'perform', i.e. perform financially.

14.2.2 The concept of social marketing

Marketing is typically defined in business terms as the planning, pricing, promoting, distribution and servicing of goods and products. It has been concerned with economic exchange of goods. As such it has been associated with business objectives to sell products and to learn about the kinds of product that the public would like to purchase. For millions of people, their leisure time is taken up with voluntary commitment to good works and social causes. Marketing could be an anathema to them. Where does it fit in? The concept of marketing, however, can be interpreted as much broader than just economic exchange and could also 'logically encompass exchanges dealing with social issues and ideas' [5]. Most people are familiar with recent attempts to project politicians and political platforms through marketing: 'For example, an individual participating in an election exchanges his vote for the promise of the enactment of a particular political platform if his candidate is elected. Thus, this situation involves exchange' [5]. Marketing, it is argued, includes the facilitating of social exchanges as well as goods and services.

Kotler and Zaltman [6] define social marketing as 'The design, implementation and control of programmes calculated to influence the acceptability of social ideas and involving consideration of product planning, pricing, communication, distribution and market research'. Marketing, then, can encompass political campaigns, community programmes and social causes, such as environmental 'green' issues, pollution control, family planning, health, stop smoking campaigns, equal opportunities, and anti-apartheid and peace campaigns. The success of BBC's *Children in Need* and ITV's *Telethon* are testimony to the power of marketing social causes in recent years.

Any new trend is likely to have both positive and negative effects. Marketing can improve the chances of useful social and community programmes coming to fruition. However, marketing can also be seen as having potential ethical problems. Those who are economically powerful could use marketing techniques to enhance ideas which may promote causes that are not socially beneficial.

Social marketing can be utilized in the leisure field for causes and community projects and to assist in recreation planning. A wide range of causes could be brought to public attention, for example, retention of open space, recreation for the disabled, health and fitness, 'sport for all', 'art for all' and 'music for all' campaigns. However, its sensitive application is enormously important, to avoid the criticism of indoctrination, for social marketing could be a powerful instrument which can affect the way people think, speak and act. This, of course, is the purpose of some marketing and this is why the causes and issues must be debated and adjudged by society to be beneficial. It is very important to put philosophy and principles first. Therefore, start any marketing strategy with a 'mission' statement which tells everybody why we are in business and what we are in business for.

14.2.3 Leisure is a marketing service

The provision of leisure, whether in the public or private sectors, should be a marketing exercise. Consider the following sequence of events:

- facilities like theatres, swimming pools and sport centres are built in locations where they are thought to be right for the market;
- programmes are designed to attract people from the catchment area;
- the activities are priced at levels to attract buyers and give value for money;

- the 'packages' of activities are promoted and targeted;
- the performance is evaluated.

This sequence illustrates the interwoven nature of management processes, marketing and programming. In other words, leisure – regardless of who manages – is a market-orientated business.

However, there will be different goals and different nuances for different markets.

14.2.4 Marketing public leisure and recreation services and facilities

Despite a radical 'sea change' by local authorities, in the wake of compulsory competitive tendering, and the advent of 'Best Value', towards a more 'commercial' stance or 'economic approach', differences of principle behind the provision of leisure still exist. The way marketing is carried out will be different; local authorities will be more sensitive to political and general public reaction and will endeavour to meet social policies.

Compulsory competitive tendering brought into public leisure management direct service organizations – DSOs. Many regard themselves, falsely, as being 'commercial', though there is a blurring of differences between public and private businesses particularly with the success of private contract companies managing local authority facilities. But local councils are still in control, accountable to the public, and managing facilities provided by tax- and ratepayers' money. Local councils have political, governmental, traditional and institutional constraints, in addition to keener social and moral obligations, compared with commercial enterprises. What has changed is the use of commercial techniques and the keener financial objectives of local authorities.

Local authorities provide a number of services such as housing, refuse collection, social services, and so on, and citizens have little choice in the matter. But they can choose whether or not to use local authorities' leisure facilities and services. The facilities are said to cater for the whole community. Clearly, they do not. Some people are not aware of their existence; others are aware but are not motivated to use the facilities – they are either not prepared or not able to exchange what they have for what is on offer. Indeed, the facilities are disproportionally used by those who are more able, more mobile and more socially and financially advantaged.

The broad conclusion of studies by Cowell [7] two decades ago was that there was 'no major evidence of marketing being applied to local authority recreation and sports centre planning and provision. However, the question now raised is whether it is reasonable to expect that marketing could and should be applied to this area.' There were exceptions to the general finding and since then marketing has received far greater attention than ever before. Even so, the overall picture is one of limited evidence of marketing application. Demand assessments were rarely undertaken before facilities were built, but the climate has now changed. However, there are few price experiments (discounts apart) or use of prices as promotional tools and promotional budgets are small and inadequate.

Cowell states that the absence of substantial marketing should not necessarily be seen as criticism. Should marketing be practised? Three main possible explanations were put forward for the relative lack of marketing: general constraints, institutional constraints and service constraints. Do these still apply today? Local authorities still want to be all things to all people.

> Providing for everybody's needs may make good political sense; it is unlikely to make sound marketing sense where segmentation is in vogue. Organizational structures too are often extended and are rarely designed for speedy response to the market place; political interests cloud issues; the committee system can delay decision making; local authorities interpret their sport, leisure and recreation responsibilities differently [7].

Many authorities see recreation as a social service. The nature of what is being 'sold', however, is only partially understood. What is actually being marketed? In the commercial sector financial profits are used as measuring criteria. In local authorities, financial pressures lead to ambivalence. Panic measures may demand that income be maximized and expenditure minimized. This may mean that expenditure in one vital area is reduced, which could then work against achieving the objectives – a treatment least likely to effect a cure.

It is clear that, while marketing may have considerable benefits in local authority provision and management of recreation, the use of marketing approaches must be adapted to suit the social, political, economic and institutional structure within the local government setting.

14.3 Customers and the influences upon them

A caption in *Advertising Age* exemplified the susceptibility and vulnerability of potential customers to persuasive promotion: 'In very few instances do people really know what they want, even when they say they do.'

Customers have many similar needs. But their demands may vary as do their levels of disposable income. In addition, in times of economic recession, the disposable income of many people diminishes, while the costs of goods and services increase. Not only do customers vary one from another, but the same customers may vary from one situation to another, from one mood to another and from one inclination to another. Therefore in leisure we must market for both the similarities and differences in customers.

Many factors affect demand, as we have seen in chapter six: social class, age, family, education, looks, personal aspirations, income, government restrictions, hire purchase, fashion, social attitudes, choices, motivations and many more.

Customers come in all shapes and sizes, from tiny gymnasts to Sumo wrestlers, and from grandparents in the over sixties' keep fit classes to their grandchildren learning piano scales. Different customers, however, may have many similar needs – young and old may be equally at home in the fitness centre using different fitness programmes. And similar types of customers may have different needs – not all young men necessarily want to play football.

Customers are a variety of people. They include:

- individuals
- friends and families
- organizations (who buy for others)
- supporters
- spectators
- schools
- parents
- visitors.

Each link in the chain is a customer. The network is wider than we at first imagine; the chain is longer. Many factors affect demand, including:

- interests and motivations
- choices available
- home and upbringing
- social groups, pressures and attitudes
- age and peers
- family and friends
- education
- looks and abilities
- personal aspirations and confidence
- income and spending power
- job and status
- fashion and trends.

Customers are under constant pressure, whether as individuals or companies. In the past, there were small, concentrated and highly profitable markets. Now there are widespread mass markets with affluence. There is far greater choice. Because of this there can be constant changes in the market and in the buying habits of customers. The leisure market has seen many shifts in demand, from ballroom dancing to step aerobics and from trampolining to bungee jumping!

Customers are not static, unquestioning beings, but dynamic and often highly irrational people. They do not remain the same. Situations can change people. Therefore there is a need for flexibility in management style. Managers must vary their responses so that they continue to be appropriate to changing situations. In leisure services we cannot satisfy all of the people all the time, but we can go a long way towards satisfying most people. As the late management trainer Ted Blake [8] believes, we can satisfy most people by treating them with importance, attention and understanding. This underlines the importance of staff training in customer care.

In leisure services there is often a tendency to treat managers, processes, systems and organizational structures as important. Such services are not customer-orientated, and may not meet customer expectations. Even in times of financial pressure, organizations should not be greedy and kill the golden goose. How many authorities are saying 'Put up the price of aerobics and fitness; there is demand; they'll pay'. This will work when demand outstrips supply; but when supply outstrips demand; then one enters a highly competitive market. In addition, the amount of one's disposable income influences decisions. But how much will they pay? How many of the young or less well-off will continue to pay? Are there alternatives or substitute activities for them?

In order to market leisure successfully, we must sell benefits to customers. These benefits go to make up the picture of success. Local authorities have special benefits to give, particularly to those who are least able to fend for themselves; special groups include the old, the young, the handicapped, the unemployed and especially the jobless school-leaver. Here the problem is compounded, in that they have more free time, less disposable income and poor mobility. Young people, for example, need a favourable image of themselves; they need to realize some of their dreams. The marketing of leisure can assist in this image seeking. Yet the young are susceptible to marketing; commercial enterprise has been quick to seize the opportunity to provide what they are looking for. Pop culture, fashion, music and drink take a massive share of leisure spending. The pub is the leisure centre for many young people.

Suffice it to say that, in terms of marketing, the customer is key. In leisure management we must therefore be customer-orientated. However, potential customers can be influenced in a variety of ways. It is worth considering therefore some of the motivating factors.

14.3.1 *Motivation and the depth approach to marketing*

All of us can be influenced and manipulated, far more than we realize, through marketing. Efforts are constantly being made to channel our unthinking habits, our buying decisions and our thought processes through the use of sciences such as psychiatry. 'Typically these efforts take place beneath our levels of awareness, so that appeals which move us are often, in a sense, hidden' [9]. Some 'manipulating' has been amusing, and some disquieting. The 'depth' approach, as Vance Packard calls it, is being used in a variety of fields and on a variety of unsuspecting people.

> The use of mass psychoanalysis to guide campaigns of persuasion has become the basis of a multi-million dollar industry. Professional persuaders have seized upon it in their groping for more effective ways to sell us their wares – whether products, ideas, attitudes, candidates, goals or states of mind [9].

The 'persuaders' are looking for the whys of our behaviour; for example why people are drawn into illogical purchases or fill shopping baskets in a supermarket as though under hypnosis, or why others buy certain drinks or cars. Packard believes that the 'persuaders' see us typically as 'bundles of day-dreams, misty hidden yearnings, guilt complexes, irrational emotion blockages. We are image lovers given to impulse and compulsive acts' [10]. It seems that our subconscious can be 'pretty wild and unruly'. The persuaders stop at nothing. Nothing is immune or sacred.

Agencies seek to discover the psychological effects of the female menstrual cycle on the purchasing of certain food products; psychiatric probing techniques have been used on impressionable young people anxious to be attractive; and public relations experts are advising church ministers on improving communications with their congregations. Cheskin [11] adds support to Packard:

> Motivation research is the type of research that seeks to learn what motivates people in making choices. It employs techniques designed to reach the unconscious or subconscious mind because preferences generally are determined by factors of which the individual is not conscious. . . . Actually in the buying situation the consumer generally acts emotionally and compulsively, unconsciously reacting to the images and decisions which in the subconscious are associated with the product.

Marketing is, then, potentially powerful and equally potentially dangerous. What people tell interviewers at a surface, conscious level could have little bearing on how they will actually behave in a buying situation. The manipulators are working beneath the surface of conscious life. Most leisure research concerned with public sector provision has been based on surface-level surveys and questionnaires and on quantitative analysis. Research which is more qualitative and looks beneath the surface is required to help to understand people's motivation in making recreation choices.

14.3.2 What motivates people to 'buy' leisure and recreation?

What motivates people in making choices? The realization that there are 'hidden persuaders' makes us aware that there are factors of which the individual is unconscious and that people do different things from what they say they will. For example, impressions could decide the customer's response. First impressions count. Leisure facilities must therefore create the right impression. Marketing slogans preach: 'it is not the product but the promise'. There is a need in leisure to be selling both the product and the promise.

Music has been used cleverly to symbolize and promote products and messages, for example, famine in Ethopia. The selling of 'pop music' singles is often marketed on what are sometimes termed 'hooks' – i.e. those lines, rhythms or jingles which you catch on to and cannot get out of your head, however hard you try. Puccini's 'Nessun Dorma' sung by Luciano Pavarotti was BBC TV's introduction to the 1990 World Cup in Italy. The single and LP were massive 'hits' both for the records and for 'selling' the BBC and the World Cup. A Eurovision Song Contest number one is another example. One of the best-selling top twenty hits of 1973, 'Tie a Yellow Ribbon', was revived in 1981 to welcome home to the United States the Iranian hostages, and again in 1985 for the hostages from Beirut. The jingle had not been forgotten and so the message had not been forgotten. The ribbon symbolism was used years later as a mark of peace on the fortieth anniversary of the dropping of the first atomic bomb on Hiroshima and again after the Gulf War in 1991.

Some marketing slogans can become part of the product itself and hence a great deal of marketing can be undertaken at very little cost. Leisure equipment, clothing and fashion can carry slogans, messages and communications which become embedded in the minds of consumers. To return from shopping in London's West End carrying a Harrod's carrier bag confers a kind of status on the carrier. The trefoil or the laurel wreath seen on a sports shirt carries the name and markets the goods: 'carrying an Adidas sports bag and wearing an Adidas sports shirt confer status beyond what might be expected from association with the names of professional sportsmen' [12]. The McDonald's 'M' and the Nike tick illustrate that we are 'symbol minded'! But, companies such as these have to be quick to change products and promotional methods – McDonald's had to deal with the United Kingdom beef scare and Nike has to deal with the footwear trend now that trainers are no longer as fashionable as they were.

Co-operative marketing spreads the burden of promotional expenditure. Kellogg's, for example, supports promotions of toys, video recorders, sports bags, tennis rackets and bathroom scales. The television and radio media are flooded with advertising jingles. The jingles may remain in the head and promote products for an appreciable length of time. Wilson and West [12] recall that, in 1971, Coca-Cola commissioned a jingle for a new advertising campaign. This was heard repeatedly on television and in cinemas throughout the world. The copyright was assigned to a musical company and a new lyric was written. The former commercial jingle entered the singles record charts as 'I'd Like to Teach the World to Sing'. But the pop song never lost its association with the Coca-Cola advertisement: 'So the company not only recovered much (if not all) of the original investment; it also continued to enjoy a promotional benefit.'

14.3.3 The leisure demotivators

Bad news travels fast. It is passed on more readily than good news. Marketers (i.e. Leisure Managers) must therefore not only have concern with what motivates people to recreation, but also with what demotivates. Nothing demotivates more than poor handling of customers: rudeness, a 'take it or leave it' attitude, ruined expectations, dissatisfactions and broken promises. The package holiday scandals of holidaymakers being sent to the wrong place, or double-bookings, demotivate.

Leisure service is primarily concerned with customers; it is about their needs. Townsend [2] believes that good service is given and things get done because of men and women with conviction. In current leisure management, the 'light of conviction' is often seen in the eyes of junior staff, who may not have the necessary experience but can, with enthusiasm, 'reach the parts others cannot reach'! They should be encouraged, for leisure can be best marketed by people who are involved, committed and who undertake their work with conviction and enthusiasm.

Satisfying customers brings benefits. Success in selling leisure and recreation lies not in leisure departments, centre management, committees or even in the facilities themselves, but out in the market, in the minds and pockets of the customers.

14.3.4 Training for customer caring

Who should do the selling to customers? The British Productivity Council estimate that in 95 per cent of cases there must be face-to-face selling. Commercial organizations spend considerable effort in training and briefing staff, teaching staff how to talk with, meet and communicate with customers.

Training of staff in public facilities is poor by comparison. Many who are in the greatest need of training are those who manage facilities and are not released by their authorities for training or those who work at a face-to-face level with customers. It is these staff at the 'sharp end' i.e. the receptionists, the caretakers, groundsmen, park keepers and supervisors of all kinds – who have the job of meeting and motivating the public. With some notable exceptions (such as many reception staff), face-to-face employees are often the least capable of communicating with and handling customers. They have not been trained, encouraged, motivated, made to feel important or supported. Yet it is they who are called upon to undertake the most important job, namely that of communicating with people. People market leisure and recreation – customers and staff. Staff need help in carrying out this important function; they need training. Regrettably many leisure services, far from motivating people, sometimes serve to demotivate them, achieving the complete opposite of that which was intended.

Customer care and quality of service in the leisure service is probably more important than in any other service because the leisure 'product' we are dealing with is providing satisfying experiences for customers. A visit to a leisure event which is badly managed and results in bad experiences is unlikely to be bought again. Now, if people are seeking satisfying experiences, they can find these in all kinds of leisure activities, not just those that your organization is promoting. At leisure facilities and events, customers need to enjoy their experience or to have found it worthwhile. If they do, they will probably come again and they will let others know about it.

14.4 The marketing mix

Marketing is concerned with providing the right products and services and then forging the best relationships between customers and products and services. The 'Marketing Mix' is the means by which that relationship is expressed. It has a number of ingredients, each of which will have a greater or lesser influence in different settings:

1   product (including service)
2   pricing
3   place
4   promotion (pre-purchase)
5   performance (post-purchase).

There are a number of factors which need emphasis in deciding how the ingredients are going to be mixed in order to be appropriate to the market. Sandy Craig [13] points to some:

Firstly, the nature of the product or service influences the balance of the ingredients. Products with a high fashion content, e.g. designer sportswear, emphasise the product itself through product development and design and promote heavily. Price and availability are not so important. By contrast, staple foods such as canteen food emphasise price and ready availability with promotion and product playing less important roles. (If the 'canteen'/cafe in your facility provides fast food the availability becomes more important, product development (including packaging) becomes more important and price less important. If it provides health food (or healthy food) then product development (including packaging and presentation) becomes even more important, and price less important.

The emphasis on leisure products in the commercial sector and on products in community recreation services will be different. The sections which follow deal with the main ingredients in the 'marketing mix' and, first, the product.

14.5 The leisure product

The product (including the service) is the basis of all marketing. It is the unit of exchange with the client or customer. If it offers the customer satisfactions, he or she may continue to buy it. Products exhibit life-cycles. With most commercial products, that life-cycle revolves around a) product start, b) growth, c) development and d) decline and the replacement by better products. In leisure services many products have been with us for decades, but even well established activities like squash may currently be on the decline and have to be packaged differently to redress the present downward trend. What is needed is product development to provide a continuous stream of new or changing products.

It may be thought that the products are facilities (squash and tennis courts) and activities (theatre-going and aerobics). Yet, in reality these are the vehicles for getting to the 'real' product – experiencing satisfaction through leisure 'participation', this is the unit of exchange with customers. If customers do experience satisfactions or worthwhileness, they will want to 'buy' them again. Hence a leisure centre's products are not just the facilities and activities on offer, but the experiences they provide and the relationships with the customers.

The leisure product we are talking about is described in chapter four. In essence, it is the satisfying or worthwhile experience derived from participation in or involvement with an activity in a person's time for leisure. Therefore the product is not goods, but the experiencing of satisfactions. Let us use the analogy of tennis. As Jim Johnson reminds us [14] you can buy a tennis racket, feel and handle it, pay for it and keep it. It is tangible. But leisure is intangible, until you experience it. The tennis racket not sold today can be sold tomorrow. The tennis court space or theatre seat not sold today is lost for ever. Its 'sell-by' date is in advance of the activity. Leisure, in this sense, cannot be stored. The product is perishable. If you are rich you might own a tennis court, but most of us simply rent it for an hour and we have a choice of waiting our turn at the park courts, booking in advance at the sports centre or taking part at a tennis club.

As well as being perishable, the product is fragile and unpredictable. It is easily damaged. John McEnroe can smash his racket on the ground and may still be able to play with it. But a customer treated rudely at reception, double-booked on the court or unable to get a drink at the bar in reasonable time, can take her or his custom elsewhere. Leisure behaviour is less predictable than work behaviour. In leisure customers have choice and they can be fickle!

The leisure 'product' therefore is somewhat of an enigma – diverse, changing, intangible, perishable, fragile and fleeting – and, in many instances, dependent on the person giving the service, namely the coach, tour guide or performer [14].

In terms of leisure participation, people are 'in it' for what they can get out of it. People want to enjoy, to be with friends, to learn, to look better, to feel better, to be somebody, to be skilful, to win. We need to sell 'success'. We have in leisure management the means to make people into better players, better coaches, better administrators, keener supporters. We can help to make people happier, healthier, slimmer, fitter. We can sell glamour, risk, excitement and adventure, particularly for the young. The potential benefits are abundant.

Capturing interest is essential. Good marketers should encourage levels of originality and be prepared to take risks. They need to explore possibilities. Originals and 'firsts' can not only capture interest, they can also create a lasting impression. Who was the first to break the four minute mile? Now who was the second? Who were the first to climb Everest? Now who were the second? The first product to find a niche in the customer's mind is difficult to dislodge. The array of synthetic sports surfaces by other manufacturers is still referred to as 'Tartan' for tracks and 'Astroturf' for artificial grass. Instant cameras by other suppliers are still called 'Polaroids'. Spa baths are called jacuzzis. Good marketers must also experiment with new ideas – fitness and swim packages, not just single lines; extending leisure self-service (early swims; late squash); and self-booking systems (after all we help ourselves to far more costly items at petrol filling stations).

Firsts are influential – for successes and for failures. Hence market research and product testing need to be undertaken to have the best chance of matching people with products. Leisure products need testing and changing to suit customer needs

Leisure products and services are provided by the public, voluntary and commercial sectors. Commercial leisure normally has a finite answer and a measurable target. For example, a health and fitness club may need to enrol 80 per cent of its projected 1,000 members on a direct debit basis at an average monthly of £35 per member. But along with this objective of selling memberships, there are many service elements – efficiency, attractive facilities, ambience – all of which go to make up the product and bring satisfaction to the user.

Demand for a product may arise out of choice, out of opportunity or from the facilities themselves. Facilities, opportunities and 'welcome' can stimulate demand and dramatically expand a leisure market. On the other hand, demand for a product can be stifled by restrictive policies, limited opportunities, highly exclusive clubs, lack of choice, vested interests and other demotivators. For example, a sports facility requiring a playing-in standard, or an enrolling fee, or a proposer and seconder on an application form, may attract better players, more affluent people and those who can handle the whole 'joining' process; others may find the joining process itself intimidating and a major stumbling block to participation. The objectives determine the leisure products and their promotion.

Most recreation programmes, even those designed with major speciality areas, tend to market more than one product; no indoor tennis centres are built today without fitness facilities. How many products are to be marketed? It has been shown in recent years, not only that a combination of facilities attracts greater use and is more economical, but also that the spin-off to other activities expands the market. Many David Lloyd centres are used more for health and fitness, swimming and social activities than tennis.

Markets rarely remain static. Managers should therefore avoid putting all their eggs in one basket. In addition, if the aim of a council is to give the public a level of freedom of choice, then it is important to give that choice and variety within the overall service.

Products exhibit life cycles. With most commercial products, their life cycle revolves around:

- a product start
- growth
- development
- decline and
- replacement by better products for today's market.

In leisure services, many products have been with us for decades: theatre, cinema, golf, swimming. But some well established activities are on the decline, for example, squash and cue sports, and may have to be packaged differently to redress the trend. What is needed is product development to provide a continuous stream of new or changing products. Cinemas have changed from single to multi-screen. Tenpin bowling and bingo have changed to social 'nights out' venues with a wider range of products. Golf is played on golf driving ranges. Swimming includes water fun, water recreation and 'swim aerobics'.

Some products will cease to contribute to 'profits' or 'benefits'. New products may be the life-blood of some static leisure services. The answer may be to introduce new looking products to create new images: 'New looking products carry advantages to stress new customer benefits' [8]. What do potential customers think the product is? Their notion of what it is and what the benefits are, is what matters.

Products may decline, but demand for the type of product may still be rising. Skateboarding's rapid growth and decline hides the creation of new looking activities on wheels such as roller hockey and roller blading, which in turn have re-kindled skateboarding.

Product development and improvement are therefore of importance. Packaging different products can generate customer benefits at all levels of participation, e.g. a daytime leisure centre package might include: sports activity, dietary clinic, sauna and a crèche for the children.

14.6 Pricing the products

We need to match people's needs with products at a price they are willing to pay. The pricing policy is an important factor in financial planning and in the overall strategy. It is a vital part of marketing. Should we price high and then reduce; price low for a quick penetration of the market; price at one rate for all the customers; or offer special rates, discounts and packages? Commercial marketing is profit orientated; therefore, it is price sensitive. Products must be gauged at the right price to attract customers to buy. Discussion is often centred on keeping prices low, but in many exclusive establishments pricing high can achieve the type of response aimed to meet objectives.

In the commercial sector, charges must be levied to ensure sufficient surplus revenue to remain solvent and in business. In the public sector a greater 'commercial reality' now exists but there are still many social service elements, and the question arises: should we charge some people at all? Many public service facilities, such as parks, remain free because they are paid for with rates and to charge could be unacceptable and uneconomic because the cost of collection may be greater than the income accrued. Pricing policies remain a thorny problem in most local authorities. The private sector has a far easier choice. It sets its prices at what is the most profitable. Whether public or private we need to ask: how can pricing help us to achieve objectives? Pricing strategies include:

- status quo
- price increase
- price decrease
- price offers.

Choice of strategy will depend on needs to:

- make financial profits
- cover costs
- cover part costs
- undercut competitors' price
- win additional market share by low pricing
- win segmented market share by pricing high.

Pricing is only one factor in making choices. Price may not be as dominant a factor as we may think. Cheapness is one criterion, especially for the financially disadvantaged, but not necessarily the only criterion. Rambling, camping, tennis, museums, theatres and athletics, for example, are relatively cheap activities, yet they attract only certain small segments of the population.

Public tastes can be notoriously fickle. We can offer 'superior' products to enhance quality of life, health and fitness and provide them at no charge, yet many will prefer mediocre, expensive, even damaging-to-health alternative products. The truism is that prevention is extremely difficult to sell; yet how easy it is to sell cures!

The level at which prices are set can also be used to control the demand for a particular activity (e.g. high pricing exclusive golf courses). On the other hand, it can be used to extend the capacity of a facility (e.g. the indoor tennis initiative with lower pricing of indoor tennis courts).

Local authority pricing is largely based on tradition, and what is an 'acceptable' level compared with other authorities. There is great similarity between authorities in terms of pricing levels, although there may be a range of charges levied for different activities or services. These can be expressed in theory along a charging continuum, which extends from a social service approach, where no charges are imposed, to a commercial approach at the other end of the continuum. Figure 14.1 illustrates this charging continuum within the public sector, together with its user implications. Where the social service type of approach exists, the basis of such a policy is based upon the belief that the intrinsic value of leisure and recreation is beneficial both to the participants and the community and that the opportunities should be equally available to all members of the community. Consequently, no charge for using the facilities and services is made. The facilities that fall within this category are the parks, the libraries and some community centres. The bulk of public sector leisure activities are priced at a subsidized level to make recreation accessible for all the community – swimming is a prime example.

The economic approach is based upon the belief that the benefits obtained are largely confined to the participants themselves, and hence the charges levied include all costs in an effort to break-even. Generally this approach is becoming

◄-- *Subsidy*   *Profit* -------------------- ►

Type of charge	No charge	Some charge	Economic charge	Commercial charge
Basis of policy	Social service – all residents have a recreational need – facilities available to all	Many people and groups have needs for specialist activities for health and recreation	Participants are main benefactors – hence have to pay full costs	Benefits participants exclusively. Charges include full costs + Profit charges based on what market can bear Profit used to subsidize other facilities
Type of facilities	Parks Libraries	Swimming pools Public tennis courts Arts centres Community centres	Entertainments Golf courses	Indoor tennis Health and fitness Squash Sauna Sunbeds
Profile of users	Representative of neighbourhood	High proportion of local population Youths/young people	Middle income groups Young adults	Middle to high income groups

FIGURE 14.1 The charging policy continuum in the public sector

more popular within the public sector and with many local authorities charging an economic rent for entertainment and facilities such as golf courses. In recent years, the high running costs of leisure services and centres, allied to competitive tendering, has called for a more objective financial appraisal. Authorities are asking themselves: is it possible to cover running costs? Should subsidy be given in greater measure to certain sectors of the community?

The profit approach is based upon the belief that the benefits obtained are exclusively restricted to the participants, hence the charges levied not only cover all costs, but also a profit that can be used to subsidize other activities. Thus at this end of the continuum, the charges made are what the market can withstand. Examples of activities that frequently fall within this category include squash and the use of sun beds.

There is fierce competition in the commercial world. Competitive pricing and good margins are valuable weapons for sales personnel. There are special bonuses for stockists; discounts apply. Attractions in the form of points, wrappers, competitions, free glasses at petrol stations, incentive schemes, holidays for two and a host of other methods are tried. The promotional inventiveness is endless. Commercial marketing is not just concerned with the product (it is often quite secondary to other factors), but with the benefits to the customers, if they buy the product and to the salespeople, if they sell it.

Price therefore may not be as important after all. Cheapness is one criterion, especially for the financially disadvantaged, but not necessarily the only criterion. Marketers (i.e. managers) have the task of creating images in order to draw people to the leisure product. The level at which prices are set can also be used to control the demand for a particular activity, while at others it may be used to extend the capacity of a facility. Pricing has always been a vitally important element in commercial business. Now it is more important for local authorities because of the financial constraints imposed on local government. Local authorities will need to examine their marketing strategies in terms of subdividing their products by price and quality and consider the advantages and disadvantages of pricing high, medium or low and the implications of these policies on the service. Maintaining a principle of accessibility for all will be sorely tested. One of the keys may be price flexibility, allowing managers to gauge the sensitivities of the market.

14.7 Place

Products – facilities, programmes, activities – need to be accessible to the people they have been developed for. Therefore, the distribution policy should be based on the market research about customers, their home and work locations, transportation and accessibility factors in addition to the products and the prices.

It is therefore very important for services and facilities to be placed in locations that customers can get to easily. We need to make the facilities both physically and socially accessible. Influence the journey with directional signs, maps and an attractive welcoming entrance. Light the parking areas and walkways. Reinforce the general awareness with attractive displays and exhibitions in public places and with leaflet distribution.

It is also important to locate key elements within facilities with customer convenience in mind, e.g. changing rooms near playing area, crèche adjacent to outdoor play space, good viewing to activities. Programming of different activities, times, space and opening hours, all need to be orientated to meet customer needs, rather than the needs of organizations and staff.

Services may well be available, accessible and at the right price but customers may still not take advantage of the opportunity. This is where promotion and communications come into play. Activities need to be in the right place at the right time. Information services often close in the evenings and weekends when they may be most needed. Many leisure facilities will be inaccessible to segments of the population. Some people will live in remote parts, some will be small children, some will be old, some will be infirm, some will have little motivation. In these cases, needs can be met, for example, by managing mobile services – library, toy library, play bus, travelling theatre and by appointing artists in residence, sports motivators, *'animateurs'* and leisure counsellors.

14.8 Promotion

Leisure provides choices. So far we have looked briefly at the customer, the products, pricing, buying, motivating and selling. Another ingredient of the 'marketing mix' is promotion. Promotion provides awareness and seeks to attract customers to a particular service or product. It is a process of familiarizing, reminding and creating favourable images, attitudes and a willingness to buy. The process is one of pulling customers to the product using words, music, pictures and symbols to present an image of the product that is attractive, if not compelling.

Promotional activity has been defined as 'an exercise in communications. Its role is to facilitate exchanges with potential client groups by communicating the benefits offered by a programme or service. It seeks to inform, persuade or remind' [15]. We now realize that there are many factors affecting demand, some which we may be unconscious of. Impressions, for example, could decide our response. Leisure facilities must, therefore, create the 'right' impression – the motivating impression. And first impressions count most! They can motivate or demotivate.

Promotion consists of four major components:

1 Personal contact – this involves a verbal 'presentation' to one or more potential customers with the objective of selling a service or a product;
2 Advertising – this represents a paid form of non-personal presentation about the organization and/or the programme of opportunities offered;
3 Incentives – these represent a financial offer or 'gift' that is made to potential customers with the objective to encourage them to purchase a particular service or product;
4 Publicity – this represents a favourable form of communication in the media (e.g. print or broadcast) at no direct cost to the organization concerned.

14.8.1 Personal selling

Leisure is 'sold' largely through people. The public's impression of a service or facility is often made on the flimsiest brush or smallest incident with a member of staff. A warm smile says, 'You're welcome'. Looking elsewhere and talking to someone else says 'You're not welcome'! Staff who are concerned with their own status often demotivate – GPs' receptionists becoming snooty medical experts; the uniformed supervisor becoming an authoritarian Colonel-in-Chief! Fortunately, in most leisure businesses the staff generally have the right attitudes and many have an outgoing personality which enables them to interact well with their customers. To be effective in personal selling, it is necessary that the person concerned does it with enthusiasm, so that he or she is perceived as being capable, efficient and caring. The function of personal selling involves a two-way communication process and can provide valuable feedback information about existing and potential recreation programmes.

A promotional strategy should be built around a proper brief taking account of:

- the benefits of the products, e.g. for fitness and health
- the target markets, e.g. children and the 'seniors'
- the information and messages to be conveyed, e.g. relieve stress; look and feel good
- the media and promotional methods to be used
- the offers and inducements.

If the message does not reach people, there is no point in sending it. And if it reaches people, do they understand it? The message must be relevant to the market and also be expressed in such a way that it attracts, rather than detracts. The media are a major vehicle by which managers can communicate their products and services. The more direct forms include television, radio, press and the cinema. The less direct include literature and packaging, sales gimmicks, incentives and sponsorship. But word of mouth and recommendation could be the most successful in that a large proportion of leisure facility users come with friends and like-minded groups of people.

Different methods of communication and different messages suit different markets. *The Sunday Times* and *Sunday Sport* newspapers need quite different forms of communication!

14.8.2 Advertising

Advertising encompasses many forms of communication and includes:

1 posters – in prominent, eye-catching locations
2 brochures and leaflets that describe the facilities, services and programmes on offer
3 advertisements placed in the local media – i.e. newspapers and radio

4   newsletters and fully paid supplements in the local newspapers
5   direct mailing enclosing new information, e.g. offers of new benefits in new programmes.

In comparison to publicity, advertising does not provide immediate feedback and can be an expensive form of promotion. Television advertisements are extremely expensive, as are paid advertisements in the press. In contrast, the local cinema can be a relatively cheap form of advertising. As cinema-going audiences are largely young people, then products, activities and services that appeal to young people could be effectively advertised in local cinemas. Local radio advertising can vary in cost but in getting across to young people local radio could pay dividends. Poster advertising can be very indifferent compared with face-to-face communication (i.e. human communication), which makes a greater impact. A 'mail shot' using an agency address list or compiling a data base is a good way of getting directly to a target audience but costs need to be compared to other methods.

The message to Leisure Managers appears to be to look at the whole variety of ways of communicating, to try out various forms and 'shop around' and then act positively, measure results and make appropriate adjustments. In order to ensure that the communication messages are effective, there are general guidelines that can be helpful in attracting the attention of potential customers.

1   Colour attracts the attention of the reader far more than black and white material.
2   Unusual or novel design catches the eye of the reader.
3   Taller shaped material appears to be more effective than wide shaped material.
4   Large materials tend to attract more attention than small exhibits.
5   Communications that involve more than one sense (e.g. sight and sound) appear to have the greatest impact.
6   Headlines attract interest (pick up any tabloid newspaper).
7   Topical features hold interest and curiosity.
8   'Strap lines' demand attention e.g. 'Free – this Week', 'Play in a Day'.

Further, in any written form the importance of the headline cannot be over-emphasized. The headline must be catchy to stimulate the reader to read the full message. Often this takes the form of a question with the answer or solution appearing in the text below. Current questions that touch on aspects of health, fitness and beauty tend to arouse adequate interest for potential customers of sports centres to read further. Also the text should be persuasive and demand action from the reader such as 'telephone now' or 'complete the attached form now'.

A self-testing criterion for an advertising communication is that it should produce positive answers to the following questions.

1   Is it eye-catching?
2   Is the layout attractive?
3   Does the headline stimulate the reader to proceed further?
4   Does it provide adequate information?
5   But at the same time, is the message clear and simple?

6   Is the text persuasive and credible?
7   Does the advertisement create a favourable public image of the organization?

14.8.3 Incentives

The 'offer' has become a prime means of persuading people to buy. In contrast to the other forms of promotional activity, incentives should not be used on a regular basis and when offered should be restricted to a limited period of time. The main objective of using incentives is to stimulate participation from identified market targets. The incentives can take the form of an introductory offer – e.g. centre tee-shirts, discounts (two tickets for the price of one), awards and badges.

Financial incentives can be persuasive. We all like to think we are getting something for nothing. The offer of discounts such as reduced off-peak pricing without adequate advertisements and publicity is unlikely to have a great impact on generating increased levels of utilization. Permanent discounts appear to have a minimum impact and can lead to questions being raised on whether the pricing levels are good value for money.

One of the cardinal principles of attracting a positive and warm response is to give freely and generously. We may give free tennis courts, but that is usually because it is more costly to collect the money. But genuine giving has both direct and indirect benefits. Leisure managers should always carry free tickets for visits to the centre, free 'have-a-go' tickets, free sampler-activity tickets, free sauna or a free second activity for those taking part in one activity only.

Promotional activity should be planned around a strategy and follow a plan. The messages must be appropriate to the target markets and the methods must be compatible to the characteristics of the market. Continued, modified promotion and sustained public relations campaigns are needed for long-term effects, with short-burst promotions for one-off events. Promotions, then, will include all the methods designed and packaged to sell the benefits of the services and products on sale. They include the marketing research information, advertising, packaging, sales promotions, public relations and in the leisure facility environment member-ship schemes, 'passport' schemes, discounted prices, price packaging and a host of others. If you don't promote the organization you either limit or diminish it.

14.8.4 Publicity

Communicating and promotion are an essential part of the marketing mix. Only a proportion of the population make use of leisure facilities provided out of public money. It could be that the products do not appeal sufficiently or that the pricing is too high in some instances. However, we know that the activities can be hugely enjoyable and beneficial and that at public facilities the costs are in most cases at subsidized levels, therefore promotional activity and conveying appealing messages need to play a more significant role in the market mix.

Since most local authority leisure services departments have a minimal promotional budget, this has resulted in many concentrating more on publicity.

This normally takes the form of press releases, feature articles and in some instances, a leisure centre may write its own weekly column in the local newspaper. It is a useful method of conveying information to customers, and potential customers, about changes in a programme and informing the community of the results of fixtures in the local leagues and competitions. To keep a facility continually in the public's mind, it is necessary periodically to have general interest stories relating to the facility in the local newspaper, since not all readers read the arts and sports pages.

Although publicity does not directly involve financial expenditure, the true cost of preparing the publicity material may be considerable, particularly if many senior personnel are involved. Also the editorial staff may reject the 'press release' or leisure centre prepared copy on the grounds that it is not adequately newsworthy.

Coverage of a leisure programme or event or issue can fix an image in the mind of the public. Such an image is difficult to eradicate, particularly if the image is a poor one. The press can give a negative image in seconds; and the press is often seen as challenging, questioning and embarrassing to the local authority. Therefore, the only effective approach is to influence the control of the image-making and take a hand in managing the coverage. This can be achieved by informing and involving them and keeping them up to date with news. Good press coverage will help the public to say that their money on a leisure facility is well spent.

This section has been concerned with a number of ways leisure can be promoted. In Table 14.1 the impact from various methods and how they compare shows that the cheapest and potentially the easiest method is when potential customers call in!

14.9 Towards a marketing plan – mission, position and segmentation

In constructing a marketing plan, an understanding is needed concerning three further concepts:

- mission – what are we in business for?
- position – how are we placed in the market?
- segmentation – what segments of the market are we to target?

14.9.1 The mission

Marketing starts with a cause – a mission. The ethos of an organization can be encapsulated in what is now being termed a mission statement. It exists to promote the organization within and without, stating why the organization exists and what it hopes to achieve, what it believes in, how it should behave, what its strategies are and what image it wants to promote. As Ted Blake puts it in his succinct manner [16]:

TABLE 14.2 Cost per communication

Type	Impact	Targeting	Person	Flow	Form	Use
Advertising in one or more of five media: TV – radio – outdoors – press – cinema/theatre	Low	Low	Cheapest	• One way • No feedback	It is fixed to all	To contact many with random(?) hits in a fast and cheap way to create leads to follow up
Personal 'face to face' 'selling': persuasion by controlling interview with questions	High – if we remember we never get a second chance to make a first impression	If first we have identified i.e. profiled most likely customers	Quite expensive in salary, travel, time, etc.	• Two way • Plenty of feedback if you ask and listen	It can be very flexible	When high impact, flexible two way feedback is necessary and can well justify the high cost and time required. Really the only way to sell enough at right prices
Direct mail: letters, etc. to houses, offices etc. informing and influencing with inducements	Medium	The list is 45 per cent of total effect	Cheaper than personal selling	• One way • A little feedback by way of response	It can be variable to various groups	To hit special groups, ie segments of the market with a special message (appropriate to them) in a fast, cheap way – but 'creams off' market (4 per cent response, 2 per cent orders) and warns people about you
Telephone *out*: Cold calling to make appointments etc.	Fairly high	High	Cheap if DIY?	• Two-way feedback by asking and listening	It can be flexible	When cost and time for the fact to face selling are expensive, but other needs are the same – set up a telesales desk for low potential A/Cs
Telephone *in*: Usually forgotten, but the target has thrown itself at the gun!	Very high	Right on	Free	• You've got it made!	Flexible	Sell all the time. Does your telephonist give right impression! Have you phoned your own office to find out? 'Add on' to orders phoned in?

From: Ted Blake: Promoting: Comparing Communication Alternatives

Everybody is looking for meaning in their lives. The right kind of mission gives this meaning. Meaning, in addition to fair pay and good working conditions, inspires greater trust, co-operation, commitment and loyalty through better job clarification and satisfaction; better decision making; clearer communication; and greater ease of delegation with less need for supervision and inspection. Recruitment becomes less subjective and the mission makes it easier to define, recruit, promote and develop the 'right kind of people'.

The 'mission statement' then becomes the organization's cause, its flag, its purpose.

14.9.2 *Position*

We then need to consider where our organization and its products and services exist in the minds of potential customers. What is our position in the market?

Positioning, like many marketing innovations, emanates from the USA with its highly competitive selling of products. 'Positions' are people's perception of products that can be retained and recalled instantly, and products with favourable positions can also be banked upon for continued sales.

Products and services have long-term 'personalities', just like people. For example, the Bank of England – safe and dependable; Wimbledon – the pinnacle, traditional values, class; or Richard Branson's Virgin products – innovative, creative, daring, adventurous. McDonald's; Levi's, Nike, Kelloggs, Heinz, Harrods, Ascot and hundreds of other 'institutions' have a position in our minds and in the market place, as has Disney and, in the United Kingdom, Center Parcs has established a firm position in a short space of time. Positions, however, can be favourable or unfavourable. Local authority leisure services are anxiously trying to throw off perceptions of yesterday. Despite many extremely successful services and good management, they are still tainted in the minds of some people with the tag of 'baths', the smell of chlorine, 'keep off the grass' and cheapness in both senses of the word.

But market positioning can be re-positioned. Lucozade used to be sold in chemist's shops for people who were ill. The Daley Thompson TV promotions repositioned Lucozade as a refreshing energy drink for athletes – from the sick to the fit. This promotional baton was taken up by campaigns with Linford Christie and other athletes. Ted Blake [16] paints the picture vividly:

Coca-Cola is teenaged, ubiquitous and very American. Hofmeister is a smart 'with it', street-wise lager. Bisto is simple, tasty and dependable like Mother. Guinness is friendly, classless with comforting strength, warmth with a touch of humour. Jerry Hall helped Bovril re-position itself as a must nutrition for the ultra-figure conscious.

Positions, however, usually take time to establish though television exposure has speeded up the process for new activity holiday resorts like Center Parcs; and insurance firms like Cornhill and Axa Equity and Law have improved their business ranking through sponsorship of cricket, as has Green Flag with football.

Positions are perceptions – feelings that linger in the public mind. They can be evoked, dramatized, and made more important and urgent by advertising and promotion. Leisure facilities that do not at present engender such perceptions need to work on their products and the presentation of them to win favourable market positioning.

14.9.3 Market segmentation

Knowing our mission and the position of our products in the minds of potential customers, we need to decide where our best future opportunities lie. Which section or segment of the population should we target? There are basically four approaches which are illustrated in Figure 14.2.

1   Selling to existing markets, which includes extending product life cycles e.g. from aerobics to step aerobics (market penetration);
2   selling to new markets e.g. incentives for new customers who try taster courses (market development);
3   selling new or re-modelled services to existing customers (product–service development);
4   selling the new services to new markets (market diversification).

It has often been claimed that the problem with municipally managed leisure facilities is that they try to cater for all the community rather than concentrate and penetrate a segment of the total market.

A painter or a potter creating a work of art for a special gift provides an exclusive service. Teaching the piano or tennis through private one-to-one tuition also provides an exclusive product designed for the individual. With mass markets, however, it is impossible to provide exclusive products for each individual, but it is possible to tailor-make products for segments of a market. Low-income earners do

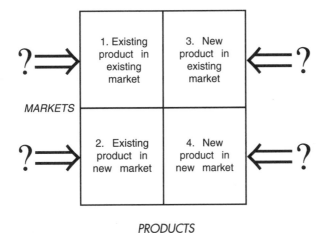

PRODUCTS

FIGURE 14.2 Increasing products and expanding markets

not buy Rolls Royce cars, nor join the most expensive golf clubs, nor book seats at Covent Garden Opera House (Sir Thomas Beecham is reported to have said: 'God has yet to invent a faster way of spending money than putting on an opera'). However, there are many dissimilar individuals who can still be segmented because of their similar characteristics – e.g. the same age, the same sex, the same fashions, similar interests, and so on. Targeting to like-minded segments, with appropriate products, is much more likely to achieve success than a hit-or-miss strategy. Local authorities tend to avoid market segmentation because they believe they should be providing for all their customers. The problem with this view is that the service given may not be wholly appropriate to any group, in particular: trying to suit everybody may suit very few.

A market segment, then, is any homogeneous subdivision of a market that is likely to be attracted to particular products or services. A local authority or a company can choose different kinds of segmentation to attract people to their products and services.

1　Differentiated markets separate products and services for each segment (e.g. junior sports and senior citizens' 'Old Time Music Hall').

2　Undifferentiated markets sell one product to all buyers within a catchment area (e.g. town festival which caters for all segments).

3　Concentrated markets focus on one or just a few lucrative or popular 'brands' (e.g. health and fitness and aerobics in a sports centre or golf and tennis at a country club).

The process of segmentation needs good market research, understanding of groups and people's life-cycle needs. It requires strategies and selection of segments which match particular products within the overall service.

14.10　Constructing a marketing plan

In order to market successfully there needs to be a marketing plan. We want to bridge the gap between where we are now and where we want to be. To do that we need to match appropriate products and services to the different segments of the market. We may need to develop or expand the market and we will need to balance the various ingredients of the marketing 'mix' to get the right results. This involves seeking answers to fundamental questions. What business are we in? What are our services and products? What is the market structure? Who are the competitors? Who are the customers? What are the products? Such an initial approach provides information. But it is only information. It will not make decisions. It represents a reconnaissance of the market. It needs to be turned into a plan of action.

Having arrived at a profile of the community or market sector or target group, the manager must then construct a marketing plan. There are no exact formulas, no off-the-shelf marketing plans, no one-way-only strategies. The marketing process is a flexible process, able to adapt to changing situations, able to respond to opportunities. After all, it is not the process that counts, but the results that are achieved. The process is also a never-ending one, constantly evolving, needing review or developing and adapting. Marketing is integral to the whole management of the leisure business.

Good marketing plans are bespoke plans. They are tailor-made. They take time, often years to get into their stride. An example of how a marketing plan for a new swimming pool can be developed is illustrated below and consists of ten distinct stages.

Marketing plan – a ten-stage plan for marketing a new swimming pool in a local authority

Stage 1 Council policy – review the purpose

- Determine council policy.
- Establish purpose of facility.
- Write the 'mission statement' or 'statement of intent' to which all are committed.

Stage 2 Market demand – analyse the current situation

- Determine potential of facility.
- Undertake demographic analysis of perceived catchment area (having taken location and accessibility into consideration).
- Study the population and market profile: use census data, which analyses ward populations and enumeration districts, and catchment databases which provide social profiles within travel distances, such as CACI 'ACORN' profiling – a system that provides detailed information about catchment populations based on types of housing and households.
- Consider the market structure and the range of competing facilities. Is the market expanding or contracting? What are the market trends? What is our share of the market? What positions do our products have on the market?
- Undertake survey of programme requirements of local clubs, schools and organizations.
- Examine competition in the area.
- Examine potential demand in the area.
- Examine competence of staff to undertake promotional tasks.
- Look into the organization – its 'position', performance, services and products; undertake a SWOT analysis (strengths, weaknesses, opportunities and threats).
- What segments of the market need to be targeted?

Stage 3 Set market objectives and targets

Having analysed the market structure, position and products and services, all we have achieved is to know where we stand! We need to decide where we want to get to and how.

- Set marketing objectives including the targets, the market segments, and the results to be achieved.

Stage 4 Market strategy

- Decide strategies, marketing 'mix' and actions to meet the objectives.
- Provide centre with identifiable logo (local competition).
- Establish programme guidelines to cover:
    casual use by public;
    education;
    range of activities to be offered;
    club usage;
    courses.
- Establish target groups:
    50 plus;
    unemployed;
    disabled;
    mother and toddler.
- Determine potential total attendances.
- Propose areas to secure sponsorship (to supplement promotional budget).

Stage 5 Programme (product)

- Produce practical suggestions for programming to meet council policy:
    range of activities;
    range and ability level of courses to be offered;
    proposed competitions;
    proposals for establishment of facility-based clubs;
    specific programme for different target groups;
    suggest role in borough/district sports development plan.

Stage 6 Pricing strategy

- Produce proposals to ensure:
    value for money image;
    maximum penetration in local catchment area;
    maximum impact on target groups.
- Consider:
    discounts for target groups;
    cost per participant for courses.
- Suggested prices for:
    peak/off peak;
    club use;
    hire for galas.
- Estimate gross profit levels on trading activities.

Stage 7 Promotions

7A Pre-opening phase

- Identify methods to create high levels of awareness amongst potential users.
- Maintain high level of press coverage throughout the development phase.
- Communicate with clubs and organizations and representatives of education service.
- Introduce newspaper pull-out supplement to enhance public image of facility (and obtain sponsorship and sale of advertising space).
- Produce brochures providing information relating to:
    - scale of facilities;
    - activities to be offered/opening hours;
    - availability of courses;
    - prices to be charged;
    - programme for target groups;
    - booking procedures.
- Distribute leaflets at locations accessible to public.
- Produce 'give-aways' e.g. stickers, badges and balloons.
- Produce design/layouts for posters and advertisements.

7B Opening phase

- Suggest programme for official opening, e.g. displays, competition.
- Obtain personality and resources to undertake official opening.
- Draw up list of official guests and VIPs.
- Suggest buffet for guests and VIPs.
- Draw up invitation list of local clubs and organizations.
- Place advertisements in local media.
- Organize house-to-house invitation drop.

7C Post-opening phase

- Consolidate early successes.
- Identify programme areas that are underperforming and reassess them.
- Organize and promote special events on regular basis.
- Review programme on regular basis and modify if necessary.

Stage 8 Estimated costs

- Estimate gross cost of:
    - printing brochures, posters etc.;
    - advertising in local media;
    - staff/personality fee;

cost of art work;
cost of promotional 'give aways';
staff costs and travel expenses.
- Estimate income from sponsorship to offset costs.

Stage 9 Project results

- Estimate:
  level of utilization;
  total attendances;
  total users – adults, juniors;
  club usage;
  attendance on courses;
  total income;
  user profile.

Stage 10 Monitor and review

- Assess effectiveness of promotional strategy.
- Compare facility performance with set objectives and targets.
- Amend programme if necessary.

14.11 Marketing conclusions

Marketing approaches to leisure products and services, using a marketing plan, will increase the probability of success in both public and private sectors. The marketing approach ensures that when a product or service is made available to the consumer, it has been planned, designed, packaged, promoted and delivered in such a manner that the customer is not only persuaded to buy, but also to repeat the experience as often as possible. While impulse buying, like attending an event or 'having a go' are important, repeat visits and repeat buying of the leisure experience are even more important. People get 'hooked' on products. Once caught with the bug of pottery, painting, jazz, playing golf, fitness, squash, snooker, sauna bathing or yoga, we are anxious to participate even more. Impulse buying may attract people but this needs to be capitalized on, for new-found satisfying experiences want to be bought again and again. They become habit-forming.

Marketing needs a budget. The amounts that local authorities spend, usually under the heading 'advertising', are minimal. Many seaside resorts, theatres and festivals are well publicized and some are marketed well; however, the general picture is poor. For example, many authorities have a revenue expenditure at leisure centres in the region of £1 million and more yet spend less than 0.5 per cent on marketing and promotion. Commercial leisure businesses will spend in the region of 5 per cent–10 per cent of turnover.

The marketing process will need to be adjusted to meet the conceptual differences to be found in private sector establishments and local authority services. Local authorities have great opportunities to market their services to meet their aims and objectives through marketing and promotion. Their services on the whole fail to attract the majority of the underprivileged and lower socio-economic groups. Indeed, one might argue that the higher up the social scale one goes, the more of one's entertainment, such as opera, ballet and music, and leisure activity such as swimming and playing sport, is paid out of public money. Opportunities exist to meet community needs and demands but sensitive, humane handling of the marketing process must be achieved.

At the start of this chapter, it was stated that marketing is concerned with voluntary exchange and that community leisure services are provided in exchange for people's money, time and rates and taxes. If the public does not want what is provided and is not prepared to pay the costs and give up the time, then local authority support could well be reduced. Therefore, Leisure Managers must be concerned with the questions: are the customers satisfied with the leisure products; are they experiencing satisfactions? It is not just how many participated, but whether the market target groups were reached with satisfying results and whether objectives were met. Community leisure and recreation marketing is concerned with identifying and responding to what the community needs and wants and is prepared to support and pay for.

In summary, marketing needs objectives, a plan, action and measurement. Marketing need not be a highly sophisticated and learned process. A marketing plan is a statement about what actions are to be undertaken to meet objectives. Marketing affects people's attitudes. It affects the way they speak, look, think and behave. Managers of leisure should encourage people to look more favourably towards themselves and towards the products and services being offered by their organizations. What is of greater importance is that managers should ascertain first what is likely to be most satisfying to customers and try to provide what is needed. This can be undertaken more successfully through marketing approaches adapted to meet the demands of the situation.

Notes and references

1 McIver, C. (1968), *Marketing* (3rd edition) (revised and edited by G. C. Wilson), Business Publications, London.
2 Townsend, R. (1970), *Up the Organization*, Coronet Books, London, p. 96.
3 Kotler, P. (1975), *Marketing for Non-Profit Organizations*, Prentice-Hall Englewood Cliffs, NJ, p. 5.
4 Blake, T. (1985), 'Image', *Leisure Management*, November, 5 (11), 14–15.
5 Laczniak, G. R. *et al.* (1979), 'Social marketing, its ethical dimension', *Journal of Marketing*, Spring, *43*, 29–36.
6 Kotler, P. and Zaltman, G. (1971), 'Social marketing: an approach to planned social change', *Journal of Marketing*, July, *35*, 3–12. Fox, K. and Kotler, P., 'The marketing of social causes: the first 10 years', *Journal of Marketing, 44*(4), 24–33.

7   Cowell, D. (1978), Marketing's Application to Public Authority Sport, Recreation and Leisure Centres. Paper presented at Marketing Education Group (MEG) Conference, Hull College of Higher Education.

8   Quoted by management trainer Ted Blake in several presentations on Marketing Sport and Recreation.

9   Packard, V. (1965), *The Hidden Persuaders*, Penguin, Harmondsworth, p. 11.

10   *ibid.*, p. 14.

11   Cheskin, L., quoted in *ibid.*, pp. 14–15.

12   Wilson, A. and West, C. (1982), 'Effective marketing at minimum cost', *Management Today*, January, 72–8.

13   Craig, S. (1989), *Marketing Leisure Services*, Leisure Futures, London.

14   See the series of articles by Jim Johnson (1987), in *Leisure Manager*.

15   Howard, D. R. and Crompton, J. L. (1989), *Financing, Managing and Marketing Recreation and Park Resources*, W. C. Brown, Dubuque, Iowa.

16   See the series of articles by Ted Blake (1990), in *Baths Service and Recreation Management*.

Recommended additional reading

Torkildsen, G. (1993), 'Marketing made simple – forget the myths and mysteries', *Torkildsen's Guides to Leisure Management*, Longman, Harlow.

Courtis, J. (1987), *Marketing Services: A Practical Guide*, for British Institute of Management, Kogan Page, London.

Kotler, P. (1990), *Principles of Marketing*, 5th edition, Prentice-Hall, Englewood Cliffs, NJ.

Lovelock, C. (1991), *Services Marketing*, 2nd edition, Prentice-Hall, Englewood Cliffs, NJ.

McIver, C. (1987), *The Marketing Mirage: How to Make a Reality*, Heinemann, London.

Stone, M. (1990), *Leisure Services Marketing*, Croner, Kingston-upon-Thames.

Chapter fifteen

Organization of major events

Events are an important part of any comprehensive leisure and recreation programme. They have appeal; they capture the imagination. Events can involve the community, increase awareness and help put an organization or an activity on the map. Some events can attract top-class performers; other events can display the talents of beginners; some provide entertainment, novelty, adventure and fun; and some bring glamour to a programme.

Well organized events can therefore be a boon to any organization; badly organized, they can detract. Being out-of-the-ordinary, they carry programme and promotional advantages. Community events, in particular, need the help of many people and usually large numbers of volunteers. They attract unwieldy committees and lots of people with very good intentions, but with variable aptitudes for organization! Well intentioned helpers also like organizing their own little bit of the event, often at the expense of the event as a whole. ('The event may have made a loss, but my cake stall made a profit!'). Some people take on too much and others let you down at the last moment. Events, therefore, need a competent co-ordinator. His or her role is of paramount importance.

The management of major events is receiving greater attention as people are increasingly exposed to professionally produced events, as the British arena event industry continues to develop and as more events are presented in the hundreds of venues throughout the United Kingdom and on television. The public has thus become more sophisticated in its taste when it comes to the organization of events whether national or local. Leisure Managers must be capable of leading or controlling the planning and execution of major events.

The management of event arenas is considered at length in the publication *Arenas* [1], so arena events as such are not covered in this chapter, though they are covered briefly in chapter thirteen on programming. Suffice it to say, however, that all events need good planning and organization. Whilst most top-level major events are organized by promoters or by governing bodies and associations outside the control of leisure facility managers, community related events, joint promotions and 'own' promotions call for considerable expertise on the part of leisure managers.

This chapter is written for Leisure Managers who have to present major events throughout the course of the year as part of the total leisure and recreation programme. The principles and many of the methods will apply to all event organizers, but it is recognized from the outset that some organizations are set up as specialized event producers. In local authorities, too, there are specialized event departments and committees to stage the county show, or annual festival. In national sports administration, committees and staff exist to administer international events. While all event organizers can learn something from this brief chapter, it is the Leisure Manager, whose special events are superimposed on all his or her other tasks, that it is primarily intended to serve. The chapter therefore focusses attention upon the management of events at a local level. For the grand, celebratory spectaculars, read, for example, *Special Events: The Art and Science of Celebration* [2].

The chapter is written in the following sequence. First, the question is raised: what is a major event and what makes it special? Second, the formulation of policies, event organization strategies and budgets are considered. Third, organization structures are discussed. Fourth, the special staffing requirements are considered. Fifth, the need for detailed and meticulous planning is shown. Sixth, all events are subject to problems – and learning from these is an important clue to better future events. Seventh, as part of the chapter summary, an event planning guideline, an event checklist and an event planning process model are put forward as an approach.

Having read this chapter, event organizers will be in no doubt as to the importance of events within a comprehensive leisure service and that they should be embarked upon with clear vision and concise objectivity. Organizers will understand that events need military precision not just in their presentation, but in their preparation; the free-rein or flexible style of management will not be appropriate. Unlike the ongoing programme, events have precise starts and finishes and are encapsulated into absolute parameters of time and space. The clearest lesson to be learned is that an event needs one co-ordinator, by whom the event organization is controlled. Events lend themselves to clear objectives, tight administration and budgets, preparation deadlines, entrepreneurial flair, excellent preparation and honest evaluation.

15.1 Special characteristics and functions of major events

What is a major event? It can be a special 'happening', project or attraction of any kind that is outside the 'run of the mill' programme. It usually has some significance. It usually attracts a crowd or an audience or draws the attention of the media. An event can be international, national, regional or local. It can include sport, art, music, drama, festival or tournament. It can be competitive, fund-raising, social or just 'plain good fun'. It can be the town annual show or the village fête, athletics championships or the Boy Scouts' sports. It can be an exhibition, a meeting, a rally or a talk. The scope of major events is as wide as the scope of the leisure and recreation spectrum.

Major events carry a number of features which distinguish them from other elements within a leisure and recreation programme, including the six outlined below.

1   Events have distinctive characteristics – all major events are perceived as being something special. All events have a starting and finishing point. They are tightly bound in time and space. They have fixed deadlines. For the Leisure Manager, these are usually superimposed on other work.
2   Events carry opportunities to improve programming and management – events can capture the imagination of 'sellers' and 'buyers'. They can be a means of promoting the organization and creating favourable images. Their organization crosses administrative and departmental boundaries; hence they can unify the organization. They call upon all the resources of an organization and test them, revealing strengths and weaknesses. They may break new ground and could present the organization as a pioneer.
3   Events must conform to regulations – most special events have to meet stringent regulations involving aspects of health and safety and police matters. Licensing issues have become more complex and obtaining licences to hold large events is now more difficult than ever before. Events such as firework displays and pop concerts have to be very carefully planned, controlled, 'policed' and monitored.
4   Events pose many problems to all organizers – events are risky, so we have to expect the unexpected. Most problems can be anticipated but many will be unforeseen. The event, unlike the normal ongoing programme, is speeded up and delivered within a short space of time; this concentrates all the advanced planning and actions into specific hours and moments. Problems can thus be dramatic and could prove devastating. One problem is that managers and event organizers cannot depend on established routines. Another is that there are dangers in dates slipping by in preparation, targets not being met and budgets being overspent. In addition, there are dangers in lack of co-ordination, bringing inadequate linkages, miscommunications, omissions, duplications, wasted effort and inadequate controls.
5   Events lend themselves to certain management styles and methods – first, events need a co-ordinator; his or her role and style are paramount. Second, they need precision, deadlines and fast decisions and this differs from most

normal programming issues. Third, tight administration, using flowchart organization and checklists can help to meet deadlines and objectives. Fourth, entrepreneurial skills, allied to good administration, can be put to best effect. Fifth, because events are task-orientated, a more authoritarian style of leadership or 'benevolent dictatorship' may be required in the late stages of detailed preparation and on the day itself, autocratic management, particularly hours before the curtain goes up.

6   Events have similarities in organization – in terms of management approaches, the similarities of different events appear to be greater than the differences. While policies, programme and content will differ, a planning sequence is the same for all.

Decision making

↓

Planning and preparation

↓

Presentation

↓

Evaluation

No one precise method of organizing a major event is best and all others second best. The method will depend on the event and the circumstances surrounding it. However, some ways are more effective than others. Events therefore are a specialized aspect of leisure and recreation management and event planning in perspective approach is outlined in the sections that follow.

15.2 Event planning stages and organization

All events need good planning and organization [3, 4]. Regrettably, all events are not well planned and organized, even many of some significance, particularly in the voluntary and public sectors. Leisure Managers must guide and support event organizers in the basic principles of planning and organization.

The management approach to an event will depend on the particular circumstances, but it is worth recognizing seven interrelated planning stages in the life-cycle of a major event:

1   formulating the proposal and the policy;
2   undertaking feasibility and making decisions;
3   forward planning, objectives and budgeting;
4   organization structure and key appointments;

5   general and detailed preparation;
6   the event presentation;
7   feedback and evaluation.

15.2.1 Policy formulation to objective setting

First, formulate the idea. Debate, reason out and answer fundamental questions: why is the event proposed? What is it for? How will the event be run? Where will it be held? Who will be responsible for its planning and operation? When will it be held? If the idea is a good one, take the idea to the next stage of considering its feasibility.

Second, in considering the feasibility of an event it is important to explore in greater depth the questions already raised. What are the benefits? What are the costs, not just in terms of money, but also in terms of personnel, time and effort? Will the effort result in meeting the aims of the event? Can the problems be overcome?

If the event is not feasible, planners should have the courage to say 'no'. Regrettably, many events have taken place without considering their feasibility and they should never have been held. If the event is feasible, and there is positive commitment to the project, then it is important to make a firm decision, allowing ample time for forward planning and detailed planning. Coinciding with the decision to go ahead, certain crucial tasks should be undertaken.

1   Announce the decision to hold the event.
2   State clearly the nature of the event and the aims of the event; commit these to paper.
3   Appoint an events main committee – a working committee.
4   Appoint the key figure in the planning and control of the event – the co-ordinator.
5   Set objectives.

In setting objectives, be clear and unequivocal in stating them as measurable targets. Make them unambiguous. Include all main areas and units of the pro-gramme. In particular, be precise about the financial estimates and budgeting. In formulating the objectives, the co-ordinator should consult with the policy makers and the key personnel involved in it, whether as representatives of organizations or as unit or team leaders. Set the dates, times, specific deadlines and critical dates in the planning stages.

15.2.2 Evaluating costs and setting budgets

All major events need a budget. The extent to which they do depends on the nature of the event and on the objectives. Is the event designed to give a free service to the public: an open day in the park, free band concert, children's festival or a sports centre open day? Is the event designed as a crowd puller on a break-even financial exercise: an entertainment talent contest or a sports tournament? Is the event a sponsored event to draw in the crowds and capture the eye of the media: a national basketball tournament? Is the event totally sponsored, such as a leisure exhibition? Is the event primarily designed to raise funds for the organization or another charitable cause?

Most local authority events are heavily subsidized (i.e. by the rates). Town shows, orchestral concerts, free pop festivals in the park, old-time music halls, painting competitions, exhibitions and many thousands of events are run because they enhance the quality of life of citizens and are part of our heritage and traditions. Two key aspects concern evaluating true costs and setting budgets.

As far as the Leisure Manager is concerned, all events, even those totally subsidized, in reality, cost money. They must all have budgets and must all achieve the income/expenditure balance or ratio set in the objectives. Even more important is that the event be run with excellence. The principle for the Leisure Manager to work to is that of being professional. Regardless of whether the event is free, the facilities are free or the staff are already paid for, the manager should always evaluate the true costs.

It will normally cost money to use, hire or acquire facilities and make them functional and attractive for the event. There will be costs for electricity, water and technical and maintenance aspects. There will be costs of transport. Equipment may need to be hired, purchased, borrowed and transported. Additional staffing, stewards, voluntary helpers and personnel connected with the event will be required. Administration costs will include not only the promotion, printing, tickets, posters, financial costing and preparations, but also the whole office backup and administrative services, such as telephone, stationery and staff resources. There will normally be costs for mounting the event itself, the programme costs, the cost of artists, hospitality, the additional insurances and legal costs. The hidden costs of most events are enormous. The good manager should know what they are. They may not be of great importance to one event, but they could be to the next.

Most events will accrue some income. Even events which are 'free' to the consumer may be raising income from some sources such as grant aid from the local authority. Income can be derived from direct methods and indirect methods. The direct methods include gate receipts, programmes, bar and catering, car parking, cloakrooms and costs of other services. The indirect methods include advertising, donations, sponsorships, sales, raffles and fund-raising of a variety of sorts. Sometimes the amount of effort put into running the annual dinner raffle is more than that put into the whole event itself!

Events, then, need a budget and all events need expenditure limits. A large proportion of events also need income targets. If budget targets are known to all from the outset and are included in the objectives of the event, then everyone is working to the agreed targets for the event. Many events lend themselves to a break-even figure: for example, an entertainment festival may cost in cash terms £2000 and is to run for one week; the objective could then be to attract a minimum of say, 2000 customers at an average spend of £1; or 1000 customers at an average spend of £2. Numbers over this become a bonus, but normally not a profit. Extra income that might accrue will normally help to meet hidden costs or help the organization or boost the funds for the charity.

The risk element with most events is very high, particularly when they are at the mercy of the weather, or the call of the television on Cup Final Day, or when new ideas are being tried or when dealing with an unknown quantity. There are risks enough without taking even greater financial ones such as overspending budgets or minimizing income. Events therefore need not only the budget but also a co-ordinator to ensure that financial targets are met.

15.3 Event organization structures

Organization is concerned with planning, establishing an organization structure and developing working relationships and methods to achieve objectives. Organizational structures cover the chains of command, the spans of control and the discrete units, teams or working parties dealing with the various areas of work. The structure must cover the broad spectrum of the event. An event such as a festival involving community groups might have several units, for example:

1   programme and content – activities, organizations;
2   budget – accounting, income and expenditure in all areas;
3   promotion – awareness, publicity, media, etc.;
4   personnel and staffing – contracts, duties, etc.;
5   administration – programmes, printing, box office, legal, etc.;
6   technical – resources, equipment, preparation, etc.;
7   services – parking, cloaks, information, first aid, etc.;
8   catering and social – routine, special entertaining, etc.

There should be a working group for each area and a section leader who accepts the responsibility and links with the main co-ordinator. It is important to agree the precise roles and responsibilities of each group and each leader; and the organization, tasks, target deadlines and dates. The events personnel structure for a large town festival [5] is shown in Figure 15.1; the organization structure for a national sports championship [5] is shown in Figure 15.2.

15.3.1 Roles and responsibilities

Everyone involved in an event should know to whom they are responsible, who is responsible to them, who they are working with and what exactly their function is in the organization. Areas of responsibility and tasks to be done should be handled in discrete units, linked together through a co-ordinated network. Key factors in the make-up of the organization are: the people carrying out the planning; the task units; the heads of the units; their span of control.

There must be sufficient, keen and knowledgeable people prepared to give time and effort to the tasks. But there must also be an efficient organization to make the best use of such people. People need an optimum amount of responsibility. In chapter eighteen on staffing, we learn that a person's span of control depends on many factors, and that there are dangers in either too wide or too narrow a span.

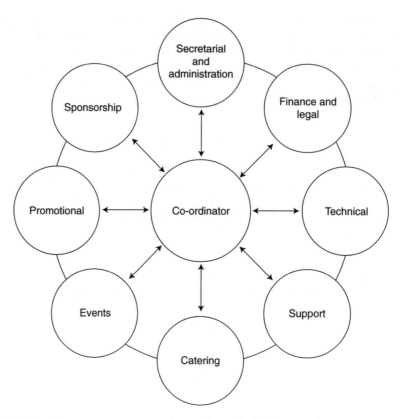

FIGURE 15.1 Major events structure with units/teams linked to co-ordinator

Source: 'Successful event management' in Torkildsen, G. (1993) *Torkildsen's Guides to Leisure Management*, Longman, Harlow

We also learn that although formal structures are important, the informal structures are also critical to the harmony and efficiency of an organization. Unfortunately, with many event organizations, the structures are poor and without co-ordination. The result is that informal dealings flourish without co-ordination; misunderstandings and miscommunications abound, leaving many parts of the planning to fall between two stools. 'It will be all right on the night' is a totally inadequate substitute for good organization. On the day, organizers have found the makings of a comedy series; examples occurring at leisure events over the period of writing these editions of the book include: there was no staging; the public address did not work, lights did not come on; the changing rooms were in the nearest school a mile away; the VIPs at a national event were standing in the rain trying to convince the doorman that they had been invited; players at an All Stars match could not get into the ground because the entrance was blocked with traffic; and the grand piano for the concert at the sports centre had been delivered to the theatre! At one national United Kingdom leisure event, catering for the conference banquet had not been arranged; the organizer in London and the hosting authority

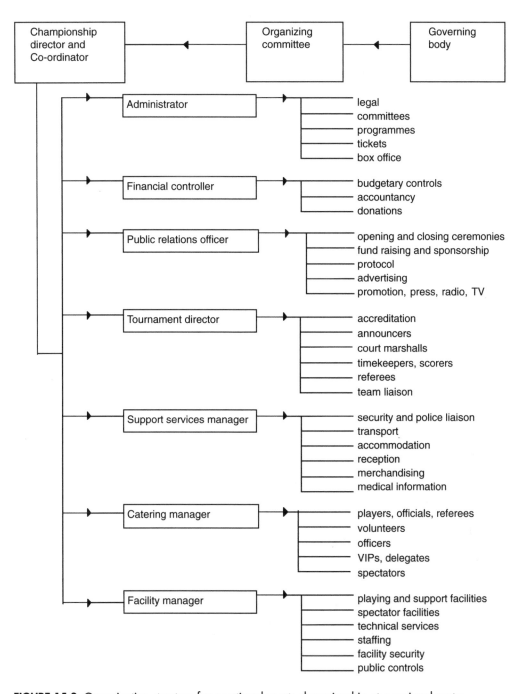

FIGURE 15.2 Organization structure for a national sports championship at a regional centre

Source: 'Successful event management' in Torkildsen, G. (1993) *Torkildsen's Guides to Leisure Management*, Longman, Harlow

in Wales had each thought the other was organizing it! The lack of co-ordination and delegated task responsibilities are evident in such situations.

15.3.2 Organization, tasks and dates

Once principles have been agreed and objectives set, then the structure for organizing the event can be put together. The use of an organization chart is helpful. It helps to clarify any ambiguities and provides an overall picture indicating the various responsibility areas. Its main disadvantage is that it shows only the formal relationships. However, this is not too limiting for events. Events are finite, fixed occasions, requiring task operations that need to be controlled and, particularly in the later stages, handled autocratically to meet deadlines. For major international events such as an international tournament, an organization handbook will be necessary, in addition to an organization chart [4].

In addition to the structure, a work flow-chart indicating critical paths will be valuable for programming and timetabling the work of committees, task units and sections. It should indicate the flow pattern, the critical dates, the deadlines, the merging of sections at appropriate times and the interrelationships between sections.

15.4 Staff and personnel

All events need personnel. The number and type will depend on the nature of the event. However, all events need a co-ordinator and support staff.

1 The co-ordinator

The co-ordinator does not organize directly. He or she is the leader, the link person, the informer, the one person who knows what is going on in each unit, section or team. The co-ordinator does not have to know every detail, but needs to know who has the knowledge and whose responsibility it is. The co-ordinator must control and monitor progress using the most efficient methods – i.e. meetings, sectional heads reporting, work flow-charts. He or she needs to be an encourager, yet firm in handling situations. Towards the later stages of the planning, in particular, the co-ordinator will have to exert pressure and make authoritative decisions in order to meet the deadlines. He or she is the key figure in any event organization – the link, the controller and the communicator. Information to all concerned throughout the planning is essential to keep people motivated, involved and committed, in addition to keeping abreast of information. So often, those in the firing line are ill-informed.

2 Support staff

For large events, the co-ordinator will normally work with a team of sectional heads. Each team head, and each discrete unit, will have its clear responsibilities, duties, times, deadlines and calendars, but all within the overall organizational design. Without linkages, it is possible for one unit to function independently, making its own contribution unilaterally, and sometimes competitively, without thought to the overall success of the project.

Events are run with many different types of staff and helpers. Large scale events will have full-time staff, part-time paid staff, paid casual staff and volunteers and will also delegate certain functions to organizations or concession others.

Paid staff will need to know well in advance their pay, the times and the conditions; trade unions may well be involved; and there will be irregular hours, different rates of pay and insurance aspects. Volunteers will also need to know exactly where they stand, what their responsibilities are and how far these extend. Legal problems are always to be borne in mind with special events; contractual problems, insurance details and promotional aspects will call for professional legal advice.

Staff and helpers need to know what their job is, what is expected of them, who they are responsible to, who is responsible to them and what they have to do to be successful. They must be highly committed and involved. This is the job of the co-ordinator and the team heads. The answer is never to be complacent, nor to take people for granted. Motivation, acknowledgement, praise and thanks are important. People want to see something of themselves in a successful venture.

15.5 Detailed planning of the event and the evaluation

The event itself should be preceded by detailed planning and rehearsals. It should be excellently presented, with a memorable start and finish. A careful evaluation and follow-up should also be part of the whole process.

The detailed planning can be assisted by the use of work flow-charts, critical paths, checklists, targets and dates. Five steps must be taken in the final stages for many major events.

1 The detailed final plan must be produced.
2 Checklists must be carefully followed.
3 Contingency plans must be formulated.
4 The event should be practised or components rehearsed, including staff duties.
5 All possible elements should be double checked.

The event itself, having been thoroughly planned, should normally go well. However, there will invariably be problems. The co-ordinator of a large event must be totally free to make objective decisions, should these be required. Section leaders also need to be relatively free to control their own sections.

The ending and closure is an important component of the whole event. Closing ceremonies, hospitality, the thanks to all, cashing up, stock checking, clearing up and motivating workers to carry things through to the end, all make for ultimate success. After the event, the accounting, reports, lessons to be learned, making good damage and writing of 'thank yous' must be undertaken. A social event to thank the workers should be considered, in addition to thanking them on the day itself.

In the cold light of day, a full evaluation is needed which assesses the preparation, the organization structure, the event, the results, the feedback from spectators, participants and staff and the lessons for future events. A report should be prepared both for record purposes (sometimes queries continue for several years) and to assist in the future planning of events.

Having considered the theoretical base from which to stage events, it is salutary to consider the range of problems that can occur leading up to events and at the events themselves. Some of these problems are raised before conclusions are summarized.

15.6 Main problem areas in staging major events

In order to run efficient, memorable events, it is wise to consider the problems of previous events. Some major and some minor faults are listed below. Ten areas have been identified. The first mentioned is possibly the most critical, yet the most frequently violated.

1   Lack of objectivity and clarity – insufficient consideration of the aims and objectives and organization structure at the outset: this invariably leads to poor communication, duplication of effort but, even more serious, lack of direction, authority and controls.

2   No appointment of a co-ordinator – this is the key figure: there are usually a chairman and heads of committees but often no co-ordinator with the authority and responsibility for planning and operational control.

3   Inadequate administration – failure to maintain accurate written records of all that transpires during the planning stages: if good records are kept, they act as reminders and checks for work to be carried out. Rarely are there flow charts with deadlines plotted. Much is kept in one's head. This leads to misunderstandings and recriminations on the day.

4   Insufficient planning time – organizations give themselves insufficient planning time. Even when they do have sufficient time so much effort is put in at the last moment. This can lead to overloading and frustration through poor planning.

5   Poor organizational structure – committee and unit structures are in many cases too narrow or too unwieldy. Many are far too large. Others leave matters to one person. These individuals invariably take on far too much. They see the event as 'their event'. They are so keen to do the job that they will not share responsibility or delegate duties. Some very busy people take on events as social obligations and over commit themselves. These problems are typical of an amateur approach but must not be part of the professional Leisure Manager's repertoire.

6   Lack of unity and co-ordination – there are often problems with 'governing' bodies. These usually stem from lack of agreement on principles and organization in the first place. There are problems with looking after guests. Relationships with staff (who have heavy additional duties in addition to their normal work) are often strained.

7   Poor anticipation of potential problems – unusual problems can be encountered. The technical problems are considerable: for example, noise from other parts of a building, the import of a whole range of additional equipment, the extra floor markings or take-up of markings, the additional stage lighting, decor, the need for additional seating and many others.

8   Insufficient prior adherence to licensing and safety regulations – certain events require licences. There are a range of health and safety regulations. The police must be informed about certain kinds of events and should be informed of all events attracting a crowd.

9   Lack-lustre, unprofessional event – poor events often lack a professional presentation, and are therefore unmemorable experiences.

10   No evaluation or learning lessons from the past – only counting numbers and income is poor evaluation. There needs to be evaluation of the planning inputs, the processes, the event and the results – particularly the satisfactions of those attending.

Any problems that spoil an event should not be tolerated; no matter what the organization, certain problems must be ironed out for the next event. They include lack of clear objectives, weak co-ordinator and sectional heads, faulty public address, keen but ineffective announcers, insufficient staff, insufficient food and drink, failure to inform the police, no first aid, no plans for inclement weather, no press coverage, no litter containers, embarrassing pauses between activities, programmes overrunning, no hospitality for visitors, untidy and careless presentations, no colour, no glamour, no heightened emotion – no umph!

Some problems can be put right immediately for the next event, others need time and consideration and planning. This is the role of the Leisure Manager. A comparison between good organization and poor organization are outlined in Table 15.1.

Event planning can be greatly assisted by a logical, simple process. But there is no 'one way only'. Whilst the event planning 'model' outlined below, and illustrated in Figure 15.3 shows a logical pattern, it must be appreciated that event management is not a straight line process from A to Z. Many steps need to be taken at the same time, working in harmony. The 'model' needs to be adapted to meet the needs of the particular event.

1. Ideas

Formulate the idea or receive a proposal: ask why, what, how, where and when? Is proposal from reputable body with financial/administrative credibility? Does event fulfil purposes of the organization? Only if it is a good idea go on to Step 2.

TABLE 15.1 Event management: good and poor organization

	Good organization	*Poor organization*
1. *Objectives and clarity*	Clear, written, agreed and all committed to	Vague aims, well intentioned hopes and dreams with no clear objectivity
2. *Co-ordinator*	Of calibre and authority	No one co-ordinator but many leading 'hands' overlapping
3. *Administration*	Skilled, organized secretarial systems, records and accounting	Unorganized and ad hoc systems
4. *Planning time*	Long lead-in time and built in contingency at each stage for slippage	Short lead time and no time for slippage leading to eleventh-hour panics
5. *Organization*	An overall structure, with discrete units for specific tasks	Organization in the hands of too many or too few with no workable structure
6. *Unity, co-ordination and communication*	Team effort, positive attitudes and enthusiasm	Many work in isolation with little corporate commitment
7. *Problem anticipation*	Potential problems identified; alternatives and contingencies planned	No agenda for anything going wrong; 'head in the sand'
8. *Licensing and regulations*	Licensing authorities, police, health and first aid consulted at the outset	Licensing an afterthought
9. *Professional presentation*	Good start, finish and timing with some glamour, novelty and surprise	No memorable start and finish; over-running and poor presentation
10. *Evaluation and lessons from the past*	All are winners. Evaluation of planning the event itself and the outcome – the result	No clear evaluation, only numbers and income and no record for future events

2. Feasibility

Consider the feasibility or evaluate proposal: what are assets, problems, support, cost in terms of money, effort, time? What is possible disruption to the normal programme/organization? Only if it is feasible, go on to Step 3.

3. Decision making

Announce decision, the event and its aims or sign contract: if 'outside' organizers, establish terms, areas of responsibility *re* staffing, equipment, accommodation, etc. and appoint representative to their committee. Sign exchange contract. Establish a monitoring, reporting and evaluation process. In-house organizers go on to Step 4.

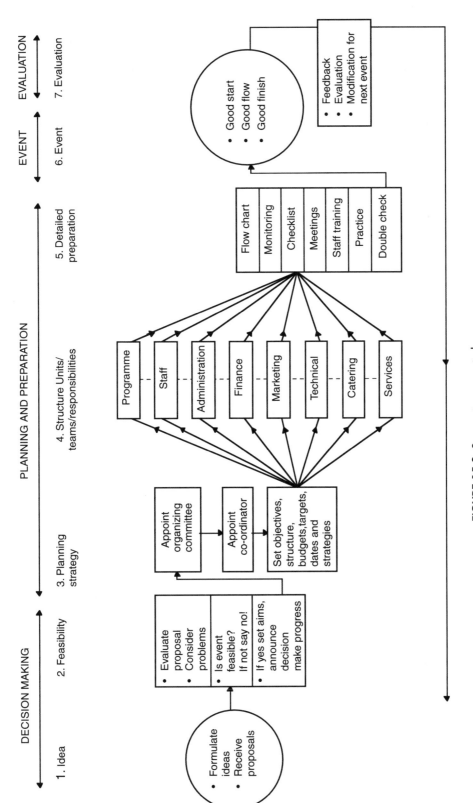

FIGURE 15.3 Seven-stage event planner

483

4. Strategy, structure and objectives

a) Appoint event committee: must include people with commitment, authority and energy.
b) Appoint the co-ordinator: give resources, authority and support.
c) Set objectives, targets, budgets: must be measurable, timed, dated; draw up draft planning flow chart.
d) Establish organization structure: fix discrete units/teams with unit leader: give roles, targets, responsibilities.

5. Planning and preparation

Detailed planning can be assisted by use of work flow charts, critical path networks, checklists, targets and dates.

a) Plan dates *backwards* from event day: agree planning flow chart with dates and use it.
b) Each key unit leader should have own calendar within agreed overall plan.
c) Fix key meetings long in advance.
d) Circulate information very regularly: communicate often.
e) Monitor progress: check meticulously.
f) Check budgets systematically.
g) Follow detailed plan: use checklists; anticipate problems, make contingency plans and emergency procedures, practice and rehearse; double check.
h) Resist afterthoughts.

6. Fine tuning and rehearsal

Professional artists who make their performance look so easy have rehearsed and rehearsed until it is perfect – it becomes second nature. Many events however cannot be rehearsed until the day itself, but the preparation, the systems and controls can be checked and double-checked and the staff trained.

a) Go over the final plan.
b) Follow checklists carefully.
c) Make fine tuning adjustments.
d) Prepare contingency plans and emergency procedures.
e) Rehearse components and practice.
f) Double check.

7. Event

An event needs 'professional' presentation. Make it memorable.

a) Open with style.
b) Present event with class, flair and imagination.

c)   Keep co-ordinator totally free for overall control and effective decisions under
      crisis or potentially difficult situations.
d)   Close event with crescendo: good impression to start and finish. End on a
      high note – a lasting memory.

8. Immediate post-event

a)   Clear the decks tidily and with precision – cashing up, stock checking,
      clearing up, making good damage.
b)   Give thanks *on the day*.

9. Evaluate and account

Thank officially; collect feedback from promoters, participants, staff, spectators;
report and record. Has the event fulfilled its purposes, met objectives? What
lessons are there for future events? A full evaluation is needed which assesses the
preparation, the organization, the event, the results and the lessons for future
events. Prepare a report.

15.6 Events checklists

Events lend themselves to organization structures, work flow charts and methods
of checking action. A checklist is one of the additional methods. However, events
vary so much that detailed checklists to cover all events would be inappropriate,
could waste time and effort, and could run into thousands of items. It is important
never to use the one checklist, without situational changes and amendment, for all
events. No two events are the same. Even twin events programmed at different
periods or at different locations will differ in some respects. A checklist summary,
however, could be of value to check up on the various areas. A detailed list or
amendments could be undertaken for each event. A general checklist is at Table
15.2.

15.7 Summary – event management

Oscar Wilde is quoted as saying, 'if a thing is worth doing, it's worth doing badly'.
Unfortunately, too many event organizers seem to have taken him literally! If you
don't plan, it won't be 'all right on the night' and, following Murphy's Law, 'If
anything can go wrong, it will!'
      Experience of running events shows that although all events differ one from
another, in terms of management approaches, the similarities are greater than the
differences. While policies, programme and content will differ considerably, a
planning sequence similar to the one proposed in this chapter serves the requirements for many events.

TABLE 15.2 A 'programme content' checklist

General checklist

Specific checklists will be needed for specialized events, eg international sports championship, concert, exhibition, fete.

Facilities for events

1	Access – check driveway, gates, paths, widths of doorways, etc.	☐
2	Alternative areas, e.g. wet weather	☐
3	Car parks – on and off site	☐
4	Changing rooms	☐
5	Control points	☐
6	Disabled access	☐
7	Exhibition areas	☐
8	Event accommodation and space layout to scale	☐
9	First aid and medical rooms	☐
10	Flooring suitability and covering	☐
11	Hospitality boxes	☐
11	Lavatories	☐
12	Loading bays	☐
13	Lost property room	☐
14	Offices	☐
15	Officials' rooms	☐
16	Performers' rooms	☐
17	Playing areas and dimensions	☐
18	Poster sites	☐
19	Press boxes	☐
20	Ramps	☐
21	Power points	☐
22	Reception areas	☐
23	Rehearsal space	☐
24	Safety – e.g. alarms, fire hoses, floor and roof loadings	☐
25	Sales points	☐
26	Seating layout	☐
27	Security rooms	☐
28	Service/delivery points	☐
29	Signposting	☐
30	Site restrictions e.g. overhead obstructions, pillars	☐
31	Social areas, bar and catering	☐
32	Sponsors' boxes	☐
33	Storage and security of valuable goods	☐
34	VIP lounges	☐
35	Warm-up/practice areas	☐

Staff and personnel (Full time, part time, casual, voluntary)

36	Administrative	☐
37	Announcers	☐
38	Attendants	☐
39	Bar staff	☐
40	Car park attendants	☐
41	Cashiers	☐
42	Caterers	☐
43	Cleaners	☐
44	Cloakroom attendants	☐
45	Doctor/medical staff	☐
46	Electricians	☐
47	Hosts	☐
48	Interpreters	☐
49	Maintenance personnel	☐
50	Master of ceremonies	☐
51	Officials	☐
52	Patrols	☐
53	Receptionists	☐
54	Safety, e.g. lifeguards	☐
55	Security guards	☐
56	Stewards	☐
57	Technicians	☐
58	Telephonists	☐
59	Traders/exhibitors	☐
60	Traffic controllers	☐
61	Ushers	☐
62	Volunteer helpers	☐

Administration, documentation and finance

63	Accounts and auditing	☐
64	Admission	☐
65	Appeals/fund raising, grants, lotteries	☐
66	Arrival/departure	☐
67	Box office	☐
68	Budget and estimates	☐
69	Cashflow/security/change	☐
70	Cleaning costs	☐
71	Committees	☐
72	Contracts	☐
73	Concessions/franchise	☐
74	Copyright	☐
75	Credit card transactions	☐
76	Documentation and name tags	☐
77	Donations – to and from	☐
78	Fees	☐
79	Hire charges	☐
80	Identification/passes	☐
81	Insurance – accident, third party, weather, equipment, theft	☐
82	Invitations	☐
83	Legal, eg contract of hire	☐
84	Licensing – bar extension, spectators, entertainment	☐
85	Organization structure	☐
86	Postage	☐
87	Printing	☐
88	Programmes – printing and sales	☐
89	Reception	☐
90	Rentals	☐
91	Repair costs	☐
92	Sales	☐
93	Seating arrangements	☐
94	Signs and maps	☐

95	Stationery ☐
96	Stock control ☐
97	Sunday trading ☐
98	Tickets – pricing, printing, sales and complimentary discounts ☐

Equipment

99	Acoustics ☐
100	Audio/visual ☐
101	Chairs and tables ☐
102	Communications – bleep system, two-way radio ☐
103	Decoration/decor/floral ☐
104	Directional signs ☐
105	Disco ☐
106	Display boards ☐
107	Fencing/barriers ☐
108	Flags ☐
109	Heating ☐
110	Hire of equipment ☐
111	Lectern ☐
112	Lighting – stage, TV, generator, emergency ☐
113	Litter bins ☐
114	Marquees ☐
115	Projection equipment – film, slide, overhead ☐
116	Public address – records, tapes, national anthems, fanfares ☐
117	Rostrum/dais ☐
118	Scoreboards ☐
119	Signs, e.g. 'No Smoking' ☐
120	Spectator stands ☐
121	Staging ☐
122	Timing system equipment ☐
123	Uniforms for staff; protective clothing ☐

Presentation and media

124	Advertising ☐
125	Appeals ☐
126	Artwork ☐
127	Badges ☐
128	Banners ☐
129	Ceremonies ☐
130	Civic officials ☐
131	Commentators/announcers ☐
132	Dress rehearsal ☐
133	Entertainment, including licensing ☐
134	Films/photography ☐
135	Interpreters ☐
136	Logo and stationery ☐
137	Marketing ☐
138	Merchandising, e.g. T-shirts ☐
139	Newsletter ☐
140	Music and music licence and performing rights ☐
141	Posters, leaflets ☐
142	Presentation – programme, timetable of events ☐

143	Press and press releases ☐
144	Prizes/medals/cups and engraving ☐
145	Protocol ☐
146	Publicity ☐
147	Public relations ☐
148	Radio ☐
149	Receptions ☐
150	Souvenirs ☐
151	Sponsorship/patronage ☐
152	Theme/logo/image ☐
153	TV/Video taping event ☐
154	VIPs

Support Services

155	Accommodation ☐
156	Ambulance service ☐
157	AA/RAC ☐
158	Agencies ☐
159	Bank ☐
160	Bar – public, guests ☐
161	Catering – public, performers, guests and licenses ☐
162	Car parking – public, special ☐
163	Changing accommodation ☐
164	Childminding/crèche ☐
165	Cleaning, before, during, after ☐
166	Cloakrooms ☐
167	Church services ☐
168	Directional signs ☐
169	Disabled support services ☐
170	Emergency procedures ☐
171	Entertainment ☐
172	Exhibition ☐
173	Health and safety ☐
174	Hospitality ☐
175	Hotels ☐
176	Information services ☐
177	Lost property ☐
178	Lost children ☐
179	Maintenance ☐
180	Medical ☐
181	Photocopier ☐
182	Police ☐
183	Post Office ☐
184	Red Cross/St John Ambulance ☐
185	Secretarial ☐
186	Security – people, property, bomb scares ☐
187	Shops ☐
188	Technicians ☐
189	Telephone/telex/fax:/Email ☐
190	Tourist information – guide books, maps ☐
191	Translation services ☐
192	Transport ☐
193	Travel agency ☐
194	Typewriters ☐
195	Visits and tours ☐

No one method of organizing a major event is best and all others second best. The method will depend on the event and the circumstances surrounding it. However, some ways are more effective than others; they are more objective, they are better planned, costed and controlled.

What experience has shown is that there has very often been insufficient thought given to the planning and organization of the event before committees are set, jobs allocated and decisions made to go ahead. Forward planning, organization structure, objective setting and communications are main issues integral to successful event management.

Well run events will have clear and agreed objectives to which all are committed; discrete units to undertake specific tasks yet work as a whole; a co-ordinator of calibre and authority; unity of effort; efficient lines of communication; and no duplication of effort or waste of time.

Events are important strings to the Leisure Manager's bow. Their organization is important to his or her repertoire of skills. Events lend themselves to certain styles of management such as Management by Objectives and strong, authoritative management. They need a sound, logical framework, with a starting point very much like an athletic race. Events need thorough planning, imaginative marketing and promotion and excellent presentation.

Notes and references

1   Shields, A. and Wright, M. (eds) (1989), *Arenas: A Planning, Design and Management Guide*, Sports Council, London.

2   Goldblatt, J. J. (1990), *Special Events: The Art and Science of Celebration*, Van Nostrand Reinhold, New York.

3   See Video Arts (1975) *What Every Exhibitor Ought to Know*, the companion booklet to their films *It'll be OK On the Day* and *How Not to Exhibit Yourself*, Video Arts Ltd, London.

4   See The Scottish Sports Council (1980), *Major Events: An Organization Manual*, SSC, Edinburgh.

5   Torkildsen, G. (1993), *Torkildsen's Guides to Leisure Management*, Longman, Harlow.

Recommended additional reading

Richards, B. (1992), *How to Market Tourism Attractions, Festivals and Special Events*, Longman, Harlow.

Health and Safety Commission/Home Office/The Scottish Office (1993), *Guide to Health, Safety and Welfare at Pop Concerts and Similar Events*, HMSO, London.

Passingham, S. (1995), *Organizing Local Events*, 2nd edition, Directory of Social Change, London.

Greater London Arts Association (1978) *Community Arts Festival Handbook*, Greater London Arts Association, London.

Institute of Municipal Entertainment (undated), *Planning Your Course or Conference*, [supplement] Institute of Municipal Entertainment London.

Amateur Swimming Association (1989), *Organizing a Swimming Competition*, Amateur Swimming Association, London.

Central Council for Physical Recreation (1989), *The Search for Sports Sponsorship*, and *Let's Make an Event of it: What, Why, When*, CCPR, London.

English Tourist Board (undated), *How to Organize an Event*, ETB, London.

Spencer, P.J. (1982), *OK On The Day*, National Association of Youth Clubs, Leicester.

Event organization information can also be obtained from the Sports Councils, Arts Councils, governing bodies of sport and many other agencies, such as the National Outdoor Events Association.

Chapter sixteen

Staffing and staff structures

Excellent staff are as important as excellent facilities. Therefore, senior professionals and managers in leisure services must have knowledge, experience and understanding of staff matters: selection, staff relations, staff motivation, organizational structures and something of the law as it relates to employment.

Staff – full-time, part-time or voluntary – are the most important resource in any leisure organization and their cost should be regarded as a highly valued investment rather than an expensive item of expenditure. The right staff need to be employed, trained, nurtured and enabled to perform well for their organizations and for themselves.

In chapter twelve we dealt with many of the general management aspects: principles of management, leadership, motivation and decision making. This chapter deals with some aspects of staffing, mainly within leisure services departments. First, staff and staffing structures within leisure service organizations are examined and emphasis is placed on the need for more effective organization. Second, the principles of management which concern staffing are considered. Third, the formulation of organization and staffing structures is examined, including departmental structures, formal and informal structures and mechanistic and organic 'models'. Fourth, some legislation relating to staff employment is summarized. Fifth, a brief analysis is made of the recruitment and selection of staff and staff appraisals; and sixth, the production and use of a staff handbook is advocated.

Having read this chapter, readers will be in no doubt that the effective handling of staff and the way the staff are organized and employed are essential for effective and efficient management. Good handling of staff is important, but needs to be structured fairly and professionally for greater effectiveness and efficiency and also for legal, economic and social reasons.

Students will learn the basic principles of staff management: 'chains of command', 'span of control' and 'logical assignment' and understand the nature of formal and informal organization structures. Readers will be introduced to a number of the laws relating to staffing and the duties of employers and responsibilities of employer and staff. They will learn how to produce and use an organization chart, formulate a staffing structure and produce an essential staff handbook.

16.1 The changing labour force

Most employers in the United Kingdom will find the labour market is changing as a result of many factors, principally changes in population and technology. This was the warning of the report *Young People and the Labour Market*, produced in 1988 by the National Economic Development Office (NEDO) and the government training agency and was followed in 1990 in the report, *Defusing the Demographic Time Bomb*. The need was shown for a better educated and trained workforce at a time when the number of young people leaving schools and colleges was falling sharply. Since then, of course, population patterns have shifted but the numbers of young people are still lower than in times past.

The leisure industry, a major employer in the United Kingdom and abroad, has become used to employing young people (and part-time female employees) often because they represent cheaper labour or availability in holiday periods and at weekends, and also because they are flexible in hours and duties and provide the energy and adaptability required in the leisure industry.

Yet the changes taking place in the labour force are about much more. Employers have to consider their future skill needs in the wider context of changes in technology and quality and competition from abroad. There needs to be a committed and highly motivated workforce, with more flexibility to respond to the challenges of the year 2000 and beyond.

16.2 Staff and staffing structure in leisure organizations

One of the key areas in the management of leisure and recreation services departments and facilities is the staffing and staffing structure. The way in which staff are organized is a crucial factor in the performance and level of success of management. The structure represents the way in which the work is organized and shared out and the manner in which an organization is managed.

Every leisure and recreation service, from the smallest to the largest, has an organization and staffing structure of some kind. Used effectively the structure provides the framework through which the work operations proceed in an orderly manner towards achieving organizational objectives.

16.2.1 Staff and structures vary

Staffing structures, the types of staff and the levels of staffing in leisure services vary considerably from authority to authority, organization to organization and from centre to centre, even where facilities are comparable and where policies appear to run parallel.

In public recreation, financed in large measure by rates and taxes and subject to bureaucratic administrative systems and standardized procedures, one might expect to find a considerable level of uniformity. However, in the United Kingdom there are almost as many different structures as there are authorities and it is difficult to find two precisely the same. While different localities have different facilities and different circumstances, it is understandable that variations exist. However, the variations in structure, methods, approaches and personnel are so wide – from a small subsection to a comprehensive department, in towns of the same size and with similar ranges of services – that comparative studies are needed to highlight the benefits and limitations of different systems. By way of illustration, at some similar, large leisure complexes in the United Kingdom, total staff numbers can vary from 50 to 100.

Not only are structures different, but also the types of staff vary. In addition, staff vary within the same organization from full-time to part-time, temporary, casual and voluntary. There are recreation executives, senior, middle and line managers, recreation officers, wardens, park-keepers, coaches, teachers, community workers, youth workers, play leaders, artists, caterers, technicians, supervisors, administrators and a wide range of technical, clerical and maintenance staff. They have variations in contracts of employment, job descriptions, training and benefits. They work different hours and different shifts and many work long, unsocial hours. With most comprehensive leisure facilities, opening hours are lengthy, as much as 100 hours a week. In these circumstances, even the most dedicated manager is in essence a part-timer!

The allocation of revenue expenditure towards staffing, particularly in public recreation facilities, takes the largest share of operating costs. For example, salaries and wages account generally for 55–60 per cent of the operating expenditure, plus the statutory and other 'on costs'. In times of economic stringency, and with competitive tendering, reduction in staff is one method of reducing deficits or increasing net returns. It is therefore important to demonstrate clearly the appropriate levels and duties of staff as a means towards achieving objectives.

16.2.2 Inadequate staff structures

In many public leisure and recreation organizations the staffing structure is inappropriate to the needs. The structure of, say, an arts centre may be unhappily embedded within a local authority departmental structure with a hierarchy, levels and status positions which have little relationship to programming needs, the needs of staff and, possibly least of all, the needs of users. Fitting new types of facility and services into outmoded structures highlights the problem even more clearly. Many new leisure centres require managers with considerable decision making powers and senior staff to take full responsibility in unsocial hours (usually peak hours, in terms of attendances, events and programme variety). They need structures which are flexible enough to respond to changes, in order to meet less predictable community demand.

Despite local government re-organization, the upsurge in facilities and the emergence of an embryo profession of leisure and recreation management, staff in some cases are having to fit into structures and systems designed in times past to suit the Victorian 'parks–pitches–pools' era. In one London borough, a vast community sports and recreation centre had its director replaced by an administrator, so that the centre's organization structure could fit into the borough's departmental structure! The bureaucracy could not handle flexibility, even at this one centre, which had demonstrated itself to be unique, something outside the normal run of things.

16.2.3 Staffing flexibility

Many leisure facilities, particularly in the voluntary sector, are managed by a leader and many volunteers. They take responsibility for facilities, plant, programme and personnel. Even in public leisure and recreation centres the level of part-time staff can be high. It is not unusual to find a leisure centre manned at 9 pm by a supervisor or receptionist and a few part-timers, managers and senior staff having long since gone.

Different forms of management will be needed to optimize, promote and encourage leisure and recreation on a broad front. Part-time paid staff, coaches, community workers and volunteers may be needed to help to meet the needs of those who find it difficult to make use of public recreation facilities.

It is apparent that leisure and recreation services call for special, sensitive handling of staff. Staff have a variety of duties and the facilities are open for long hours. The nature of the job – that of creating satisfaction for people in their leisure time – requires that good staff have personal commitment and an understanding of customer requirements: if staff flexibility is required, then organization and employer flexibility are also required.

16.3 Staffing and principles of management

Some top-level managers and senior personnel are concerned with the formulation of policies and organizational structures. Most managers, however, are appointed to positions in existing organizations, to which they have to adapt. It is important that managers at all levels understand the organization structure, the principles on which it is based and the components which go to make it up.

According to the International City Management Association [1], three basic principles of management must be considered in establishing an organizational structure, namely: unity of command; logical assignment; span of control; and to these can be added: authority and power.

1. Unity of command

The principle states that each individual in an organization should be responsible to only one superior. Adherence to this principle establishes a precise chain of command within the organization.

Situations exist in recreation organizations which do not follow such a principle. For example, at one recreation centre the head groundsman is answerable both to a centre manager and to an assistant technical officer at the town hall. At another, a recreation manager is responsible both to a centre director and to a borough recreation officer. At another recreation and leisure establishment, while the principle of unity of command exists (in that the centre manager is responsible to only one person), he is answerable not to the borough director of recreation, but to the chief executive!

In these examples, a key member of staff has been able to leap-frog or by-pass his or her senior officer. The formal structure has not worked and possibly more importantly, the essential informal structure has not been established because of envy and personality clashes and the guarding of territory.

2. Logical assignment

The principle states that staff doing the same work should be grouped together and that work is planned and scheduled in a logical order.

Situations exist in leisure management where structures and departmentalism are put first, and the job in hand second. Without logical assignment, there will be duplication, overlap, confusion, resentment, power struggles, drawing in of responsibilities to heighten status, keeping things close to the chest, and not sharing, which all lead to poor performance. Here again, personalities are blamed but the greater responsibility rests with those responsible for the structure and its implementation.

3. Span of control

The principle is something of a misnomer. The principle states that there are limiting factors which must be considered in deciding the number of subordinates a member of staff can effectively handle. Span of control may be more accurately defined as span of management because the limiting factors are many. They include the number of people that can be supervised, depending on the quality of staff and level of delegation, the distance over which control can be exercised, the amount of time in which to exercise control, and the number of activities that a manager can effectively manage. The span of management is, then, a statement of those limitations.

It is not possible to state the exact number of people a manager should 'control'. Much depends on the competence of subordinates and the manager's own knowledge, ability, time, energy, personality, leadership style and the environment and situation in which work must be undertaken. The type of work, in addition to the capacities of the manager, must also be considered. Organizations with narrow spans of control have the potential for good control and close supervision of staff (Figure 16.1). However, managers tend to get involved in the work of their subordinates. Narrow spans of control are often found in hierarchical organizations where the many tiers of management will incur high staff costs and the distance between the top and lower levels can make communication difficult.

Too many staff, on the other hand will limit a manager's efficiency and effectiveness. Some public authorities put one senior manager in control of sport, arts, community, environment, youth, libraries, cemeteries, catering (including meals on wheels) and entertainment (Figure 16.2). For many the span of control is too wide and managers become ineffective and inefficient. There is a tendency for the manager to become overloaded. However, with a manager that can communicate well, delegate clearly and select appropriate and capable subordinates, the organization can work efficiently and at a lower cost than an organization with a hierarchy and with a smaller span of control. Further, the climate within the organization is more likely to encourage innovation and creative thinking with a concentration on achieving the organization's objectives and not upon the means of achieving them. Innovation needs delegated authority and the freedom of action.

4. 'Authority' and 'power'

Too often these words are mistakenly treated as being synonymous. Authority within an organization is based upon a person's position within the organizational structure and incorporates the person's responsibilities, tasks, etc. and is accepted by his/her subordinates as having 'legitimate' authority. Power on the other hand is a much broader concept and relates to the person's ability to influence or persuade others to take a particular course of action. Power can come from being a leader, even without positional authority, and power can also come from being an expert – the power of knowledge. Hence, in a more organic structure, the power within the organization can change, depending on the task or function being undertaken.

A narrow span of 'control' makes it possible to supervise work tightly but it does not give assistant staff the opportunity to make decisions or feel a sense of commitment and achievement. Recreation needs highly motivated staff. Recreation also needs many specialists such as coaches, community leaders, park wardens and outdoor activity specialists, some literally 'paddling their own canoes', who need guidelines of principle and support, but also a level of autonomy rather than overt control and supervision. These staff develop skills peculiar to the job and special expertise. This technical know-how can be harnessed to improve motivation, job

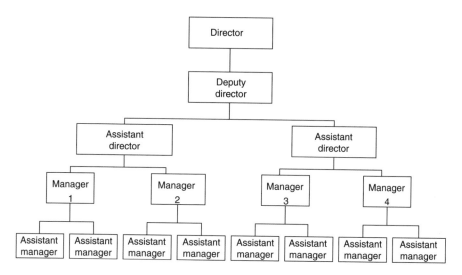

FIGURE 16.1 An organization with narrow spans of control

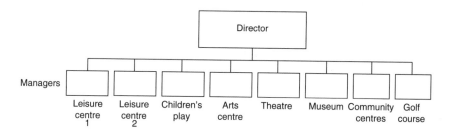

FIGURE 16.2 An organization with a wide span of control

satisfaction and involvement in decision making processes, which impinge on their area of work.

In local government recreation services many managers have responsibility for a large geographical area. Members of staff directed by a specific manager should not be situated too closely if this results in over-supervision. However, they should not be located too far away as this can lead to under-supervision.

Time is a very limiting factor. Every manager has to allocate time to: routine work which is usually delegated but must be monitored; regular work a manager must do himself or herself; special work and assignments and creative work. Executives and senior managers often give very little time to the routine super-visory work, the kind of face-to-face work with the workforce. Many pool supervisors, green-keepers, community art workers and play leaders would not be able to recognize the director of leisure services if he or she walked into their work situation. Hence, structures are needed in which the workforce feel involved. It seems logical therefore to have as broad a span as possible because fewer tiers reduce the remoteness of managers from staff; the lines of communication are shortened; broad spans tend to stretch and develop future managers; and fewer tiers of structure should save money and time.

16.4 Organization and staffing structures

It is important for managers in leisure services to have knowledge, experience and understanding of staff, staff relations and organizational structures. Managers will have to work within structures, often not of their choosing; they will have to be negotiators, decision makers, communicators and understanders of a wide variety of professional and lay staff. An appropriate staff structure will assist the manager in the achievement of the goals of any organization. However, it is not a panacea or alternative to good management. Rather, it is a means to an end. A 'good' structure as such does not exist in isolation; it is only good if it is good for the organization it serves. Furthermore, organization structures provide only a framework for management and staff to work within. The type of structure will depend on several important factors:

1   The nature of the controlling body (local authority; commercial entrepreneur; private club).
2   Aims and objectives of the organization (profit making; service orientation).
3   The stability of the environment in which the organization operates.
4   Distribution of facilities (localized; widespread).
5   Financial targets (subsidy; break-even; profit-making).
6   Scale and nature of the facilities and resources (sport or art-specific; multi-leisure).
7   Layout and design of facilities (compact; separated elements).
8   Nature of the service to be provided (community-based; sports development).
9   Levels of performance (top level; casual; formal; informal; beginners or a comprehensive range).
10 Quality of management and staff and the level of delegation possible.
11 The hours of operation.

Structured, well managed organizations can achieve more than a collection of individuals. Through the organization's pool of knowledge and resources, the necessary tasks can also be accomplished more quickly and efficiently. Further, organizations can meet many of the basic needs and requirements of its staff whilst at the same time giving them greater security.

16.4.1 Formal and informal organizations

There is a need to distinguish between informal and formal organizations.

A formal organization is a clearly defined structure that establishes relationships and differences in status, role, rank and levels of authority, in a controlled environment where rules exist with regard to channels of communication, accepted forms of behaviour and the manner in which key tasks have to be undertaken.

Additionally, such organizations have defined outcomes and in order to achieve these the overall work is divided amongst the workforce in a co-ordinated way so that they function as a unit or a department.

In contrast an informal organization has a much less defined structure. It is also likely to be much smaller in size, have a shorter life span and on occasions be composed of individuals who have made no conscious effort in forming a group. In certain circumstances an informal organization will be converted into a formal one, e.g. a collection of friends with a similar interest forming a club or society with rules and a constitution.

It is important for leisure managers to be aware that in every formal organization there is likely to be at least one informal organization that draws upon its 'membership' from different management levels and departments. Hence formal organizations also incorporate informal organizations. It is the informal relationships which provide for lateral communication rather than 'going through the channels' and where two-way communication leads to improved understanding. Much of the important 'human' work which makes an organization 'tick' is undertaken through cross-communication. While formal structures are required, managers should also encourage effective informal structures to enable the essential human dimension in organizations.

16.4.2 *Designing formal structures*

Forming an organization structure is like creating a building structure from building blocks – the work unit or the job of an individual worker is the smallest building block in the structure as a whole. Organizing is the process of dividing up the work in a structured framework. Managers have six distinct tasks in setting up the staffing structure:

1   Dividing the work or tasks into jobs.
2   Grouping similar tasks – usually by forming departments.
3   Specifying and controlling the relationships between the groups.
4   Delegating authority for carrying out the jobs or group of jobs; this is normally done via 'chains of command'.
5   Specifying the authority or control over the groups, which can be centralized or decentralized to varying levels.
6   In organizations like a large leisure centre, local authority department, theatre or park, creating 'line-and-staff' relationships.

Dividing the work up into jobs is easier when jobs are specialized or the tasks are narrow – grass cutting, ski instruction, cleaning, accounting. Specialization is essential for many tasks but leisure personnel are increasingly 'generalists' with specialist leanings – personnel officer-cum-duty officer. And also at a grass roots level, we have trainees at poolside who also carry out sports coaching and act as duty supervisors. Leisure jobs call for greater flexibility than factory jobs.

In some situations staff structures have been charted even before an organization has outlined its policies, objectives and target programmes. These are usually a copy of a structure elsewhere that may not even be appropriate. Such mismanagement is born out of the belief that it is the way in which squares and rectangles fit neatly into a comprehensive family tree and which lends support to the status quo that will find favour. But the first step should not be the discussion of a structure, rather an analysis of the organization and its policies which the structure is to serve.

Many leisure centres in the United Kingdom have tried to copy or to emulate a structure which has been developed elsewhere. Some standardization is useful and makes for efficiency. However, different areas have different priorities; each has its own identity; each has its own budget targets; and each has its own style. Structures must be developed which meet the needs of the situation. It is true that commercial chains provide a standardized structure, e.g. McDonald's, but they provide a standardized product also. Leisure services, which have a myriad of permutations, call for appropriate situational solutions.

Organization and staff structure should not be static, determined and fixed for ever. Structures must be changed to meet changing situations. For example, a manager usually comes into a structure previously determined, and finds ways of improving performance or ways in which the staff will respond to his or her ideas. Programmes will change; staff will develop and some will move on; and financial forecasts will alter. Therefore, appraisals, say, after one or two years should be undertaken and changes implemented to meet the new situation. It is said that we can be certain of only one thing – change. Changes in structure, changes in style and changes in objectives are always necessary over a period of years, but seldom implemented in public recreation services.

The staffing structure has an effect on the management of the organization, just as the activities themselves affect the programme and the organization. That is not to imply that the more staff one has, the better the management or more varied the programme. Rather the way staff are organized, deployed and motivated will have decided effects on the results.

Staff structures should be tailor-made to be appropriate. They also need to be altered to respond to situational changes

16.4.3 Departmental structures

Historically, departmentalization by numbers was the most frequent method in the organization of tribes and armies, but with the need for specialized staff, this method appears to be confined to the lower tiers of an organization, e.g. the army; factory production line; cleaning staff at a major event stadium.

To be effective, managers must divide the workload into manageable parts. The main purpose of dividing the work is to establish methods of determining individual groups, and section responsibilities, the distribution of authority to individuals and the processes of delegation. The most used method of dividing work is departmentalization, that is dividing the workforce into units and departments.

According to Grossman [2], there are four avenues managers can follow in creating departments.

1   *Function* – These are departments in which staff are grouped according to function, for example: sports coaching; arts and crafts; and maintenance.
2   *Clientele* – These departments are grouped according to the clientele they are to serve, for example: junior; youth; and senior citizens.
3   *Geographic* – Staff are grouped according to the area in which they work, for example: a large borough could have area or district departments.
4   *Process* – These are usually service-giving departments and grouped according to the process used in providing the particular services, for example an information service or counselling.

And to these can be added:

5   *Time or shift* – Staff are grouped in shifts to cover all the hours that a service or facility is open.

1. Functional departments

Functional departments are a logical and time-proven approach and are the most common method used in the leisure industry, e.g. parks department, arts and entertainment department. They encourage the use of specialization and hence make for the efficient use of staff. Also, authority is vested with the managers who are responsible for the organization's major functions.

Unfortunately, when different departments are competing for increased budgets the organization's objectives can be forgotten and greater loyalty given to the department, as distinct from the organization. All too frequently in public authorities, we find that the finance department is in the driving seat, with the emphasis being given to providing an efficient service at the expense of providing an effective service, concerned with meeting the needs of the community.

2. Client departments

Clientele departments encourage the staff to concentrate on clients' needs. Staff can develop an expertise within areas of specialization. They can also give confidence to the customers in that they feel they are being served by an understanding organization.

This method, however, can have its disadvantages. Some client groups may be difficult to clearly define, e.g. 'ethnic minorities', and they may feel patronized. Further, certain client groups may require specialist staff, e.g. counsellors, who may not necessarily be found among the organization's personnel. Service-giving departments, however, will need to have personnel – in house or external – who are both qualified and capable of giving the service.

3. Geographic departments

The advantages of geographic departments include decentralizing the service and placing responsibility with the managers and staff at lower tiers of the organization;

this gives these personnel the opportunity to take higher levels of responsibility and achieve job satisfaction. The staff involved in the decision making process, 'at the coal face', are likely to be aware of the needs and demands of their particular area and will be more accessible to their customers. Hence, the service provided is likely to be far more effective, given good staff with delegated powers.

This method of departmentalization, however, may require managers to have interdisciplinary knowledge, that in the leisure field covers sports, arts, play, entertainment, etc. It is also likely that there will be a degree of duplication of services with both the area management office and the Central Office having their own purchasing and promotion sections. Geographic departments require very reliable and capable staff or, because of their remoteness, regular and costly monitoring will need to be put in place.

4. Service or process departments

Some areas of work lend themselves to another word rather than 'department'; for example, counselling is better described as a service. Some local authorities use names which provide immediate recognition, e.g. youth service; access.

5. Departments based on time or shift patterns

These are usually at the lower levels of an organizational structure where the service extends well beyond the normal eight-hour working day. For example, a leisure centre that is open for some 100 hours per week will usually require three distinct shifts to cover the service it provides for the public. Problems can arise over co-ordinating of staff and with communication of information and instructions, whilst on a practical side, the hand-over by one shift to another can be problematical if tight procedures are not maintained. Running three shifts at a centre is a very expensive exercise. In the private sector, full staff shifts are used less. Managers and core staff work long hours and use support staff for essential peak times and for specialist timetabled services, e.g. fitness testing for two hours each evening.

The manager needs to understand the alternatives to develop the most appropriate departmental structure.

16.4.4 Formal and informal structures

Once the work is departmentalized, managers must make decisions relating to levels of authority. It is these decisions which establish chains of command within an organization. Authority levels establish the organization's power structure. Staff appointed to high authority levels have a greater say in group management decisions.

Inflexible, bureaucratic adherence to chains of command, however, is inappropriate for much of the 'gelling' of an organization. The structure is there as a framework. Within and around the formal structure there is very soon built up an informal structure: 'It is the informal structure which provides for cross-communication rather than going through the channels' [3]. Much of the important 'human' work which makes an organization 'tick' is undertaken through cross-communication. A recreation department and youth department, for example, often work out joint problems without going through their department channels.

An example of good cross-communication is shown at a leisure centre in Essex. Daytime integrated sports coaching classes are run for the community and college pupils – i.e. within the same space/time allocation, utilizing coaches from either organization. The possibility of these classes being held would have been remote if procedures and communications had been conducted through the formal structures of the county council and the technical college. The informal structure and communications network enabled those with first-hand knowledge to make decisions relating to work, which they are the best to advise upon. This informal process cuts across organizational boundaries, budgets, space and time allocations, staff and administrative red tape. One of the skills of the good manager is to permit, within certain limits, a level of face-to-face work which in essence bypasses the chain of command.

Nancy Foy [4] believes that it is time we 'humanized' our systems. We need not scrap them, as long as they remain human in scale. While organizations and the people in them need rituals and regular checkpoints, they also need information about their own work groups, their own outputs, and so on: 'A lot of information that can't be transmitted can normally flow informally, with complete credibility and confidentiality, once people believe they are hearing the truth and able to tell it as well.'

16.4.5 Line and line-and-staff organizations

Organizational charts normally depict 'line' organizations in which authority is passed on from the highest to the lowest levels via a chain of command. In line-and-staff organizations staff personnel are incorporated, in addition to 'line' staff. 'Staff' personnel are frequently specialists who service 'line' personnel, for example, financial, programming and personnel specialists. In many recreation organizations 'staff' sections have line staff under the direction of a sectional head. The principle of 'logical assignment', however, needs sensitive manipulation. The financial and technical officers at one leisure centre carry out their 'staff' functions in office hours, and their 'line' functions as duty managers in the evenings and at weekends.

'Line-and-staff' organizations are more flexible than 'line' organizations (Figure 16.3). They permit 'line' personnel to carry out the regular work – the use of the resources and the facilities by the public – leaving certain specialist functions to 'staff' personnel. Table 16.1 shows how the International City Management Association [5] differentiates the functions of line and staff.

Separate staff function advantages include: reduction in costs (one finance officer for several sections); an arm's-length objectivity; longer term stability; and specialist inputs into the organization. This provides service, advisory and planning information for managers and the organization [6]. A potential disadvantage is that

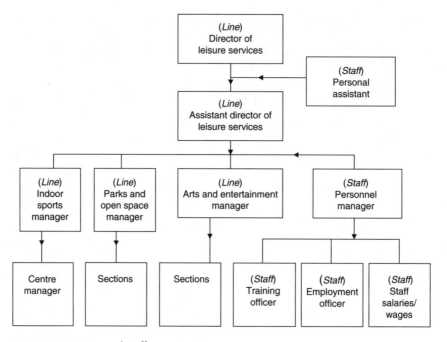

FIGURE 16.3 Line-and-staff organization

staff departments tend to grow at a faster rate than other departments, leading to greater overheads, administration and 'tail-wagging-the-dog' inclinations. Staff sections such as finance and planning can also gather undue power and influence.

In highly technical or bureaucratic organizations, line management and staff management equate to 'workers and staff'. The nature of a leisure service organization is suited to 'line-and-staff' systems, which create greater opportunities for all staff to provide customer service.

16.4.6 The organization chart

The organization chart is the most common approach to portraying the organization's structure. It illustrates the hierarchy, functions and chain of command. Strict adherence to charts and family trees is not advocated, but as a general framework it helps staff within an organization to visualize and understand, to see clear lines of authority and communication. Where a recreation service is geographically spread, or where there is difficulty in perceiving the roles of particular departments, the organization chart has considerable advantage. The organization chart, however, must not be given permanent status, as though it was indestructible. It portrays the organization, acts as a framework for sharing the work and indicates levels of responsibility. It should be used to further the work of the organization.

TABLE 16.1 Line functions and staff functions

Line functions	Staff functions
• Line directs or orders	• Staff advise
• Line has responsibility to carry out activities from beginning to end	• Staff studies, reports, recommends, but does not carry out
• Line follows chain of command	• Staff assists line but is not part of chain
• Line decides when and how to use staff for line use	• Staff always available
• Line is doing part of the organization	• Staff is the assisting part of the organization

Source: International City Management Association (1965), *Basic Concepts of Organization*, ICMA, Washington, DC

The structure, however, is not infallible; it has limitations. First, it is skeletal, in static form. It is representative only as long as the status quo remains. Second, it has little flesh about the skeleton; it is not precise about amounts of authority and responsibility. Third, and most important, it does not portray the essential informal structure and relationships.

The organizational structure, used wisely, is one of the tools to promote successful management performance. Because structures emphasize hierarchies, they confer status and 'pecking orders'. Some managers therefore become over concerned with preserving and enhancing the organization structure itself, rather than using it to help to serve the principles, aims and objectives of the organization. Organization charts serve a useful function in visualizing and reinforcing the organization and its structure. The picture-image, however, only illustrates a framework and should not become a sacred cow for bureaucracy.

16.5 Mechanistic and organic organizational models

The various organization structures used in the delivery of leisure services fall on a continuum between a mechanistic model which is rigidly structured, at one extreme to an organic model which is flexibly structured at the other (Figure 16.4).

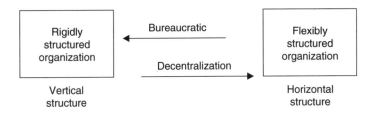

FIGURE 16.4 The mechanistic/organic continuum

The different models are outlined below, together with the characteristics; either more 'vertical' or more 'horizontal', and more or less 'bureaucratic'.

1. Mechanistic organization

- Operates more effectively when the environment is stable.
- Formal structures predominate.
- Control, authority and communication usually follow hierarchical patterns.
- The work is broken down into differentiated tasks with precise instructions that become highly standardized.
- Interaction tends to follow hierarchical lines between superior and subordinate.
- There is a general assumption that those higher up the hierarchy are better equipped to make the more important decisions.
- Operational actions tend to be governed by instructions issued by superiors.

2. Organic organization

- Better suited to operate in an environment where change is a factor – it is adaptable to changing conditions.
- Informal structures are permitted.
- One's special knowledge and experience are looked at in terms of what they can contribute to the overall task.
- Problems are not pushed upward, downward or sideways – i.e. 'buck-passing' is discouraged.
- Control, authority and communications move through a wide network rather than a single hierarchical structure.
- Communication tends to be more lateral than vertical and content consists of information and advice rather than instructions and handed-down decisions.
- Leadership in a given situation tends to fall to the person with the most appropriate expertise and ability in that field.

3. Vertical and horizontal structures and decentralization

Vertical organizations tend to be highly structured and the role expectations of staff strictly controlled, leaving little room for individual discretion and initiative. In contrast, horizontal organizations tend to be more loosely structured, with fewer constraints, leaving staff with considerable discretion to define their own roles in achieving the overall objectives. The right balance for maximum effectiveness must be achieved.

Peter Drucker [6] has often spoken of the need to decentralize structures: 'performance will be improved by de-centralization. It will make it possible for good men, hitherto stifled, to do a job effectively. It will make better performers out of mediocre men by raising their sights and the demands on them. It will identify the poor performers and make it possible for their replacement.

Decentralization can lead to decisions being made more quickly and nearer to the point of action. It reduces lines of communication, reduces status problems and provides greater job satisfaction [7]. However, decentralization is not appropriate to all situations.

4. Bureaucracy

Large organizations in the United Kingdom, including local authority services exhibit the culture of organizations based on bureaucracy. The turn-of-the-century German sociologist and politcal economist Max Weber extolled the virtues of organizations based on his 'bureaucratic' model, with principles of fixed rules, office hierarchy, levels of graded authority and written documents (files) which make up the 'bureau' – the office. Once established, organizations are difficult to dismantle. The bureaucratic model is the most widely implemented form of organization. It is a vertical structure. Authority is located at the top of the hierarchy and flows downwards through the organization. The division of labour emphasizes the hierarchical structure and establishes a superior/subordinate relationship. This allows the various activities to be subdivided into a specific set of tasks with the roles of individuals clearly defined.

5. The pyramid

Laurence Peter, a Canadian famous for coining the term 'the Peter Principle' (an individual in a hierarchy tends to rise to his or her level of incompetence) demonstrates in *The Peter Pyramid* [8], the ways in which profilerating bureaucracies sap human resources. Dr Peter perceives that the problem with major organizations is that they are constructed upside down, with the point of the operation almost invisible underneath the baggage of top-heavy administration.

A leisure service operation, looking to prune expenditure, often cuts away at jobs at the lower, delivery levels – the customer service elements: receptionists, grounds staff, coaching staff, cleaners, attendants – a solution least likely to effect a cure! It cuts off the hands that actually provide the service.

There is nothing wrong with an organizational model like a pyramid but, as Kenneth Blanchard and Patricia and Drea Zigarmi point out in *Leadership and the One Minute Manager* [9],

> The trouble comes when you think in a pyramid. . . . When you think in a pyramid, the assumption is that everyone works for the person above them on the organizational ladder. As a result, managers are thought to be 'responsible' for planning, organizing, and evaluating everything that happens in the organization while their staff are supposed to be 'responsible to the directives of management'. . . . I prefer to turn the pyramid upside down so that top managers are at the bottom. . . . When that happens there is a subtle, but powerful, twist in who is responsible and who should be responsive to whom.

Another problem with hierarchies is the belief that those at the top, who get paid more, are more essential to the organization than the staff below. This is mistaken, leads to poor use of human resources and is a recipe for job dissatisfaction.

6. The matrix organization

The matrix organization is a grid organization (Figure 16.5). Normally it is a combination of a functional departmentalization structure with an overlay of project managers, who are responsible for completing specific topics, e.g. feasibility study for a swimming pool. In this example the project manager can call upon the expertise in the different departments to assist in the production of the feasibility study: personnel on staffing aspects; technical services on producing the designs and projections and capital costs etc. The advantage associated with this structure is that it concentrates on the task in hand; staffing levels are minimal and technical experts are used as and when required.

Unfortunately, many problems can be encountered when using this form of organization such as role conflict and role ambiguity, which can produce tensions and possible work overload, or providing inadequate authority and power to the project managers, which can delay the project and result in time-consuming negotiation and meetings.

In order to make a matrix organization effective, objectives need to be clearly defined and known by all and delegated authority given at a senior level.

7. Leisure service delivery

The delivery of leisure services calls for flexibility and adaptability – different forms of organizational structure may suit different situations. Trust management,

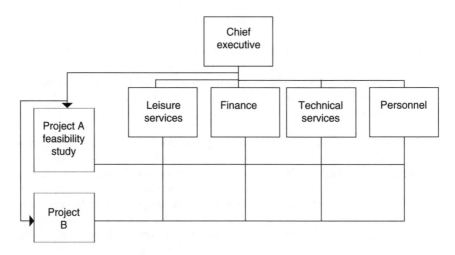

FIGURE 16.5 Matrix organization

partnership management or volunteer management, with different needs and resources, will require different structures. Sports, arts and outdoor leisure often call for specially created forms of 'looser' organizational structures. In such leisure environments with outreach workers, wardens, coaches, teachers and voluntary support groups, there will be a need to cultivate a management organization specially adapted for such situations.

Although leisure departments in local authorities appear, on paper, as clear-cut family trees, the extent of overlap and duplication and cross communications can be considerable. In some cases, the work gets done *despite* the constraining structure. Leisure service delivery sometimes calls for hybrid staffing structures, tailor-made for situations not normally found in other industries because leisure behaviour is different from work behaviour; it is far less predictable.

16.6 Staffing and legislation

The employment of staff and staff relations are governed, to a considerable extent, by government legislation. In recent years, there have been fundamental changes in the law in the United Kingdom, which have far-reaching consequences for employers and employees. Legislation has set new standards in personnel policies and in employer–employee relationships and has provided statutory bodies to enforce the new standards.

There are in the region of forty Acts of Parliament which have a bearing on staff relations and employment, most of which have been introduced or have been changed in the past three decades. Most legislation has put obligations and constraints on employers and extensive rights have been given to the employees. An exception was the *Industrial Relations Act 1971*, which, while imposing restrictions on management, had far more effect on unions; this Act, however, was repealed in 1974.

The new Acts have undoubtedly improved the working conditions and job security of employees in general (outside times of recession). The effects of the new legislation have been most dramatic on industry. They have been less dramatic in the public sector where many of the new obligations were already being practised, for example, equal pay. For all employers and employees, the position is now much clearer than in times past. Employees now have a much clearer idea of their position within their authority or place of employment; employers have a detailed procedural guide to employment matters. In theory, if the procedures are carefully and sensitively followed, there should be less conflict. However, despite legislation, tribunals and procedural guidelines, problems of employment and staff relations seem always to exist. They are primary factors in poor public relations, poor communications, mismanagement and low morale, all leading to less successful business enterprises, whether in the private, commercial or public sectors and whether in the context of factory, school, swimming pool or opera house.

Problems still arise and statutory bodies have been appointed to ensure that the law is adhered to. For example, Industrial Tribunals were established by the *Industrial Training Act 1964* as a type of court which is suitable for hearing matters of industrial relations legislation. The tribunals cover not only matters arising from that Act, but also the *Equal Pay Act 1970*, the *Sex Discrimination Act 1975*, the *Employment Protection Act 1989* and the *Race Relations Act 1976*, as well as several others. Appeals go before the Employment Appeals Tribunal.

Much of the work carried out in the field of recreation and leisure is subject to these Acts. Unsocial hours, special duties and overtime hours of full-time staff have to be handled along with part-time staff, volunteers and temporary staff. The kinds of work and the complex nature of recreation programmes often produce the pressures which cause tensions and can lead to disputes. Managers should be aware of the laws which regulate staff relations. A thumbnail sketch of some of the relevant Acts of Parliament follows.

1   The *Sex Discrimination Act 1975* makes it unlawful to discriminate in employment, education and training in Britain on grounds of sex, or marriage. The Equal Opportunities Commission was established to enforce the legislation and individuals have the right to complain to courts and industrial tribunals. The law covers recruitment and existing employees in matters like promotion. The employment provisions were amended by the *Sex Discrimination Act 1986* to bring legislation in line with the European Community directives on equality and restrictions on the maximum hours of women employed in industrial undertakings were repealed.

The *Employment Act 1989* amends the *Sex Discrimination Act 1975*, in pursuance of the directive of the Council of the European Communities, on the implementation of the principle of the equal treatment for men and women as regards access to employment, vocational training and promotion and on working conditions.

2   The *Race Relations Act 1976* makes it unlawful to discriminate on grounds of colour, race, nationality or ethnic origin. Individuals have access to civil courts and industrial tribunals. The Commission for Racial Equality was established to enforce the legislation.

3   The *Health and Safety at Work Act 1974* has the purpose of 'securing the health, safety and welfare of people at work and to provide for the protection of the public whose health and safety might be affected by work activities'. The 1974 Act is superimposed on previous acts of legislation, some of which still apply. Previous legislation, however, only covered two-thirds of the labourforce; now everyone, except domestic staff, is covered. The general principle underlying the Act is that employers, in consultation with their employees, will draw up health and safety arrangements, within the broad obligations of the law to suit their own work areas.

The 1974 Act established the Health and Safety Commission, responsible for developing policies, including guidance, codes of practice and proposals for regulations. The Act also set up the Health and Safety Executive, which includes a government inspectorate covering a number of work activities. Regulations introduced in 1988 to control exposure to nearly all substances hazardous to health in all places of work represent the most significant health and safety legislation since the 1974 Act.

4   The *Equal Pay Act 1970*, amended by the *Equal Pay (Amendment)*

Regulations 1988, requires men and women to be paid the same rates of pay for doing the same or broadly similar work, or work of equal value. The purpose of the Act is to eliminate discrimination in pay and other employment matters: holidays, sickness benefit, bonus, overtime, etc.

5   The *Employment Protection Act 1975* and the *Employment Protection Consolidation Act 1978* (as amended by the *Employment Act 1982*) provide the machinery for promoting good industrial relations and give employees certain rights, including: maternity rights; rights for time off work either paid or unpaid for certain reasons; written statements of main terms and conditions of employment; an itemized pay statement for employees; and protection against unfair dismissal. The 1975 Act also set up ACAS, the Advisory, Conciliation and Arbitration Service.

6   The employment of young people and children in certain occupations is governed by the *Young Persons Employment Act 1938* and the *Employment of Children Act 1973*. These Acts make provision for the employment of young people under the age of 18. These are divided into two groups: young people over school-leaving age but under 18, and children below school-leaving age. Section 10 of the *Employment Act 1989* makes amendments relating to the employment of young persons.

7   The *Industrial Training Act 1964*, amended by Acts in 1973 and 1981, was consolidated by the *Industrial Training Act 1982* which is the principal Act relating to industrial training.

8   Two Acts were passed in 1969, the *Employers Liability (Compulsory Insurance) Act*, which stated that all employees must be insured, by the employers, against industrial injury or disease; the certificate must be placed where all can see it. The *Employers Liability (Defective Equipment)* Act stated that any injury suffered by an employee, through defective equipment was deemed to be the employer's fault. The employer can counter-claim against the supplier or employee for negligence.

9   Major changes to trade union legislation have been introduced by the government through four Acts: the *Employment Acts 1982, 1988* and *1989* and the *Trade Union Act 1984*. During much of the twentieth century, trade unions and their officials and members have enjoyed immunity from legal action when organizing certain industrial activities. The *Trade Union Act 1984* removed legal immunity from trade unions which call a strike without first holding a properly conducted secret ballot of members concerned and securing a majority vote for this action. The *Employment Act 1988* provided for the removal of the remaining statutory support for the closed shop. The *Employment Act 1989* removed civil law immunity from those organizing certain forms of secondary action and limited lawful picketing to peaceful picketing at the pickets' own workplace.

10 The *Employment Rights Act 1996* consolidated a number of enactments including *Employment Acts 1980, 1982, 1989, 1990, Wages Act 1986* and the *Betting, Gaming and Lotteries Act 1963*. Under the Act, employees must be given a written statement of particulars of employment. Minimum periods of notice must be given. Contracts must give details of dates, rates of pay, hours, holidays, sick leave, pension rights and discipline and grievance procedures.

The Act establishes the right of employers and employees to a minimum period of notice.

11   The *Disabled Persons (Employment) Act 1944*, supplemented by the *Disabled Persons (Employment) Act 1958*, imposed upon employers of 20 or more employees a duty to employ a quota of disabled persons. These provisions were repealed by the *Disability Discrimination Act 1995*, which establishes a statutory right of non-discrimination for disabled people in employment.

Not included in this section are a range of other Acts of Parliament that affect the leisure industry and thus the people working in it. For example, the Acts relating to compulsory competitive tendering have had a profound effect. The pending legislation relating to 'Best Value' will also have far reaching effects on local government and, hence, leisure personnel. The *Education Reform Act 1988* (see Section 9.5) introducing local management of schools and legislating on the community use of schools, and *The Children Act 1989* (see Section 9.6) providing duties and powers in the way children's activities are regulated, have also had substantial effects on the employment of personnel. The range of Acts impinging on leisure include legislation on: office premises; fair trading; consumer safety; supply of goods; public health; town and country planning; water resources; the countryside; licensing and lotteries; gaming; fire precautions; football spectators; and others.

In summary, these Acts of Parliament and other legislation illustrate the legal and contractual implications of employer and employee and these laws affect leisure organizations. What follows – the recruitment of staff and production of a staff handbook – are thus of relevance.

16.7   Staff recruitment and selection

Staff selection is one of the most important functions of employers and managers. Successful management is dependent on good staff. Good staff assist in leading an organization towards its goals. They work together to achieve objectives; they overcome difficulties, they solve problems. They are flexible in both spirit and deed.

Poor staff are a millstone. They make for ineffective organizations and lack flexibility and create blockages in the system; they become a heavy burden for the organization, resulting in redundancies, at best, and to ineffective organizations at worst; and they expend considerable funds of energy of the organization, which could otherwise have been effectively applied to meeting objectives. It is important therefore to select staff wisely [10].

16.7.1   Methods of selection

Selecting the right people for the right jobs is of crucial importance to an organization's prosperity. Selecting staff is basically about judging other people and their abilities and their appropriateness for the job. In addition to the standard letters, curricula vitae and application forms, there are many methods or combinations of methods for shortlisting or selecting staff:

1   promotion internally
2   on recommendation
3   'head hunted'
4   written presentations
5   verbal presentations
6   discussion groups
7   personality testing
8   agency shortlisting or recruitment
9   consultancy advice
10 interview.

Personnel selection has become a major sphere of management and has been subject to considerable 'scientific' investigation. Measuring the qualities of leadership potential, emotional stability, and the like, have been part and parcel of civil service selection boards, for example, throughout this century. However, in spite of the research and development of psychological tests of intelligence and personality, the job of selection remains inexact and subjective. The interview, in spite of its critics, remains the primary method of assessing and selecting staff. The standard local government format with leisure and recreation posts is that of: application form; shortlist; references; and a half-hour interview by a panel. The task is to match the person to the job.

1. The right man or woman for the right job

Who will make the judgement? People's innate skills in judging and selecting staff varies and some, given the responsibility, are wholly inadequate. Finding the right person for the job is a time-consuming and expensive business. It becomes even more expensive when tackled badly because the wrong person may be selected.

Two of the main problems employers bring on to themselves is either choosing a poor candidate or finding a good candidate, but one who does not fit the post. This may mean changing the job to meet the qualities of the candidate or living with a mismatch.

In leisure, wages, salaries and associated costs form a significant proportion of operational costs. The efficient recruitment and utilization of manpower is an important management responsibility and can offer scope for both improved performance and cost savings.

2. Job descriptions, conditions and person profiles

The job 'description', 'conditions' and the 'specification' of the qualities needed to fit the job are quite distinct. The job description describes the job, its functions, responsibilities and what the employers' expectations are in terms of carrying out the job. Its major concerns are with the nature of the work itself and the achievements necessary to meet the goals of the organization. Job descriptions for senior posts should never be fixed and strictly demarcated, or they will become a straitjacket, limiting the development of the job and the person. They should serve as parameters and guidelines encouraging initiative, growth and job enrichment. Staff should have titles and job descriptions which give them a broad scope of duties and which do not limit their function.

The person specification sets out the ideal credentials required from candidates to fit the job. The specification is not a detailed description of the job. The job conditions set out what the employer has to offer in terms of conditions of service, pay, benefits and prospects. The 'person specification' and the 'job description' are often combined in one document, but selection panels ought to match personal credentials to the requirements of the job.

3. Learning from professional selectors

The leisure industry has much to learn from professional selectors of people. Leisure employers, by the nature of their function, usually lack the continuous interviewing experience and the knowledge needed to probe the job market effectively. Too often local government interview panelists, local authority members, for example, pride themselves on their ability to make instant decisions about people. They work on feelings and hunches. With good judges of people's character and ability that may be fine, but with biased or poor judges the results can be disastrous both for the organization and the new employee. Interviewing and selecting staff are difficult and inexact exercises, but guidelines or 'outside' or 'informed' help can reduce uncertainties and chance. For example, a good agency or consultancy service will have a selection procedure which has been rigorously tested through practical experience and good results.

16.7.2 A selection process

Selecting the right person is made more effective if a logical sequence is followed, which is based on proven successful methods. Video Arts films [10] illustrate selection techniques and the need for a methodical process. In simple terms, there are five key steps:

1   *Describe and define the job* – Should you fill the old one? Should you create a new one? Can you re-allocate the workload? It is wise to avoid seeking a replica of the previous job holder as no two people are alike and the job will have changed. Instead use the vacancy to bring about necessary change and improvement. The job description defines the job.

2   *Specify or 'profile' the person whose qualities are likely to meet the requirements of the job* – Detail the expertise, experience, skills and qualifications that are likely to fit the job. Describe the personal qualities being sought, the demands of the job and the people already working in the team.

3   *Set out the conditions of the job* – i.e. pay, benefits and prospects.

4   *Choose methods of communicating and publicizing the job vacancy, seeking to match the person to the job* – This may require a range of internal

communications, outside advertising and professional advice from specialist recruitment sources.

5   *Select sensitively, carefully and methodically* – Haphazard selection can be ineffective and unfair. Probe, search and enable candidates to express their capabilities, enthusiasm, weaknesses and strengths. Selection is choosing the right and best person who fulfils the needs of the job, the tasks and the relationships with others and who is well satisfied with the conditions for employment.

Selectors need to satisfy themselves on these main points.

1   Is the candidate capable of doing the job?
2   Does he or she have the qualities and real credibility in the field?
3   Will the candidate fit well into the organization and get on well with people?
4   Is he or she the best of the capable candidates?
5   Is it the right person for the right job?
6   Does he or she have the courage to do the right things, not just the ability to do things right and so assist the organization towards its goals successfully?
7   Is the candidate happy with the terms and conditions?

Investment in people pays off. Staff employed will require a high level of dedication if the full potential of leisure service and facilities are to be realized. They will also need to be appraised as part of their development and for the good of the organization.

16.8   Staff appraisal

Staff need to be effective. If they are also motivated, they will experience a sense of worthwhileness, a value far beyond salaries and conditions. Being effective does not mean having certificates hanging on the office wall, it means meeting in full measure the requirements of the job. Therefore, staff need to know exactly what is required of them and how they are performing. Appraisal provides the opportunity to achieve better results. However, a formal system is no substitute for on-the-spot action. Appraisals, used inappropriately, can become mechanical and ineffective; there is no need to wait for the appraisal day to offer counsel and feedback. Most people want to do a good job and to be valued. Sometimes, appraisals have been used for discipline, with staff being 'hauled over the coals'. Immediate problems – sloppiness and poor service – should be dealt with here and now. The appraisal system, in contrast, should be positive and constructive, measuring performance against management expectations, over time.

There are different appraisal systems. The system which is chosen should meet the objectives. 'Comparative' systems compare one employee's performance with others; they do not allow for two-way communication. 'Absolute' methods are more independent. They include: writing a report on the employee, which is limited by subjectivity; appraising an individual against specified traits such as initiative; rating an employee on a numerical or alphabetical scale; and a range of more sophisticated techniques. Peer group appraisal is one method which has advantages but employees tend to band together in collectives supporting each other. In this atmosphere of pulling together, it is awkward and perceived as disloyal to single out work colleagues. Results-orientated appraisals focus on performance against set objectives. They are less open to subjectivity and bias and are more amenable to performance improvement. Key determinants are the job objectives themselves. The appraisal system needs to fit into the culture of the organization. Some organizations keep results close to their chests; others have an openness which enhances mutual trust and respect.

Operating an appraisal system requires resources, time and effort. The investment needs to be justified. The specific benefits will depend on the objectives. There can be benefits to the person being appraised – the appraisee, to the person doing the appraisal – the appraiser, and to the organization.

The benefits to the appraisee are several. Employees need to know how well they are doing. On-going feedback tends to be task-specific; the appraisal, on the other hand, is concerned with the overall performance over time. Overall achievements can be formally recognized and documented. While somewhat contrived, an appraisal system is above board. It is better than conducting an unstructured appraisal behind closed doors, without the employee knowing anything about it. Staff are affected by the way in which they are managed. Employees may not be given enough attention, sufficient resources or authority or may not have had their jobs clearly explained. Some staff are unclear as to the objectives of their job; when these are clarified, accepted and owned, priorities can be set far more easily.

The appraisal system has benefits to the appraiser. It provides a structured way to feed back to each of the team; any criticisms will be in the context of the job as a whole; objectives and priorities can be clarified by two-way communication. The line manager has a means of forward planning, setting each team member individual targets.

Managers need feedback on their own styles of management and the appraisal system should enable employees to talk frankly about how a manager's style affects their work.

Hence, feedback to the manager can explore opportunities, resolve problems, obtain commitment and, by tackling contentious issues, staff turnover could be reduced. Opportunities are provided also to discuss the chances of promotion. Frank assessments as to one's prospects can be made and advice as to further career counselling can be given, though this should be outside the focus on current and improved performance.

There are also benefits to the organization. If organizations value their employees and show commitment to them, improved performance should result. The system will identify and collate training needs. It can help to measure the strengths of the staff, whether the right people are in the right jobs, whether they can fill vacancies, and who is right for promotion. Staffing strategies can be determined. Without appraisal, some key issues might be overlooked.

The appraiser needs to be someone who knows about the appraisee and the job description and must be skilled in listening and dealing with sensitive issues, and have the ability to review successes and areas for improvement, looking forward with confidence. Focussing on the past tends to be negative. The appraisal should not dwell on pay or conditions, except where these adversely affect the job. Performance related pay (PRP) is a reasonable proposition – the higher the performance, the higher the pay. However, in leisure management, with complex permutations in the measurement of outputs, it can be insensitive to single out particular performances from the overall accomplishments. Pay reviews are best left out of staff appraisals.

Appraisal reports could include: measurement of current duties; professional and technical competence; approach to work; loyalty; supervision of staff; upward and downward communication; interpersonal skills; achievements since previous appraisal; overall performance; and readiness for further responsibilities.

The appraisal should end on a positive note and an unambiguous agreement between appraiser and appraiseee as to the goals and expectations between now and the next appraisal. A succinct report should be filed and it is wise to review the report with the member of staff and for both to sign it. The report should be used to check the employee's progress until the next appraisal interview. It is a means of motivating, improving performance, inculcating positive attitudes and planning for the future.

Staff appraisals are largely private affairs, kept to a core group: appraisee; appraiser(s); and legal/personnel manager. The system must be, and must be seen to be, fair, non-discriminatory and equal. In a climate where there is greater supply of personnel than demand, and where jobs for life no longer apply, procedures are needed to deal with promotions and, regrettably, redundancy. Faced with these difficult circumstances, managers having to make painful judgements about who to keep and who to let go can be aided by sound appraisal systems. Appeals procedures must be known to all and carried out by managers at a level to overturn previous decisions.

16.9 Staff handbook

The right staff need to be employed, trained, nurtured and enabled to perform well for the organization and themselves. A staff handbook is a useful communications document but only if it is read, understood, accepted and used, and as long as it is sufficiently flexible to meet changing circumstances. Working by the rule-book can be like 'working to rule' – the kiss of death to an organization, if ever there was one. Many organizations have wonderful personnel policies on paper; unfortunately, that is *all* they appear to be.

The information-giving handbook can provide a valuable source of reference for managers and staff. It should back up and support the face-to-face, two-way communications and staff training. It should welcome, introduce, inform, explain and give new and existing staff a picture of a businesslike, friendly organization that cares about its customers, its staff, its products and services.

The handbook's production should be clear, unambiguous and authoritative. It should be attractive and well produced, but not expensive, impracticable or glossy. It needs to be indexed for easy reference, personal and friendly in its style and suited to its readers, yet factual and concise. The handbook is basically an exercise in communication. It is essential therefore that management and staff are consulted fully as to its contents and style and its distribution, in order to achieve cooperation and acceptance. An *aide-memoire* for producing a comprehensive handbook [11] is set out below.

Producing a handbook for staff – a guideline with twenty key sections

1. Introduction and welcome

- personal message of welcome from Chairman or Chief Executive
- general aims of organization, its background and history, the current position and priorities
- the products and services and their value to the customers
- the organization structure and committee, departmental and staffing structure
- an employment and personnel policy statement
- a policy statement on excellence in relationship with the public and customer care

2. Recruitment and selection

- documentation required – references, medical certificate, etc.
- personnel records and notification of changes
- probationary or trial periods

3. Contract of employment

Inform new employees they will receive a written statement within the legally permitted time and what that statement will cover. Inform staff of their legal rights in these matters.

4. Induction, training and assessment

The sooner a new employee can be used effectively, the greater the organization's effectiveness. The job and the environment are inextricably linked.

- induction and familiarization systems
- essential training provided and additional training opportunities
- methods of appraisal and assessment
- job evaluation and review
- opportunities for promotion
- career development

5. Salaries and wages

The legalistic mind of the employer is matched by that of the employee. The handbook must be unambiguous.

- statement on payment system
- precise methods of payment
- deductions – e.g. income tax (PAYE), national insurance contributions and any others
- additional payments – e.g. special, overtime, bonus
- allowances for particular duties or circumstances of unsocial hours
- expenses – e.g. travel, car, refreshment
- procedures relating to pay reviews, alterations to pay, etc.
- incentive pay or bonuses

6. Hours of work

- normal working hours
- flexitime
- timekeeping, starting and finishing times
- evening, weekend, overtime and other special hours
- meal and rest entitlements
- variation of hours
- time off in lieu

7. Time off and absence

- procedures for notification of absence
- time off and under what terms for public duties – e.g. political, magistrates, jury service
- maternity and paternity rights
- sick pay scheme and Statutory Sick Pay (SSP) entitlements
- medical certificates
- unauthorized absence
- requests for special unpaid leave
- hospital, dental and other personal appointments

8. Holidays

- annual holiday entitlements
- holiday increases for long service
- public holidays and 'in lieu' entitlements
- holiday pay and special pay on termination of employment

9. Fringe benefits

Fringe benefits are part of the total job environment. The handbook should set out in general terms the opportunities and benefits open to the staff as a whole.

- housing scheme
- insurances
- medical scheme
- car purchase
- educational and training opportunities
- social, leisure and recreation opportunities
- incentive schemes and other benefits

10. Amenities and facilities

Leisure organizations will have services and amenities to offer employees. These benefits make up the job environment and can help maintain harmony and goodwill. They can also be a source of discontent if handled unfairly or perceived to be unfair. The handbook should set out:

- use of the telephone – a statement to say in what circumstances
- use of 'company' facilities and products
- personnel, welfare, medical and information services
- staff meals and refreshments
- free memberships or use of leisure facilities
- discounted services and facilities
- 'company' clubs and societies
- social amenities
- use of amenities by family members and friends

11. Trade unions

- the right to join or not to join a trade union
- the unions and their position within the organization
- trade union representatives

12. Health and safety

Responsibility, legally, falls on both employer and employee. Set out those responsibilities.

- policy statement, including safety officer role
- general procedures and sources of information
- safety regulations
- fire precautions and drills
- hospital, doctor, first-aid procedure
- emergency procedures

13. Property

- security of the business plant, supplies, equipment, money and property within and outside the premises
- security of personal belongings
- the right of search
- lost property procedures for public and staff

14. Disciplinary rules and procedures

Rules are needed for safety, fairness and efficiency. However, careful and sensitive wording is needed to convey collective responsibility and good individual conduct, rather than penalites for misconduct.

15. Grievances

The law sets out procedures to enable staff to seek redress of any grievance. The handbook should set out the legal procedures and the three grievance stages that must be followed.

16. Staff counselling, mentoring and personal problems

Problems may stem from inside or outside the job. In the work situation counselling is needed before rules and procedures come into play. Home circumstances or personal and domestic problems can lead to low morale and poor efficiency. Good listeners are essential. The organization may have established a mentoring system, in which case employees can be informed how they go about participating in the scheme. Counselling, far from offering advice, is non-directive – i.e. a counsellor or mentor helps a colleague to come to terms with the situation and find the solution himself or herself. The handbook should inform staff where to go for help and what to do.

17. Staff involvement

It is good practice to involve staff in the decision making process. Marketing a successful organization with a good public image makes for a high staff morale and *esprit de corps*. The handbook should explain the ways in which staff can take a 'share' in shaping and keeping a successful organization:

- 'shares' in the success of the organization
- joint consultative committees
- staff representation
- meetings

- suggestion schemes
- notices
- 'in house' magazine
- 'company' events – for itself, staff families, charity, etc.

18. Retirement and pensions

Organizations should prepare staff for retirement.

- retirement policy and entitlement
- voluntary early retirement and benefits
- pensions
- retirement courses and planning

19. Termination of employment

- notice entitlements
- redundancy
- discharge

20. New clauses and changes

16.10 Leisure service and facility guidelines

Outlined below are twenty suggestions for improving leisure service staffing.

Guidelines for facility staffing and staff structures

1   *Understand the aims and objectives of the organization*
2   *Select staff wisely and logically* – Match the qualities of the candidate to the job – the right person for the right job.
3   *Train and deploy* – The way staff are trained and deployed affects results.
4   *Study legislation* – Legislation affects both employer and employee.
5   *Understand management principles* – Recognize the limitations of span of control and use of 'unity of command' and 'logical assignment'.
6   *Create formal structures* – Provide for clear lines of authority. People like to know 'where they stand'.
7   *Flatten hierarchies* – Horizontal structures encourage empowering staff to take on responsibility.
8   *Permit informal structures* – Recognize the importance of cross-communications.

9   *Construct departments and decentralize* – Divide the work into units and identify functions. Identify tasks and responsibilities attached to each position. Encourage decentralization.

10 *Start with essential staff* – When opening new facilities, start with essential staff and then build up as needs dictate. The full-time staff positions should be limited to immediate recognizable functions. To cope with initial, additional demands, core staff should be encouraged to 'go the extra mile' led by the manager, and use trainee and part-time staff.

11 *Create team management* – Recognize the value of team management to co-ordinate long hours and a varied programme.

12 *Use 'line-and-staff' approaches* – Avoid rigid 'line' structures. Consider appropriate hybrids to meet particular situations.

13 *Make conditions flexible* – The complexity, hours and patterns of use of leisure facilities call for flexible conditions which encourage initiative and do not limit staff functions.

14 *Consider alternative structures* – Appraise the relative value of additional, different forms of community recreation management – train and support voluntary assistants, outreach service workers, animateurs, etc., consider job sharing. Consult with trade unions.

15 *Produce staff handbook*

16 *Establish management information systems* – Use the organization structure to best effect in disseminating information and in communications.

17 *Establish an appraisal system*

18 *Use structures as means, not ends* – A structure chart is a management tool. It must be used. It must be changed to meet changing situations. Do not be preoccupied with structures and family trees. Structures are means towards ends, not ends in themselves.

19 *Empower staff* – Many management gurus believe that tomorrow's business organizations will be non-hierarchical and where a wide range of talented staff will be 'empowered' to handle resources and make managerial decisions.

20 *Reward staff collectively for successes* – From time to time, say twice a year, when excellent results or efforts have been made, reward the staff with a party, a gift or some novel 'event'.

16.12 Summary – staffing

This chapter has been concerned with staff and staffing structures within leisure and recreation organizations. It is clear that Leisure Managers should understand the way in which staff are employed, trained and deployed in order to maximize efficiency, bring out the best in staff and lead the organization towards its goals.

The manager should understand relevant employment legislation and the principles of management as they relate to staffing, the formulation of organization structures and the specialist responsibilities of selection and staffing functions within leisure and recreation services and facility management. However, managers should not be preoccupied with organizational charts and family trees.

The organization chart must not be given permanent status, as though it were indestructible. Jobs need to change because situations change. Structures therefore must also change or adapt.

Leisure organizations deal with people in their leisure time, who have a variety of choice. Leisure organizations therefore need to be sufficiently flexible to be appropriate to the needs and demands of their customers. They have to be more organic in structure than most other industries and businesses. They have more scope to pursue greater results than purely financial bottom-line policies. Clearly, organizations such as Leisure Services businesses, are more than structures and systems. Strategies and processes should come before structures.

Notes and references

1   International City Management Association (1965), *Basic Concepts of Organization. Bulletin 3, Effective Supervisory Practices.* ICMA, Washington, DC.
2   Grossman, A. H. (1980), *Personnel Management in Recreation and Leisure Services*, Groupwork Today, South Plainfield, NJ, p. 64.
3   *ibid.*, p. 65.
4   Foy, N. (1981), 'The human side of information', *Management Review and Digest*, October.
5   International City Management Association (1965), *Basic Concepts of Organization*, (3), p. 5.
6   Drucker, P. F. (1955), *The Practice of Management*, Pan Books, London.
7   e.g. Elliott, G. (ed.) (1989), *The Manager's Guidebook*, Longman, Harlow, Section 4.6 (Instalment 5); for other personnel aspects, see section 9.
8   Peter, L. (1986), *The Peter Pyramid*, Allen & Unwin, London.
9   Blanchard, K., Zigarmi P. and Zigarmi D., (1986), *Leadership and the One Minute Manager*, Collins, London.
10 See Video Arts films, and read Briefcase booklets, Davies, C. (1988), *When Can You Start?*, Tietjen, T. (1978) *How Am I Doing?*, and Honey, P. (1987) *Can You Spare A Moment*, Video Arts, London.
11 Specific practical evidence was gained from the general manager and staff at Harlow Sportcentre.

Chapter seventeen

Leisure and recreation management education and training

Leisure is a growth industry of national significance both in social and economic terms. Jobs in tourism and leisure amount to approximately 2.5 million, 6 per cent of the workforce in the United Kingdom. Employment on this scale raises substantial questions about training and career development in the emerging profession of leisure and recreation management. In a time of change, growth and complexity, there need to be sound principles, objectivity and excellent leadership. In a relatively new industry, without adequate professional foundation stones, these factors are of significance in establishing a professional ethos.

Education and training therefore are of vital importance at all levels of leisure and recreation management. Without men and women of vision and standing at top management level, and without qualified and trained staff at all levels, no leisure service can hope to be efficient, let alone effective in meeting the needs and aspirations of its customers.

There exists some confusion over the use of the three terms 'management training', 'development' and 'education'. At times these terms appear to be interchangeable, and sometimes one term may be all embracing, encompassing three meanings in one. Management education may be seen as a process of active learning and enquiry (including learning from one's peers), with learner input a necessary part of this process. Management training may be seen as an input process from teacher to learner, whereby the learner is equipped with the specific job-related knowledge and skills needed to carry out his or her job successfully. Management development may be seen as encompassing both management education and training, increasing the manager's adaptability and flexibility, maximizing his or her strengths and overcoming weaknesses.

Although all three terms are identified here, for the sake of simplicity when discussing the issues, the term 'training' will be used to embrace all three, although it is recognized that it is a far from satisfactory description.

First, the potential market for training is identified. Second, a brief historical record is noted of the ways in which government and its agencies have tried to establish training in the field. Third, the need for training and the content of courses – in broad principle – is considered. Fourth, government initiatives are described: National Vocational Qualifications; national training organizations; modern apprenticeships; national traineeships; and 'New Deal'. Fifth, training in the Hospitality Industry is mentioned briefly; and sixth, the question of whether leisure management is an emerging or an emerged profession is discussed.

Having read this chapter, readers will appreciate the need for training in order to help establish professional – trained and competent – men and women in leisure management. They will understand that a need exists for education, training and career development and that it is only through a systematic process that the needs of staff and the organizations can be met effectively. Readers will become aware of the shortcomings of a number of current courses in the United Kingdom and should be challenged as to how best to provide training which is good for students, trainees and the leisure business.

17.1   Potential training market

Any coherent system of training must be structured around the needs of the people it is intended to serve. If training is to be effective we need to ask, 'who is it for?', before we can ask, 'what should it be?'

The leisure industry is a vast one; and the number of people employed both as managers and subordinates has increased substantially over the past thirty years. Although it is difficult to determine the precise number of people employed in the leisure industry, in 1988 it was estimated that this was in the region of 1.6 million (excluding the voluntary sector), of which approximately 1 million were in what one may loosely term 'tourism' [1]. The approximate breakdown of the employees is shown in Table 17.1.

Since that time, the leisure industry has expanded but the general picture appears to be similar. In 1990 [1], it was estimated that there were over 750,000 leisure 'managers' in the voluntary sector, nearly all of whom are unpaid and occupy official posts such as chairmen and women, secretaries, treasurers, and so on. Hence, the current and potential training market is exceptionally large and so is the range of courses required to meet the training needs of many different personnel. It can be subdivided into three main categories:

TABLE 17.1 Employees in employment in Great Britain 1996

Categories of leisure management	Numbers employed – full-time equivalents
Hotels and accommodation	338,000
Bars	398,000
Restaurants	341,000
Canteens	183,000
Recreational, cultural and sporting activities	530,000

Source: *Annual Abstract of Statistics*, (1997)

1   *Personnel employed within the leisure industry* – This includes people involved in the public, voluntary and commercial sectors, covering arts, sports, play, entertainment, etc; and it also includes a range of posts in junior, middle and top management, supervisory level staff, technical/manual staff (incorporating bar, catering staff, etc.) and administrative/reception staff.
2   *Personnel in other industries* – Many related industries and professions have connections with or require leisure management knowledge and skills; this category includes managers and staff employed in education, dual use centres, industrial sports clubs, outdoor pursuit centres, community centres and youth clubs, etc.
3   *Individuals seeking employment within the leisure industry* – These include school-leavers without leisure qualification, college students with a qualification, and those wishing to change career.

This illustrates something of the range of courses required to meet the training needs of many different personnel.

17.2   Recent history in an emerging profession

The concept of leisure and recreation management, as we know it today in the United Kingdom, has only emerged since the mid-1960s, as a direct result of the development of indoor sport and recreation centres. Prior to that time, various 'professional' bodies had been running training courses and awarding institution qualifications for many years, with some institutions going back to the 1920s. However, these qualifications were of a technical nature and did not cover the broad spectrum of leisure and recreation management. One long-standing institution, the Institute of Sport and Recreation Management (ISRM; formerly the Institute of Baths Management), has not only survived, but also prospered, with an extensive programme of training courses and its own qualifications.

The need for professional management of recreation centres prompted the Sports Council to set up a working party that reported its findings, *Professional Training for Recreation Management*, in 1969 [2], which led to the first postgraduate/post-experience courses and qualifications.

The reorganization of local government in 1974 brought about new comprehensive leisure departments and a greater awareness was created as to the benefits of improved management of recreation in the public sector. There was also a growing realization that recreation management should be applied to a much broader field than was once appreciated. This growth led to the instigation of a government working party. The Recreation Management Training Committee (the Yates Committee) was appointed in 1977 by the Secretaries of State for Education and Science and for the Environment [3]. The report called for a co-ordinated, strategic approach to the planning of recreation management training. It took several years to produce the final report and its actual publication [4] was further delayed until 1984, which reduced the expected impact. Moreover, its recommendations were never implemented. One of its cornerstones – the enhancement of Regional Management Centres (RMCs) – was thwarted, with the demise of many of the RMCs. Further, another of the recommendations of creating a single professional institute had been overtaken with the formation of the Institute of Leisure and Amenity Management (ILAM), although the industry is still some way from establishing a single, all-embracing institute for leisure management. (ILAM today has its own Training Unit and has great demand for its courses).

Since then, a number of initiatives in training for leisure management have emerged. However, despite the expansion of courses in the 1980s, particularly those at the lower ranges of operation and management, with the introduction of City and Guilds, and the Business and Technician Education Council (BTEC) courses, criticism was still levied at the range, quality, relevance and accessibility of training opportunities available. Cited were: the lack of adequate resources, with only a limited range of literature available in the library and a general lack of simulated practical material such as case studies and management games on the courses; the lack of relevance of many of the courses related to the limited knowledge and experience of many tutors; and the general lack of leisure management content within the syllabuses. All too often, commercial financial management techniques were taught on courses targeted to public sector employees, while other courses conveyed false levels of expectations to potential students about the quality of the course and the type of post they might expect upon successful completion of the course. The distribution of courses was not made on any strategic basis and hence access to certain categories of courses in different areas of the country was not available. Additionally, the concentration of full-time courses in middle and top management restricted courses for many potential students.

However, the 1990s saw a sea-change, particularly in business management, quality standards and the range of national initiatives. The introduction of compulsory competitive tendering played a big part in a call for management efficiency and productivity. The rapid pace of change in local government leisure services, as a consequence of the demands of CCT, meant that there was a need for an up-to-date analysis of training needs in local government. Several surveys were undertaken [5] and the Sports Council published the CELTS Report, *Recreation Management Training Needs*, in 1990 [6].

In recent times, the most significant change has come about with the introduction of National Vocational Qualifications (NVQs), the leisure industry lead bodies (LIBs) and the creation of national training organizations (NTOs), all of which we turn to later in this chapter.

17.3 The need for training

The need for training is generally described as the need for employees to learn new areas of knowledge and skills, so that they undertake the tasks associated with their posts more effectively. In this way, the needs of both the individual and the organization are fulfilled. However, not only is it necessary to provide training for staff to acquire new skills to meet the requirements of new technology such as computerized booking systems, there is also a need for the key personnel to acquire the necessary knowledge (e.g. about the leisure product, factors that influence or inhibit participation, etc.) to ensure that the service provided is effective. There is also a moral responsibility for the organization to develop its staff (in respect of their abilities and skills) and motivate them through more challenging areas of responsibility and experience. This will give employees the opportunity to achieve a greater self-worth in the job, while the organization will benefit through having a more productive and flexible workforce. The staff further benefit if the courses they successfully complete are recognized by the leisure industry as they form an integral part of the person's career structure.

17.3.1 What kind of training?

There are many kinds of training. Here, we touch on just four types: full-time; part-time; distance learning; and in-house training.

1. Full-time training

Undoubtedly, full-time courses that are relevant, accessible and appropriate to the ability and skill level of the person concerned can be the most effective method of acquiring new knowledge and skill. On such courses, the students are able to concentrate fully on their course work and their attention is not diverted to problems associated with their work.

With the current emphasis of central government on producing an 'economic service' and reducing operational costs in real terms, it is unlikely that many staff in the public sector will be given secondment to attend such courses. Likewise, full-time management courses for middle and top managers are normally of a postgraduate level, and as such local education authority students' grants fall into the category of a discretionary award; and in the present economic climate, such a grant is unlikely to be forthcoming. Consequently, students able to undertake full-time courses are school-leavers who are eligible for mandatory grants.

2. Part-time training

Part-time or day release courses that lead to nationally recognized qualifications or to membership of professional institutions have certain advantages. Students can benefit from mixing with students from other organizations, which can broaden their perspective. However, off-the-job training can be difficult in transferring skills and knowledge learnt in the classroom, unless the examples given and the problems set are provided in a simulated working environment.

Other forms of 'off-the-job training' can be seminars organized by professional institutions (such as ILAM and ISRM) and national agencies (such as the Sports Council, Arts Council and Tourist Boards). However, in some circumstances, these may be expensive, they are often one-offs, and because such training tends to lack reinforcement and evaluation, it is unlikely that direct learning from the lectures and talks is cost effective.

3. Distance learning

The potential of distance learning material has never been exploited sufficiently by the leisure industry. The advantages of this method are that it can make courses accessible in geographical areas that do not offer such courses and gives the individual the freedom to choose the time he or she wishes to study. The disadvantages associated with this method are that it can be costly to produce materials and will require amendments and updating from time to time, although the biggest disadvantage is probably the absence of the discipline associated with a formally structured course with its programme of learning and assignments.

4. In-house training

'On-the-job training' is preferred by commercial leisure organizations, particularly among its manual and 'lower-level' staff where skills are learned by doing. The public sector is beginning to follow suit and many local authorities have recently organized 'in-service' training in such areas as: health and safety; budgeting; customer care, marketing, first-aid, and so on, but unlike the commercial sector, these are often haphazard and lack continuity, reinforcement and monitoring of results.

17.4 Content of college training courses

The basis of most arguments on what to train essentially revolves around how specialist or how general such training should be, with the arguments tending to fall into one of three categories:

1   that leisure management is composed of two separate elements – recreation and management – and that the management element is applicable to any management situation (this seems to be the present basis of most academic college courses);
2   that leisure management is an area of knowledge within its own right, with a set of specialist skills that are applicable across the recreation sphere;
3   that leisure management is composed of specialist management subdivisions (e.g. sports management, countryside management, arts management), with particular skills unique to that subdivision.

1. Leisure management is composed of two separate elements

The arguments in favour of this concept tend to perceive the leisure element as comprising an essentially technical body of knowledge, and that the management element will be applicable in varying degrees to all management situations. Drucker [7] states that 'Businesses are different, but business is much the same regardless of size and structure of products, technology and markets, of culture and management competence. There is a common business reality'.

On many college courses, the management and leisure elements are treated independently, taught by separate staff from separate departments with little effort made to integrate the two. Many of the management elements are taught in a way that has limited relevance to leisure situations.

2. Leisure management is an area of knowledge in its own right

This viewpoint holds that management skills are not necessarily applicable to any situation, but are specific to the context in which they are being used. Rosemary Stewart [8] states that:

> The job of the manager is varied; the differences may be as much, if not more than, the similarities. These lists of management functions ignore the diversity of management; the job of the top manager bears little resemblance to that of the junior manager, or that of being a coke manager in a steel mill is hardly comparable with being an advertising manager to a popular shoe manufacturer. These jobs differ because they have different functions, but even more because the situation of the firm is so dissimilar.

A possible explanation for the different interpretation of the functions of management as perceived by Drucker and Stewart [7,8] is that the former is basically concerned with efficiency – i.e. the optimum use of the resources that are at the disposal of the organization – while in a service industry the emphasis is on effectiveness, which can be seen as providing a service that meets the needs of the community it is to serve – i.e. providing the right service in the right place at the right time. It is possible to manage a service efficiently while failing to meet the needs of a community – i.e. not effectively. In this sense, effectiveness is the more important goal for leisure managers.

If the argument that management training needs to be specialist in nature is accepted, then the degree to which specialization is necessary has to be determined. Some see general recreation management skills as being applicable to a wide range of subdivisions. Pick [9] believes that the old distinctions between heritage arts, leisure activities, community arts, sports and games do not now apply to what is actually happening in Britain:

> In a conversation between myself and two theatre administrators we listed the various events we had helped to promote in the last five years. Answers included sky diving, bingo, beagling, flower show, go-go dancing, rush

weaving course, basketball tournament, kinetic sculpture, fancy dress parades, cookery demonstrations and pop concerts. Is there, I wonder, any substantial organization now which does not offer food and drink, a spread of activities, but which exists solely for one form of entertainment?

Viewed in this way, there would appear to be considerable overlap between the leisure subdivisions, particularly with regard to programming and promotional skills. Further areas of common interest may be identified by looking at an analysis of the topics most requested by arts administrators for inclusion in training schemes [9]. These were book-keeping, fund-raising/grant applications, contract characteristics (performers), law affecting venue and performance, publicity, catering management, event festival planning, box office systems analysis, print buying, inter-personal skills, wage and salary administration and communities and facilities. Nearly all these topics could be relevant equally to syllabuses for the training of leisure centre managers, community centre wardens or organizers of outdoor events in parks and the countryside and, consequently, would seem to indicate that the training requirements of a number of the subdivisions are similar in a number of ways.

3. Recreation management is composed of specialist subdivisions

This argument takes the viewpoint that management skills are specific to the management situation; the various subdivisions are the specialist management situations, rather than recreation management as a whole. It sees the management training requirements of a swimming pool manager to be different from those of a countryside manager; or those of a sports hall manager to be different from those of an entertainments manager. This would appear to be true to an extent since the lack of specialist technical knowledge about swimming pools, horticulture, countryside maintenance, and so on, could have a noticeably adverse effect on the efficient and effective functioning of a manager involved with any of these recreation subdivisions.

One of the major problems in interpreting leisure management as a series of specialisms is that training may become supervisory or technically-orientated instead of management-orientated. The theory put forward by Kahn and Katz [10] suggests that as one ascends the managerial ladder the amount of technical skill and knowledge required decreases, while the conceptual skills and knowledge requirement increases. This implies that the higher management skills need not be specialist and are relevant to most top management situations within the leisure industry. A further criticism of the specialist approach is that it becomes too facility-orientated.

The CELTS study [6] collected information on the nature and relative importance of skills and knowledge required for jobs related to sport and recreation, the in-service training needs and the education and training needs. It concluded that job-related skills and training requirements are best regarded as a continuum, rather than a series of distinct grade-related breaks. Further, the high priority given to the basic management skills indicates the widespread lack of formal management training among leisure service personnel. Given the presumed radical changes associated with compulsory competitive tendering (CCT) (contractor–client relationships; performance monitoring and evaluation; increased consumer orientation; and stricter financial management), the need for these skills has become more urgent.

The study found that local authorities appeared to regard training as a cost, while commercial organizations regarded training as an investment. However, it was suggested that because of CCT, local government leisure services were shifting from a vague philosophy of public service to a more precise statement of aims, objectives and values:

> The bureaucratic and fragmented approaches of local government needed to be replaced by a more coherent, integrative organisational culture – one based on approaches and values described variously as 'consumer orientation', 'entrepreneurialism', 'enterprise' or 'commercial attitudes'.
>
> CELTS (1990), *Recreation Management Training Needs*

Clearly, competition in the industry has increased. In local government there are pressures on managers to become more entrepreneurial and to compete with private contractor companies. These developments have implications for the current and future roles of leisure managers.

Over the past twenty five years in the United Kingdom, there has been a confusing plethora of courses in recreation management. This complex picture has been streamlined of late, with the standardization of some of the qualifications. However, the courses tend to be taken up more by the public sector and many commercial leisure companies run their own courses. Courses provided in the institutional sector can be loosely grouped under 'further education', 'higher education' or 'continuing education':

1 *Further education* includes courses at a basic level of entry, run by colleges of further education or technical colleges; further education courses include BTEC First and National, as well as City and Guilds courses and SCOTVEC National Certificate modules.
2 *Higher education* includes courses entered at post A-level (or Scottish Higher) standard, run by polytechnics, colleges of higher education and universities. Higher education courses include Higher National courses, degrees, higher degrees and postgraduate diplomas.
3 *Continuing education* includes courses entered by mature students who have some management experience and wish to study on a part-time basis. The BTEC Continuing Education Certificate (Leisure Management) courses are run by a range of educational institutions. There is a significant move towards practice and competence-based qualifications, following the establishment of the National Council for Vocational Qualifications, and the implications for leisure awards and courses are considerable.

17.5 Government initiative on training

A programme was initiated under the auspices of the Department of Employment Training Agency, designed to provide a trained and qualified workforce to meet the demands of a changing society. The programme applies to all sectors of industry, including the leisure industry. Each section of industry has an industry lead body (ILB). There are approximately one hundred and fifty, 4 per cent of which have a direct involvement in leisure: amenity horticulture, arts and performing arts, hotels and catering, museums and art galleries, retail travel, tourism and leisure, and sport and recreation.

The programme is designed to improve work performance through a system of vocational qualifications and training. National Vocational Qualifications (NVQs, or SVQs in Scotland) have been developed, based on 'standards of competence agreed and accepted by both employers and employees from the industry'. These vocational qualifications are being designed to demonstrate what an individual can do at work and how well he or she can do it.

The NVQs are approved by the National Council for Vocational Qualifications (NCVQ), and SVQs are approved in Scotland by SCOTVEC. They reflect the standards of work performance set by each industry; NVQs are grouped into a framework which identifies the level of work for which a person is qualified – i.e. from basic tasks to supervisory and management skills. Armed with NVQs as an acknowledgement of their skills, it will be easier for employees to progress within an industry and it will help employers to select the right people with the right skills for the right job [11].

The 'competence standards' are the tasks an employee undertakes at work and the skills and knowledge the employee requires to fulfil these tasks. The industry lead bodies believe that setting standards will benefit employee, employer and customer.

1   For the employee, there will be
     • qualifications and training geared to the needs of the industry
     • better employment prospects
     • clear career progression
     • recognition of experience and ability.

2   For the employer, there will be
     • a properly trained workforce
     • qualifications relating to the industry
     • a consistent national standards framework
     • the right people applying for the right jobs.

3   For the customer, there will be
     • a better trained and qualified workforce which will mean an improved quality service.

However, the leisure industry is, as we have pointed out, vast, volatile and managed by so many different sectors that uniformity and standardization may be inappropriate in many respects, primarily because leisure behaviour is different from work behaviour which is far more predictable and far less discretionary.

The NVQ also presupposes that all tasks can be predetermined and hence will not take into consideration the unusual situation where a degree of flexibility is required. Also the system does not adequately reward the individual who uses his or her initiative. Indeed, it tends to reinforce the bureaucratic type of organization, with emphasis on job demarcation, the means to undertake a task as opposed to the end result and upon efficiency rather than effectiveness. This situation could have a detrimental effect upon staff initiative, morale and motivation which, in turn, can influence the quality of the service offered and the level of productivity of the staff.

17.5.1 *National training organizations*

National training organizations (NTOs) provide a United Kingdom focus and lead for 'human resource development' in their sectors, as the national sector partners of government. NTOs set and implement standards; represent, consult and lead employers; maintain labour market information and analysis; develop and promote national initiatives such as S/NVQs, modern apprenticeships and national traineeships; and promote the 'Investors in People' standards and good practice. There are six NTOs directly related to leisure: Arts; Heritage and Museums; Media; Hospitality; Tourism; and Sport Recreation.

Since the last edition of this book, there has been a substantial increase in the training and career development strands of leisure and recreation management, none more so than the creation of SPRITO, the National Training Organization covering the fields of Sport, Recreation, Playwork, Outdoor Education and Development Training, Fitness and Exercise. The market is growing, with an estimated 433,000 in the leisure industry segment represented by the NTO, with over two million volunteers in the United Kingdom and consumer expenditure of £12 billion, according to SPRITO.

In brief, NTOs are employer-led membership organizations representative of the industry with responsibility for leading the industry. SPRITO was created in 1994 and recognised on a United Kingdom basis by the Department for Education and Employment and the United Kingdom Sports Council as the National Training Organization in 1997. SPRITO has the remit to provide and oversee:

1   national occupational standards
2   Scottish and National Vocational Qualifications
3   modern apprenticeships and national traineeships
4   direct representation to government on all education and training issues
5   nationally recognized, industry-wide quality control on qualifications and training
6   employer input to full-time education courses – content, funding and delivery.

Full membership of SPRITO is open to operators (i.e. organizations providing opportunities for people to take part in sport and recreation activities) and approved S/NVQ Assessment Centres. Associate membership is open to training providers and other interested parties. In becoming an NTO, SPRITO encompassed the role of the former Sport and Recreation Lead Body and formed new partnerships with the trades unions, the Local Government Management Board and the Convention of Scottish Local Authorities. The remit was expanded when the employers installing synthetic surfaces and play equipment, SPRINT, formed under the NTO banner, broadening the range of organizations across all sectors of the industry.

The NTO presents its national programme under two main headings: human and skill development, and organization and sector development. The former is concerned with understanding, qualifying and developing the workforce and entry into the industry. The latter is concerned with strengthening and supporting the industry. Skills and qualifications leading to employment are a major strand of current government policy. The NTO is heavily involved in establishing clear entry and career progression routes into the industry:

> Amongst young people there is a high level of interest in working in the industry, particularly in sport. Higher education and further education programmes have expanded rapidly to meet this demand, making sport and recreation related qualifications the most popular provision. The popularity of the GNVQ in Leisure and Tourism is further evidence of this interest, and the NTO has recently been involved with QCA in revising the advanced level GNVQ. Sport and physical education is a key part of the school curriculum and the educational and development benefits of play and outdoor activities are widely acknowledged.
>
> National Training Organization for Sport, Recreation and Allied Occupations (undated), *Putting Quality into Life*, SPRITO, London.

The NTO is also assessing potential for a Graduate Apprenticeship to stimulate the employment market in the industry for graduates. The issue of graduate employability has been the subject of a two year study funded by the Department for Education and Employment, which was undertaken by the NTO and the UK Higher Education Standing Conference on Leisure, Recreation and Sport (SCLRS). The work involved consulting with 200 employers and their staff and 500 students in five higher education institutions.

For graduates the conclusions of the study are positive in that there is a good employment record for sport and recreation graduates, even though there is generally a low level of interest from industry in graduate recruitment and development. As Professor Peter Taylor at Sheffield University points out:

> In fact there is a significant short-termism in employer practices – recruiting for immediate attributes and ineffective utilization of graduate skills. Employers are looking for technical/professional qualifications and relevant experience, as well as or even in preference to a degree. . . . One of the problems with employers in the sport and recreation industry is that they are a diverse set, with at least four main sub-sectors identified in the project – sport and leisure; outdoor activities; playwork; and health and fitness – each with its own expectations of and attitudes to graduates from sport and recreation degrees. [11]

The lessons appear to be that graduates need practical skills and job-seeking skills and that employers need to take a longer-term view of graduate developments. A new factor which now comes into the debate, the decision by government to substitute grants to students with student loans, is likely to muddy the waters in the short term. This could mean that some potential students will be attracted to other avenues to training and employment.

17.5.2 Modern apprenticeships

Modern apprenticeships have been designed by employers to train young people at junior management, technician and craft levels. Modern apprenticeships are work-based and develop occupational, team work and problem solving skills. The programme provides a national structure and entry programme for 16–24 year olds. All the training leads to a National Vocational Qualification at Level 3 or above. Unlike the old apprenticeship schemes, there are no restrictions on the duration of training or start dates and they are available to all new and existing employees who can complete their modern apprenticeship by the age of 25. They are subsidized by training and enterprise councils. The benefits include: a flexible, tailor-made training package; the opportunity to recruit and train young people to nationally recognized standards; and support from quality assured training organizations.

Employers are expected to employ new recruits, and provide on-the-job training and supervision. Typically, the modern apprenticeship will take up to three years to complete, for which employers could receive a contribution of between £2,500 and £8,000, dependent upon the training costs and the time the young person needs to achieve the qualification.

The modern apprenticeship programme in sport and recreation was launched in August 1995. There are now more than 1,200 people enrolled nation-wide. It was developed by the Local Government Management Board, supported by SPRITO and its partners. The programme provides training to match what the business requires, to raise the levels of customer service and competitiveness and provide structured career routes. There are three strands to the training: the needs of the organization; occupational development; and the industry.

1   *Organization awareness* focusses on understanding the employing organization, its aims and objectives, products and services, marketing, customer care, health and safety issues and understanding basic financial and human resource matters.
2   *Occupational development* provides the knowledge, skills and competencies required for the job and to take steps towards positions with greater responsibility. Candidates have to achieve a minimum NVQ Level 3 from the SPRITO framework, as well as NVQ Key Skills in information technology, application of number, communication and working with others. Industry skills, such as first aid, National Pool Lifeguard or Coaching Awards are also completed under this strand.
3   *Industry awareness* provides a feel for the industry, its history and recent trends within trainees' own specific sector, for example, health and fitness or outdoor education.

The availability of nationally recognized awards has been an important step in developing professionalism in the leisure industry. Modern apprenticeships are one route to training and career development available, with the added advantage of government funding available through the training and enterprise councils (TECs). Their success, however, as with any other training programme, depends on the commitment of employers and their policy towards investing in their people.

17.5.3 National traineeships

National traineeships are the latest government-backed hospitality training initiative for England and Wales. Developed in 1997 (operational in April 1998) by the Hospitality Training Foundation (HtF), the national training organization for hospitality, they offer a way into the industry for 16–17 year old school or college leavers.

Training and enterprise councils are the first step towards getting involved in national traineeships. There are two options: training the candidate in-house and developing key members of staff qualified to assess the candidates. In this case, funding can usually be obtained from the TEC. Alternatively, a local college or training provider can be used to help with training and assessment, and then the college would receive the funding. It is also possible to have a combination of both.

Candidates who have achieved their national traineeship can continue in full-time employment, and could also study for a modern apprenticeship and further NVQs, or undertake further or higher qualifications. An average traineeship will take about two years to complete, but like NVQs and modern apprenticeships, there is no time limit for completion. Credits towards traineeship awards are possible through a system called accreditation of prior learning (APL).

17.5.4 Quality and best practice

Another essential strand of the NTO is to identify and promote best practice in support of continuous improvement in the quality of performance in the workplace. In partnership with the company, Associated Quality Service Ltd (AQS), a quality scheme called Quest (United Kingdom Quality Scheme for Sports and Leisure) was designed as the Business Excellence Model for the industry. The NTO is working on integrating Quest with the government's concept of 'Best Value' in local authority services to replace compulsory competitive tendering.

In 1993, the Sports Council, through the British Quality Association Committee for Leisure and Tourism embarked on defining standards of performance in the delivery of leisure services. The Sports Council commissioned a study looking into a specific 'quality scheme'. This resulted in Quest, a system which enables continuous improvement of leisure organizations, using four basic 'tools': 1) a managers' guidance pack; 2) self-assessment; 3) assessments; and 4) improvement reports.

The managers' pack includes an 'excellence model' of principles and assessment criteria which are linked with the United Kingdom business excellence model, depicted in Figure 17.1.

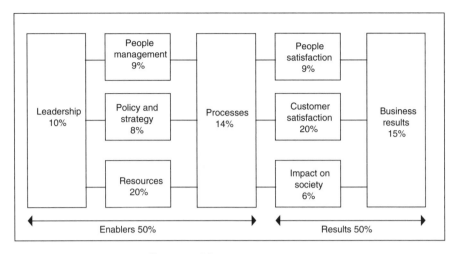

FIGURE 17.1 Business excellence model

A self-assessment quality questionnaire and workshop approach involving staff representatives to arrive at consensus is used. To measure progress against industry best practice Quest offers an external assessment process involving 'mystery customer visits' and on-site inspection. At all stages of the process, improvement reports are used. The NTO also supports the performance standard Investors in People which, together with Quest, will enhance quality of service in the industry. The NTO is cognizant of recent government initiatives, 'Welfare to Work', the 'New Deal' for the long-term unemployed and the 'National Childcare Strategy'. The NTO will be working with the Department for Education and Employment to help provide appropriate training and qualifications for those working with children in out-of-school initiatives.

17.5.5 'New Deal'

The White Paper, *Lifelong Learning* [12], was presented to Parliament by the Secretary of State for Education and Employment in February, 1998. The White Paper follows reports by Sir Ron Dearing, Dame Helena Kennedy and Professor Bob Fryer. The promise of 500,000 new students by the millennium was made. One approach has been launched – 'New Deal'.

'New Deal' offers colleges access to £700 million of funding over three years. Colleges have to demonstrate their ability to deliver high-quality programmes to attract 'New Deal' places. With significant new resources obtainable, it matters to colleges, lecturers and students how institutions address the challenge. 'New Deal' requires innovation to meet the requirements of new students with specific needs. It raises several questions. Will people who do not engage in lifelong learning be attracted? Will it make a difference to them? Secretary of State, David Blunkett, believes that skills and employability are the keys.

We must equip men and women now with the capability to be able to take on new jobs and encourage them to use their creativity and innovation to develop the jobs they are in. We must ensure that those who are unemployed have the skills they need to take up the jobs of tomorrow.

Labour Conference publicity material

A very high number of 'New Deal' candidates will be unemployed. Over 280,000 students in colleges were on courses in 1996/97 while they were unemployed, according to the Further Education Funding Council (a substantially higher figure than previous records have shown). As these claimants are called for 'New Deal' interviews, many risk having to end their courses in order to take up employment. A strongly held view, particularly by colleges bidding to run the education and training strands of 'New Deal', is that students should be given a choice between education and employment, rather than be pressed into work.

'New Deal', with the goal of employment, will put an emphasis on people and their employability. Colleges and universities will need to prove that a high proportion of the 500,000 new students are coming from previously under-represented groups and also that they are going to be more employable after the courses.

17.6 The hospitality industry

The hospitality industry estimates that the industry employs more than two million people – around 7 per cent of the United Kingdom workforce, in more than 250,000 locations. The Hospitality Training Foundation forecasts that 310,000 new jobs will be created by the year 2004, with the largest growth in restaurants, pubs and hotels.

The industry provides a wide range of jobs in the leisure sector for qualified and unqualified people, in full- or part-time jobs. There are three main routes into hospitality: finding a job; becoming an apprentice or trainee; or working for a qualification at college or university, full- or part-time.

The majority of young people will work towards NVQ/SVQ Level 1 (operative) or Level 2; those with experience will work to Level 3. Level 4 is for 'advanced craft' and supervisory management; Level 5 is for senior management.

There are five modern apprenticeships for the hospitality industry: chef, pub, restaurant, accommodation and fast food. Each consists of three phases. The induction phase is common to all routes. The intermediate phase involves further development of practical job skills. The final phase leads towards a Level 3 NVQ/SVQ.

For those in work, there are a number of professional and other qualifications which can be studied on a part-time or distance-learning basis for the qualifications of the industry's professional management associations: the Hotel and Catering International Management Association (HCIMA) and the British Institute of Innkeeping. The institute is currently offering free training for 1,500 employees in the licensed sector under their 'Better Business Initiative', to make professional training more accessible.

17.6.1 A university on the internet

The tremendous scope for training and education using the internet is just beginning to gain a foothold in the leisure and recreation field. The United Kingdom
hospitality industry has launched a university on the internet with qualifications on
offer designed to be useful in the workplace. It is called 'Our University for Industry
– Hospitality Worldwide' (Ufi-hw) and is designed to lead to the award of academic
degrees (Bachelors and Masters) for work-based rather than academic-based
projects and is run via the internet.

Partnered by the British Hospitality Association, and the Hotel and Catering
International Management Association, Ufi-hw

> seeks to provide a radically different form of educational development for
> managers and supervisors working in the hospitality industry which is based
> on action learning – the way in which individuals and teams solve problems
> and find answers to the challenges and opportunities they face at work.
> Learner resources, Internet-based tutoring and mentoring are supplied
> directly to the workplace. [13].

The new programme is organized by International Management Centres (IMC), a
global business school dedicated to action learning, Oxford Brookes University,
and MCB University Press, said to be the world's largest publisher of academic and
professional journals.

17.7 The 'professional' bodies representing leisure managers

Leisure and recreation attract large numbers of representative bodies, including
associations and institutes with many overlapping interests. Trained and/or
qualified leisure and recreation personnel and some in training are likely to join a
professional association or institute, initially for what they can get from it, including
status and recognition. For a number of professional bodies, there are strict entry
qualifications. The link between new national training qualifications and entry into
professional organizations is very much at a wait-and-see stage. The professional
bodies in the United Kingdom include:

* Institute of Leisure and Amenity Management (1983) (an amalgamation of the
  former Association of Recreation Managers, Institute of Leisure Management,
  Institute of Park and Recreation Administration and Institute of Municipal
  Entertainment)
* Institute of Sport and Recreation Management (originally Institute of Baths
  Management) (1921)
* Chief Leisure Officers' Association (1976)
* Tourism Society (1977)
* Library Association (1877)
* Museums Association (1989)

- Leisure Studies Association (1975)
- Institute of Entertainments and Arts Management (1982)
- The Physical Education Association (1899)
- Recreation Managers' Association (1956) (formerly Industrial Sports Clubs)
- Association of Playing Fields Officers (1958)
- Hotel and Catering International Management Association (1971)
- British Institute of Innkeeping (1981).

Many of the above, including ILAM and ISRM, have their own training programme and career structure and make a valuable contribution to the training of their members.

17.8 Leisure and recreation management – an emerged profession in the United Kingdom?

Previous editions of this book placed leisure and recreation management as an emerging profession. Have we now arrived? Whether the managers in the leisure industry consider themselves to be professionals is dependent upon their perception of the nature of their work and its value to society, and their capability and standing within the community. Not surprisingly, personnel within the industry perceive themselves as professionals. It is, however, questionable whether the rest of society view them in the same light as the high-status professions or occupations. Although there is no generally accepted definition of the word 'profession', there appears to be an acceptable criterion for evaluating whether an occupation is of professional standing.

Sessoms [14] writing about the evolution of recreation professionalism in the United States, has described a profession as implying 'a defined and distinctive body of knowledge attained through a disciplined, formal education process prior to sanction for practice. It bridges technique and immediate application with theory, sets standards and serves social needs'. Murphy [15], in 1980, claimed that while accepting the concept that recreation management encompasses a relevant body of knowledge, it is not adequately defined and lacks 'a formal education process for entry into the occupation'. But that was twenty years ago; things have moved on since then.

Although both 'recreation' and 'management' tend to be regarded as secondary disciplines, they do however draw on other disciplines such as sociology and psychology. Entrance to some of the main leisure and recreation management institutes is by means of a formal examination, or equivalent qualification and in the case of ILAM proof of practical competence is also required. It would thus appear that the leisure and recreation management occupation has significantly advanced towards or along the professionalization continuum. However, it has some way to go and it could be argued that recreation is becoming more occupational rather than professional.

The church, law and medicine are often considered as the original 'professions'. Other professions like education and accountancy are placed somewhere on a continuum between these originals and those which are classed as 'occupations', like advertising and coaching. Leisure and recreation management, as an emerging profession, albeit with a growing body of knowledge, does not yet fit into the main strands of the professional continuum. The service areas and job tasks have been identified, public recognition is very slowly coming about and formalizing structures and training is beginning through the government's national initiatives. However, there is a wide gap between leisure management and the original professions with their adoption and enforcement of ethical codes. Indeed, the wide interpretation of what is, and what is not, acceptable leisure, make the enforcement of ethical codes difficult.

With the widening of knowledge and the dawn of the technological and computer age, many emerging professions have been slowed down in their professional recognitions. The profession of physical education, for example, is increasingly being challenged by the advance of professional coaches, sports psychologists, fitness experts and aerobics teachers. Similarly, in the arts and music, professional artists have an important role to play in teaching. The self-governance of schools, the involvement of parents and the heightened use of volunteers can fill gaps, normally the province of the 'professionals'.

In this book we have shown that provision for, and management of, leisure and recreation is made by major sectors: public, institutional, voluntary and commercial. The Leisure Managers represented by the institutions and associations discussed in this chapter and the managers that emerge from the courses and training schemes represent only a small part of the world of leisure and recreation and its management, primarily those areas in the hands of public or semi-public bodies. The range and scope of leisure and recreation requiring management, however, is very wide. The non-public sector, made up of thousands of voluntary organizations and commercial bodies, is barely touched by current levels of leisure management training. Even in the public sector many areas of leisure and recreation are not encompassed, for example, in the education-related leisure field.

Whether working in the public or non-public sector, Leisure Managers are concerned with creating opportunities for people to have satisfying leisure experiences. They must attract the public or fail. Leisure and recreation is a 'people-orientated' business, i.e. giving a people-orientated service. Training is a means of acquiring new skills and new knowledge. Managers and organizations must evolve as demands change, rather than simply becoming more efficient, consolidating the status quo and thus becoming less expansive and less attractive to the many thousands entering the field. No amount of training and management education will guarantee making a successful manager, but with education and training, leisure personnel are more likely to become good managers.

Leisure and recreation management education, training and development, with advanced technologies and the internet, is at the threshold of yet another giant step towards the realization of a future profession of great import in the United Kingdom and beyond.

Notes and references

1   Central Statistical Office, *Annual Abstract of Statistics* (1997 edition), The Stationery Office, London.

2   Sports Council (1969), *Professional Training for Recreation Management: Report of a Working Party* (Chairman, D. D. Molyneux), Sports Council, London.

3   Department of the Environment (1978), *Recreation Management Training Committee: Interim Report* (A Discussion Paper) (Chairman, Anne Yates), HMSO, London.

4   Department of the Environment (1984), *Recreation Management Training Committee: Final Report*, HMSO, London.

5   For example, MSc/Mid-Kent College Local Collaborative Project (c. 1989), *Training Needs and Training Provision Requirements in Sports/Recreation Centres in Kent*, Mid-Kent College of Higher and Further Education, Maidstone.

6   CELTS (Centre for Leisure and Tourism Studies) (1990), *Recreation Management Training Needs*, London, Sports Council.

7   Drucker, P. F. (1969), *Managing For Results*, Pan Books, London.

8   Stewart, R. (1970), *Managers and their Jobs*, Pan Books, London.

9   Pick, J. (1978), 'Training: the future', *Municipal Entertainment*, 5, 10, June, 11.

10   Kahn, D. and Katz, R. L. (1966), *The Social Psychology of Organizations*, Wiley, New York.

11   Taylor, P. (1998), 'Making the grade', *Leisure Opportunities* 6–7.

12   National Council for Voluntary Qualifications (NCVQ), *Lifelong Learning*, publicity literature.

13   Our University for Industry – Hospitality Worldwide, http://hcima.org.uk.

14   Sessoms, H. D. (1975), 'Our body of knowledge: myth or reality?' *Parks and Recreation*, November, 30 (USA).

15   Murphy, W. (1980), Professionalism and Recreation Management, Occasional Paper, unpublished.

Chapter eighteen

Towards effective leisure and recreation management: some conclusions

This book set out to further an understanding of leisure and recreation and improving its management. This fourth edition has also sought to revise, update and improve upon previous editions. Substantial changes have been made.

This edition has been written in four main parts. The first part concerned leisure and the needs of people, spanning chapters two to five. The second part, chapters six to eight, looked at the trends in leisure, planning for it and the main agencies involved. The leisure providers in the public, voluntary and commercial sectors were covered in part three, chapters nine to eleven. The fourth part addressed the range of topics under the umbrella of management, including in chapters twelve to seventeen general management, programming, marketing, events, staffing and training. In this concluding chapter, the strands are drawn together and some conclusions are reached.

18.1 'Pleisure' at the heart of leisure

The difference between this book and other books on management is that it deals as much with the nature of the leisure experience and the needs of people in leisure as it does with the process and practice of management, although management takes up the greater part of the book and permeates throughout.

My concern is with effectiveness rather than efficiency alone. Effectiveness is concerned with meeting the goals of an organization *and* the needs of people. An effective service for the greater good of the greater number of people needs to be based on four foundations: leisure opportunity; meeting needs of different people; sound planning and provision; and management excellence, including organizational policies, aims and objectives and outstanding service delivery.

Potentially, leisure can provide experiences and satisfactions which enhance the quality of people's lives. In chapter four, for individual people, leisure was perceived as experiencing activities, chosen in relative freedom, that are personally satisfying and innately worthwhile and that can lead to self-actualization and, ultimately, to a self-fulfilling life. By 'self-actualization' (a word borrowed from Abraham Maslow), I mean realizing fully our potential, to be or become what we are capable of becoming. Leisure then, ideally, can be an integral part of our way of living.

Alas, most of us do not live in an ideal world and many of us choose not to accept the gift of leisure, nor to sacrifice what we already have for something which, potentially, could be far better. This may be because we have not had the opportunity, nor seen the potential of leisure (or, like the author, we have been too busy!) This is where the leisure professional comes in.

In terms of planning for and managing leisure services and facilities, Leisure Managers can perceive leisure as a framework of opportunity for people to be attracted, to choose and to experience satisfactions, which lead to interests and life-enhancing pursuits. Satisfying people's needs is also a very powerful means of making good business, as the commercial sector is quick to realize.

Leisure's potential includes the possibility of achieving innate experiences through chosen activities, very similar in quality and feelings that can be found in the experiences of play and 're-creation'. I invented a new word and called this wordless experience, 'pleisure', a derivative of the words 'play', 'recreation' and 'leisure' (Figure 18.1).

If, as leisure professionals, we want to provide a choice of activities and opportunity for people to experience and develop leisure potential, then such experiences are more likely to occur for individual people if the setting and

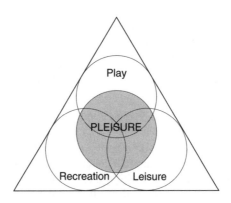

FIGURE 18.1 'Pleisure' at the heart of play, recreation and leisure

circumstances are favourable. For such experience to occur, we need to provide the right conditions – levels of freedom and choice; satisfaction in the doing; and positive outcomes such as well-being, achievement and self-esteem.

These innate, worthwhile, experiences give satisfactions. Satisfactions lead to consuming interests. Interests help people to realize their potential. However, most people are not free agents to enjoy leisure as they might. Indeed, it is clear that leisure is linked inextricably to other elements of life, many of which are far more pressing and constraining. Therefore, leisure professionals need to know something about the needs of people in order to manage appropriately. The needs of people and the factors which influence their participation in leisure were addressed briefly in chapter five.

People have diverse needs, and different people have different needs, which change according to their circumstances and stage in life. Leisure needs, as such may not exist, but some of the needs of people can be met through involvement in leisure pursuits. Some needs are basic to survival, some are essential to cope with living in an uncertain social world, and others are at the apex of living life to the full, seeking to find balance, harmony and self-worth. People want to be 'somebody'; it is therefore in this latter category that leisure opportunity can help people to meet some of their needs, to find themselves and have a favourable personal identity.

However, emotional stress, financial and family worries, work obligations and crisis points in life may dominate to the extent that leisure becomes peripheral. For example, leisure for many disadvantaged people is likely to remain low, while major life constraints persist such as lack of income, poor housing, poor mobility and unrelieved pressures of parenting. These life factors support my contention that leisure cannot be divorced from other elements of life. Therefore, effective public leisure services require local authorities to play enabling and supporting roles, examples of which have been given in chapter four.

18.2 Planning, providing and governing

In times past, life used to be lived on fixed timetables, with patterns of work, shopping and leisure which provided structures to live by – a time to reap and a time to sow. These building blocks are disappearing and we are moving to flexible work patterns, twenty-four hour shopping, home banking and the internet. The pace of change has been rapid. Most of us – though not all – are enjoying higher standards of living filled with goods, services, activities and opportunities that in past years seemed unimaginable. Chapter six showed some of the trends in leisure with more people taking some active recreation, a greater interest in health and fitness and an even greater interest in social activities such as going to the cinema, 'clubbing' for young people, the second holiday and in hoping for life in the lap of luxury once we have won on the National Lottery.

In chapter seven on planning, a need was shown for a greater interrelationship between planners, leisure professionals and the community. 'Putting people into the plans' was a developing theme. The likelihood is strong that all local authorities in the United Kingdom will need to have in place leisure strategies or local leisure plans using nationally devised facility planning models as part of the process.

One of the most significant changes in leisure in the broadest sense has been the creation of a United Kingdom government department – the Department for Culture, Media and Sport – as an umbrella for leisure-related activities including arts, sports, libraries, museums, heritage, tourism, broadcasting and more. Government direction and policy has seen changes to the Arts Council and Regional Arts Boards, the creation of the United Kingdom Sports Council and the English Sports Council, influential reports such as *Raising the Game* and *England the Sporting Nation*, and the prominence given to Sports Development and the involvement of young people through the National Junior Sport Programme. Of great importance also for arts, sports, heritage, charities and millennium projects has been the National Lottery and the introduction of a sixth 'good cause' including advocating healthy living centres. The Leisure Manager has an important role to play in all these new and demanding initiatives.

Leisure facilities are provided in the public, institutional, voluntary and commercial sectors. Each has an important role to play. The public sector has been and continues to be under great pressure to deliver greater efficiency and effectiveness. Leisure in England and Wales is a non-statutory service and, therefore, is vulnerable to cuts in funding. Increasingly, the public sector is having to compete with the private sector. Competitive tendering, local management of schools, education reform, externalization of services and the introduction of 'Best Value' have changed local government dramatically, and perhaps for all time. The Leisure Manager has a key role in managing leisure services in a highly professional manner. Links with the voluntary sector and the commercial sector are becoming essential in many of the services. With the constraints on local government, the voluntary sector is having to take on greater responsibility for community recreation and is also being asked, into the bargain, to become more 'professional' in its management. Clearly, the field of leisure management is expanding by the year, if not by the season.

Chapters nine to eleven dealt with the major providers of leisure services and facilities – public, voluntary and commercial. Choice is essential, but planners, providers and managers need to be aware of the implications of making certain choices. Powerful commercial attractions have a magnetic draw and successful products will also have significant value for jobs and the economy; yet there is a need for people to learn to choose not only activities which are superficially pleasurable alone, but also activities which are intrinsically worthwhile. Leisure advocates must not lose sight of, or inadvertently destroy, the leisure 'gift' which is there for the taking. In chapter four, the concept of 'serious leisure' was introduced – a kind of positive, enhancing participation.

Each of the providers has valuable contributions to make. The commercial sector can provide pleasurable social, physical and entertaining activities and the infrastructure for attractions and tourism. The public sector, despite changes and the constraints upon it, still has many roles to play, namely those of planner, provider, enabler and manager and increasingly, co-ordinator boroughwide. The voluntary sector, in particular, provides great opportunity for many millions of people to develop consuming interests and to express themselves in company with like minded people and to achieve together the goals of their organizations.

18.3 The management of leisure

If leisure is a freedom to choose, then personal management is of greater importance than management by someone else, particularly a faceless 'someone' like a local authority or another organization or a third party – a Leisure Manager! However, this book has shown that effective 'professional' management is needed to open up opportunity, create the right environments and manage situations so that more people can be attracted to and benefit from leisure. Chapters twelve to seventeen covered a number of general and specific management topics.

Effectiveness is measured by the degree to which an organization achieves its goals and objectives. This applies to all organizations, whether in commerce or leisure. In public leisure services, effective community leisure management can be measured, in part, by the degree to which a reasonable balance of market segments has been attracted. For example, if a leisure centre purports to be a centre for the community, it follows that it should attract a cross-section of the local community.

Two key elements are a) the interaction between the organization and those who use the services – i.e. it is a people-orientated business, and b) managers are involved in the achievement of goals. A leisure and recreation organization is a business whose functions include the creation and distribution of services, programmes and activities that are used by individuals and groups during their time for leisure. Leisure and recreation management is, therefore, the process whereby a manager works with resources – especially human – to achieve goals and objectives. Good leisure and recreation management must include qualitative as well as quantitative objectives.

Good management is largely the result of good managers – they are individuals who are responsible and have authority for providing direction to their organization and who also have the ability to move it towards its goals. Managers are, therefore, directly responsible for much of the success or failure of an organization. Management, to be effective, needs to be flexible enough to accommodate changing circumstances and to meet the different needs of different people. Managers, therefore, have substantial influence not only in what they do, but in *the way* they do it. They have influence on the objectives and targets, programmes, activities and the results; their style of management can influence dramatically both staff and customers.

During the course of writing this book, in examining the operation of scores of leisure establishments, invariably it was found that programmes were built upon lettings policies and centrally directed approaches. Community-initiated programmes were not greatly in evidence.

Another problem found was that the evaluation of services and programmes was almost entirely quantitative. Evaluations based on a number–income obsession led to less energy being directed towards meeting the needs of some market sectors. Unless the goals of an organization include qualitative aspects, which are measured, then a community leisure facility cannot be said to be managed effectively. The goal of leisure – i.e. that of self-actualization and psychological well-being – is often dependent on *other* more basic needs than the activity itself, for example, the need to feel welcomed, to be with friends, to feel at ease, to feel capable of taking part and to be helped to achieve. The right atmosphere and the appropriate encouragement may be all that is needed to overcome a person's anxiety. Sensitive, appropriate and capable management is, therefore, one of the keys to opening up leisure opportunity for each person. Such an opening door can help people towards achieving their potential.

Programming is the key element in the delivery of services and goes hand in hand with marketing. Programming was covered in chapter thirteen, Marketing in chapter fourteen. Marketing, promotion and customer service have received a good deal of attention of late within the field of leisure and recreation management. The concept of marketing is relatively simple: it is academics who have made it something complex. It is about understanding the needs of potential customers, the needs of the organization and then matching markets to products.

Events, too, are an important part of any comprehensive leisure programme. Well organized, they can be a boon; badly organized, they can spell disaster and detract. Leisure Managers must be capable of leading or controlling the planning and staging of events. Ways of doing this were shown in chapter fifteen.

Staff are the most important resource in any leisure organization and their cost should be regarded as an investment rather than an expensive item of expenditure. The right staff need to be employed, trained, nurtured and enabled to perform well for their organization and for themselves. If not, then they are an expensive liability. Chapter sixteen was concerned with staffing and chapter seventeen with training.

Leisure professionals must manage with excellence, inspire, lead, teach and instil values, so that work is done gladly, with energy and enthusiasm. Leisure has an abundance of positive selling points. People want to work for more than money. The motivation must come from the job itself, not just from salaries and fringe benefits. Work, therefore, should be satisfying in the doing. Attitudes, in delivery, can often be the ingredients that turn an average service into a great one. We don't want to churn out professionals, so called, on a conveyer belt of certificates, but develop competent, confident people at all levels of service, able to enhance their organizations and the lives of their customers.

Training has been a major growth factor since the last edition. It is a huge field and is changing with the introduction of National Vocational Qualifications, National Training Organizations and Quality Schemes. New legislation has provided universities and colleges the opportunity to set up new courses and attract new students. Leisure is one of the most attractive fields for young people to study in and, hence, a plethora of courses in leisure now exist. We are also on the verge of leisure management training on the internet as demonstrated by the hospitality industry. Whether there will be enough sustainable jobs in the field is a question still to be answered.

18.4 Towards a theoretical framework for effective community leisure management

Since the last edition of this book, government direction and competition have put emphasis on efficiency – financial efficiency. This book has been preoccupied with *effectiveness*, on the presumption that it is no use having super-efficient services that are ineffective, i.e. that fail to meet the needs of the people they are intended to serve.

To improve the management of community leisure, an approach towards a theoretical framework in the form of a conceptual 'model' was designed for the third edition of this book. The premises on which it was constructed have changed little since then. An outline of the assumptions on which it is based follows.

Leisure management is concerned with four main basic ingredients:

1   *The concept of leisure* Leisure can provide satisfying and intrinsically worth-while activities and experiences.
2   *People's needs* Leisure Managers deal with people's wants, wishes and demands, and importantly, with needs, which are more complex to uncover.
3   *Leisure management* This involves management across a wide range of elements – planning, providing, operationally managing and delivering services and programmes.
4   *Aims and objectives* Underpinning the whole 'box of tricks' is the organization itself that is responsible for the services and facilities, its philosophy, aims and objectives.

Now, how do we 'manage' to put all these things together? I visualize a model – a pyramid – depicted in Figure 18.2. Picture, if you will, the model as a transparent triangular pyramid, which has three sides, or planes, and a base:

1   leisure plane
2   needs of people plane
3   management plane
4   the base of the pyramid represents the aims of the organization.

The triangular pyramid represents and illustrates the bonding of leisure, people's needs and management based upon principles and objectives of an organization.

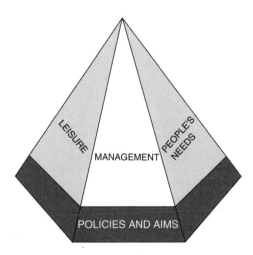

FIGURE 18.2 Conceptual model for leisure management – leisure, policies, needs and management

For management effectiveness, the three planes must function in balance and harmony. Balance points will differ depending on the goals of the organization, the situation and the current emphasis. Therefore, for efficiency and measurability each of the three planes will need to contain levels of performance to meet objectives and targets. For simplicity and illustration only, this is represented in the 'model' as three levels: the lower tier or basic level, the middle tier or secondary level and the upper tier or primary level, Figures 18.3 and 18.4.

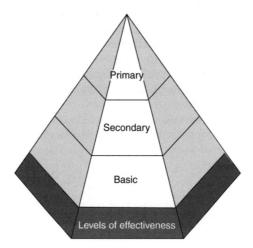

FIGURE 18.3 Conceptual model for leisure management – levels of performance

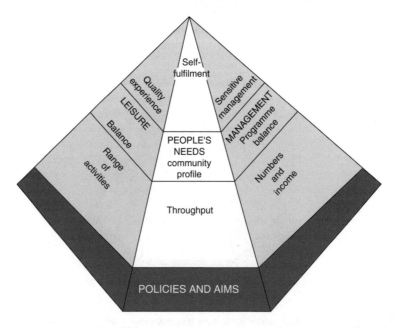

FIGURE 18.4 Conceptual model for leisure management – performance and effectiveness

1. Basic level

At the lower, basic, level managers would seek to achieve a wide range of choice of activities, general service efficiency, high levels of throughput and income and a broad programme of casual, 'club' and special programmes and events. The basic level therefore represents the numbers game – i.e. an activities, head-counting and money-counting exercise. Many authorities and organizations measure success only at this point – i.e. an organization survival level. They stop at this point!

2. Secondary level

At the secondary level we could expect to see, in public services, a user profile reflecting broadly the catchment population and the target markets which the organization is aiming to attract. At this level, managers would seek to have a balanced programme to meet some of the needs of the different people and groups of like-minded people in the area. Greater emphasis will be given to customer service, the encouragement of community initiative and meeting the standards and quality of service expected by the manager, organization and community.

3. Primary or upper level

At the top level, the manager will be concerned with individual customer and group needs, sensitive handling of customers, the needs of the disadvantaged, the quality of experience of the individual and the encouragement of long-lasting activities that are perceived by the individuals to be personally worthwhile and of importance.

The apex of the pyramid serves to illustrate the goal of leisure management – i.e. personal self-actualization or self-fulfilment of individual people through leisure opportunity. It thus represents the highest quality of leisure experiences that people will want to 'buy' again and again, the satisfactions that can lead to an enhancing of the quality of life. It is to this goal of quality leisure and recreation that a manager must strive in order to give a service that can truly be called 'excellent leisure management'.

18.4.1 Value of the model

This skeletal, conceptual model serves as an illustration only of the essential components which go to make up effective management of leisure facilities open to all. It is also illustrative of the theory that an individual is like all people in having the same basic needs (the basic level of the pyramid), like some other like-minded people in sharing the same interests (the secondary level) and like no other person – a unique individual at the apex of the pyramid. At the top point of the pyramid there is no room for more than one.

To make operational sense of the various elements within the framework, the ideas and themes can be incorporated from various starting points, placing greater emphasis on one of the 'planes' depending on the circumstances. From whatever direction, there will be a sequential and continuing process of providing levels of balance to meet both the goals of the organization and the needs of the people to be served. The framework also allows for maximum flexibility, so that Leisure Managers can vary their responses to be appropriate to given situations. Good management needs to be flexible management, but the greater the flexibility, the greater the need for management excellence.

In summary, the first tenet of management is to know what we are in business for, i.e. what it is we are supposed to be managing. Leisure Managers are not only managing parks, pitches, pools, theatres and sports centres, but creating opportunities for people to experience leisure in ways satisfying to them. Therefore, there must be effective management – i.e. management concerned with what is below the surface as much as what is above it. Measures of effectiveness must therefore include not only throughput, income and expenditure, but the range of people, the scope of the activites and the quality of the experience. Managers must ask themselves: 'to what extent have we met the needs of the people we are here to serve?'

To provide more effective community leisure management, a theoretical framework has been built upon the three interlocking aspects of people, leisure and management, visualized as the three planes of a triangular pyramid, with the base of the pyramid as a representation of the purposes of the organization. Hence a new approach to community leisure and recreation management has been fashioned which calls for a re-orientation towards a better people and process management approach.

One of the purposes of this book has been to examine the linkages between leisure philosophy, resources and management and to build bridges between them in an attempt at improving the management of community leisure services and facilities. At the outset, three propositions were put forward.

- The first was that providers and managers should be concerned with the quality of experience for the individual and not just with the quantity of facilities and numbers attending.
- The second was that leisure opportunity can lead to satisfying leisure and recreation experiences which, in turn, have positive effects on the quality of life of individual people.
- The third was that management policy and performance can be powerful influences on both people's participation and non-participation.

The study undertaken in writing this book confirms these three propositions. The theoretical framework illustrates, in conceptual form, the components which make for effective community leisure management. The value of a theory is the degree to which it explains and predicts and is of practical use. The adage holds true: there is nothing more practical than a good theory – as long as you put it into practice! Indeed, if it is no good in theory, it will be no good in practice.

18.5 Discussion

If leisure management is to blossom into a profession with a philosophy, an ethic and professional standing, it needs to establish itself as a discipline with a basic framework of terminology and understanding. At present, leisure theory, and consequently leisure planning, appear to be flowing in several diverse directions in search of such a cohesive perspective. If we can understand what it is and why people play, we shall then have a fundamental basis upon which planning should be based. If we know what motivates people to participate, then conflicts over priorities and facilities would be quickly resolved. On the other hand, if we have no basic insights into why people play and find recreation, then we cannot have any confidence either in the facilities we produce or the programmes we manage, for we will not know whether they are relevant or appropriate.

Leisure has emerged over recent history as an important sphere of life. It now has less to do with former definitions of time and specified activities and more to do with satisfying experiences. As a choice of life-style and a form of personal expression, it should now become less a reflection of demographic and socio-economic status and more a reflection of who we are and what leisure means to us.

Leisure consumption is one of the few growth areas in the current economic climate in the United Kingdom. Well into the foreseeable future, there will be continued demand for centres of interest to satisfy the rising expectations of people in all walks of life and all sections of the community. Well researched patterns of social change show that the trend will continue well into the twenty-first century. Therefore, new facilities specially selected for their leisure and social value – in partnerships between public, institutional, voluntary and commercial sectors – should be developed. In addition, existing services, facilities and operations should be improved to take full advantage of a positive leisure climate.

The benefits of providing for these trends will include, it is hoped, a healthier and more relaxed population, more effective use of leisure time and, above all, greater personal fulfilment. The case for leisure and recreation investment and support is well made. I believe, and evidence exists in this book to show, that leisure opportunity can be the vehicle through which people can play and find recreation and in so doing meet some of their human needs.

The correlation between leisure and recreation participation and variables, such as social class, education and income, though far less obvious, still remains. The extent to which participation is influenced or conditioned by such factors is not absolutely clear and the question is raised whether leisure and recreation policies and management can overcome many of the apparent constraints to wider participation. I believe that good management can remove many of the artificial barriers and that planning, location, perception, accessibility, choice, social acceptance, the attitude of managers and the quality of management, have very important effects. In a social and community context, leisure can help to give people self-worth and confidence; all people appear to have a quest for personal identity. Moreover, resourceful people are those who can overcome obstacles and find preoccupying activities and interests. Leisure and recreation management has much to offer in the way of enabling people to develop skills, to discover themselves and reach beyond their immediate grasp.

Whether Leisure Managers operate in the public, voluntary or commercial sector, a part of their job is to provide people with opportunities to experience satisfactions through leisure activities. Managers must understand the nature of the leisure experience and what motivates people to leisure and recreation. They must create environments in which leisure can flourish. Then they can define managerial objectives, develop skills for the job and utilize the resources at their disposal. Managers need multi-skill qualities for both general and specialist management. All providers and managers must attract people or fail. Leisure and recreation is a people-orientated business.

In essence, Leisure Managers are no different from other managers. Leisure Managers must, above all else, be good managers. They need an understanding of general management principles, processes, practices and the ability to handle people. They must have skills of leadership, decision making, communications and administration. They have to choose, train and deploy staff wisely. They need objectivity, financial acumen, marketing, programming and operational ability. Management must be appropriate to different situations, and the manager must adapt his or her style of management to be appropriate to changing situations.

As pointed out earlier, a Leisure Manager is not someone who comes out of college with a certificate. Nor is he or she someone who, through experience, can operate a facility but fails to appreciate what it means to achieve an effective service. A grasp of theory can accelerate the learning through job experience. However, the opposite is not necessarily true. Job experience may, or may not, accelerate a grasp of theory. In this book, a theory–practice orientation is advocated to produce the most effective Leisure Managers. Yet no amount of training will guarantee to make the manager: he or she is someone with a mixture of ability, objectivity, craft and humanity.

There is much to be said for practical, simple, common-sense approaches to management. We have somehow managed to make management something academic and difficult, particularly in the public sector, with many levels of bureaucracy. Mechanistic and institutionalized systems are still prevalent. Some institutional managers get stuck in a rut; then they do not respond positively to change and far from enhancing leisure, they may well militate against effective management. While knowledge, logic and technical ability are important, there is also an important place for enthusiasm and empathy, even charisma. There is room for belief and conviction.

Leisure opportunity is a tangible means of improving the lot of individuals in society. The message to policy makers is clear: make savings on capital if you must, but never on good management. A great deal can be done without major capital expenditure. In many circles, there still exists a gulf between well-meaning public providers and the actual public themselves; often there is inarticulateness and miscommunication at the interface between people and providers. Leisure Managers can help to mesh together the resources that already exist, help to make the connections and the linkages. Enabling, encouraging and supporting can be achieved in a thousand and one small ways. 'Small things make a big difference', particularly when it is people's feelings that we might be dealing with and personal satisfactions with which leisure management is ultimately concerned.

Leisure professionals must develop a 'helicopter' view of their leisure services: the higher they go, the greater the vision. They need to view not just the array of facilities but also the interconnections, the junctions of the various pathways, the fuels that make the processes effective, and the blockages that cause the hold-ups.

Leisure Managers should continue to develop people-serving concepts, with an emphasis on concern for the client and customer. Policy makers, planners and managers should continually question the assumptions on which we plan and manage. Policy makers and managers must focus their leisure orientation within the context of the total human experience. Such a perspective broadens the basis of leisure expression.

Here, then, is the conflict, the dilemma: leisure and recreation are concerned with human experience. It defies management. But management is the instrument by which environments can be shaped, opportunities can be given and people can be enabled or taught to cope. The challenge therefore is not just in facilities, programmes, costs, income or even in numbers, but whether leisure services can provide opportunities for leisure and re-creation to occur for people, and where individuals can choose, learn, find pleasurable and satisfying experiences and control the content of their leisure activity and participation. These objectives apply to all sectors of leisure – public, voluntary and commercial.

In this book, emphasis has been placed on effectiveness. We desperately need a method of evaluation that permits a social cost–benefit analysis. We do not want to promote the slogan 'Leisure for all – who can afford it'! Allowing the accounting mind to dictate social policy will be a tragedy for people, for art, for sport and for the nation.

At the community level, the major resource that this world has is people. Many of our social systems – including leisure – make people dependent on directed programmes and services, without the inputs from community groups. Building on the theme of Nellie Arnold (from her pre-Commonwealth Games address in Brisbane) our untapped resources are in the community sector. We need to create: an enabling environment, returning much leadership to the community – play, leisure and recreation are born at the grass-roots level; a supporting environment, providing a resource, an economic and administrative base; and a connecting environment, linking people to agencies, clubs and voluntary and commercial bodies. Our role as advocates is crucial.

'Leisure for all', should be concerned with individual people achieving a personal harmony through satisfaction in participating in art, music, sport and recreation. Those who can experience the joy of play, participation and exhilaration of movement, and who can reach beyond the ordinary, have greater opportunity to find a better and more satisfying life.

In these days of standardization, bureaucratic institutions, financial accountability and competitive tendering, our attention is being drawn towards mathematical results and quantitative performance ratios. Facilities are being planned for entertainment, eating and drinking and 'all the fun of the fair' because these attractions achieve volume traffic and greater spends per head – the right mix for profitability. But other provision (often unprofitable) is also needed to help to meet the goal of leisure. Furthermore, too much time and energy is being spent on who is going to do the managing – public departments or private companies. But it should not matter who is managing, but rather what is being managed and how, and what are the benefits. Disney has taught us that treating customers with attention, understanding, consideration and courtesy – 'quality services' – brings quality results. Let us focus on the results for people – locally for communities, nationally for each nation, and internationally for a 'Leisure for all' movement worldwide.

While leisure is personal, it is also universal. The fiftieth anniversary of the United Nations Universal Declaration of Human Rights including the rights of all people to leisure was in 1998. The World Leisure and Recreation Association, in the prologue to its *Charter for Leisure*, states:

> All societies and all cultures increasingly recognize people's right to certain periods of time during which they can choose freely to occupy themselves and which experiences to select to further their quest for self-fulfilment and to improve the quality of their lives. Peace, a minimum of social stability, the opportunity to establish meaningful inter-personal contacts, and the reduction of social inequality, are some of the major prerequisites for the full implementation of that right.

Leisure is not new. 'With what activity should we occupy our leisure?' asked Aristotle. 'Let each become all he or she is capable of being' could have been his modern-day slogan. Jacob Bronowski believed that leisure activity has potential for a deep sense of appreciation which can lift us to a higher plane, where we discover peace, beauty and joy in this world. This can carry over to an increased appreciation of life itself. Julian Huxley, in the *Bulletin of Atomic Scientists* states: 'The leisure problem is fundamental. Having to decide what we shall do with our leisure is inevitably forcing us to re-examine the purpose of human existence, and to ask what human fulfilment really means.' I believe that leisure management should be concerned with such fulfilment, with a love of life, for people and for the human expression that leisure opportunity affords. At the end of the day, it is about one person and his or her experience, and the knock-on effect to communities living in harmony.

A House of Lords Report written twenty-five years ago captured the belief and the spirit in which this book is written:

> Many people suffer from a lingering feeling that leisure is something of a luxury. As an escape from the commendable pursuits of earning a living and making a contribution to the national economy, leisure seems tainted. When carried to excess it is called idleness. But the Committee believe that it is time for the puritan view of leisure to be jettisoned. Leisure is as much a part of life as work and it plays an equally important part in man's development and the quality of his life. . . . In its own way it is almost as important to the well-being of the community as good housing, hospitals and schools.

The world may change, but some things are changeless; we have been given creative, changeless gifts. It is through play, recreation and leisure that our talents for discovery, invention, music, art and sport are realized. My hope for leisure providers and managers is that they will not just concentrate on efficiency, finding more administration to satisfy less activity, but to aim for effectiveness and put their talents into ideas and activities for more people to find self-fulfilment. The spirit of the world cannot be changed through money, facilities or bureaucracy, nor by government, but by imagination and ideas. Those ideas need the backing of our enthusiasm, confidence and vision – and our advocacy and management expertise.

The leisure experience which I have described in this book stems from intrinsic, rather than extrinsic rewards: it is person-centred. Each society should respect the individuality of each of its people. Society, in turn, will benefit, for people who function at their optimal potential can help society to reach a far better level of collective well-being. As the Select Committee of the House of Lords put it: 'When life becomes meaningful for the individual then the whole community is also enriched.'

Index